Working with Lotus 1-2-3 (Version 2.2)

Bruce J. McLaren

Indiana State University

HarperCollins*Publishers*

Sponsoring Editor: Rick Williamson

Development Editor: Liz Lee

Project Coordination: BMR of Corte Madera

Text and Cover Design: Gary Palmatier, Ideas to Images

Cover Photograph: Murray Alcosser

Photo Research: BMR of Corte Madera

Production: Michael Weinstein

Compositor: Ideas to Images

Printer and Binder: Courier Corporation

Cover Printer: The Lehigh Press, Inc.

Lotus and 1-2-3 are trademarks of Lotus Development Corporation.

For permission to use copyrighted material, grateful acknowledgment is made to the copyright holders on pages 369 and 370, which are hereby made part of this copyright page.

Working with Lotus 1-2-3 (Version 2.2)

Copyright © 1992 by HarperCollins Publishers Inc.

All rights reserved. Printed in the United States of America. No part of this book may be used or reproduced in any manner whatsoever without written permission, except in the case of brief quotations embodied in critical articles and reviews. For information address HarperCollins Publishers Inc., 10 East 53rd Street, New York, NY 10022.

Library of Congress Cataloging-in-Publication Data

McLaren, Bruce J.
    Working with Lotus 1-2-3 (version 2.2) / Bruce J. McLaren.
        p.   cm.
    Includes index.
    ISBN 0-06-500530-9
    1. Lotus 1-2-3 (Computer programs) 2. Business—Computer programs.
3. Electronic spreadsheets   I. Title.
HF5548.4.L67M36   1991
650'.0285'5369—dc20   91-34551
                                                          CIP

91 92 93 94 9 8 7 6 5 4 3 2 1

Contents

Preface xi

1 Microcomputer Software Applications 2

INTRODUCTION 4

BUSINESS APPLICATIONS SOFTWARE 4

MICROCOMPUTER EQUIPMENT 7

Computer System Unit 7
    The Microprocessor 8
    Primary Memory: RAM and ROM 10
    Input/Output (I/O) Ports: Parallel, Serial, Game 10
    Expansion Slots 11

Peripheral Hardware 12
    Disk Storage Devices 12
    Floppy Disks 12
    Hard Disk Drives 14
    Hard Disk Backup Devices 15
    Video Adapter 16
    Video Monitor 16
    The Keyboard 17
    Pointing Devices: Mouse, Joystick, Trackball, Light Pen 18
    Printing Devices 18
    Connecting to Other Computers 21
    Expansion Alternatives 24
    Miscellaneous Supplies and Accessories 25

CHAPTER REVIEW 25
KEY TERMS 26
DISCUSSION QUESTIONS 26
CHAPTER 1 PROJECT: COMPUTER CONSUMER GUIDE 27

2 The Operating System: DOS and Utility Software 28

INTRODUCTION 30

ELEMENTARY DOS COMMANDS 30

Getting Started: Booting Up the Computer 30
    Example: Booting Up the Computer 30
    Changing the Date and Time 32
    Changing Disk Drives 33
    Removing the Diskette 33

The Keyboard and Correcting Mistakes 33
    Warm Boot: Restarting the Computer with Ctrl-Alt-Del 35
    Screen Print Commands 35
    Example: Printing the Screen's Contents 35

Working with Files 36
    File Names and Terminology 36
    Wildcard File Name Templates 37
    Initializing a Blank Disk: FORMAT 37
    Example: Formatting a Blank Floppy Disk 37
    The Disk Directory 38
    Listing File Names: DIR 40
    Copying a File: COPY 40
    Displaying the Contents of a File: TYPE 41
    Example: Display the AUTOEXEC.BAT File 41
    Printing the File: PRINT 41
    Removing a File: DEL 42
    Changing a File's Name: RENAME 42

DOS Disk Commands 42
    Copying an Entire Disk: DISKCOPY 42
    Comparing Two Disks: DISKCOMP 43
    Checking the Disk: CHKDSK 43

CONTENTS

Example: Checking Your Disk   44

WORKING WITH HARD DISKS 44

Using Subdirectories   44

     Making a New Subdirectory:
MKDIR or MD   46

     Changing to a Subdirectory:
CHDIR or CD   46

     Removing a Subdirectory: RMDIR or RD   46

     Displaying the Subdirectory
Name: PROMPT   47

**DOS Pathnames:
Drive, Directory, and File Name**   47

     Pathname Rules   47

     Setting a Search Path: PATH   47

Backing Up a Hard Disk   48

     Copying the Hard Disk: BACKUP   48

     Restoring the Hard Disk: RESTORE   49

     Copying Files and Directories: XCOPY   49

File Storage and Disk Fragmentation   50

ADVANCED DOS CONCEPTS 50

User-Prepared Startup Files   50

     The CONFIG.SYS File   50

     Example: Creating a CONFIG.SYS
File with COPY CON   50

     The AUTOEXEC.BAT File
and TSR Programs   51

DOS Command Keys   52

     The Command Line Template   52

Other DOS Commands   52

File Attributes   53

CREATING AND EXECUTING
DOS BATCH FILES 53

Batch Command Files   53

Creating a Batch File with COPY CON   54

     Example: Creating a Batch File
with COPY CON Filename   54

Using EDLIN to Create a Batch File   55

**Creating a Batch File with
Your Word Processor**   55

Example Batch Files   55

NON-DOS UTILITY PROGRAMS 56

File Management and DOS Shell Programs   56

     The Norton Utilities   56

     PC-TOOLS   57

     Mace Utilities   58

Hard Disk Backup and Restore Utilities   58

**Multitasking Environments:
Windows and DESQview**   58

DOS, OS/2, AND OTHER
OPERATING SYSTEMS 59

Other DOS Versions   59

OS/2—The Multitasking Software   59

Unix   60

DOS COMMAND SUMMARY 61

CHAPTER REVIEW   61

KEY TERMS   63

DISCUSSION QUESTIONS   64

EXERCISES   65

CHAPTER 2 PROJECT: GRAPHICAL USER INTERFACES   66

3   Spreadsheets:
The Manager's Tool 68

INTRODUCTION TO SPREADSHEET
APPLICATIONS AND LOTUS 1-2-3 70

Spreadsheets   70

Learning Lotus 1-2-3   70

LOTUS 1-2-3 QUICKSTART 71

Starting Lotus from a Floppy Disk   71

Starting Lotus from a Hard Disk   71

The Lotus Access Menu and 1-2-3   72

     The 1-2-3 Module   72

     PrintGraph Module   72

     Translate Module   72

     Install Module   72

The Lotus 1-2-3 Control Panel   73

     Spreadsheet Modes   74

     Lotus Lock Indicators   74

     Other Status Indicators   74

     Lotus / Command Display   75

CONTENTS

Moving Around the Worksheet   76

Obtaining Help in Lotus 1-2-3   77

Making Cell Entries   77
     Lotus Formulas   78
     Correcting Errors   79
     Example: Building the SMITHTON RV Spreadsheet   79
     Specify the Print Range   83

Printing the Worksheet   83
     Send Output to the Printer   84
     Example: Printing the Smithton Worksheet   84

Saving the Worksheet   85

Retrieving a Worksheet from the Disk   86

Leaving Lotus 1-2-3   86
     Example: Saving the Smithton Worksheet   86

The Lotus / Command Menu   87
     The /Worksheet Menu   87
     The /Range Menu   87
     /Copy and /Move Menus   87
     The /File Menu   87
     The /Print Menu   87
     The /Graph Menu   88
     The /Data Menu   88
     The /Add-in Command   88
     The /System Command   88

Lotus Function Keys   88

CHAPTER REVIEW   88
KEY TERMS   91
DISCUSSION QUESTIONS   92
EXERCISES   93
CHAPTER 3 PROJECT: CAMPUS NETWORKING   97

4 Building Lotus 1-2-3 Worksheets 98

INTRODUCTION 100

WORKING WITH ROWS, COLUMNS, AND CELLS 100

Design Considerations   100

Inserting and Deleting Rows and Columns   101
     Example: Inserting a Single Row   101
     Inserting a Single Column   102
     Example: Inserting a Column   102
     Inserting Multiple Rows or Columns   103
     Deleting Rows and Columns   103
     Example: Deleting a Column   104

Copying and Moving Cells   104
     Example: Copying Cell Formulas   104
     Example: Moving Cell Formulas   105
     Relative and Absolute Cell Addresses   106
     Example: Using Absolute Cell Addresses   106
     Types of Absolute Cell References   106
     Example: Entering an Absolute Cell Reference with F4   107

Working with Lotus Cell Range Names   108
     Creating Range Names   108
     Example: Creating Range Names   108
     Using Range Names in Expressions and Commands   108
     Example: Using the Range Name in a Command   109
     Other Range Name Options   109
     Example: Placing a Range Name Table in the Worksheet   109

Formatting Cell Appearance: Formats and Column Width   109
     Numeric Cell Formats   109
     Assigning a Format to Cells   111
     Example: Formatting the Smithton Spreadsheet   112
     Converting Formulas to Text Format   113
     Example: Displaying the Worksheet as Text Format   114

Changing Column Widths: Global, Individual, and Column-Range   114
     Changing the Global Column Width   114
     Changing an Individual Column or Column-Range   115

Label Prefixes: Left, Right, Center, and Repeating   115
     Types of Label Prefixes   115
     Changing the Global Label Prefix   116
     Changing the Label Prefix for a Range of Cells   116
     Label Prefixes for Value Cells   116

Recalculation in Lotus 1-2-3   116

Changing the Recalculation Mode 117
Performing a Manual Recalculation 118

Protecting Cell Formulas 118
Example: Protecting Cell Expressions 118

Working with Large Spreadsheets: Titles and Windows 119
Creating Titles 119
Example: Creating a Horizontal Title 119
Removing a Title 120
Creating Lotus Windows 120
Example: Creating a Vertical Window 120

LOTUS @-FUNCTIONS 121

Statistical Functions 121

Mathematical Functions 122

Financial Functions 123
Time-Value Functions 123
Lotus Depreciation Functions 124

Date and Time Functions 125

Logical Functions: Conditional Values 126
The @IF Function 126
The @HLOOKUP and @VLOOKUP Functions 127

String Functions: Manipulating Labels 129

CHAPTER REVIEW 130

KEY TERMS 133

DISCUSSION QUESTIONS 134

EXERCISES 136

CHAPTER 4 PROJECT: PINE FARM APARTMENTS 141

5 Advanced Lotus File and Print Commands 142

INTRODUCTION 144

LOTUS FILE OPERATIONS 144

Changing the Default Directory 144
Changing the Directory for One Command 144
Temporarily Changing the Default Directory 144
Example: Temporarily Changing the Default Directory 145
Permanently Changing the Default Directory 145
Example: Permanently Changing the Default Directory 145

Retrieving and Saving Worksheet Files 145
Retrieving an Existing File 146
Saving a Worksheet File 146

Working with Other Files 147
Listing File Names 147
Erasing Files 147
Saving a Portion of the Worksheet 149
Example: Saving a Portion of the Worksheet 149
Combining Two Worksheet Files 150
Example: Combining Two Worksheet Files 151
Linking Data from Another Worksheet (Release 2.2) 151
Example: Using a Link Formula 152
Importing Data from Non-Worksheet Files 153
File Commands for Temporarily Entering DOS 153

PRINTING THE WORKSHEET—ADVANCED COMMANDS 154

Main Print Menu Choices 154

Print Options Submenu 155
Example: Creating a Print Header 155
Example: Using Print Borders 156

Other Submenu Choices—Printing Cell Formulas 157
Example: Printing Cell Formulas 157
Forcing a Page Break 158

Printing to a File 158
Example: Printing the Worksheet to a Text File 158

Other Printing Features—Allways 160
Example: Using Allways Features to Print a Worksheet 161

CHAPTER REVIEW 163

KEY TERMS 164

DISCUSSION QUESTIONS 164

EXERCISES 165

CHAPTER 5 PROJECT: SCHOOL OF BUSINESS BUDGET 168

6 Lotus Graphs ... 170

INTRODUCTION ... 172

CREATING LOTUS GRAPHS ... 172

Graphing Basics 172
- X and Y Variables: Data Ranges 172
- Graph Types 173

Creating the Graph 176
- *Example:* Creating a Bar Graph 176

Graph Settings 178
- Titles, Legends, and Data Labels 178
- *Example:* Adding Titles and Data Legend to the Graph 178
- Scales and Formatting the Axes 179
- Drawing Grid Lines 180
- Other Graph Options 181

Naming and Saving the Graph 181
- *Example:* Saving the Graph Settings 182

PRINTING THE GRAPH: LOTUS PRINTGRAPH MODULE ... 182
- Selecting the Graph Image 183
- Selecting PrintGraph Options 184
- Printing the Graph 185
- *Example:* Creating and Printing a Graph 186

PRINTING GRAPHS WITH ALLWAYS ... 189
- *Example:* Printing a Graph with Allways 189

CHAPTER REVIEW 192
KEY TERMS 193
DISCUSSION QUESTIONS 193
EXERCISES 194
CHAPTER 6 PROJECT:
HCP INCORPORATED ANNUAL REPORT 197

7 Data Management with Lotus 1-2-3 ... 200

INTRODUCTION ... 202

LOTUS DATA MANAGEMENT ... 202

Databasics with 1-2-3 202
- Data Storage in the Worksheet 202

The /Data Menu 202
Filling Data Cells 203
Sorting Data Records 203
- *Example:* Sorting in Lotus 204

CREATING DATA QUERIES ... 205
- Query Data Ranges: Input, Criteria, Output 206
- *Example:* Building a Query Find 207
- Advanced Criteria Expressions 208
- *Example:* Building a Query Extract 210
- Database Statistical @-Functions 211
- *Example:* Using Database Statistical Functions 211

DATA TABLES ... 211
- *Example:* One-Parameter Data Table 212
- *Example:* Two-Parameter Data Table 213

OTHER DATA COMMANDS ... 215

Regression with 1-2-3 215
- Performing a Simple Regression 216
- Interpreting the Regression Results 217
- Performing a Multiple Regression 218

Data Distribution 219
- *Example:* Using the Data Distribution Command 219

Parse and Matrix Commands 220

CHAPTER REVIEW 220
KEY TERMS 221
DISCUSSION QUESTIONS 222
EXERCISES 223
CHAPTER 7 PROJECT:
PEAK STATE BANK MORTGAGE LOAN DEPARTMENT 227

8 Lotus Macros and Advanced Spreadsheet Topics ... 228

INTRODUCTION ... 230

MACROS AND THE LOTUS COMMAND LANGUAGE ... 230

Overview of Macro Applications 230
Creating a Simple Macro 231

Executing a Macro 231
Example: Simple Range Formatting Macro 232
Example: Modifying a Simple Macro 233
Example: A Printing Macro 234

Release 2.2 Learn Feature 234
Example: Creating a Macro Using the Learn Feature 235

Debugging a Macro 237

The Lotus Command Language 238
Keyboard Macro Commands 238
Advanced Macro Commands 238

Creating a Menu Macro 241
Overview of Menu Macros 241
The Print Macro 242
The Save Macro 242
The Exit Macro 242
The Quit Macro 243

Autoexecute Macros 243

COMPANION SPREADSHEET PRODUCTS 244
Allways 244
Sideways 244
HAL—The Natural Language Analyzer 244
Spreadsheet Notes and Word Processors 244
Database Linkers 244
Spreadsheet Analyzers 245
Graphing Packages 245
Spreadsheet Compilers 246
Decision Analysis Tools 246
Optimizing Products 246
Financial Add-Ins 246
Forecasting Add-Ins 246
Other Utilities 246

COMPATIBILITY WITH OTHER LOTUS 1-2-3 VERSIONS 247
Earlier Releases: 1a, 2, 2.01 247
Release 2.2 247
Release 3.0 247
Release 3.1 and 3.1+ 248

OTHER SPREADSHEET PROGRAMS 249
Lotus Work-Alikes: VP-Planner and Twin 249
Quattro and Quattro Pro 249
Microsoft Excel 249
SuperCalc 250
Other Spreadsheets 250

CHAPTER REVIEW 250
KEY TERMS 252
DISCUSSION QUESTIONS 252
EXERCISES 254
CHAPTER 8 PROJECT:
PORT HURON INVESTMENT GROUP 257

9 Integrating the Tools 260

INTRODUCTION 262
Exchanging Data Between Software Packages 262
Types of Data Transfers 262

TRANSFERRING DATA FROM WORDPERFECT 263
Saving Documents in Text (ASCII) Format 263
Example: Creating a Text File with WordPerfect 263

WordPerfect CONVERT Program 263
Example: Converting a WordPerfect Merge File to DIF Format 265
Example: Create a WordPerfect Secondary Merge File from a Mail Merge File 266

TRANSFERRING DATA TO WORDPERFECT 267
Reading a Text File with WordPerfect 267
Example: Reading a Lotus Text File 268
Example: Reading a Text File with Soft Returns 268

Importing a Lotus Worksheet File Directly   269

Example: Importing a Spreadsheet into a WordPerfect Table   270

Inserting a Lotus Graph Image into a Graphics Box   270

Example: Importing a Lotus Graph into WordPerfect   270

TRANSFERRING DATA FROM LOTUS 1-2-3 272

Creating a Lotus Text (.PRN) File   272

Example: Printing to a Disk File   272

Using the Lotus Translate Module   273

Example: Translating from DIF to WK1 Format   274

Example: Translating from WK1 to DBF Format   276

TRANSFERRING DATA TO LOTUS 1-2-3 277

Combining Information into a Lotus 1-2-3 Worksheet   277

Importing Text Information into a Lotus 1-2-3 Worksheet   278

Example: Importing a Text File into 1-2-3   278

Example: Parsing Data with 1-2-3   278

TRANSFERRING DATA FROM dBASE IV 281

Using the COPY TO Command to Export Data   281

Example: Create an SDF Text File with the COPY TO Command   282

Example: Create a WKS File with the COPY TO Command   282

Creating a Text File with the dBASE IV LIST TO FILE Command   282

Example: Create a Text File with the LIST TO FILE Command   282

Exporting Data from the dBASE IV Control Center   284

Example: Create a Delimited (Mail Merge) File   284

TRANSFERRING DATA TO dBASE IV 286

Using the APPEND FROM Command with Other Files   286

Importing Data from Other Files   286

Example: Adding Records from Another dBASE File   288

Example: Adding Records from a Text File   290

CHAPTER REVIEW   291
KEY TERMS   291
DISCUSSION QUESTIONS   292
EXERCISES   292
CHAPTER 9 PROJECT: STUDENT VOLUNTEER AGENCY   296

10 Working with Lotus 1-2-3 Release 2.3 and 3.1 298

INTRODUCTION 300

LOTUS 1-2-3 RELEASE 2.3 300

System Requirements   300
Overview of New Features   300

LOTUS 1-2-3 RELEASE 3.1 304

System Requirements   304
Overview of New Features   304

New File Types   304

Multiple Worksheets Per File   304

Example: Preparing a Multiple Worksheet   305

WYSIWYG Graphical Display   306

Example: Creating a WYSIWYG Worksheet   309

New Graph Features   312

Print Features   314

Worksheet Analysis and Debugging Features   315

Automatic Cell Formatting   316

New /Data Options   317

Release 3.1 Macro Changes   317

Other Changes   318

Compatibility with Other Lotus Versions   318

Lotus 1-2-3 Release 3.1 Plus   319

CHAPTER REVIEW 319

KEY TERMS 322

DISCUSSION QUESTIONS 322

EXERCISES 323

CHAPTER 10 PROJECT:
HCP INCORPORATED ANNUAL REPORT 325

Appendices 327
A: **A PC BUYER'S GUIDE** 328
B: **DOS COMMANDS** 339
C: **LOTUS 1-2-3 COMMANDS** 341

Index 361

Preface

TEXT'S FOCUS

Virtually all people in the business environment need to know how to use a computer to assist in decision making and—more importantly—to boost their productivity. *Working with Lotus 1-2-3 (Version 2.2)* offers a comprehensive introduction and keystroke tutorials for the best-selling spreadsheet program, Lotus 1-2-3.

HARDWARE REQUIREMENTS

This book targets the IBM-compatible microcomputer as the standard hardware. There are many excellent computers that meet this standard. Each machine should be equipped with a hard drive or connected to a local area network that provides the Lotus application software from a file server. While Lotus 1-2-3 Release 2.2 does not require a hard drive, it operates better if a hard drive is present. Each machine should have at least 512 KB of random access memory, preferably 640 KB. A graphics monitor will allow the display of graphs. A printer is essential.

FEATURES

In addition to covering the most popular spreadsheet package, *Working with Lotus 1-2-3 (Version 2.2)* offers these features:

- The book begins with a discussion of the use and expansion of microcomputers, their application in business today, and an overview of products currently on the market. It is supplemented by Appendix A, a Buyer's Guide to evaluating and choosing new software and hardware.

- Detailed, step-by-step keystroke tutorials lead students through the software; they learn by actual hands-on experience.

- The writing style in *Working with Lotus 1-2-3 (Version 2.2)* is clear and friendly.

- The text contains thorough explanations of the various commands, with realistic screen displays that illustrate their use.

- One chapter contains numerous examples of integrating data between Lotus 1-2-3, WordPerfect, and dBASE.

- The last chapter provides an overview of the two newest Lotus versions, 2.3 and 3.1.

ORGANIZATION

The textbook consists of 10 chapters:

- Chapter 1 contains an overview of microcomputer applications and a discussion of microcomputer hardware components. Chapter 2 deals with the DOS operating system and utility software programs such as Windows, PC-Tools, and Norton Utilities.

- Chapters 3 to 8 teach Lotus 1-2-3 Version 2.2. The first Lotus chapter contains a concise QuickStart section, designed to get new users into the software as quickly as possible. Remaining chapters cover worksheet design, Lotus functions, advanced file and printing commands, graphing, data management, and Lotus macros.

- Chapter 9 is a comprehensive presentation of transferring data between Lotus 1-2-3 and two other popular programs, WordPerfect and dBASE. Chapter 10 provides an overview of the features in the newer Lotus releases, 2.3 and 3.1, for those instructors who want to cover those versions.

APPROACH

Working with Lotus 1-2-3 (Version 2.2) presents a thorough and comprehensive view of this application. While the beginning chapter of each module presumes little knowledge by the user, later chapters present commands and techniques that advanced users will find useful in the business environment.

The discussion questions and exercises are designed to thoroughly test the student's knowledge. Exercises are graded by difficulty, and are organized by increasing degree of challenge.

LEARNING AIDS

Each chapter contains a number of learning aids for students:

- **Learning objectives,** five to fifteen per chapter, are placed at the beginning of each chapter.

- **Hands-on examples** and illustrations are used to demonstrate specific computing tasks. These clearly explained examples feature numbered steps and multiple screen illustrations. Most chapters have at least six examples.

- **Content summary,** one to three pages long, concludes each chapter and is organized by main chapter headings.

- **Key terms** list the commands and essential vocabulary covered.

- **Discussion questions** appear at the end of each chapter. These are suitable as short-answer examination questions or for class discussions.

- **Exercises** are challenging hands-on tests of knowledge—six to fifteen per chapter—that are presented in order of increasing difficulty for each chapter topic.

- **Chapter projects** are content-inclusive tasks concluding each chapter. Projects may be assigned for group solution, as extra credit, or as less-structured yet comprehensive exercises.

- **Appendices** include a Buyer's Guide, a DOS command summary, an alphabetical Quick Reference Guide to Lotus commands, a graphical command tree for the 1-2-3, PrintGraph, and Allways modules, and a summary of @-functions.

Chapter Exercises

A critical part of any software tutorial is the opportunity for students to test their skills. *Working with Lotus 1-2-3 (Version 2.2)* includes several hundred discussion questions and hands-on chapter exercises. Most are designed with business situations in mind, yet require little prior business knowledge. These challenging exercises appear in increasing order of difficulty so that instructors can choose the proper level.

A floppy disk containing data files is available with this textbook. The data disk includes text files, Lotus 1-2-3 spreadsheet and graph files, and various other files needed to solve the exercises. Use of the data disk enables students to focus on the assigned software task rather than on data input. Solutions to all discussion questions and chapter exercises are provided in the Instructor's Manual and its accompanying solutions disk.

Comprehensive Chapter Projects

Each chapter ends with a comprehensive project. The project offers the student an opportunity to use the applications software to solve a realistic business problem. The projects are less structured and are more challenging than other chapter exercises. The project places the student in the role of a consultant retained to solve a particular problem. In this role the consultant must define objectives, consider alternatives, and build the model using the tools within the software package.

Extensive PC Buyer's Guide

Appendix A is included as a supplement for those interested in purchasing a new computer or upgrading existing equipment. It offers advice to the new buyer and goes into more detail about hardware components than Chapter 1 does. The five-step purchasing procedure will be helpful for those who aren't sure where to start. This Buyer's Guide will assist the course instructor who is constantly asked, "What shall I buy?"

SUPPORT PACKAGE

Each adopter of the text will receive an Instructor's Manual. The manual contains sample course outlines and numerous teaching suggestions for using the textbook. Each chapter has learning objectives, a detailed chapter outline, teaching hints, and complete solutions to all discussion questions and chapter exercises. Hints for solving chapter projects are also included. The solutions disk accompanying the manual has over 50 files containing solutions to each chapter exercise and most of the example files used within the text. A set of transparency masters and the data disk are included with the manual. A test bank is also included with the Instructor's Manual.

TO THE STUDENT

The material covered in this textbook is easily grasped if you practice on the computer while reading the chapter. First, read through the hands-on examples and the accompanying explanations. Then, while sitting at the computer, follow the same steps. Review your progress after each step when doing the examples. Compare your screen with the one in the textbook. Write down any differences or print a copy of the screen to discuss with your friends and the instructor.

Like any other learned skill, your computer knowledge will fade away if it is not used. Take every opportunity to practice using the software in other courses, your job, and in other applications. This book will serve as a reference in the future when you need to learn more of the Lotus commands and functions.

ACKNOWLEDGMENTS

Without the help of many people a project of this nature could not be completed. These individuals include colleagues, family, friends, students, reviewers, and publisher staff members.

My appreciation goes to the School of Business at Indiana State University and Dean Herb Ross for their support. In particular, I would like to thank Professors Belva Cooley, Dennis Bialaszewski, Jim Buffington, Kwang Soo Lee, Jennifer Lee, Billy Moates, and Ross Piper of the Systems and Decision Sciences Department at Indiana State University for their cooperation in reviewing the manuscript and using a previous version of this material in the classroom. Professors Sandy Barnard, John Swez, and Chat Chatterji gave valuable assistance.

Paul Hightower provided some of the photographs used in the textbook. Emily Varble offered many suggestions for the manuscript.

I am grateful to numerous students at Indiana State University who used various drafts of the manuscript. Thanks go to Jim Hannem of the Douglas Stewart Company for providing examination copies of Lotus Releases 2.3 and 3.1.

I would like to thank Vice President Anne Smith and CIS Editor Rick Williamson of HarperCollins for their support in this project. Business Media Resources and Gary Palmatier of Ideas to Images produced the text. My thanks go also to Liz Lee for her assistance in the development of the manuscript.

Many thanks go to the reviewers of this manuscript and its predecessor version. Reviewers included:

    Robert M. Adams, Clarke College
    William E. Burkhardt, Carl Sandburg College
    Jason Chen, Gonzaga University
    Amir Gamshad, Tennessee State University
    Franca Giacomelli, Humber College
    Douglas A. Goings, University of Southwest Louisiana
    James Hanson, Cleveland State University
    Ernest Harfst, Kishwaukee College
    Ann W. Houck, Pima Community College
    Anne M. Knicely, DeVry Institute
    Carroll L. Kreider, Elizabethtown College
    Patricia Laffoon, Union University
    Dennis H. Lundgren, McHenry County College
    Gretchen Marx, Saint Joseph College
    Jeanne Massingill, Highland Community College
    Cathleen C. McGrath, Highland Community College
    Carl M. Penzuil, Corning Community College
    Marilyn J. Pulchaski, Bucks County Community College
    Tom E. Rosengarth, Westminster College
    Laura Saret, Oakton Community College
    James B. Shannon, New Mexico State University
    Steven Silva, DeVry Institute
    Richard G. Stearns, Parkland College
    Susan V. Wiemers, McHenry County College

Finally, special thanks go to my wife, Professor Connie McLaren, for her steady encouragement and careful reading of everything associated with this manuscript. Without her support this book would not exist.

                                                         Bruce J. McLaren

Working with Lotus 1-2-3
(Version 2.2)

Microcomputer Software Applications

Objectives

After completing this chapter, you should be able to:

- Describe the categories of microcomputer applications in business.
- List the components of the system unit and describe their functions.
- Describe the three types of secondary storage devices.
- Discuss the various video options.
- List the types of printers and describe uses for each.
- Discuss connectivity options.
- List the steps in buying a personal computer (covered in Appendix A).

INTRODUCTION

In the few short years since 1982, personal computers (PCs) have changed the way computing is done. No longer are we tied to large, shared-use computers. Inexpensive personal computers have brought affordable computing to the desktops of all organizations. The more than seventeen million personal computers in use have dramatically increased the productivity of students, managers, office workers, and users of all kinds. Low cost and powerful software has enabled us to accomplish tasks directly, without going through the computer department. PCs can save time and make our work more accurate.

Chapter 2 will cover the disk operating system (DOS) and some utility programs. Coverage of the Lotus 1-2-3 Release 2.2 spreadsheet package begins with the Chapter 3 QuickStart section and proceeds in increasing detail in the following chapters. Chapter 9 details transfer of information between Lotus 1-2-3, WordPerfect 5.1 and dBASE IV. Chapter 10 provides an overview of other versions of Lotus 1-2-3. The Appendix contains a Buyer's Guide for selecting personal computing software and hardware as well as summaries of Lotus commands and functions.

Some chapter material, like that in this chapter, is designed to be read traditionally. At other times you will be reading along as you follow steps at the PC. Each hands-on application section is clearly marked as an **Example:**, with important actions highlighted in color. Of course, you will want to try many of the techniques on your own as you read about them. Remember, the more you experiment with and use an application, in this course and in others, the more skill you will develop!

BUSINESS APPLICATIONS SOFTWARE

Word processing software enables us to create documents—letters, reports, proposals, invoices—electronically (see Figure 1-1). Corrections are easily made, and letter-perfect copies can be quickly produced on a variety of printers and paper. Authors can make changes in page format and content rapidly, resulting in improved documents. Word processing software is able to correct spelling errors or offer suggestions for alternative wording. Personalized form letters can be prepared for a few or hundreds of people. Phrases can be highlighted for emphasis. With a laser or other high-quality printer, near-typeset documents can be produced quickly.

Electronic **spreadsheet software** is used for representing row-and-column worksheets of numbers (values) and words (labels) and has nearly replaced the calculator for many business applications (see Figure 1-2). You can create worksheets that will add columns of values, calculate percentages of a total, and prepare a graph of the values, all from the same program. Spreadsheets can be used to answer "what-if" questions—change a value and the spreadsheet will immediately recalculate the worksheet and display the results. Spreadsheets can be used to prepare budgets, accounting statements, sales forecasts, price lists, and financial ratio analyses. Extensive financial planning can be accomplished with spreadsheets, including loan amortization, present values, and depreciation. Professors use spreadsheets to calculate student grades and statistics. We can store data in spreadsheets and recall values that match certain criteria; for example, we might retrieve real estate listings that match a buyer's criteria. Spreadsheets can be used to quickly create bar and line graphs, and pie charts.

Database management software is used to store large amounts of data and permit us to recall certain records when needed (see Figure 1-3). Databases can be sorted on different data values (called key fields) and reports can be printed in the desired order. You can build forms electronically to enter data directly into the database, without transcribing from paper records. A user can build a

BUSINESS APPLICATIONS SOFTWARE

```
Microcomputer Applications in Business

    Word processing software enables us to create documents --
    letters, reports, proposals, invoices -- electronically.
    Corrections are easily made, and letter perfect copies can be
    quickly produced on a variety of printers and paper. Authors can
    make changes in page  format and content rapidly, resulting in
    improved documents. Word processing software is able to correct
    spelling errors or offer suggestions for alternative wording.
    Personalized form letters can be prepared for a few or hundreds
    of people. Phrases can be highlighted for emphasis. With a laser
    or other high-quality printer, near-typeset documents can be
    produced quickly.

    Electronic spreadsheet software is used for representing row and
    column worksheets of numbers (values) and words (labels) and has
    nearly replaced the calculator for many business applications.
    You can create worksheets that will add columns of values,
    calculate percentages of a total, and prepare a graph of the
    values, all from the same program. Spreadsheets can be used to
    answer "what-if" questions -- change a value and the spreadsheet
    will immediately recalculate the worksheet and display the
    results. Spreadsheets can be used to prepare budgets, accounting
    statements, sales forecasts, price lists and financial ratio
D:\WP51\1-01.WP                              Doc 1 Pg 1 Ln 1.33" Pos 2.5"
```

FIGURE 1-1

Screen Showing WordPerfect 5.1 Word Processing Software

```
A1: [W13] 'SMITHRV -- B. McLaren  6/27/89                          READY

          A         B         C         D         E         F         G
1   SMITHRV -- B. McLaren  6/27/89
2
3                SMITHTON RECREATIONAL VEHICLE SALES, INC.
4
5                          1987      1988      1989
6                         ----------------------------
7   SALES                  1405      1205      1150
8   EXPENSES
9     Cost of Vehicles     786.8     674.8     644
10    Commissions          47.208    40.488    38.64
11    Salaries             120       130.8     142.572
12    Administrative       175       175       175
13    Marketing/Adv.       180       220       250
14                         ----------------------------
15    Total Expenses       1309.008  1241.088  1250.212
16
17  GROSS PROFIT           95.992    -36.088   -100.212
18
19
20
01-Nov-90   04:32 PM
```

FIGURE 1-2

Screen Showing Lotus 1-2-3 Spreadsheet Software

query to retrieve records that match specific criteria and output the information in sophisticated reports. Databases are used for storing medical information, lists of textbooks required for college courses, inventories of video tape libraries, student records, and much more. Data can be retrieved from the database and transferred to spreadsheet programs for further analysis. Data for form letters can be retrieved from the database and transferred to the word processor for printing. Some database management programs can be used to create full information systems, such as a cable television rental and billing system.

FIGURE 1-3

Screen Showing dBASE IV Database Software

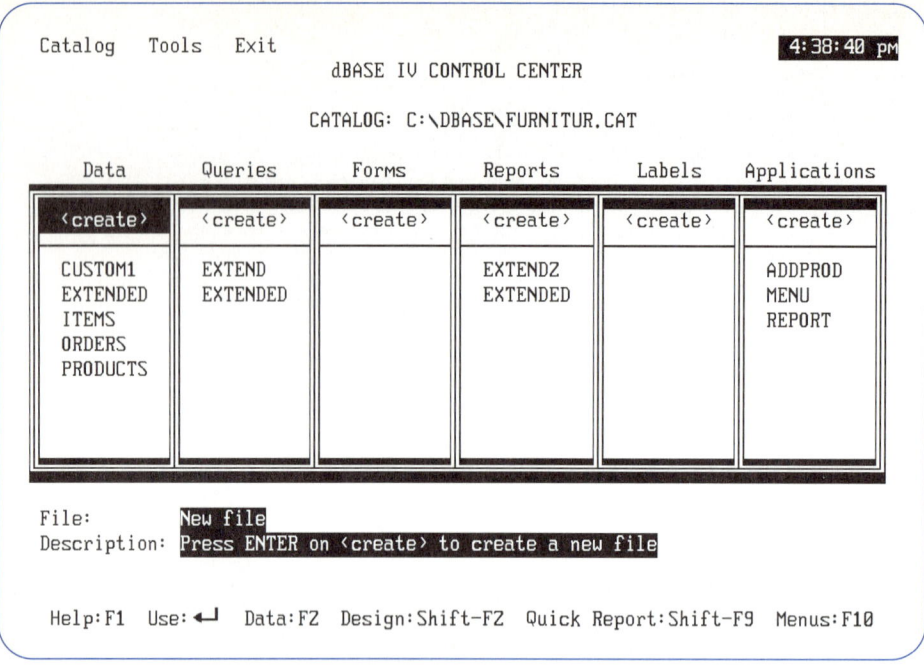

Sophisticated business graphics are possible with **graphing application programs.** You can start with basic data from a spreadsheet program, or add data directly. Existing graphs can be annotated for emphasis. Three-dimensional, shaded, and multiple graphs can be created on the same page. Output can go to high-resolution black-and-white printers, to color printers, or to color slides. **Presentation graphics** are used to create text graphics with large letters for group presentations. Formal documents prepared with a word processor can include imported graphics. **Desktop publishing programs** produce reports and brochures that closely resemble typeset quality. Graphs and artwork can be included within such documents. Freehand artwork can be accomplished with paint packages. **Computer-assisted design (CAD) software** has all but replaced mechanical drawing with pencil and paper. Figure 1-4 shows a sample graph from the Harvard Graphics software package.

Personal computers are frequently used as **terminals,** communicating with remote-host computers over telephone lines. Users are able to check electronic mail and perform other tasks from home, on the road, or from the office. **Accounting applications** are often implemented on personal computers with inventory, accounts receivable and payable, general ledger, order entry, and more modules. Many taxpayers save time by using income tax software applications on a microcomputer. Not only is the process automated, but errors are avoided and you can quickly make changes if another deduction or inventory item is discovered. **Project management software** can assist the manager to oversee projects with long durations. Tasks can be entered into the project database and a critical path calculated. Progress against plan can be plotted, with tasks that have fallen behind schedule highlighted for attention.

Many **recreational applications** for microcomputers have been created. You can fly realistic airplanes and helicopters, skipper submarines, or handle air-traffic-controller duties. You can chase criminals in a world-wide pursuit; search for clues in a "who-dunnit"; play chess, bridge, football, golf, and baseball against the computer; or improve your SAT score. Many **personal improvement programs** are available, including packages that teach children math, language, and other skills. Library-type databases are available for microcomputers,

MICROCOMPUTER EQUIPMENT

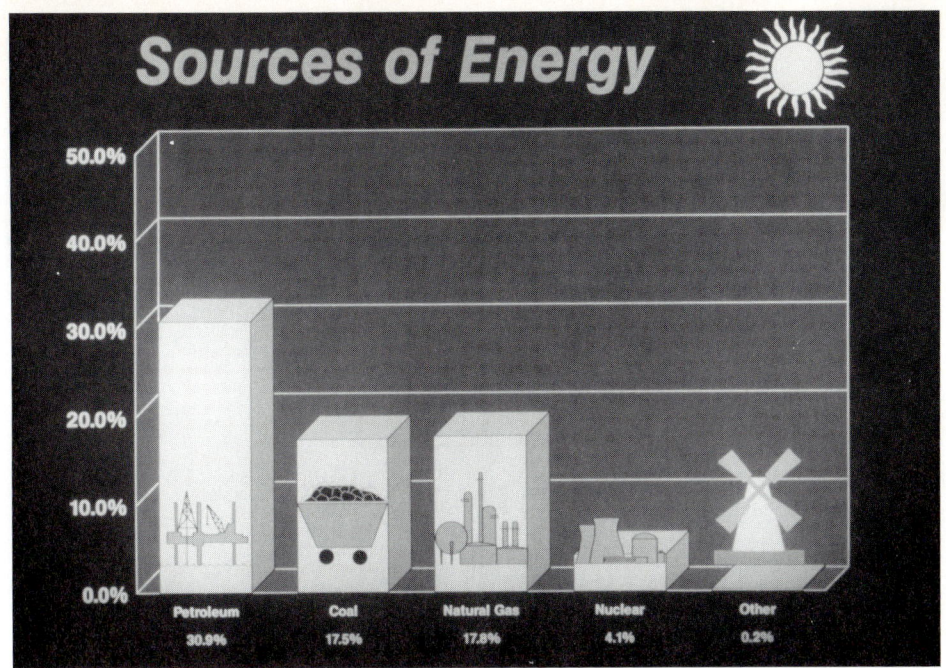

FIGURE 1-4

Sample Graph from the Harvard Graphics Software Package

including annotated and indexed Bible programs, demographic data, financial and stock market data, and industry statistics.

Programmers have access to the entire range of languages on microcomputers. BASIC is often included with the computer, and full-feature versions of all major languages—Pascal, COBOL, FORTRAN, C—are available. The personal computer is especially convenient for writing and debugging (correcting mistakes) programs in that it frees the programmer from relying on a large shared-use computer called a mainframe.

Each application improves the productivity of the user, and enhances the ability to do his job effectively. Many applications did not exist before microcomputers achieved widespread distribution, but are firmly entrenched today. In fact, the ease of use and friendly interface with the computer has affected the way mainframe computing applications are written today.

MICROCOMPUTER EQUIPMENT

Several different families of microcomputers are available today, but each shares a common set of system components. The computer consists of the system unit, some peripheral devices for input, output, and storage, various printing devices, and communications and expansion items. Figure 1-5 shows a schematic diagram of these components.

Figure 1-6 shows a typical IBM personal computer, and Figure 1-7 shows an Apple Macintosh computer. These represent the most popular business microcomputers available today.

Computer System Unit

The main module of the microcomputer is the system unit, consisting of a **microprocessor, primary memory** (RAM and ROM), **I/O ports** (input and output), and **expansion slots.** The components are mounted on a large electrical circuit board (called the **motherboard**) along with the power supply, on/off and reset switches, disk drives, and the video adapter board. The components are connected electrically to the **signal bus,** where the data, address, and control signals travel between parts of the computer. Figure 1-8 (on page 10) shows the inside of the system unit.

FIGURE 1-5

Microcomputer System Components

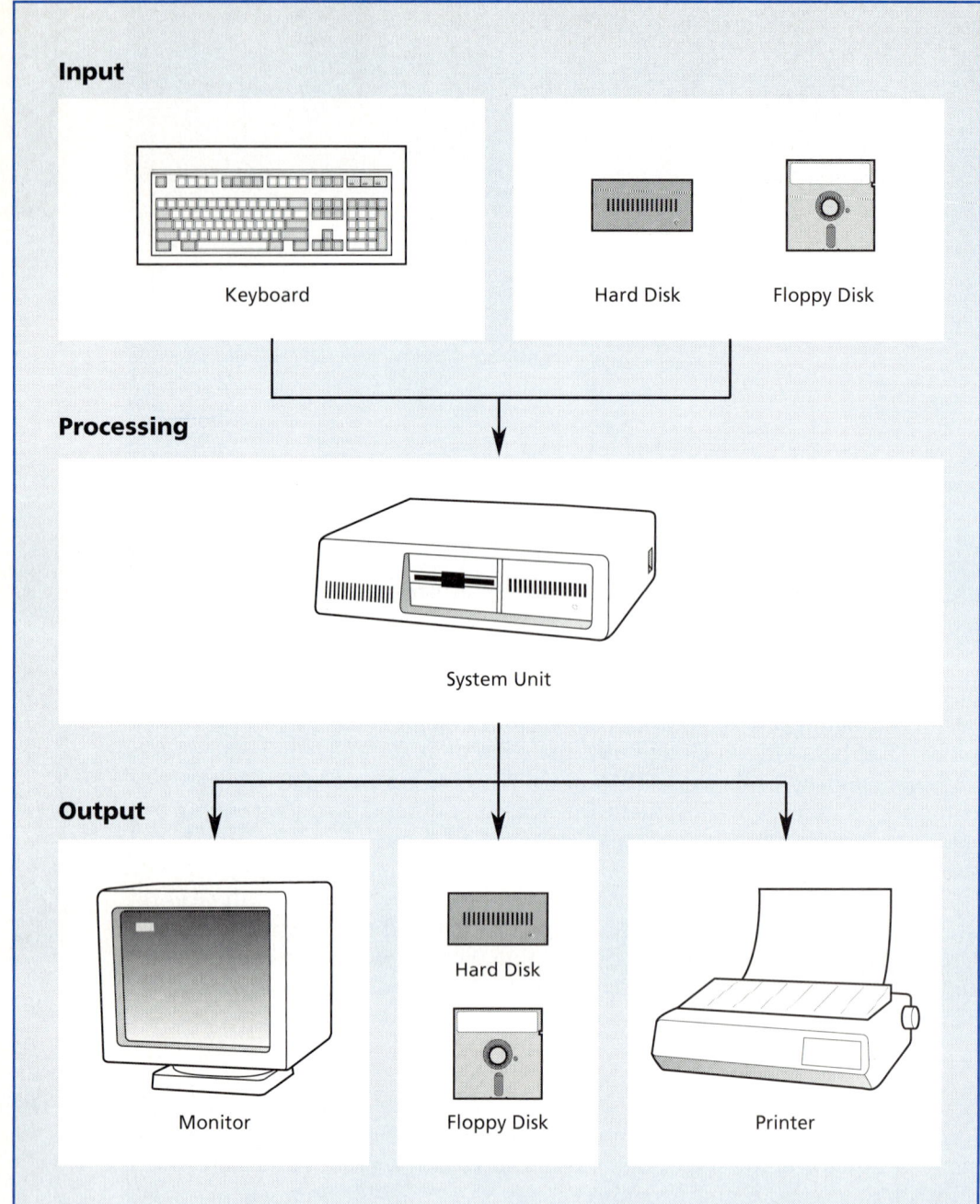

The Microprocessor

The microprocessor is a thumbnail-sized integrated circuit (chip) and is responsible for calculations and processing. IBM-compatible computers use the Intel family of microprocessors (8088, 8086, 80286, 80386SX, 80386, 80386SX, and 80486) while Apple Macintosh computers use Motorola microprocessors (68000, 68010, 68020, and 68030). The speed of the microprocessor is expressed in megahertz, or millions of clock cycles per second. Computers with faster processors are able to process more data but also cost more. Figure 1-9 shows an Intel 80486 microprocessor. Most computers have a socket for installing a **numeric coprocessor chip,** useful for speeding up numeric operations such as found in spreadsheet and graphics applications. Further discussion of these components is contained in the Buyer's Guide supplement in the Appendix.

FIGURE 1-6

IBM Personal Computer

FIGURE 1-7

Macintosh Personal Computer

FIGURE 1-8

The Inside of the System Unit

Primary Memory: RAM and ROM

Primary memory is used to temporarily store the application programs and data while the programs execute. **Random access memory (RAM)** chips are volatile—that is, they only "remember" their contents while power is on in the computer. **Read-only memory (ROM)** chips are non-volatile, and programs stored in these chips are permanent. ROM chips are used for controlling the internal functions of the computer, not for applications programs. The BIOS (Basic Input-Output System) is stored on ROM chips.

The amount of RAM is measured in bits and bytes. A **bit** is a single storage point with a value of 0 or 1 and comes from the words "**b**inary dig**it**." A **byte** is a group of 8 bits, and represents one character of storage. The prefix *kilo-* in front of bit or byte means approximately one thousand; the *mega-* prefix means one million. Individual RAM chips are typically sold in 256-kilobit or 1-megabit sizes, but 4- and 16-megabit chips are on the horizon. DRAM stands for dynamic random access memory. Nine DRAM chips are needed for a complete set. A SIMM is a single in-line memory module consisting of nine DRAMs mounted on one carrier. Both types of RAM chips are common today.

The total amount of RAM in IBM-compatible computers is usually 640 kilobytes (640 KB) or more. Computers with more RAM can run larger programs and may execute these programs faster. The newer 80286 and 80386 computers may be ordered with 4 or more megabytes (MB) of RAM.

Input/Output (I/O) Ports: Parallel, Serial, Game

The system unit also contains the Input/Output (I/O) ports for the computer. Parallel interfaces use 8 wires to send all 8 bits (1 character) at the same time. The serial interface uses a single wire and sends the 8 bits one after another.

MICROCOMPUTER EQUIPMENT

FIGURE 1-9

An Intel 80486 Microprocessor

Parallel interfaces transfer data much quicker than serial. **Parallel ports** are used for most printers. IBM-compatibles may contain up to three parallel ports (named LPT1, LPT2, and LPT3). **Serial ports** may also be used for printers, but are more often used for other peripherals such as an external modem or a mouse. IBM-compatible computers usually come with two serial ports (named COM1 and COM2) but newer computers may have COM3 and COM4 ports. A joystick can be connected to the **game port;** the game port is an extra-cost item in most computers. Many game programs can use a joystick to make inputs easier. Other ports in the system unit include connectors for the keyboard and monitor.

Expansion Slots

The system unit usually contains room for expansion cards that support additional features. These add-on cards are plugged into slots at the left rear of the system unit. The slots are attached directly to the **signal bus** of the computer, and thus can be accessed by the microprocessor and other circuits. The signal bus refers to the connections between various parts of the system unit. The edge of an expansion card protrudes from the rear of the computer and may have a cable connector for attaching a peripheral device. IBM has changed the type of expansion slots with each new personal computer family. The PC/XT models use the most common style that transfers 8 bits at a time. The AT model uses 8 additional data lines to transfer 16 bits at a time. The PS/2 line introduced the micro channel architecture (MCA) where 16 or 32 bits are transferred at a time. While PC/XT cards may be inserted into AT slots, the opposite is not true. And PC/XT/AT cards are not compatible with MCA cards. A typical expansion card is shown in Figure 1-10.

Chapter 1 — *Microcomputer Software Applications*

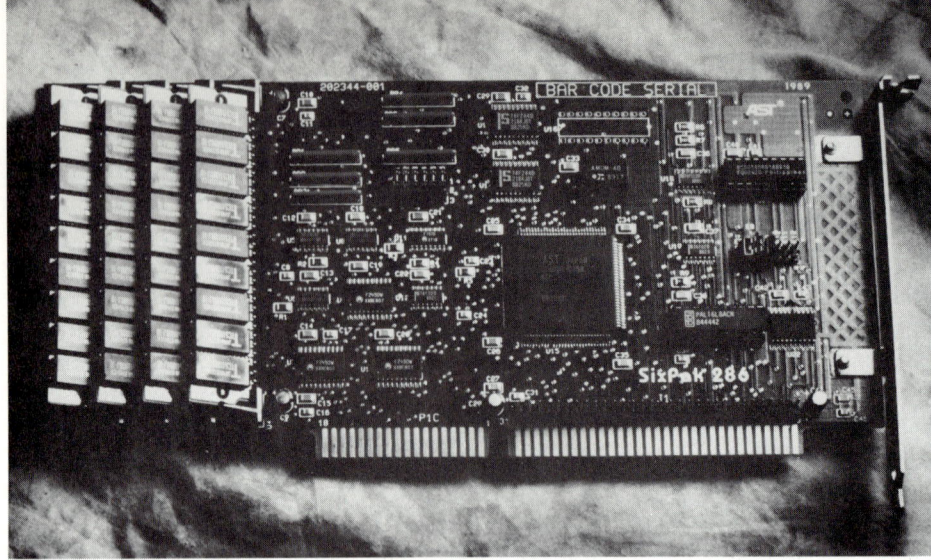

FIGURE 1-10

A Typical Expansion Card

Peripheral Hardware

Usually contained within the system unit are the data storage devices, floppy and hard **disks.** The **video adapter** and **video monitor** are used for visual output of text and graphics. The **keyboard** contains the usual typewriter keys, laid out in QWERTY fashion (top row letter keys begin with QWERTY), plus additional function and control keys used for entering commands. The **mouse** and **joystick** are pointing devices used to facilitate input. **Magnetic tape drives** are increasingly used to back up the contents of a hard disk drive to protect data in the event of a failure of the hard drive.

Disk Storage Devices

Floppy and hard disks are considered non-volatile (permanent) secondary storage units. Hard drives hold more data than RAM, and, because they use a magnetic code for storage, will retain their contents when power is removed from the computer. **Hard disks** are usually fixed within the computer and cannot be removed without disassembly. **Floppy disks** are used to distribute software, and can be moved from computer to computer. Common storage capacities of floppy disks range between 360 KB and 1440 KB (1.44 MB). The two most common floppy disk sizes (given as the diameter of the disk) are 5.25 inches and 3.5 inches. The earlier 8-inch size has been discontinued in favor of smaller disks. Most computers are being sold with the 3.5-inch disk drives. Notebook-size computers use 2-inch disks. Figure 1-11 shows several different floppy disk sizes. Figure 1-12 illustrates the capacities associated with various sizes of floppy disks.

Floppy Disks

Floppy disks are relatively inexpensive, yet provide secure storage of data if handled properly. Data are stored on a circular disk of mylar plastic that is coated with a magnetic material similar to that used in audio tapes. Figure 1-13 shows the construction and features of the two most popular types of floppy disks.

The 3.5-inch disks come with a hard-plastic case and a spring-loaded sliding door covering the area where data is written on the disk. The case is constructed so that the disk can be inserted only in the proper manner (the

MICROCOMPUTER EQUIPMENT

13

FIGURE 1-11

Different Floppy Disk Sizes

Disk Size (diameter)	Type*	Capacity (bytes)**	
2 inches	DD	730,112	(720 KB)
3.5 inches	DD	730,112	(720 KB)
3.5 inches	HD	1,457,664	(1.44 MB)
5.25 inches	DD	362,496	(360 KB)
5.25 inches	HD	1,213,952	(1.2 MB)

* DD is Double Density, HD is High Density
** KB mean kilobytes, MB means megabytes

FIGURE 1-12

Capacities Associated with Various Sizes of Floppy Disks

5.25-inch disk could easily be misinserted in the drive). The disk also contains a write-protect window in the lower left corner. If the slide in the window is closed, the disk may be read from and written on normally. When the slide is moved and the window is open, the disk cannot be written on, a safety feature designed to protect valuable data.

The 5.25-inch disk has a rectangular slot in the upper right side. If the slot is open, the disk may be read and written on normally. When the slot is covered with an opaque metallic tape, the disk is write-protected. Unfortunately, the tape can loosen and fall off, rendering the write-protection inoperative. Because the jacket on a 5.25-inch disk is thin, never write on the disk or on the label attached to the disk except with a felt-tip pen. The pressure from the pen or pencil point could damage the surface of the disk, causing lost data. The hard case of the 3.5-inch disk allows the user to write safely on an attached label.

When carrying floppy disks, especially the 5.25-inch variety, protect them from becoming pinched (as in a three-ring binder) or from other physical

FIGURE 1-13

The Construction and Features of Floppy Disks

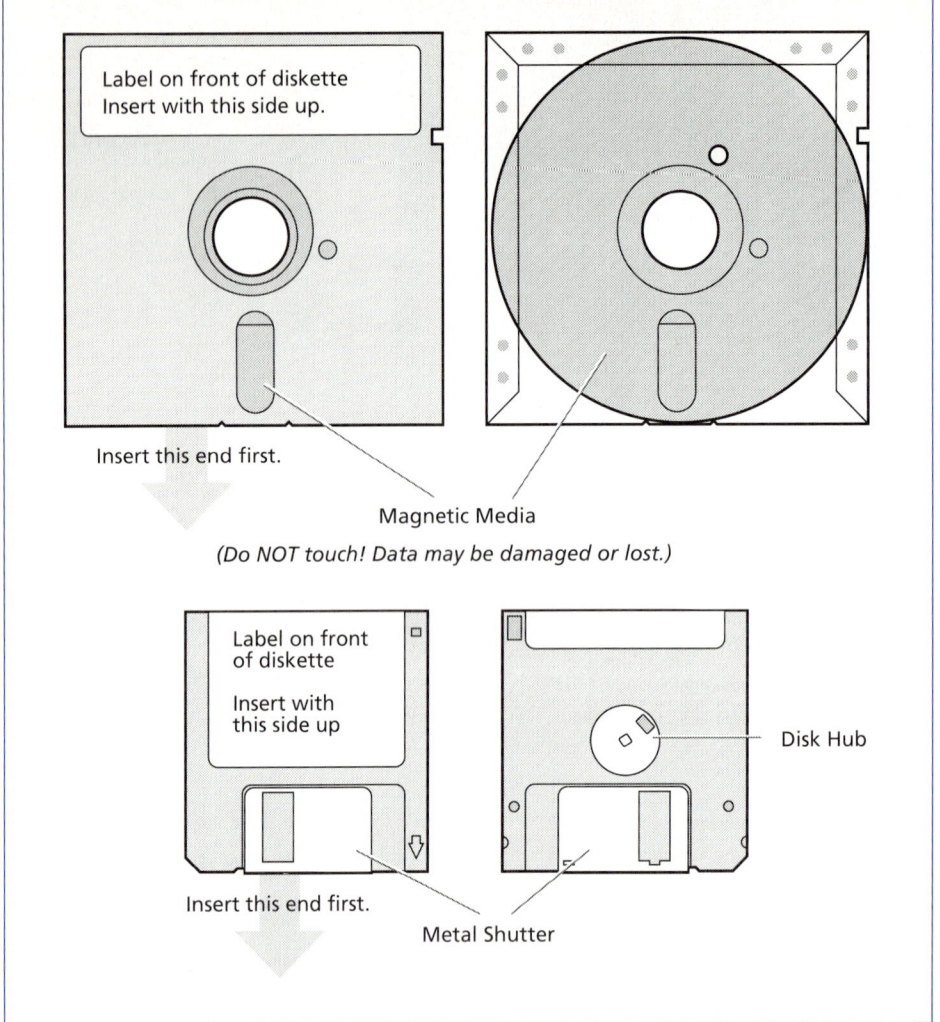

damage. Avoid magnetic fields of all kinds—even a tiny magnetic charge can erase your disk. Magnetic paper clip holders can ruin a disk. Never paper-clip a disk to other items. Avoid leaving disks in hot places, especially automobiles. Heat can damage or destroy the contents of a disk. Extreme cold and liquid spills can also harm a disk.

Hard Disk Drives

Hard disk drives provide spacious storage with very fast retrieval speeds. Storage capacities range from 20 MB to 100 MB or higher, representing the storage of 30 or more floppy disks. New computers designated for local area networks can range to 300 MB or more per drive, providing storage equivalent to many minicomputers. Hard drives use two or more highly polished, coated aluminum disks that spin at 3600 RPM. Hard drives provide access to data at ten times the rate of floppy disks. Most business computers use floppy disks for transferring software onto the hard disk, then programs and data are permanently stored on the hard drive.

Figure 1-14 shows the physical design of a typical hard disk drive. Each disk surface has its own read/write head, and there is a high-speed data link between

MICROCOMPUTER EQUIPMENT

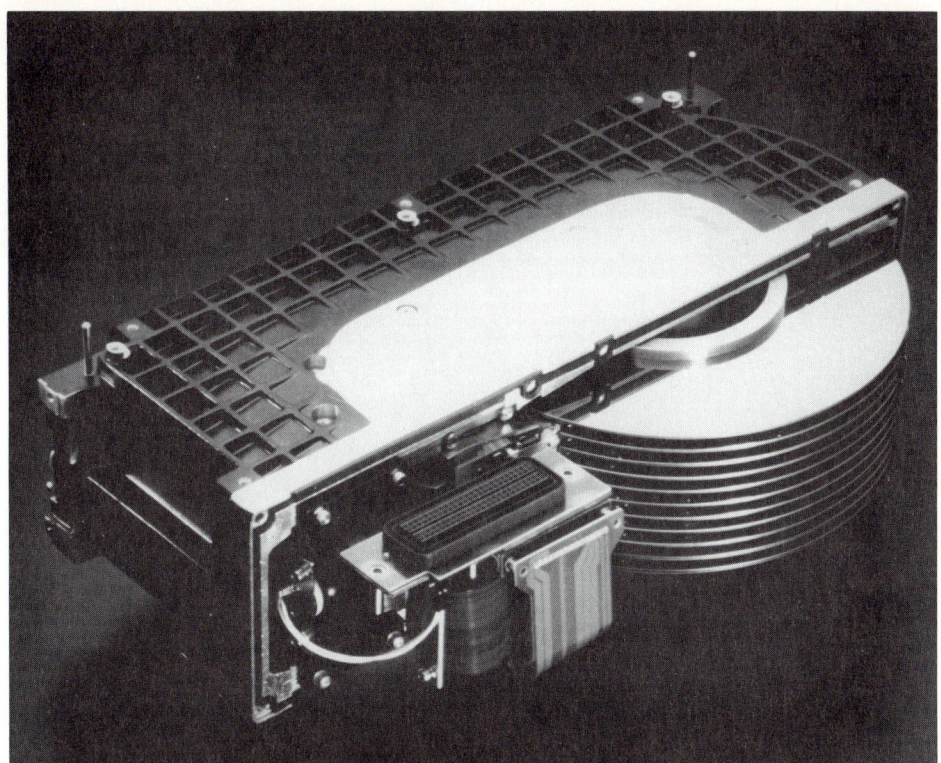

FIGURE 1-14

The Physical Design of a Typical Hard Disk Drive

the hard drive and its controller board, located inside the system unit in an expansion slot or built into the motherboard. The distance between the head and the disk surface is only a few millionths of an inch, allowing dense storage and high capacity on the drive. This small clearance is the reason why damage to the disk's surface may occur if the drive is jostled while spinning. Care must be taken when working with a hard drive. This is one of the most expensive parts of the computer and the one part most likely to fail over the computer's lifetime due to its mechanical complexity and close working tolerances.

Hard Disk Backup Devices

Hard disk drives must be regularly copied onto a **backup device** to protect against lost data in the event that the drive malfunctions. The usual medium for these backups is the floppy disk, but for large hard drives this requires many floppy disks, even if the high-density versions are used. Backing up on floppy disks is time consuming and requires that the user be physically present to exchange floppy disks. For example, a full 30 MB hard disk might require as many as 25 1.2 MB floppy disks and take 30 minutes or more to back up. There is a section in the DOS chapter on backing up and restoring hard drives using floppy disks.

A higher capacity backup scheme uses a **cartridge,** or **cassette tape,** unit for storage, and permits the user to use a single tape for a backup, rather than several boxes of floppy disks. The tape units come with backup software that allows automatic after-hours backups, saving work time. The tape drives are small, usually fitting in the same space as a floppy disk drive. Some units are designed to be moved from computer to computer and come with an external box and external power supply. There must be a separate tape-controller card for each computer used with a portable tape unit. Figure 1-15 shows a tape cartridge holding 60 megabytes of data, equivalent to more than 50 floppy disks.

FIGURE 1-15

A Tape Cartridge Holding 60 MB of Data

Video Adapter

Also located inside the system unit is the **video adapter** for the computer. This circuit board's role is to convert the video instructions of the program into a video signal that the monitor can understand. IBM has introduced several video standards, each one requiring a different video adapter-and-monitor combination. Attaching the monitor into the wrong type of video board can result in permanent damage to the monitor.

The earliest video standard, monochrome text, is obsolete today. It was replaced by the **monochrome graphics (MGA) standard,** also known as the Hercules monochrome standard, and offers 720 x 348 pixels (horizontal x vertical) resolution. A **pixel** is the smallest point of light on the screen that can be turned on or off independently. The first color standard, **color graphics adapter (CGA),** offered low-resolution color (320 x 200 pixels in 4 colors and 640 x 200 in 2 colors).

The next video adapter introduced by IBM was the **enhanced graphics adapter (EGA).** It offered substantially higher resolution at 650 x 350 pixels in 16 colors. The EGA video adapter could also be used with the monochrome and CGA monitors. The newest widely accepted video standard is the **video graphics array (VGA)** offered by IBM when they introduced the PS/2 microcomputer line. At 640 x 480 pixels and up to 256 colors, this video standard offers higher resolution for graphics and CAD (Computer-Assisted Design) applications. Higher video resolution may become standard in the near future: Super VGA is 800 x 600, and the IBM 8514A and XGA video offers 1024 x 768 pixels.

Video Monitor

The monitor is the primary output device of the microcomputer. Figure 1-16 shows a typical monitor. It must match the video adapter (monochrome, CGA, EGA, VGA, Super VGA, 8514A) installed in the computer. **Ergonomics** is the study of how individuals can work more effectively with devices in the workplace. Monitors are designed with ergonomic features such as low glare, tilt and swivel

MICROCOMPUTER EQUIPMENT

17

FIGURE 1-16

A Typical Video Monitor

base, good contrast, and low radiation emissions. Most users place the monitor on top of the system unit, although floor-mounted (tower) computers allow the monitor to sit flat on the desk. Ergonomic studies show that the ideal height of the center of the monitor is 13 inches above the table. Color monitors offer easier viewing than monochrome monitors. Creative use of color makes a program easier to learn and use.

The Keyboard

The keyboard for IBM-compatibles is the primary input device and contains 84 or 101 keys, depending on the layout. Figure 1-17 shows a typical **PC keyboard.** The white keys in the middle represent the typical keys found on a typewriter, while the gray keys are those with special functions. The numeric keypad at the right edge does double duty—those keys can be used as a number keypad, similar to a calculator layout, or for moving the cursor around on the screen. In numeric keypad mode many numbers can be entered quickly. The **function keys** at the left edge of the keyboard have special meaning within each software application, and will be defined in later chapters. The special keys on the keyboard are illustrated in Figures 2-4 and 2-5, and include **Enter, Tab, Ctrl, Shift, Alt, Esc, BkSp, NumLock, ScrollLock, PrtSc, Ins, Del, Home, End, PgUp, PgDn,** and the four arrow keys.

Most keyboards have LEDs (red or green light emitting diodes) to show the status of the **CapsLock, NumLock,** and **ScrollLock** toggle keys. With the toggle keys, the first keypress activates the feature, and the second releases it. In addition, many applications will have on-screen indicators for these. The **Ctrl** and **Alt** keys work in a similar fashion to the **Shift** key. They are used in combination with another key: hold down the **Ctrl** or **Alt** key, then press another key. These keys are used extensively with word processing and database software applications, and in recreational software. The 101-key enhanced keyboard has the function keys across the top of the keyboard instead of at the left, and duplicates the cursor control keys between the regular keyboard and

FIGURE 1-17

A Typical 84-key PC Keyboard

the numeric keypad. The latter allows full-time use of the numeric keypad at the same time as cursor control keys.

Pointing Devices: Mouse, Joystick, Trackball, Light Pen

Pointing devices like the mouse, joystick, trackball, and light pen are designed to make input easier and more natural. Rather than force the users to the keyboard and character input, the users can move the **mouse** as if they were pointing to a menu item on the screen with their fingers. With a little practice, most users find the mouse permits them to pick from menu items with speed and is faster than using the keyboard to type in commands. Figure 1-18 shows a typical mouse, so named because of its shape and the cable which resembles a mouse tail. Mice have 1 to 3 buttons on top for entering commands, and a ball that rolls inside a collar as it is moved across the table. The user moves a pointer on the screen to a predetermined target by moving the mouse on the table in the same direction. The pointer, often called the **cursor,** will stop when the mouse stops moving. Depressing a mouse button (clicking) while the cursor is in a menu box will activate that menu choice. The **joystick** is more difficult to use because the cursor will continue to move as long as the joystick is held in one direction.

The **trackball** is a kind of upside-down mouse mounted so that the ball rotates in a collar. The user can roll the ball with his hand in any direction, causing the cursor to move in that direction on the screen. The trackball saves desk space in that it needs no extra room, unlike the mouse. The **light pen** is a wand that the user touches against the screen to make menu choices. Special software is able to convert the touch into a row-and-column location. A more expensive kind of pointing device is the touch-sensitive screen which requires special hardware. The user can simply touch the screen with a finger and the location is noted for menu choices.

Printing Devices

While the video display is the primary output device, most users will need to print final results at the end of a session. Printers can be classified by print speed and print quality. Cost is usually dependent on these characteristics. Draft quality **dot matrix printers** are the mainstay of the microcomputer world (refer to Figure 1-19). Fast, reliable, and versatile, these printers can produce draft versions of documents and reports, as well as graphics. Most dot matrix printers have a dual-pass mode in which the characters are double-struck, producing

MICROCOMPUTER EQUIPMENT

19

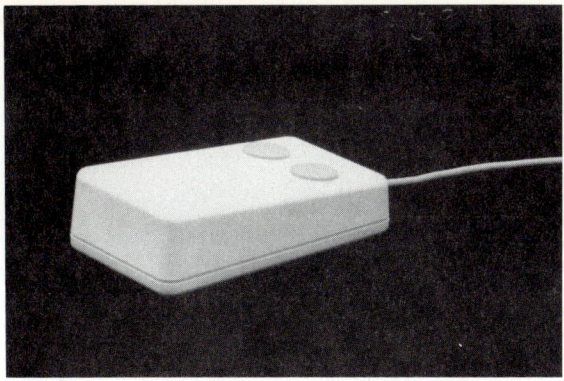

FIGURE 1-18

The Mouse, One Type of Pointing Device

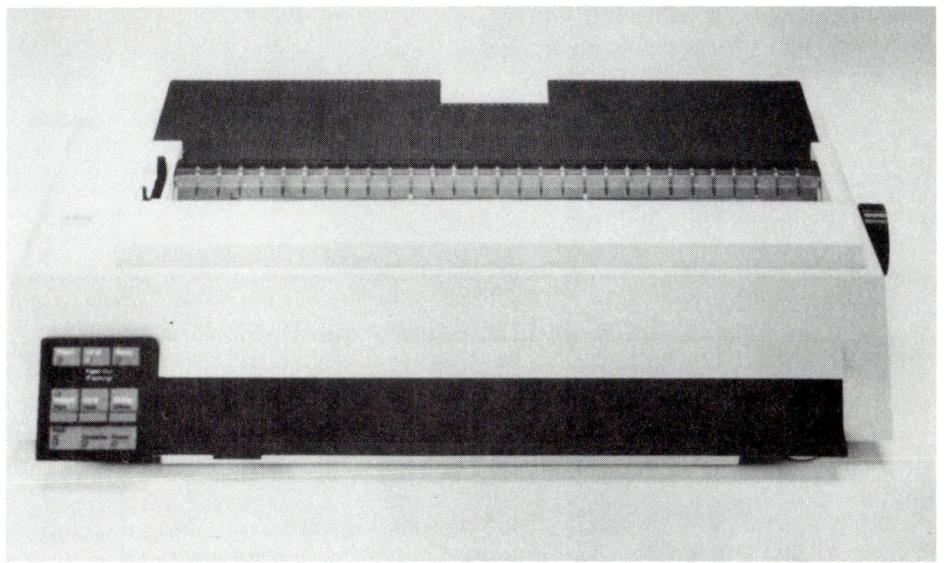

FIGURE 1-19

Dot Matrix Printer

near-letter quality, which is acceptable for most purposes. Dot matrix printers use a print head consisting of 9, 18, or 24 pins which are fired electrically against a ribbon and onto the paper, leaving an image of closely spaced dots. Print heads with more pins produce images with less space between dots, improving print quality. Printers with 24 pins cost $100-$200 more than 9-pin printers. Dot matrix printers can be programmed to produce different print styles or fonts by changing the spacing between characters and the dot pattern. Print speeds range from 100 to 400 characters per second in draft mode, and 20 to 120 characters per second in near-letter-quality mode.

A relatively recent technology offers high print quality and faster print speeds. **Ink jet printers** work by squirting a fine droplet of ink against the paper, making no impact and little noise. New models print up to 300 characters per second and offer high resolution graphics capabilities. These printers are also available in higher-cost color versions, providing full-color output at high speed.

The high end of microcomputer printers is the **laser printer.** Using a low-power laser and technology taken from the copier industry, the laser printer "paints" tiny dots on a light-sensitive drum which picks up black toner particles where it was exposed. Paper is given a small electrical charge, and the toner is transferred from the drum to the paper. The final step is to fuse the toner onto the paper by heating it as it exits the printer. Laser printers offer near-typeset

Chapter 1 — *Microcomputer Software Applications*

FIGURE 1-20

Two Models of the Hewlett-Packard Laserjet

quality at high dot resolutions, with 300 or more dots per inch. Because the printer uses the dot approach to forming characters, different print styles and sizes can be easily programmed and printed. Thus the laser printer is very versatile. Its graphics capabilities exceed those of dot matrix printers in quality and speed. Laser printers have enabled many users to do desktop publishing, an application where documents and reports can be composed and printed in final form without going to a typesetter. Two models of the Hewlett Packard Laserjet are shown in Figure 1-20.

For high quality printing, **daisy wheel printers** offer typewriter-like features but print much slower than ink jet or laser printers—15 to 70 characters per second. The name comes from the arrangement of the print wheel, with molded characters at the end of "petals" of a daisy. The printer works by rotating the print wheel until the correct character appears at the top, then striking the petal with a small hammer, pressing the "petal," or print element, against the ribbon and ultimately against the paper. The character is fully formed, not composed of dots, and resembles the output of an electric typewriter. Many electric typewriters now use daisy wheel print technology. Daisy wheel printers are not as versatile as other printers. Each typeface requires that the user change print wheels, and these printers cannot print graphics. Daisy wheel printers have become less popular since ink jet and laser printers were introduced.

Plotters are used to print graphic images; a variety of plotter types are shown in Figure 1-21. Moving a pen against the paper in the horizontal and vertical directions, the flatbed plotter is able to print images directly, much as a human would draw them. A plotter is rather slow at printing characters, but is able to draw arcs and diagonal lines directly and continuously without approximating the line with dots as the dot matrix, ink jet and laser printers would do. Some plotters are able to exchange pens for different line widths or more colors. Large-scale plotters move the pen in the vertical direction, and move the paper in the horizontal direction to create images. Plotters are useful for creating high-quality, colorful images for CAD (computer-assisted design) and for business graphics. Although plotters are relatively expensive, other kinds of printers can produce only single-color images. Plotters are

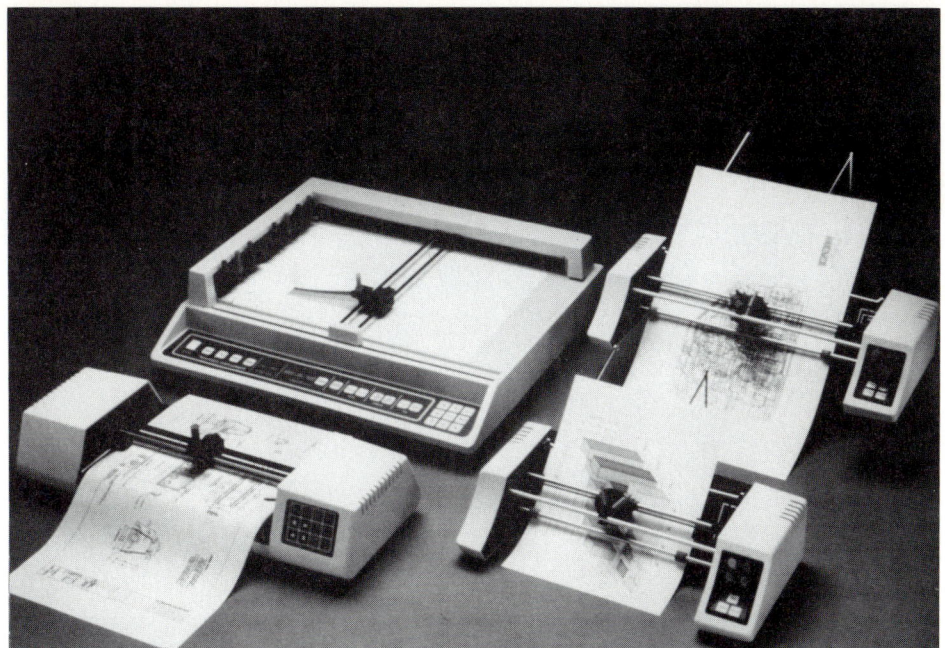

FIGURE 1-21

Four Types of Pen Plotters

sometimes used to create graphics on transparency film for presentations with an overhead projector.

Another kind of output device is the **film recorder.** This device produces high-quality color images on 35 millimeter slide film for presentations with a slide projector. Although expensive, these devices can produce better-quality images at higher resolutions and less distortion than is possible when taking a photograph of the monitor's screen. Some companies will accept print files by disk or via telephone, and can expose, develop, and return the slides by overnight express.

Connecting to Other Computers

Modems connect computers over telephone lines, permitting remote computing and exchange of data. A modem takes digital (0 or 1) signals from the computer and converts them to analog signals for transmission over the telephone. At the other end is a compatible modem which will convert the analog signal back into a digital format for the other computer. If you listen to a modem while it is transmitting, you'll hear a high-pitched whine, the carrier signal, signifying the two modems are communicating, and a series of whistles or tones representing the data being transferred between modems. The most popular speeds today are 1200 and 2400 bits per second, representing about 120–240 characters per second. Faster modems are available for high-volume situations. Voice-grade telephone circuits support speeds up to 9,600 bits per second.

Internal modems are built into an expansion card and are installed in an expansion slot in the system unit. They come with a built-in serial port. **External modems** connect to a serial port, so one must be available. External modems cost more because they need a case, an extra power supply, and a serial cable to connect to the computer (see Figure 1-22). The telephone line plugs directly into the modem, and most modems will automatically dial a number or answer the phone. No telephone is needed, although one can be plugged into the modem for normal use of the phone line. Most modems require that a private, single-line telephone connection be available; party lines are not allowed for

FIGURE 1-22

An External Modem

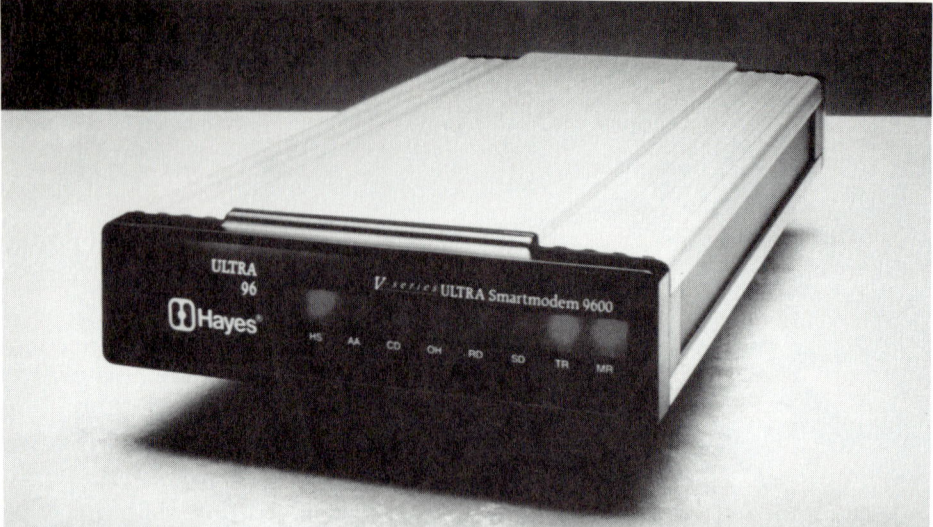

FIGURE 1-23

An Internal Modem with Communications Software

data communications. To use a modem with a PC, you must use communications software that converts the microcomputer into a terminal. Many modems come with free communications software; Figure 1-23 shows an internal modem package that includes software.

A new kind of modem is the **fax card,** which converts the PC into a facsimile machine. The fax card is able to receive fax messages over the telephone from other fax machines and stores them on the disk in graphics format. You can print them out on a compatible dot matrix or laser printer. You can create a message with a word processor, store it on the disk, then use the fax card to send the message to other fax machines. If the outgoing fax message is already in hard copy form, an **optical scanner** can be used to convert the image into a graphics format which is stored on the disk for transmission. The scanner reads the light and dark areas on a document, converting these areas to a digital (on or off) pattern of dots which can be manipulated by graphics programs.

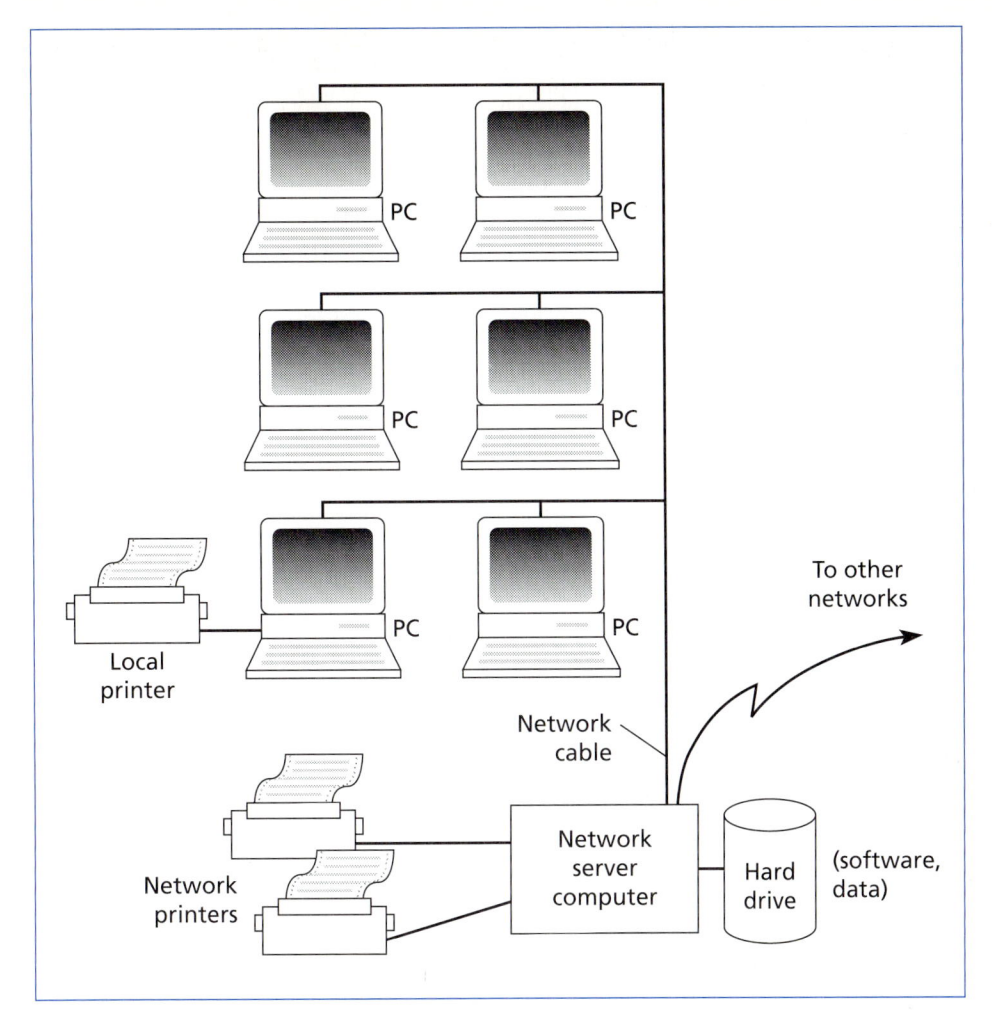

FIGURE 1-24

A Local Area Network (LAN) Used to Link Individual Microcomputers

A **local area network (LAN)** is a group of microcomputers connected to each other and to a **server computer,** sharing the server computer's hard disk and printers. LANs permit each user to access common programs and data. A high-end PC acts as a dedicated network file server and is connected to the shared hardware. Expensive resources such as laser printers, scanners, and tape drives may be used as though they were attached to each user's machine. Less expensive computers may be used as workstations because they can share the more expensive hardware attached to the server. Each station must have a **network interface card** connecting it to the network cable and a network software license. While personal computers are usually thought of as being independent, stand-alone machines, when included in a LAN they have the capability of shared computing power much greater than any individual component and at a fraction of the cost of a multi-user computer. Figure 1-24 shows a local area network used to link microcomputers in a classroom.

Local area networks carry some disadvantages. They can be complex to install and configure, requiring significant technical expertise. Because network users depend on the server and the network cable for access to data and resources, failures in these components can render the entire network inoperative. Stand-alone versions of some software packages will not run properly on a network, requiring either a network version or that the software be installed on each user's hard drive. Because network users have potential connections to data on the server, it is important to safeguard sensitive data with appropriate access privileges.

Expansion Alternatives

All IBM-compatible personal computers are capable of addressing at least 1 MB of memory; 640 KB of this is **conventional read/write RAM,** and the remainder **(high memory)** is used for the BIOS read-only memory (ROM), video memory, and hard disk controller ROM. For applications requiring extra memory, several types of RAM are available. **Expanded memory (EMS)** is used with 8088 processors to provide additional RAM—EMS RAM is "swapped" through a 64 KB-window above 640 KB, with conventional RAM in the first 640 KB. Applications programs like Lotus 1-2-3 that have been programmed to take advantage of expanded memory can handle larger problems. **Extended memory** is used with 80286, 80386, and 80486 processors which are capable of addressing more than 1 MB of RAM. Extended memory addresses begin at 1 MB. Figure 1-25 shows how memory is subdivided. Most memory expansion boards can be set up to handle conventional, expanded, or extended RAM. Some memory management programs can convert extended memory into expanded memory without changing the board's settings. For example, with an 80386 processor all expansion memory (beyond 640 KB) should be configured as extended memory; the memory manager program should be installed in the configuration file to enable the use of EMS memory.

Accelerator boards with a faster microprocessor can be added to older computers to speed up their operations. Rather than replace the entire computer, an 80286 processor can be added at a cost of 20% of the new computer. All the

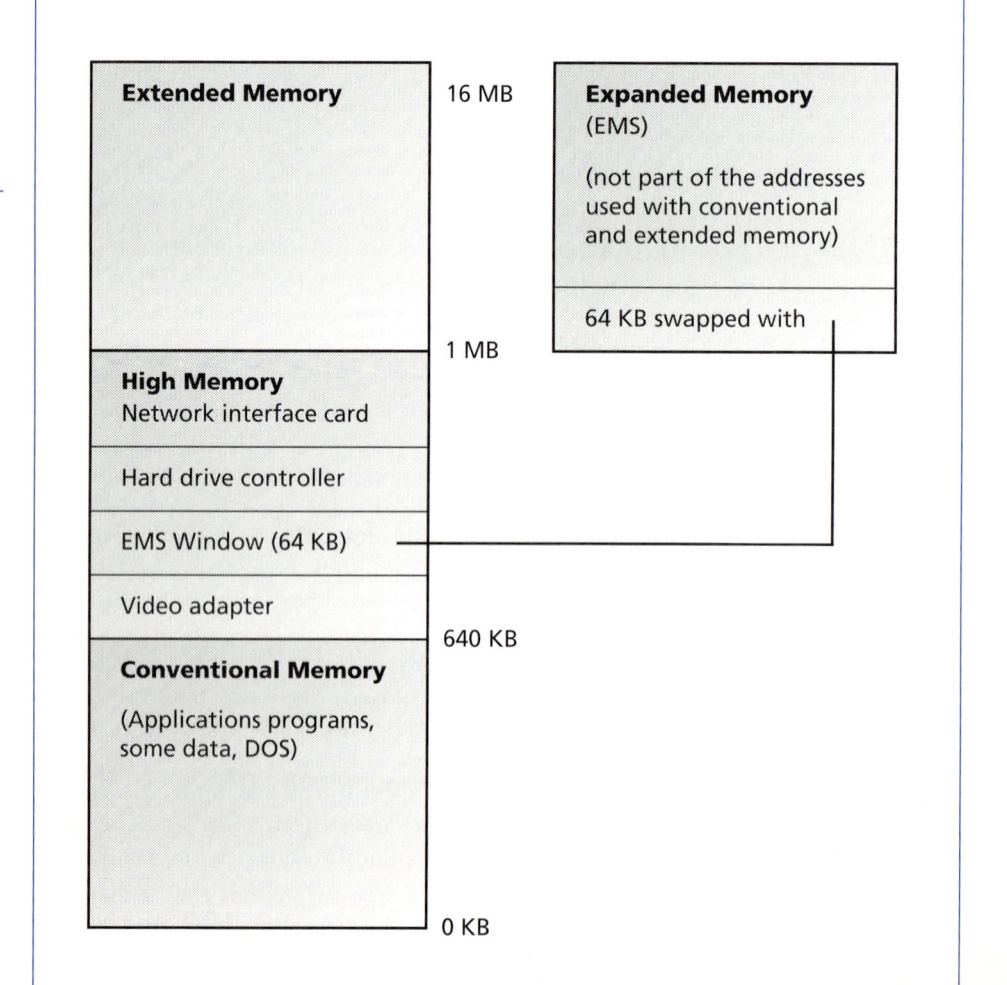

FIGURE 1-25

Memory Allocation in IBM-Compatible Computers

old peripherals can be used with the accelerator board, but there is a speed penalty because the new processor cannot take advantage of newer devices and a faster signal pathway or bus. For 80286 owners, accelerator boards featuring the 80386SX processor provide many advantages of the 386 chip without the full expense of replacing the entire computer. While 286 and 386 processors are able to access more memory than the 8088, most DOS programs are written for the 8088. The 286 and 386 simply run the same applications faster. This is likely to change in the future as more applications are written for the newer processors. The OS/2 operating system, Lotus 1-2-3 Release 3, and Microsoft's Excel spreadsheet are examples of software that will not operate on 8088 machines.

Miscellaneous Supplies and Accessories

Blank disks are required for all computers, even those equipped with hard disks. Diskette storage boxes are useful for keeping floppy disks organized and stored properly. Printers require paper and printer ribbons or ink cartridges. Laser printer toner cartridges must be replaced every 3000–5000 pages. Cables are needed to attach peripherals to the computer. Adapters are often needed to convert cables to fit a specific port. Many users struggle to find enough power outlets for their equipment—power strips with multiple outlets can solve that problem. Some power strips come with a **surge protector** in case there are power surges on the line. Caution is in order—never operate a computer during a thunderstorm. The best surge protection is to unplug the computer from all power outlets *and* unplug the telephone line from the modem. For critical applications, particularly in local area networks, you may install an **uninterruptible power supply (UPS)** to assure uninterrupted operations, even during a power outage.

CHAPTER REVIEW

Microcomputer Applications in Business

Microcomputers have dramatically increased our productivity. Word processing, electronic spreadsheets, database managers, graphics and desktop publishing applications make our work easier, improve accuracy, and save time. Telecommunications software allows us to connect our personal computers to larger computers and share data effectively. Recreational software provides entertainment and can help us learn.

Microcomputer Equipment

The microcomputer's system unit contains the microprocessor, primary memory, input/output ports, video adapter, and expansion slots. Secondary storage devices such as floppy and hard disk drives are used for permanent storage of data and programs. Other standard peripherals include the keyboard and video monitor. Accessories include a mouse and other pointing devices, a tape drive for disk backups, and a printer. Dot matrix printers provide good quality text and graphics at a reasonable price. For better print quality choose an ink jet or laser printer. Plotters produce high-quality graphical output in many colors. Film recorders produce images directly on 35 millimeter slide film for slide presentations.

Modems are used to connect computers over standard telephone lines. Local area networks provide the opportunity to share expensive hardware resources like laser printers and to share programs and data electronically.

When buying a microcomputer, analyze needs and applications before comparing prices. Mail order suppliers can save money but may not provide a suitable level of support. Choose your vendor carefully.

KEY TERMS

accelerator board	floppy disk	personal improvement
accounting applications	function keys	programs
backup device	game port	pixel
bit (**b**inary dig**it**)	graphing application	plotter
byte	programs	presentation graphics
cartridge (cassette tape)	hard disk	primary memory
color graphics adapter	high memory	programmers
(CGA)	I/O ports	project management
computer-assisted design	ink jet printer	software
(CAD) software	joystick	random access memory
conventional read/write	keyboard	(RAM)
RAM	laser printer	read-only memory (ROM)
cursor	light pen	recreational applications
daisy wheel printer	local area network (LAN)	serial port
database management	magnetic tape drive	server computer
software	microprocessor	signal bus
desktop publishing	modem (internal,	spreadsheet software
program	external)	surge protector
dot matrix printer	monochrome graphics	terminals
enhanced graphics adapter	(MGA) standard	trackball
(EGA)	motherboard	uninterruptible power
ergonomics	mouse	supply (UPS)
expanded memory (EMS)	network interface card	video adapter
expansion slots	numeric coprocessor chip	video graphics array VGA
extended memory	optical scanner	video monitor (display)
fax card	parallel port	word processing software
film recorder	PC keyboard	

DISCUSSION QUESTIONS

1. Contrast word processing, spreadsheet, and database management applications. When is each useful?

2. List at least three graphics applications packages.

3. Define desktop publishing.

4. List and describe the major components of the microcomputer system unit. What is the function of each?

5. Contrast floppy and hard disks. Are there situations in which the floppy disk is preferable? Explain.

6. Compare parallel and serial I/O ports. What peripherals are typically attached to the I/O ports?

7. List the advantages of each of the following printers: dot matrix, ink jet, laser, and plotter. When is each most likely to be used?

8. Describe the purpose of a modem. Can you think of reasons when an external modem is preferred to an internal modem that plugs into an expansion slot?

9. Compare the four kinds of memory: conventional RAM, expanded memory (EMS), extended memory, and ROM.

10. List at least three kinds of pointing devices. When are pointing devices more useful than the keyboard?

11. What is a fax card? How does it differ from an ordinary fax machine?

12. Describe a local area network and discuss the advantages of connecting microcomputers with a LAN.

13. What functions does an accelerator card perform?

14. Why is a numeric coprocessor useful for business computing?

15. Contrast mail order and local vendors for computer hardware and software. What are the advantages of each?

16. Contact a local computer store and find out the prices of blank floppy disks in the four standard sizes: 360 KB, 720 KB, 1.2 MB, and 1.44 MB. Calculate the cost per 1000 characters of storage. Which is most economical?

CHAPTER 1 PROJECT
COMPUTER CONSUMER GUIDE

For this project you should prepare a comprehensive report on at least three different personal computer models. Assume that the buyer is a college sophomore majoring in Business. The three models should be from the following categories:

- Laptop computer
- 8088-based desktop computer
- 80286-based desktop computer
- 80386-based desktop computer
- Macintosh computer

Before gathering data you should compile a list of features for the computer system. The list might include some of these items:

- Floppy disk size, capacity
- Hard disk capacity
- Amount of system RAM
- Speed of the microprocessor
- Type of video (video adapter, monitor)
- Type of keyboard (84 or 101 key)
- I/O ports
- Number and type of expansion slots

Peripheral devices on your list might include some of these items:

- Mouse
- Printer type, speed, print quality
- Modem (internal, external) and speed
- Miscellaneous equipment

Your report should include a comparison of product features, specifications and prices. Local computer stores and your college computer center may have special pricing programs for college students. Don't forget to ask about warranty and service information.

2

The Operating System: DOS and Utility Software

Objectives

After completing this chapter, you should be able to:

- Explain the purposes of an operating system.
- Describe the purpose of the special keys on the keyboard.
- List the steps necessary to boot the computer.
- Format a blank floppy disk.
- Discuss the elementary DOS file commands.
- Discuss hard disk subdirectory commands.
- Describe how to backup and restore a hard disk.
- Explain how to create a DOS command batch file.
- Describe the capabilities of utility programs.
- Discuss DOS shells for multitasking and OS/2.

INTRODUCTION

The **operating system** is a collection of system programs that manage the computer's resources. These programs perform such tasks as scanning the keyboard to see if a key has been pressed, displaying information on the monitor, sending characters to the printer as it is able to print them, handling disk allocation and read/write requests, performing housekeeping duties for applications programs, and communicating with the user through keyboard commands. You must have an operating system and it is usually purchased with the computer. The operating system for IBM compatibles is called **PC-DOS** or **MS-DOS;** only IBM brand computers use PC-DOS but for most purposes they are nearly identical. We will use the single abbreviation **DOS** (Disk Operating System) to describe both. This book will assume DOS version 3.3 or higher.

The operating system is stored in a number of places in a PC. A portion of it is permanently stored in the BIOS read-only memory, instantly available at power-up. **BIOS** stands for **Basic Input/Output System.** The purpose of the BIOS is to interpret the specific hardware configuration for DOS functions, allowing the same DOS to be used on almost any IBM-compatible computer. The BIOS in each IBM-compatible machine is slightly different, corresponding to design differences between machines. The remainder of the operating system is stored on the **boot disk,** the disk which contains DOS and is used to start up the computer; the term "boot" comes from "pull yourself up by your bootstraps."

The boot disk can be a floppy disk or a hard disk, and contains special programs stored in three files. Two of the files are hidden and don't appear in file (directory) listings. These two files must be placed in the boot tracks, the first two tracks of the disk. During boot-up they are automatically loaded into the RAM of the microcomputer by the BIOS program and, when they are successfully loaded, control is passed to these programs contained in the RAM. The third file, COMMAND.COM, is the command interpreter. Together, the two hidden files and COMMAND.COM comprise much of the operating system. Additional utility programs are stored as separate files, not part of the previous built-in set, to save memory space. These external commands are described later in the chapter, and summarized in the command summaries at the end of the chapter.

ELEMENTARY DOS COMMANDS

Getting Started: Booting Up the Computer

To start the computer, the system or boot diskette must be in the boot drive. This drive is the top or left drive in a floppy-disk machine, called the A drive. In a hard disk machine the boot disk is the internal drive, called the C drive. Because hard drive computers will boot automatically without inserting the floppy disk, we will describe the floppy configuration steps that the user must take and point out differences for hard drive machine users where needed. Network users may follow a different procedure, but in most cases it is similar to the hard disk procedure. Figure 2-1 shows the location of the boot drive in a typical floppy-drive PC.

Example: *Booting Up the Computer*

1. If you do not have a hard disk, insert the diskette into the A drive with the label up and the read/write window facing into the machine. 3.5-inch diskettes can be inserted only the proper way; the drive will grab the disk from the user and seat it if the disk is inserted correctly. Push the disk in slowly until it slips into place. The 5.25-inch diskette, however, *can* be inserted incorrectly, so take care to orient the disk properly. Before the diskette can be read, the door on a 5.25-inch drive must be closed after the disk is in place. Most 5.25-inch drives use a lever or door that is moved 90 degrees to close the opening. Practice opening and closing the door.

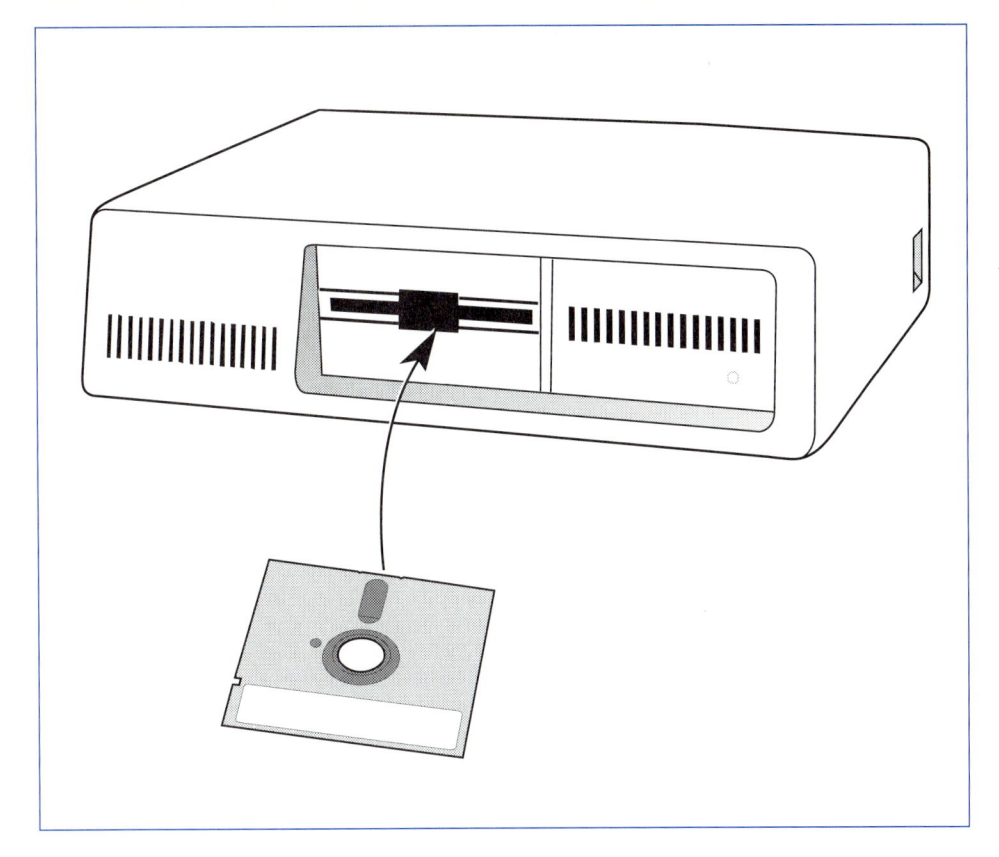

FIGURE 2-1

Location of the Boot Drive in a Typical Floppy-Drive PC

2. With the boot disk in position in the A drive, (not necessary with a hard disk computer—see step 5 below) turn on the power to the computer. The power switch is usually located in the right front or right side. Some computers also require that the monitor power switch be activated.

3. The PC will go through a power-on self-test (POST) procedure, taking several seconds. When it determines internal circuits and memory are functioning properly, the computer will begin to boot, reading the two hidden files from the boot disk. These files, called IO.SYS and MSDOS.SYS on most non-IBM brand machines, and IBMBIO.COM and IBMDOS.COM on IBM machines, contain the bulk of DOS. When the two files have loaded properly from the boot disk, those programs begin to execute.

4. If the wrong disk has been inserted in the boot drive, an error message like "Non-system disk—insert proper disk and press any key to continue" is displayed.

5. With a hard disk machine the boot disk is always in place inside the computer. When starting a hard disk computer, do *not* put any disk in the A drive before turning the power on.

6. The system will display the log-on message shown in Figure 2-2 and may ask the user to set the proper date and time. If the date and time are correct, press the Enter key; otherwise enter the correct values in the format shown on your screen.

7. Figure 2-3 shows the screen after the boot process has been completed. The A> prompt indicates that DOS is ready for you to enter a command or run a program. Hard disk computer users will see the C> prompt. Network users may see a C> prompt or the F> prompt.

FIGURE 2-2

DOS Initial Log-On Message

```
Current date is Tuesday  5-16-1989
Enter new date (mm-dd-yy):
```

FIGURE 2-3

Boot-up Screen for DOS 3.3

```
Current date is Tuesday  5-16-1989
Enter new date (mm-dd-yy):
Current time is  10:21:18.55
Enter new time:

Microsoft(R) MS-DOS(R)   Version 3.3
         (C)Copyright Microsoft Corp 1981-1987

A>
```

Changing the Date and Time

Many personal computers have a built-in battery-operated clock, and the current date and time are displayed during the boot procedure. Because date and time information are maintained for files that are stored on the disk, you should always enter the correct date and time. If the wrong date or time is entered, you can use the DOS **DATE** and **TIME** commands to make changes. These commands display the current date and time, and provide a guide for you to enter correct values. With most computers, these commands do not *permanently* change the date or time, merely the in-memory values. Because it varies from model to model, you should refer to the computer operations manual for the command that will update your computer's internal clock.

At the DOS prompt type **DATE** and you will see the following message from DOS. Input the correct date in the same manner as the current value.

```
Current date is Tue 5-16-1989
Enter new date (mm-dd-yy): _
```

Changing Disk Drives

The DOS prompt indicates the **default disk drive,** and signifies that you may enter commands. Any disk command issued will apply to the default drive, unless the command includes a different drive designator. Disk drives are lettered, starting with A and ending with the last drive. Hard disk users will probably see C> in the prompt line, indicating the default drive is C, the hard drive. Network users will find drive letters beyond A, B, and C, indicating connection to the network server's hard disks. Floppy-disk users see the default drive as A. To change the default drive, simply enter the desired drive letter followed by a colon, then press **Enter.** For example, **B:** will cause the default drive to become B, the second floppy drive. When changing to a new drive, be certain there is a diskette in the drive first or you will get a "Drive not ready" error message. In this case, place the disk in the drive and press **R** to retry the command.

Removing the Diskette

For computers with a 3.5-inch drive, press the small button on the face of the drive to eject the diskette. To release a 5.25-inch disk, open the drive door or lever and pull out the diskette. Some drives have a small spring which will eject the disk when the door is opened.

The Keyboard and Correcting Mistakes

The original IBM PC and XT models came with the standard 84-key keyboard with function keys at the left side, pictured in Figure 2-4. The IBM AT and later models came with the enhanced keyboard, with function keys across the top and an extra set of cursor control keys, allowing simultaneous use of the numeric keypad and arrow keys. An enhanced keyboard is pictured in Figure 2-5. Commands are entered much as you would with an electric typewriter. After you have typed the command, press the **Enter** key to execute that command. The Enter key may be labelled with an L-shaped left arrow instead of the word "Enter."

DOS normally requires that you press the **Enter** key to complete a response or command, providing an opportunity to make changes before the Enter key is pressed. If you make a mistake in typing, erase any incorrect characters with the **Backspace** key, located above the **Enter** key at the upper right side of the keyboard. The Backspace key may be designated by a left-facing arrow, or the abbreviation "BkSp." To make a correction, backspace until you erase the incorrect character, then retype the remainder of the response or command correctly, and press the Enter key.

Some other keys of interest include the **Tab** key, sometimes labelled with two opposite facing arrows. The Tab key works in the same way as on a typewriter, moving the cursor over several spaces (usually five) to the right. Some software provides for a backwards Tab, by pressing **Shift-Tab.** The four arrow keys on the numeric keypad will move the cursor around the screen in the desired direction, although only the left arrow functions in DOS, where it acts as a destructive Backspace, erasing characters as the cursor moves left. In an application like

FIGURE 2-4

The 84-Key PC Keyboard

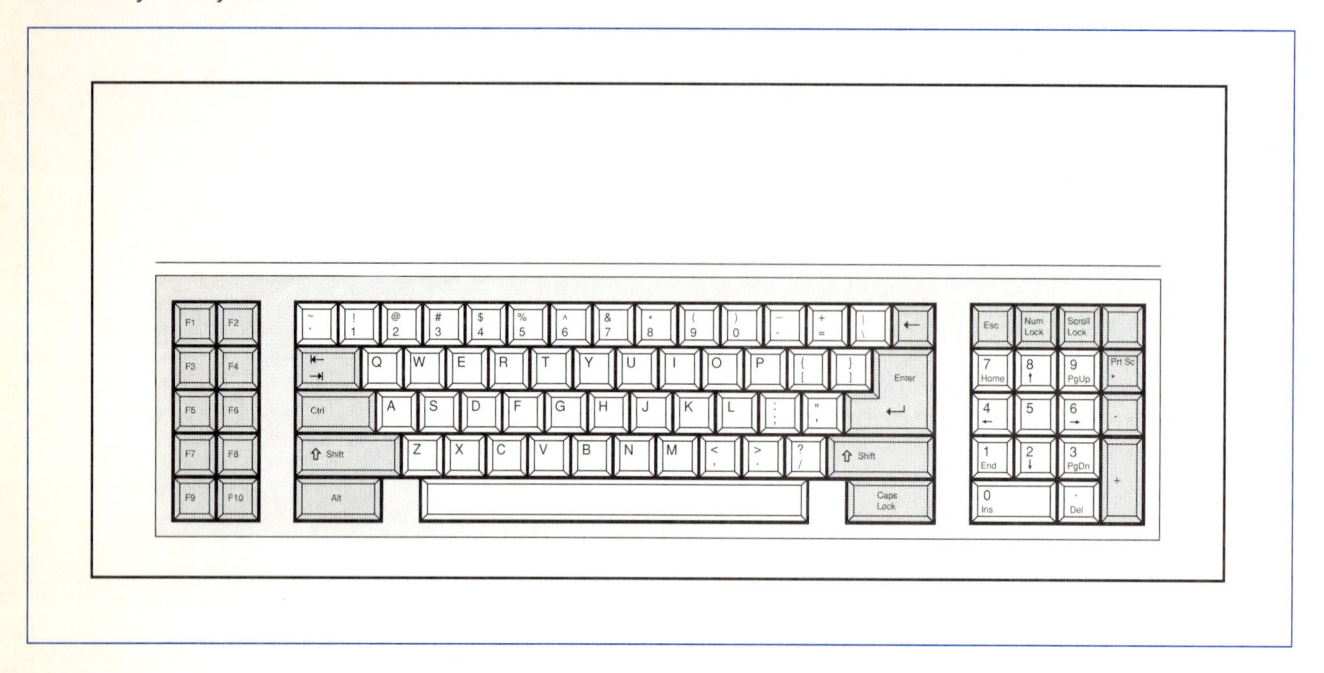

FIGURE 2-5

An Enhanced Keyboard

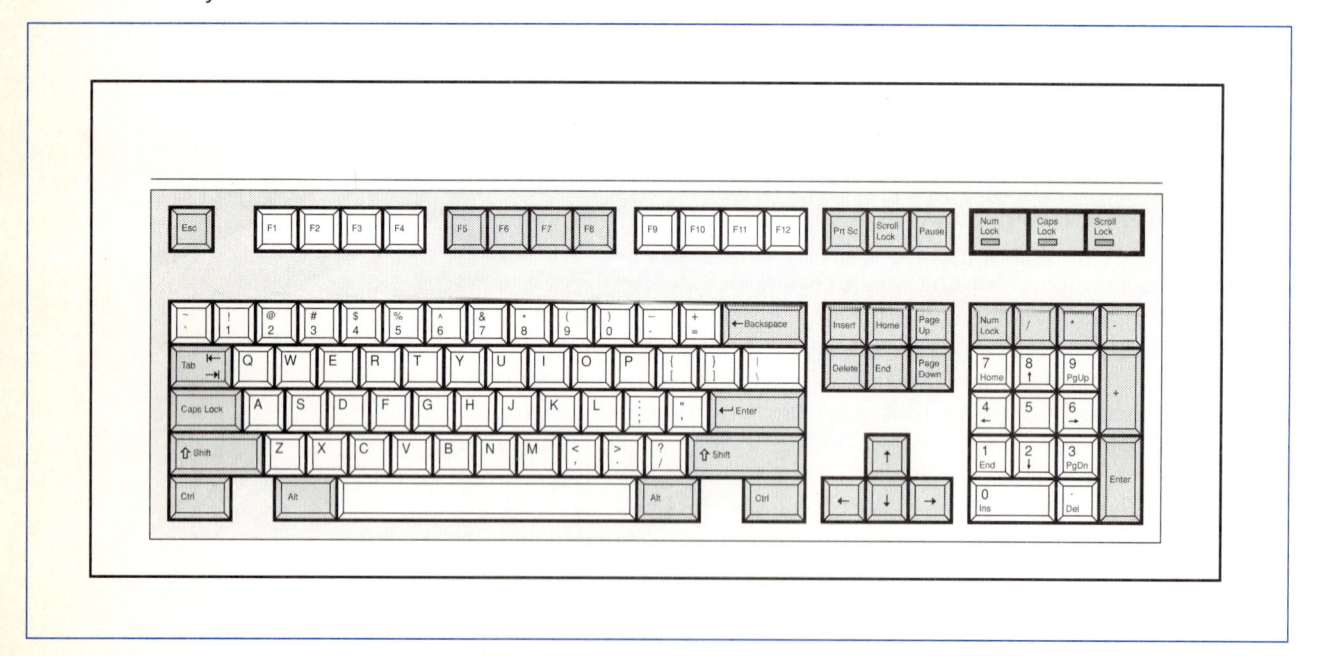

WordPerfect, these keys move the cursor without deleting any characters. In Lotus 1-2-3 the arrow keys move the cursor to new locations, again without erasing any characters.

The numeric keypad normally is set for cursor control, using the lower symbol on each key. However, if the **NumLock** key is pressed once, the keypad functions are shifted to the upper symbol on each key, representing the numbers and decimal point. Most keyboards have a **light-emitting diode (LED)** to indicate whether the keypad is set for numbers or cursor control. **CapsLock** causes a capital letter to be entered when an alphabetic key is pressed. It has no effect on other keys; it is not a Shift Lock key. A second press of CapsLock returns the keyboard to normal lowercase mode.

The other keys on the keypad (**Home, End, PgUp,** and **PgDn**) have different functions depending on which application is running. These keys are used to move the cursor around the screen in larger jumps than the arrow keys provide. The **Del** key is used to delete the character beneath the cursor, but normally has no function in DOS. The **Ins** key is a **toggle** key—one key press switches the setting and the second key press switches it back to the original setting. The **Ins** key switches the PC between overtype and insert modes. In overtype mode, new characters typed in replace characters already in that screen position. In insert mode, new characters typed in "push" existing characters over, making room for the new ones to be inserted. The function of these two keys depends on the specific application package.

Warm Boot: Restarting the Computer with Ctrl-Alt-Del

There are several other useful key combinations available through DOS. The **warm boot** sequence of **Ctrl-Alt-Del** will cause the computer to restart and go through a normal boot process. The warm boot is quick because it does not go through a memory check as is done when the machine is powered up. You may need to perform a warm boot if a program "hangs," or is no longer working. To perform a warm boot, hold down the **Ctrl** and **Alt** keys, then depress the **Del** key. A **cold boot** occurs when the machine's power switch is turned on, or when the Reset button is pressed. If Ctrl-Alt-Del has no effect, press the Reset button. If your machine does not have a Reset button, turn the power off and wait until the disk drives stop spinning (no noise is coming from the system unit). Then turn the power back on and the computer will boot again.

Screen Print Commands

Each of the applications packages has its own printing menus and procedures. However, the PrtSc key has two printing functions within DOS.

- When used in combination with the Ctrl key, **Ctrl-PrtSc** will toggle the printer on so that anything that is subsequently displayed on the screen will also be printed on the printer. This is a useful way to get a printed copy of a disk directory, or to document a sequence of complicated commands. Press **Ctrl-PrtSc** again to disable the print echo.

- **Shift-PrtSc** will cause a "snapshot" of the screen's present contents to be sent to the printer. Only text mode screens can be captured in this fashion unless the DOS GRAPHICS command is used first. Most screens in DOS, WordPerfect, Lotus 1-2-3, and dBASE appear in text mode. On enhanced keyboards you may press **PrtSc** or **Shift-PrtSc**.

Example: *Printing the Screen's Contents*

1. Insert your data disk in the A drive, type **DIR A:** and press **Enter**.

2. Make sure the printer is attached and turned on.

3. When the DOS prompt reappears, press **Shift-PrtSc** to copy the contents of the screen to your printer.

Working with Files

File Names and Terminology

DOS **file names** are used when retrieving or saving files on the disk. File names consist of several parts: optional drive letter and optional subdirectory path, the name, and an optional file extension. If present, the drive letter is followed by a colon and gives the drive on which the file is located. Subdirectories are discussed later in this chapter. The **name** is descriptive and can be from one to eight characters long. Allowable characters are A–Z, a–z, 0-9, and $ % ' - @ { } ~ ` ! # ( ) &. The name is chosen by the user and should describe its contents. The **extension** is optional, and contains from one to three characters, preceded by a period. Some programs add an extension to file names while others let the user pick one if desired. Figure 2-6 shows a sample of some standard file extensions and their meaning.

In DOS, files with .COM and .EXE extensions represent executable programs, and can be executed just by typing the file name. Files with a .BAT (batch) extension represent sets of user commands that have been stored in a file for later execution. These may also be executed by giving the file name. Many software packages use .BAT files to install software and start the program with ease. Figure 2-7 shows examples of valid and invalid DOS file names.

FIGURE 2-6

Sample File Extensions

Extension	Program	Meaning
.EXE	DOS	Executable program
.COM	DOS	Executable program
.BAT	DOS	Batch file of DOS commands
.WPM	WordPerfect	Macro file
.BK!	WordPerfect	Backup file
.WK1	Lotus 1-2-3	Spreadsheet file
.PIC	Lotus 1-2-3	Graph image file
.PRN	Lotus 1-2-3	Text file
.DBF	dBASE	Database file
.MDX	dBASE	Multiple index file
.PRG	dBASE	Program file
.CHT	Harvard Graphics	Chart file

FIGURE 2-7

Examples of Valid and Invalid DOS File Names

Valid File Names	Invalid File Names	Reasons
DEMO.BAT	FILE 1.JKL	Space in file name
ACE123.XYZ	INCOMESTMT.FIL	Name > 8 characters
FILENAME.EXT	DESKTOP.FILE	Extension > 3 chars.
A:199.000	BJM.123.456	Two periods in ext.
MCTAVISH	CFILENAME.EXT	No : after C, 9 characters long
BUDGET89.WK1		
1239-16.DBF		
C:WP{WP}.SET		
WP.EXE		

Wildcard File Name Templates

When copying or deleting files, the file names may be spelled out precisely, or an abbreviation for the file name may be created using a DOS **wildcard template.** The * and ? are special wildcard characters which allow matching of any character. The ? represents a single character position, while the * represents any characters which follow. For example, ABC?F.EXT would be matched by ABCDF.EXT, ABC9F.EXT and ABC-F.EXT, but not by ABCDE.EXT or ABCF.EXT. WP*.* would be matched by any file starting with the letters WP. WP{WP}.SET, WP.EXE and WP{WP}US.THS all match. The ? may be used in any position in the name or extension, but the * must always come at the end of the name or the extension. Wildcards are especially useful when referring to an entire group of files with a single command. For example, you could copy all of the WordPerfect program files that begin with WP with the command, **COPY WP*.*.**

Initializing a Blank Disk: FORMAT

Before a blank floppy diskette can be used to store data, it must be **formatted.** The formatting process scans the disk for bad data storage regions and **initializes** the disk's file directory and file allocation table (FAT). The FAT tells the computer where on the disk each file is stored. This command's syntax is

```
FORMAT drive: /switches
```

The switches include formatting a low-density 5.25"-disk in a high-capacity disk drive (/4), adding a volume label of up to 11 characters (/V), and making this a system (boot) disk (/S). The boot switch must appear last in the list, if used. Other FORMAT switches are described in your DOS manual. The volume label is recorded magnetically in the disk's directory. You should also place a sticky label on the disk identifying its content and giving your name. Unless you use a felt-tipped pen, never write directly on this sticky label when it is attached to the disk—write on the label, then peel it off and affix to the diskette. Examples of the FORMAT command include:

FORMAT A: /V   Format a blank disk in drive A to its standard capacity. If drive A is a high-capacity drive (1.2 MB or 1.44 MB), high-capacity media must be used. DOS will ask you to provide a volume label (up to 11 characters) which is displayed whenever the disk's directory is listed. DOS 4.01 will automatically use **/V** by default.

FORMAT B: /4   Format a 5.25-inch blank disk in drive B to low-density capacity (360 KB). The /4 is not necessary if the B drive is a 360 KB drive.

FORMAT A: /N:9   Format a 720 KB diskette (using 9 sectors per track) on a 3.5-inch high-capacity A drive. The /**N:9** is not necessary if drive A is a 720 KB drive.

FORMAT A: /S   Prepare a system (boot) disk in drive A using standard drive capacity.

Example: *Formatting a Blank Floppy Disk*

Before trying this example, you will need to obtain a blank disk of the size and capacity appropriate for your computer system. For this example we will assume you are formatting a diskette that matches your drive. (Remember that formatting a disk will erase any information previously stored on it, so if you don't have a blank floppy, be sure to pick a disk that you wish to erase.)

1. Make sure the computer has started up, with the A> or C> prompt displayed on the screen.

2. Next issue the command **FORMAT A:** and press the **Enter** key. We will not place the DOS boot files on this disk, leaving more room to store programs and data.

3. DOS will next instruct you to insert the blank floppy disk into drive A. If you issued the wrong command, pressing **Ctrl-C** will abort the command and return you to the DOS prompt. Make sure the disk is *not* write protected:

   - On 5.25-inch disks, remove the tape covering the slot on the right edge of the diskette.
   - With 3.5-inch diskettes, slide the small plastic cover in the disk's lower-left corner so that the write-protect window is closed.

4. When prompted, properly insert the blank disk in drive A and close the door. [Note: 3.5-inch drive doors do not have to be closed.] For most disk drives, you will place the thumb of your right hand on the diskette's label and insert the sliding window edge (for 3.5-inch disks) or read/write window (for 5.25-inch disks) into the drive, label up. 3.5-inch diskettes have a small arrow in the upper left corner to help you orient the disk.

5. Press **Enter** to begin the formatting process. The disk drive activity light will indicate that the disk in that drive is being accessed. After a few moments, DOS may display the progress of the format.

6. When the formatting is finished, a "Format complete" message will be given, along with the space available on the disk. [Note: if there are fewer bytes available than total disk space, DOS may have found bad spots on the disk and locked them out. DOS 4.01 users will see additional information about the number of allocation units on the disk and the volume serial number.]

7. At the question "Format another (Y/N)?" reply **N** and press **Enter** to return to the DOS prompt. Figure 2-8 shows a similar command.

The Disk Directory

The **disk directory** contains information about the files stored on that disk. File name, file size bytes (characters), and date and time of the file's creation are displayed for the user. The directory also contains information about where on the disk that file is stored, and the status of the **file attributes,** but this information is not displayed to the user. A file directory of the DOS 3.3 boot disk is shown in Figure 2-9. DOS 4.01 adds the volume serial number to the display.

To display the directory for the default drive, enter the **DIR** command. The disk's **volume label,** MS330PP01, is shown at the beginning of the listing. The remainder of the entries are data or program files. The date and time that each file was created or last changed is shown in the last two columns of the directory listing. The final entry displays the amount of free space remaining on the disk, approximately 5,000 characters in this instance.

ELEMENTARY DOS COMMANDS

```
C:\>FORMAT A: /N:9
Insert new diskette for drive A:
and strike ENTER when ready

Format complete

    730112 bytes total disk space
     20480 bytes in bad sectors
    709632 bytes available on disk

Format another (Y/N)?n
C:\>
```

— This disk has some bad sectors.

FIGURE 2-8

Formatting a Blank Floppy Disk (720K Format)

```
Volume in drive A is MS330PP01
Directory of  A:\

4201     CPI    17089   7-24-87   12:00a
5202     CPI      459   7-24-87   12:00a
ANSI     SYS     1647   7-24-87   12:00a
APPEND   EXE     5794   7-24-87   12:00a
ASSIGN   COM     1530   7-24-87   12:00a
ATTRIB   EXE    10656   7-24-87   12:00a
CHKDSK   COM     9819   7-24-87   12:00a
COMMAND  COM    25276   7-24-87   12:00a
COMP     COM     4183   7-24-87   12:00a
COUNTRY  SYS    11254   7-24-87   12:00a
DISKCOMP COM     5848   7-24-87   12:00a
DISKCOPY COM     6264   7-24-87   12:00a
DISPLAY  SYS    11259   7-24-87   12:00a
DRIVER   SYS     1165   7-24-87   12:00a
EDLIN    COM     7495   7-24-87   12:00a
EXE2BIN  EXE     3050   7-24-87   12:00a
FASTOPEN EXE     3888   7-24-87   12:00a
FDISK    COM    48919   7-24-87   12:00a
FIND     EXE     6403   7-24-87   12:00a
FORMAT   COM    11671   7-24-87   12:00a
GRAFTABL COM     6136   7-24-87   12:00a
GRAPHICS COM    13943   7-24-87   12:00a
JOIN     EXE     9612   7-24-87   12:00a
KEYB     COM     9041   7-24-87   12:00a
LABEL    COM     2346   7-24-87   12:00a
MODE     COM    15440   7-24-87   12:00a
MORE     COM      282   7-24-87   12:00a
NLSFUNC  EXE     3029   7-24-87   12:00a
PRINT    COM     8995   7-24-87   12:00a
RECOVER  COM     4268   7-24-87   12:00a
SELECT   COM     4132   7-24-87   12:00a
SORT     EXE     1946   7-24-87   12:00a
SUBST    EXE    10552   7-24-87   12:00a
SYS      COM     4725   7-24-87   12:00a
       34 File(s)     5120 bytes free
```

FIGURE 2-9

Directory of the DOS 3.3 Boot Disk

FIGURE 2-10

Wide Directory of the DOS 3.3 Boot Disk

```
A>DIR /W

 Volume in drive A is MS330PP01
 Directory of  A:\

4201     CPI     5202     CPI     ANSI     SYS     APPEND   EXE     ASSIGN   COM
ATTRIB   EXE     CHKDSK   COM     COMMAND  COM     COMP     COM     COUNTRY  SYS
DISKCOMP COM     DISKCOPY COM     DISPLAY  SYS     DRIVER   SYS     EDLIN    COM
EXE2BIN  EXE     FASTOPEN EXE     FDISK    COM     FIND     EXE     FORMAT   COM
GRAFTABL COM     GRAPHICS COM     JOIN     EXE     KEYB     COM     LABEL    COM
MODE     COM     MORE     COM     NLSFUNC  EXE     PRINT    COM     RECOVER  COM
SELECT   COM     SORT     EXE     SUBST    EXE     SYS      COM
       34 File(s)      5120 bytes free

A>
```

Listing File Names: DIR

The directory list command **DIR** can be used to list all files, or can show a subset. DIR B: will list only the files stored on the disk in the B drive. DIR WP* will show all files beginning with WP on the default (A) drive. An abbreviated directory listing showing only file name and remaining space is available with the **DIR /W** command, the /W meaning "wide." The same directory from above, but with the wide listing, looks like that of Figure 2-10.

The **DIR /P** command is used to automatically pause the directory listing when the screen is filled. Pressing any key will display the next page of file information.

Copying a File: COPY

The **COPY** command is used to copy a file from one disk to another, or to make a new copy on the same disk with a different name. The format of this command is:

    COPY [d:]oldfilename [d:]newfilename

If you include a new drive letter without a newfilename, the file is copied with the same name onto the new drive. The [d:] parameters are used to optionally provide the drive letter for each file. If no drive letter is specified, DOS assumes the file is located on the default drive. Some examples:

COPY ALPHA B:	Copies a file called ALPHA from the default drive to the B drive using the same name.
COPY B:BUDGET C:TEMP	Copies a file called BUDGET from the B drive onto the C drive as TEMP.
COPY *.* B:	Copies all files from the default drive to the B drive.

ELEMENTARY DOS COMMANDS

```
C>TYPE AUTOEXEC.BAT
PATH C:\DOS;C:\WP;C:\DBASE;C:\PCPLUS;C:\
PROMPT $P$G
MSMOUSE
MIRROR
SETUP HP.PMF
C>
```

FIGURE 2-11

Displaying the Contents of AUTOEXEC.BAT File with TYPE

COPY OLDONE NEWONE Copies a file called OLDONE under the new name NEWONE on the default drive.

COPY P&L8? C: Copies all five-character file names starting with P&L8 onto the C drive. Any character matches the ? in the template.

Displaying the Contents of a File: TYPE

The **TYPE** command is used to display the contents of a text file on the screen. (It gives unpredictable results on other file types such as WordPerfect, Lotus 1-2-3, or dBASE files.) For example, the command **TYPE AUTOEXEC.BAT** will display the contents of the AUTOEXEC.BAT file, as shown in Figure 2-11, although your AUTOEXEC.BAT file will probably not be the same.

Example: *Display the AUTOEXEC.BAT File*

1. If you booted from a floppy, make sure that the boot disk you used is in the A drive. Issue the command **TYPE AUTOEXEC.BAT** and press **Enter.**

   OR

1. If you booted from the hard drive, enter the command **TYPE C:\AUTOEXEC.BAT** and press the **Enter** key.

2. If there is an AUTOEXEC.BAT file on your boot disk, its contents will be displayed on the screen.

Printing the File: PRINT

While the TYPE command displays the contents of a text file on the screen, the **PRINT** command will send the file to the printer for hard copy. PRINT works in the background, sending characters to the printer as it is able to print them, while you can continue working with the PC on another task. The format of this command is

```
PRINT filename /switches
```

Switches include such features as number of copies to print, which printer to send the file to, line length, page length, and more. See your DOS manual for details.

PRINT C:LETTER.TXT　　Will send file LETTER.TXT to the default printer.

PRINT BID C:PAYLIST　　Will print files BID and PAYLIST on the default printer.

Removing a File: DEL

To delete a file, use the DOS **DEL** or **ERASE** command. DEL permits you to delete a single file, or a group of files by specifying a wildcard template. Every file can be deleted with the *.* template, but care should be given when using this command. It is sometimes possible to "undelete" a file using a utility program such as PC-TOOLS or Norton Utilities, but only if no other files have been created or altered on that disk since the deletion. See the last section of this chapter for details.

Examples of the DEL command are shown below.

DEL SHARKS.TXT　　Deletes file SHARKS.TXT from the default drive.

DEL B:*.DBF　　Delete all files with a .DBF extension from the B drive.

DEL A:*.*　　An extremely dangerous command, this will erase all files in the current directory from the A drive. DOS will ask you to confirm all *.* deletions.

Changing a File's Name: RENAME

The **RENAME** command is used to change a given file's name to something new. The format is

```
RENAME oldfilename newfilename
```

Only one file may be renamed at a time, so wildcards are not used. RENAME may be abbreviated as REN for faster typing.

RENAME FREDDY JOHNNY　　Renames FREDDY on the default drive to new name JOHNNY.

DOS Disk Commands

Copying an Entire Disk: DISKCOPY

The **COPY A:*.* B:** command can be used to copy all files from one drive to another, but the **DISKCOPY** command is more efficient. This command copies all information between two compatible (same density, size) disks, track by track. Several files are copied at once, being stored in RAM, to reduce the number of disk swaps. The syntax of this command is

```
DISKCOPY sourcedrive: targetdrive: /switches
```

The sourcedrive is typically A: or B:, and the targetdrive may be the same drive. If you specify only one drive, it is used both as source and destination, and DOS prompts you when to switch disks. This version is most often used when there is only a single floppy drive in the system, or when the two drives are different types. DISKCOPY will automatically format the destination disk if it is not already formatted, saving time. The most often used switch is /V, verify that all files are copied properly. Examples of this command:

DISKCOPY A: B: Copy all information from drive A to drive B. Source disk goes in drive A and target disk in drive B.

DISKCOPY A: A: /V Copy all information from the source disk to the target disk, verifying that the two disks agree. DOS prompts the user to alternately place source or target disk in the A drive.

Comparing Two Disks: DISKCOMP

DISKCOMP is used to compare two disks to see if they contain the same data. An explanatory message is given if the disks are not the same.

```
DISKCOMP sourcedrive: targetdrive:
```

DISKCOMP compares the disks track by track, reporting any differences. It will only compare compatible media, meaning the size and capacity must be the same. Examples:

DISKCOMP A: B: Compare disks in drives A and B.

DISKCOMP A: A: Compare disks using only drive A; DOS will prompt the user to switch disks as needed.

Checking the Disk: CHKDSK

Occasionally the disk's directory may be logically damaged. That is, the directory does not accurately depict the location of files stored on that disk. The most common cause for such errors is removing the disk at the wrong time. Stray magnetic fields may also induce random errors on the disk. The **CHKDSK** command will check the directory and file allocation table (FAT) for consistency, and report any errors found. It will also show statistics about disk usage, space remaining, and RAM usage. The format for this command is:

```
CHKDSK drive: /switch
```

Directory errors are serious and may jeopardize the contents of a disk. It is a good idea to run this command frequently, and fix any errors that are found. In particular, you should not continue to use a disk with directory errors because new files saved on the disk may not be safely stored. It is also a good idea to make more than one copy of important work—keep current copies of your files on two diskettes. Output from the CHKDSK command on a hard drive might look like Figure 2-12. DOS 4.01 displays some additional information.

The /F switch instructs DOS to attempt to correct the errors it encounters. Do not try to use a disk with a damaged directory—seek assistance when your disk has CHKDSK problems. Do not use the CHKDSK command on a computer attached to a local area network because it does not work with network drives. CHKDSK errors generally indicate lost data. Disk repair utility programs such as Mace Utilities and Norton Utilities may help in recovering lost data.

FIGURE 2-12

Status Report from the CHKDSK Command

```
C>CHKDSK

Volume HARD_DRIVE  created Sep 17, 1988  4:54p

 33435648 bytes total disk space
    47104 bytes in 4 hidden files
    96256 bytes in 32 directories
 28776448 bytes in 1440 user files
    10240 bytes in bad sectors
  4505600 bytes available on disk

   655360 bytes total memory
   540288 bytes free
```

Example: Checking Your Disk

Make sure your data disk is in the A drive (or whatever is appropriate for your computer).

1. Enter the command **CHKDSK A:** and press **Enter.** DOS will examine the disk's directory and display a report of disk space and RAM usage.

WORKING WITH HARD DISKS

A hard disk offers a large storage space and much quicker retrieval and storage of files without the disk swapping that occurs with floppies. Many software packages require use of a hard disk drive. WordPerfect is distributed on 10 or more floppy disks and works more effectively on a hard drive machine. The procedure to install, or initialize, and implement a hard disk drive is shown in Figure 2-13. See your DOS manual for specific instructions.

Using Subdirectories

Because of the immense storage space of a hard disk, from 50 to hundreds of times more storage than on a floppy disk, the storage space should be well organized. The DOS subdirectory technique is used to subdivide the hard disk (or a floppy disk) into smaller, more manageable sets of files. A **subdirectory** is a grouping of related files and is specified by the user. The **root directory,** designated with a back-slash (\), is the beginning point for subdivision. The root directory contains the system tracks and other start-up files. Each software application is typically given its own subdirectory when the package is installed. Thus to use a particular package you should first change to that subdirectory, then execute the program.

Some packages create further subdirectories within the application subdirectory to store certain files. For example, you might have a WordPerfect subdirectory called WP51 and within it, have subdirectories called LEARN and

Three steps are required to prepare the hard drive for use after it is physically installed in the system unit:

- The DOS **FDISK** command will **partition** the drive for use with DOS, as described in the instructions that accompany the drive. This step involves assigning certain cylinders of the drive as a DOS partition (usually the C drive), and setting up the boot partition. The FDISK program will provide default values which are usually correct.

- After partitioning, **low-level formatting** (sometimes called preformatting) is done. This step may be done automatically, or you may have to go through another utility program, depending on specific hard drive and controller used. This step also permits you to enter any bad cluster numbers — DOS will automatically lock these clusters out and not use them for storage. The CHKDSK command's status report includes a line for "Bad Sectors."

- The third step involves using the FORMAT program to **initialize** the drive. The /S switch is chosen to copy the hidden system files onto the drive and make it ready as a boot drive.

FIGURE 2-13

Steps in Initializing a Hard Disk Drive

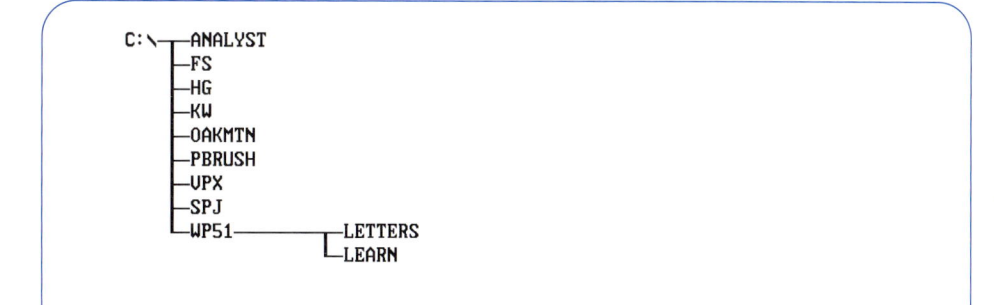

```
C:\──┬──ANALYST
     ├──FS
     ├──HG
     ├──KW
     ├──OAKMTN
     ├──PBRUSH
     ├──UPX
     ├──SPJ
     └──WP51──┬──LETTERS
              └──LEARN
```

FIGURE 2-14

Graphical View of Subdirectory Structure

LETTERS. When viewed, the subdirectory organization resembles a tree lying on its side. The DOS **TREE** command will display the directory structure in a hard-to-read fashion. There are better utility programs for this, such as Norton Utilities. DOS 4 presents a graphical view of the subdirectory structure, shown in Figure 2-14.

Making a New Subdirectory: MKDIR or MD

To create a new subdirectory, use the DOS **MKDIR** command, abbreviated **MD.** This will create a subdirectory with the specified name within the *current* directory. This command does *not* change to the new subdirectory, however. Use the **CD** command to change to a specified directory. Directory names follow DOS file name rules without extensions. At the C> prompt, type:

MD WORDPROC   Create a new subdirectory called WORDPROC within the current directory.

Changing to a Subdirectory: CHDIR or CD

The DOS **CHDIR** command, abbreviated **CD,** is used to change the current or default directory to a specified one. For example, at the C> prompt type:

CD WORDPROC   Change the default directory to WORDPROC.

MD REPORTS   Create a new REPORTS (child) subdirectory within the WORDPROC (parent) directory.

MD SCHOOL   Create the SCHOOL subdirectory, also within the WORDPROC subdirectory.

CD . .   DOS uses the special file name ". ." to represent the parent of the current subdirectory. If you are in the SCHOOL subdirectory, this command changes to SCHOOL's parent, WORDPROC. The special file name "." represents the name of the current directory.

The subdirectory structure for the example is shown in Figure 2-15.

Removing a Subdirectory: RMDIR or RD

RMDIR (abbreviated **RD**) will remove an existing subdirectory, provided it is empty or contains no files or subdirectories. To remove a directory, use the CD

```
C:\—WORDPROC─┬─REPORTS
             └─SCHOOL
```

FIGURE 2-15

Example of a Subdirectory Structure

command to change to the *parent* directory of the one you wish to delete. For example, to remove the last directory added above (SCHOOL), first change to the WORDPROC subdirectory, then remove the SCHOOL directory. At the C> prompt type:

CD \WORDPROC You must specify the *complete* subdirectory path when changing the subdirectory.

RD SCHOOL Remove the subdirectory SCHOOL. If SCHOOL contains any files or subdirectories DOS will not complete the removal. Delete all files in the SCHOOL subdirectory before issuing the RD command.

Displaying the Subdirectory Name: PROMPT

DOS provides the **PROMPT** command to help you know which subdirectory is the default one. The command

    PROMPT PG

will change the DOS prompt from C> to C:\WORDPROC>, indicating that WORDPROC is the current directory. Each time you change directories, the DOS prompt will give your location. The PROMPT PG command can be added to the AUTOEXEC.BAT file; when the computer boots and the AUTOEXEC.BAT file is executed, the PROMPT command will automatically take effect for that session.

Pathname Rules

The full DOS **pathname** consists of **drive:\path\name.ext.** Drive and path are optional parts of the pathname if you are referring to files within the current default subdirectory. The pathname is used to completely identify a file and its storage location. It is possible for files *in different subdirectories* to have the same file name. But two files cannot share the same pathname. Here are some examples of pathnames that could be used in commands such as COPY, REN, DEL, and TYPE.

C:BOOKS.DBF Here the path is omitted, so file commands default to the current subdirectory.

C:\DBASE\BOOKS.DBF The DBASE subdirectory is given first, then the file name itself.

WP\CH2 The drive designator is optional, defaulting to the default drive. In this case WP is the subdirectory name.

C:\WP\LETTERS\OTOOLE Here the path refers to the file called OTOOLE in the LETTERS subdirectory within the WP subdirectory of the C drive.

DOS Pathnames: Drive, Directory, and File Name

Setting a Search Path: PATH

When issuing a file command, DOS will first look in the default subdirectory, then any other subdirectories that appear in the **search path.** The **PATH** command is used to create the search path. In the AUTOEXEC.BAT file illustration given earlier in this chapter, the search path command was:

```
PATH C:\DOS;C:\WP;C:\DBASE;C:\PCPLUS;C:\
```

DOS will first look in the current subdirectory for files to load. If the files are not there, DOS will look in each of the subdirectories shown in the PATH command, in the order listed. If the same file name exists in more than one subdirectory, the first one encountered is loaded. Be cautious when naming more than one file with the same name.

Backing Up A Hard Disk

Hard disks are subject to occasional failure, jeopardizing the disk's contents. Prudent users will conscientiously practice a program of regular backups on floppy disks or a tape backup unit. There are two kinds of DOS backups: you could use the COPY command to copy specific files to formatted diskettes, or use the DOS **BACKUP** command. The COPY technique is useful when working on a particular assignment, and it is simple to copy your file to a floppy disk. This chapter is copied onto a floppy disk at the end of each writing session. However, COPY becomes tedious when there are many files to copy.

Copying the Hard Disk: BACKUP

The BACKUP command copies a file, a group of files, a subdirectory and all its files, or an entire disk's contents onto one or more floppy disks. The syntax of this command is

```
BACKUP fromdrive:[pathname] todrive: /switches
```

The "fromdrive" gives the letter of the drive to be backed up; the "todrive" gives the drive location to which the files are copied. The optional pathname identifies the location (subdirectory name, file name) of the file(s) you wish to save on the floppy disk. Wildcard templates may be used to specify groups of files. The floppy disk in the "todrive" does not have to be formatted unless you are using an older version of DOS that does not offer a built-in formatting option, requiring that a sufficient number of formatted disks be available before the BACKUP is begun. BACKUP will prompt you to insert additional disks as needed until all of the specified files are backed up. The disks should be numbered consecutively on the disk's external label. The most commonly used optional switches are:

/A Add newly backed-up files to other files already on the floppy disk. If not specified, any information previously stored on that diskette is destroyed.

/D Back up those files dated on or after a certain date (/D:date). Date is entered as mm-dd-yy form.

/F Format destination disks without prompting. This could destroy data if the wrong disk is inserted.

/S Back up files in subdirectories of the current directory.

/M Back up only those files modified since previous backup. The DOS archive attribute is used to indicate if the file has been changed since the last backup.

Some examples of the BACKUP command follow.

BACKUP C:WP*.DOC A: /A	Back up all files ending with the .DOC extension from the WP subdirectory of the C drive. Append these files to any already on the backup disk in drive A.
BACKUP C: A: /D:05-17-89	Back up all files dated after 5/17/89 in default subdirectory of the C drive onto the A drive.

Restoring the Hard Disk: RESTORE

The counterpart to the BACKUP command is the DOS **RESTORE** procedure. Files saved with BACKUP must be accessed with RESTORE. You must use the same DOS versions of BACKUP and RESTORE. The syntax for this command resembles that for BACKUP:

```
RESTORE fromdrive: todrive:pathname /switches
```

The "fromdrive" indicates where the floppy disk containing the backed-up files is located; the "todrive" gives the drive where the files are to be restored. Pathname is optional, and indicates which files or groups of files to restore. If pathname is omitted, all files on the backup set are restored to the hard drive. Switches include /B and /A (restore files before/after a given date), /M (restores only those files modified since the last backup), and /S (restores subdirectories also). Your DOS manual has additional details.

RESTORE will re-create subdirectories on the hard disk with the same organization that existed when they were backed up unless overridden by the user. Some examples:

RESTORE A: C:\DBASE	Restore all files from the A drive to the DBASE subdirectory.
RESTORE A: C: /S	Restores all files to the C drive, including those in subdirectories, from the backup disks in the A drive.

Copying Files and Directories: XCOPY

The COPY command is used to copy a file, or a group of files, from a single directory to a single directory. The DOS **XCOPY** command will copy files and the underlying directory structure (including lower-level directories if they exist) from one drive to another. If the directories on the target disk do not already exist, DOS will create them before copying files to them. The format of this command is:

```
XCOPY [d:][path][filename] [d:][path][filename] /switches
```

The /S switch will force XCOPY to copy lower-level subdirectories; otherwise only the current directory and its files are copied. The /D switch copies files that were modified on or after a specified date. The /M switch copies only those files that have been modified since the last time they were backed up or copied with XCOPY. Some examples:

XCOPY A: B: /S	Copies all the files and subdirectories from the A drive to the B drive. Lower-level directories are copied.
XCOPY A:\UTIL B:	Copies the \UTIL directory and its files from the A drive to the B drive.

File Storage and Disk Fragmentation

Files are stored in clusters; a cluster is a unit of disk space amounting to 2048 characters on a hard disk, or 512 characters on a floppy disk. In DOS 4.01 clusters are known as disk allocation units. As old files are deleted from the disk, that space is made available for new files. If a new file is larger than the next set of contiguous clusters in the directory, the file is stored in two or more non-adjoining clusters on the disk. Over time the files on the disk become fragmented and access times slow considerably as the disk heads are moved back and forth to retrieve a file. To remedy this situation, files should be repositioned to contiguous, or adjoining, clusters. Although there are no DOS programs to accomplish this, you can copy the files to a newly-formatted disk and the files will not be fragmented. Both Norton Utilities and PC-TOOLS offer utilities that can "defragment," or compress, an existing disk, improving performance significantly.

ADVANCED DOS CONCEPTS

User-Prepared Startup Files

Part of the boot-up process utilizes two special user-created files, **CONFIG.SYS** and **AUTOEXEC.BAT.** These optional files are placed in the root directory of the boot disk and are processed automatically after the other system files are loaded. These files are used to create special hardware and software configurations that are not a standard part of DOS.

The CONFIG.SYS File

CONFIG.SYS contains special configuration commands that are loaded into memory for the duration of the session. Installation instructions for new application packages frequently mention adding lines to the CONFIG.SYS file. Some installations do this automatically while others ask the user to do so manually. For example, WordPerfect recommends the following in your CONFIG.SYS:

```
FILES=20
BUFFERS=20
```

These commands instruct DOS to handle up to 20 open files simultaneously; 6 is the default number with no FILES= command in the CONFIG.SYS file. The BUFFERS command reserves a certain amount of RAM to speed up disk accesses. DOS will transfer several consecutive clusters at the same time, placing them in the **disk buffer** in memory. Fewer disk accesses are usually needed with more buffers, improving efficiency. The installation program that comes with some software packages may automatically modify your CONFIG.SYS file. Knowledge of *how* the CONFIG.SYS commands work is not critical to successful use of the application, but be sure your CONFIG.SYS matches the requirements of your software.

Example: Creating a CONFIG.SYS File with COPY CON

If the CONFIG.SYS file does not exist, you can create one with the COPY CON command. CON is a special DOS reserved word that refers to the system console, or keyboard. The COPY CON command will copy the keyboard keystrokes to the designated file. Its usage is:

```
COPY CON filename
```

The entries to create the CONFIG.SYS file are shown in Figure 2-16.

1. Type the three lines shown in the figure, then press **Enter.** The **^Z** (Ctrl-Z) at the end of the last line tells DOS to terminate the copy operation and create the new file.

```
A:\>COPY CON CONFIG.SYS
    FILES=20
    BUFFERS=20^Z
        1 File(s) copied

A:\>
```

FIGURE 2-16

Results of COPY CON CONFIG.SYS Command

2. If there was an existing CONFIG.SYS file on the default drive, its contents have been replaced by the lines that you entered with this command.

The AUTOEXEC.BAT File and TSR Programs

The AUTOEXEC.BAT file contains DOS commands and other programs that should be run every time the computer is booted up. Some typical AUTOEXEC commands set up the search path, change the DOS prompt, initialize certain print utilities such as a print spooler, load the **driver software** that controls the mouse, and load other **terminate-and-stay-resident (TSR) programs.**

Also called memory resident programs, TSR programs reside in RAM and can be called into action from within other programs with a special keystroke, called the **hot key sequence.** PC-TOOLS has a set of desktop utilities that can be used at any time, even while another program is running. TSR programs provide useful functions but occasionally can interfere with each other or with applications software. Many technicians suggest removing some or all of the TSR programs if a newly purchased package doesn't work properly.

A **print spooler** uses a portion of RAM to hold output characters for the printer. Because the computer can generate output much faster than the printer can accept it, the spooler allows the software to work ahead of the printer. Most printers can be equipped with an internal or external buffer, but the print spooler offers more features and typically more capacity. Expanded or extended memory can be used for the print spooler, conserving conventional RAM for regular applications.

A **RAM disk** can be established to emulate a speedy disk drive in RAM. By copying an application to the RAM disk, then executing it from that drive, it may execute much faster than from a floppy drive or hard drive. Of course, RAM disks do occupy memory that might be better used for ordinary storage. DOS provides a means of creating a RAM disk in extended memory, saving conventional RAM for applications programs and data.

DOS Command Keys

The Command Line Template

The previous DOS command line is automatically saved in a portion of memory. You can re-run the same command, or modify parts of it, without having to retype the entire command. The function keys at the left side or top edge of the keyboard and the numeric keypad keys have special meanings in DOS. The function keys are identified as F1–F10. These keys can save time by repeating or making changes to the previous command. Use of the keys in DOS is explained below. [Note: the meanings of these DOS function keys change when a specific application program is loaded.]

F1 Copies the characters from the previous command, one at a time. You can copy a few characters, make a change, and then copy the remaining characters.

F2 char Copies all characters up to the specified character, and places them on the command line.

F3 Copies the entire previous command to the command line.

F4 char Skips over the characters from the previous command to the character specified.

F6 Places an end-of-file character (Ctrl-Z) in the command line. This is useful when creating a file with the **COPY CON filename** command.

Esc Voids the current command line and lets you start over again.

Ins Enter insert mode with the first keypress; return to normal mode with second keypress. Allows insertion of characters into previous command line template.

Del This key passes over characters from the previous command line, one at a time. It "removes" characters from the previous template.

You can enter repetitive commands using the **F3** key without retyping them, or make slight changes to commands that are similar. For example, you might be looking through a stack of diskettes for a certain file called CRIB.TXT. Put the first disk in the A drive, and type **DIR CRIB.TXT**. The DIR command will search the disk and indicate whether the file resides on that disk. If the file is not on that diskette, insert the next one and press **F3** instead of typing in the whole DIR command. Press **Enter** to execute the command.

Other DOS Commands

The MS-DOS 3.3 manual lists over 50 commands, most of which are not used by the typical user. Some of the commands are used for creating DOS batch files as described in the next section. A few of the more useful commands are briefly described below. Some versions of DOS may contain additional commands, or more options within existing commands. For more details, see the command summaries at the end of this chapter or your DOS manual.

ATTRIB Display file attributes or change attributes such as **read-only** or **hidden** file. See section below.

CLS Clears the screen. This is useful when finishing an application and leaving the computer's power on. Avoid leaving the same image on the screen—it can become "burned in" on the inside of the screen, causing permanent damage.

FC Display differences between two files.

GRAPHICS Allows printer to print certain graphical images from the screen.

LABEL Allows a disk's volume label to be changed.

MODE This is a multi-purpose command that enables you to configure the equipment attached to your computer. The MODE command can divert printer output from one port to another, configure the screen mode, and on some Zenith computers can turn the modem on or off, adjust the clock speed, and set the time until the screen goes blank (for battery operated computers).

RECOVER Upon a CHKDSK or other disk read error, this command can be used in an attempt to recover readable portions of a damaged file.

VER This will display the DOS version number on the screen.

VOL Display the disk's volume label. The label is also displayed when the directory of that disk is retrieved.

File Attributes

DOS maintains four file attributes which normally are not displayed with the directory listing. The attributes can be changed with the DOS ATTRIB command, but this is more handily done with a utility program such as PC-TOOLS or Norton Utilities, described later in this chapter.

- The **hidden** attribute will cause the file to not appear in a directory listing.
- The **read-only** attribute permits normal file access but prohibits the file from being changed or deleted.
- The third attribute, **system** status, describes a file as being a special system file, used in the boot process.
- The final attribute, **archive,** is used to indicate that the file has been modified since the last time it was backed up. This attribute is used when a partial backup of only changed files is desired; the normal backup procedure is to copy all files to backup media.

CREATING AND EXECUTING DOS BATCH FILES

Batch Command Files

Batch files contain DOS commands and calls to other programs that you might type from the prompt line. Putting frequently-used commands together in a batch file permits them to be executed with one command, instead of keying in the individual lines. AUTOEXEC.BAT is the most commonly used batch file. It was described earlier. AUTOEXEC.BAT is automatically executed by DOS if it is stored on the boot disk in the root directory. Any DOS command can be placed in a batch file with appropriate options specified.

Batch files can accept parameters and can execute different sections depending on the values of these inputs. These parameters are entered after the name of the batch file, and are numbered by DOS. The name of the batch file is %0, the first parameter is %1, and so on. Some commonly used batch file DOS commands include:

ECHO text This command will display the words found in "text" on the screen as the batch file executes.

ECHO OFF This will suspend the normal display output from most DOS commands so the user does not view each command as it is executed. **ECHO ON** will resume output from commands.

REM [text] This is a remark statement, useful for describing the batch file. They are optionally displayed on the screen as the batch file executes unless ECHO OFF is entered before the REM line.

PAUSE [text] PAUSE will cause the batch file to stop executing and prompt the user to press a key to continue. If text is included after PAUSE, that text will also display unless ECHO OFF appeared first.

CLS CLS will clear the screen and place the cursor in the upper left corner.

:label Indicates the start of a particular section in the batch file. The IF and GOTO statements will send execution to the section of the macro that has a matching label.

GOTO label Transfer execution to the named label.

IF .. GOTO .. The IF command compares two character strings; if they are identical, control in the batch file is passed to a specific line. For example,

```
IF "%1"=="B" GOTO BACK
```

compares the first parameter entered in the batch file command line to "B". If it is B, control goes to a line in the batch file containing :BACK; if not, it goes to the next line of the file.

Creating a Batch File with COPY CON

Batch files can be created in several ways. The simplest is to use the **COPY CON filename.BAT** command. This command provides for any characters entered on the console device (the keyboard) to be placed in the named file. Care should be taken in entering each line of the batch file because once a line is entered, it cannot be changed without a word processor or creating the entire file again. The last line of the batch file must end with the **F6** or **Ctrl-Z** character, the standard DOS end-of-file character.

Example: Creating a Batch File with COPY CON Filename

In this example we will create a small batch file called SHOW.BAT which will display all of the files on the default drive whose names begin with A, B, or C.

1. At the DOS prompt type **COPY CON SHOW.BAT** and press **Enter**. You will not see any prompt after pressing the **Enter** key.

   ```
   C:\>COPY CON SHOW.BAT
   ```

2. Next type in the following three lines:

   ```
   DIR A*
   DIR B*
   DIR C*
   ```

3. After you have typed in the last line above, press the **F6** key and **Enter**. You will see the characters "^Z" appear at the end of the last line. DOS will issue a message, "1 File(s) Copied," indicating that the new file has been created.

4. Issue the command **TYPE SHOW.BAT** to see if the file displays properly.

5. To execute the batch file, at the DOS prompt type **SHOW** and press **Enter**.

   ```
   C:\>SHOW
   ```

Using EDLIN to Create a Batch File

DOS includes a rudimentary line editor called EDLIN. This program allows you to create a file line by line, and to make corrections to existing files. EDLIN is described in the DOS manual.

Creating a Batch File with Your Word Processor

One common way to create a batch file is with the ASCII text or non-document file feature of your word processor. WordPerfect uses the Text In/Out command (**Ctrl-F5**) to create text files. Don't use the regular document editing portion of WordPerfect—DOS cannot recognize the special file format used by the word processor. WordStar uses the **Non-document mode** for creating text files; its **Document mode** creates a special file format that DOS cannot read. See your word processor manual, or the WordPerfect section of this textbook, for instructions on creating a text file.

Example Batch Files

Simple batch files can be great time savers. Suppose you have two printers attached to your computer, one a dot matrix and the other a daisy wheel printer. The MODE command can be used to divert normal output from the dot matrix printer, usually attached to parallel port 1 (LPT1), to the daisy wheel on serial port 1 (COM1). Figure 2-17 shows two simple batch files that activate the proper printer port within DOS. To turn on the parallel port, simply type **DOT** at the DOS prompt. To use the daisy wheel printer on the serial port, type **DAISY** at the DOS prompt.

A more complicated batch file, shown in Figure 2-18, uses a single batch file to do both jobs depending on the parameter added to the end of the command. Specify DOT (uppercase) and the batch file will select the dot matrix printer; otherwise the daisy wheel printer will be chosen.

To make installing software packages easier, many publishers include complex batch files. The user is asked questions about his computer configuration, and the batch file copies the appropriate files from the distribution disks to the user's own disks. For a simple installation batch file see Figure 2-19. What does each line accomplish?

```
REM ** DOT.BAT ** Divert printer output to LPT1
MODE LPT1

REM ** DAISY.BAT ** Divert printer output to COM1
MODE LPT1=COM1
```

FIGURE 2-17

Sample Batch Files

```
REM ** PR.BAT ** Divert printer output to proper port
IF "%1"=="DOT" GOTO DOT
:DAISY
MODE LPT1=COM1
GOTO END
:DOT
MODE LPT1
:END
```

FIGURE 2-18

Printer Setup Batch File

FIGURE 2-19

Software Installation Batch File

```
C:
CD\
COPY A:KWMAIN.BAT
MD KWTRACK
CD KWTRACK
COPY A:*.* C:
CD\
```

FIGURE 2-20

Floppy Copy Batch File

```
DEL C:\DTEMP\*.*
CD DTEMP
PAUSE  Insert the source disk in A:
COPY A:*.* C:
PAUSE  Now insert the destination disk in A:
COPY *.* A:
CD \
REM  Finished ... returning to root directory
```

Another batch file example (Figure 2-20) is a set of commands to copy one floppy disk to another by temporarily storing the files in a special subdirectory on the hard drive. What does each line accomplish?

NON-DOS UTILITY PROGRAMS

DOS has its roots in the microcomputer operating system called CP/M, popular more than 10 years ago. While internal DOS operations have continually changed, the user interface has remained consistent, and many think it to be rather "unfriendly." To solve this problem, and to provide additional functions not previously available with DOS, several vendors have developed excellent companion utility products. These utility programs offer a better user interface and additional functions, provide much-improved disk backup and restore, and permit multiple programs to be loaded in memory at the same time for rapid switching, also known as **multitasking.**

File Management and DOS Shell Programs

A **DOS shell** is a program that presents menus for managing files and entering DOS commands. Because the normal DOS commands may be difficult for new users to learn and use, DOS shells were designed to replace the usual DOS interface. The two best-known packages are Norton Utilities and PC-TOOLS. Originally sold as tools to undelete files that were erased accidentally, these utilities have grown into much larger, more comprehensive products. In fact, DOS 4.0 was developed, in part, to provide some of the ease of use and additional functions provided by these packages.

The Norton Utilities

Norton Utilities provide more than 20 utility programs to do such things as sort directories, test the disk, find a file by matching text within the file or by file name, maintain and display a graphical directory tree, give disk and file statis-

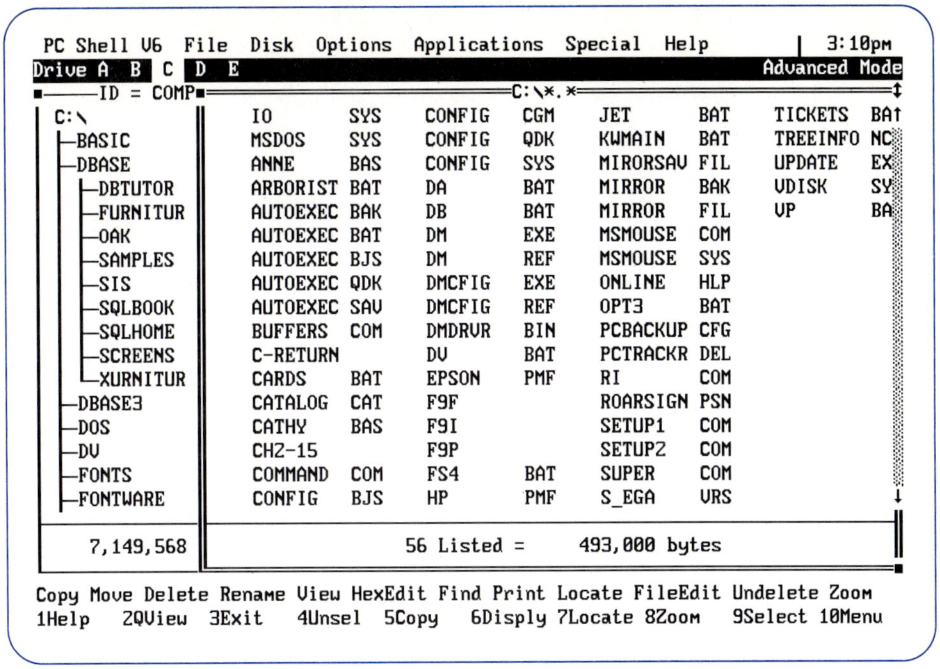

NON-DOS UTILITY PROGRAMS

FIGURE 2-21

PC TOOLS V6 Shell

tics, attach comments to files, and defragment a hard disk, as well as the well-known Norton Unerase facility. The Norton Commander shell acts as an easy-to-use substitute for the DOS command interpreter. You can select subdirectories and files by choosing from menus rather than typing in a sometimes hard-to-remember command. DOS 4.0 offers a similar shell.

PC-TOOLS

PC-TOOLS (version 5 or higher) has evolved into a full-function package offering most of the same features as Norton Utilities, plus a set of desktop tools. The desktop contains notepads and an outline facility, an appointment scheduler and a telecommunications package for accessing remote computers using a modem, a simple editor for creating batch and other text files, three calculators (algebraic, financial using a Hewlett-Packard 12C keyboard, and hexadecimal for programmers), and a database function that will read and write dBASE formatted data files. The PC-TOOLS shell offers menus for various file and DOS functions, as well as offering additional functions. Included in this package are a high-speed backup/restore program to replace the sluggish DOS equivalent, a replacement formatting program that permits reversal of an accidentally-formatted hard disk, a file undelete function, and a program which copies the directory and FAT to a safe spot on the disk, permitting the disk to be rebuilt in case of damage to the directory. The shell is shown in Figure 2-21.

The PC-TOOLS shell allows you to **tag** groups of files that will undergo the same file operation. Using a mouse or the cursor control keys, you can move the cursor to each file desired in the group. Then using the pull-down menu at the top of the screen, perform such file operations as copy, move, delete, change attributes, and more. Most DOS features are available through the shell, and some users rarely use DOS commands. One useful capability is directory maintenance—the ability to change the subdirectory structure quickly. The prune-and-graft option permits you to move a subdirectory from its original location to another parent. PC-TOOLS provides mapping functions to visually depict the disk's physical layout and show where individual files are stored.

Mace Utilities

Mace Utilities is another useful add-on utility package. It offers assistance in rebuilding damaged files and disk directories. This package is also useful at recovering lost data from dBASE data files. The cost of this kind of software is easily justified if lost data is retrieved.

Hard Disk Backup and Restore Utilities

With larger hard drives and heavy reliance upon them for vital business data, systematic backups are mandatory. The DOS BACKUP/RESTORE programs do work, but are cumbersome to use, relatively slow, and require a large number of floppy disks. Even with the higher-capacity 1.2 or 1.44 MB diskettes, many are needed to do a full backup. Fortunately, there are alternative backup programs that make this task somewhat easier. It is likely that backups will be done more often if they are less taxing!

The better backup programs are able to fit 30% more data on the same diskette than usual, so fewer disks are needed. They use a proprietary data compression algorithm and special file format for storing data, and the backup disks can only be read by the accompanying restore utility. These programs maintain a file log, similar to a disk directory. Backups and restorations are done visually, using a menu and graphical display of subdirectories and files. You can select files to be backed up or restored from the screen instead of having to list them on the DOS BACKUP command line. These packages offer multiple options for backups, and are highly recommended. PC-TOOLS contains an advanced backup program. Fastback-Plus is another popular backup package.

For large hard drives, backups on floppy disks take an excessive amount of time. For these users, a cartridge tape drive is recommended both to save time and reduce the effort spent in doing backups. The tape cartridge can be loaded into the computer and the backup can be timed to occur overnight; the user need not be present if the tape will hold the entire disk's contents. Otherwise the user must continually insert and remove a seemingly endless number of floppy disks.

Multitasking Environments: Windows and DESQview

With the popularity of the Macintosh graphical operating system and users' requests for running more than one program at a time, Windows and DESQview provide an alternative **environment** to DOS. These programs load into RAM when the computer boots up, and provide a graphical shell for the user. But their real advantage comes when running programs. With a few keystrokes, you can switch from one program to another, exchange data between programs, and even run two programs at the same time. These environments require additional RAM be installed in the computer beyond 640 KB to hold the programs.

For example, someone running a database application may need to retrieve data from another computer over a telephone line. He could open a second window from the database for the telecommunications program, initiate the communications session, then retrieve the data. Then he can quickly switch back to the database, where nothing has changed since he left. In another case a user might be preparing a report using a word processor, and need to go into the spreadsheet program to do additional analysis, then import the spreadsheet into the report. Windows and DESQview offer similar capabilities but require a fast computer with plenty of RAM to work effectively. If the RAM is not large enough to hold all the desired programs, the hard disk is used to temporarily hold portions of memory, called **pages.** Thus a fast-access-time hard disk speeds up the switching process. Figure 2-22 shows a Windows 3 session with several applications running concurrently.

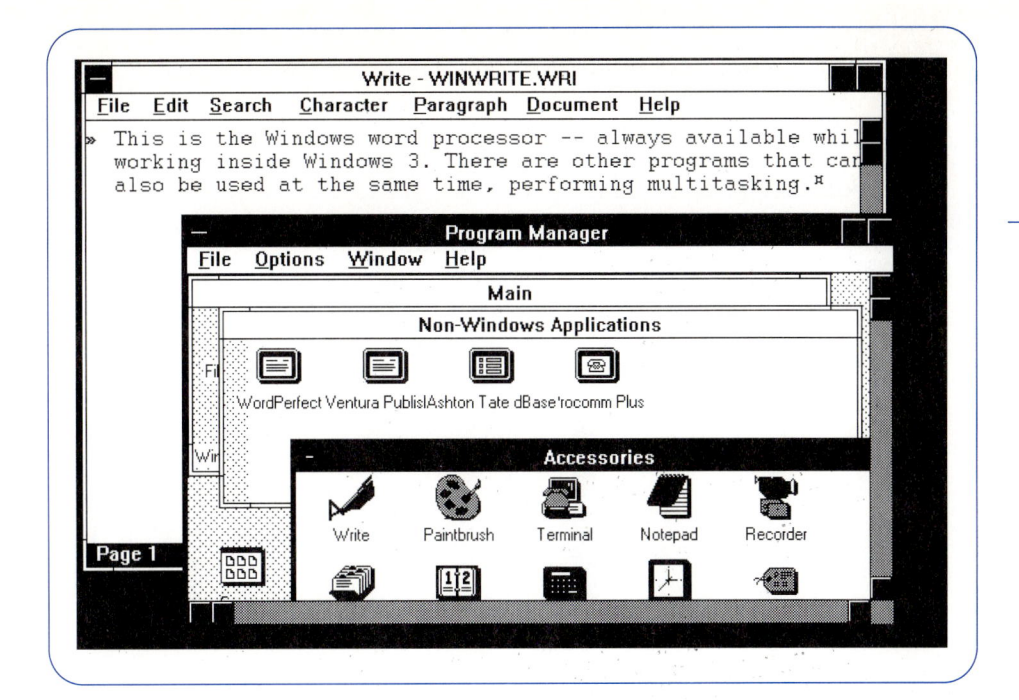

FIGURE 2-22

Sample Windows 3 Screen Display

DOS, OS/2, AND OTHER OPERATING SYSTEMS

Other DOS Versions

When the IBM PC was developed, the prevailing microcomputer operating system was called CP/M. Running on 8080 microprocessor computers, CP/M had to fit into a small amount of RAM. The earliest version of DOS (version 1.0) was introduced in 1981 with the IBM PC. Version 1.0 assumed a minimal memory and secondary storage configuration. Version 1.1 added support for double-sided floppy disks. Later versions of DOS grew larger and more capable. Version 2.0 accompanied the hard disk-based IBM XT. This version supported hard disks and additional file manipulation commands.

DOS 3.0 appeared in 1985 with the introduction of the 80286-based IBM AT personal computer. This version supported the high-density 1.2 MB floppy diskette, and used the setup configuration stored within the computer to determine the type of disk drives attached. DOS 3.1 was introduced shortly after with support for local area networks through the NetBIOS commands.

Support for 3.5-inch drives appeared in DOS 3.2. In 1987 DOS 3.3 extended that support to 1.44 MB 3.5-inch drives, along with the ability to handle different national languages through the use of country codes. Display, keyboard, and printer codes can be modified for certain special language characters.

In 1989 DOS 4.0 was released with improvements in several areas. This version permitted hard disk drives to be larger than 32 MB without special software drivers. DOS 4.0 also came with an optional graphical shell, shown in Figure 2-23, that replaced the DOS prompt and keyboard-entered commands. DOS 4.0 also supports higher-resolution video modes, including the ability to print high-resolution graphics screen images. DOS version 4.01 was released to fix some errors. DOS 5.0 was released in 1991. This version provides more free conventional memory by loading itself in extended memory (286 or higher). Faster than previous versions, it also provides online help.

OS/2—The Multitasking Software

When IBM introduced the PS/2 microcomputer family in 1987, they also announced a new operating system that would solve many problems inherent with DOS and the 8088 microprocessor family. **OS/2** leaps past the 1 MB RAM limitation but requires an 80286 or 80386 microprocessor; 8088/8086 computers

Chapter 2 — *The Operating System: DOS and Utility Software*

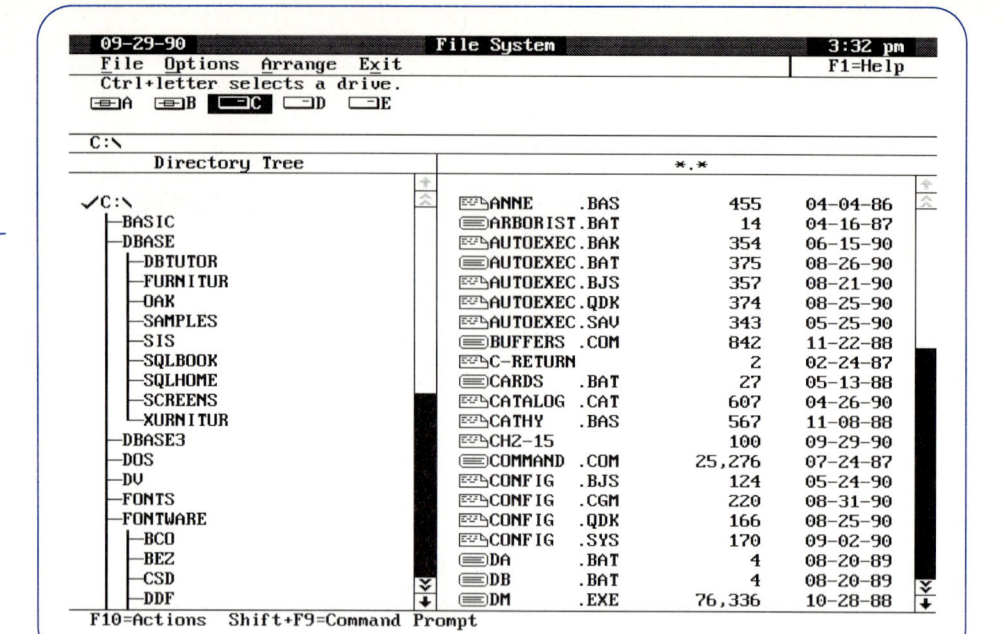

FIGURE 2-23

DOS 4 Graphical Shell

```
09-29-90                    File System                     3:32 pm
 File  Options  Arrange  Exit                               F1=Help
 Ctrl+letter selects a drive.
   A     B    ■C■    D     E

C:\
            Directory Tree                      *.*
   ✓C:\                            ≡ANNE     .BAS       455   04-04-86
    ├─BASIC                        ≡ARBORIST.BAT        14   04-16-87
    ├─DBASE                        ≡AUTOEXEC.BAK       354   06-15-90
    │  ├─DBTUTOR                   ≡AUTOEXEC.BAT       375   08-26-90
    │  ├─FURNITUR                  ≡AUTOEXEC.BJS       357   08-21-90
    │  ├─OAK                       ≡AUTOEXEC.QDK       374   08-25-90
    │  ├─SAMPLES                   ≡AUTOEXEC.SAV       343   05-25-90
    │  ├─SIS                       ≡BUFFERS .COM       842   11-22-88
    │  ├─SQLBOOK                   ≡C-RETURN             2   02-24-87
    │  ├─SQLHOME                   ≡CARDS   .BAT        27   05-13-88
    │  ├─SCREENS                   ≡CATALOG .CAT       607   04-26-90
    │  └─XURNITUR                  ≡CATHY   .BAS       567   11-08-88
    ├─DBASE3                       ≡CH2-15             100   09-29-90
    ├─DOS                          ≡COMMAND .COM    25,276   07-24-87
    ├─DV                           ≡CONFIG  .BJS       124   05-24-90
    ├─FONTS                        ≡CONFIG  .CGM       220   08-31-90
    ├─FONTWARE                     ≡CONFIG  .QDK       166   08-25-90
    │  ├─BCO                       ≡CONFIG  .SYS       170   09-02-90
    │  ├─BEZ                       ≡DA      .BAT         4   08-20-89
    │  ├─CSD                       ≡DB      .BAT         4   08-20-89
    │  └─DDF                       ≡DM      .EXE    76,336   10-28-88
 F10=Actions  Shift+F9=Command Prompt
```

cannot run OS/2 without an accelerator card which replaces the original processor.

With OS/2 software developers can design much larger programs, and accomplish multitasking in a sophisticated manner. OS/2 requires significantly more memory and disk space, generally twice as much as DOS. Thus a computer needs 2+ MB of RAM and a 40 MB or greater disk drive to effectively use OS/2. The complexity of this advanced operating system delayed its introduction for many months, and as of this writing only a portion of software publishers have shipped OS/2 compatible software. While OS/2 will run regular DOS programs, only those programs especially written for OS/2 can be run in the larger memory space and with multitasking.

The OS/2 Presentation Manager is a graphics-oriented environment similar to Windows and to the Macintosh user interface. Users running this version of OS/2 would initiate commands by using a mouse to move the pointer to the screen icon (picture) representing that function. Graphical user interfaces may be easier for new users to master. Users would be able to move between different programs more readily if they shared the same basic user interface.

Some experts predict that both DOS and OS/2 will exist in the future. Users with less demanding needs would use DOS on a smaller computer, while those with sophisticated applications would have OS/2 running on powerful computers. Software publishers may support applications in both environments, or there may be less-powerful versions (or even different programs) for DOS users.

Unix

The **Unix** operating system is widely used in multiple-user minicomputer applications. Because there is a great deal of general Unix software in the public domain, Unix is an attractive environment for those who wish to use that software. Several Unix versions have been created for microcomputers, including SCO Unix and Microsoft Xenix. These versions share the same rich set of programmer tools with the larger Unix implementations, and can also be used for multi-user applications with the 80286 or 80386 microcomputer as host CPU.

Some DOS packages are able to run under Unix. Software written expressly for Unix can be run in a multitasking mode. The user is able to switch quickly from one program to another while the switched-out program continues to run (albeit more slowly) in the background.

DOS COMMAND SUMMARY

Internal DOS commands are always available at the DOS prompt, and are the most commonly used commands. **External commands** are stored as separate files on the DOS disk, and are executed by typing their name. However, DOS must be able to locate the file containing the instructions for that command or you will get the error message, **Bad command or file name,** indicating the file could not be located. For hard disk users, be sure to include in a PATH command the name of the subdirectory where the external DOS commands are located. While this text assumes you are using DOS 3.3, these commands are nearly identical on most versions of DOS. Figures 2-24 and 2-25 contain a summary of the most useful commands.

CHAPTER REVIEW

Elementary DOS Commands

The operating system is a set of utility programs that manage the computer's resources. When the computer is powered up, DOS is loaded from the boot disk into RAM. The AUTOEXEC.BAT and CONFIG.SYS files contain important start-up commands for the computer. DOS file names consist of a name of up to

Command	Purpose
BREAK	Allows or disables Ctrl-C interrupt of program
CHDIR (CD)	Change default directory
CLS	Clear the display screen
COPY	Copy specified file(s)
d:	Change default drive to specified letter
DATE	Display and set the current date
DEL (ERASE)	Delete specified file(s)
DIR	List files in a directory
EXIT	Exit the command processor
MKDIR (MD)	Create a new subdirectory
PATH	Set command file search path
PROMPT	Change DOS command prompt
RENAME (REN)	Rename a file
RMDIR (RD)	Remove a subdirectory
SET	Set environment variable
TIME	Display and set the current time
TYPE	Display contents of a file on the screen
VER	Show the DOS version number
VOL	Display the disk's volume label

FIGURE 2-24

Internal DOS Command Summary

FIGURE 2-25

External DOS Command Summary

Command	Purpose
APPEND	Set a search path for data files
ASSIGN	Assign a drive letter to a different drive
ATTRIB	Set or display file attributes
BACKUP	Back up files from one disk to another
CHKDSK	Check directory for errors, also display free RAM and disk space remaining
COMMAND	Start the DOS command processor
COMP	Compare the contents of two files
DISKCOMP	Compare the contents of two disks
DISKCOPY	Copy contents of one disk
EXE2BIN	Convert .EXE files to binary format
FC	Compare files, display differences
FDISK	Configure and initialize hard disk
FIND	Locate a specific text string
FORMAT	Prepare a new disk for storing data
GRAFTABL	Load a table of graphics characters
GRAPHICS	Prepare DOS to print graphics screens
JOIN	Join a disk drive to a path
LABEL	Display and change disk volume label
MODE	Set operating characteristics for devices such as monitor and I/O ports
MORE	Display screen of output at a time
PRINT	Print contents of file
RECOVER	Recover from errors in file
REPLACE	Replace previous version of file with new version of same name
RESTORE	Restores files that were previously backed up
SORT	Sorts data in ascending or descending order
SUBST	Substitute a string for a path
TREE	Display subdirectory structure and file names
XCOPY	Copies files and subdirectories

8 characters and an optional 3-character extension preceded by a period. The * and ? wildcard characters let you refer to groups of files sharing common name elements.

Working with Files

The directory of a disk contains information about the files stored on that disk, including the date that each file was last changed. Files can be copied, renamed, printed, or deleted from the disk. Blank disks must be formatted prior to being used. Data disks are used to store programs and data, while system disks can boot the computer.

Working with Hard Disks

Hard disks offer large storage capability and fast storage and retrieval of information. They should be organized into separate subdirectories for each application. Disk backups are necessary in case the disk drive should fail. DOS offers built-in programs to back up and restore hard drives, but improved packages are available from other vendors for this important task.

Creating and Executing DOS Batch Files

DOS batch files are used to automatically execute sequences of commands. Virtually any DOS command can be placed in a batch file, and additional batch file commands are available to accomplish various programming tasks.

Non-DOS Utility Programs

Several utility programs that augment DOS functions are available from other vendors. For instance, a deleted file can be undeleted if certain conditions are met. DOS shells offer an alternative user interface to the DOS command interpreter. Some utility programs can offer multitasking capabilities, running two or more programs in memory at the same time.

DOS, OS/2, and Other Operating Systems

OS/2 was announced at the time the IBM PS/2 line of personal computers was introduced. OS/2 offers multitasking capabilities, along with a graphical user interface similar to that of the Macintosh computer. However, OS/2 requires an 80286 or higher microprocessor and much more RAM than does DOS. Programs must be written especially for OS/2, and software producers have been slow to produce new OS/2 programs. At this writing it appears that DOS applications will exist alongside OS/2.

KEY TERMS

archive
AUTOEXEC.BAT
Backspace key
BACKUP
Basic Input/Output System (BIOS)
boot disk
CapsLock key
CHDIR (or **CD**)
CHKDSK
cold boot
CONFIG.SYS
COPY
DATE
default disk drive
Del key
DEL (or **ERASE**)
DIR
disk buffer
disk directory
Disk Operating System (DOS) (MS-DOS, PC-DOS)
DISKCOMP
DISKCOPY
DOS shell
driver software
End key
Enter key
environment
Esc key
extension
external commands
F1 key
F2 key
F3 key
F4 key
F6 key
FDISK
file attributes
file names
FORMAT
formatted disk
hidden file
Home key
hot key sequence
initialize
Ins key
internal commands
light-emitting diode (LED)
low-level formatting
MKDIR (or **MD**)
multitasking
name
NumLock key
operating system
OS/2
pages
partition
PATH
pathname
PgDn
PgUp
PRINT
print spooler
PROMPT
PrtSc key

RAM disk
read-only file
RENAME
RESTORE
RMDIR (or **RD**)
root directory
search path
Shift-PrtSc

subdirectory
switches
Tab key
tag
terminate-and-stay-
    resident (TSR) programs
TIME
toggle

TREE
TYPE
Unix
volume label
warm boot
wildcard template
XCOPY

DISCUSSION QUESTIONS

1. Explain the purpose of an operating system. What is the operating system used with IBM-compatible microcomputers?

2. What are the differences between a system (boot) disk and a data disk?

3. Why do we format blank disks before they are used? Explain how to format a data disk.

4. Explain the use of the following keys: Backspace, left arrow, Esc, NumLock, CapsLock, Shift, F3, Shift-PrtSc, Control-PrtSc.

5. Which of the following DOS file names and pathnames are not valid?

   ```
   HECTOR.123      FILENAME         B:SPECIAL.FILE
   ACCOUNTING      ACTG.A           C:\WP\FILE99.CHK
   123.BILL        BILL.123         A:DATADISK
   BUDGET89.WK1    DOCUMENT.45      C:/LOTUS/LOTUS.COM
   ```

6. Which command is used to erase a file permanently?

7. Which command is used to display the contents of a file on the screen? On the printer?

8. Which command can be used to display the disk's file directory? Explain the information contained in the disk directory. Which command can be used to verify that the directory is logically correct?

9. Discuss the usefulness of organizing hard disks into subdirectories. Which commands are needed when working with subdirectories?

10. Explain the purpose of the DOS search path. How can one be set up?

11. Discuss the special files AUTOEXEC.BAT and CONFIG.SYS. What role do they play with the microcomputer?

12. Give at least two ways to copy all the files from one disk to another.

13. Define disk fragmentation and discuss how to resolve this problem.

14. What is a DOS batch file? Why are they useful?

15. Why do we need to do hard disk backups? How are they accomplished in DOS?

16. What is meant by the term *multitasking*? What tools are available to do multitasking on a personal computer?

17. Why are programs such as PC-TOOLS and Norton Utilities useful? Discuss their features that are absent from DOS.

18. What is OS/2? Discuss its future use. Will it replace DOS?

EXERCISES

1. Format a blank floppy disk as a data disk. Then obtain a directory of that disk. You'll get a "File not found" message. A printed copy of your screen may be obtained by using the **Shift-PrtSc** command after the directory is displayed on the screen.

2. Use the DOS DATE and TIME commands to change the date and time on your PC, then change them back to the correct values.

3. Using the wildcard technique, obtain a directory of only the .COM files on the boot disk.

4. Change the default drive to the drive where your data disk resides. Then copy all of the .COM files from the boot disk to your floppy disk using the wildcard template procedure.

5. Create the following file on your data disk by using the **COPY CON TEST** command. The last thing to enter is the F6 command which will produce a ^Z on the screen. ^Z is the representation for **Ctrl-Z,** and is *not* created by typing the ^ key and Z.

   ```
   This is a sample file created from the console.
   It consists of three lines.
   This is the last line
   [F6]
   ```

6. Copy the TEST file to another file, SECOND. Are their directory entries identical?

7. Rename the TEST file as FIRST.

8. Delete the SECOND file from the disk.

9. Apply a write-protect tab over the notch of the data disk if it is a 5.25-inch diskette. For 3.5-inch disks open the small sliding window in the lower-left corner. Reinsert the disk in the drive. Then attempt to delete the FIRST file. What does the message mean? [Be sure to remove the write protect tab or close the slider window on your data disk before attempting to save anything else.]

10. Use the CHKDSK program to verify that the directory of your data disk is correct. What other information is displayed?

11. On your data disk, create a directory called PAPERS. Within the PAPERS subdirectory, create two more subdirectories called MIS and ENGLISH. Copy the FIRST file from the root subdirectory into the MIS subdirectory.

12. Use the DOS PRINT command to obtain a printed copy of the FIRST file on the printer.

13. Use the DOS VER command to display the version of your operating system.

14. If you have a hard disk on your computer and a sufficient supply of floppy disks, use the BACKUP command to make a backup copy of the root subdirectory of the hard disk. Use the /D switch to backup only those files created or changed during the current year (after January 1 of this year).

FIGURE 2-26

Sample Batch Files for Exercise 15

```
ECHO OFF
REM  ** Menu Program for Exercise 15
ECHO 1. WordPerfect Subdirectory
ECHO 2. Lotus Subdirectory
ECHO 3. dBASE Subdirectory
ECHO Enter the number of the desired choice and press Enter


ECHO OFF
REM ** 1.BAT   To switch to the WP Subdirectory
CD \WP

ECHO OFF
REM ** 2.BAT   To switch to the LO Subdirectory
CD \LO

ECHO OFF
REM ** 3.BAT   To switch to the DB Subdirectory
CD \DB
```

15. Use the COPY CON command to prepare batch files for the following menu exercise. The menu file, MENU.BAT, should display the following menu:

    ```
    1. WordPerfect directory
    2. Lotus directory
    3. dBASE directory
    ```

    The user then will press **1, 2, or 3** (and press **Enter**) to switch to the appropriate directory.

    Enter the MENU.BAT file and the three batch files 1.BAT, 2.BAT, and 3.BAT as shown in Figure 2-26. Before running these files, be sure to create the WP, LO, and DB subdirectories on the default drive.

CHAPTER 2 PROJECT
GRAPHICAL USER INTERFACES

There has been considerable discussion of the differences between the DOS command-line interface and graphical interfaces such as the icon-driven Macintosh operating system. This project is intended to highlight many of the differences between DOS and other operating system environments. You will need to do additional research on some of the products discussed in the chapter. Your report should focus on the following issues:

- Other user interfaces (DOS 3.x shells, DOS 4, Windows, OS/2 PM, Unix, Macintosh)

- Ease of learning with graphical user interfaces (GUI)

- Ease of use with GUI

- Comparison of common DOS commands with Macintosh equivalents

- Future directions for IBM-compatible operating system and user environment.

3

Spreadsheets: The Manager's Tool

Objectives

After completing this chapter, you should be able to:

- Describe an electronic spreadsheet and discuss spreadsheet applications.
- Explain how to load Lotus 1-2-3.
- Start the 1-2-3 spreadsheet module from the Lotus Access Menu.
- Make cell entries in the spreadsheet and move the cursor around the worksheet.
- Access the Lotus Help System.
- Explain how to correct errors in worksheet cell formulas.
- Print the worksheet contents.
- Save the worksheet in a disk file.
- Retrieve a previously saved worksheet from the disk.
- Discuss the Lotus Control Panel and key status indicators.
- Bring up the Lotus / Command menu and explain the various / commands.
- Exit from 1-2-3 and from the Lotus Access Menu.

Chapter 3 — Spreadsheets: The Manager's Tool

INTRODUCTION TO SPREADSHEET APPLICATIONS AND LOTUS 1-2-3

Spreadsheets

Just as the calculator quickly replaced hand calculations for doing calculations, so has the spreadsheet augmented the manager's ability to make decisions quickly and effectively. Electronic spreadsheets permit the rapid development of row and column models, using the ability of the microcomputer to do recalculations whenever a value is changed.

The simplest definition of a spreadsheet is a representation of data that can be presented in row and column fashion. The **cells** in the spreadsheet contain data or represent some calculation based on nearby cells. Spreadsheets frequently have column or row totals. Of course, if anything changes in the sheet the totals must be recalculated. We have used paper spreadsheets for hundreds of years, often for accounting purposes.

The advent of the electronic spreadsheet in the late 1970s and early 1980s heralded a new way of looking at information. Spreadsheet programs like VisiCalc were designed for use with inexpensive personal computers by relatively untrained, non-computer specialists. The era of "end-user computing" gained significant support with the development of electronic spreadsheet products. Lotus 1-2-3 was released in the early 1980s, shortly after the IBM PC was introduced. It quickly became the single most popular application program available.

An **electronic spreadsheet** utilizes the same rows-and-columns approach as the paper variety, but stores data and cell formulas electronically and does the calculations automatically. Row and column totals can be inserted at the touch of a few keys. Whenever a numeric value in the range of cells referenced in a formula changes, the computer automatically recalculates the designated function. One of the major advantages of a spreadsheet is the ability to do "what-if" calculations. If the analyst wants to know the effects of a different assumption, he can change the spreadsheet cell containing that assumption and immediately see the bottom-line results.

The best-selling spreadsheet product for IBM and compatible PCs is **Lotus 1-2-3.** For the remainder of this chapter, we'll refer to Release 2.2 of Lotus 1-2-3 as Lotus. Lotus features include a fully functional spreadsheet, a database, and integrated graphics. The "1-2-3" name comes from the combination of these three capabilities in one package. The **database module** allows storage and retrieval of data records according to user criteria. The **graphing module** permits display of data from the spreadsheet and database for easy review and analysis. All three functions are integrated for ease of learning and to facilitate transfer of data between modules.

Built into the spreadsheet module are nearly 100 preprogrammed **@ functions** that make it easier for the user to accomplish complicated calculations. Lotus includes mathematical, financial, date and time, logical, trigonometric, and string functions. While use of functions is described in more detail in the next two chapters, a simple example will be provided in the QuickStart section of this chapter.

You can solve many problems using Lotus without having to know how to write a traditional program. In fact, Lotus was designed specifically for use by the business decision maker. No other single software category is more responsible for creating the multibillion-dollar personal computer market.

Learning Lotus 1-2-3

The best way to learn Lotus, like WordPerfect, is to try it out alongside your textbook. Use the command tree and quick reference guide found in the back of your text as we demonstrate various features. You may wish to make notes on the command tree or mark the most frequently used commands and functions.

Many successful Lotus users have placed their pocket calculators in a drawer, using Lotus for day-to-day calculations as well as the heavy-duty jobs.

Because Lotus lets you lay out a problem in a fashion similar to solving it by hand, the row and column format is a familiar one. Try using Lotus to solve some of your own problems that you might have used a calculator for.

LOTUS 1-2-3 QUICKSTART

Starting Lotus from a Floppy Disk

We will assume that Lotus has been configured for the computer, display, and printer you are using. Although displaying graphs requires a graphics adapter in your personal computer, you can create and print graphs without a graphics adapter.

The computer must be booted up with a DOS disk in the A drive. With the A> prompt on the screen, insert the Lotus system disk in the A drive and a formatted data disk in the B drive and type **LOTUS** and press the **Enter** key. The data disk will hold your spreadsheet and graph files as they are saved. You can change the default disk drive for storing data files from within Lotus.

Lotus will load from the floppy disk in the A drive in a few seconds and present the Lotus Access System Menu shown in Figure 3-1. The cursor highlights the first choice, **1-2-3**. Press the **Enter** key and the 1-2-3 module will be loaded into RAM. You will see the 1-2-3 worksheet screen.

When using other Access modules such as PrintGraph or Translate, Lotus will prompt you to place the proper disk in the A drive, replacing the System disk. Keep your boot disk handy in case Lotus prompts you to replace the A disk with one containing the COMMAND.COM DOS file. Other than loading from the A drive and specifying the location of user files, the remainder of the Lotus instructions are the same for hard and floppy disk users.

Starting Lotus from a Hard Disk

Turn the computer on and allow the boot process to complete. With the C> prompt, type **CD 123** [or the appropriate directory name] to switch the default subdirectory to Lotus. The default location for storing files will also be the C drive unless you modify it within Lotus. Check with your lab assistant for more help. Type **LOTUS** and press **Enter**. In a few seconds the Lotus Access Menu will

```
1-2-3   PrintGraph   Translate   Install   Exit
Use 1-2-3

              1-2-3 Access System
             Copyright  1986, 1989
           Lotus Development Corporation
                All Rights Reserved
                   Release 2.2

  The Access system lets you choose 1-2-3, PrintGraph, the Translate utility,
  and the Install program, from the menu at the top of this screen.  If
  you're using a two-diskette system, the Access system may prompt you to
  change disks.  Follow the instructions below to start a program.

  o   Use → or ← to move the menu pointer (the highlighted rectangle
      at the top of the screen) to the program you want to use.

  o   Press ENTER to start the program.

  You can also start a program by typing the first character of its name.

  Press HELP (F1) for more information.
```

FIGURE 3-1

Lotus Access System Menu

appear on the screen as shown in Figure 3-1 The cursor highlights the first choice, **1-2-3**. Press the **Enter** key and the 1-2-3 module will be loaded into RAM. You will see the 1-2-3 worksheet screen and the cursor will be blinking at cell A1, the intersection of column A and row 1.

When using other Access modules such as PrintGraph or Translate, Lotus will automatically load them from the hard disk, so no Lotus disk swaps will be necessary. Keep your data disk handy so that you can make a backup copy of any spreadsheet files saved during this session.

The Lotus Access Menu and 1-2-3

Because Lotus was originally designed for use with minimally equipped PCs, the complete system was broken into smaller modules. Each module fit onto one floppy disk, and the system would unload one module and replace it with another when the user needed the additional functions. The common menu of the Lotus Access System permitted return to any of the modules as needed. For floppy disk users, this meant some disk swapping was necessary. Hard disk users didn't notice the disk swapping inconvenience because the entire system resided in the Lotus subdirectory.

The 1-2-3 Module

The first choice in the Lotus Access Menu shown is **1-2-3**, the module where spreadsheets are created and databases are stored. Graphs are created and displayed in the 1-2-3 module. This module is the most commonly used and appears first in the list. Use the 1-2-3 module for almost all spreadsheet operations, including saving a spreadsheet, printing a spreadsheet, and creating the graph settings.

PrintGraph Module

PrintGraph is used for printing the Lotus graphs that were created and saved within the 1-2-3 module. While PrintGraph has some settings, most of the graph decisions must be made while in the 1-2-3 module. Versions of Lotus newer than 2.2 do not require use of PrintGraph—the graph can be printed directly from the spreadsheet module. Graphing is covered in Chapter 6.

Translate Module

The Lotus designers have provided a means of transferring data from and to other major programs, and the **Translate module** will do the necessary modifications to the data files so that the transfer can take place. Translate does not do the actual transfer—there are routines within the 1-2-3 module for reading outside files, or for creating an external file. Chapter 9 in this book discusses transferring data between WordPerfect, dBASE, and Lotus.

Install Module

The **Install module** is not for the inexperienced user. It permits Lotus to be customized to work with the particular hardware attached to the computer. The primary choices deal with type of display adapter, monitor, and printer. Most schools will pre-install Lotus in a lab so that the students will not need to make any adjustments with Install.

LOTUS 1-2-3 QUICKSTART

FIGURE 3-2

Sample Lotus 1-2-3 Worksheet

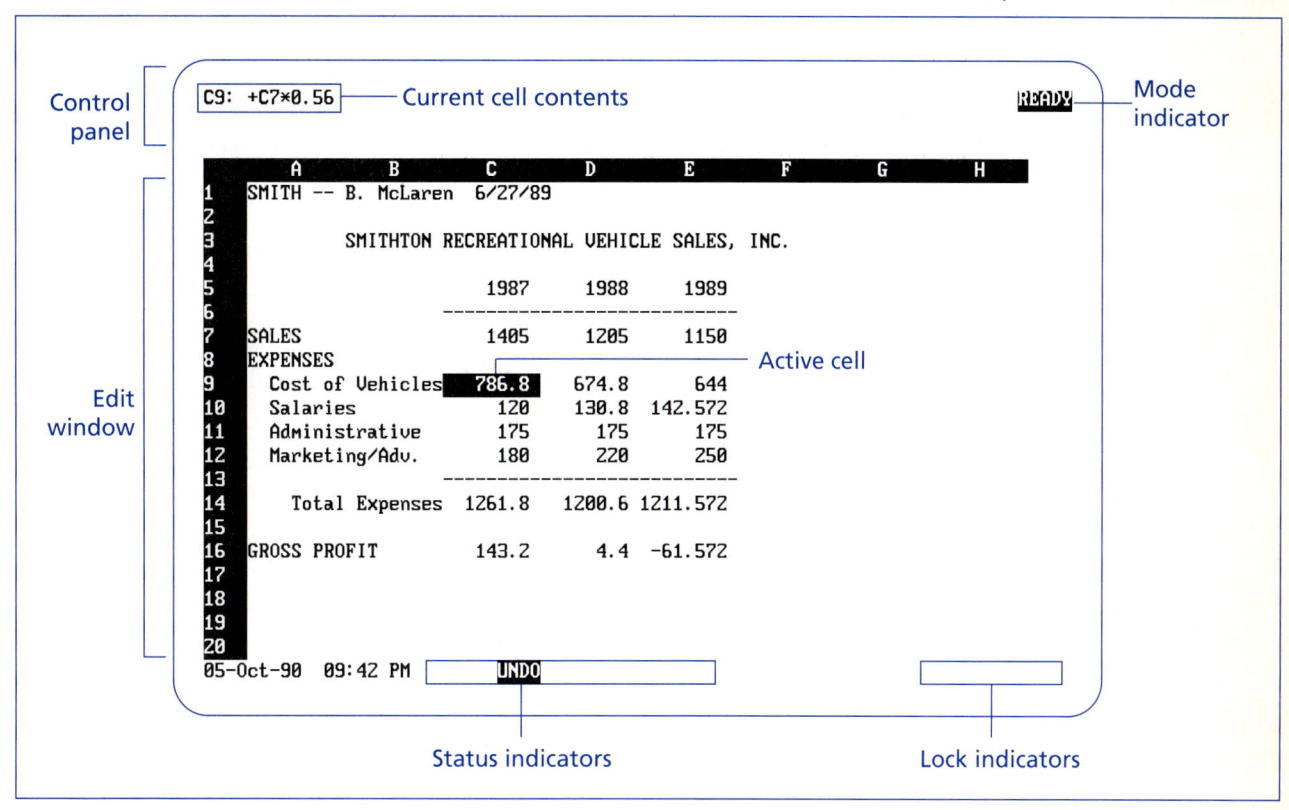

```
C9: +C7*0.56  — Current cell contents                    READY — Mode indicator

      A       B          C          D       E       F       G       H
 1 SMITH -- B. McLaren  6/27/89
 2
 3           SMITHTON RECREATIONAL VEHICLE SALES, INC.
 4
 5                      1987       1988    1989
 6                      ----------------------------
 7 SALES                1405       1205    1150
 8 EXPENSES                                          — Active cell
 9   Cost of Vehicles   786.8      674.8   644
10   Salaries           120        130.8   142.572
11   Administrative     175        175     175
12   Marketing/Adv.     180        220     250
13                      ----------------------------
14   Total Expenses     1261.8     1200.6  1211.572
15
16 GROSS PROFIT         143.2      4.4     -61.572
17
18
19
20
05-Oct-90  09:42 PM        UNDO
```

- Control panel
- Edit window
- Status indicators
- Lock indicators

The typical Lotus screen with a small sample spreadsheet is shown in Figure 3-2. You will build this spreadsheet later as the chapter progresses. Now, we will use it to locate features of the Lotus display. Cells are numbered with the column letter first, followed by the row number. Thus cell **G9** represents the intersection of column G and row 9.

The Lotus 1-2-3 Control Panel

- At the top left is the **current cell indicator** and the contents of that cell. In this case the cursor is in cell C9, which has the formula +C7*0.56, meaning the contents of cell C7 are to be multiplied by the cost factor of 0.56.

- The **cell contents** displayed in the worksheet are the value of the formula, or 786.8.

- The **mode indicator** appears in the upper right corner, in this case READY. The mode indicator is used to show status of the worksheet. Typical values for the mode are shown below.

- The screen displays 20 rows and approximately eight columns of the worksheet in the **edit window**. The number of columns depends on the user-adjustable width of each column. If the full width of a column will not fit on the screen, Lotus will not display any of the column on the current display window.

- The **lock indicators** in the lower right corner show the status of the keyboard lock keys, described below.

- Several worksheet **status indicators** may appear in the bottom part of the 1-2-3 screen. These are described below.

Spreadsheet Modes

The **spreadsheet mode** depends on what Lotus is doing and how the user has entered commands. The mode is displayed in the upper right corner of the screen. Some modes include:

READY The normal message indicating Lotus is ready for you to enter a command or make a cell entry.

WAIT The computer is working on a previous task and will not accept further commands until finished with that task.

VALUE The content of the cell being entered is a numeric value or formula (see section below on Making Cell Entries).

LABEL The content of the cell being entered is a label.

EDIT Lotus has entered Edit mode for the current cell. You could have pressed the **Edit key, F2,** or Lotus may enter Edit mode automatically if there is a mistake in the cell's formula.

HELP A Help screen is being displayed, the result of pressing **F1** for Help.

ERROR An error has occurred and Lotus will wait until you have pressed the **Enter** key to acknowledge the error.

POINT Lotus allows you to make a cell reference by moving the cursor and "pointing" to the desired cell range.

FILES Lotus indicates you are to select a file from a list of files.

MENU You are working with one of the Lotus / menus.

Lotus Lock Indicators

The status of the three Lock keys is displayed at the lower right corner of the Lotus screen. This information is useful for those users whose keyboards do not have indicator lights for these keys. [Note: It is possible on rare occasions for the keyboard to not agree with a Lotus indicator. Use the Lotus indicator in this instance. The next time you re-boot the computer, the problem will clear up by itself.]

The **NumLock** key toggles the numeric keypad between cursor and numeric modes. If NUM is lit, the keypad will return numbers instead of arrow cursor movements. Users with the enhanced keyboard have an extra set of cursor keys to the left of the keypad and should not need to toggle the keypad away from numeric mode. In NUM mode the arrow keys may still be used by holding down the Shift key and pressing an arrow key.

The **CapsLock** key is used to select only capital letters from the keyboard, useful for typing titles and some column headings. To improve legibility of the worksheet, you should not use capital letters for all cell labels. CAPS appears in the indicator area if the CapsLock key is on.

The **ScrollLock** key's function is described in detail in the section on Moving Around the Spreadsheet. Instead of just moving the cursor, the entire display window is moved when in ScrollLock mode. When on, the word SCROLL will appear in the indicator area.

Other Status Indicators

Depending on the worksheet status, there are several more status indicators that can appear in the lower screen section.

- **OVR** will appear when the Ins key has been pressed, indicating Lotus is in **overtype mode**. Press **Ins** again to return to the normal insert mode, where no indicator is lit.

- **CALC** indicates that the spreadsheet has changed since the last recalculation was done, and you should press the **Manual Calculate** key, **F9**, before viewing the results shown on the screen.

- The **END** indicator is lit when the **End** key has been pressed. The cursor moves to the end of the filled or unfilled cell (depending on the cell in which the cursor was positioned when END is pressed), when one of the arrow keys is pressed after End.

- If **CIRC** appears in the indicator area, Lotus has detected a **circular reference** in your spreadsheet. This condition occurs when a cell references a cell that directly or indirectly references the first cell. For instance, cell H82 might contain the formula, **+L89/J67** while cell J67 might contain a formula such as **+H82*1.05**. Every time the spreadsheet is recalculated the values in these cells change because they refer to each other. Cell formula expressions are discussed shortly.

- The current date and time are shown in the lower left corner of the display. If these are incorrect, the DOS **DATE** and **TIME** commands can be used to set the proper system values. Because files are marked with the system date and time when they are first saved or later modified, it is important to keep the date and time correct. You can remove the date and time from the display if desired.

- If **MEM** appears in the status area, Lotus has detected that fewer than 4096 bytes of memory are available for storing new cells in the worksheet. You should save your work and refer to Appendix C of the Lotus Reference Manual for ways to increase the amount of memory available.

- The **UNDO indicator** of Lotus 2.2 shows that you can erase the effects of any changes made since the last time the spreadsheet was in the READY mode. Press **Alt-F4** to execute UNDO. Because UNDO stores a complete duplicate of your spreadsheet in memory, it may be disabled at your computer lab in order to conserve RAM space.

Lotus / Command Display

When first introduced, the Lotus **moving bar menu** system was an innovative way to communicate with the user. Many programs have followed the Lotus method. The command menu is brought to the display with the / key, and is displayed on the second line from the top of the screen. The cursor highlights a choice on the menu, and the third line of the display is a sub-menu with a descriptive message about the highlighted command. Some menus provide this help for the indicated command, while others show the menu that will *follow* if the highlighted choice is taken.

The display in Figure 3-3 shows the default command menu with the word **Worksheet** highlighted. The third line of the display shows the various choices possible in the Worksheet submenu to follow if the Worksheet choice is taken. You can move the cursor to other choices in the command menu line with right and left arrow keys. Each menu option will present a different message on the help line below.

To execute a command, move the cursor to that command choice and press the **Enter** key. For new users this is the preferred method because it

FIGURE 3-3

Lotus / Command Menu (Press /)

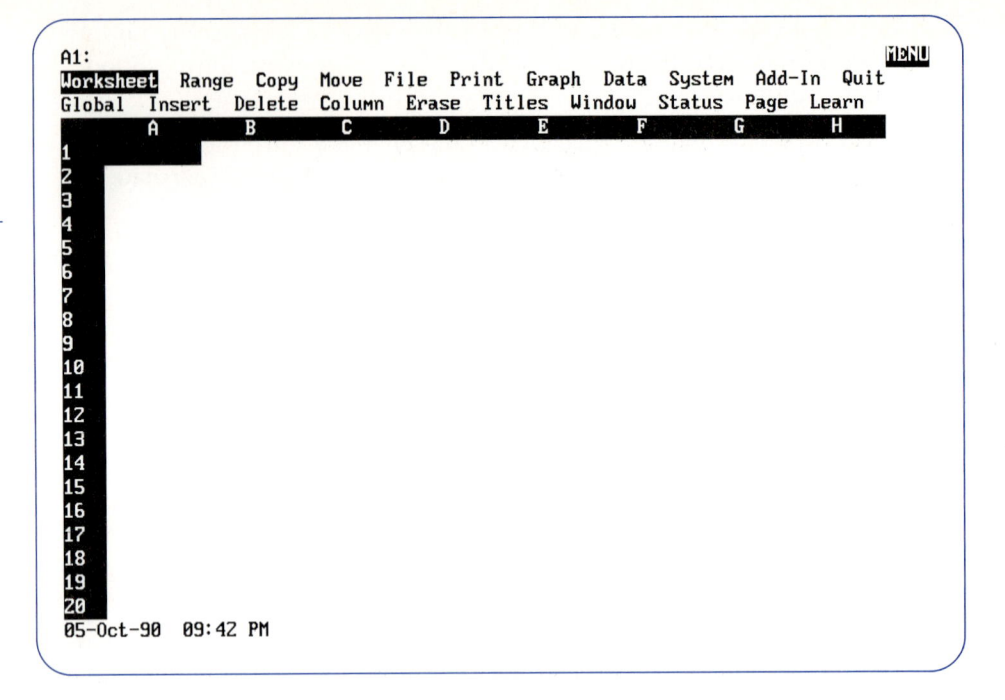

```
A1:                                                                    MENU
Worksheet  Range  Copy   Move    File   Print  Graph   Data   System  Add-In  Quit
Global     Insert Delete Column  Erase  Titles         Window Status  Page    Learn
     A          B           C          D         E          F          G          H
 1
 2
 3
 4
 5
 6
 7
 8
 9
10
11
12
13
14
15
16
17
18
19
20
05-Oct-90   09:42 PM
```

permits you to examine the help line before taking the command. Experienced users may simply press the first letter of the desired command and Lotus will immediately execute that command. More details are provided in the section below on Lotus commands.

Moving Around the Worksheet

The primary means of moving the cursor to new cells in the worksheet is with the **arrow keys** in the keypad to the right of the Enter key. The upper left corner of the Lotus display gives the current cursor cell location; the cursor is located in cell A1 in Figure 3-3 above. Each arrow press will move the cursor one cell up, down, left, or right. The **PgUp** and **PgDn** keys will move the display window up or down 20 rows at a time, the size of the window. To move the display window right or left a screen at a time, use **Ctrl-<arrow>** with the left or right arrow keys. [Note: The equivalent **Ctrl-↑** and **Ctrl-↓** keystrokes have no effect—use **PgUp** and **PgDn** instead.] **Tab** and **Shift-Tab** work like **Ctrl-→** and **Ctrl-←**.

The **Home** key will return the cursor to the home position in the upper left corner, cell A1. **End** with **Home** moves the cursor to the lower right-hand corner of the entered spreadsheet. The **End** key, together with one of the arrow keys, can be used to quickly move the cursor to the edge of the worksheet. Pressing **End** lights the END indicator in the lower right corner of the screen. Lotus waits for you to press an arrow key and moves the cursor in that direction. It will go to the edge of the worksheet if there is no non-empty cell before the edge is reached. If the cursor is in a non-empty cell, using the **End** key will move the cursor to the last non-empty cell in that direction. If the cursor begins in an empty cell, it will move to the first non-empty cell in that direction.

Normally the arrow keys move the cursor within the display window while the window remains in one place. When the cursor reaches the edge of the window, continued presses of the arrow key will "push" the window in that direction. The **ScrollLock** key changes slightly the function of the arrow keys. When this key is pushed, the SCROLL indicator lights in the lower right corner of the screen. The arrow keys move the entire display window a cell at a time when SCROLL is lit, regardless of the cursor's position in the window. You can move the display window to the desired location, then toggle SCROLL off; the

FIGURE 3-4

Cursor Movement Commands

Command	Meaning
↑	Move cursor up one row
↓	Move cursor down one row
←	Move cursor left one column
→	Move cursor right one column
PgUp	Move display up 20 rows (one screen)
PgDn	Move display down 20 rows (one screen)
Ctrl-←	Move display left one screen
Ctrl-→	Move display right one screen
Home	Move cursor to A1 cell location
End Home	Move cursor to lower right corner of sheet
End ↑ / ↓	Moves cursor to last (un)filled cell in the up/down direction from current cell
End ← / →	Moves cursor to last (un)filled cell in the left/right direction from current cell
(F5) <cell>	Go directly to indicated cell address
ScrollLock "on"	When ScrollLock is on, arrow commands cause the screen to move instead of the cursor.

arrow keys again work normally, moving the cursor within the new window location. Figure 3-4 summarizes the 1-2-3 cursor movement commands.

Obtaining Help in Lotus 1-2-3

The Lotus menu system contains a built-in help message for the current choice in the third line of the display. As you move the cursor through various commands the message specific to that choice appears.

If you would like more help on the current command choice, press the **F1** Help key at the point where you need more information. The Help screens are context-specific: the help message applies to the current menu. Other related Lotus help screens are available for many topics and may be accessed by moving the cursor to the desired Help block and pressing **Enter**. To exit from the Help system at any time, press the **Esc** key.

In case you need help for a topic that is not shown, press the **F1** key and select the **Help Index** choice. You'll see a screen similar to Figure 3-5. Choose the topic and press **Enter**.

Making Cell Entries

To enter something into a worksheet cell, first use the arrow keys to move the cursor to the desired cell. Lotus provides 256 columns numbered A to Z, AA to AZ, BA to BZ, ... and IA to IV. Spreadsheets may use up to 8192 rows, although memory limitations prevent using *all* 2,097,152 cells (256 * 8192) at the same time.

To continue the cell entry process, begin typing in the cell. The Lotus Control Panel will display your entry in the upper left corner of the screen as you type. To correct mistakes, use the backspace key to erase characters and retype the correction. When you are finished with the cell entry, press the **Enter** key. Lotus will display the cell's contents on the screen in the worksheet area, and the entry that created that cell in the upper left corner.

FIGURE 3-5

Lotus Help Index Screen (Press **F1**)

```
A1:                                                                      HELP

1-2-3 Help Index
     About 1-2-3 Help      Linking Files           1-2-3 Main Menu
     Cell Formats          Macro Basics            /Add-In
     Cell/Range References Macro Command Index     /Copy
     Column Widths         Macro Key Names         /Data
     Control Panel         Mode Indicators         /File
     Entering Data         Operators               /Graph
     Error Message Index   Range Basics            /Move
     Formulas              Recalculation           /Print
     @Function Index       Specifying Ranges       /Quit
     Function Keys         Status Indicators       /Range
     Keyboard Index        Task Index              /System
     Learn Feature         Undo Feature            /Worksheet

To select a topic, press a pointer-movement key to highlight the topic and then
press ENTER.  To return to a previous Help screen, press BACKSPACE.  To leave
Help and return to the worksheet, press ESC.

05-Oct-90  09:43 PM
```

Lotus cells may contain numbers, text characters, formulas, and @-functions. Based upon the first key typed in a cell, Lotus determines whether the cell is to be a **value** or a **label**. Values can be used in arithmetic operations. Formulas representing numbers are evaluated to a numeric result. Labels represent all other types of data. Common examples of labels are titles, column headings, underlines for column totals, and character data.

If the first key you press in making a cell entry is one of the numeric characters (0–9, plus or minus sign, decimal point, left parenthesis) the cell is considered to be a value. The @ ("at" sign) is also used in functions representing numbers. When entering a formula that refers to other cells be sure to use the + sign or left parenthesis to begin the entry. For example, the entry **B5-B4** would be considered a label by Lotus because the first character typed, the letter B, is not one of the value characters. However, if you entered **+B5-B4** or **(B5-B4)** in the cell, Lotus would calculate the difference between the values in cells B5 and B4 and place that result in the cell. VALUE or LABLE appears in the upper right corner to indicate the cell type.

Lotus Formulas

The usual addition, subtraction, multiplication and division operations are represented by the symbols **+**, **–**, *****, and **/**. Exponentiation uses the **^** symbol. Thus **4^2** represents 4*4 or 16. Parentheses can be used to designate groupings in formulas. For example, the expression **(C1+C2)*(H1–H2)** implies that the contents of cells C1 and C2 would be added together, then H2 is subtracted from H1. Finally the results of these two operations are multiplied together.

Formulas are evaluated by Lotus from left to right. The highest level operations, those within parentheses, are done first. Within the same level, exponentiations are done first. Following that, multiplication and division operations are done. Finally, any additions or subtractions are done.

For example, the expression (1+2^3)*(4+5/2) would be evaluated as follows:

1. The first expression in parentheses, (1+2^3), is evaluated.

2. Within that expression, the exponentiation is done first. Thus 2^3 yields 8.

3. Next (1+8) is evaluated, yielding 9.
4. Then the second expression in parentheses, (4+5/2), is evaluated.
5. Within that expression, the division is done first. Thus 5/2 yields 2.5.
6. Next (4+2.5) is evaluated, yielding 6.5.
7. Finally, the two quantities are multiplied. Thus 9*6.5 yields 58.5.

Correcting Errors

Errors in cell expressions may be corrected in several ways. If you haven't yet pressed the **Enter** key when making the cell entry, use the backspace key to erase the incorrect characters. Retype the remainder of the cell to complete the entry. Alternatively, for short cell expressions, you can simply move the cursor to that cell and retype the entry. Pressing **Enter** will replace the old cell's contents with what was just typed.

For making minor corrections in the cell's contents, move the cursor to the cell and press the Lotus Edit key, **F2**. The mode indicator in the upper right corner will display EDIT and the cell entry will be displayed in the upper left corner of the screen. Use the arrow keys to move the cursor as needed within the expression to make corrections. Lotus is always in Insert mode when you enter Edit. To change to overtype mode, press the **Ins** key and OVR will light up in the lower right corner of the screen.

If you make a mistake in entering a Lotus / command, press the **Esc** key. Lotus will ignore the command just given and return to the previous menu. Successive **Esc** key presses will return to higher menu levels until the / command menu disappears and the READY mode returns. To **abort** the command menu and return directly to READY mode, press **Ctrl-Break**.

Example: *Building the SMITHTON RV Spreadsheet*

The first step is to start Lotus and enter the 1-2-3 module as described earlier in this chapter. You should see a blank worksheet, with the cursor in cell A1. Let's examine the contents of several cells from our example spreadsheet. The modified view in Figure 3-6 shows the actual cell expressions used in this spreadsheet. Columns were widened and reformatted to show complete formulas where needed. Your screen will *not* look like this one. You should enter the cell expressions as you follow along.

1. For documentation purposes, we will put the name of the spreadsheet and its author in the upper left cell of the worksheet. In this instance cell A1 contains:

    SMITH--B. McLaren 6/27/89

    Enter **SMITH--**, your own name, and the date in the format of the above phrase and press the **Enter** key to store the cell contents. This cell expression is wider than the default 9 character width of column A and "spills over" into column B. As long as there are no entries in cells to the right of a long cell expression, it will display fully in adjacent cells.

2. Another long title is to be placed in cell B3. Press the → key then press ↓ twice to move the cursor to that cell . Type **SMITHTON RECREATIONAL VEHICLES SALES, INC**. in the cell and press **Enter** to store the results in the worksheet.

80   Chapter 3 — Spreadsheets: The Manager's Tool

FIGURE 3-6

Sample Worksheet with Cell Formulas

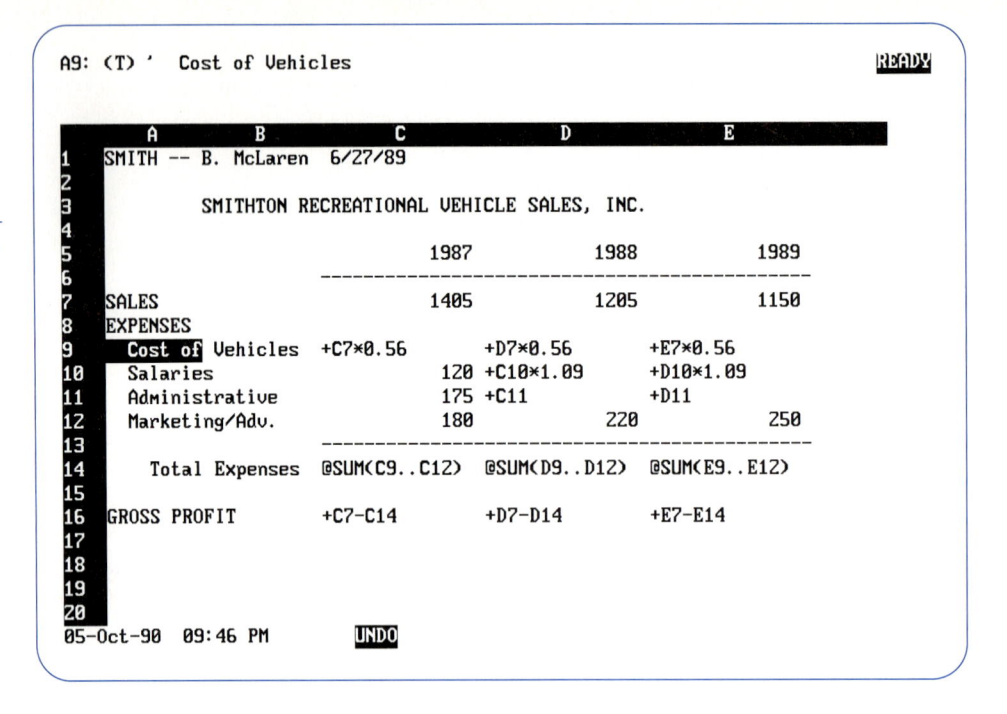

```
A9: (T) '  Cost of Vehicles                                    READY

           A          B            C            D            E
 1  SMITH -- B. McLaren  6/27/89
 2
 3              SMITHTON RECREATIONAL VEHICLE SALES, INC.
 4
 5                          1987         1988         1989
 6              ----------------------------------------------
 7  SALES                   1405         1205         1150
 8  EXPENSES
 9    Cost of Vehicles   +C7*0.56     +D7*0.56     +E7*0.56
10    Salaries              120      +C10*1.09    +D10*1.09
11    Administrative        175      +C11         +D11
12    Marketing/Adv.        180         220          250
13              ----------------------------------------------
14    Total Expenses   @SUM(C9..C12) @SUM(D9..D12) @SUM(E9..E12)
15
16  GROSS PROFIT       +C7-C14       +D7-D14      +E7-E14
17
18
19
20
05-Oct-90  09:46 PM           UNDO
```

3. Use the arrow keys to move the cursor to cell C5. Type **1987** and press **Enter** to store the cell. Use the arrow keys to move to cell D5 and enter **1988**. Finally, move the cursor to cell E5 and enter **1989**. The three Year column headings were entered as numbers, but they could have been labels. Generally, use numeric values only for cells that are to have arithmetic operations.

4. All the cells in column A are text labels. Use the ← and ↓ keys to move to cell A7. Enter **SALES** and press the **Ente**r key.

5. Use the arrow key to move to cell A8. Enter **EXPENSES** and press the **Ente**r key.

6. Use the ↓ key to move the cursor to cell A9. Notice that the cursor highlights cell A9 in Figure 3-6. The A9 cell contents appear in the upper left corner of the display.[1] The entry there is:

    ' Cost of Vehicles

    The single quote or apostrophe preceding the label is automatically added by Lotus and indicates the label is to appear in the left portion of the cell, similar to a left-justified tab in WordPerfect. The label in this cell begins with two spaces to slightly indent the expense category beneath the EXPENSES label. Press the space bar twice and type **Cost of Vehicles.** Press **Enter** to store the cell in the worksheet.

7. Move the cursor to cell A10. Press the space bar two times and type **Salaries**, then press **Enter**. In a similar fashion, move the cursor to cells A11 and A12 and enter the labels **Administrative** and **Marketing/Adv.** respectively. Remember to press the space bar twice to indent each entry.

---

[1] The **(T)** indicates this cell is a Text format type, made to display the complete cell expression and ordinarily are absent. They are *not* part of the cell expression. The next chapter discusses changing cell formats and column widths.

LOTUS 1-2-3 QUICKSTART   81

```
E13: \-                                                              READY

       A       B        C       D       E       F       G       H
1  SMITH -- B. McLaren  6/27/89
2
3             SMITHTON RECREATIONAL VEHICLE SALES, INC.
4
5                      1987    1988    1989
6                      -------------------------
7  SALES
8  EXPENSES
9     Cost of Vehicles
10    Salaries
11    Administrative
12    Marketing/Adv.
13                     -------------------------
14    Total Expenses
15
16
17
18
19
20
05-Oct-90  09:49 PM           UNDO
```

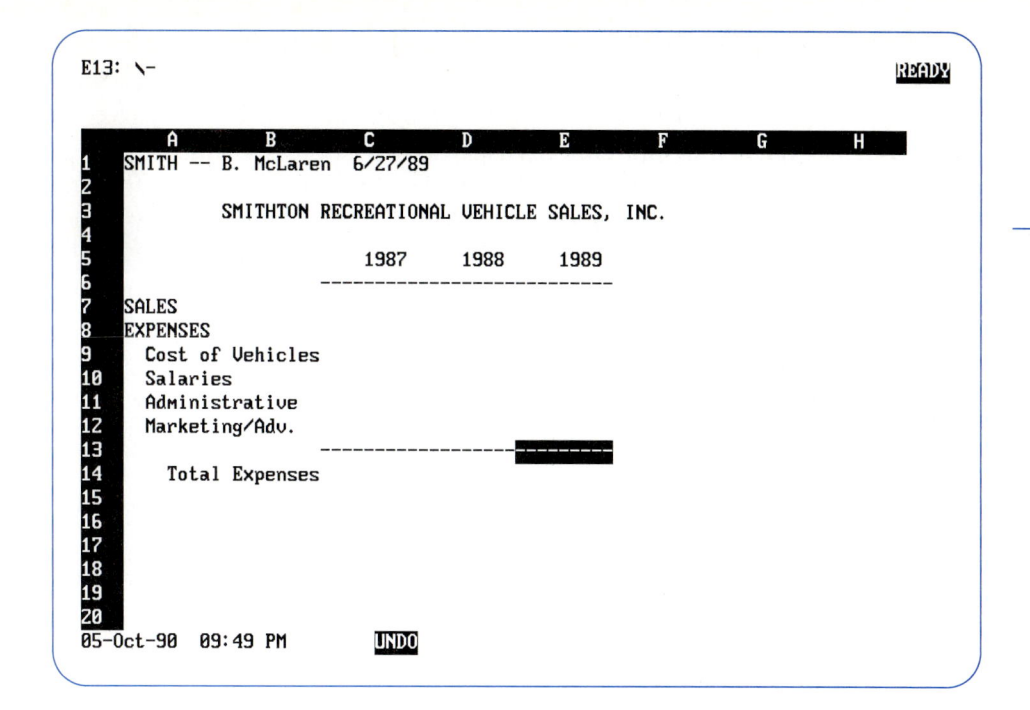

FIGURE 3-7

Sample Worksheet After Step 9

Move to cell A14. Press the space bar four times, then enter **Total Expenses.**

8. The dashed lines separating the Sales amounts and the Total Expenses are easily prepared with Lotus. Move to cell C6 and type \– as the cell entry. Press **Enter** to store the expression in the worksheet. Lotus will fill the entire cell with hyphens. Be sure to use the backslash (\) key, *not* the forward slash (/) key. Press the hyphen, not the underline key, after the backslash. If you ever change the width of the column containing this entry, Lotus automatically extends the hyphens to fill out the new cell width. Any other character or characters can be substituted for the "–". For example, an entry of _– would produce these characters in the cell: _–_–_–

9. Repeat this \– entry for cells D6, E6, C13, D13 and E13. The worksheet should look like Figure 3-7.

10. The three sales amounts in cells C7, D7, and E7 are entered as numeric values. Move the cursor to cell C7 and enter **1405**. Next move the cursor to cell D7 and enter **1205**. Finally move to cell E7 and enter **1150**. After each entry press **Enter** to store the cell in the worksheet.

11. The Cost of Vehicles amount is a percentage of Sales, in this case 56%. The formula for cell C9 is

    +C7*0.56

    The + in front of C7 indicates to Lotus that this is to be a value expression. The contents of cell C7, the 1987 Sales amount, is multiplied by the vehicle cost percentage, 0.56. Notice that even though there is a formula typed into the cell, the value that displays on the screen is 786.8. Move to cell C9 and type **+C7*0.56** and press **Enter**.

12. Move to cell D9 and enter the formula **+D7*0.56**. Likewise, move to cell E9 and enter **+E7*0.56**.

13. The 1987 Salaries, Administrative, and Marketing/Adv. expenses are all entered as numbers, not formulas. Move to cell C10 and enter **120**. Move to cell C11 and enter **175**. Move to cell C12 and enter **180**.

14. For 1988 the expression for Salaries reflects the 1987 amount (C10) multiplied by 1.09, reflecting a 9% increase in personnel costs for that year. Move to cell D10 and enter **+C10*1.09**. Lotus will calculate the result, 130.8, and place it in the worksheet.

15. Likewise, the 1989 amount is the 1988 amount (D10) multiplied by the same factor, 1.09. Move to cell E10 and enter the expression, **+D10*1.09**. Lotus will calculate the result and place 142.572 in the cell.

16. The Administrative expense cell in 1988 is equal to the 1987 amount, or +C11. Move to cell D11 and enter +C11. The 1989 Administrative expense is also equal to the previous year, or +D11. Place **+D11** in cell E11.

17. The Marketing/Adv. expense for 1989 is 220. Move to cell D12 and enter **220**. Place **250** in cell E12.

18. Totals are calculated using the built-in @SUM function. The notation (C9..C12) refers to the cell range from C9 to C12. In this case the expression in cell C14 adds up the cell values in cells C9, C10, C11, and C12, placing the total in cell C14. Move to cell C14 and type the expression, **@SUM(C9..C12)** and press **Enter**. Lotus will place 1261.8 in the display.

19. Similar totals are found in cells D14 and E14. In cell D14 enter **@SUM(D9..D12)** and in cell E14 enter **@SUM(E9..E12)**. The worksheet should look like that shown in Figure 3-8.

20. Finally we are ready to add row 16 for Gross Profit. Move to cell A16 and type **GROSS PROFIT** and press **Enter**. Move the cursor to cell C16 and enter the expression, +C7–C14. Lotus will subtract Total Expenses from Sales and place the result, 143.2, in cell C16.

21. Move to cell D16 and enter **+D7–D14**. Enter **+E7–E14** in cell E16. The finished worksheet is shown in Figure 3-9.

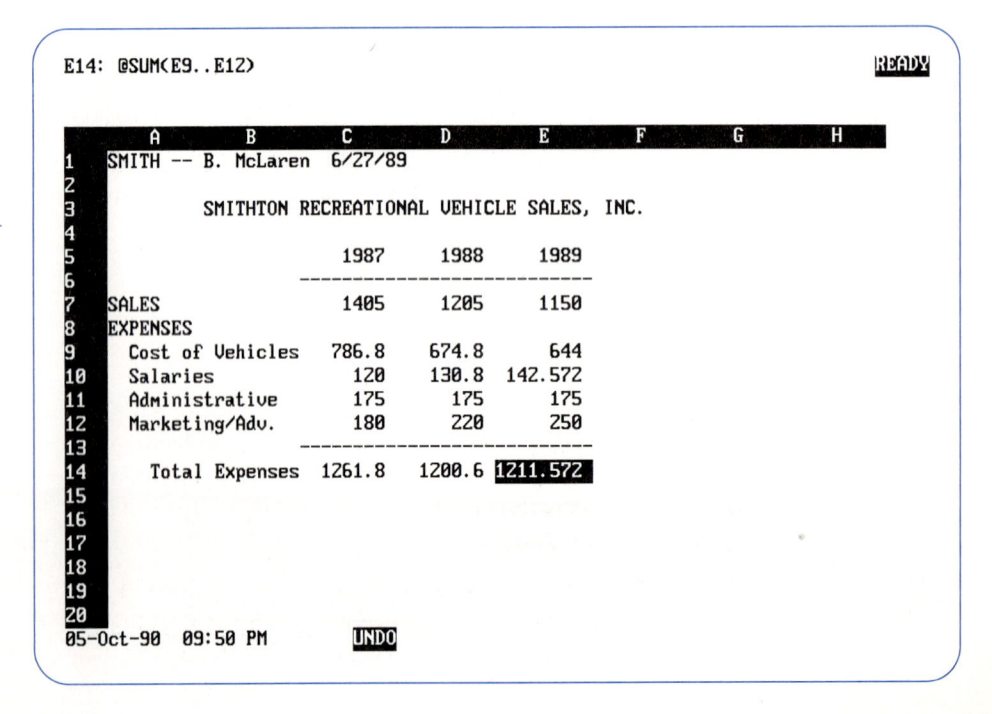

FIGURE 3-8

Sample Worksheet After Step 19

LOTUS 1-2-3 QUICKSTART

Your worksheet can serve as an estimate of Expenses and Gross Profit for the three-year period. Lotus will recalculate the Expenses and Gross Profits if any of the Sales figures are changed. It is easy to see the effect on Gross Profit of any other assumptions. For example, what is the Gross Profit in 1989 if the Sales for that year are changed from 1150 to 1100?

Printing the Worksheet

Press **Home** to move the cursor to cell A1. To print the worksheet you must give the **/Print** command. Press the **/** command and enter a **P** to bring up the **print menu.** We will be printing this worksheet on the printer, so enter a second **P** to indicate you want the worksheet sent to the printer. (Entering an **F** to the second menu would send the worksheet to a file instead.) You should see the Print menu in Figure 3-10, with the Settings Sheet below. The Settings Sheet is new with Release 2.2, and summarizes the print settings on one screen. When you choose a print option, the settings sheet disappears and the worksheet reappears. To temporarily turn off the display of the Settings Sheet, press the **F6** key.

Specify the Print Range

The first choice from the Print menu is to specify the Range of cells to be printed. Press the **Enter** key to bring up the range prompt. The range always specifies a rectangle to be printed by the cell coordinates of the upper left corner and the lower right corner. The periods between the cells indicate the range of cells between the two corners. Type in the cell coordinates directly, **A1..F16,** when prompted to enter the **cell range.**

An alternative way of specifying the cells to be printed is the point method. You will notice the POINT mode indicator (in the upper right corner of the display) when you first get the enter range prompt message. With the cursor at cell A1, **anchor** the cell range by pressing the period (.) key. Cell A1 will be highlighted and the cell range will change to A1..A1. You should use the arrow keys to move the cursor to the lower right corner of the spreadsheet to be printed. As you move the cursor all cells between the A1 cell and the cursor

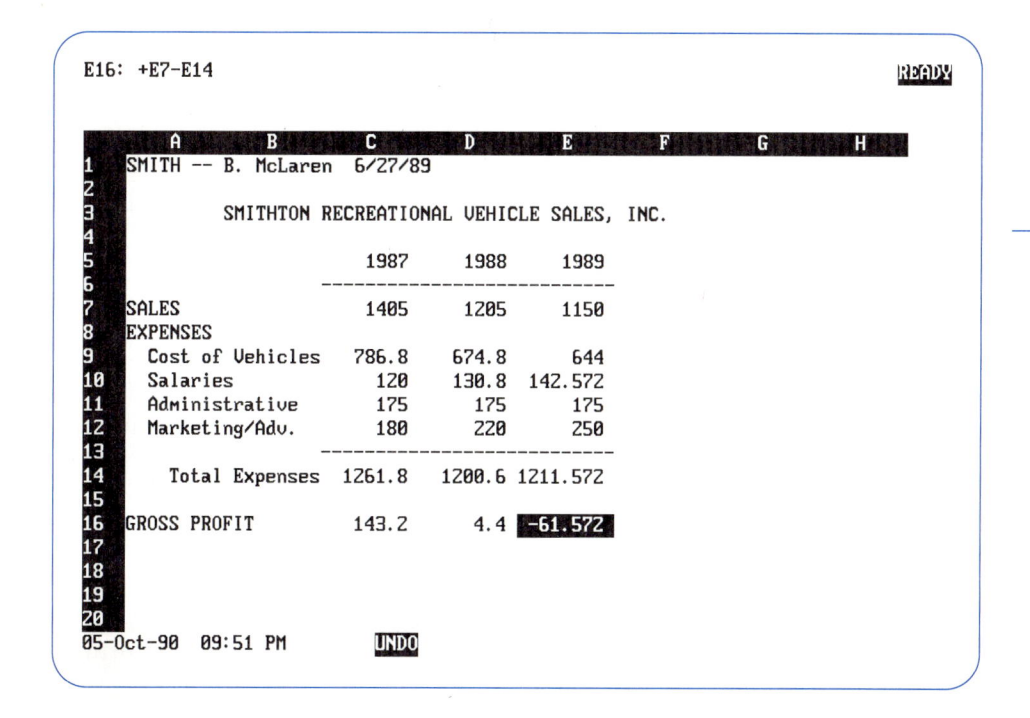

FIGURE 3-9

Completed Sample Worksheet

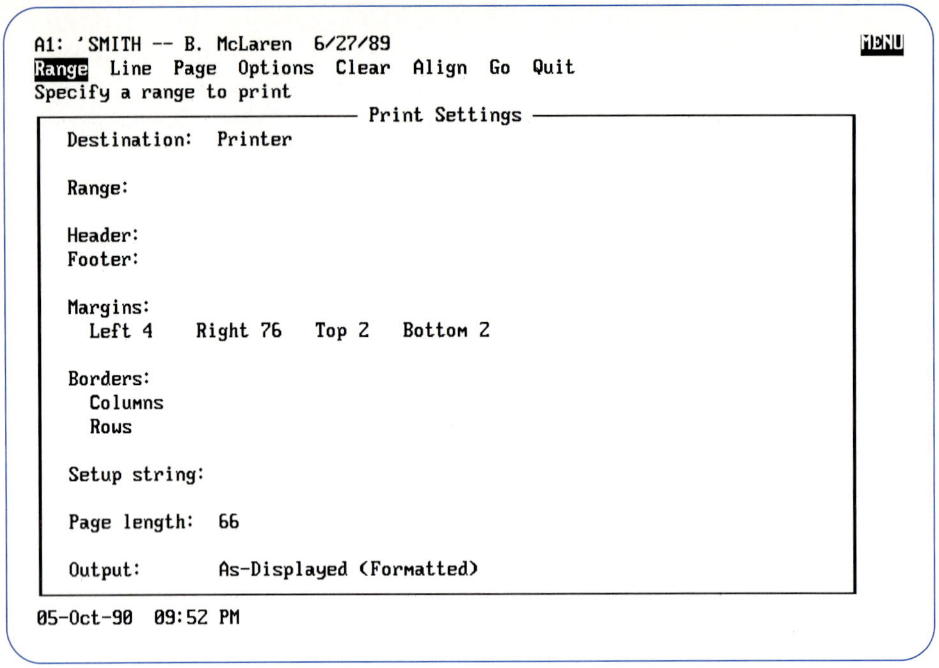

FIGURE 3-10

/Print Command Settings Sheet

```
A1: 'SMITH -- B. McLaren  6/27/89                              MENU
    Range  Line  Page  Options  Clear  Align  Go  Quit
Specify a range to print
                        ─── Print Settings ───
     Destination:  Printer

     Range:

     Header:
     Footer:

     Margins:
       Left 4     Right 76    Top 2    Bottom 2

     Borders:
       Columns
       Rows

     Setup string:

     Page length:  66

     Output:       As-Displayed (Formatted)


05-Oct-90  09:52 PM
```

location will be highlighted. When you have adjusted the range to match A1..F16, press the **Enter** key.

Send Output to the Printer

First press **A** to reset the line counter. To send the output to the printer, press the **G** key (for Go) from the main Print menu. Lotus will blink the WAIT mode indicator while it is printing your report. Lotus will put two blank lines above your spreadsheet as the default top margin, and the report will be printed below. The row and column borders will not display on the printed report.

If this is the only report to be printed at this time, press the **P** key to send a Page Feed to the printer. Lotus will skip the proper number of blank lines to feed the report through the printer. Press **Q** for Quit to leave the Print menu and return to READY mode.

Example: *Printing the Smithton Worksheet*

We will follow the procedure outlined above to print the worksheet. It is assumed that your computer is attached to a printer and that the printer is on-line, ready to accept print output. Ask your lab assistant for help if you are not sure about the printer's status.

1. With the cursor in cell A1, press the / slash key to activate the Lotus command menu. Press **P** to select the Print menu, and type a second **P** to send the printed output to the printer.

2. The cursor will highlight the Range option in the Print menu. Press **Enter** to select this option. When prompted, enter A1..F16 as the cell range to print. Press **Enter** to complete the range entry.

3. We will use the default values for all of the other print settings. Press **A** to align the top of the paper in the printer, then press **G** for Go. The printer should begin printing the Smithton worksheet.

LOTUS 1-2-3 QUICKSTART

```
A1: 'SMITH -- B. McLaren  6/27/89                                    MENU
Retrieve Save Combine Xtract Erase List Import Directory Admin
Erase the current worksheet from memory and display the selected worksheet
        A          B          C        D        E        F        G        H
 1   SMITH -- B. McLaren  6/27/89
 2
 3              SMITHTON RECREATIONAL VEHICLE SALES, INC.
 4
 5                        1987     1988     1989
 6                       ---------------------------
 7   SALES               1405     1205     1150
 8   EXPENSES
 9     Cost of Vehicles  786.8    674.8    644
10     Salaries          120      130.8    142.572
11     Administrative    175      175      175
12     Marketing/Adv.    180      220      250
13                       ---------------------------
14     Total Expenses    1261.8   1200.6   1211.572
15
16   GROSS PROFIT        143.2    4.4      -61.572
17
18
19
20
05-Oct-90  09:52 PM
```

FIGURE 3-11

/File Command Menu

4. When the printer has finished, press **P** to advance the paper to the top of the next page so it can be torn off. Depending on the kind of printer you are using, a second P command may be needed to advance the paper far enough. Tear off the printed copy of your worksheet.

5. To complete the print procedure, press **Q** to Quit from the /Print menu. You will return to the **READY** mode.

Saving the Worksheet

So far everything that has been created still resides in the computer's primary storage. To make a permanent copy we need to save it to the disk. Press the / command key to bring up the Command menu. Press **F** to enter the /File menu. Remember that you can undo mistakes by pressing the **Esc** key and enter the correct command.

The /File menu is shown in Figure 3-11. The first choice shown, **Retrieve,** is used to load a worksheet file from the default disk drive. We'll choose the second option, **Save.** Press **S** to activate Save.

Lotus will present a prompt for the file name which will include the default disk drive and possibly a subdirectory for hard drive users. Assuming that this directory is the proper place for storing the file, simply type in the new file name. Follow the usual DOS naming conventions with up to 8 characters in the file name. Call this file **SMITH** as documented in the A1 cell and press **Enter.** All of the spreadsheet settings are saved in the file, including the print range you used when printing the worksheet. When you retrieve the worksheet later, everything will be as you left it then, with the cursor in the same cell.

Lotus will automatically add the .WK1 extension to the file when it is stored. Previous versions of Lotus used a different file extension: Lotus 1a used .WKS, Lotus Student Edition used .WKE, and Lotus 2.01 and 2.2 use .WK1 as the extension. Lotus 3.0 and 3.1 use the .WK3 extension.

If a file by the same name already exists on the default disk drive, Lotus will ask whether you wish to **Cancel** the save command, **Replace** the previous file, or **Backup** the previous file. If you type **C,** Lotus will *not* save the worksheet. Type **R** if you wish to replace an older version with this revision, or **B** if you want to rename the previous version with the .BAK extension and save the current version with the usual .WK1 extension. While Lotus is saving your file it will blink the WAIT indicator. After a few seconds the READY mode indicator will appear, and you may enter another command or make more changes to the worksheet.

Example: *Saving the Smithton Worksheet*

For this example we will save the worksheet as a disk file on the default drive and directory. If your computer is configured for saving files on a floppy disk, place a formatted disk in the proper drive.

1. Activate the command menu by pressing the / key. Choose File by pressing **F**.

2. From the /File menu shown next select the Save option by pressing **S**. Lotus will display names of other files stored on the disk. Type the name of your spreadsheet, **SMITH** and press **Enter** to complete the entry.

3. If there is an existing copy of the SMITH file on the disk, Lotus will display the Cancel-Replace-Backup message. Select Replace by pressing **R**. Lotus will save a copy of the worksheet on your disk.

4. When the /File Save command is complete, you will return to the READY mode automatically.

Retrieving a Worksheet from the Disk

Like WordPerfect, Lotus does not save your work unless you direct it to do so. [Note: dBASE automatically saves your work as you create it.] Assuming you have previously saved the worksheet, you can use the /**File** command to retrieve it. Press / to bring up the Command menu, then **F** for the File menu. The first choice in the File menu is Retrieve. Press **R** to activate the retrieve menu.

When prompted for a file name, Lotus examines all the .WK? files stored on the default disk. Recall from the DOS chapter that the ? is the single-character-match wildcard. Thus any file whose file name extension begins with .WK will match. The applicable files will be displayed in alphabetical order along the top of the screen, below the file name prompt. If you recognize the name of the file, use the arrow keys to move the cursor to the desired file and press **Enter**. Additional file names that do not appear on the screen can be accessed by using the → key to move past the rightmost file name. You could also directly enter the name of the file at the file name prompt.

The selected file will be copied from the disk and put into the worksheet. Caution: any cells in a current worksheet will be erased before the new file is loaded. *Make sure the current worksheet has been saved before you retrieve another worksheet.* If you want to **combine** the two worksheets, the /File Combine command will accomplish this task. The Combine command is discussed in a later chapter.

Leaving Lotus 1-2-3

After printing and subsequently saving your worksheet, it is time to exit from Lotus 1-2-3. Press the / key to bring up the Command menu. The last option is Quit. Press **Q** to leave the 1-2-3 module. Lotus will ask you to confirm that you do wish to leave. Remember that any unsaved work will be irrevocably lost if it is not saved, so never treat this question lightly. Reply **Y** to confirm the Quit command. If you have accidentally gotten to this prompt and don't wish to quit, press **N** for No.

After a few seconds the Lotus Access Menu will reappear on your display. In this instance we have no graphs to print and so will leave the Lotus Access System as well. Press **E** to Exit this menu, and you will be returned to the DOS prompt. [Note: Floppy disk users may need to replace the Lotus System disk with a boot disk containing the COMMAND.COM file.]

The choices in the / command menu are discussed in greater detail in later chapters. This section provides a brief introduction to other commands.

The Lotus / Command Menu

The /Worksheet Menu

This menu allows you to adjust worksheet settings that affect the entire worksheet. You can insert or delete rows or columns, erase the entire worksheet, and create a split-screen effect where two parts of the worksheet are displayed on the screen at the same time. Other Worksheet commands adjust the column widths and default display format for value and label cells. The Lotus recalculation scheme is also set in this menu. Default values for printer and disk drive/directory are also established in this menu.

The /Range Menu

This command is similar to the commands available in the Worksheet menu, except that commands from this menu apply to a specific range of cells rather than the whole spreadsheet. Ranges can be formatted for more pleasing display. Cell formulas can be protected so that their contents cannot be inadvertently erased. Names can be assigned to cell ranges for easier reference in formulas and commands.

/Copy and /Move Menus

These similar commands are used to mark a cell or block of cells to be copied or moved. The Copy command makes a duplicate set of cells while the Move command erases the original cells after they have been copied to another place in the worksheet. Lotus knows to adjust the coordinate references of any cells that have been moved. For example, suppose cell G9 contained +B6/B12. If cell B12 is moved to B15, the formula in cell G9 is automatically changed to +B6/B15. The Copy command can automatically duplicate cell expressions and save significant keying time.

The /File Menu

Discussed earlier in this chapter, the File menu provides for saving and retrieving worksheet files. Other options include combining two worksheet files, extracting a portion of a worksheet file and saving it to a disk file. This menu also lets you see a list of files on your disk and has a file erase feature.

The /Print Menu

There are many optional choices in the Print menu that are discussed in a later chapter. This menu lets you change margins, provide for page headers and footers, adjust the page size, establish border rows and/or columns for large printouts, and set up special printing characteristics.

The /Graph Menu

One of the most valuable features of Lotus 1-2-3 is its graphing facility. The Graph menu provides a means of setting up various graph parameters and specifying which cell ranges are to be graphed. Through this menu you can choose the graph type. Numerous graphing options such as titles, data labels, legends, horizontal and vertical grids, and various scale features can be selected. Lotus versions 3.0 and later also permit plotting of the graph from within the 1-2-3 module. Graphing is covered in Chapter 6.

The /Data Menu

The Lotus Database capability is another popular feature of the package. From this menu you can sort rows in the worksheet, perform a linear regression (fitting a straight line to a set of X-Y coordinates), fill sections of the database with consecutive numbers, and do certain matrix operations.

The Data Query operations provide a very powerful data retrieval mechanism. After specifying the range where the database is stored, you can extract or delete data records that match user-supplied criteria.

The Data menu also provides a means of processing data imported from another application program. Lotus Data operations appear in Chapter 7.

The /Add-in Command

This command allows you to manage Lotus add-in products. Release 2.2 comes with two add-ins, the Macro Manager and Allways. Allways is discussed in Chapter 5. Other products are available from third-party sources. See the Lotus reference manual for an explanation of this command.

The /System Command

This command provides a temporary exit to DOS when you need to execute another program while keeping Lotus in the computer's memory. For network users, this command might be a means of releasing printer output from the network print spooler to the printer.

Lotus Function Keys

The Lotus function key assignments are shown in Figure 3-12. To execute the command in the F-Key Alone column, press the indicated function key by itself. To execute the command in the Alt+F-Key column, hold down the Alt key and press the appropriate function key. Although some of these commands are available through the / command menus, the function key equivalent may be faster. Most users do not need to have a keyboard template while using Lotus 1-2-3. Most of these function key commands are explained in later chapters. The two covered in this chapter are **F1**, the Help key, and **F2**, the Cell Edit key.

CHAPTER REVIEW

Spreadsheets

A spreadsheet is a representation of data in tabular manner, presented as rows and columns. Spreadsheet cells contain data or calculations based on other cells. Electronic spreadsheet programs like Lotus 1-2-3 store the data electronically and can quickly recalculate the cell expressions whenever values change. Spreadsheets like Lotus were designed for use by the end-user, not computer specialists.

CHAPTER REVIEW

Key	F-Key Alone	Alt+F-Key
F1	Help	Compose
F2	Edit	Step
F3	Name	Run
F4	Absolute	Undo
F5	Goto	Learn
F6	Window	
F7	Query	Appl 1
F8	Table	Appl 2
F9	Calc	Appl 3
F10	Graph	Appl 4

FIGURE 3-12

Lotus 1-2-3 Release 2.2 Function Keys

Lotus 1-2-3

Lotus 1-2-3 is the best-selling spreadsheet program, far surpassing sales of competing packages. Nearly 100 preprogrammed @ functions augment user-created formulas. Functions are available for mathematical, financial, date and time, logical, and other purposes. Lotus provides the spreadsheet, database, and graphic features that are reflected in its name, 1-2-3.

The Lotus Access Menu and 1-2-3

The starting point in Lotus is the Access Menu, a common way of accessing the 1-2-3 Spreadsheet, PrintGraph, Translate, and Install modules. Most activity takes place in 1-2-3. PrintGraph is used to print graphs created in 1-2-3. Translate converts files between several common file formats for use by Lotus and other packages. Install is used to customize Lotus to the types of display and printers used.

The Lotus 1-2-3 Control Panel

The Lotus Control Panel contains numerous informative indicators and messages. The mode indicator in the upper right corner shows the overall status of Lotus. Values for the mode indicator include READY, WAIT, VALUE, LABEL, EDIT, MENU and ERROR. The lower right corner of the display shows the status of the three Lock keys—CapsLock, NumLock and ScrollLock—along with several other indicators. The OVR indicator means that characters entered will overtype (replace) characters already in the cell; the default condition is insert mode, indicated by the absence of OVR. UNDO shows that any changes made since the previous READY mode can be undone.

The Lotus / Command Display

The Lotus moving-bar menu uses the top three lines of the display to present commands. Line 2 contains the actual menu of choices available to the user, and the third line presents an informative help message about the highlighted command. Move the cursor with the left and right arrow keys to other choices, the third line changes to reflect messages about that command. To execute a particular command, move the cursor to that command and press the **Enter** key. Experienced users can simply type the first character of the command. To void a command entry, press the **Esc** key and you will return to the previous menu. **Ctrl-Break** will abort the command altogether and return to Ready mode.

Moving Around the Worksheet

The four arrow keys are used to move the cursor around the worksheet. **PgUp** and **PgDn** move the display window up or down one screen. **Ctrl**-<arrow> will move the display a screen at a time to the left or right, depending on which arrow key is pressed. The up and down arrow keys have no effect when used with the **Ctrl** key. The **End** key is used to send the cursor to the end of the spreadsheet when used with one of the arrow keys. The ScrollLock mode causes the cursor to move the display window when an arrow key is pressed. Ordinarily the cursor moves within the display window until it "bumps" into a border, at which point the window moves a cell at a time.

Obtaining Help in Lotus 1-2-3

You can obtain Help from Lotus by pressing the **F1** function key. Context-specific help appears according to the status of your current command entry. Thus if you forget the meaning of the /File options appearing on the screen, press **F1** and the resulting Help screen should explain the choices. There is a Help Index that can direct you to the appropriate Help screen for dozens of topics. The moving-bar menu concept also provides help on the third line of the screen when using / command menus.

Making Cell Entries

The worksheet columns are indicated by letters, and rows are indicated by numbers. Cells in Lotus are identified by their column and row coordinates: G9 is the cell in column G, row 9. The typical Lotus screen shows 20 rows and 8 columns, depending on the width of the columns. Lotus provides up to 8192 rows and 256 columns, but the maximum worksheet size depends on the amount of RAM installed in the computer.
   Cell entries are considered either as value or label type. Values can be used in numerical calculations, while labels are strings of characters. The first character entered into a cell determines the cell type. Cell entries can be constants or expressions. Numeric expressions use an algebraic notation with +, −, *, and / symbols for the four basic math operations and ^ for exponentiation. Parentheses can group certain operations together.

Correcting Errors

Errors may be corrected by backspacing if still entering the cell contents. The F2 Edit key permits you to modify cell contents without retyping the entire cell. Pressing the **Enter** key will terminate the edit mode and save the current contents of the cell. Some changes may be accomplished more easily by retyping the cell rather than editing its existing contents.

Printing the Worksheet

Your worksheet is printed by using the /Print command. Before sending the worksheet to the printer you must specify the range of cells to be printed. The range is selected by providing the upper left corner and lower right corner cells.

You can type in the cell coordinates directly or use the Point mode and the arrow keys to highlight the proper cells. The Go command sends a copy of the worksheet to the printer.

Saving and Retrieving the Worksheet

The /File Save command is used to save the worksheet as a disk file. You can provide a name or use the default name if the file has already been saved. Lotus will ask if you wish to backup or replace a file if it already exists on the default disk drive. The /File Retrieve command will clear the worksheet space and load the designated file from the default disk drive. Be sure to save the current worksheet before retrieving a new one.

Leaving Lotus 1-2-3

The /Quit command causes you to leave 1-2-3 and return to the Lotus Access Menu. Lotus always asks you to confirm that you really want to leave the 1-2-3 module. The Exit command in the Access Menu will terminate Lotus and send you back to the DOS prompt.

The Lotus / Command Menu

The /Worksheet commands are used to adjust settings that affect the entire worksheet. The /Range commands accomplish many of the same functions as in the /Worksheet menu, but will modify ranges of cells, not the whole spreadsheet.

The /Copy and /Move commands are useful tools to manipulate the worksheet cells and reduce the amount of typing necessary to make cell entries.

The /Graph menu allows you to create and display Lotus graphs. Graph images are saved as .PIC files for actual printing by the Lotus Access PrintGraph program. The /Data commands manipulate data records and provide sorting and query/retrieval operations. The /System command can provide a temporary DOS prompt for executing a DOS command while Lotus remains resident in memory.

KEY TERMS

@-functions
1-2-3
Abort command
   (**Ctrl-Break**)
anchor cell range
arrow keys
cell
cell format
cell range
circular reference (CIRC)
combining files
/Copy menu
current cell indicator
/Data menu
database module
EDIT indicator
Edit key (**F2**)

edit window
EDIT mode
electronic spreadsheet
End command
ERROR indicator
Esc key
/File command
FILES mode
/Graph menu
graphing module
Help command (**F1**)
Help index
HELP mode
Home key
Install module
label
LABEL mode

lock indicators
Lotus 1-2-3
Manual Calculate key (**F9**)
MEM mode
MENU mode
mode indicator
/Move menu
moving-bar menu
Overtype mode (OVR)
PgDn
PgUp
POINT mode
/Print menu
PrintGraph
/Quit option
/Range menu
READY mode

row and column	status indicators	value
coordinates	**/System** command	VALUE mode
ScrollLock	Translate module	WAIT mode
spreadsheet mode	UNDO indicator	worksheet

DISCUSSION QUESTIONS

1. Describe an electronic spreadsheet. What are its advantages over a paper spreadsheet?
2. List at least four applications for a spreadsheet.
3. Discuss the purposes of the four modules in the Lotus Access System.
4. Explain how to start Lotus 1-2-3 and bring up the READY mode indicator on the display.
5. Explain briefly the meaning of the following Mode indicators:
   a. MENU
   b. VALUE
   c. POINT
   d. EDIT
   e. ERROR.
6. Explain the function of the **ScrollLock** key in Lotus.
7. What is a circular reference in your spreadsheet? How does Lotus indicate one exists?
8. Explain the function of the Lotus moving-bar menu. Discuss two ways of invoking a command with this menu.
9. How are cell locations identified in 1-2-3? What are the maximum number of rows and columns?
10. How is the cell type (value or label) determined by Lotus?
11. Indicate the cell type of the following cell expressions:
    a. B6-B9
    b. @SUM(A12..A99)
    c. 1990
    d. 1990 (space precedes the 1)
    e. +A14/A99
    f. EXPENSES.
12. Explain the cursor movement function of the following commands:
    a. Home
    b. ↑
    c. ↑ Scroll on
    d. PgDn
    e. Ctrl-→.
13. Discuss the use of the **End** key in quickly moving the cursor around the worksheet.
14. Explain how you would find Help about a function like @SUM within the Lotus system.

15. Suppose you had entered the / Command menu and made an incorrect choice. How do you "undo" that last command?

16. List, in proper order, the steps in printing your worksheet. Assume that the spreadsheet is finished and ready to be printed.

17. How would you retrieve a saved Lotus file called GRADES.WK1 from your default drive from within 1-2-3? List each step.

18. List the steps you would follow to leave Lotus. Assume you have created a worksheet but have not yet saved it.

19. Explain the purpose of the UNDO command, and how it is used.

EXERCISES

1. Practice starting Lotus and getting to the READY mode. What is the default disk drive where your files will be stored? [Hint:The **/Worksheet Global Default** command will give you many of the default settings for the worksheet.]

2. Prepare a spreadsheet table that will show current sales of Consolidated Industry's products by region and by product group. There are three regions (East, Midwest, West) and four product groups (Paper, Porcelain, Pipe, and Pigments). Sales amounts are shown in Figure 3-13. Include a proper title for your spreadsheet. Provide totals for each row and column, along with a grand total. Save a copy of your worksheet as **CONSOL.**

3. Prepare a monthly budget for someone who is starting a new job. The budget items include rent ($245 per month), car loan ($95), food ($150), gasoline and parking ($35), entertainment ($60), insurance ($35), student loan ($40), taxes ($90), clothing ($105), and miscellaneous ($120). Your budget categories should be listed down the worksheet, with total monthly expenses at the bottom. Also calculate each item's percentage of the total monthly expenses and display to the right of the expense column. Save your worksheet as **BUDGET.**

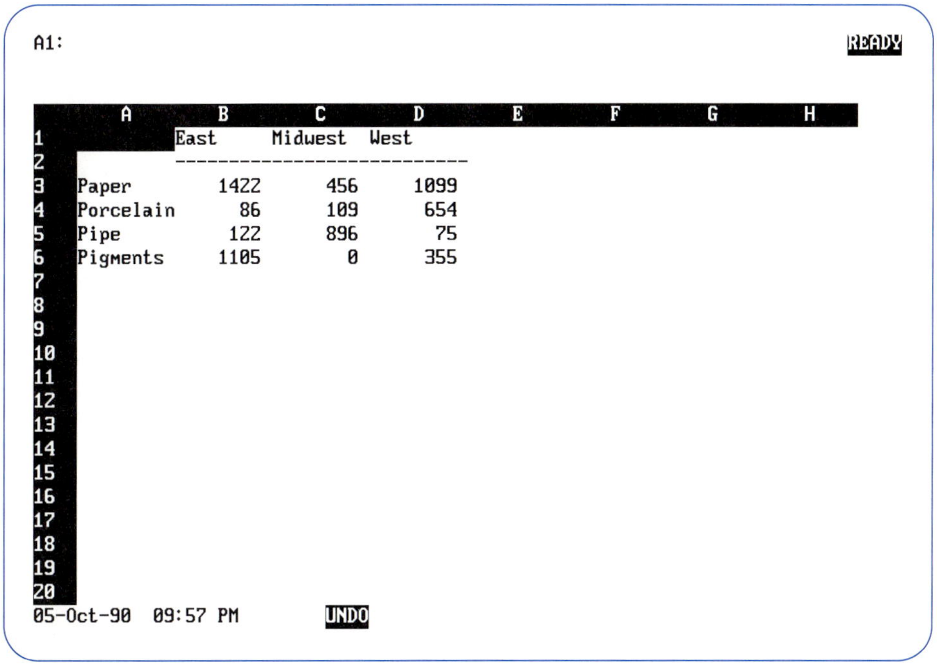

FIGURE 3-13

Sample Data for Exercise 2

```
A1:                                                              READY

          A         B         C         D      E      F      G      H
                  East     Midwest    West
       ---------------------------------------
    3  Paper      1422       456      1099
    4  Porcelain    86       109       654
    5  Pipe        122       896        75
    6  Pigments   1105         0       355

   05-Oct-90  09:57 PM           UNDO
```

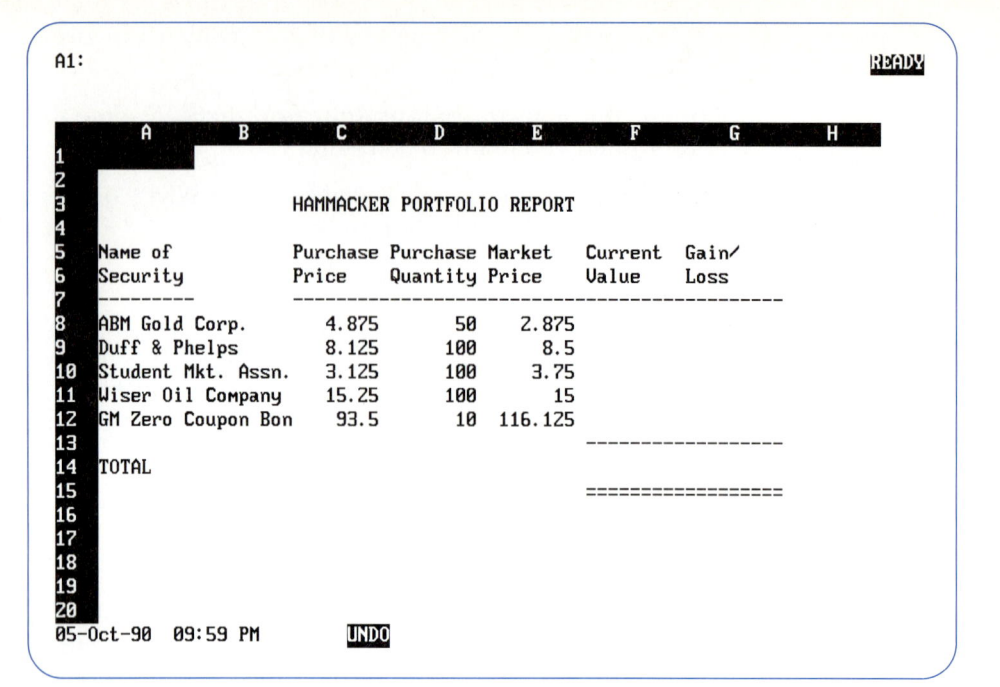

FIGURE 3-14

Sample Data for Exercise 4

```
A1:                                                                    READY

      A          B         C         D        E        F        G       H
 1
 2
 3                    HAMMACKER PORTFOLIO REPORT
 4
 5   Name of         Purchase Purchase Market    Current  Gain/
 6   Security       Price    Quantity Price     Value    Loss
 7   ---------------------------------------------------------------
 8   ABM Gold Corp.    4.875       50   2.875
 9   Duff & Phelps     8.125      100   8.5
10   Student Mkt. Assn. 3.125     100   3.75
11   Wiser Oil Company 15.25      100   15
12   GM Zero Coupon Bon 93.5       10   116.125
13                                              -------------------
14   TOTAL
15                                              ===================
16
17
18
19
20
05-Oct-90  09:59 PM             UNDO
```

4. Start Lotus 1-2-3 and create the spreadsheet in Figure 3-14. The Hammacker Corporation wishes to prepare a Portfolio Statement as shown above. You should fill in columns F and G with appropriate expressions. Column F is calculated by multiplying the number of shares by the market price. Column G is the total gain or loss, Current Value less Purchase Cost. Calculate the investment in each security based upon purchase price and number of shares and calculate the gain or loss in that security. Save the worksheet under the name **HAMMPORT.**

Your share prices in the spreadsheet will not align on the decimal point unless those cells are formatted with a fixed number of decimal places. We'll cover formatting in the next chapter.

5. The Midwest Entrepreneurship Center is developing a business plan for one of their clients, and you have been asked to build a simple income estimate for the next three years, 1990–1992. This worksheet will be similar in appearance to the Smithton worksheet used in this chapter. Use column A for the account categories; place 1990 figures in column C, with 1991 and 1992 in columns D and E. Sales in 1990 start at 1500, and increase by 12% each year. Thus the 1991 sales would be 1.12*(1990 sales). Expenses can be broken down into Cost of Goods Sold (COGS), estimated at 45% of that year's sales; Administrative Costs (Admin) are $200 in 1990, $220 in 1991, and $205 for 1992; Overhead is estimated at 15% of sales in 1990, dropping to 13% of sales in 1991 and 1992.

Calculate Total Expenses and determine Gross Profit by subtracting Total Expenses from Sales. Taxes are based upon 36% of gross profit. Finally, Net Profit is found by subtracting taxes from gross profit. Use dashed lines (\–) and blank rows to separate parts of the worksheet and to improve readability. Save your worksheet as **MIDWEST.** A sample screen is shown in Figure 3-15.

6. Professor Sheppard recently purchased a personal computer to store students' grades. He is just learning how to use Lotus 1-2-3 and wants your

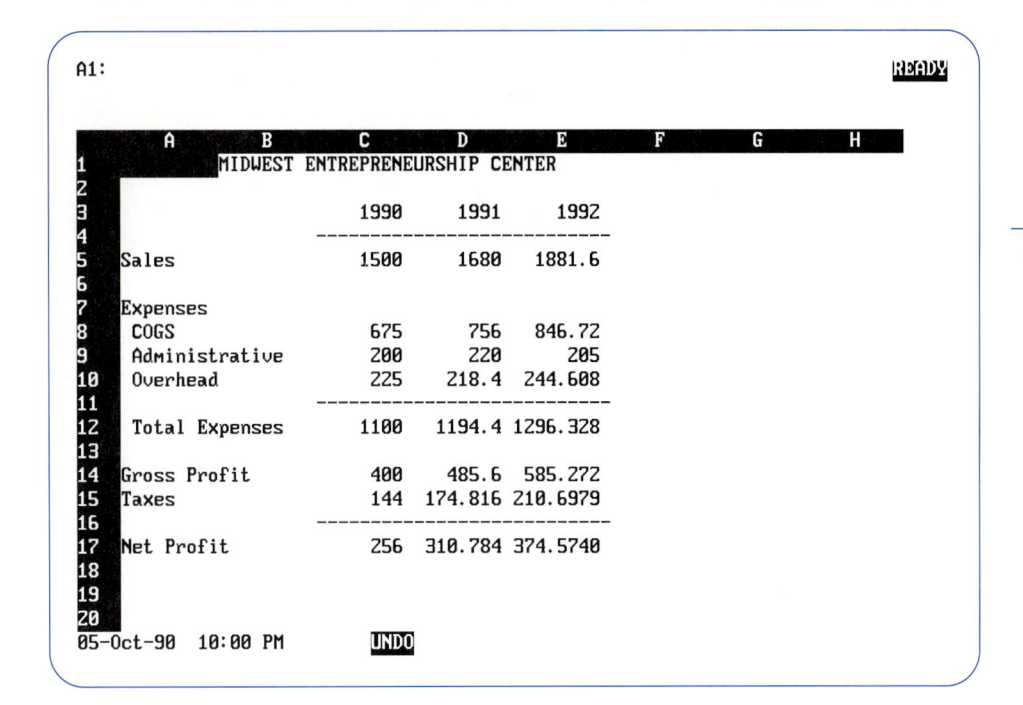

```
A1:                                                     READY

      A       B       C       D       E       F    G    H
 1            MIDWEST ENTREPRENEURSHIP CENTER
 2
 3                    1990    1991    1992
 4                   --------------------------
 5    Sales          1500    1680    1881.6
 6
 7    Expenses
 8     COGS          675     756     846.72
 9     Administrative 200    220     205
10     Overhead      225     218.4   244.608
11                   --------------------------
12    Total Expenses 1100    1194.4  1296.328
13
14    Gross Profit   400     485.6   585.272
15    Taxes          144     174.816 210.6979
16                   --------------------------
17    Net Profit     256     310.784 374.5740
18
19
20
05-Oct-90  10:00 PM         UNDO
```

FIGURE 3-15

Sample Data for Exercise 5

```
STUDENT          EXAM 1   EXAM 2   EXAM 3   QUIZZES

Smith, Brenda      90       87       79       88
Taggart, Louis     67       76       82       71
Evans, Harry       62       46       68       45
Meeks, Mike        93       85       88       91
Krum, Dennis       80       74       85       78
Palmer, Chris      92       96       80       92
```

FIGURE 3-16

Sample Data for Exercise 6

help in building a gradebook worksheet. First enter the students' names and grades for the semester. The values are shown in Figure 3-16.

Prepare a spreadsheet model for Prof. Sheppard that will display the name and four grades for each student. Add the total points together for each student. Also display the decimal percentage of the possible 400 points earned. Don't change the order of the students in the gradebook. Save your worksheet as GRADBOOK.

7. Prepare an invoice for the PSC Plumbing Supply Company, similar to that shown in Figure 3-17. The client is Mechanical and Electrical Corporation, 1817 College Avenue, Howard, OH 44136. Be sure to calculate the extended price (quantity times unit cost) and total that column. The Sales Tax Amount is 5% of the Total Merchandise Amount. Amount Due is the sum of the Total Merchandise and Sales Tax amounts.

Your spreadsheet should resemble this one, but does not have to match it exactly. The top two title lines have one space between letters and three spaces between words. Put each heading line in a single cell, letting it spill over into adjacent cells. Skip a row between lines. Underlines for column headings (with the \– command) can extend all the way across a column if

FIGURE 3-17

Sample Data for Exercise 7

```
P S C    P L U M B I N G    S U P P L Y    C O M P A N Y

         I N V O I C E    S T A T E M E N T

Mechanical and Electrical Corporation
1817 College Avenue
Howard, OH 44136    PO#: A6513245-1    DATE: July 25, 1989

PART NO.      DESCRIPTION          QTY    PRICE     EXTENDED
--------      -----------          ---    -----     --------
X12344        PVC Pipe 3/4"         16     0.24
CPU7291       Pipe stretcher         1    11.92
IS8256U       Washer gasket         15     2.14
                                                    --------
              TOTAL MERCHANDISE AMOUNT
              SALES TAX AMOUNT (5%)
                                                    --------
              AMOUNT DUE
                                                    ========
```

FIGURE 3-18

Sample Data for Exercise 8

```
Item                          Cost        Sales Price
-------------------------------------------------------
Yellow Highlighter            0.56
Pentel leads                  0.88
Calculator                    9.56
3.5-inch Diskette             1.20
10 3.5-inch Diskettes         9.44
Box of #2 pencils             2.65
Stapler, Standard             7.33
Stapler, Mini                 3.12
Breath Mints                  0.37
```

desired. Column widths may vary from these. (Chapter 4 discusses ways to modify column headings.) Save your worksheet as **PSCINV**.

8. The college bookstore has asked you to assist in preparing sales prices for items in its catalog. The standard markup percentage is 25%. Thus an item that costs the bookstore $15 will sell for 15*1.25, or $18.75. Prepare a spreadsheet model that uses an input cell for the markup percentage, and calculate selling prices for the items listed in Figure 3-18. Save your worksheet as **MARKUP**.

9. You have just read about a financial aid opportunity that requires a good grade-point average, and a history of your college work by semester. The results of the first few semesters are shown in Figure 3-19 and you are to calculate *semester and cumulative* grade point averages after each semester. Grade point average is calculated by dividing Grade Points by Credit Hours. (Grade points were determined by multiplying each course's credit hours times 4.0 for an A, 3.5 for a B+, and so on.) Use your ingenuity in

Semester	Credit Hours	Grade Points
Fall, 88	15	55
Spring, 89	17	55
Summer, 89	6	24
Fall, 89	16	50
Spring, 90	14	39

FIGURE 3-19

Sample Data for Exercise 9

designing an appropriate format to display the transcript data. Be sure to place your name, address, and student identification number prominently in the report. Save your worksheet as **GPA**.

CHAPTER 3 PROJECT
CAMPUS NETWORKING

The campus Networks Committee has been meeting for about six months in an effort to develop a master plan to connect personal computers in various departmental offices to the network. Among the committee's early accomplishments were a prioritized list of campus groups that are scheduled to be added to the campus network and approximate costs for various data communications components. The list of departments and schools is shown in Figure 3-20 with the number of local area network connections needed for each group.

Costs are based upon several factors, including the cost per station of $500 (includes cabling and a network interface card) and the cost per network server of $8800. Installation costs $1100 per server plus $50 per station.

The committee needs an estimate of the total cost for purchasing and installing all the equipment. Because only $250,000 is available in the first year, the committee wishes to know how far down the priority list those funds will serve. So also calculate the cumulative cost through each group on the list.

Use Lotus 1-2-3 to prepare an estimate of the costs for the networks committee.

Campus Group	No. of Servers	No. of Stations
Root Hall	4	129
Business	2	65
Education	2	80
Phys. Plant	1	10
Science	2	124
Technology	2	45
Classroom	1	35
Journalism	1	20
HPER	1	60
Purchasing Dept.	1	25
Administration	2	55
Nursing	1	35
Residence Halls Lab	1	20
Fine Arts/Music	1	40

FIGURE 3-20

Sample Data for Campus Networking Project

4

Building Lotus 1-2-3 Worksheets

Objectives

After completing this chapter, you should be able to:

- Discuss spreadsheet design considerations.
- Insert and delete rows and columns in the worksheet.
- Copy and move cell ranges.
- Explain the differences between relative and absolute cell references, and how to convert from one to the other.
- List the nine types of numeric cell formats available in Lotus 1-2-3 and give an example of each.
- Format a range of cells.
- Explain the differences between Global and Range cell characteristics.
- Change the Global default column width, and change the width of a specific column.
- Explain why automatic recalculation is not desirable in all situations, and how to change to manual recalculation mode.
- Discuss the use of Lotus titles and windows for large worksheets.
- List the five categories of Lotus @-functions, and explain the role of @-functions in a spreadsheet.

INTRODUCTION

In the previous chapter we learned how to start Lotus 1-2-3 and build a simple worksheet. This chapter will explain how to use the Lotus /Copy command to duplicate cell formulas in other areas of the worksheet, saving much time and reducing typing errors. Other spreadsheet functions are explained, including row and column insertion and deletion.

Cell formats are introduced, along with an explanation of how formats are used in a worksheet. You will see how the /Worksheet Global commands can be used to modify the default settings for the entire worksheet, and how to override the default settings for certain columns or cell ranges. We will explain how to change the column width to accommodate wider or narrower values.

Recalculation options are explained, along with how to change from automatic recalculation. The use of Titles and Windows to accommodate large spreadsheets is presented.

The Lotus @-functions are introduced, along with examples in each of the categories: mathematical, financial, date/time, logical, and string functions.

WORKING WITH ROWS, COLUMNS, AND CELLS

Design Considerations

As the spreadsheet solution to a problem begins to take shape it is important to keep the **worksheet design** in mind. Most spreadsheets are larger than a single display window, and many are too large to fit on a single sheet of paper. There are several important design considerations as you build the worksheet.

- Identify the purpose, author, and revision data for the worksheet in a consistent spot.

- First, lay out the spreadsheet *on paper* with the general location for various portions indicated. Keep in mind where the report layouts are located within the spreadsheet.

- For large spreadsheets with several tables, generally place them on a diagonal, from cell A1 to the lower right, so that they do not share common rows or columns. Then, if any rows or columns are added or deleted, those rows affect only a single part of the worksheet.

- Whenever possible, use range names in cell expressions rather than raw cell addresses. Document range names in a standard way in a portion of the worksheet. Range names are explained in this chapter.

- When a spreadsheet is finished, protect the cell formulas and provide a data input area for the user. Cell protection is discussed later in this chapter.

- Use adjacent cells for documentation to remind the reader what certain cells contain; any unusual cell expressions should be fully explained.

- **Macros** (stored sequences of Lotus commands that can be "replayed") are appropriate for large spreadsheets, particularly when the actual user will not be fully conversant in Lotus 1-2-3. Macros are explained in Chapter 8.

Poorly designed spreadsheets are difficult to work with and may present problems when changes are made. While most spreadsheets can be modified to fit these general design guidelines, it is easier to build them properly in the first place.

WORKING WITH ROWS, COLUMNS, AND CELLS

101

One advantage of an electronic spreadsheet is the ability to manipulate and change the spreadsheet configuration. If a paper spreadsheet is missing a row, it is difficult to squeeze one in or tedious to recopy all the rows below it to make room. With Lotus, inserting a row or column is simple. First, move the cursor to the cell where the insertion is to take place. Lotus will insert a row *above* the cursor cell or a column to the *left* of the cursor cell.

Inserting and Deleting Rows and Columns

Example: *Inserting a Single Row*

The Smithton firm wishes to add another expense category called Commissions to the worksheet. It should be inserted between Cost of Vehicles and Salaries. Unfortunately, there is no room there now. Let's recall the example spreadsheet from the last chapter. It is called SMITH.WK1 and is stored on the data disk.

1. Load 1-2-3, then use the **/FR** command to retrieve the worksheet file. It is shown in Figure 4-1.

2. To insert a row, move the cursor to any cell in row 10, say A10. Recall from the last chapter how to enter a Lotus / command. Press the / key to bring up the / Command menu. Press **WIR** (**Worksheet Insert Row**) and press the **Enter** key to execute the command at the current location. Lotus moves everything in rows 10–16 down one row and automatically adjusts all the formulas that refer to any of the moved cells. There is a new blank row at row 10, waiting for the Commissions data to be entered.

3. Assume that the Commissions are based on 6 percent of the Cost of Vehicles Amount (not based on Sales). The cursor is at cell A10. Enter the Expense category name, **'   Commissions**. (Don't forget to leave two spaces before the first letter to indent the label two spaces.)

```
A1: 'SMITH -- B. McLaren  6/27/89                              READY

        A         B         C         D         E         F         G         H
1   SMITH --  B. McLaren  6/27/89
2
3               SMITHTON RECREATIONAL VEHICLE SALES, INC.
4
5                         1987      1988      1989
6                         ----------------------------
7   SALES                 1405      1205      1150
8   EXPENSES
9     Cost of Vehicles    786.8     674.8     644
10    Salaries            120       130.8     142.572
11    Administrative      175       175       175
12    Marketing/Adv.      180       220       250
13                        ----------------------------
14    Total Expenses      1261.8    1200.6    1211.572
15
16  GROSS PROFIT          143.2     4.4       -61.572
17
18
19
20
05-Oct-90  10:10 PM           UNDO
```

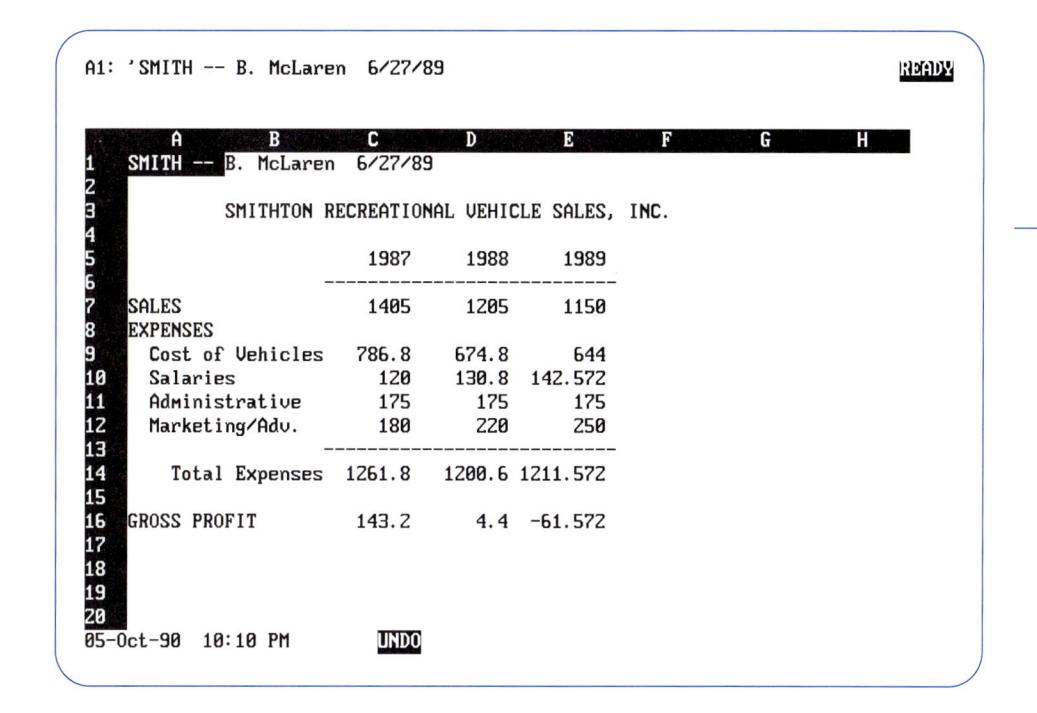

FIGURE 4-1

Original Smithton Sample Worksheet SMITH.WK1

FIGURE 4-2

Smithton Worksheet with Inserted Row (Press **/WIR**)

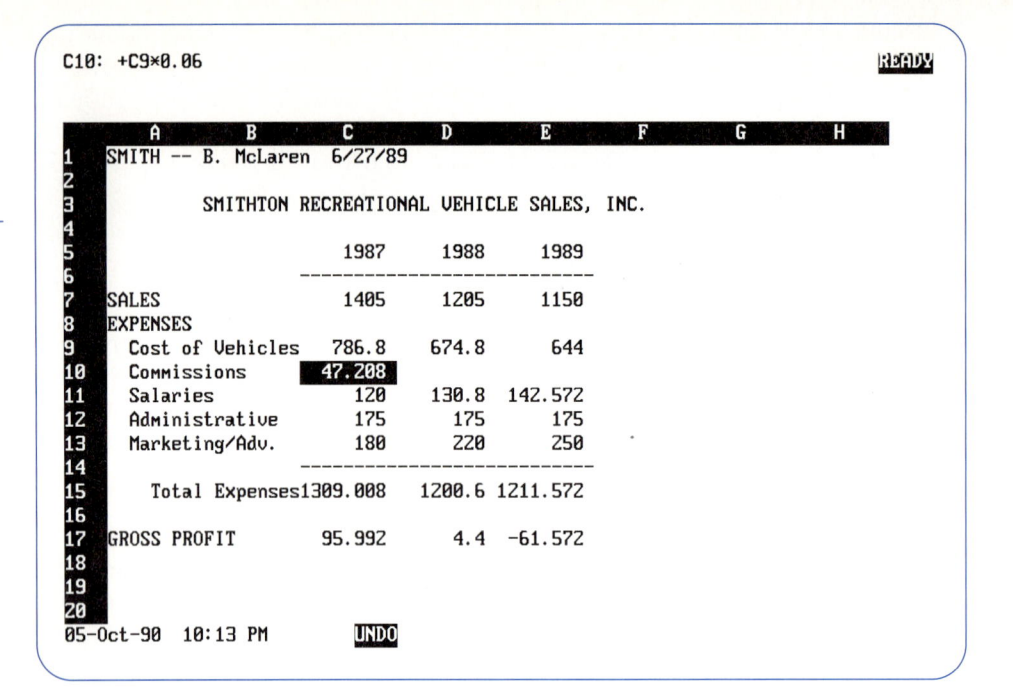

```
C10: +C9*0.06                                              READY

         A         B         C         D         E      F    G    H
 1  SMITH -- B. McLaren  6/27/89
 2
 3                 SMITHTON RECREATIONAL VEHICLE SALES, INC.
 4
 5                           1987      1988      1989
 6                         ------------------------------
 7  SALES                   1405      1205      1150
 8  EXPENSES
 9    Cost of Vehicles      786.8     674.8      644
10    Commissions            47.208
11    Salaries               120      130.8    142.572
12    Administrative         175      175        175
13    Marketing/Adv.         180      220        250
14                         ------------------------------
15    Total Expenses1309.008 1200.6  1211.572
16
17  GROSS PROFIT             95.992     4.4    -61.572
18
19
20
05-Oct-90  10:13 PM           UNDO
```

4. Next move the cursor to cell C10, type the formula **+C9*.06**, and press **Enter**.

5. You should see the spreadsheet in Figure 4-2.

6. You will fill in the other two columns shortly as you learn how to copy formulas. Notice that the Commissions amount for the first year is not rounded off—its value is 47.208. This cell has not been formatted and shows the number as it would appear on your calculator without fixing the number of decimal places.

Inserting a Single Column

To insert a column the same technique is used. Move the cursor to the cell to the right of where you would like a column inserted. Columns are inserted to the left of the cell pointer. Press the **/WIC** command (**Worksheet Insert Column**) and press **Enter** to signify the location of the column is the cursor cell.

Example: *Inserting a Column*

Suppose you wanted to insert a column in the SMITH.WK1 spreadsheet to hold the 1986 Sales data. Retrieve the SMITH.WK1 spreadsheet from the data disk.

1. Move the cursor to any cell in column C, say cell C5.

2. Type the command **/WIC** (/Worksheet Insert Column) and press **Enter** to signify you wish to insert a column before the current cell location.

3. Lotus will open up a blank column where column C used to be. All former cells in columns C–E have been moved over to columns D–F and the cell expression adjusted as needed.

WORKING WITH ROWS, COLUMNS, AND CELLS

```
C5:                                                          READY

     A      B         C       D       E        F      G       H
1  SMITH -- B. McLaren  6/27/89
2
3             SMITHTON RECREATIONAL VEHICLE SALES, INC.
4
5                            1987    1988    1989
6                         ------------------------
7  SALES                    1405    1205    1150
8  EXPENSES
9     Cost of Vehicles      786.8   674.8    644
10    Salaries              120     130.8   142.572
11    Administrative        175     175      175
12    Marketing/Adv.        180     220      250
13                        ------------------------
14    Total Expenses       1261.8  1200.6  1211.572
15
16 GROSS PROFIT             143.2    4.4    -61.572
17
18
19
20
05-Oct-90  10:15 PM         UNDO
```

FIGURE 4-3

Sample Spreadsheet with New Column C Inserted (Press **/WIC**)

4. You may now insert data into column C to represent 1986 Sales. The new spreadsheet is shown in Figure 4-3.

Inserting Multiple Rows or Columns

To insert multiple columns or rows, follow the same approach by moving the cursor to the desired location. Press **/WIR** to activate the row-insert command. When Lotus asks for the row insert range, use the arrow key to highlight the rows to be inserted. The new rows will be inserted *above* the first row highlighted in the row insert range. To insert three rows above row 10, move the cursor to cell A10 and press **/WIR**. When asked to identify the row insert range, press the down arrow twice, highlighting cells A10..A12 and press **Enter**. Lotus will insert three rows above row 10, and will renumber cells in rows below accordingly.

Deleting Rows and Columns

The command to delete rows and columns is similar to the Insert command. To delete a row, move the cursor to any cell in the row to be deleted, then press **/WDR (Worksheet Delete Row)**. When Lotus asks you to highlight the range of rows to delete, highlight cells in those rows by moving the cursor with the arrow keys, and execute the command by pressing **Enter**. To delete a column, follow the same procedure except press **/WDC (Worksheet Delete Column)** instead of /WDR.

Caution is necessary when deleting rows or columns. Unless you have Undo enabled, Lotus cannot recover deleted cells, so be sure that the range you have entered is indeed that which you wish to delete. Because the cells are highlighted on the screen you can have visual confirmation that the correct range is entered. Also remember that the row or column you delete extends all the way to the end of the worksheet. Other tables off-screen which share the same row or column will also be affected when that row is deleted. The **diagonal design rule** is a good one to follow to avoid this problem.

Example: Deleting a Column

In this example you will delete the 1986 Sales column introduced in the previous example. If you have not already inserted a new column C into your spreadsheet, please go through the previous example now.

1. Make sure the SMITH worksheet with the new column C is in memory.

2. Move the cursor to any cell in column C, say C6. Be certain the cursor is in the column to be deleted.

3. Press /**WDC** (Worksheet Delete Column).

4. When Lotus prompts for the range of columns to be deleted, press **Enter** to confirm that column C is to be deleted. (You could also type the column range directly at this prompt.)

5. The worksheet should appear as it did originally, with the new column C deleted and the information from columns D–F moved back to columns C–E.

Copying and Moving Cells

Lotus is able to immediately recalculate cell values whenever you change a cell in the worksheet, but entering formulas is sometimes tedious or error prone. The /**Copy** command is used to duplicate cell formulas in other places on the worksheet, while the /**Move** command moves the formulas from one cell to another.

The /Copy command has two parameters: you must specify the "FROM:" range of cells that you wish to copy, and the "TO:" range of cells where you want the From cells duplicated. The usual technique is to position the cursor in the upper left corner cell in the FROM range, then begin the /Copy command. Each range is in the format "cell1..cell2" where cell1 is the beginning cell of the range and cell2 is the ending cell of that rectangular range.

Example: Copying Cell Formulas

In this example you will duplicate the Commissions expression in cell C10 (+C9*.06) by copying it into cells D10 and E10. Lotus will adjust the cell references automatically and calculate the commissions for the two new cells.

1. Use the previous SMITH worksheet. Move the cursor to cell C10 which contains the expression to be copied (the FROM cell).

2. Press /**C** (Copy) to activate the copy command. The FROM: range already has C10..C10 filled in, so just press **Enter** to finish the FROM: specification.

3. Lotus next asks you to enter the TO: range. The simpler technique is to use the right arrow key to highlight the desired range of cells, in this case D10..E10. Press → once, highlighting cell D10.

4. Press the period to anchor the beginning of the range, then tap the → key once more to highlight both cells (D10 and E10). Press **Enter** to lock in the TO: range.

WORKING WITH ROWS, COLUMNS, AND CELLS

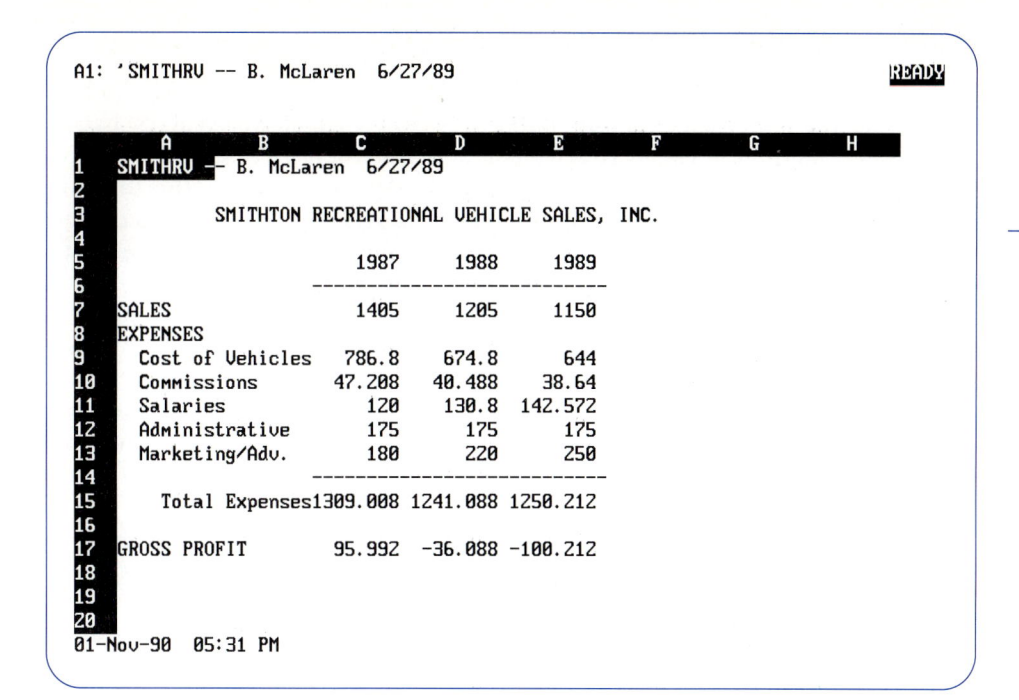

```
A1: 'SMITHRV -- B. McLaren  6/27/89                           READY

       A          B         C         D         E      F      G      H
 1  SMITHRV -- B. McLaren  6/27/89
 2
 3              SMITHTON RECREATIONAL VEHICLE SALES, INC.
 4
 5                         1987      1988      1989
 6                        ------------------------
 7  SALES                  1405      1205      1150
 8  EXPENSES
 9    Cost of Vehicles    786.8     674.8       644
10    Commissions        47.208    40.488     38.64
11    Salaries              120     130.8   142.572
12    Administrative        175       175       175
13    Marketing/Adv.        180       220       250
14                        ------------------------
15    Total Expenses   1309.008  1241.088  1250.212
16
17  GROSS PROFIT          95.992   -36.088  -100.212
18
19
20
01-Nov-90  05:31 PM
```

FIGURE 4-4

Smithton Worksheet with Commissions Row

5. Lotus will immediately insert the proper formulas into the two cells and recalculate all the cells whose values depend on the new cells. This recalculation is done very rapidly.

6. To distinguish this worksheet from the previous one, move the cursor to cell A1 by pressing the **Home** key. Then press **F2** to edit this cell. Use the arrow keys to move the cursor to the character following H in SMITH. Add the letters **RV** to the worksheet name and press **Enter** to complete the edit. The finished SMITHRV worksheet is shown in Figure 4-4.

Example: *Moving Cell Formulas*

This example shows how you can move cells with the /Move command. If it is not already in the edit window, retrieve the SMITHRV.WK1 worksheet from the data disk.

1. Move the cursor to cell C15 which contains the expression to be moved (the FROM cell).

2. Press **/M** (Move) to activate the move command. The FROM: range already has C15..C15 filled in, so just press **Enter** to finish the FROM: specification.

3. Press the ↓ key three times, moving the cursor to cell C18. Press **Enter** to complete the TO: specification.

4. Examine the contents of cell C18 in the control panel. Notice that the cell expression remains the same, @SUM(C9..C13). Also notice that cell C15 is now empty. When Lotus moves cells it does *not* adjust cell references within the cell expression as /Copy does.

5. Move the contents of cell C18 back to cell C15 using the **/M** command. The FROM: range is C18..C18 and the TO: range is C15.

Relative and Absolute Cell Addresses

Notice that the Total Expenses in Figure 4-4 are automatically adjusted to account for the increased expenses, and the Gross Profit is lowered accordingly. Lotus uses a technique called **relative cell address** when it copies the formula from cell C10. If you move the cursor to cell D10, you'll notice the formula there is **+D9*.06** and the expression in cell E10 is **+E9*.06**. When Lotus copied the formula, it adjusted the column letter for each column. Formulas copied to different rows will also have the row addresses adjusted properly.

For example, suppose you copy a cell expression from cell A25 to cell C28, two columns over and three rows down. Any cells referenced in the "FROM" expression will be adjusted in cell C28 such that they refer to 2 columns to the right and three rows below the original reference. Thus if A25 contains the expression +B24/A24, then C28 would contain D27/C27. Students often have trouble understanding relative cell addresses until they practice copying cell formulas on the computer.

Using the relative cell address in copied formulas is appropriate most of the time, and that is the default treatment. However, there are some instances when you do not want the cell address to be adjusted automatically. When calculating percentages of a total, you want to divide each item by the same amount. We can add a column to the Smithton example to illustrate this principle.

Example: *Using Absolute Cell Addresses*

Suppose we want to calculate 1989's percentages of Sales for each expense item.

1. Move to cell F5 and add the new column label by typing **Percent of Sales**.

2. Move the cursor to cell F9 and insert the following formula: **+E9/$E$7**. The dollar signs signify to Lotus that when that formula is copied to other rows, the E7 absolute cell reference is not to be changed. What would be the result if you omitted the dollar signs in the formula and copied it to the other rows?

3. Next use the /Copy command to copy that formula to cells F10 through F13: **/C Enter** ↓ **.** ↓ ↓ ↓ **<Enter>.** (Make sure the cells F10..F13 are highlighted before pressing the last Enter key.)

4. Lotus will copy the formula to rows 10 through 13, each time dividing the expense item by the Sales.

5. Let's rename this worksheet: press **F2** to edit the cell; type **SMITHRVP** in cell A1, and save it with the **/FS** command. The finished worksheet is shown in Figure 4-5.

We had to enter the formula in one cell, then were able to copy it quickly to other cells. Lotus automatically adjusted other cell references in the new formulas. For example, cell F13's formula is **E13/$E$7**, reflecting the percentage from row 13.

Types of Absolute Cell References

There are four types of **relative** and **absolute cell addresses,** or references. The dollar sign preceding the row or column reference indicates which absolute cell reference is desired. Example expressions are explained below.

WORKING WITH ROWS, COLUMNS, AND CELLS

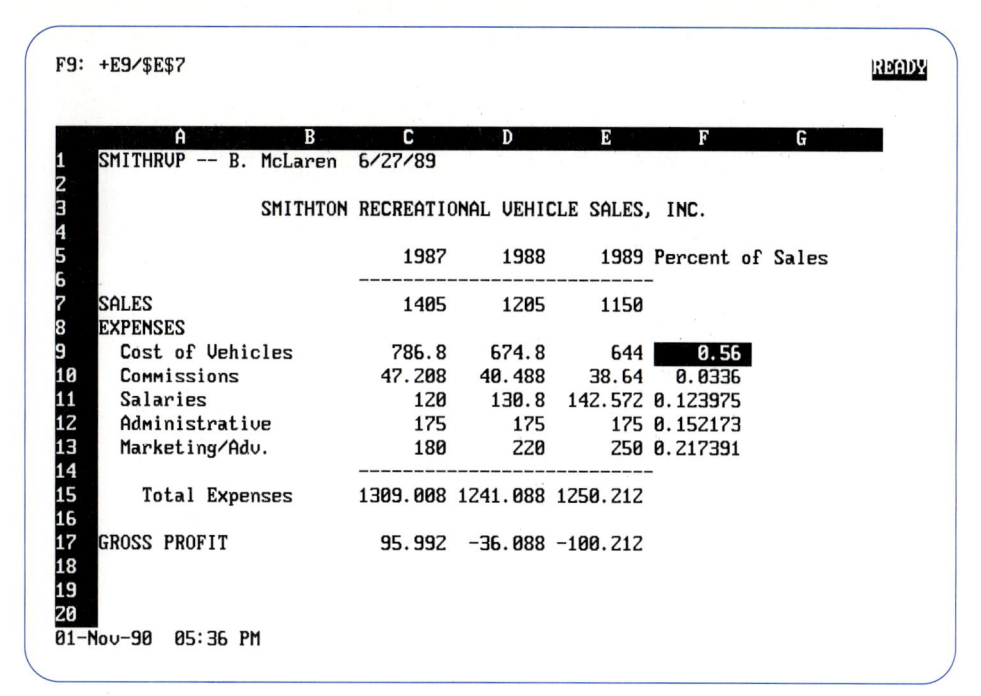

```
F9: +E9/$E$7                                                    READY

           A         B       C         D       E       F         G
 1  SMITHRVP -- B. McLaren   6/27/89
 2
 3                SMITHTON RECREATIONAL VEHICLE SALES, INC.
 4
 5                          1987      1988    1989 Percent of Sales
 6                         --------------------------
 7  SALES                   1405      1205    1150
 8  EXPENSES
 9     Cost of Vehicles     786.8     674.8    644    0.56
10     Commissions          47.208    40.488   38.64  0.0336
11     Salaries             120       130.8    142.572 0.123975
12     Administrative       175       175      175    0.152173
13     Marketing/Adv.       180       220      250    0.217391
14                         --------------------------
15     Total Expenses       1309.008  1241.088 1250.212
16
17  GROSS PROFIT            95.992   -36.088  -100.212
18
19
20
01-Nov-90  05:36 PM
```

FIGURE 4-5

Results of Copying the Percent Expression (Press /C)

E7   This is a relative cell address. Both the row and column are adjusted when the expression is copied.

$E$7 This is the full absolute address. Neither row nor column is adjusted when the expression is copied.

$E7 This is a partial absolute address. The column is not adjusted when the expression is copied, but the row is adjusted.

E$7 This is another partial absolute address. When the expression is copied, the row is not adjusted but the column is adjusted.

Example: *Entering an Absolute Cell Reference with F4*

When making a cell entry or editing a cell, you can place the cursor on any part of the cell reference and change it to one of the four types. In this example you will use the F4 function key to cycle between the four types of cell references.

1. Move the cursor to a blank cell in the worksheet, say cell A22.

2. Enter the cell expression **+A21** but do not press Enter. The cell input area in the upper left corner of the control panel will show the expression, +A21.

3. Press the **F4** key one time. The cell entry will change to +$A$21.

4. Press the **F4** key again. The cell entry will change to +A$21.

5. Press the **F4** key again. The cell entry will change to +$A21.

6. Press the **F4** key once more. The cell entry will return to the starting point, +A21.

Working with Lotus Cell Range Names

Lotus has the capability of naming ranges of cells. Once named, these cells can be referenced by that range name in other cell expressions, as a print range, and in other Lotus commands. When cells are moved, the named range is automatically updated for the new location. With range names in cell expressions, it is easier to get the correct cell range specification. Cell expressions are easier to check when they refer to named ranges and not just cell coordinates.

Creating Range Names

Creating the **range name** requires two steps: naming it, then specifying the range. First issue the **/Range Name** command (**/RN**). The menu is shown below.

MENU

Create Delete Labels Reset Table
Create or modify a range name

When you select the Create option, Lotus will ask you to name the range. Range names may be up to 14 characters long, and embedded spaces are permitted. Avoid the special range names A, B, ..., Z and 0 for now—they are used for naming Lotus macros, described in Chapter 8. Then you will be asked to provide the cell range for that name. The example below demonstrates creating two named ranges.

Example: *Creating Range Names*

In this example you will create range names to represent the Sales amounts and the entire worksheet.

1. First retrieve the SMITHRVP.WK1 worksheet with the **/FR** command.

2. The three sales cells in the example worksheet occupy cells C7..E7. To name this range, enter the **/Range Name Create** command (**/RNC**). When Lotus prompts for the range name, type in **Sales** and press **Enter**. When asked to provide the cell range, type **C7..E7** and press **Enter**.

3. It is also possible to name a larger range of cells, such as the whole sales table. Type the Range Name Create Command **/RNC**, enter the name **SALES TABLE**, and make its range **A1..G17**. Now, to specify the print range for this table we could enter the range name **SALES TABLE** instead of the cell coordinates.

Using Range Names in Expressions and Commands

Range names may be substituted whenever Lotus asks for a cell range entry. Suppose we wanted to add together the three sales figures and place this in cell G7. First move the cursor to cell G7, then type in the formula **@SUM(SALES)** (explained below under Statistical Functions). This is equivalent to entering @SUM(C7..E7), and is easier to read and verify than using the actual cell coordinates directly. Even though cell ranges have been named, they may still be referenced by their cell coordinates. Placing a dollar sign ($) before the range name has the effect of making that an absolute cell reference.

Example: *Using the Range Name in a Command*

1. To print the sales table worksheet using the range name, type the print command below. Do not put spaces before and after **SALES TABLE**; here they are for clarification only.

    /PPR SALES TABLE <Enter>AG

2. After the printer finishes, press **Q** to quit the print menu.

Other Range Name Options

The complete set of range name options are described below.

- The **Create** option allows you to assign a name to a range of cells.
- The **Delete** option will delete the range name but will not erase any cells from your worksheet.
- The **Labels** option allows you to create range names for single cells from the labels in adjacent cells in the worksheet.
- The **Reset** option will delete all range names with a single command.
- You may pick an empty spot on the worksheet and have Lotus insert a reference **Table** of named ranges and their names.

Example: *Placing a Range Name Table in the Worksheet*

Make sure there are enough empty cells for this list because Lotus will overwrite any existing cells without warning. The table is two columns wide and occupies one row for each range name.

1. To insert the **range name table** in your worksheet, first move the cursor to an empty space, cell A20, then issue the **/RNT** command.
2. When Lotus prompts for the location of the table, press the **Enter** key. The table will look like the one in Figure 4-6.

Formatting Cell Appearance: Formats and Column Width

The default conditions for **cell format** and **column width** depend on the settings made in the /Worksheet Global menu. If no changes have been made in your computer, columns are 9 characters wide and the **General cell format** is used. Numbers always appear at the right side of the cell, with one blank in the last position of the cell. Labels generally appear at the left side of the cell. You may need to change these settings to accommodate large numbers or long labels, or to display a consistent number of decimal places.

Numeric Cell Formats

The most commonly used numeric cell formats in business spreadsheets are **Fixed**, **Comma**, and **Currency**. Each provides for a fixed number of decimal places in the displayed value. Values are rounded to display the desired number of decimal places; however, the *unrounded* original value remains in the cell and is used in all calculations. In fact, using the unrounded values in calculations could lead to confusion. Suppose two cells each contain 0.225. If you add them together, the result is 0.450. However, if they are displayed with two decimal places, each display would be rounded to 0.23, leading to the appearance of 0.23 + 0.23 equals 0.45. While this is not a significant error, it could lead to questionable results.[1]

The **Comma** and **Currency** formats insert commas into large numbers to improve readability. Currency format also adds a floating dollar sign in front of the left-most digit in the number.

Another common format is **Percent**, used to display percentages with a percent sign. You can fix the number of decimal places shown in the percentage. Thus 0.123 would display as 12.3% if you choose thePercent format type with 1 decimal place.

The **General** format type displays as many decimal places as needed for the value in the cell, up to the width of the column. Very large or very small numbers are automatically displayed in scientific notation with the General format type.

The **+/− format** creates a kind of horizontal bar graph in the cell. For positive numbers it displays a series of "+" signs in the cell equal to the magnitude of the number. For negative values it displays "−" signs. The value 6.3 would display as six plus signs, or ++++++.

The **Hidden format** causes that cell to display as a blank cell on the screen and in printed output, but the value remains in the cell and is used in any calculations involving that cell. This might be useful for hiding key assumptions such as markup or cost factors and other proprietary information. If someone has a copy of the worksheet file they could easily change the format type from hidden and see the information stored in that cell. Thus only printed spreadsheets should be distributed when you don't wish others to have knowledge of the cells' contents.

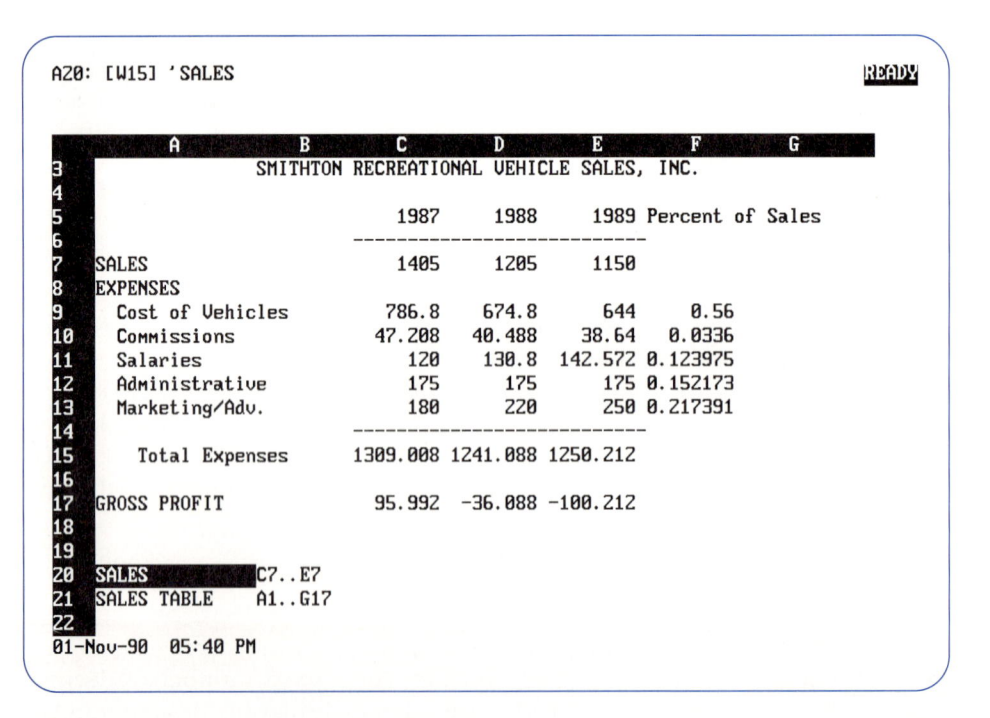

FIGURE 4-6

Example Range Name Table Beginning in Cell A20

```
A20: [W15] 'SALES                                          READY

         A            B         C         D         E         F       G
                    SMITHTON RECREATIONAL VEHICLE SALES, INC.

                              1987      1988      1989 Percent of Sales
                              ----------------------------
    SALES                     1405      1205      1150
    EXPENSES
       Cost of Vehicles       786.8     674.8      644    0.56
       Commissions            47.208    40.488    38.64   0.0336
       Salaries               120       130.8    142.572  0.123975
       Administrative         175       175       175     0.152173
       Marketing/Adv.         180       220       250     0.217391
                              ----------------------------
       Total Expenses         1309.008 1241.088 1250.212

    GROSS PROFIT              95.992   -36.088  -100.212


    SALES          C7..E7
    SALES TABLE    A1..G17

01-Nov-90  05:40 PM
```

---

[1] In this case you could use the @ROUND function to round off the internal cell values so that the internal values agree with those displayed on the screen. See Mathematical Functions section following for a discussion of the @ROUND function.

WORKING WITH ROWS, COLUMNS, AND CELLS

The table below shows example formats for two different values. The first value is a large number, and the second a smaller, negative value. The default of two decimal places was selected for most formats (as indicated by the "2" in F2, S2, C2, etc. below) and Lotus produces similar results with other choices. The format abbreviation, shown in parentheses after the format type, is displayed in the upper left corner of the control panel when the cursor is moved to a cell with that format.

Format Type	Example	Format Type	Example
General (G)	185435.678	General (G)	–6.0234
Fixed (F2)	185435.68	Fixed (F2)	–6.02
Scientific (S2)	1.85E+05	+/– (+)	– – – – – –
Currency (C2)	$185,435.68	Currency (C2)	($6.02)
Comma (,2)	185,435.68	Comma (,2)	(6.02)
Hidden (H)	(blank cell)	Percent (P1)	–602.3%

Lotus maintains dates as numeric values representing the number of days since December 31, 1899 to that date. Date numbers may be left as numbers, or formatted as dates. The example below shows the five date format types and how the date value for July 8, 1989, would be displayed with each type. The @DATE function, described later in this chapter, is used to enter the date into Lotus.

Format Type	Template	Example
General	none	32697
Date (D1)	DD-MMM-YY	08-JUL-89
Date (D2)	DD-MMM	08-JUL
Date (D3)	MMM-YY	JUL-89
Date (D4)	Long Intn'l	07/08/89
Date (D5)	Short Intn'l	07/08

Lotus maintains time of day as a decimal percentage of the 24-hour day. Thus 9:00 a.m. would be represented as 9/24, or 0.375. Because the date number is stored as an integer, the decimal fraction time of day may be added to it. Thus 9:00 a.m. on July 8, 1989, could be represented as 32697.375.

For the time of day 9:36:20 (36 minutes and 20 seconds after 9:00 a.m.) Lotus will display four different time formats, as shown below.

Format Type	Template	Example
General	none	0.400231
Date (D6)	HH:MM:SS AM/PM	09:36:20 AM
Date (D7)	HH:MM AM/PM	09:36 AM
Date (D8)	Long Intn'l	09:36:20
Date (D9)	Short Intn'l	09:36

Assigning a Format to Cells

The worksheet's global format is assigned to all cells as they are filled. To view the default global format use the /**Worksheet Status** command and examine the Cell Display section in Figure 4-7.

Changing the global format will change all cells that have *not* been individually formatted with the /Range Format command. To change the global format, type /**WGF** and you'll see the format menu:

```
                                                                    MENU
Fixed  Sci Currency , General +/- Percent Date Text Hidden Reset
Fixed number of decimal places (x.xx)
```

Move the cursor to the desired format type and press **Enter** to activate that format. (Alternatively, press the first character of the format type.) For format types Fixed, Scientific, Currency, Comma, and Percent, you must also supply the number of decimal places, with the default being 2 places.

Range formats are applied in a similar fashion to global formats, although the cell range must be specified. Move the cursor to the first cell in the range you wish to format, and type **/RF**. You will see the menu below:

```
                                                                   MENU
Fixed Sci Currency , General +/- Percent Date Text Hidden Reset
Fixed number of decimal places (x.xx)
```

Select the desired format type and specify the number of decimal places, if necessary. If you're formatting a single cell, just press **Enter** when prompted for the cell range. Otherwise use the arrow keys to highlight the desired cell range (or type in the cell coordinates or range name directly) and press **Enter** to terminate the cell range. You will immediately see the results of the new cell formats.

Range formats take precedence over global formats. In other words, if you have applied a range format to a cell, it will not change if the global format is changed. The range format is shown in parentheses in the control panel as described earlier. (If you have inadvertently range formatted some cells and wish to remove the range format, use the **/Range Format Reset** command and indicate the range to reset; the cells indicated will revert to the current global format type.)

Example: *Formatting the Smithton Spreadsheet*

So far each view of the Smithton spreadsheet has shown the cell values in the default format type, General. We will format the Sales and Expense numbers in the table as Comma type with no decimal places. The Percent values will be formatted as Percent type with 1 decimal place.

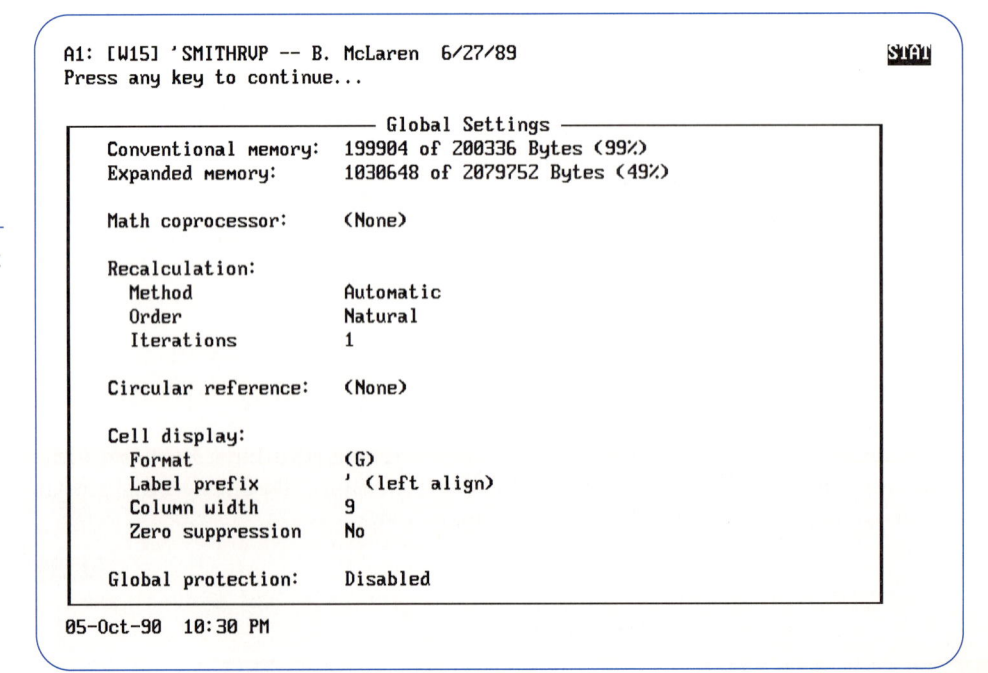

FIGURE 4-7

Global Status Settings Sheet (Press **/WS**)

```
A1: [W15] 'SMITHRUP -- B. McLaren  6/27/89                    STAT
Press any key to continue...
                           ┌──────── Global Settings ────────┐
   Conventional memory:    199904 of 200336 Bytes (99%)
   Expanded memory:        1030648 of 2079752 Bytes (49%)

   Math coprocessor:       (None)

   Recalculation:
      Method               Automatic
      Order                Natural
      Iterations           1

   Circular reference:     (None)

   Cell display:
      Format               (G)
      Label prefix         ' (left align)
      Column width         9
      Zero suppression     No

   Global protection:      Disabled
                           └─────────────────────────────────┘
05-Oct-90  10:30 PM
```

1. First use the /**FR** command to retrieve the **SMITHRVP.WK1** worksheet. If you did not create this file in a previous example it may be found on the data disk.

2. Move the cursor to cell C7, then give the /**RF** command to format a range of cells.

3. When Lotus asks the format type, press the comma key and reply to the number of decimal places prompt by typing **0**, then press **Enter**.

4. When asked to enter the range to format, reply **C7..E17** and press **Enter**.

5. Next we must format the percent column. Move the cursor to cell F9, and issue the /**RF** command again. This time pick the **P** (Percent) option, and reply with **1** decimal place and press **Enter**. The range to format is **F9..F13**. Note that the control panel in the upper left corner shows (P1) +E9/$E$7. The (P1) indicates Percent type with 1 decimal place. The numbers in the worksheet will be reformatted as shown in Figure 4-8.

6. Move the cursor to cell A1 and change the name of the worksheet to SMRV. Then press /**FS** to save the formatted worksheet. Use the name **SMRV**.

Converting Formulas to Text Format

It is possible to display the cell formulas instead of the formatted values in the cells. One method, invoked through the /Print command, is described in Chapter 5. You can also change the format type to **text**, where the formulas appear as they were entered instead of the value that the formula represents. The text format can be helpful for spotting errors in cell expressions because the worksheet appears in row-and-column orientation. You will probably have to make the columns wider to display the entire formula. It is recommended that you save the worksheet *before* converting cells to text format. Then do the conversion and print a copy of the formulas. Finally, retrieve the original saved spreadsheet file if modifications are needed.

FIGURE 4-8

Smithton Worksheet with Formatted Cells

114　Chapter 4 — Building Lotus 1-2-3 Worksheets

FIGURE 4-9

Smithton Worksheet with Cell Formulas Displayed (Press **/RFT**)

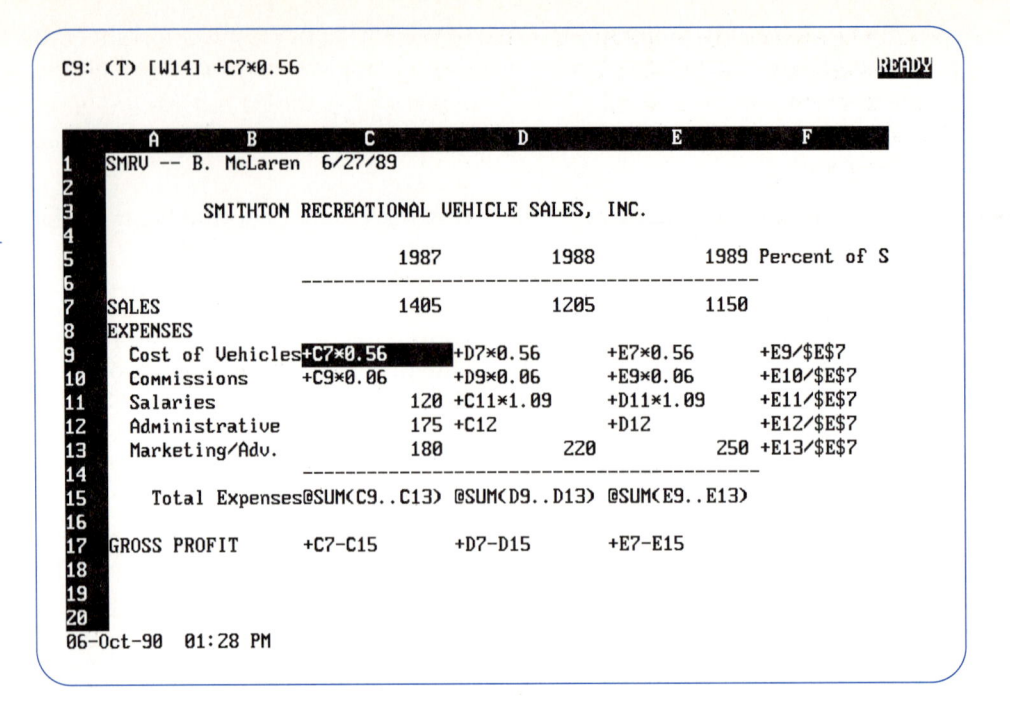

```
C9: (T) [W14] +C7*0.56                                    READY

       A         B         C              D              E              F
 1  SMRV -- B. McLaren  6/27/89
 2
 3               SMITHTON RECREATIONAL VEHICLE SALES, INC.
 4
 5                        1987           1988           1989 Percent of S
 6                   ------------------------------------------
 7  SALES                 1405           1205           1150
 8  EXPENSES
 9    Cost of Vehicles +C7*0.56      +D7*0.56       +E7*0.56       +E9/$E$7
10    Commissions      +C9*0.06      +D9*0.06       +E9*0.06       +E10/$E$7
11    Salaries              120     +C11*1.09      +D11*1.09       +E11/$E$7
12    Administrative        175     +C12           +D12            +E12/$E$7
13    Marketing/Adv.        180           220            250       +E13/$E$7
14                   ------------------------------------------
15    Total Expenses @SUM(C9..C13) @SUM(D9..D13) @SUM(E9..E13)
16
17  GROSS PROFIT      +C7-C15       +D7-D15        +E7-E15
18
19
20
06-Oct-90  01:28 PM
```

Example: *Displaying the Worksheet as Text Format*

1. To change the entire spreadsheet to text format, enter the **/RF** command and press **T** for text.

2. Specify the entire worksheet's range (**A1..F17**) and press **Enter**.

3. Next set the width of columns C–E so that the entire cell expression in those columns will display. Press **/WCC** to set the width of a range of columns. Press **S** to indicate Set-width, then enter **C9..E9** to select columns C, D and E. At the column width prompt use the right arrow key to enlarge the cells until the @SUM expressions display fully in row 15, in this case **14**. Then press **Enter** to complete the entry.

4. The text-formatted Smithton worksheet would look like Figure 4-9. Only the heading in cell F5 is cut off at the edge of the screen.

Changing Column Widths: Global, Individual, and Column-Range

If Lotus cannot display all the desired characters with the selected format type in a numeric cell, it will fill the cell with asterisks, *********, rather than chop off trailing characters. If General format is used, it will attempt to display the value in scientific notation if the cell is too narrow. Of course, long labels will "spill over" into adjacent empty cells, or will appear chopped off if the cell to the right is occupied. However, the full cell contents still exist and will display properly if the cell is widened.

Changing the Global Column Width

To change the **global column width**, type **/WGC** and specify the number of characters. Press **Enter** to complete the entry. Any column that has not been individually adjusted to a new width will immediately be adjusted to the new global width. Columns that have been individually adjusted have [Wn] appearing in the control panel; "n" represents that column's width in characters.

Changing an Individual Column or Column-Range

To change an individual column or range of columns, first move the cursor to any cell in that column. Then type **/WC** and you'll see the columns menu:

MENU

Set-Width Reset-Width Hide Display Column-Range

- The **Set-Width** option allows you to change the column width of an individual column.

- **Reset-Width** erases the individual setting for that column, returning it to the global setting.

- **Hide** will cause the column width to appear as zero, hiding the entire column from view. Its contents still exist, and all expressions using cells from that column are properly calculated. [Note: You cannot use the Set command to hide a column by making the column width narrower than one character.]

- **Display** is the opposite of Hide—it will turn hidden columns back on.

- **Column-Range** will let you set or reset the width of one or more adjacent columns. This feature was not available prior to Release 2.2 of 1-2-3.

Select **S** to change a column's width. You can type in the desired width, or experiment a character at a time with the right and left arrow keys until the desired column width is set. Press **Enter** to terminate the entry. Lotus will immediately display the column in its new width.

Types of Label Prefixes

Cells containing labels also have a format type, although it is not called "format". The default **label prefix** also depends on the settings made in the /Worksheet Global menu, and is displayed in the Status screen. Press **/WS** to view the default label prefix. The usual default value is for left-justified labels.

- Labels that are *left justified* begin at the left-most edge of the cell and start with the single quote character, '.

- *Right-justified* labels begin with a double quote character, ". These labels are placed at the right edge of the cell.

- *Centered labels* start with a caret symbol, ^. Centered labels always remain centered in the cell, even if the cell width is changed.

- *Repeating labels* begin with the backslash character, \. The label is repeated across the cell.

A prefix can be entered with the contents of the cell to override the default prefix. Otherwise, Lotus will place the default prefix with the label.

The worksheet in Figure 4-10 shows the results of different prefix characters on the position of the label in the cell. Column B was widened to illustrate the different positions.

Label Prefixes: Left, Right, Center, and Repeating

FIGURE 4-10

Effects of Label Prefix on Location

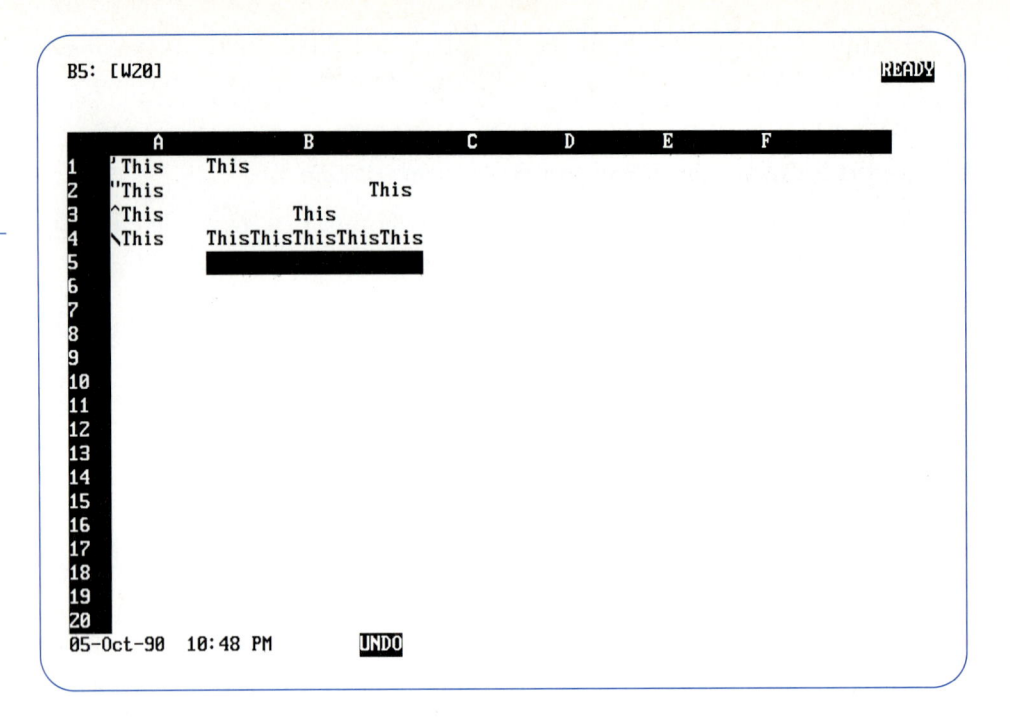

Changing the Global Label Prefix

To change the global default label prefix, use the /**WGL** command and choose **L**, **R** or **C** to indicate left, right or centered labels. You can change the label prefix for a range of cells that are already entered with the /Range Label command. Changing the global prefix has *no* effect on cells that already exist.

Changing the Label Prefix for a Range of Cells

To change the label prefix for existing cells, enter /**RL** and choose **L**, **R** or **C** to indicate left, right or centered cells. You must specify the range of cells to be changed. Cells that have a prefix (either entered as part of the cell expression or changed with the /**RL** command) take precedence over the global prefix.

Label Prefixes for Value Cells

Because Lotus places expressions that represent values in the right of each cell, it is generally wise to right-justify column heading labels for numeric columns so they are aligned. The example in Figure 4-11 shows how different label prefixes affect the placement of the label. The column width is 14 characters, and the value appears in positions 8–13 of the cell.

It is preferable to use label prefixes when positioning labels in the cell, rather than adding blanks. When the column width for the cell is changed, the label moves automatically if center or right-justify label prefixes were used. If spaces were typed in, they must be adjusted to compensate for different column widths.

Recalculation in Lotus 1-2-3

Lotus normally recalculates all cell formulas in the worksheet whenever you enter a new cell expression anywhere in the spreadsheet. With Release 2.2 **minimal recalculation** was introduced in which only cells dependent on the just-entered cell expression are recalculated. Minimal recalculation saves time.[2]

---

[2] Minimal recalculation is available only when Natural recalculation order is selected.

WORKING WITH ROWS, COLUMNS, AND CELLS

FIGURE 4-11

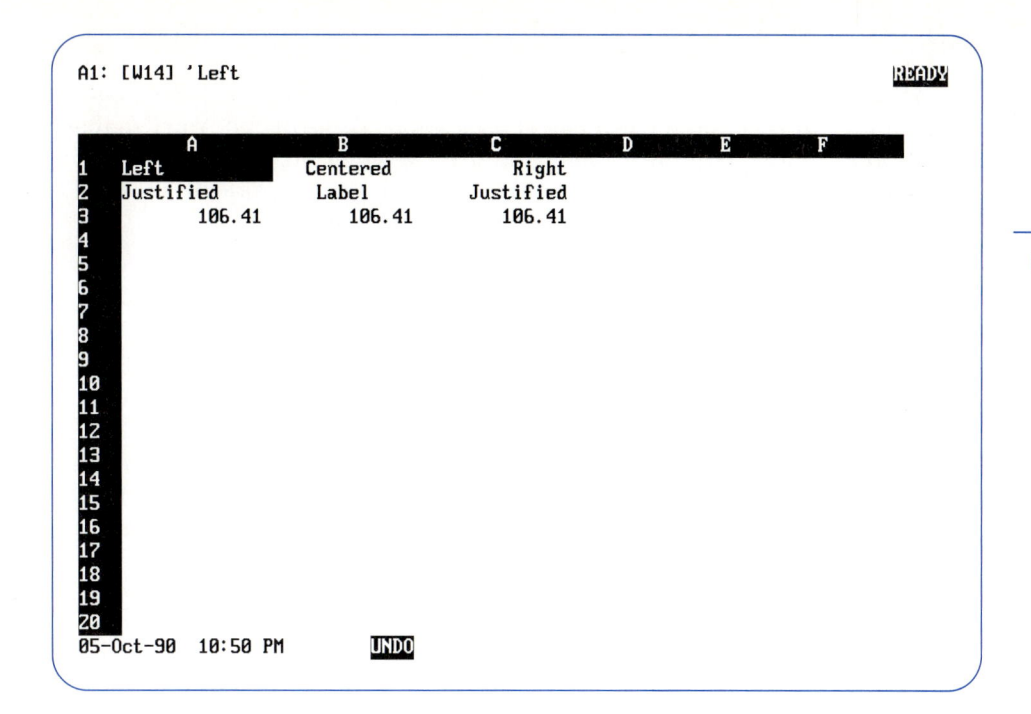

Examples of Label Prefixes with Numeric Cell Values

For small worksheets **automatic recalculation** takes very little time, but for large spreadsheets and for those with complex formulas the time delays may be excessive while the computer does recalculations. Computers with slow microprocessors such as the 8088 are especially prone to these delays. To speed up the cell entry process, Lotus provides a **manual recalculation** mode in which only the current cell is modified after its entry. The **CALC** message appears in the indicator area at the bottom right of the screen to warn that you must do a manual recalculation (press the **F9** key) before viewing any other cells.

Changing the Recalculation Mode

The / **Worksheet Global Recalculation** command brings up the calculation choices for the spreadsheet. The menu is:

MENU

Natural Columnwise Rowwise Automatic Manual Iteration
Recalculate in natural order

Automatic is the default value, using the natural sequence. Choosing Manual from this menu will select the manual recalculation mode in which the **F9** function key must be pressed to recalculate worksheet cell expressions.

The order in which cells are recalculated can make a difference in the values generated. Natural order is the normal choice in which Lotus first recalculates those cells which are referenced in another expression. Suppose cell F9 contains the formula **+E9/$E$7**. Before this cell can be calculated, Lotus must calculate values for cells E9 and E7. Cell E9 also depends on the value in cell E7. Because E7 contains a constant, 1150, it is already determined and doesn't need to be recalculated. The next cell would be E9, and finally cell F9.

It is recommended that you not choose rowwise or columnwise options unless necessary. See the Lotus manual for situations in which such a choice is warranted.

Performing a Manual Recalculation

The **F9** function key is the Lotus recalculation key—press this key when the CALC indicator is lit and the worksheet cells will be recalculated. You can make several entries in a large worksheet, then do a single manual recalculation, saving time. It is not necessary to do a manual recalculation if the CALC indicator does not appear.

Protecting Cell Formulas

Only the results of a cell expression are normally displayed on the spreadsheet (unless the text format type is used). It is easy to inadvertently "type over" a cell expression, replacing a formula with a value or incorrect formula. This kind of error then spreads into other cells that reference the current one, and often the user is unaware the change has even occurred.

Lotus allows you to protect ranges of cells. Once protected, you cannot make any changes to the contents of these cells—the computer will beep if you do so and reject the change. **Protected cells** have **PR** appearing in the control panel before the cell formula.

If you wish to protect all cells in the spreadsheet not specifically unprotected, issue the **/Worksheet Global Protection Enable** command, **/WGPE**. Lotus will display **PR** in the control panel next to the cell expression to indicate that a particular cell is protected. Because protection can be temporarily turned off with one simple command, you can revise portions of the worksheet quickly and re-establish the protection. To remove global protection, type **/WGPD**.

To unprotect a particular cell range within a protected worksheet, move the cursor to the first cell in that rectangular range. The **/Range Unprot** command will cause the computer to ask you to enter the cell range to be unprotected. Use the arrow keys to highlight that range, or type in the cell coordinates or range name directly. Press **Enter** to terminate the range. Lotus will display **U** next to the cell expression in the control panel in unprotected cells, and will display the cell entry in bold (green on a color monitor). The **/Range Prot** command can only be used to protect a range of cells after it has been unprotected.

Example: *Protecting Cell Expressions*

Suppose we wish to protect all the cells in the current Smithton worksheet. This example will demonstrate how to enable global protection, and to unprotect a range of cells.

1. Issue the **/WGPE** command to enable global protection.

2. To test the protection, move the cursor to any of the protected cells, say C9. Try to change the expression, erase the cell, or change the cell format. What does Lotus do in response?

3. Next move the cursor to cell C9 and press **/RU** to unprotect that cell. At the cell range prompt press **Enter**. The cell entry in the Control Panel will show a **U** to indicate the cell is unprotected.

4. Now try to enter something into that cell. What does Lotus do in response?

5. To disable global protection, press **/WGPD**. Cell expressions may be changed when global protection is disabled. Note that the cell entry for cell C9 continues to show the **U** even when global protection is disabled.

WORKING WITH ROWS, COLUMNS, AND CELLS

Working with Large Spreadsheets: Titles and Windows

Because most spreadsheets are larger than a single display window, it becomes more difficult to work in the screen size of 20 rows and 8 columns. Although some high-resolution monitors allow you to display more cells on the screen at a time, Lotus has a mechanism to freeze certain rows or columns on the screen at all times, or to split the screen into two windows for easier viewing of information.

Suppose you have prepared a loan amortization report consisting of one row for each loan payment. The report shows the crediting of each payment amount toward interest and principal, and shows cumulative interest and remaining balance of the loan after each payment. Because the table is so large, the column headings disappear as you scroll down in the report. Lotus **titles** can be used to freeze the column heading rows on the screen as the rest of the spreadsheet scrolls off the top of the display. Titles can be rows, columns, or both at once.

Lotus **windows** can be used to freeze the loan parameter section in one window, and the monthly payment schedule in the other window. You can scroll to the bottom of the payment schedule and examine the cumulative interest effects of changing a loan parameter such as annual interest rate and length of loan. Windows can be horizontal or vertical.

Creating Titles

To establish the rows and/or columns to become fixed titles on the display, move the cursor to the "corner" cell where the titles are to begin. Any rows or columns above and to the left of the corner cell will be fixed in place when the titles command is executed. With the Smithton spreadsheet, a candidate corner cell is C7. If we select **horizontal titles**, the cells *above* C7 (including the year labels) become column heading titles. If we were to add more Sales and Expense categories to the spreadsheet and move the cursor below row 20, the title rows will remain on the screen. If you choose **vertical titles**, the columns to the *left* of C7 become permanent titles. If we add more Years to the table and extend the worksheet past column H, the vertical titles will remain on the screen as we scroll the display to the right. Another setting allows us to activate both horizontal and vertical titles.

Example: *Creating a Horizontal Title*

In this example you will create horizontal title lines that will always appear at the top of the screen, even if you scroll down below row 22.

1. First retrieve the **SMITHRVP.WK1** worksheet with the **/FR** command.

2. Move the cursor to cell C7, and enter the **/Worksheet Titles** command, **/WT**. You will see the menu:

   `MENU`

   `Both` Horizontal Vertical Clear
   Freeze all rows and columns above and to the left of the cell pointer

3. Press **H** to activate a horizontal title consisting of the rows above row 7.

4. To explore how this title works, press the **PgDn** key. Notice that rows 1–6 remain fixed at the top of the screen even though the cursor has moved to row 21. Next press **Ctrl-→**. Did the horizontal titles remain fixed in place?

5. Next try to use the arrow keys to move the cursor to cell A1 which is inside the title. While you cannot move the cursor into the title area with the arrow keys, you can get there by pressing **F5**, the Lotus GOTO key. Specify **A1** as the cell address and press **Enter** to complete the entry.

Removing a Title

To remove a title from the worksheet display, use the **/WTC** (**/Worksheet Titles Clear**) command. The display will return to normal. If you set another title, even without using the **/WTC** command, it will replace the existing title settings.

Creating Lotus Windows

To open a second display window into the same spreadsheet use the **/Worksheet Window** command (**/WW**). To move the cursor from one window to the other press the **F6** function key. The /Worksheet Window menu appears below.

```
                                                                    MENU
    Horizontal Vertical Sync Unsync Clear
    Split the screen horizontally at the current row
```

- For **horizontal** windows, cells above the current cell will appear in their own Lotus window.

- If you choose a **vertical** window, cells to the left of the current cell will appear in a second Lotus window with their own row and column markers.

- **Synchronized** windows scroll simultaneously when you move the cursor in either window. This is the default setting.

- **Unsynchronized** windows move independently. That is, as you move the cursor in one window, the rows and columns in the other window will not move.

Example: *Creating a Vertical Window*

In this example you will create a vertical window for columns A and B in the Smithton worksheet.

1. Make sure you have retrieved the **SMITHRVP.WK1** worksheet with the **/FR** command.

2. Next move the cursor to cell C6. Press **/WW** to activate the Worksheet Window menu, then select **V** to place a vertical window to the left of column C. You will see two sets of row markers, and the cursor will be in cell B6 in the first window.

3. Press **F6** to move the cursor into the second window. Press **PgDn** and you will notice that both windows scroll synchronously.

4. To demonstrate the other setting, press **/WW** and select **Unsync**. Now press **PgUp** and you will find that the windows do not scroll together. See Figure 4-12.

LOTUS @-FUNCTIONS

There are nearly 100 built-in functions available in Lotus 1-2-3 that aid in the development of complicated worksheets. These functions accomplish various tasks that might ordinarily require a sophisticated calculator. Each function is preceded by the **@** character (Shift-2) to distinguish it from a text label. Some functions return label results, but most provide a numeric value. A few of the more useful **@-functions** are described in this section. A complete list is included in the Lotus manual.

Statistical Functions

The **statistical functions** in this section operate upon a range of cell values. The parameter "range" can be a range name, a cell range reference, a list of cells separated by commas, or a list of value constants. Refer to Figure 4-13.

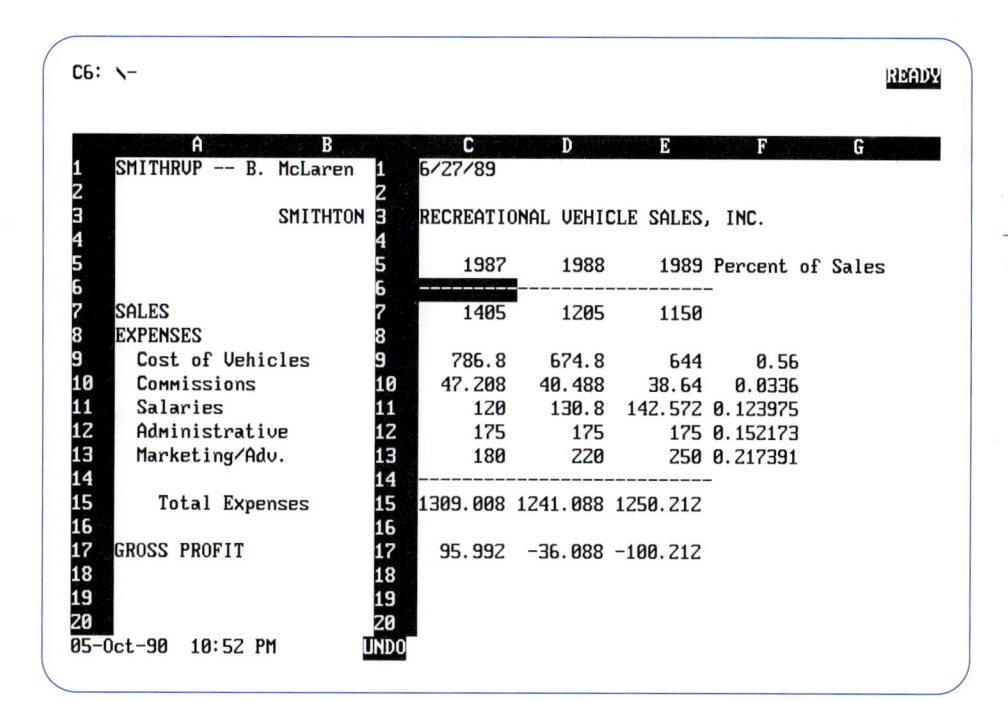

```
C6: \-                                                           READY

        A           B        C         D         E         F        G
 1  SMITHRUP -- B. McLaren  1  6/27/89
 2                          2
 3              SMITHTON    3  RECREATIONAL VEHICLE SALES, INC.
 4                          4
 5                          5    1987      1988      1989 Percent of Sales
 6                          6  --------------------------
 7  SALES                   7    1405      1205      1150
 8  EXPENSES                8
 9    Cost of Vehicles      9    786.8     674.8      644   0.56
10    Commissions          10   47.208    40.488    38.64   0.0336
11    Salaries             11      120     130.8   142.572  0.123975
12    Administrative       12      175       175       175  0.152173
13    Marketing/Adv.       13      180       220       250  0.217391
14                         14  --------------------------
15    Total Expenses       15  1309.008 1241.088 1250.212
16                         16
17  GROSS PROFIT           17   95.992   -36.088  -100.212
18                         18
19                         19
20                         20
05-Oct-90  10:52 PM                                              UNDO
```

FIGURE 4-12

Creating a Vertical Window (Press **/WW V**)

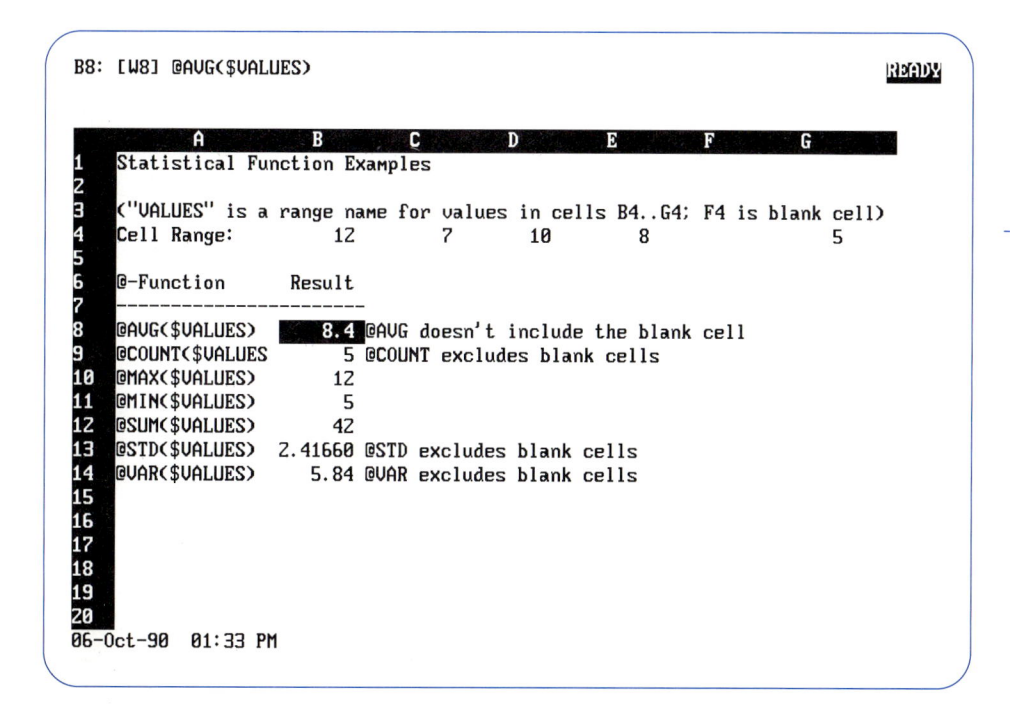

```
B8: [W8] @AVG($VALUES)                                           READY

        A           B        C         D         E         F        G
 1  Statistical Function Examples
 2
 3  ("VALUES" is a range name for values in cells B4..G4; F4 is blank cell)
 4  Cell Range:       12        7        10        8                 5
 5
 6  @-Function     Result
 7  ---------------------
 8  @AVG($VALUES)    8.4  @AVG doesn't include the blank cell
 9  @COUNT($VALUES)    5  @COUNT excludes blank cells
10  @MAX($VALUES)     12
11  @MIN($VALUES)      5
12  @SUM($VALUES)     42
13  @STD($VALUES)  2.41660 @STD excludes blank cells
14  @VAR($VALUES)    5.84  @VAR excludes blank cells
15
16
17
18
19
20
06-Oct-90  01:33 PM
```

FIGURE 4-13

Examples of Statistical Functions

FIGURE 4-14

Examples of Mathematical Functions

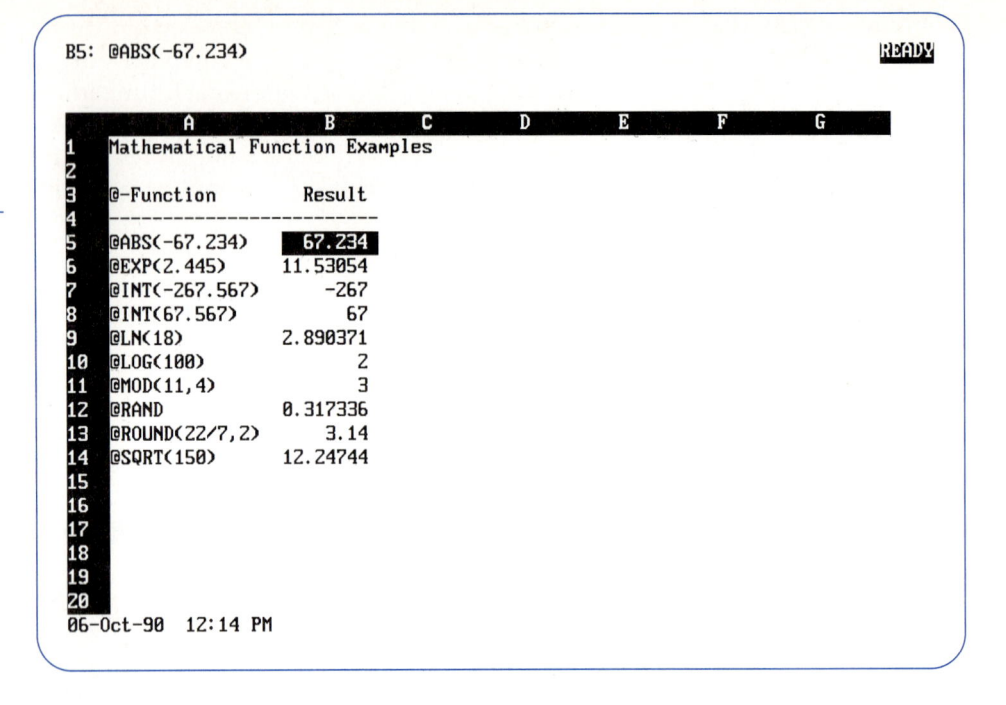

```
B5: @ABS(-67.234)                                          READY

          A           B           C       D       E       F       G
 1   Mathematical Function Examples
 2
 3    @-Function       Result
 4   ─────────────────────────
 5    @ABS(-67.234)    67.234
 6    @EXP(2.445)      11.53054
 7    @INT(-267.567)   -267
 8    @INT(67.567)     67
 9    @LN(18)          2.890371
10    @LOG(100)        2
11    @MOD(11,4)       3
12    @RAND            0.317336
13    @ROUND(22/7,2)   3.14
14    @SQRT(150)       12.24744
15
16
17
18
19
20
06-Oct-90  12:14 PM
```

@AVG(range)	Calculates the average (mean) of the non-blank cells in the range.
@COUNT(range)	Counts number of non-blank cells in the range.
@MAX(range)	Returns the maximum value in the range.
@MIN(range)	Returns the minimum value in the range.
@STD(range)	Calculates the population standard deviation of cells in the range.
@SUM(range)	Sums cell values in the range.
@VAR(range)	Calculates the population variance of cells in the range.

Mathematical Functions

These functions provide typical mathematical operations that are commonly found in a scientific calculator. The four basic arithmetic operations and exponentiation are already available directly with the usual symbols: +, −, *, /, ^. In the following examples, the "value" parameter can refer to a numeric cell, an expression, or a numeric constant. The functions operate upon a single value (see Figure 4-14).

@ABS(value)	Absolute value of a number.
@EXP(value)	Take e to the power in value. (e^{value})
@INT(value)	Take integer part of value (largest integer less than or equal to value.)
@LN(value)	Natural logarithm (base e) of value.
@LOG(value)	Common logarithm (base 10) of value.
@MOD(value, divisor)	Returns remainder of value divided by divisor.
@RAND	Random number between 0 and 1.

@ROUND(value, places)   Rounds value to the indicated number of decimal places.

@SQRT(value)   Square root of value.

Lotus also includes a complete set of trigonometric functions for scientific and engineering applications. The scientific format type is useful when dealing with very large or very small numbers.

One of the most useful components of Lotus 1-2-3 is the group of **financial functions.** Functions include net present value of a series of uneven cash flows, calculations for the payment necessary to amortize a loan, determining the number of periods in an annuity, several interest rate formulas, and three depreciation methods.

    These functions assist in financial analysis and capital budgeting decisions. All the other Lotus 1-2-3 capabilities are available, including the graphing features. Because most of the formulas involved in these functions are complex, many analysts welcomed Lotus' ability to speed up their work.

Financial Functions

Time-Value Functions

Each of these functions uses the principle of compounding money over time to arrive at answers. Otherwise known as the time value of money, some functions assume a periodic payment or cash flow, while others assume a single initial deposit is made.

    A number of parameters are used in several functions. "Payment" refers to a periodic payment or equal cash flow in each period. "Term" is the number of periods for that payment or cash flow, or the number of periods for a deposit to grow to a larger value. "Interest" refers to the periodic interest rate, and must be matched to the same time base as term. If monthly payments are made, term should be given in months and interest should be the monthly interest rate. "PV" (present value) is the initial deposit or amount borrowed in a loan. "FV" is a future value that the deposit or series of cash flows will grow to with compounding.

@CTERM(interest,fv,pv)   The number of periods at the given interest rate for an initial present value to grow to a future value; there are no periodic cash flows with this function.

@FV(payment,interest,term)   The future value amount equivalent to making the indicated payment each period for term periods at the interest rate given; this assumes periodic cash flows.

@IRR(estimate,cashflow range)   Lotus converts a series of uneven cash flows in the given range to an annual rate of return, using the estimate as a starting point.

@NPV(rate,cashflow range)   Net present value of a series of cash flows in the cell range given a discount rate.

@PMT(principal,interest,term)   Periodic payment to amortize a loan over term periods at the given interest rate for the principal amount borrowed.

@PV(payment,interest,term) Calculates the present value of term equal payments at the specified interest rate.

@RATE(fv,pv,n) Returns the periodic interest rate for an initial present value to grow to a future value over n periods.

@TERM(payment,interest,fv) Calculates the number of periods necessary for periodic payments to grow to a future value at a given interest rate.

Examples of financial functions appear in Figure 4-15. This example uses cell references whenever possible. You could use range names in place of cell addresses. The @-functions may also be used by specifying a constant for one or more financial parameters.

Lotus Depreciation Functions

When an organization purchases a long term asset such as a piece of equipment or a building, it is customary to allocate a portion of its cost to each year of its expected life. Lotus offers three **depreciation methods** for this purpose. The straight-line method assumes equal depreciation in each year. The other two methods, double-declining balance and sum-of-the-years-digits, are accelerated methods: they charge more depreciation in the early years of the asset, and less in later years. Examples appear in Figure 4-16.

Depreciation parameters include "cost," the amount initially paid for the asset, and "salvage," the expected residual (or salvage) value at the end of its useful life. "Per" refers to the specific year for which the depreciation amount is desired, and "life" is the number of years in the expected lifetime of the asset.

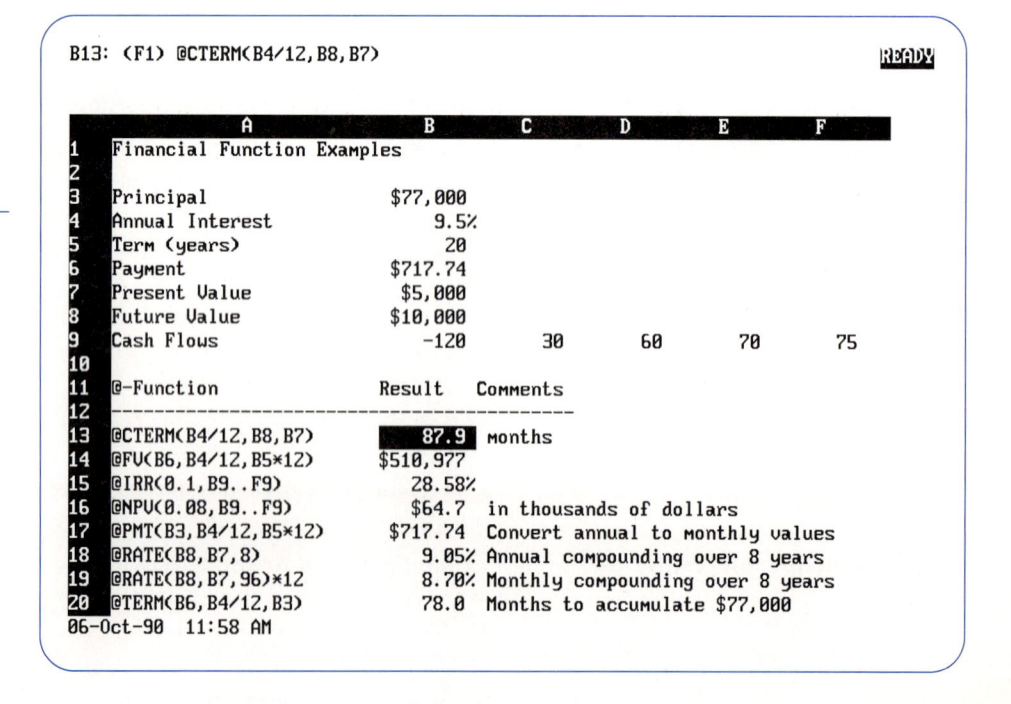

@SLN(cost,salvage,life) Returns annual depreciation for an asset of given cost and residual salvage value over life years, using the straight-line method.

FIGURE 4-15

Examples of Financial Functions

```
B13: (F1) @CTERM(B4/12,B8,B7)                              READY

              A              B         C        D        E        F
 1  Financial Function Examples
 2
 3  Principal          $77,000
 4  Annual Interest       9.5%
 5  Term (years)           20
 6  Payment            $717.74
 7  Present Value       $5,000
 8  Future Value       $10,000
 9  Cash Flows            -120        30       60       70       75
10
11  @-Function         Result    Comments
12  ------------------------------------------
13  @CTERM(B4/12,B8,B7)   87.9    months
14  @FV(B6,B4/12,B5*12) $510,977
15  @IRR(0.1,B9..F9)     28.58%
16  @NPV(0.08,B9..F9)    $64.7    in thousands of dollars
17  @PMT(B3,B4/12,B5*12) $717.74  Convert annual to monthly values
18  @RATE(B8,B7,8)        9.05%   Annual compounding over 8 years
19  @RATE(B8,B7,96)*12    8.70%   Monthly compounding over 8 years
20  @TERM(B6,B4/12,B3)    78.0    Months to accumulate $77,000
06-Oct-90  11:58 AM
```

@DDB(cost,salvage,life,per)   Returns depreciation for a specific period using the double-declining balance method.

@SYD(cost,salvage,life,per)   Returns depreciation for a specific period using the sum-of-the-years-digits method.

Date and Time Functions

As described earlier, Lotus stores dates and times as numbers, with the general form of date.time. The date portion (integer part) measures the number of elapsed days since December 31, 1899. The fractional part represents the time, expressed as a proportion of the 24 hour clock. Thus 10:00 p.m. is 22/24, or 0.916667.

There are several ways to enter a date. The @DATE function has separate parameters for day, month, and year. The @DATEVALUE uses a string version of the date, "DD-MMM-YY". Lotus handles dates from January 1, 1900, to December 31, 2099. @NOW returns the current date and time. Once a date has been placed in a cell, it can be formatted to appear in different ways, according to preference.

@DATE(year,month,day)   Converts the year value, month value, and day into a Lotus date number. Year is entered as the last two digits, and the month is entered as a number from 1 to 12. For years above 1999, add 100 to the last two year digits. Lotus handles dates through December 31, 2099.

@DATEVALUE(datetext)   Converts date text to a Lotus date number. Date is entered as "DD-MMM-YY" where MMM is the three-letter month abbreviation and YY is the last two digits of the year. The quotes must be included.

@NOW   Returns current date and time as a Lotus date number. The value changes every time the spreadsheet is recalculated.

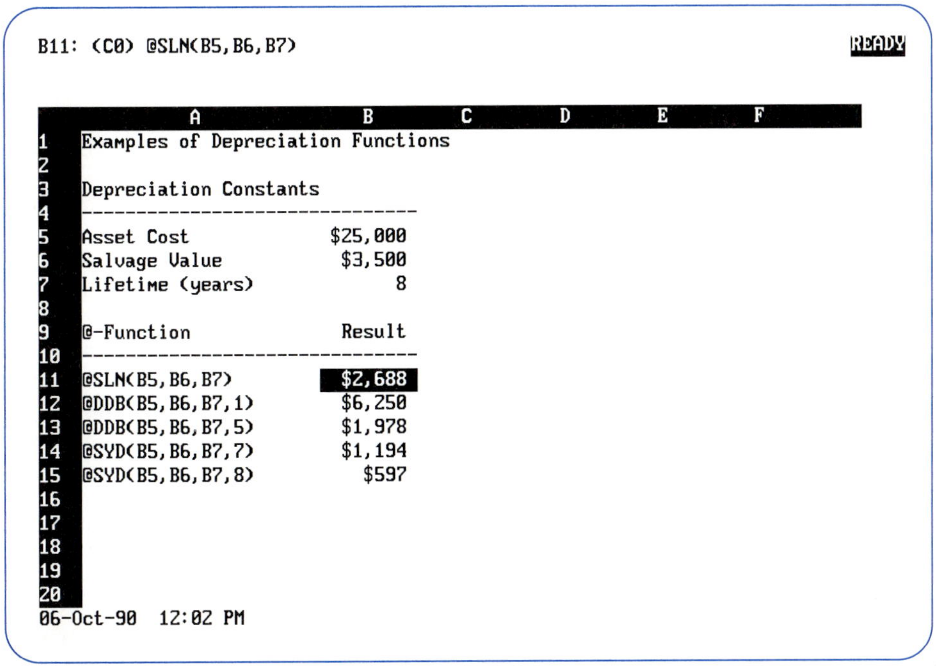

```
B11: (C0) @SLN(B5,B6,B7)                                    READY

            A                   B          C       D       E       F
   1   Examples of Depreciation Functions
   2
   3   Depreciation Constants
   4   ------------------------------------
   5   Asset Cost              $25,000
   6   Salvage Value            $3,500
   7   Lifetime (years)              8
   8
   9   @-Function              Result
  10   ------------------------------------
  11   @SLN(B5,B6,B7)          $2,688
  12   @DDB(B5,B6,B7,1)        $6,250
  13   @DDB(B5,B6,B7,5)        $1,978
  14   @SYD(B5,B6,B7,7)        $1,194
  15   @SYD(B5,B6,B7,8)          $597
  16
  17
  18
  19
  20
  06-Oct-90   12:02 PM
```

FIGURE 4-16

Examples of Depreciation Functions

FIGURE 4-17

Examples of Date and Time Functions

```
C6: (D1) [W14] @DATE(90,10,6)                              READY


         A            B         C          D         E
 1  Date and Time Function Examples
 2
 3                 Numeric   Formatted
 4  @-Function      Result     Result  Comments
 5  -----------------------------------------------------
 6  @DATE(90,10,6)   33152   06-Oct-90
 7  @DATEVALUE("6-OCT-90")  33152  06-Oct-90
 8  @NOW          33152.50   06-Oct-90  (date only)
 9  @NOW          33152.50   12:10:27 PM (time only)
10  @TIME(9,30,45)  0.396354  09:30:45 AM
11  @TIME(21,30,45) 0.896354  09:30:45 PM (hour > 12 = PM)
12  @TIMEVALUE("21:30:45") 0.896354 09:30:45 PM
13  @SECOND(A12)       45        45
14  @MINUTE(A12)       30        30
15  @HOUR(A12)         21        21
16  @DAY(A6)            6         6
17  @MONTH(A6)         10        10
18  @YEAR(A6)          90        90
19
20
06-Oct-90  12:10 PM
```

@TIME(hour,minute,sec)	Converts the hour value, minute value, and second value into a Lotus time number.
@TIMEVALUE(timetext)	Converts time text to a Lotus time number. Time text is entered as "HH:MM:SS" and quotes must be given.
@SECOND(timenumber)	Converts a time number into the number of seconds (0–59).
@MINUTE(timenumber)	Converts a time number into the number of minutes (0–59).
@HOUR(timenumber)	Converts a time number into the number of hours (0–23).
@DAY(datenumber)	Converts a date number into the day (1–31).
@MONTH(datenumber)	Converts a date number into the month (1–12).
@YEAR(datenumber)	Converts a date number into the year (0–199).

Examples of various date and time functions appear in Figure 4-17.

Logical Functions: Conditional Values

There are certain situations in which the precise cell expression used depends on certain conditions. Lotus offers three functions that examine certain conditions before returning a value or expression. The @IF function uses a notation somewhat like a programming language to determine whether a condition is true and substitutes one of two expressions. The two **LOOKUP functions,** @VLOOKUP and @HLOOKUP, check a cell value against a table and return the matching value.

The @IF Function

The @IF function parameters include the condition, a "True" expression for the cell, and a "False" condition for the cell. Lotus conditions are expressed with

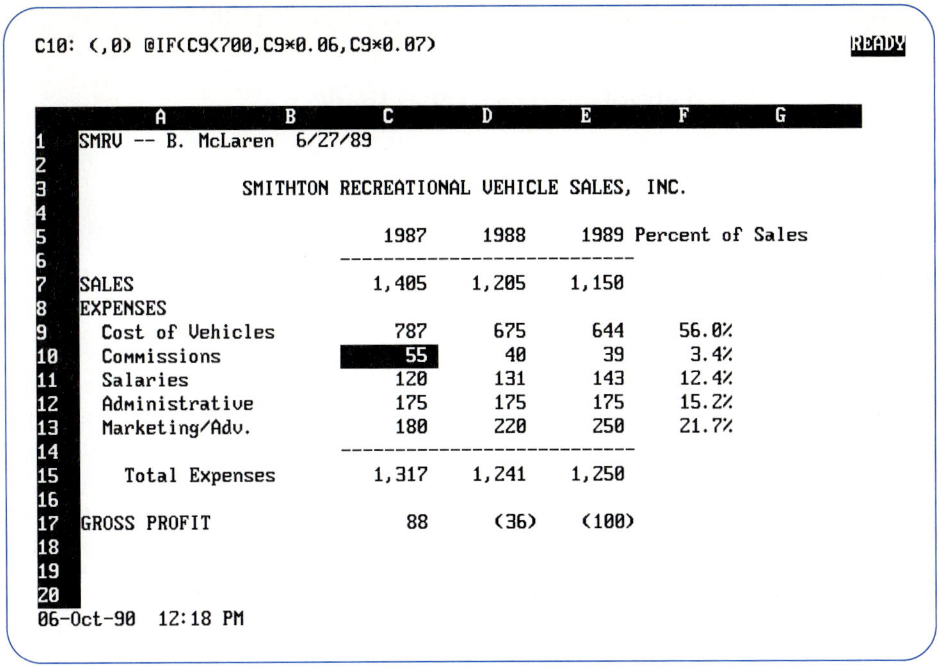

FIGURE 4-18

Example of the @IF Function

```
C10: (,0) @IF(C9<700,C9*0.06,C9*0.07)                    READY

          A         B        C        D        E    F        G
 1  SMRV -- B. McLaren  6/27/89
 2
 3                    SMITHTON RECREATIONAL VEHICLE SALES, INC.
 4
 5                              1987     1988     1989 Percent of Sales
 6                             ------------------------
 7  SALES                       1,405    1,205    1,150
 8  EXPENSES
 9      Cost of Vehicles          787      675      644    56.0%
10      Commissions                55       40       39     3.4%
11      Salaries                  120      131      143    12.4%
12      Administrative            175      175      175    15.2%
13      Marketing/Adv.            180      220      250    21.7%
14                             ------------------------
15      Total Expenses          1,317    1,241    1,250
16
17  GROSS PROFIT                   88     (36)    (100)
18
19
20
06-Oct-90  12:18 PM
```

inequality signs: <, <=, =, >=, > and <> (not equal to). For example, suppose the sales commission in the Smithton worksheet is 6% of cost for Vehicle Cost under $700, and 7% of cost for Vehicle Cost amounts $700 and over. Thus the entry in cell C10 (now +C9*.06) would become:

    @IF(C9<700,C9*.06,C9*.07)

The condition **C9<700** is true whenever the value in cell C9 is less than 700. The cell expression **C9*.06** is used whenever the condition is true; the cell expression **C9*.07** is used when the condition is false. If you copy the @IF function in cell C10 to cells D10 and E10, the worksheet would change slightly, as the condition is applied to cells D9 and E9. See Figure 4-18.

The @IF function can include references to other functions, including other @IF functions, in its cell expressions. Consider an alternative @IF function for cell C10 in the Smithton worksheet. Assume it is copied to cells D10 and E10. In this instance we model the commission rate change *only* for years after 1987.

    @IF(C5>1987,@IF(C9<700,C9*.06,C9*.07),C9*.06)

Notice that the highlighted section is another @IF function, called a nested IF. How does Lotus interpret this second @IF expression? Remember that it is the "true" expression for the first condition. Thus only when C5 is after 1987 will the second @IF be evaluated: if C9 is less than 700 then the commission rate is 6 percent; otherwise it jumps to 7%. The last parameter is the "false" expression for the original C5>1987 condition: if it isn't after 1987, the commission rate remains at 6% regardless of the cost figure. [Note: We will not make this a permanent change in the Smithton worksheet.]

The @HLOOKUP and @VLOOKUP Functions

These useful functions cause Lotus to match a value in a table, and will "look up" a corresponding value from that table. For example, suppose a professor wishes to determine a letter grade for the students in a class. The grade is based upon the percentage of total points: 90% or better is an "A", 80% is a "B", and so on. That table could be represented with two columns:

Percentage	Letter Grade
0	F
.60	D
.70	C
.80	B
.90	A

To use this vertical lookup table, we need to calculate the student's actual percentage. To look up the matching value in the first column of the table, Lotus starts in the first row and moves down row by row until the table percentage exceeds the lookup value. The correct row is one above that row. Suppose the student's percentage is .84. Start with the first row and move down until the table percentage (.90) exceeds the lookup value. Then move back up one row, and read the value (B) from the second column. The format of the @VLOOKUP function is

```
@VLOOKUP(value,table range,offset column)
```

The *value* is the lookup figure, in this case the student's calculated percentage. The *table range* is a cell range or range name for the lookup table, the first column of which contains the lookup values. The table range begins with the first row below the column headings (which aren't part of the table). The *offset column* gives the number of columns over from the lookup column where the value or label is to be retrieved. In this case the offset column would be 1.

The @HLOOKUP function works identically, except that the table appears on its side, horizontally. The table below shows the same data as before, except in a horizontal lookup table format.

Percentage	0	.60	.70	.80	.90
Letter Grade	F	D	C	B	A

The format of the @HLOOKUP function is

```
@HLOOKUP(value,table range,offset row)
```

You should provide a starting value in the lookup column (or row) that is *less than* any possible lookup value. If you use the lookup functions and give a value that is lower than the initial value in the table, Lotus will place **ERR** in the cell. One cause for this can be misspecifying the table range in the middle function parameter.

Illustration: The White Accounting Company has recently agreed to prepare a customized tax table for a client using Lotus 1-2-3. The table in question uses different percentages, depending on the taxable amount. Ranges are shown below.

Taxable Amount	Percentage
negative	0.0
0 – 1,000	2.0
1,001 – 5,000	2.5
5,001 –10,000	3.0
over 10,000	3.5

The Lotus spreadsheet model for this problem appears in Figure 4-19.

FIGURE 4-19

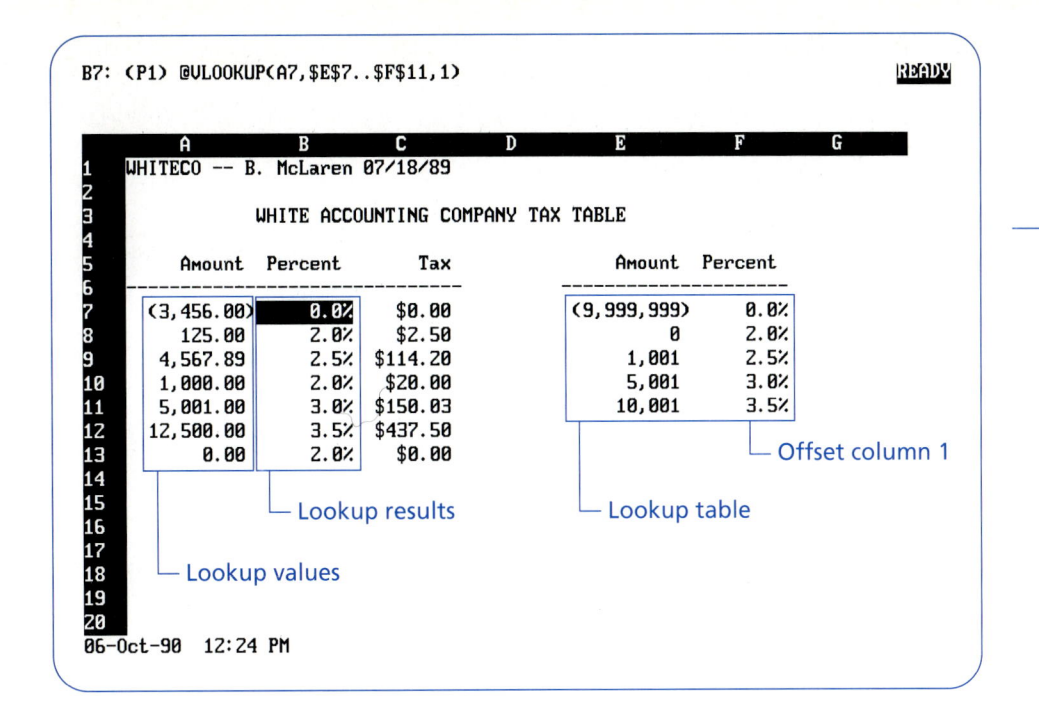

Example of the @VLOOKUP Function

The lookup table resides in cells E7..F11. The lookup values are shown in column A, with several examples displayed. The actual @VLOOKUP function for cell B7 is shown in the Control Panel. The value to look up is in cell A7, and the intermediate result is shown in cell B7. The final tax amount is shown in cell C7. The formulas in cells B7 and C7 were copied through row 12 for different lookup amounts. Notice that the lookup table range was given as an absolute cell range with the dollar signs; this allows the range to be copied to other cells and assures the table reference remains the same, not offset. Columns A, C and E are formatted in (,2) type (Comma with two decimal places) for clarification. Column B and F values are formatted as (P1) type (Percent with one decimal place).

String Functions: Manipulating Labels

These advanced functions are useful for manipulating Lotus labels—strings of characters. The term *string* will refer to a sequence of text characters residing in a spreadsheet cell. Many of these functions are useful when manipulating text data, particularly with a Lotus database. These functions are related to programming, and are often found in macros. **String functions** include operations for:

- finding a substring within a larger string
- extracting a substring from a larger string
- extracting a certain number of characters from the left or right side of a string
- determining the number of characters in a string
- converting the characters in the string to upper- or lowercase
- capitalizing the first letter of each word in the string
- creating a new string by repeating a group of characters
- trimming blank characters from end of a string
- converting between value and string cells.

In the function parameters below, "string" refers to a label cell reference, a string @-function, or a label constant; "start" and "stop" refer to a character position within a string, counting from the first character in the string; "length" is the number of characters; "number" is a value cell reference, numeric @-function, cell expression or numeric constant.

@FIND(str,string,start)	Locate the starting position of substring **str** in overall **string**, beginning in start position. Returns 0 if str is not found.
@LEFT(string,length)	Returns the left-most **length** number of characters from **string**.
@LENGTH(string)	Number of characters (including embedded blanks) in **string**.
@LOWER(string)	Converts **string** to all lowercase characters.
@MID(string,start,length)	Returns substring of given **length** from specified **string** beginning at **start** position.
@PROPER(string)	Converts character at beginning of each word in **string** to uppercase.
@REPEAT(str,number)	Repeats given string **str** a specified **number** of times.
@REPLACE(string,start,length,str)	Replaces **length** characters in **string** with **str** beginning at **start**.
@RIGHT(string,length)	Returns right-most **length** characters from **string**.
@STRING(number,places)	Converts the value in **number** to a string with specified decimal **places**.
@TRIM(string)	Trims trailing blanks from **string**.
@VALUE(string)	Converts a string to a value. The **string** must be an acceptable number form. (Example: "1989")

There are many more string functions available in Lotus. Their use is illustrated in the Lotus manual. A few examples are shown in Figure 4-20.

CHAPTER REVIEW

Building the Worksheet

When building large spreadsheets, it is important to design the spreadsheet with certain principles in mind. The author, purpose, and revision dates should be stored in the spreadsheet. Laying out the spreadsheet on paper before entering cell expressions will reduce the need to do major changes to the spreadsheet later. Worksheets with several tables should be laid out in a diagonal fashion so that rows and columns could be inserted or deleted without affecting other tables. Use range names whenever possible in cell expressions. Protect cell ranges so that formulas aren't inadvertently changed. Document the spreadsheet carefully, explaining unusual formulas.

Inserting and Deleting Rows and Columns

It is possible to insert rows or columns with the /**WI** command. Rows or columns are inserted above or to the left of the cursor location. All cell expressions are

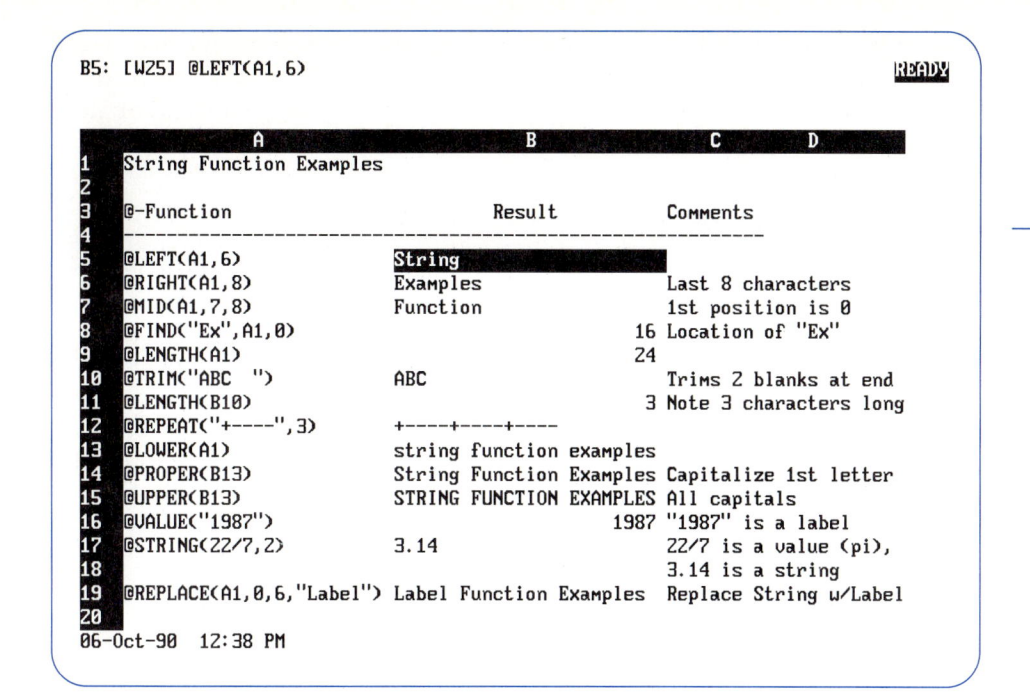

```
B5: [W25] @LEFT(A1,6)                                           READY


               A                    B                 C              D
 1  String Function Examples
 2
 3  @-Function                  Result            Comments
 4  ------------------------------------------------------------
 5  @LEFT(A1,6)                 String
 6  @RIGHT(A1,8)                Examples          Last 8 characters
 7  @MID(A1,7,8)                Function          1st position is 0
 8  @FIND("Ex",A1,0)                           16 Location of "Ex"
 9  @LENGTH(A1)                                24
10  @TRIM("ABC   ")             ABC               Trims 2 blanks at end
11  @LENGTH(B10)                                3 Note 3 characters long
12  @REPEAT("+----",3)          +----+----+----
13  @LOWER(A1)                  string function examples
14  @PROPER(B13)                String Function Examples Capitalize 1st letter
15  @UPPER(B13)                 STRING FUNCTION EXAMPLES All capitals
16  @VALUE("1987")                           1987 "1987" is a label
17  @STRING(22/7,2)             3.14              22/7 is a value (pi),
18                                                3.14 is a string
19  @REPLACE(A1,0,6,"Label")    Label Function Examples  Replace String w/Label
20
06-Oct-90  12:38 PM
```

FIGURE 4-20

Examples of String Functions

automatically adjusted to account for additional rows or columns. Similarly, rows and columns can be deleted with the **/WD** command. Be careful when making such changes, especially with other tables in the spreadsheet in an area that doesn't display on the current screen.

Copying Cells

The Lotus **/Copy** command can be used to duplicate cell formulas in nearby cells, saving time and improving accuracy of the expressions. Unless you specify otherwise, Copy operations are done using relative cell addresses, adjusting references to other rows or columns by the distance away from the cell(s) that are copied. Lotus uses the $ to indicate absolute cell addresses in formulas. When cells containing absolute cell references are copied, the new expressions will refer to the original cells. You can put a $ in front of the column letter, the row number, or both. The **/Move** command enables you to move a block of cells to a new location in the worksheet. The cell references are not adjusted with the /Move command.

Lotus Cell Range Names

Lotus range names are a shorthand way of referring to ranges of cells. Range names may refer to a single cell, a row or column of cells, or a block of cells. Range names may be used whenever Lotus expects a cell address. Pressing the **F3** key in 1-2-3 will display the range names currently defined in the worksheet. You can use the **/RNC** command to create a range name. Other commands will delete a range name, reset the range name, or place the range names in a table somewhere in the worksheet.

Formatting Cell Appearance: Formats and Column Widths

Lotus uses two kinds of cell formats, Global and Range. The Global format is applied to all cells as they are created, and is set in the **/WGF** menu. The usual default Global format type is General, where the number of decimal places varies according to the value itself. Cells that have been Range formatted will not respond to changes made in the Global format. The range format for a cell is shown in the control panel by a coding system in parentheses.

Numeric Cell Formats

Currency and Comma format types insert commas into large numbers to improve readability. Fixed, Currency, and Comma format types allow you to control the number of decimal places that are displayed. The Percent format type displays decimal values as percentages, also with a fixed number of decimal places. The +/− format converts the magnitude of values into an equivalent number of + signs (positive numbers) or − signs (negative numbers) in the cell. There are several formats for date numbers and time numbers that allow you to display dates and times in various ways. Scientific format type is used to display very large or very small numbers in scientific notation. The Hidden format type will temporarily cause a cell to disappear, but its value will still be used in cell expressions referring to it.

Converting Formulas to Text Format

You can convert a cell formula from its calculated value to the cell expression itself by using the Text format type. This is useful for documenting the expressions used in a worksheet.

Changing Column Widths

Column widths are set Globally through the **/WGCS** command. The usual default value is 9 characters wide, and individual columns are set with the **/WCS** command. Certain format types require wider cells to display all the characters. Cells that contain all asterisks (*********) are too narrow to fully display the value in that cell in the range format specified. The **/WCH** command can be used to temporarily hide a column so that none of the cells in that column appear in a display or printed output. **/WCD** will display a hidden column.

Label Prefixes

The Lotus label prefix character determines the placement of the label in a cell. The single quote character indicates a left-justified label, while the double-quote sets the label as right-justified. Centered labels are preceded by the carat character. The **/RL** command is used to set the label prefix for a range of cells.

Recalculation

Lotus normally recalculates each cell value every time a new cell entry is made. For large spreadsheets and those with complex formulas, this automatic recalculation may cause undesirable delays. You can select the manual recalculation mode whereby formulas are only evaluated when you press the **F9** recalculation key. The CALC indicator tells you when you must do a manual recalculation.

Protecting Cell Formulas

Cell formulas are protected in a two-step process. First you must enter all the cell expressions as usual, then enable global protection with the **/WGPE** command. Protected cells cannot be changed or erased, and prevent inadvertent erasure or replacement of formulas. It is wise to protect formulas in a worksheet that is to be used by people other than its developer.

Working with Large Spreadsheets: Titles and Windows

Titles are used to provide row or column headings that are frozen on the screen as you scroll the display window to other parts of the spreadsheet. Titles are useful with large spreadsheets when the rows or columns in a particular table extend past the boundaries of the display area. You can establish two editing windows at one time with the **/WW** command. The cells in one window can be synchronized with the other window as you scroll through the worksheet, or remain in place. Windows are useful when comparing two portions of a large spreadsheet at the same time.

Lotus @-Functions

There are nearly 100 built-in @-functions to provide specialized calculations in cell expressions. Mathematical functions are used for such purposes as absolute value, logarithms, exponentials and square roots. Statistical functions calculate average, standard deviation, minimum, maximum, and variance for a range of cell values. Financial functions include payment, present value, rate of return, term, and future value in time-value-of-money calculations. There are three types of depreciation functions. There are numerous functions to enter and manipulate date and time data.

The @IF and Lookup Functions

The @IF function offers conditional cell expressions that depend on the result of a logical condition. The two lookup functions match a value against a table of values, returning conditional information from the table that depends on the lookup value.

String Functions: Manipulating Labels

There are numerous string functions that manipulate strings of text characters. These functions are especially useful with text data in a Lotus database. Functions include locating certain text strings, converting between upper and lower case, determining the length of a string label, and extracting substrings from within larger strings.
+/– format

KEY TERMS

@-functions	financial functions	minimal recalculation
absolute cell address	Fixed cell format	/Move command **(/M)**
automatic recalculation	General cell format	Percent cell format
cell format	global column width	protected cell
centered label	GOTO command **(F5)**	/Range Format command
clear titles	Hidden format	**(/RF)**
column width	horizontal title	range name
Comma cell format	label prefix	range name table
/Copy command **(/C)**	left-justified label	recalculation mode
Currency cell format	lookup functions	relative cell address
date and time functions	macro	right-justified label
depreciation functions	manual recalculation **(F9)**	statistical functions
diagonal design rule	mathematical functions	string functions

Chapter 4 — Building Lotus 1-2-3 Worksheets

time-value functions
title
vertical title
window
window command **(F6)**
/Worksheet Delete Column
   command **(/WDC)**

/Worksheet Delete Row
   command **(/WDR)**
worksheet design
/Worksheet Insert Column
   command **(/WIC)**
/Worksheet Insert Row
   command **(/WIR)**

/Worksheet Status
   command **(/WS)**
/Worksheet Titles
   command **(/WT)**
/Worksheet Window
   command **(/WW)**

DISCUSSION QUESTIONS

1. List at least five principles of good spreadsheet design. Why must we *design* a spreadsheet before creating it?

2. Explain what happens when you insert a column between existing columns D and E. Where should the cursor be before entering this command?

3. In the Smithton spreadsheet we indented certain row headings. Explain how this is done, and list other layout appearance considerations when entering text labels as column or row headings.

4. Why is caution necessary when inserting or deleting rows in a large spreadsheet?

5. Discuss the differences between relative and absolute cell addresses. How are absolute cell references indicated?

6. Suppose you need to copy or move the formulas shown below to new locations. Without trying them on the computer, indicate the exact formula that will appear in the new location.
   a. Copy **+C9+C8** from cell C12 to cell E12.
   b. Move **@SUM(B4..G4)** from cell H4 to cell L9.
   c. Copy **(A1+A2+A3)/$A$6** from cell A7 to cell B7.
   d. Move **@PMT(1000,.01,36)** from cell G14 to cell A14.
   e. Copy **(A1+A2)** from cell A3 to cell B2.
   f. Move **+G300/$G301** from cell G302 to cell H302.
   g. Move **+G300/G$301** from cell G302 to cell H302.

7. How do you create and use range names in Lotus cell expressions? Why are they useful?

8. If a cell formula containing a range name is copied, should the range name be preceded by a dollar sign? Why?

9. Explain the *differences* between global and range formats. Which takes precedence?

10. Define the characteristics of the following format types, and briefly explain when each should be used:
    a. Currency
    b. +/−
    c. Percent
    d. Comma
    e. Fixed
    f. General
    g. Date

h. Text

i. Hidden

j. Scientific.

11. Give the format type for the following formatted values:

    a. (12,345.34)

    b. - - - -

    c. $254.25

    d. 1,836.99

    e. 1836.9877564

    f. 12.4

    g. 21-JUL-89

    h. +G24/12

    i. <empty cell on display>

    j. 10:26:11 AM

    k. 6.02E+23.

12. Describe how the label prefix can affect how a label is displayed in a cell.

13. Suppose you have just changed the global column width from 9 to 14 characters, and all columns *except* column C have changed. What went wrong with column C? Can it be remedied?

14. What is meant by the term "natural order recalculation"?

15. List reasons why you would want to change from automatic to manual recalculation.

16. List the Lotus 1-2-3 functions of the following function keys:

    a. F1

    b. F2

    c. F3

    d. F4

    e. F5

    f. F6

    g. F9.

17. Why should cell formulas be protected? What does "protection" mean in this instance?

18. List the 1-2-3 commands needed to accomplish the following:

    a. Change the global column width to 14 characters.

    b. Format cells A9..H9 as comma type with 2 decimal places.

    c. Change the label prefix to right-justified for the labels in cells C1..C15.

    d. Change to manual recalculation mode.

    e. Display the global spreadsheet settings on the screen.

    f. Protect the cell formulas in cells A1..G99.

    g. Create a range name called COSTS for cells H14..M14.

    h. Obtain a help screen for cell format types.

19. Explain the situation in which Lotus titles or windows would be desirable. Describe the differences between these two features.

20. Briefly define the calculations done by the following Lotus @-functions, showing the results where applicable:

a.	@INT(436.5)	m.	@DATE(90,2,25)
b.	@LOG(14.23)	n.	@DATEVALUE("25-FEB-90")
c.	@ROUND(3.14159,3)	o.	@NOW
d.	@SQRT(2344)	p.	@TIME(17,48,40)
e.	@AVG(1,4,5)	q.	@HOUR(0.25)
f.	@MAX(1,4,5)	r.	@DAY(15682)
g.	@STD(1,4,5)	s.	@YEAR(15682)
h.	@CTERM(.11,50,25)	t.	@IF(5<6,100,200)
i.	@NPV	u.	@VLOOKUP
j.	@PMT(1000,.01,12)	v.	@FIND("AN","GIANT",1)
k.	@TERM(100,.01,12)	w.	@LEFT("PERSONAL COMPUTER",5)
l.	@DDB(2500,0,5,3)	x.	@STRING(124.35,2).

EXERCISES

1. The Crowfly Construction Company has assembled data for making an estimate for construction projects. The table below summarizes one such job, project number WW47809-89, for remodeling a dental office.

DESCRIPTION	MATERIALS	LABOR
Hardware	2,450	0
Lumber	12,888	0
Framing	0	6,250
Electrical	1,000	1,200
Carpeting, Tile	2,400	1,400
Permits	1,000	0
Clean Up	0	2,000
Supervision	0	4,500

   Contracting Fee (20% of total)

   a. The client for this job is Michael D. Litner, DDS, 175 Deming Avenue, Clay City, Indiana 47867. Prepare a spreadsheet showing the estimate, totalling each construction category across (materials plus labor) as well as column and grand totals. The job carries a 20% contracting fee, based upon the total job cost. All numbers should be formatted with the comma format, with no decimal places. Do not type the comma when you enter the numbers. Column totals should use the currency format with no decimal places. Print the spreadsheet.

   b. After printing the spreadsheet it was realized that several expense categories were omitted from the original worksheet. Insert them between Framing and Electrical without retyping the other rows.

Painting	2,390	7,145
Concrete	14,000	6,000

   Print the revised spreadsheet.

2. Prepare a family income table that would help determine if school children qualify for free or reduced-cost lunches. If the family income is at or

below the table figure, the child may qualify for this program. The table has the following columns:

| Family Size | Annual Income | Monthly Income | Weekly Income |

The table is based upon a figure of $11,306 per year for a family size of one, and $3,704 per additional member. Prepare the chart for 2 through 12 family members. Monthly income is determined by dividing annual income by 12. Weekly income is annual income divided by 52. Use appropriate titles to illustrate the meaning of the chart. Use currency cell formats.

3. Prepare a worksheet to display the annual professional society budget data, a portion of which is shown below.

	1987	1988	1989	1990
RECEIPTS				
Meetings	1800	2893	1848	3000
Raffle	68	99	106	125
Membership Rebate	795	660	390	660
Seminar	1344	3796	530	3500
Other	86	20	12	459
EXPENSES				
Dinner	1733	2325	1446	450
Speaker	90	250	80	545
Region Meetings	322	1067	295	1100
Postage	163	320	165	407
PO Box	29	29	29	29
Education/Seminar	32	2308	388	2900
Officer Expenses	14	182	38	160
Other	125	707	570	709

Total the Receipts and Expenses for each year, and prepare a Net Gain (Total Receipts minus Total Expenses) figure for each year. The first budget item in each list should be displayed with currency format, and all others with comma format. The total figures should also be displayed with currency format.

4. Using the professional society data from the previous problem, insert an additional column between each two years. Then calculate the net increase or decrease and display this figure as a percentage, using Percent format. For example, between 1987 and 1988 the Meetings category increased by (2893-1800)/1800 or 60.7%. Also calculate percentage changes for the total figures.

5. Using the quality control statistical data below, answer the following questions by coding the proper @-functions. The numbers below (read them across) represent measurements taken over time from a manufacturing operation. Place the numbers in a single column of the worksheet. Properly label your answers with the letter of the problem.

3.45 3.23 3.47 3.49 3.52 3.51 3.49 3.55 3.58 3.62 3.65 3.64 3.69
3.75 3.81 3.75 4.06 3.88 4.01 4.08 4.12 4.06 3.44 3.43 3.51

a. What is the largest measurement?
b. What is the average measurement?
c. Calculate the standard deviation of this sample of 25 measurements.
d. Add another column next to the measurement data, filling each cell with the quotient of the measurement from that period divided by the average measurement.
e. What is the range of the measurements (maximum − minimum)?

6. Use Lotus 1-2-3 functions to solve the date and time questions included below.

   a. Enter the date, December 17, 1978, as a Lotus date number using the @DATE function. Enter the same date using the @DATEVALUE function. Compare the date number with the one from the first function.
   b. Format the date number, 32666, as D1, D2, D3, D4, and D5 format types in consecutive cells.
   c. Enter the time, 11:09:20 a.m., using the @TIME and @TIMEVALUE functions. Compare the time numbers from the two functions using the D6 and D9 time formats.
   d. What date is 180 days after August 22, 1981?
   e. Prepare a Lotus date number for 1:30 p.m. on December 17, 1989. Format it appropriately.
   f. Use appropriate functions to determine the month, day of the month, and year of the Lotus date number, 15317.
   g. Use proper functions to determine the hour, minute, and second of the Lotus time number .1234567.

7. Use Lotus 1-2-3 functions to solve the following financial questions. Place your answers on a single spreadsheet, with the letter of the question in column A, the properly formatted answer in column B, and any descriptions necessary in column C. The questions are independent of one another unless otherwise indicated.

   a. What is the monthly payment for a $7,000 loan for 30 months at 7.9% annual percentage rate?
   b. How many months will it take to pay off a $25,000 loan (present value) if each payment is $275 and the APR is 8.5%?
   c. Suppose $5,000 is deposited in a financial institution at 7.5% annual percentage rate. Interest is compounded *quarterly*. How many *years* will it take for that deposit (plus interest) to grow to $10,000?
   d. What is the cumulative interest paid in the loan from part (a) above? (Hint: subtract Principal from total payments.)
   e. A company has agreed to accept 60 monthly payments of $1,000 each as compensation for a piece of equipment they sold. If their internal rate of return is 11%, what is the present value of these cash flows?
   f. What is the future value of the cash flows from part (e)?
   g. The Anders Machine Shop is considering a new venture. The cash flows (in thousands of dollars) over the next five years are estimated as −150, −10, 40, 100, 150. Assuming a discount rate of 13%, what is the net present value of the cash flows?
   h. The Lost Creek State Bank has announced a new investment opportunity. For an initial deposit of $2,500 the bank will pay you $5,000 in

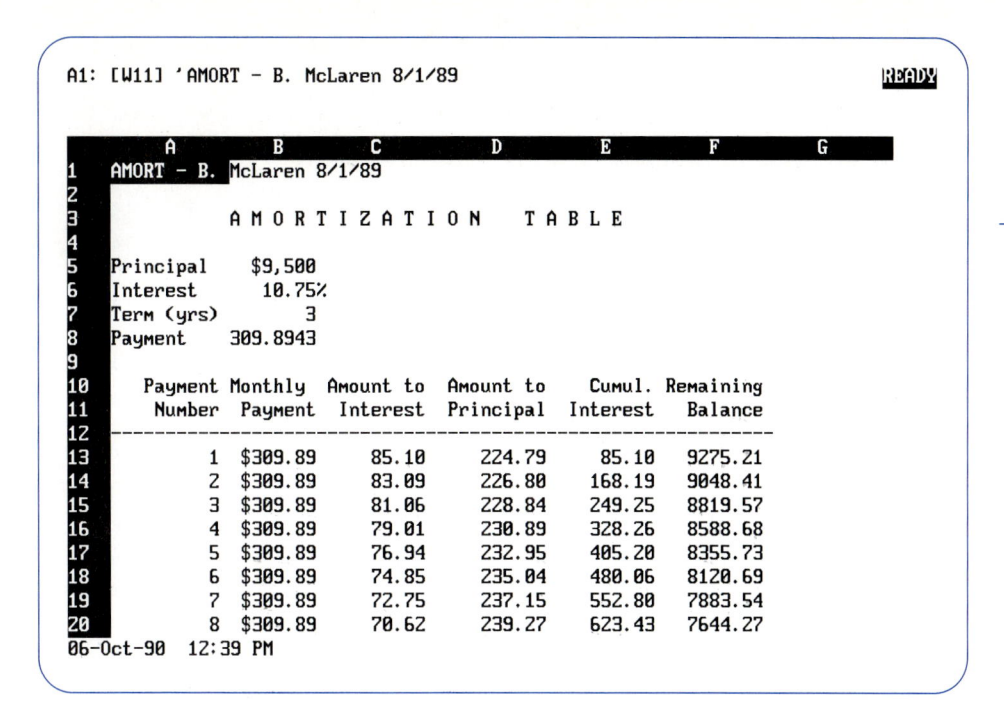

```
A1: [W11] 'AMORT - B. McLaren 8/1/89                                    READY

         A          B         C          D          E         F        G
 1  AMORT - B. McLaren 8/1/89
 2
 3              A M O R T I Z A T I O N    T A B L E
 4
 5  Principal    $9,500
 6  Interest     10.75%
 7  Term (yrs)       3
 8  Payment     309.8943
 9
10       Payment Monthly  Amount to  Amount to  Cumul.  Remaining
11       Number  Payment  Interest   Principal  Interest Balance
12  ------------------------------------------------------------
13          1   $309.89    85.10      224.79     85.10   9275.21
14          2   $309.89    83.09      226.80    168.19   9048.41
15          3   $309.89    81.06      228.84    249.25   8819.57
16          4   $309.89    79.01      230.89    328.26   8588.68
17          5   $309.89    76.94      232.95    405.20   8355.73
18          6   $309.89    74.85      235.04    480.06   8120.69
19          7   $309.89    72.75      237.15    552.80   7883.54
20          8   $309.89    70.62      239.27    623.43   7644.27
06-Oct-90  12:39 PM
```

FIGURE 4-21

Sample Amortization Table for Exercise 9

eight years. Assuming annual compounding, what is the implied annual percentage rate for this investment?

8. Use Lotus 1-2-3 functions to solve the following depreciation questions. Place your answers on a single spreadsheet, with the letter of the question in column A, the answer in column B, and any descriptions necessary in column C. The questions are independent of one another unless otherwise indicated.

   a. Assume that a piece of equipment has an initial cost of $30,000 and a salvage value of $5,000 after five years of useful life. What is the annual straight-line depreciation amount?

   b. For the same piece of equipment, determine the depreciation for year 2 using the double-declining balance method.

   c. Use the sum-of-the-years-digits method to determine the second year depreciation for the same piece of equipment.

   d. Prepare a separate table comparing depreciation in each year between the three methods. Your table should have the years 1–5 in five rows, with separate columns for the three depreciation methods. Also compare total depreciation with the three methods.

9. Prepare an amortization table for a 36-month consumer loan using the @PMT function to determine the payment. Build into the worksheet the following as parameters (refer to cells B5–B8 in the formulas beginning in row 13 of Figure 4-21. Your spreadsheet should allow new parameters to be entered in cells B5–B7):

   Term = 3 years   APR = 10.75%   Principal = $9,500

   Columns for your table include Payment Number, Monthly Payment, Amount to Interest, Amount to Principal, Cumulative Interest, and Remaining Balance for the loan. [Hint: The Amount to Interest is calculated by multiplying the previous month's Remaining Balance by the monthly interest rate. Amount to Principal is Payment – Amount to Interest.] Figure 4-21 shows the first few lines of your worksheet.

FIGURE 4-22

Sample Data for Exercise 10

Freehafer, J.	6	8	3	9	10	12	14	15	16	15	9	75	64	109
Smith, L.	7	9	6		10	14	14	15	14	12	13	87	89	130
McTavish, S.	8	10	10	10	9	14	15	13	13	15	11	82	87	141
Gravvit, M.	9	9	9	9	10	15	14	13	12	13		92	74	100
Hassler, MJ	4	6	7	6	8	12		14	15	15	7	65	59	111
Walker, G.	6	5	8	9	9	10	11	14	14	14	12	71	78	90
Katt, T.	10	8	9	9	8	15	15	15	13	13	13	90	95	135

10. Professor Kantkount's Gradebook. You are to prepare a gradebook for the professor that will store records for the class and will provide the usual gradebook calculations—total points, and percentage of total possible points. Data for the gradebook are shown in Figure 4-22. Assume there are 5 quizzes worth 10 points each, 6 computer projects worth 15 points each, and three exams worth 100, 100 and 150 points, respectively. Thus total points are 490.

    Also report the average score for each item beneath the column. Be sure to consider only those who turned in the item. Ignore blank scores for purposes of calculating the average. Of course, blanks count as a zero toward the semester grade.

    Adjust column widths to fit all the data onto the worksheet. Use a Vertical Title in the column following the student name so that the scores can be entered for the proper student. Design a pleasing appearance for your gradebook.

11. Using the data and your gradebook worksheet from the previous problem, determine semester letter grades for the students. Letter grades are based upon a lookup table using 60% as the minimum D grade, 65% for a D+, etc. Don't forget to include a category for F grades. Your spreadsheet would allow for a 1/2 percent roundup factor: a percentage of .745 should be rounded up to .75, thus qualifying for a C+ grade. Place the letter grade after the last column in the worksheet.

    a. Print a copy of the worksheet. Include all columns of the gradebook, and the lookup table.

    b. Use the /Range Format Hidden command to hide the students' names. Reprint the worksheet without the names showing so that the professor can post grades anonymously. (Assume a graduate assistant will write code numbers in by hand.)

12. You have been asked to help the Registrar's office prepare a tuition and fees table for the fall semester. The University is using a bracket fee system, based upon credit hours taken and residency status.

    For 0 to 9.5 credit hours, fees are assessed per hour. In-state residents pay $71 per credit hour; non-residents pay $165 per hour.

    Full-time students, 10 or more hours, pay a flat fee. In-state students pay $996 while non-residents pay $2,363.

    Using the @IF function, calculate the total fees for the following students. Number of credit hours and residency status are indicated for each student.

Format the information properly. Print the worksheet and cell formulas. [Hint: Ignore the residency status at first while developing the @IF expression. You will have several @IFs within the same expression.]

STUDENT NAME	HOURS	RES STATUS
Halter, B.	13	Resident
Jones, J.	18	Resident
Parren, A.	6	Non-resident
Conable, B.	9	Resident
McInver, F.	12	Non-resident
Waters, M.	21	Non-resident
Green, J.	10	Resident

CHAPTER 4 PROJECT
PINE FARM APARTMENTS

A group of local investors is analyzing an apartment complex investment opportunity. You have been retained as a consultant in the project, and intend to use Lotus 1-2-3 to evaluate the desirability of the investment. Some of the financial data is shown below. Some may not be relevant, and you may need to make an informed assumption about missing information. Because the analysis is done with an electronic spreadsheet, it should be easy to change those assumptions by inserting a new value into a parameter cell.

The cost of the land is estimated at $320,000. The building costs are estimated at $41 per square foot for the basic building, plus $6,000 per apartment for appliances, furnishings and decorating. The general contractor will add 10% to the building costs. Additional parking lot and driveway construction will cost $32,000. Landscaping will cost $35,000 in the first year, plus $10,000 in each of the next two years. A 15-year mortgage is available at 9.7%, with 2.5 points plus $4,000 closing costs. The bank requires at least 15% down payment on commercial loans.

Apartments are now estimated at 1000 square feet each, with twelve apartments per building. Each building will have another 1200 square feet of common area. At the present time eight buildings are planned. Rents for two-bedroom apartments currently average $475 per month, although some complexes are able to charge an additional $50 for premium accommodations. Current occupancy rates for similar complexes run about 83%; ten percent lower rents would probably increase that number to 90%. Rent is expected to increase by seven percent annually.

The operating costs are more difficult to estimate. Maintenance costs are expected to run around ten percent of rent receipts. Utilities will run approximately $6,000 per month for the complex, plus $45 per apartment each month. Renters are responsible for telephone and electricity, but the complex will provide gas heat and cable television. Insurance will run about $25,000 per year, but may increase in the future. The investment group expects to claim straight-line depreciation over 27.5 years. The partnership tax rate is estimated at 36%.

The partners wish to know if this is a good investment, and the expected after-tax cash flow for the next ten years. They realize that the first few years may be unprofitable, but hope to recover their costs and turn a profit as soon as possible.

5

Advanced Lotus File and Print Commands

Objectives

After completing this chapter, you should be able to:

- Change your default disk drive and directory for storing Lotus files.
- Display names of Lotus worksheet, print, graph, and linked files.
- Explain how to erase Lotus worksheet, print, graph, and other files.
- Discuss the ways to combine two or more worksheets into a single worksheet.
- Create a cell expression to link a value from another worksheet into the current worksheet.
- Explain the steps in printing a Lotus worksheet, including Options.
- Describe how to print cell formulas instead of the values of the cells for auditing purposes.
- Discuss the benefits of using the Allways spreadsheet publishing module.

Chapter 5 — Advanced Lotus File and Print Commands

INTRODUCTION

This chapter will discuss the use of /File command options to save and retrieve worksheets, and to save a portion of the worksheet. Options for combining two or more worksheets are covered, along with the procedure to link a value from another spreadsheet to the current worksheet.

The /Print options are covered in depth, including changing margins, print fonts, printing to a file and printing cell formulas instead of values.

LOTUS FILE OPERATIONS

In the Lotus QuickStart chapter we discussed how to save a finished worksheet and how to retrieve an existing worksheet. Lotus also allows you to combine information from other worksheets and even from non-worksheet files. You can extract information from the current worksheet and save it to another worksheet file. The /File menu for file operations looks like:

```
                                                                  MENU
Retrieve Save Combine Xtract Erase List Import Directory Admin
Erase the current worksheet from memory and display the selected worksheet
```

Changing the Default Directory

All of the Lotus /File operations are done with files in the **default directory.** The default directory is stored in a configuration file that is read when 1-2-3 begins. There are three ways to change to a different directory:

- in effect for the current file command (press /F, then a file option, then Esc key)
- temporarily for the current 1-2-3 session (use /FD command)
- permanently (use /WGDD command).

Changing the Directory for One Command

This change allows you to change the directory when doing a single file operation such as Save, Retrieve, or Erase. Begin the operation as usual with the /**F** command and the appropriate option. When Lotus prompts you for a file name press the **Esc** key twice. The first press will erase the current file name, leaving just the current default drive and directory. A *second* press of **Esc** will erase the drive and subdirectory names and you can fill in another drive, subdirectory and file name. You may then complete the file operation with the new directory. Although most subsequent /File commands will default to the initial directory, the /File Save command will continue to use the file name you previously provided.

Temporarily Changing the Default Directory

To temporarily change the default drive and directory for the current 1-2-3 session, use the /**File Directory** command (/**FD**). When Lotus prompts for the new directory information, type in the drive letter and a colon, followed by the subdirectory on that drive, if any. For example, to change to the B drive, enter /**FD B:** and press **Enter**. The new directory will be the default location for /File operations until you quit 1-2-3. The next time you start 1-2-3 the original directory will be the default.

LOTUS FILE OPERATIONS   145

Example: *Temporarily Changing the Default Directory*

This example will demonstrate how to change to the MIS376 subdirectory within the Lotus directory on the C drive. This example assumes that such a directory already exists.[1]

1. Enter **/FD** to activate the File Directory command.

2. When Lotus prompts for the new directory name type **C:\123\MIS376** and press **Enter**.

Permanently Changing the Default Directory

The permanent change is accomplished through the **/Worksheet Global Default** menu. Enter **/WGDD** command to select the Directory option. When prompted for the new directory name, enter the appropriate drive and directory path and press **Enter**. From the next menu press **U** to update the configuration information, then press **Q** to quit the default menu. From this point onward you will default to the new directory in this and future 1-2-3 sessions. It can be overridden during a session by either of the preceding methods.

Example: *Permanently Changing the Default Directory*

In this example you will change to the C:\123\MIS376 directory. This example assumes that such a directory already exists.

1. First type **/WGDD** to activate the Worksheet Global Default Directory menu.

2. Type the new directory path **C:\123\MIS376** and press **Enter** to complete the entry.

3. At the next menu press **U** to Update the configuration file. If this step is omitted the change will not be permanent.

4. Finally press **Q** to Quit the Global Default menu.

You should recall that Lotus does not automatically save the worksheet file for you. Rather, the worksheet is held in RAM and is subject to erasure and complete loss when you quit the 1-2-3 module or whenever there is a power interruption to the computer. For this reason it is a good practice to save your worksheet file frequently while entering the worksheet cell formulas. As with WordPerfect, a good rule of thumb for the frequency of your saves depends upon your typing speed and the difficulty of re-entering all the information should the spreadsheet somehow get "lost."

Retrieving and Saving Worksheet Files

---

[1] To create a subdirectory from the DOS prompt, change to the parent directory with the **CD\123** command. Then issue the **MD MIS376** command to make a new directory called MIS376 within 123 directory on the C drive.

FIGURE 5-1

Lotus File Type Extensions for Various Versions

Version	File Extension
1a	.WKS
2, 2.01, 2.2	.WK1
Student	.WKE
3.0, 3.1	.WK3 or .WK1

Retrieving an Existing File

The /**File Retrieve** command (/**FR**) will display all the worksheet files in the default directory. Because each version of Lotus 1-2-3 uses a different file type and file extension (see chart in Figure 5-1), Lotus uses the (*.WK?) wildcard file name template and shows all matching files. When you retrieve a different version worksheet file, Lotus will do file conversion automatically. In most cases a *later* version of Lotus is able to retrieve and convert an *earlier* file type. You should not attempt to retrieve a *later* file type with an *earlier* Lotus version without using the Translate facility, available with the Lotus Access Menu and discussed in Chapter 9.

To retrieve a file, move the cursor to the desired file in the menu and press **Enter**. If you know the proper spelling of the file name, you can type it in at the file name prompt, followed by **Enter**. The retrieved file will replace the current worksheet in memory, so be sure you have saved this worksheet before issuing the Retrieve command.

To retrieve a file from a different directory, press the **Esc** key one or more times to erase the default drive and directory names. Then enter the proper pathname, ending with the file name. For example, to retrieve a file called MYFILE.WK1 from the A drive, enter /**FR**. Because Lotus will display the worksheet files in the default directory, press **Esc** twice. The first press will erase the *.WK? template, and the second press will remove the current drive and directory names from the file name prompt line area. Then enter **A:MYFILE** and press **Enter**. Lotus will temporarily switch to the A drive for this command only. To change the default directory for this 1-2-3 session, use the /FD command described earlier.

Saving a Worksheet File

To save the current worksheet, enter the /**File Save** command (/**FS**). Lotus will prompt you to enter the file name. There are several ways to specify the file name, depending on whether the file was previously saved:

- You may enter a file name of up to eight characters long, followed by **Enter**. Use the customary DOS file name conventions. If you do not enter a file extension, Lotus will use the default .WK1 extension. Because Lotus displays only file names with the default extension in the /File Retrieve, it is better to not specify a different file extension.

- If the worksheet has been previously saved, Lotus will display the previous name and give you the opportunity to change it. Press **Enter** to use the existing name, or type in a replacement name and press **Enter** to complete the entry.

- You may temporarily select another drive or directory by pressing the **Esc** key one or more times to remove the default values. Then enter the proper directory and file name.

After you provide the file name, Lotus will check the current directory for any files with the same name. If such a file already exists, you'll see the following menu:

MENU

Cancel Replace Backup
Cancel command--Leave existing file on disk intact

- Pressing **Cancel** will cancel the Save command, leaving the existing file intact, and *not* save the current worksheet.

- Pressing **Replace** will save the current worksheet and replace the previously saved worksheet with the same name.

- The **Backup** option will first rename the older worksheet with the .BAK extension, then save the current worksheet version with the .WK1 extension. Lotus versions before 2.2 did not have the backup feature.

Working with Other Files

Lotus has commands to list and erase files on the default directory, and to change the default directory. You can combine two or more worksheet files. There are /File commands to import data from a text (non-worksheet) file, and to save a portion of the spreadsheet to another worksheet file. You can also enter DOS commands temporarily as described in the last section.

Listing File Names

To display the names of files stored on the default drive, use the **/File List** command (**/FL**). You'll see the following menu.

MENU

Worksheet Print Graph Other Linked
List worksheet files

The first menu choice will display all the Worksheet files in the default directory, using the .WK? wildcard template. Other file types include:

- The **Print** choice displays the .PRN files (worksheets printed to a file instead of the printer).

- The **Graph** option will list all the .PIC files (graph image files, discussed in Chapter 6).

- The **Other** selection will display all files, using the *.* wildcard template.

- The **Linked** option will list all files that are linked (with a link cell expression) to the current worksheet in memory.

Figure 5-2 shows a typical File List screen for worksheet files. The first entry in the file list is highlighted at the top of the display with its date, time and size in characters shown. As you move the cursor to another file name in the list, its detailed information will be displayed near the top of the table.

Erasing Files

The **/File Erase** command (**/FE**) will permanently delete a file from the default disk directory. It has no effect on the worksheet currently in the 1-2-3 workspace.

Chapter 5 — Advanced Lotus File and Print Commands

FIGURE 5-2

Worksheet File List Screen (Press **/FLW**)

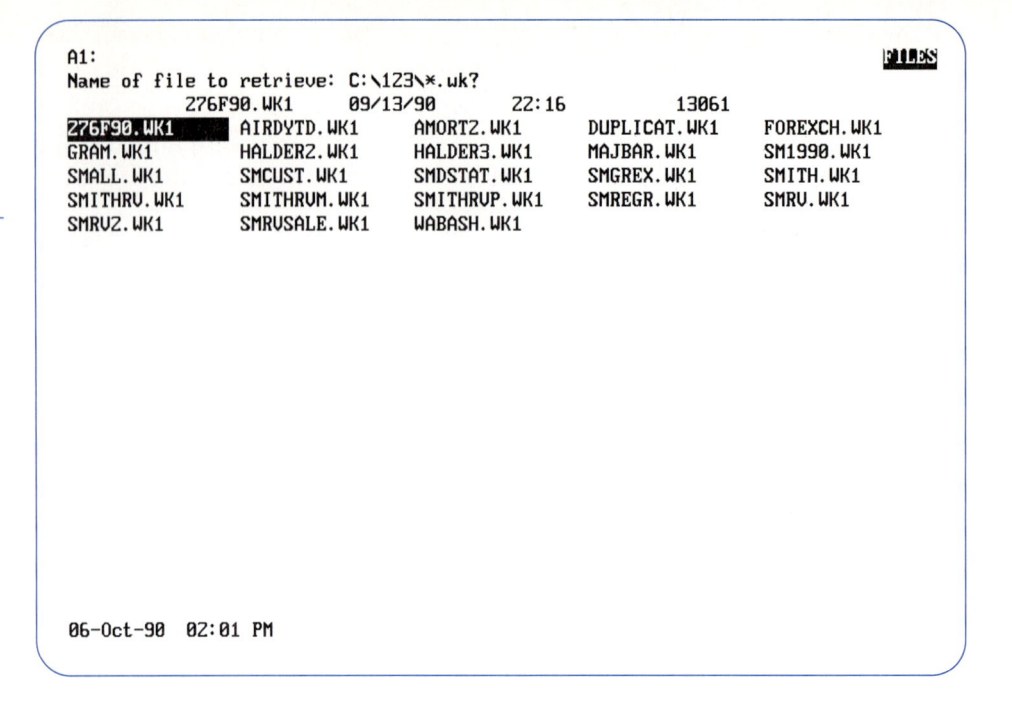

```
A1:                                                               FILES
Name of file to retrieve: C:\123\*.wk?
                276F90.WK1    09/13/90       22:16        13061
276F90.WK1     AIRDYTD.WK1   AMORT2.WK1    DUPLICAT.WK1   FOREXCH.WK1
GRAM.WK1       HALDER2.WK1   HALDER3.WK1   MAJBAR.WK1     SM1990.WK1
SMALL.WK1      SMCUST.WK1    SMDSTAT.WK1   SMGREX.WK1     SMITH.WK1
SMITHRV.WK1    SMITHRVM.WK1  SMITHRVP.WK1  SMREGR.WK1     SMRV.WK1
SMRVZ.WK1      SMRVSALE.WK1  WABASH.WK1




06-Oct-90  02:01 PM
```

FIGURE 5-3

Worksheet File Erase Display (Press **/FEW**)

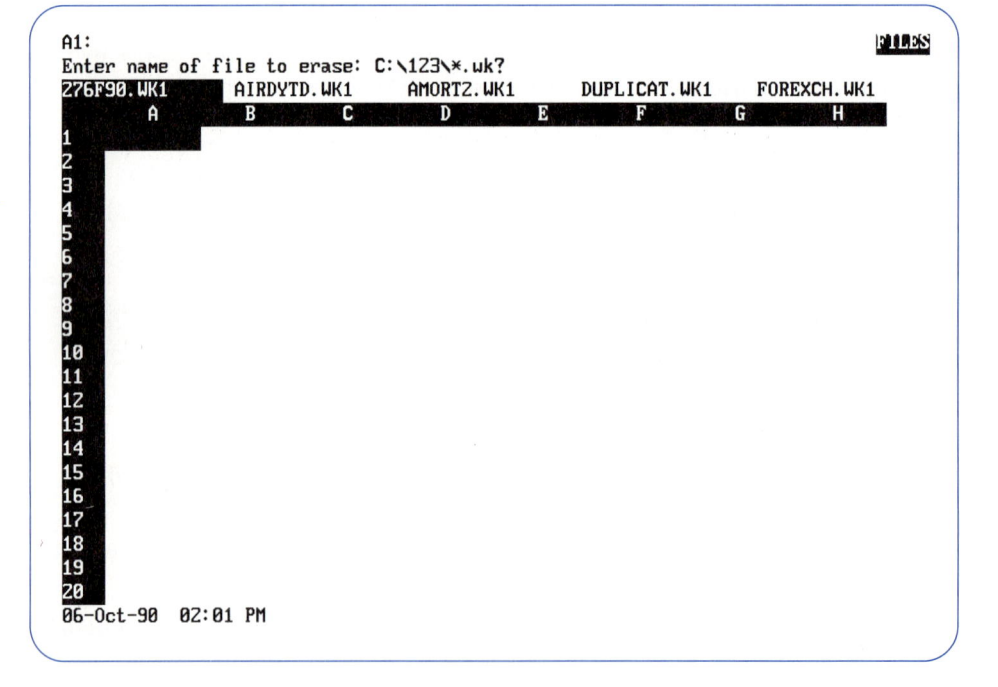

```
A1:                                                               FILES
Enter name of file to erase: C:\123\*.wk?
276F90.WK1     AIRDYTD.WK1   AMORT2.WK1    DUPLICAT.WK1   FOREXCH.WK1
        A       B       C       D       E       F       G       H
 1
 2
 3
 4
 5
 6
 7
 8
 9
10
11
12
13
14
15
16
17
18
19
20
06-Oct-90  02:01 PM
```

The erase menu is very similar to the List menu.

MENU

Worksheet Print Graph Other
Erase a worksheet file

After you select the type of file to erase (worksheet .WK?, print .PRN, graph .PIC, other *.*), Lotus presents a menu of file names. You can use the left and right arrow keys to move the cursor to the desired file, then press **Enter** to select a file to be erased. You must confirm the choice before Lotus will delete the file.

```
A1:                                                              FILES
Enter name of file to erase: C:\123\*.wk?
             276F90.WK1      09/13/90      22:16         13061
276F90.WK1      AIRDYTD.WK1    AMORT2.WK1    DUPLICAT.WK1   FOREXCH.WK1
GRAM.WK1        HALDER2.WK1    HALDER3.WK1   MAJBAR.WK1     SM1990.WK1
SMALL.WK1       SMCUST.WK1     SMDSTAT.WK1   SMGREX.WK1     SMITH.WK1
SMITHRV.WK1     SMITHRVM.WK1   SMITHRVP.WK1  SMREGR.WK1     SMRV.WK1
SMRV2.WK1       SMRVSALE.WK1   WABASH.WK1




06-Oct-90  02:04 PM
```

FIGURE 5-4

Worksheet File Erase Extended Display (Press **/FEW F3**)

The display in Figure 5-3 appears first. If you would like to see more information about the files before selecting one to erase, press the **F3** function key and the second display in Figure 5-4 will appear. The files are shown in alphabetical order, helping you find the file to select. The file name, date, time, and file size are displayed on line 3 for the currently highlighted file.

Saving a Portion of the Worksheet

Lotus permits you to save just a part of the current worksheet to another worksheet file by using the **/File Xtract** command. The regular /File Save command saves *all* of the current worksheet. The commands are similar, although the **/File Xtract** command (**/FX**) also prompts you for the range of cells to be saved. Move the cursor to the beginning cell of the range we wish to save. Enter the **/FX** command, and you'll see the following menu.

```
                                                              MENU
Formulas Values
Save data including formulas
```

The **Formulas** choice will save the cells exactly as they were entered, including cell expressions with cell references relative to their position on the spreadsheet. Thus if a cell referred to a cell two rows above it, the formula would refer to cells 2 rows above it when combined with another spreadsheet. If the extracted worksheet is later combined into another worksheet, these cells would be recalculated according to the cell expressions. If you save **Values**, only the results of the current cell expressions are saved. Thus the values would not change if combined into another worksheet.

Example: *Saving a Portion of the Worksheet*

For example, suppose we want to save the Gross Profit row of the Smithton spreadsheet to another file.

FIGURE 5-5

Example of /File Xtract Command (Press **/FX**)

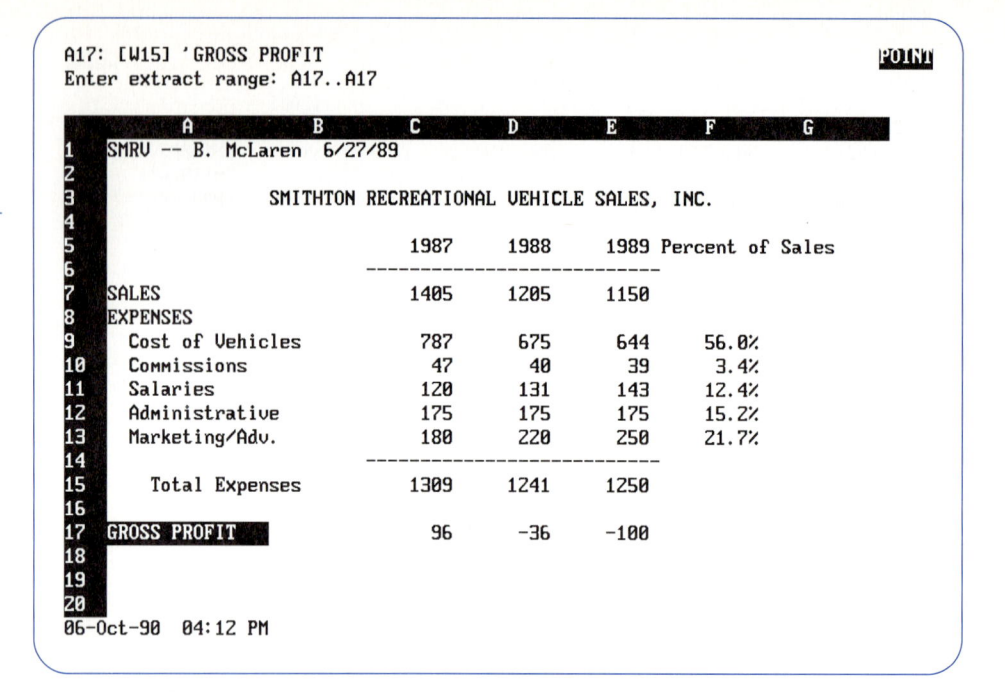

```
A17: [W15] 'GROSS PROFIT                                          POINT
Enter extract range: A17..A17

        A         B         C         D         E         F         G
 1  SMRV -- B. McLaren  6/27/89
 2
 3                    SMITHTON RECREATIONAL VEHICLE SALES, INC.
 4
 5                        1987      1988      1989 Percent of Sales
 6                        ----------------------------
 7  SALES                 1405      1205      1150
 8  EXPENSES
 9    Cost of Vehicles     787       675       644     56.0%
10    Commissions           47        40        39      3.4%
11    Salaries             120       131       143     12.4%
12    Administrative       175       175       175     15.2%
13    Marketing/Adv.       180       220       250     21.7%
14                        ----------------------------
15    Total Expenses      1309      1241      1250
16
17  GROSS PROFIT            96       -36      -100
18
19
20
06-Oct-90  04:12 PM
```

1. Make sure you have started Lotus and entered the 1-2-3 module. Retrieve the Smithton worksheet with the **/FR** command. The file name is **SMRV**.

2. Move the cursor to cell A17, the first cell in the Gross Profit row that we wish to save.

3. Press **/FX** to activate the File Xtract command.

4. You'll be asked whether to save Formulas or Values. For this example, let's select **Values**.

5. The next menu prompts you to select the save-to file name. Type the name **SMGRPR** and press **Enter**. You'll see the screen shown in Figure 5-5.

6. Highlight the range of cells we wish to extract by moving the cursor to cell **E17**. The cell range should be A17..E17. Press **Enter** to complete the entry.

7. Lotus will save those 5 cells to a second worksheet file called SMGRPR.WK1 (or whatever worksheet extension your version of Lotus uses). You can examine that file by retrieving it in the usual way.

Combining Two Worksheet Files

You can combine the contents of two worksheet files with the Lotus **/File Combine** command (/**FC**). First you must retrieve the base worksheet. Move the cursor to the desired location in the base worksheet. You can then combine all or part of the second worksheet into the base worksheet. Lotus provides three options for combining files:

MENU

Copy Add Subtract
Copy data from a file on disk to the worksheet

You must instruct Lotus how to handle cells the two files have in common.

- The **Copy** option will replace cells in the base worksheet with the cells from the file being combined.

- The **Add** option will add the numbers from the file to the numbers in the base worksheet. Cells with labels are not affected.

- The **Subtract** option will subtract file cell values from the base worksheet cells. If the cell in the base worksheet is empty, the file cell is subtracted from zero. Cells with labels are not affected.

One application of the /**File Combine** command is to consolidate spreadsheets from different divisions, product lines, or time periods. The **Add** option is used to add values together from these worksheets. In this case the previous cell values of the current worksheet are lost when they are combined; they still exist, however, in the saved copy of that worksheet.

Lotus will next ask whether you wish to combine the entire file or a specified range, as shown below. You may specify a range name from the saved file or give the actual cell range reference.

MENU

Entire-File Named/Specified-Range
Incorporate entire file into worksheet

The specified portion of the file will be inserted into the base worksheet at the cursor location. Cells are *not* matched by absolute address, but are inserted relative to the cursor location in the base worksheet. In the example below, the cursor is moved to cell F5. The first cell in the combined file, C5, will be placed in cell F5. Cell C6 of the combined file is placed in cell F6, and so forth.

Example: *Combining Two Worksheet Files*

Suppose we wish to add the 1990 Income Statement results to the Smithton spreadsheet. The results are stored in a file called **SM1990.WK1** on the data disk.

1. First retrieve the **SMRV.WK1** base worksheet file from the data disk with the /**FR** command. This is the formatted worksheet with the inserted Commissions row.

2. Move the cursor to cell **F5**. You will place the column of 1990 sales results at this location, replacing the present column.

3. Press /**FC** to activate the /File Combine menu. At the next menu select the **Copy** option. Lotus will ask if you wish to incorporate the entire file or a name specified range. Select the second option by pressing **N**.

4. When prompted for the range name or address, enter **C5..C17** and press **Enter**. At the prompt enter the file name **SM1990.WK1**. Lotus will immediately load the cell expressions from the SM1990.WK1 file into the base worksheet. The resulting worksheet appears in Figure 5-6.

Linking Data from Another Worksheet (Release 2.2)

Release 2.2 introduced a useful feature in the ability to **link** a cell value from another worksheet saved on disk to the worksheet currently in memory. A linking formula has the format +<<**filename**>>**cellref**. The **filename** is

FIGURE 5-6

Combined Spreadsheet Example (Press **/FC**)

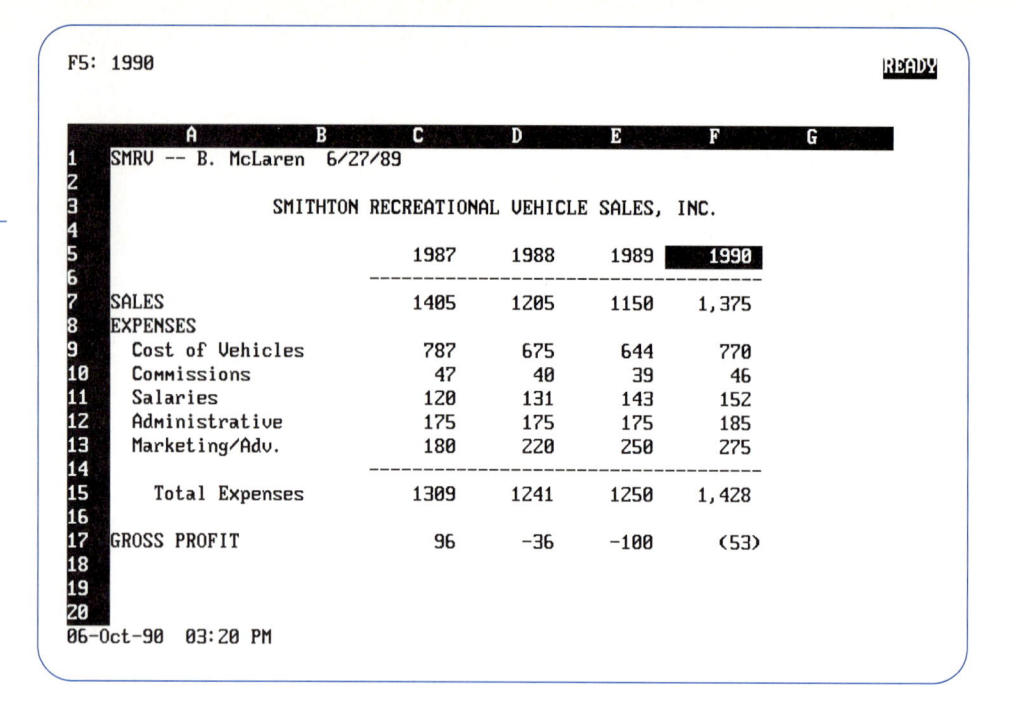

```
F5: 1990                                                      READY

         A          B          C         D         E         F         G
 1  SMRV -- B. McLaren  6/27/89
 2
 3                     SMITHTON RECREATIONAL VEHICLE SALES, INC.
 4
 5                              1987      1988      1989      1990
 6                              ----------------------------------
 7  SALES                       1405      1205      1150     1,375
 8  EXPENSES
 9    Cost of Vehicles           787       675       644       770
10    Commissions                 47        40        39        46
11    Salaries                   120       131       143       152
12    Administrative             175       175       175       185
13    Marketing/Adv.             180       220       250       275
14                              ----------------------------------
15    Total Expenses            1309      1241      1250     1,428
16
17  GROSS PROFIT                  96       -36      -100      (53)
18
19
20
06-Oct-90  03:20 PM
```

the pathname of another worksheet file, including the file extension. The **cellref** is the cell address or range name of the cell value in that file name that is to be linked to the current worksheet.

Examples of link formulas are shown below.

```
+<<SMRV.WK1>>A14              .WK1 is optional
+<<A:LANCOST>>SERVER_COST     SERVER_COST is range name
+<<C:\123\89SALES.WKS>>J22    Full pathname given
```

Example: Using a Link Formula

Suppose you wanted to use the gross profit data from the Smithton worksheet in another spreadsheet without going through the /File Combine procedure. This example will demonstrate how to use the Release 2.2 link feature.

1. Begin 1-2-3 as usual and start with an empty worksheet. You can use the **/WE** command to erase the worksheet if necessary. The new worksheet will be called SMLINK.

2. We will use the three gross profit cells, C17–E17, from the SMRV.WK1 worksheet stored on the data disk.

3. In cell A1 enter **SMLINK--** and add your name and the date.

4. In cell A3 enter **Year** and in cell B3 enter **Gross Profit**.

5. In cells A4–A6 enter **1987, 1988,** and **1989**.

6. In cell B4 enter the first link expression **+<<SMRV>>C17** and press **Enter**. You should notice disk activity as Lotus temporarily opens the SMRV worksheet and copies the value in cell C17 into your current worksheet. Lotus will display 95.992 in cell B4.

7. In cell B5 enter **+<<SMRV>>D17** and in cell B6 enter **+<<SMRV>>E17**. Your worksheet should look like the one in Figure 5-7.

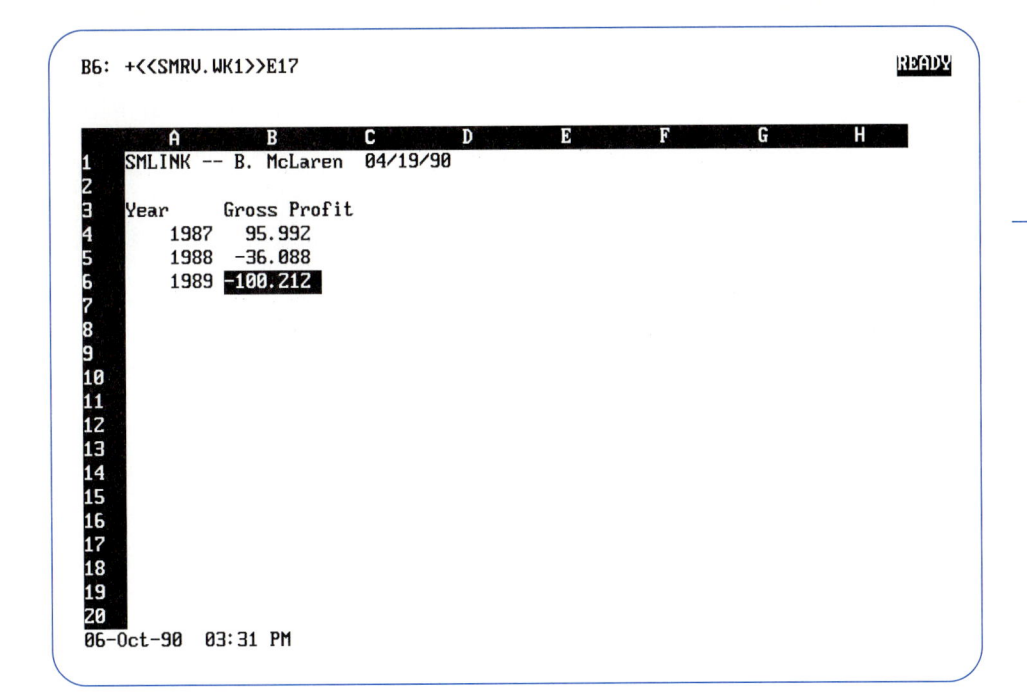

```
B6: +<<SMRU.WK1>>E17                                    READY


         A         B         C         D         E         F         G         H
  1  SMLINK -- B. McLaren  04/19/90
  2
  3  Year      Gross Profit
  4     1987      95.992
  5     1988     -36.088
  6     1989    -100.212
  7
  8
  9
 10
 11
 12
 13
 14
 15
 16
 17
 18
 19
 20
 06-Oct-90   03:31 PM
```

FIGURE 5-7

Example Showing Link Cell Expressions

Importing Data from Non-Worksheet Files

Because valuable data may reside in non-Lotus file formats, you may need to import this data directly into Lotus. The Lotus Translate module can be used to convert certain well-known file formats, and is described in Chapter 9. The **/File Import** command (**/FI**) will accept data in **ASCII format**—that is, standard text characters and digits. ASCII is the name of the character coding system used in personal and some larger computers. If you can use the **TYPE** command to display the file from the DOS prompt and it displays properly on the screen, it is probably an ASCII file. WordPerfect files are not ASCII files, although you can use the Text In/Out command (**Ctrl-F5**) in WordPerfect to save a file in ASCII format.

One way to transfer data from a database to Lotus is to prepare an ASCII file in the database program and import it into 1-2-3. Chapter 9 will go into more detail on transferring data to Lotus 1-2-3 from dBASE and other sources. That chapter contains several examples.

File Commands for Temporarily Entering DOS

While Lotus does not have a file copy command, you may always use the **/System** command to temporarily return to DOS, execute DOS commands, and return to Lotus.

To temporarily leave Lotus 1-2-3, use the **/System** command (**/S**). If your computer is properly set up with a copy of the DOS COMMAND.COM file available, you will see the DOS prompt. If the computer prompts you to insert a disk containing a copy of COMMAND.COM, insert the boot disk in the A drive and press the **Enter** key. On floppy-only computers the DOS prompt will likely be A>. On hard disk machines this will probably by the C> prompt, and on network computers it might be the F> prompt. In any event, you can type in the usual DOS commands while your spreadsheet and Lotus remain in memory. For example, if you run out of room on the current disk, you can use a **temporary DOS session** to format a new blank diskette. Then return to Lotus and save the file on the new disk.

Chapter 5 — Advanced Lotus File and Print Commands

When finished with this temporary DOS session, type **Exit** and press **Enter** at the DOS prompt to return to Lotus. Remember that there is less memory available than usual because Lotus is still loaded in RAM, so you may not be able to execute programs that require more memory than is available.

PRINTING THE WORKSHEET— ADVANCED COMMANDS

We covered the basics of printing a Lotus worksheet in the QuickStart chapter. This section will explore more details of the printing process, including options. Recall that the **/Print Printer** command menu and settings sheet look like the example in Figure 5-8. The Settings Sheet summarizes the various print settings. To temporarily remove the settings sheet from the display, press the **F6** key; it will reappear when you press **F6** again, or the next time you activate the /Print menu.

Main Print Menu Choices

Several of these /Print options were discussed in the previous chapter.

- **Range** allows you to specify the range of cells you wish to be printed. The range must be specified or nothing will be printed. A shorthand way of specifying the entire worksheet is the range:

    Home..End Home

- **Line** causes the printer to advance one line in the printed output. Lotus keeps track of the number of lines that have been printed so far on the current page, and will automatically skip to the top of the next page when the bottom of the page is reached.

- **Page** will instruct the printer to skip to the top of the next page and reset the line counter.

- **Align** is used to reset the line counter when you have manually adjusted the printer to the top of the page, such as by pressing the printer Form Feed button. If you forget to use the Align command after manually

FIGURE 5-8

Print Menu and Print Settings Screen (Press **/PP**)

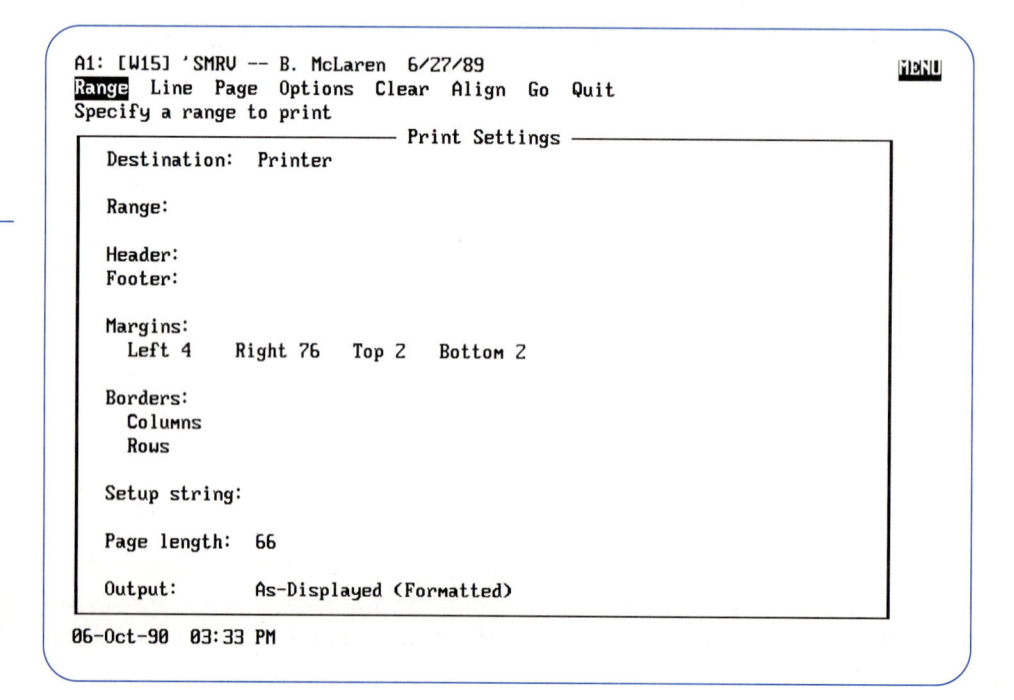

```
A1: [W15] 'SMRU -- B. McLaren  6/27/89                           MENU
Range Line Page Options Clear Align Go Quit
Specify a range to print
                          ─── Print Settings ───
   Destination:  Printer

   Range:

   Header:
   Footer:

   Margins:
     Left 4      Right 76    Top 2    Bottom 2

   Borders:
     Columns
     Rows

   Setup string:

   Page length:  66

   Output:       As-Displayed (Formatted)


06-Oct-90  03:33 PM
```

PRINTING THE WORKSHEET — ADVANCED COMMANDS

155

advancing the paper, Lotus may produce a page break in an unexpected place. Align also resets the page counter to 1 for automatic page numbering.

- **Clear** allows you to reset some or all of the printer settings. The Clear menu looks like this:

  MENU

  All Range Borders Format
  Return all print settings to defaults

  The Clear subchoices include:
  - **All** will reset all print settings.
  - **Range** will clear the print range.
  - **Borders** will cancel border rows or columns (described under Options below).
  - **Format** will reset any page format changes made such as Margins, Pg-length, and Setup strings (also described below).

- **Go** will send the output to the printer.

- **Quit** will leave the /Print menu and return to the READY mode. If you re-enter the /Print menu, Lotus remembers how many lines have been printed, along with all other print settings. Retrieving a new worksheet will clear all settings except the lines-printed counter.

The **Print Menu Options** choice allows you to modify some of the optional print settings. The Options menu is illustrated below.

Print Options Submenu

MENU

Header Footer Margins Borders Setup Pg-Length Other Quit
Create a header

- The **Header** and **Footer** choices create a one-line phrase to appear at the top or bottom of each page, similar to WordPerfect. Lotus inserts two blank lines between the header and body of the report, and likewise for the footer. If you place the **#** character in the header or footer, Lotus will print the page number in its place. The **@** character instructs Lotus to print the current date in its position.

Example: *Creating a Print Header*

In this example you will create a print header that will print at the top of each page of a multi-page printed report.

1. Retrieve the file **AMORT2.WK1** from the data disk. This file contains bi-monthly payment figures for a home mortgage and takes two pages to print. Only the first three years (78 payments) are calculated in this file.

2. Press **/PP** to activate the print menu. The **Range** is **Home..End Home** or **A1..F90**.

3. Press **O** to enter the Options Menu, then **H** to specify a one-line header phrase. At the prompt, type **Bi-Monthly Amortization Schedule** and press **Enter**.

4. To print the report, press **Q** then **AG**. You'll see the phrase at the top of both pages of the report. When the printer finishes, press **PQ** and tear off the output.

- The **Margins** option is used to set top, bottom, left, and/or right margins for the page. The default margins are shown in the **/Worksheet Status** screen (**/WS**). If they have not been changed at your site, the defaults are:

    ```
    Top Margin = 2 lines
    Bottom Margin = 2 lines
    Left Margin = 4 characters
    Right Margin = 76 characters
    ```

- The **Borders** option is used to select certain rows and/or columns that will be printed on each page. Borders are typically used as row or column headings. Similar to worksheet Titles, Borders help the reader follow tables that are larger than one page size.

Example: Using Print Borders

This example will print ten rows from the worksheet as a border at the top of each printed page in the output.

1. Again retrieve the **AMORT2.WK1** worksheet from the data disk. This step will clear the header created in the previous example. (Conversely, you can use the **Clear** command in the main /Print menu and select **All** to delete the header and other print settings.)

2. Press **/PP** to activate the print menu. The print **Range** will be **A13..F90**. Do *not* include the top portion of the worksheet (rows 3–12) in the print range or it will be printed twice on the first page.

3. Press **O** to go to the Options menu, then **B** to select Borders.

4. Press **R** to designate Rows as borders. When prompted for the border cell range, type **A3..A12** and press **Enter**.

5. Press **Q** to quit the Options menu, then **AG** to print the report. Lotus will print the ten border rows at the top of each page.

6. Press **PQ** to eject the page and leave the /Print menu.

- **Setup** is used to send printer control codes directly to the printer, controlling such printer settings as type size, font, draft or near letter quality, and page orientation (for laser printers). The specific codes used with your printer depend on the kind of printer you have. A common **setup string** that is used with Epson-compatible printers is **\015**. This code tells the printer to switch to compressed print mode and will print more than 80 characters on a line. [Note: If you switch to compressed mode you should also change the right margin to 132, corresponding to the new maximum number of characters per line.] The setup code for Epson-compatible printers to return to normal print mode is **\018**. Your computer lab will have the correct setup strings for your printer.

- The **Pg-Length** option lets you adjust the current page length, in lines. The default length is 66 lines (11 inches at 6 printed lines per inch). The number of lines printed on one page is equal to the Pg-Length minus Top-margin and Bottom-margin (PL – TM – BM). If you change the

PRINTING THE WORKSHEET — ADVANCED COMMANDS   157

paper length, adjust the Pg-Length accordingly. Another change to Pg-length is necessary if you use the Setup code to change the vertical line spacing, say to 8 lines per inch, or from 8 back to 6 lines per inch.

- **Other** choices are discussed in the next section.

Other Submenu Choices—Printing Cell Formulas

The **Other** choice brings you to another menu where you may elect to print the cell formulas instead of the values they represent. Similar to the **Text** format type, cell formula outputs are useful for debugging spreadsheet models—checking for errors—and for documentation purposes. The output from this command is displayed in a single column, with one cell per row of output. It is more difficult to interpret the output obtained by the cell-formulas method than converting the cells to text format but much easier to create. The Other menu looks like:

```
                                                        MENU
As-Displayed Cell-Formulas Formatted Unformatted
Print range as displayed
```

- The default choice, **As-Displayed**, produces the standard output with cell values presented as they are displayed on the screen.

- **Cell-Formulas** will produce the detailed output for cell formulas, formats, column widths, and protection status for all cells in the print range indicated. An example of a portion of the Smithton spreadsheet is shown in Figure 5-9.

- The **Formatted** option produces the normal output with headers, footers, and banners.

- If **Unformatted** is chosen, no headers, footers, or page breaks will be generated. The Unformatted option is generally used when you print the spreadsheet to a disk file, in preparation for inserting it into a word processing document.

Example: *Printing Cell Formulas*

In this example you will print the cell formulas from the Smithton worksheet. Remember that Lotus will print one cell per line, and will show the cell's location, its column width, cell format (if any), protection status, and the cell expression. The report is presented by row, starting at the top of the worksheet. Only cells that have non-blank entries are shown.

1. Be sure that Lotus 1-2-3 is loaded. Retrieve the **SMRV.WK1** worksheet from the data disk. This is the formatted version of the worksheet.

2. Enter the command sequence **/PP** to activate the main /Print menu. Press **R** to select the print range, then enter **A1..G17** as the print range. Press **Enter** to complete the entry.

3. Press **O** to select Options, then press **O** to select Other. Press **C** to choose the Cell-Formulas mode.

4. Press **Q** to quit the Options menu. Press **A** to Align the printer at top of page, then press **G** to Go.

5. When the worksheet has finished printing, press **P** to clear the printer to top of the next page, then press **Q** to quit the /Print menu.

6. The output is shown in Figure 5-9. In cell A1 the [W15] means column A has a width of 15 characters. In cell C7 the (F0) means this cell is formatted in Fixed type with 0 decimal places.

Forcing a Page Break

Lotus 1-2-3 counts the number of lines printed on a page, comparing it to the page length and top and bottom margins. The default values for these of 66, 2, and 2, respectively, allow 62 printable lines on a normal page. When the page is full, Lotus sends several line feeds to the printer and subsequent output appears on the next page.

If you wish to force part of the output to start at the top of a new page, move the cursor to the cell you want to be on the new page and give the **/Worksheet Page** command (**/WP**). Lotus will insert a blank row above the cell and place the :: symbol in the blank row. When you print the worksheet, your printer will interpret this character as the code for skipping to the top of the next page. To issue the /WP command you must be in READY mode, not within the /Print menu.

Printing to a File

As mentioned in the previous section, Lotus provides a way to "print" the spreadsheet to a text file that can be read by other programs. This file, with a .PRN extension, is a standard ASCII file that can be printed from DOS with the **Print** command or inserted into a word processing document. The command to create a print file is /Print File, or **/PF**. All the usual /Print options apply when printing to a file, and the resulting output will be identical to the printed copy. You may wish to change the margins before printing to the file, or there will be several blank lines above the table, and each line will have spaces in front, corresponding to the usual left margin.

Example: *Printing the Worksheet to a Text File*

Let's practice printing the Smithton spreadsheet to a file, then try to retrieve it into a WordPerfect document. The worksheet will be saved in a text file with the .PRN extension.

1. If the **SMRV** worksheet is not already in the Lotus workspace, use the **/FR** command to retrieve it from your data disk.

2. At the READY mode, enter the **/P** command, then select **F** to print to a file. You'll see the prompt to enter the file name. The default *.prn file template is used.

   `FILES`

   ```
   Enter print file name: C:\LOTUS\*.prn
   FIFUNEX.PRN  SMITHCF.PRN
   ```

3. If there are any other files with the .PRN extension in the default directory, they'll be shown in the third line of the FILES screen, as the two files above. Type in the name **SMRV** and press **Enter**. Will Lotus replace the SMRV.WK1 file with this one? (No, because this SMRV file has the .PRN extension.)

PRINTING THE WORKSHEET — ADVANCED COMMANDS

```
A1: [W15] 'SMRV--B. McLaren 6/27/89
B3: 'SMITHTON RECREATIONAL VEHICLE SALES, INC.
C5: 1987
D5: 1988
E5: 1989
F5: 'Percent of Sales
C6: \-
D6: \-
E6: \-
A7: [W15] 'SALES
C7: (F0) 1405
D7: (F0) 1205
E7: (F0) 1150
A8: [W15] 'EXPENSES
A9: [W15] ' Cost of Vehicles
C9: (F0) +C7*0.56
D9: (F0) +D7*0.56
E9: (F0) +E7*0.56
F9: (P1) +E9/$E$7
A10: [W15] ' Commissions
C10: (F0) +C9*0.06
D10: (F0) +D9*0.06
E10: (F0) +E9*0.06
F10: (P1) +E10/$E$7
A11: [W15] ' Salaries
C11: (F0) 120
D11: (F0) +C11*1.09
E11: (F0) +D11*1.09
F11: (P1) +E11/$E$7
A12: [W15] ' Administrative
C12: (F0) 175
D12: (F0) +C12
E12: (F0) +D12
F12: (P1) +E12/$E$7
A13: [W15] '   Marketing/Adv.
C13: (F0) 180
D13: (F0) 220
E13: (F0) 250
F13: (P1) +E13/$E$7
C14: (F0) \-
D14: (F0) \-
E14: (F0) \-
A15: [W15] '    Total Expenses
C15: (F0) @SUM(C9..C13)
D15: (F0) @SUM(D9..D13)
E15: (F0) @SUM(E9..E13)
A17: [W15] 'GROSS PROFIT
C17: (F0) +C7-C15
D17: (F0) +D7-D15
```

FIGURE 5-9

Partial Listing of Cell Formulas
(Press **/PPROOCQAG**)

4. At the next menu you will see the usual /Print menu choices. Select **Range** and specify that the entire spreadsheet is to be printed. This is **A1..G17**. Press **Enter** to complete the range entry.

5. Then press **G** for Go, and the spreadsheet will be saved in a file called SMRV.PRN on the default directory. Note the current subdirectory where the SMRV.PRN file is stored—when you retrieve the file in WordPerfect, you'll have to specify where the file is stored.

6. Press **Q** to quit the Print menu to the READY mode.

7. Let's temporarily go to DOS and make sure it was saved properly. Enter **/S** to go to DOS. At the DOS prompt, enter **TYPE SMRV.PRN** and press **Enter**. You should see the contents of the spreadsheet scroll down the screen. What happens if you enter the **TYPE SMRV.WK1** command from the DOS prompt? Lotus uses a non-ASCII file format for saving worksheet files which prevents display of the contents of the worksheet file.

8. To re-enter Lotus, type **EXIT** and press **Enter**. Quit 1-2-3 by typing **/QY** and then **Exit** the Lotus Access Menu to DOS.

9. Change to the WordPerfect subdirectory (or follow local instructions for starting WordPerfect) and load WordPerfect.

10. When WordPerfect has loaded, you have two ways to retrieve your spreadsheet .PRN file. Because it is a text file, use the WordPerfect Text In/Out command, **Ctrl-F5**, then press **1** to specify DOS Text and **2** to Retrieve the text file.

11. When the computer prompts for the text file's name, enter the appropriate drive and subdirectory pathname for the SMRV.PRN file. For the illustration above, this file's pathname would be **C:\123\SMRV.PRN**. Your path depends on where you stored the text file, in this case the 123 subdirectory on the C: drive.

12. Use the usual WordPerfect commands to view the document. If you had first retrieved a document, you could insert the spreadsheet file at a certain point in the document.

Other Printing Features—Allways

Lotus 1-2-3 comes with an add-in product called **Allways** that provides **spreadsheet publishing** capabilities. This product provides special formatting and presentation-quality printing capabilities with Lotus worksheets and graphs. Because it installs as an add-in, Allways can be called up like other Lotus commands, usually with the **Alt-F7** keystroke. Allways requires at least 512K of conventional memory and a hard disk. It must be installed before it can be used. Check with your computer lab consultant for availability at your site. You may have to disable Undo (**/WGDOUD**) to provide enough RAM for Allways.

Allways provides desktop-publishing qualities for your worksheets, including multiple typeface fonts, different character sizes, and special print features such as bold, underline, and italics. Print sizes as small as 6-point allow you to pack a great deal of information inside the spreadsheet. Larger type sizes provide headline capabilities for emphasis and report titles. With Allways you can add vertical and horizontal lines, boxes, and shading to worksheets. You can print the worksheet and associated graph on the same page. Another advantage is the ability to print Allways graphs without leaving the 1-2-3 module, instead of the conventional procedure using the PrintGraph module which is explained in Chapter 6. An Allways command tree appears in the Appendix.

Allways will work with most printers that support graphics, including dot matrix printers. It works best with printers that can print downloaded fonts, such as laser and ink jet printers. Allways supports proportionally-spaced text and includes three standard sets of downloadable soft fonts. Users with graphics video displays can view the Allways worksheet in **WYSIWYG** fashion—"what you see is what you'll get"—before printing.

An example of output using Allways is shown as part of the next example. It demonstrates Allways fonts, shading, and line drawing. The Lotus Reference Manual includes a detailed explanation of how to use Allways.

Example: *Using Allways Features to Print a Worksheet*

In this example you will activate the Allways **add-in module** (/A) and use it to enhance the Smithton formatted worksheet. Although Allways uses a similar set of menus to 1-2-3, you should not confuse the two: Allways commands cannot be executed while in 1-2-3. The upper right corner mode indicator shows which module is in use: READY indicates 1-2-3 and ALLWAYS indicates Allways is active. (You may need to disable undo with /WGDOUDQ.)

1. If you haven't already started Lotus, enter the 1-2-3 module. Retrieve the **SMRV** worksheet file with the **/FR** command.

2. Next you will attach the Allways module. Press **/A** to activate the Add-In menu. Select **Attach** from the menu, and select **ALLWAYS.ADN** from the list of add-in modules. At the next prompt, choose **7** to indicate that Alt-F7 is the keystroke to activate Allways.

3. You will see a brief Allways screen as it is loaded into memory from the disk drive. At the next menu press **Q** to return to READY mode. You will see the Smithton worksheet.

4. To invoke Allways, press **Alt-F7**. You will see the screen shown in Figure 5-10. The mode indicator shows that this is the main ALLWAYS display screen.

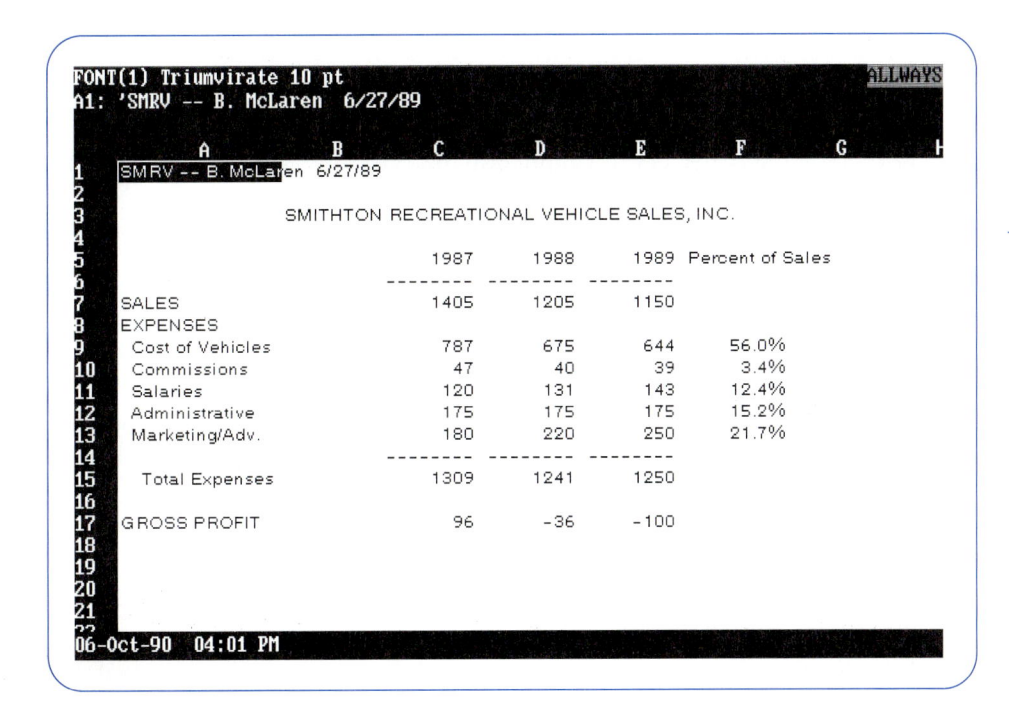

FIGURE 5-10

Allways Display

5. First we will mark the title to appear in a larger font. Move the cursor to cell **B3** and press **/F** to activate the Format menu.

6. From the Format menu press **F** to select the Font option. Next move the cursor to font **3**, Triumvirate 14 point, and press **Enter**.

7. At the next prompt use the → key to highlight the **B3..F3** cell range. Press **Enter** to complete the entry. The worksheet title will appear in a larger font, but no longer is centered over the spreadsheet.

8. To remedy the centering problem, press the **Esc** key to return to the 1-2-3 READY mode. Then use the **/M** command to move the title from cell **B3** to cell **A3**. Then press **Alt-F7** to return to Allways mode. The title should now be centered over the report.

9. Next you will use the italic font for the column headings and expense category labels. Move the cursor to cell **C5**. Press **/F** to activate the Format menu. Press **F** to select the Font option. Move the cursor to font **2**, Triumvirate Italic 10 point, and press **Enter**. At the next prompt use the → key to highlight the **C5..F5** cell range and press **Enter** to complete the entry.

10. Repeat the previous step for the expense category labels. Move the cursor to cell **A9**. Press **/FF** to activate the Font menu, and select font 2, Triumvirate Italic 10 Point by pressing **Enter**. At the next prompt move the cursor to cell **A15**, highlighting the **A9..A15** cell range and press **Enter** to complete the entry.

11. Now we will draw a box around the numbers in the worksheet. Move the cursor to the first cell to be included, **C5**. Next press **/FL** to activate the Line menu. Select **Outline** from that menu. Then use the arrow keys to mark the **C5..E17** cell range, and press **Enter** to complete the entry. Allways will draw a box around the figures in that range.

12. You can use Allways to shade sections of the worksheet. Move the cursor to cell **C5**. Press **/FS** to activate the Shade menu. Press **Enter** to select the Light shading. When prompted, use the arrow key to mark the **C5..C17** cell range and press **Enter** to complete the entry. Allways will shade the entries in column C. Repeat with cells **E5..E17** to shade column E.

13. Move the cursor to cell **F5**. Use the **/WCS** command to adjust the width of column F. At the column width prompt, enter **14** and press **Enter** to complete the entry. (You could also use the arrow keys to adjust the column width.)

14. Move the cursor to cell **C6**. We want to remove this row and replace the row of hyphens by underlining row 5 entries. Press **Esc** to return to the 1-2-3 READY mode. Press **/WDR** to delete row 6. Press **Enter** to confirm that C6..E6 is the correct entry. Move the cursor to cell **C13** and repeat the procedure to delete row 13: **/WDR Enter**.

15. Press **Alt-F7** to return to ALLWAYS mode. Move the cursor to cell **C5**. Then press **/FL** to activate the Line menu. Select **Bottom** from the menu, then enter **C5..E5** as the cell range. Move the cursor to cell **C13** and press **/FL** to activate the Line menu. This time select **Top**, then enter **C13..E13** as the cell range.

16. To further highlight the middle year, we will add vertical lines to the left and right of the 1988 figures. Move the cursor to cell **D5**, then press **/FL** to activate the Line menu. Select **Left**, and enter **D5..D15** at the cell range

CHAPTER REVIEW

FIGURE 5-11

Output from Allways Add-in Module

SMITHTON RECREATIONAL VEHICLE SALES, INC.

	1987	1988	1989	Percent of Sales
SALES	1405	1205	1150	
EXPENSES				
Cost of Vehicles	787	675	644	56.0%
Commissions	47	40	39	3.4%
Salaries	120	131	143	12.4%
Administrative	175	175	175	15.2%
Marketing/Adv.	180	220	250	21.7%
Total Expenses	1309	1241	1250	
GROSS PROFIT	96	−36	−100	

prompt. With the cursor still in cell D5, press /**FL** and select **Right**. Specify **D5..D15** as the cell range and press **Enter** to complete the entry. Allways will place vertical lines between the columns. [Note: You could also use the Outline choice for cell range D5..D15 and achieve the same results.]

17. Finally we are ready to print the worksheet with Allways. Press /**P** to activate the Print menu. Press **RS** to Set the range, then enter **A3..F16** as the print range. Allways will highlight the printed portion of the worksheet. Then press **G** for Go, and Allways will print the worksheet. Because it will be printed in graphics mode on a dot matrix printer, it may take longer than usual to print. The completed worksheet as printed by a laser printer appears in Figure 5-11.

18. To complete the work, press **Esc** to return to 1-2-3. Because you have made changes to the worksheet in 1-2-3, you must Save it to make the changes permanent. Press /**FS** and enter the new name **SMRV2** as the name for the file. Lotus will create two files: the normal SMRV2.WK1 worksheet file, and a second file called SMRV2.ALL which contains your Allways worksheet instructions.

CHAPTER REVIEW

Lotus File Operations

Besides the usual Save and Retrieve File operations, Lotus offers functions to List file names, Erase files, change the default drive and directory, and exchange information with other programs. You can extract a portion of the worksheet, saving it to another worksheet file. You can combine a base worksheet with another worksheet file, useful for consolidating several worksheets together into a large worksheet. You can import ASCII (text) data from other files directly into the current worksheet.

Chapter 5 — Advanced Lotus File and Print Commands

Printing the Worksheet

Lotus keeps a counter for the number of lines printed on the current page. There are /**Print** commands to advance one line or go to the top of the next page, and to reset the line counter if you have manually set the printer to top of page. You can clear some or all of the print settings. The /Print Options menu contains commands for setting one-line Header and Footer, and for adjusting the four page Margins and Page length. You can also send printer Setup codes to activate specialized printer functions such as compressed print. Other options include printing Cell-Formulas instead of the regularly displayed values, and for suppressing page Formatting, especially useful when printing the spreadsheet to a file.

Printing Cell Formulas

Lotus also provides a way to print cell expressions, one cell to a line, by using the /**PPROOCQAG** command. The latter is more difficult to use because the cells are not in their usual spatial relationship with other cells.

Allways

Allways is a spreadsheet publishing add-in product that is included with Release 2.2. With Allways you can add different size print fonts, bold, underlining, italics, shading, and horizontal and vertical lines. An Allways .ALL file is automatically created when the worksheet file is saved.

KEY TERMS

/Add-in command (**/A**)
Allways
ASCII format
As-Displayed option
backup file option
border
cell values
Cell-Formulas option
default directory
/File Combine command
  (**/FC**)
/File Directory command
  (**/FD**)
/File Erase command (**/FE**)

/File Import command (**/FI**)
/File List command (**/FL**)
/File Retrieve command
  (**/FR**)
/File Save command (**/FS**)
/File Xtract command (**/FX**)
file name
formatted option
linked file
margin
page footer
page header
print cell formulas

Print options
setup string
spreadsheet publishing
/System command (**/S**)
temporary DOS session
Unformatted option
/Worksheet Global Default
  command (**/WGD**)
/Worksheet Page
  command (**/WP**)
/Worksheet Status
  command (**/WS**)
WYSIWYG

DISCUSSION QUESTIONS

1. Explain the three methods for changing the default disk drive and directory in Lotus 1-2-3. What are the commands needed to change to the 123\FINANCE directory on drive C?

2. Describe the differences between the /**Print File**, /**File Save**, and /**File Xtract** operations. When would the Xtract be used?

3. Describe the differences between the /**File Retrieve**, /**File Combine**, and /**File Import** operations. When would the Combine and Import operations be used?

4. Discuss the link feature of Release 2.2. How is it different than using the /File Combine command?

5. Describe the *two* ways to print a worksheet's cell formulas. Which method is preferred, and why?

6. Briefly define the purpose of the following /**Print** commands or options:
   a. Align
   b. Page
   c. Header
   d. Margins
   e. Pg-Length
   f. Setup
   g. Borders
   h. Cell-Formulas
   i. Unformatted
   j. Page.

7. List the reasons for printing the worksheet to a file instead of the printer.

8. Discuss the advantages of using Allways to print the worksheet file. What features does it add to Lotus 1-2-3?

EXERCISES

1. Starting with a clean worksheet, retrieve the stored worksheet for Smithton, SMITHRV.WK1 from the data disk or from your previous work. The worksheet is reproduced in Figure 5-12.
   a. Extract just the Gross Profit line (row 17) and store that in a file called SMGREX.WK1 on your disk drive. Use the values option to save the numbers, not the cell expressions. Remember, don't save the entire worksheet.
   b. To test whether that range was saved properly, use the /File Combine command to bring that file's contents back into the same spreadsheet. Place the results in cell A18, using the Copy option to the Combine command.

2. The Air Direct Company flies several small aircraft in a variety of situations. This exercise will combine several worksheets together.
   a. Create the following worksheet showing second quarter sales results for the Air Direct Company. Save the worksheet as the file named **AIRDQ2.WK1**. The worksheet is shown in Figure 5-13.

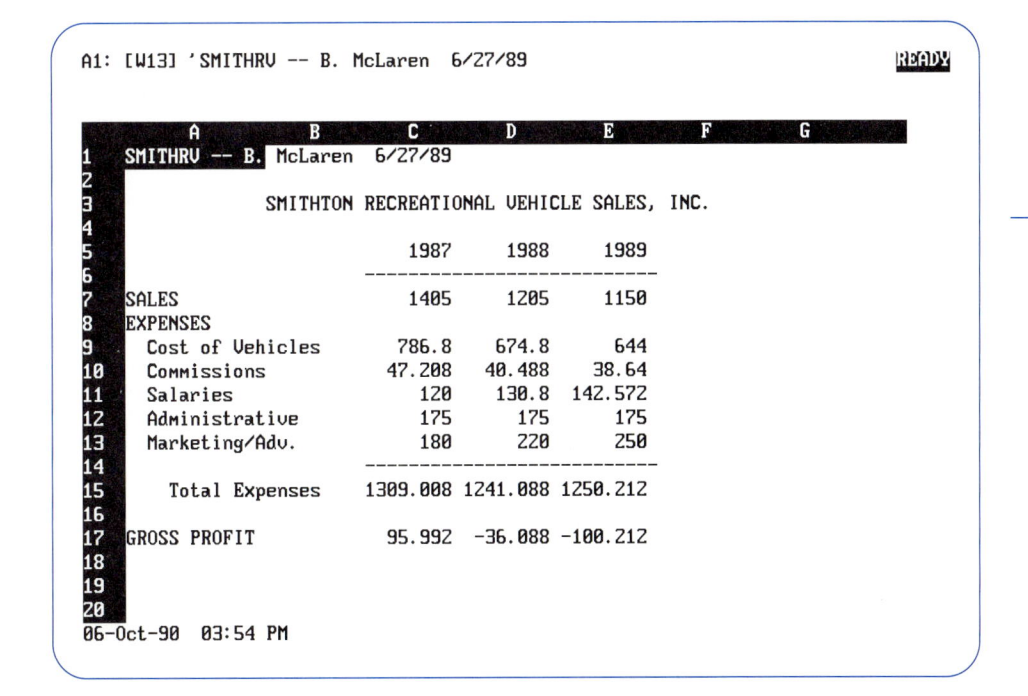

```
A1: [W13] 'SMITHRV -- B. McLaren  6/27/89                          READY

        A          B       C        D        E       F       G
 1  SMITHRV -- B. McLaren  6/27/89
 2
 3                 SMITHTON RECREATIONAL VEHICLE SALES, INC.
 4
 5                         1987     1988     1989
 6                         ------------------------
 7  SALES                  1405     1205     1150
 8  EXPENSES
 9    Cost of Vehicles     786.8    674.8    644
10    Commissions          47.208   40.488   38.64
11    Salaries             120      130.8    142.572
12    Administrative       175      175      175
13    Marketing/Adv.       180      220      250
14                         ------------------------
15    Total Expenses       1309.008 1241.088 1250.212
16
17  GROSS PROFIT           95.992   -36.088  -100.212
18
19
20
06-Oct-90  03:54 PM
```

FIGURE 5-12

Spreadsheet for Exercise 1

FIGURE 5-13

Worksheet for Exercise 2a

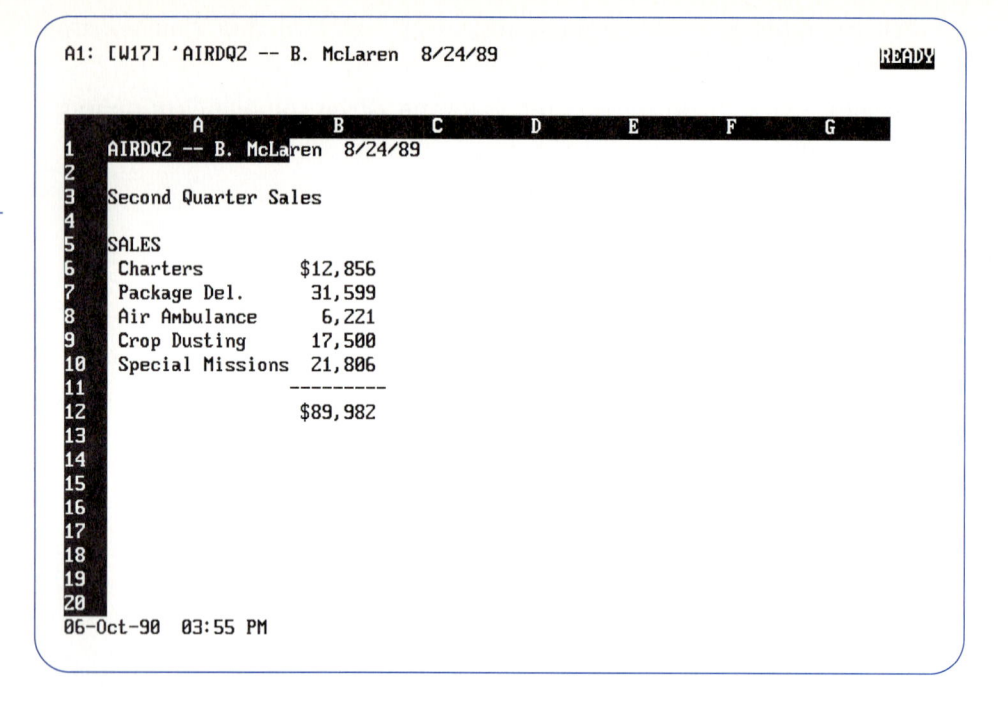

```
A1: [W17] 'AIRDQ2 -- B. McLaren  8/24/89                          READY

              A            B         C       D       E       F       G
 1    AIRDQ2 -- B. McLaren  8/24/89
 2
 3    Second Quarter Sales
 4
 5    SALES
 6      Charters       $12,856
 7      Package Del.    31,599
 8      Air Ambulance    6,221
 9      Crop Dusting    17,500
10      Special Missions 21,806
11                     ---------
12                     $89,982
13
14
15
16
17
18
19
20
06-Oct-90  03:55 PM
```

FIGURE 5-14

Worksheet for Exercise 2b

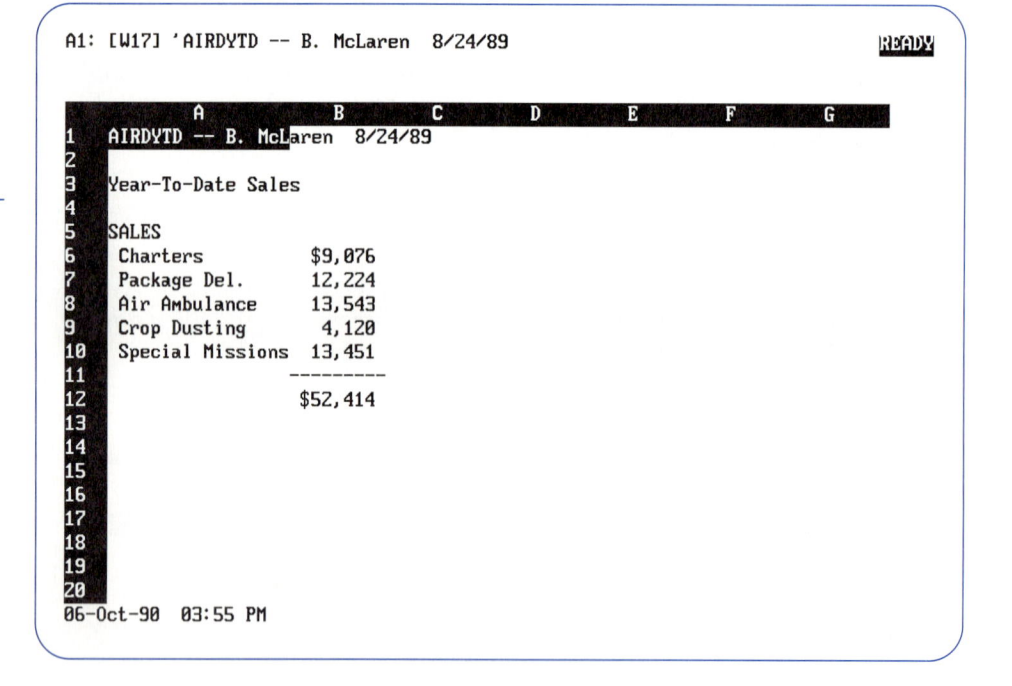

```
A1: [W17] 'AIRDYTD -- B. McLaren  8/24/89                         READY

              A            B         C       D       E       F       G
 1    AIRDYTD -- B. McLaren  8/24/89
 2
 3    Year-To-Date Sales
 4
 5    SALES
 6      Charters        $9,076
 7      Package Del.    12,224
 8      Air Ambulance   13,543
 9      Crop Dusting     4,120
10      Special Missions 13,451
11                     ---------
12                     $52,414
13
14
15
16
17
18
19
20
06-Oct-90  03:55 PM
```

    b. Next retrieve the file called **AIRDYTD.WK1** from the data disk. It is shown in Figure 5-14 if you don't have the data disk. This year-to-date file will be used to accumulate the cumulative sales amounts in each category. It already contains the first quarter sales results.

    c. Move the cursor to the A1 cell by pressing the **Home** key. Use the /**File Combine** command to **Add** the entire contents of the AIRDQ2.WK1 worksheet to the base worksheet. Print the contents of the combined spreadsheet.

    d. Next create a slightly different combined worksheet. Again retrieve the AIRDYTD.WK1 worksheet file. Move the cursor to cell B1, one column over from the previous problem. Use the /**File Combine** command to **Add** the entire contents of the AIRDQ2.WK1 file to the base worksheet. Print the combined worksheet. How does it differ from the previous combined worksheet? Explain.

3. In this exercise you will use link expressions to copy data from the AIRDQ2.WK1 worksheet to the AIRDYTD worksheet.

   a. First retrieve the original AIRDYTD.WK1 worksheet which contains just the first quarter sales results totalling $52,414.

   b. Move the cursor to cell C6 and use a link expression to copy cell B6 from the AIRDQ2.WK1 worksheet. Repeat the process for cells C7–C10 in the base worksheet. You may use the /**Copy** command to copy the link expression from cell C6. Print the worksheet containing the linked values.

4. Retrieve the worksheet file GRAM.WK1 from the data disk. This file consists of 60 rows of price data for farm products collected over time, and will require more than one page when printed.

   a. Prepare a Lotus print Header to state **GRAM QUOTATION SERVICES** on the top of each page.

   b. Adjust the bottom margin to 8 so that 50 lines print per page. Keep the page length at 66 lines per page.

   c. The print Border will be the title and column headings in cells A3..E7. They will print on all pages, including the first page.

   d. Print the spreadsheet, but print *only the data rows*, beginning with the August 24 data.

5. Print the GRAM.WK1 worksheet to a file called GRAM.PRN (Lotus will add the .PRN extension automatically). Use the Unformatted option. Be sure to clear all previous print settings before printing this worksheet. All rows in the worksheet are to be printed for this problem.

6. Print a Cell-Formulas listing of the SMITHRV.WK1 worksheet file. All cells should be printed.

7. Retrieve the gradebook worksheet that you created in exercise 11 of the previous chapter. Use the Setup option of the /Print menu to print the gradebook in compressed print. Many Epson-compatible printers use the **\015** setup code to compressed print, and **\018** for normal print width.

8. This exercise requires that Allways be installed for your computer. Retrieve the GRAM.WK1 worksheet file from the data disk. If Allways has not already been attached, use the /**A** command to place it in memory and assign it to the **Alt-F7** key. Use Allways to prepare the following items:

   a. Use the 14-point Triumvirate font for the two title lines. Keep them roughly centered over the report. You may need to return to 1-2-3 to move the first title cell expression to the column A. Leave the second title in column B.

   b. Delete the row of hyphens beneath the column headings within the 1-2-3 module. Use Allways to place a line below the column headings.

   c. The column headings should be in italics.

   d. Alternating sets of five price lines of the report should be shaded to improve viewing legibility. That is, the August 24–28 lines should appear unshaded, August 29–September 2 lines should be shaded, and so on.

e. Place an outline around the highest price cell in each column.
f. Print a copy of the worksheet with Allways.
g. Save the worksheet under the name, **GRAM2**.

CHAPTER 5 PROJECT
SCHOOL OF BUSINESS BUDGET

The 1992 budget has been prepared by three departments. You should develop a means of combining the three spreadsheets into one School of Business spreadsheet without rekeying the individual cell expressions into the master spreadsheet.

The budgets should be stored in three spreadsheets called ACCT.WK1, MGT.WK1 and MIS.WK1. Each spreadsheet contains account titles and the 1992 budget items in separate columns. A sample departmental worksheet is shown in Figure 5-15 for the MIS Department.

Develop budget worksheets for the other departments, then build a master worksheet to hold the consolidated information from all departments. Each department should have a column in the master worksheet. You should use a range name for the 1992 amount column in each departmental worksheet and combine that specified range into the master worksheet in the appropriate department's column.

Print the master worksheet.

FIGURE 5-15

Sample Worksheet for the MIS Department

```
MIS Department 1992 Budget

Account                  Amount
------------------------------
Admin. Assistant         11,350
Benevolence                 500
Equipment                12,500
Maintenance               2,250
Office Supplies           4,500
Recruiting                6,000
Student Workers          12,500
Telephone                 3,500
Training                  1,000
Travel                    6,000
                       ---------
Total                    60,100
```

6

Lotus Graphs

Objectives

After completing this chapter, you should be able to:

- List the various types of graphs available with Lotus 1-2-3.
- Discuss the X- and Y-variable graph parameters.
- Create, save, and print a simple Lotus graph.
- Explain titles, legends, and data label graph settings.
- Discuss how to select different print sizes, printers, and printer fonts for your graph.
- Explain how to create and print a graph with Allways.

INTRODUCTION

An important feature of Lotus 1-2-3 is its ability to quickly create and display graphs of data contained in a worksheet. This chapter introduces graphing with Lotus, the "2" part of the 1-2-3 product name. Various graph options are presented, along with a discussion of how graphs are named and saved in Lotus. The chapter explains how to display and print graphs with Lotus. The chapter concludes with an example of how Allways is used to print a graph along with a worksheet.

CREATING LOTUS GRAPHS

There is an old saying that "a picture is worth a thousand words." This saying is most applicable to numerical data in electronic spreadsheets. The ease of creating numerous tables of numbers with a spreadsheet may hinder the interpretation of the meaning of the data. The ability to quickly create graphic presentations of data in the worksheet propelled Lotus 1-2-3 to the top of personal computing software. Once the data values have been stored in the worksheet, only a few keystrokes are needed to display a graph of the same data.

Graphing Basics

X and Y Variables: Data Ranges

The usual two-dimensional graphing model is used in Lotus graphs. The **X-axis** goes across the screen horizontally, while the **Y-axis** goes up the screen vertically, as shown in Figure 6-1. Lotus graphs use an X and a Y value for each point that is plotted. From one to six different **data ranges**, or variables, can be plotted on a single graph. These are designated by the letters **A** through **F**. The letter **X** stands for the X-axis variable.

A typical graph for the Smithton spreadsheet might involve plotting Sales, Total Expenses, and Gross Profit for the three years, 1987–1989. The X-variable for this example would be the year, contained in the three cells C5..E5. There are three Y-variables to be plotted on the graph, represented by the letters A, B and C. The A-range (Sales) is contained in cells C7..E7. The B-range (Total Expenses) occupies cells C15..E15. The C-range (Gross Profit) is in cells C17..E17.

FIGURE 6-1

Two-Dimensional Graph with X- and Y-Axes

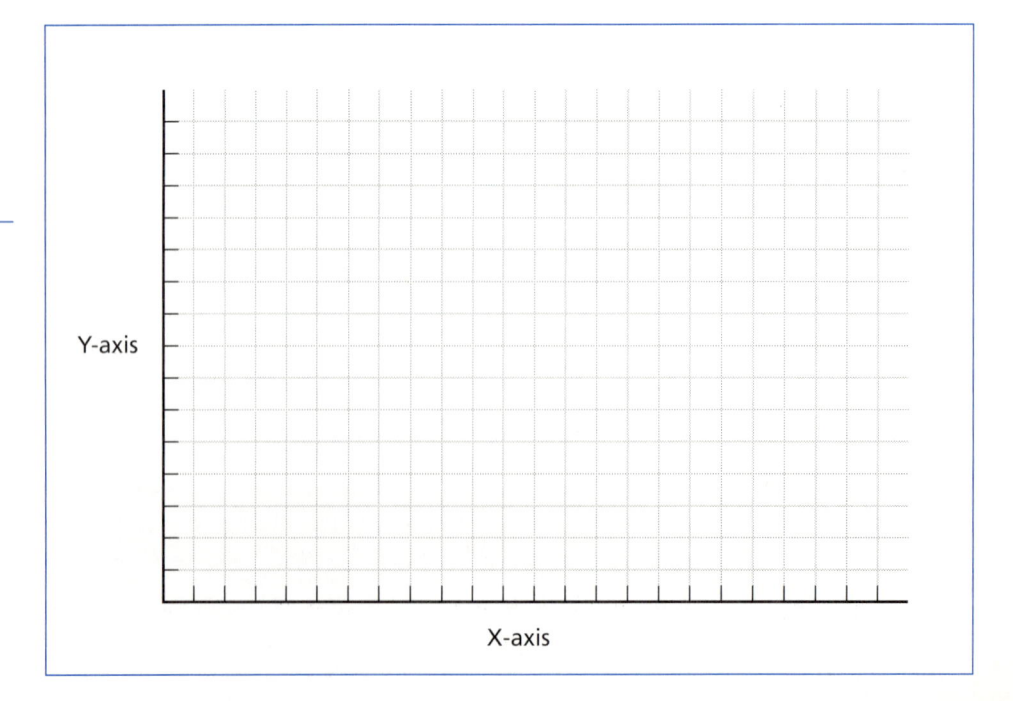

Graph Types

Because many types of data can be modeled in a spreadsheet, Lotus provides several **graph types** that best display the data. Final versions appear as samples.

- The **line graph** is useful for showing how one or more variables move over time; plotted points are usually connected with a line segment. The **X-range** is typically a time period, and the **Y-range** contains the values of the points appearing in the graph in each of those periods. The points are automatically spaced along the X-axis according to the number of cells in the range. An example of this graph type is shown in Figure 6-2.

- The **bar chart** presents data as vertical bars whose height reflect their magnitude. It is useful for comparing values from one or more data ranges over several periods or from different divisions, product groups, etc. **Stacked bar charts** present data for each observation by "stacking" bars from different data ranges on top of one another; this graph type is only meaningful if the data can be added together. Bar chart examples are shown in Figures 6-3 and 6-4.

- A **pie chart** is used to compare items that comprise a whole as wedge-shaped pieces of a mythical pie. The size of each piece is proportional to the percentage each cell in the A-range is to the sum of those cells. This graph uses the X-range to give labels for the values to be plotted; the A-range contains the values. The B-range can be used to determine special plotting instructions such as different colors or shading patterns, or to "explode" that segment of the pie for special emphasis. Ranges C–F are not used with pie charts. A pie chart is shown in Figure 6-5.

- The **X-Y graph** plots points according to their X- and Y- coordinates. An example of this graph type is a plot of unit selling price versus annual sales of that product. A sample X-Y chart is shown in Figure 6-6.

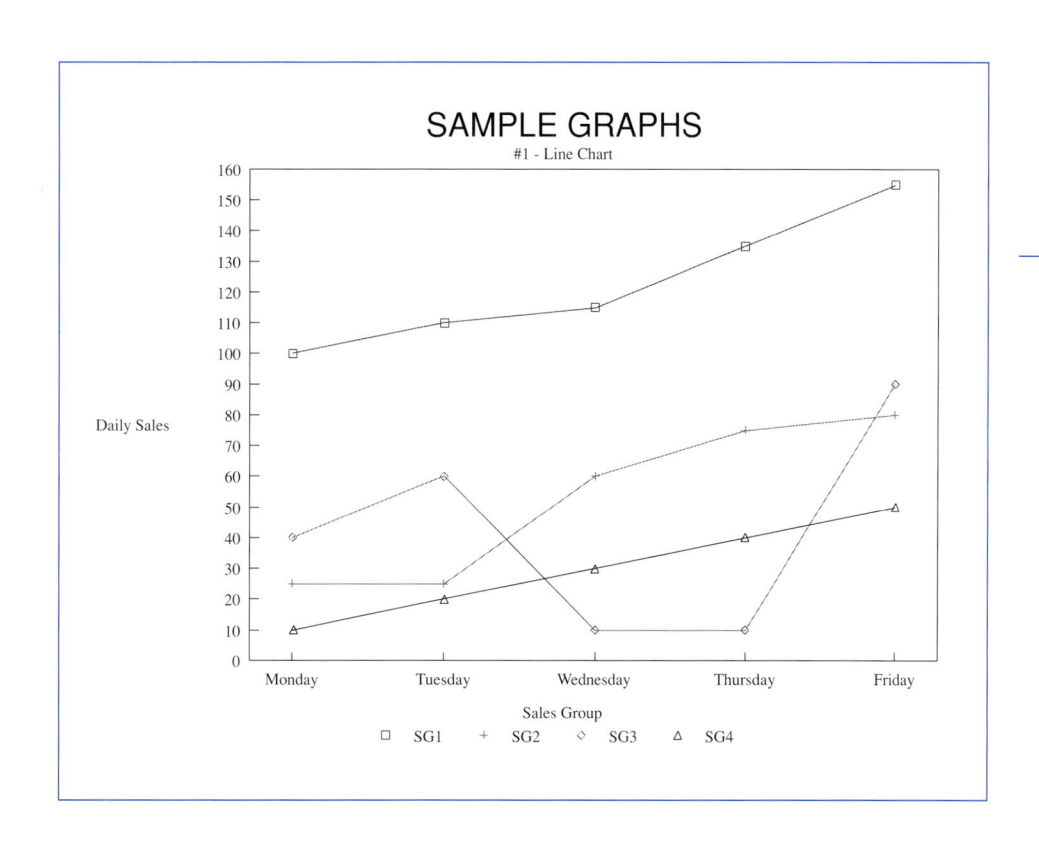

FIGURE 6-2

Sample Lotus Line Graph

FIGURE 6-3

Sample Lotus Bar Graph

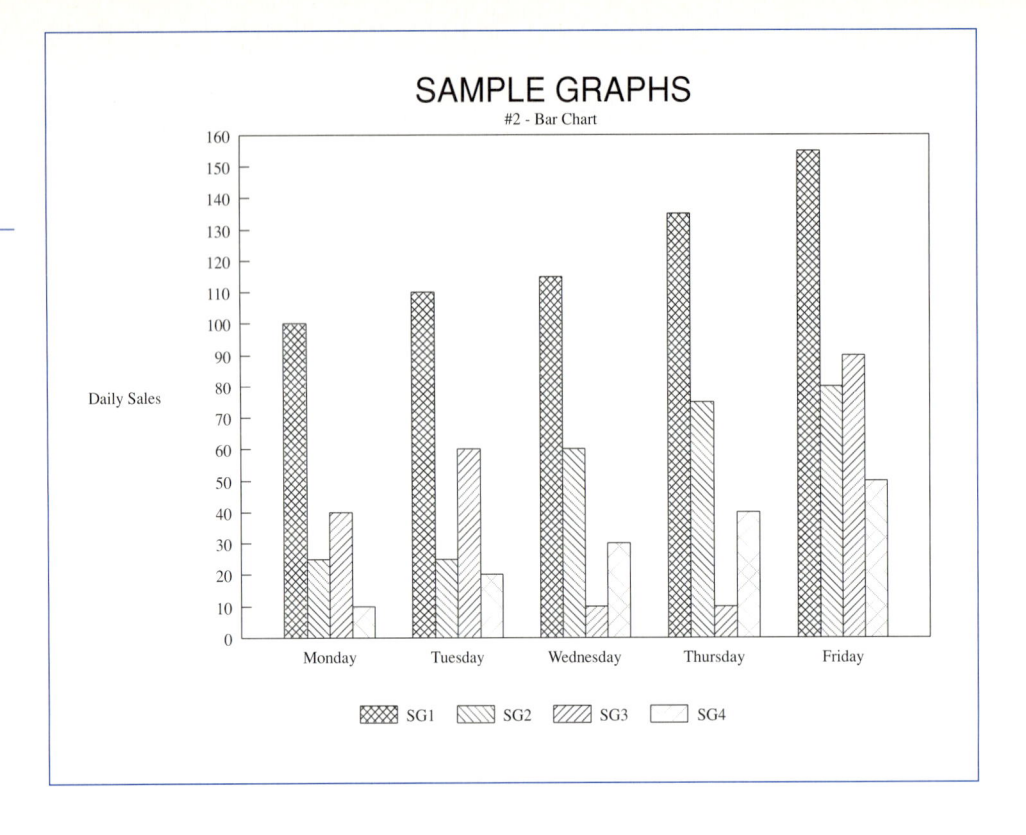

FIGURE 6-4

Sample Stacked Bar Graph

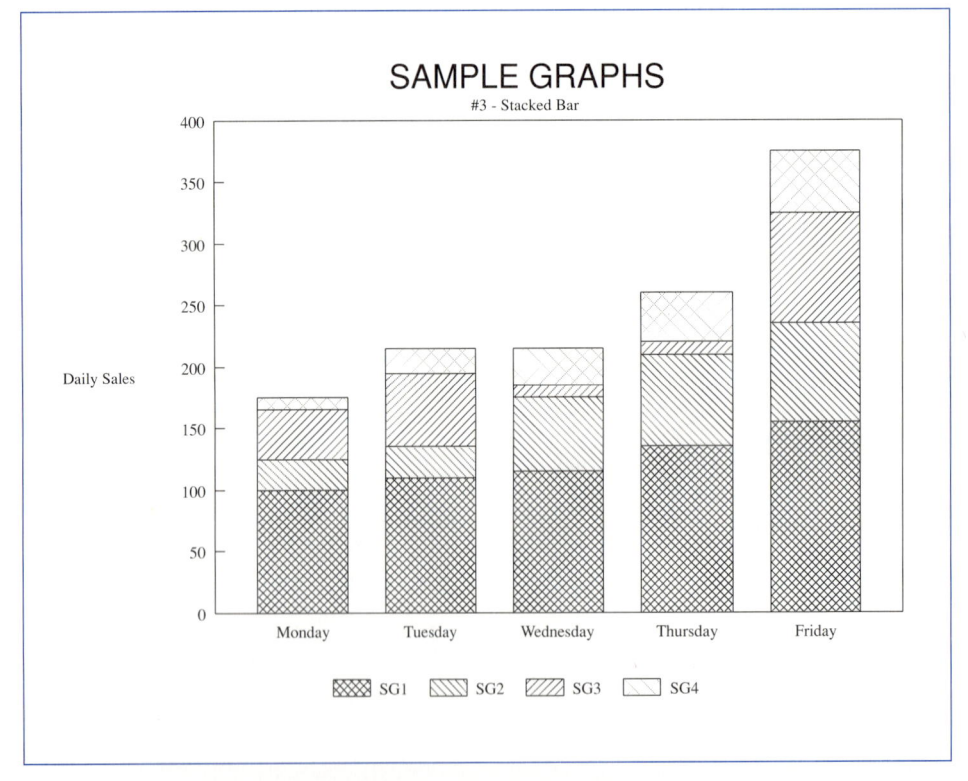

Lotus Release 3.1 offers additional graph types, as described in Chapter 10. These new types include a **high-low-close graph** (useful for displaying security prices), and a **mixed graph** that includes both bar and line graphs. Release 3.1 includes the ability to have a second Y-axis on the same graph.

CREATING LOTUS GRAPHS

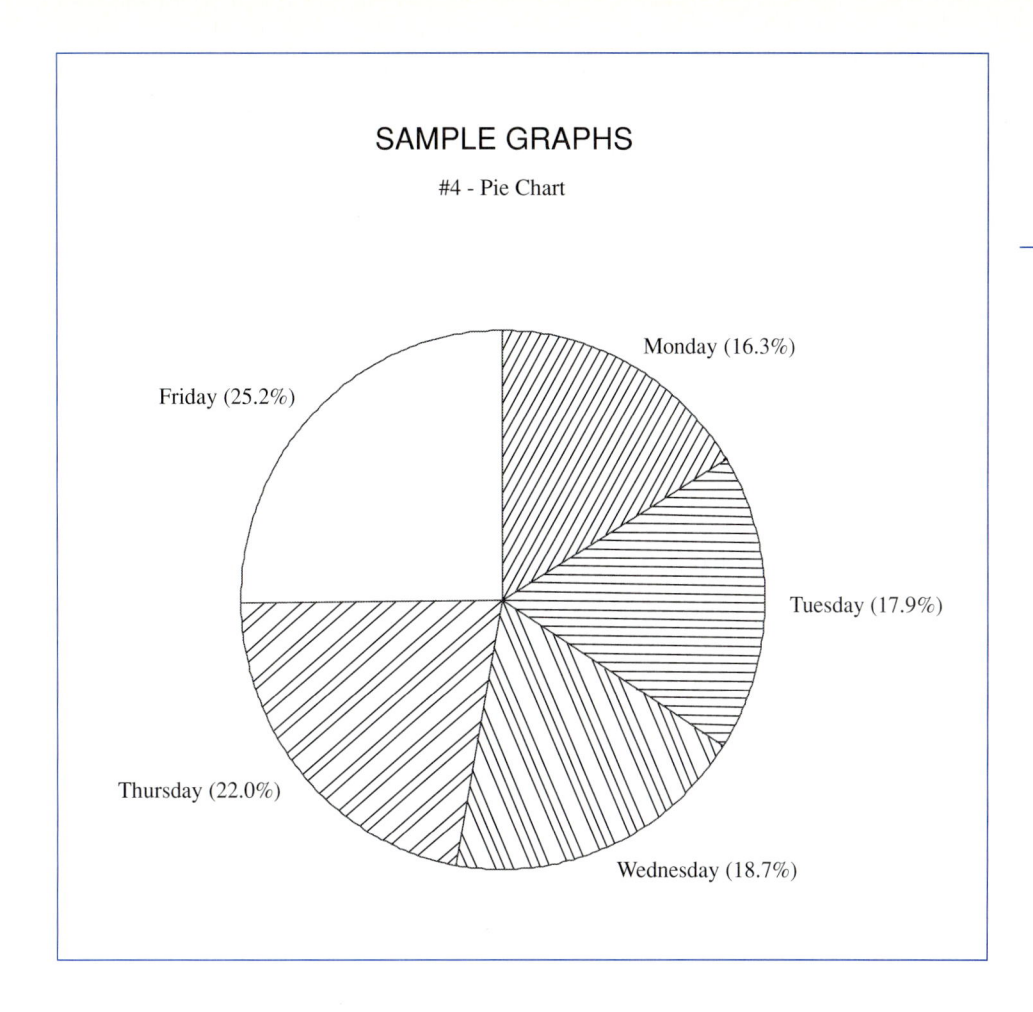

SAMPLE GRAPHS

#4 - Pie Chart

Monday (16.3%)
Friday (25.2%)
Tuesday (17.9%)
Thursday (22.0%)
Wednesday (18.7%)

FIGURE 6-5

Sample Pie Chart

Sample X-Y Graph

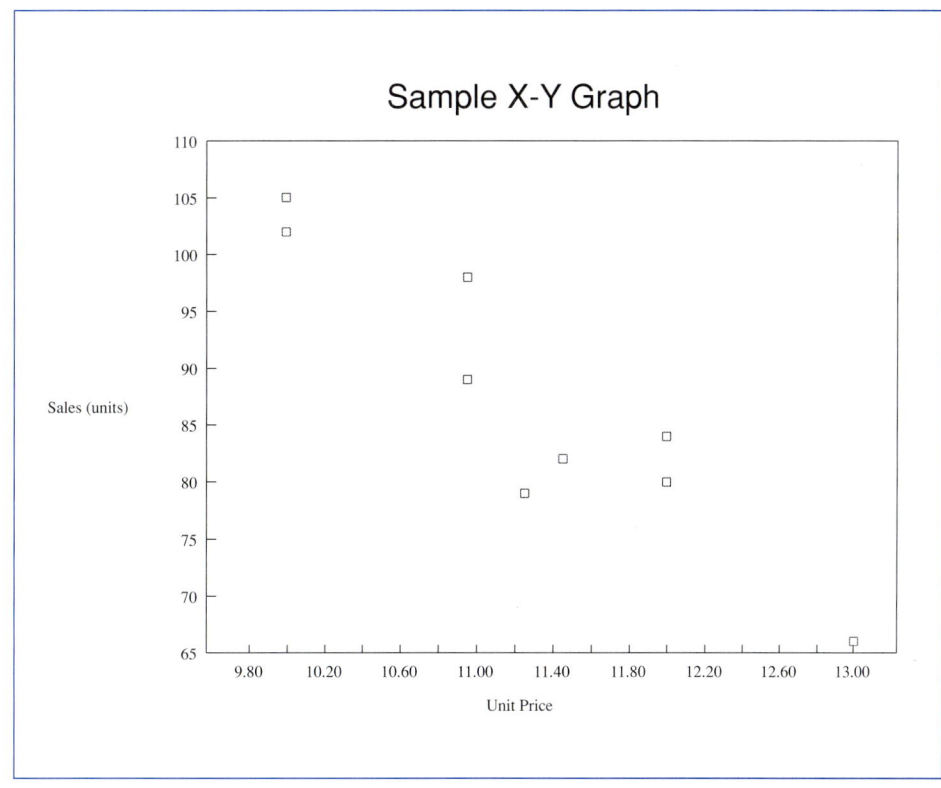

Sales (units)

Unit Price

FIGURE 6-6

Sample X-Y Graph

Chapter 6 — Lotus Graphs

Creating the Graph

Normally you will have the worksheet values that are to be plotted before creating the graph. However, you can change those values at any time, even after the graph is created, and display the new graph immediately. The **F10** function key can be used to display the current graph at the READY mode.

Example: *Creating a Bar Graph*

Let's use the Smithton spreadsheet to create this graph. If you wish to follow along, retrieve the file called SMITHRV.WK1 from the data disk that accompanies this text. See Figure 6-7.

The spreadsheet appears with no cell formatting so that the precise value of each cell is apparent. Our first graph will be a simple graph showing sales in each of the three years.

1. To begin, press the /**G**raph (/**G**) command. You will see the main graphing menu and Settings Sheet shown in Figure 6-8.

2. The highlighted choice, **Type**, allows you to choose the graph type. Select this option by pressing the **Enter** key or by typing the first letter of the option, **T**. The Graph Type menu appears.

   MENU

   Line Bar XY Stacked-Bar Pie
   Line graph

3. Choose **Bar** from this menu.

4. Next we will choose the X-range and A-range cells to be plotted. The X-range represents the three years, in cells C5..E5. Press the **X** key, then enter **C5..E5** as the range. If Lotus displays a different highlighted range, press the **Esc** key to remove the previous range and enter the proper range. Press **Enter** after the correct range is selected to complete the entry.

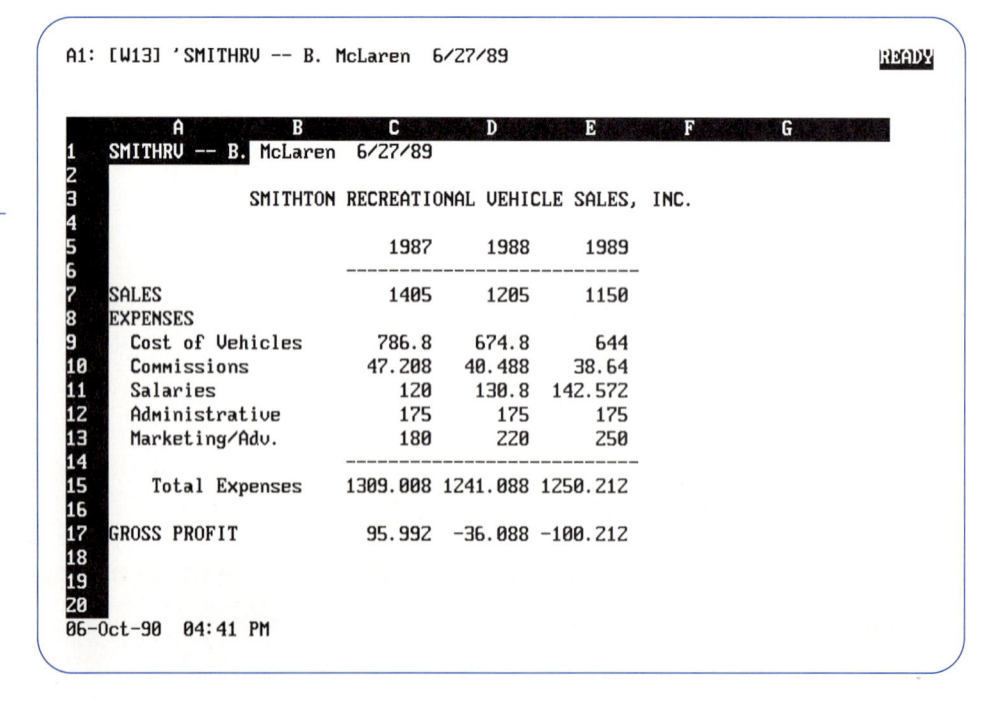

FIGURE 6-7

Sample Smithton Worksheet (Press **/FR**)

```
A1: [W13] 'SMITHRV -- B. McLaren  6/27/89                              READY


         A         B         C         D         E         F         G
 1  SMITHRV -- B. McLaren  6/27/89
 2
 3                    SMITHTON RECREATIONAL VEHICLE SALES, INC.
 4
 5                              1987      1988      1989
 6                            ------------------------------
 7   SALES                     1405      1205      1150
 8   EXPENSES
 9      Cost of Vehicles       786.8     674.8      644
10      Commissions            47.208    40.488    38.64
11      Salaries               120       130.8     142.572
12      Administrative         175       175       175
13      Marketing/Adv.         180       220       250
14                            ------------------------------
15      Total Expenses        1309.008 1241.088 1250.212
16
17   GROSS PROFIT               95.992  -36.088  -100.212
18
19
20
06-Oct-90  04:41 PM
```

5. Next press the **A** key to enter the A-range cells. Enter **C7..E7** for the cell range, and press **Enter**.

6. To display the graph, enter the **View** command (press **V**). You should see the graph shown in Figure 6-9. Press any key to return to the /Graph menu.

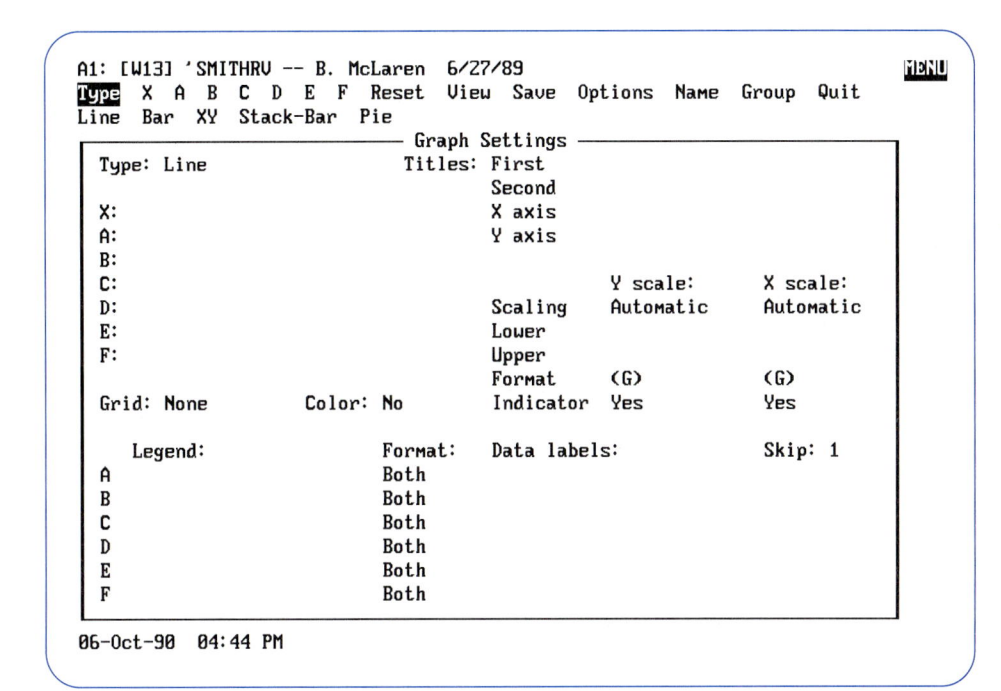

```
A1: [W13] 'SMITHRV -- B. McLaren  6/27/89                          MENU
Type  X  A  B  C  D  E  F  Reset  View  Save  Options  Name  Group  Quit
Line  Bar  XY  Stack-Bar  Pie
                        ┌──── Graph Settings ────┐
  Type: Line              Titles: First
                                  Second
  X:                              X axis
  A:                              Y axis
  B:
  C:                                      Y scale:      X scale:
  D:                              Scaling  Automatic     Automatic
  E:                              Lower
  F:                              Upper
                                  Format    (G)          (G)
  Grid: None      Color: No       Indicator Yes          Yes

    Legend:              Format:  Data labels:           Skip: 1
  A                      Both
  B                      Both
  C                      Both
  D                      Both
  E                      Both
  F                      Both

06-Oct-90  04:44 PM
```

FIGURE 6-8

Graph Settings Sheet (Press **/G**)

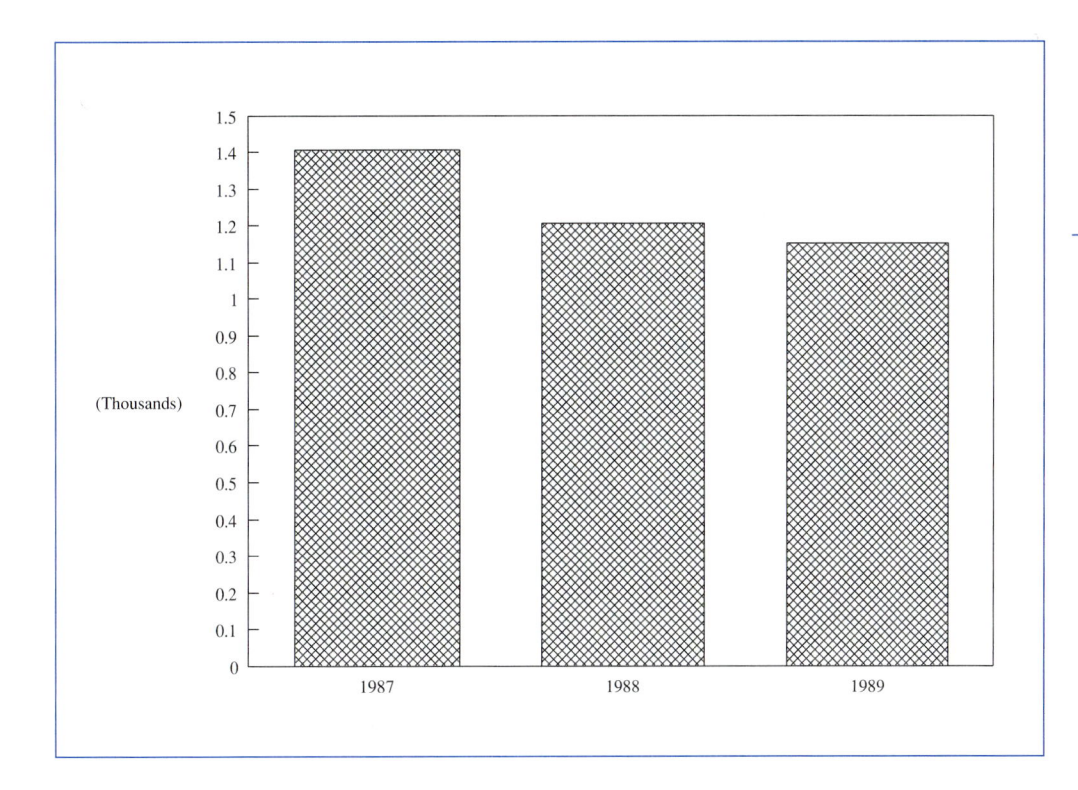

FIGURE 6-9

Sample Bar Graph with No Titles or Data Legends

Graph Settings

The previous graph is very simple and takes only a few keystrokes to create. We can add features to make the graph more readable, and to convey more meaning to the reader. These graph settings can be activated through the /Graph Options menu.

Titles, Legends, and Data Labels

Every Lotus graph should have a **title** at the top, explaining the overall meaning of the graph. Lotus provides four title positions.

- First   Top of graph, centered automatically
- Second   Just below Title 1, smaller size, centered
- X-Title   Below X-axis, describing X-axis range
- Y-Title   To left of Y-axis, describing Y-axis ranges

The first two titles are centered above the graph, and should be used to convey overall meaning to the graph. The X and Y titles are used to describe the X- and Y- axis ranges. For example, in the Smithton graph above, a good first title is **SMITHTON RECREATIONAL VEHICLE SALES**, and the second title might be **Projected Sales, 1987–1989**. Because the first title appears in a larger type size when printed, you might need to shorten it to fit small graphs. The first title is most important and should be descriptive.

The X-axis range for this example is the year for the income projection; an appropriate X-axis title is **Year**. Because the Y-axis title represents thousands of dollars, you might wish to use that as the Y-title: **(Thousands of Dollars)**. However, Lotus will automatically scale all quantities over 1,000 and may produce undesired results. You might be tempted to use the A-range variable, Sales, as the Y-title. But we will be adding more ranges to our graph and the Y-axis title should be descriptive for all the Y-ranges. We will use the data legend to individually describe each Y-range variable graphed, instead of labelling the axis.

Data legends are used to identify each data range that is plotted. The legends appear beneath the graph, below the X-axis. You should choose a short phrase, particularly if there are several ranges in the graph. Lotus Release 2.01 truncates those legends that don't fit, while Releases 2.2 and 3 place them on alternating lines so they don't overlap.

Example: Adding Titles and Data Legend to the Graph

1. To add titles to our graph, press **O** to activate the **Options** selection from the main /Graph menu. You should see the following screen.

   MENU

   Legend Format Titles Grid Scale Color B&W Data-Labels Quit
   Create legends for data ranges

2. Press **T** for Titles and you'll see the Titles screen.

   MENU

   First Second X-Axis Y-Axis
   Assign first line of graph title

3. Press **F** for First and enter the title, **SMITHTON RECREATIONAL VEHICLE SALES**, followed by **Enter**.

4. To enter the Second title, again press **T** to enter the titles screen, and press **S** for Second title. The second title is **Projected Sales, 1987-1989**. Again press **Enter** to complete the entry.

5. Press **T** to enter the titles menu, and press **X** for the X-axis title. Type **Year** and press **Enter**.

6. To view the titles, press **Q** to quit the Options menu, and press **V** to view the graph. Notice a difference? Press any key to leave View.

7. To enter a legend for Sales, from the main /Graph menu press **O** to enter the Options menu. Then press **L** for Legend and you'll see the Legend menu.

```
                                                              MENU
A B C D E F Range
Assign legend for first data range
```

8. You can type an **A** to enter the A range legend. At the next prompt, type **Sales** followed by **Enter** to complete the entry. Figure 6-10 shows the Graph Settings sheet after you have made these changes.

9. An alternative way of entering legends is to type a backslash character (\), immediately followed by the cell address of the label cell which you wish to use as the legend. In this case, we could have entered **\A7** to use cell A7 (SALES) as the legend. A nice feature of the alternative method is that you can change that cell's contents at the READY mode, thus changing the graph setting, without actually going into the /Graph menu. Titles can also be entered with the \ and a cell reference.

Data labels are used to place the value of the cell in the graph itself, near the plotted value. Labels may be placed to the left, above, to the right, or below the plotted point, or centered atop the point. A graph with data labels is shown in Figure 6-11 as it will appear in 1-2-3, before final printing.

Scales and Formatting the Axes

Lotus chooses the scale for the axes automatically to best fit the data values plotted. You may choose to set the axes' upper and lower limits manually, using

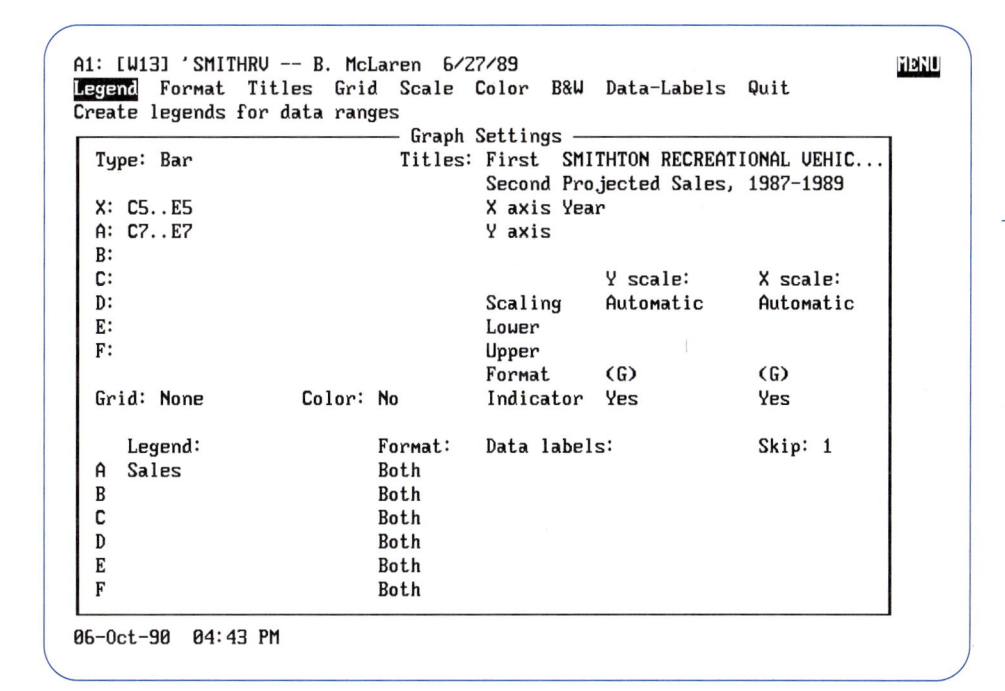

```
A1: [W13] 'SMITHRV -- B. McLaren  6/27/89                         MENU
Legend Format Titles Grid Scale Color B&W Data-Labels Quit
Create legends for data ranges
                        ─── Graph Settings ───
   Type: Bar              Titles: First    SMITHTON RECREATIONAL VEHIC...
                                  Second   Projected Sales, 1987-1989
   X: C5..E5                      X axis   Year
   A: C7..E7                      Y axis
   B:
   C:                                      Y scale:     X scale:
   D:                             Scaling  Automatic    Automatic
   E:                             Lower
   F:                             Upper
                                  Format    (G)          (G)
   Grid: None     Color: No       Indicator Yes          Yes

      Legend:           Format:   Data labels:            Skip: 1
   A  Sales             Both
   B                    Both
   C                    Both
   D                    Both
   E                    Both
   F                    Both

06-Oct-90  04:43 PM
```

FIGURE 6-10

Graph Settings Sheet After Adding Titles, Data Legend

FIGURE 6-11

Example Graph with Titles, Legend, Data Labels

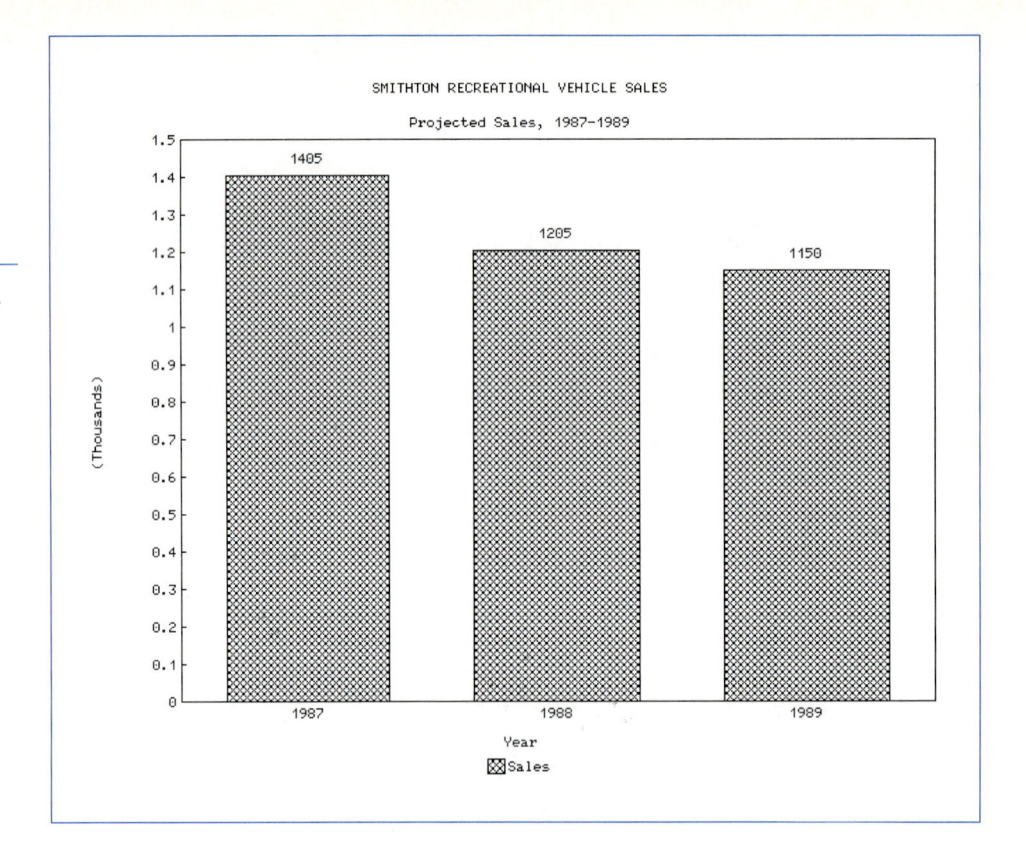

the **/Graph Options Scale** command (**/GOS**). You must choose the **Y**-axis or **X**-axis option next, depending upon which axis you wish to manually scale. The menu for either axis looks like:

MENU

`Automatic Manual Lower Upper Format Indicator Quit`
`Scale automatically based on data ranges`

If you choose **Automatic**, Lotus will choose upper and lower limits for the axis that fit the largest and smallest value plotted against that scale. If you choose **Manual**, you must also select values for the **Lower** and **Upper** limits for that scale.

The **Format** option from this menu lets you choose the way Lotus displays numbers on the axes, similar to doing a range format. You can fix the number of decimal places, add a dollar sign and/or commas in large numbers, or place a percent sign at the end of percentages. The default axis format is usually Fixed, but the number of decimal places depends on the numbers plotted. The **Indicator** option is used to allow or suppress the scale units indicator. In this example the Y-axis indicator is (Thousands).

Drawing Grid Lines

The default condition is to not display **grid lines** on the graph, but Lotus will draw horizontal and vertical lines across the graph if desired. Grid lines may help the reader follow the graph's axes more easily, especially where many points are plotted. Grid lines are especially useful with Line and X-Y graph types. To invoke grid lines, enter the **/Graph Options Grid** command (**/GOG),** at the READY prompt. You'll see the Grid menu.

FIGURE 6-12

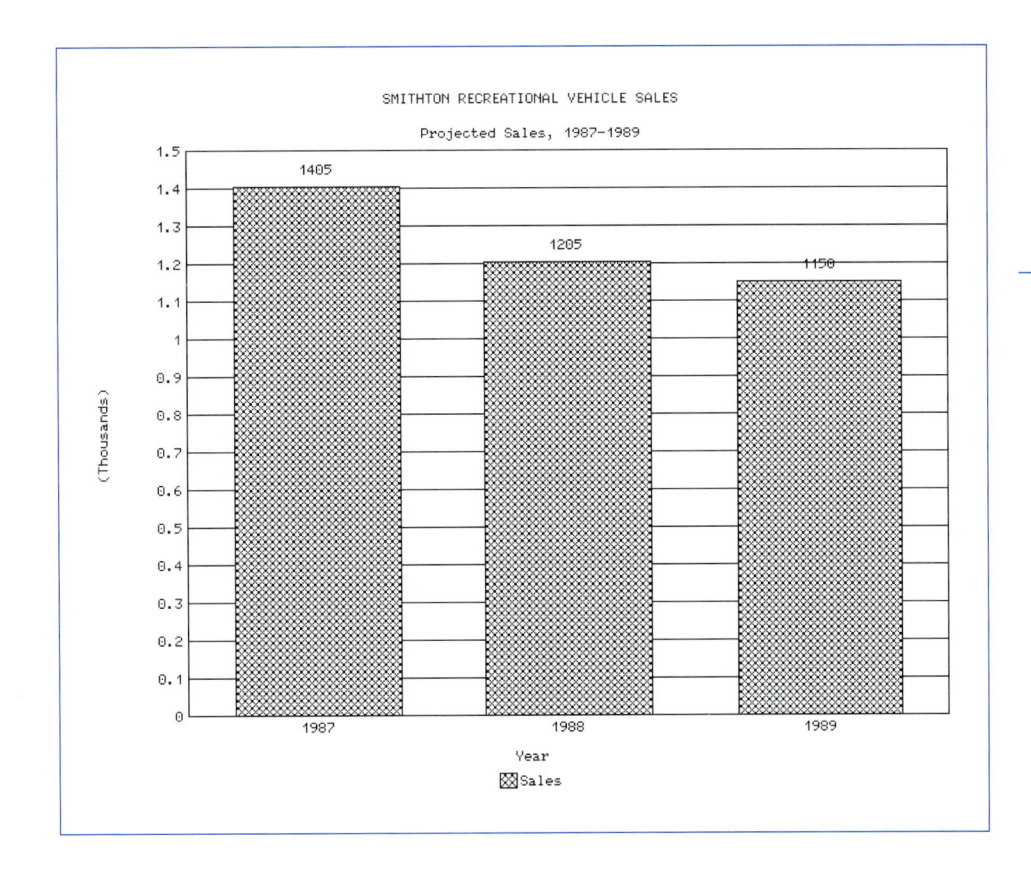

Example of Graph with Horizontal Grid Lines

```
Horizontal Vertical Both Clear
Draw grid lines across the graph
```

Enter **H** for horizontal lines, drawn across the graph. Enter **V** for vertical grid lines, drawn down the graph. **B** invokes both horizontal and vertical, and **C** will clear grid lines from the current graph. The Smithton graph with horizontal grid lines appears in Figure 6-12.

Other Graph Options

The **Format** command can be used to choose how a cell value will be plotted. The default choice is to use a symbol for the point, and connect the points with a straight line. You can omit the line or the symbol, or both, if desired.

Color and **B&W** can be used to toggle the display between colors and cross-hatching for bars and lines. The default is usually B&W. Note that this option affects the display only; colors for printing are determined in the PrintGraph program. Color graphs will print as a solid block.

Naming and Saving the Graph

Lotus offers a peculiar method of keeping track of graphs, and it frequently confuses new users of 1-2-3. Release 2.2 and earlier versions require that you create a **picture file** (**.PIC** extension) of the graph before it can be printed. Release 3.1 provides for printing the graph directly from 1-2-3, eliminating the need to save a picture of the graph. Nonetheless, you should follow a three-step process after having created the graph itself:

1. **Save** a picture of the graph for later printing. This copy can *only* be printed—you cannot change any graph settings with this version of the

graph. Follow DOS file name rules, using no more than 8 characters with no embedded spaces. Lotus will add the .PIC extension to the name. This file will be used for printing purposes later, from the PrintGraph module.

2. **Name** the graph settings for use within Lotus 1-2-3; like range names, this graph name can be up to 14 characters long and may contain spaces. Naming the graph settings is optional, but advisable. Lotus allows you to have up to 10 graphs in one worksheet, and you access them by name. If you neglect to name them, only the last graph settings used will be saved in the worksheet.

3. **Quit** from the /Graph menu and **Save** the entire worksheet again. This is a *critical step:* unless the worksheet file is saved, the graph settings will be irrevocably lost should you wish to make changes, even if the .PIC file is saved and the graph has been named.

Example: *Saving the Graph Settings*

In this example you will save the graph settings within the SMITHRV worksheet and save a picture of the graph in a .PIC file.

1. The first step is easy. From within the /**Graph** menu, press **S** for Save. Lotus will prompt for a DOS file name, using the current default subdirectory. For the Smithton spreadsheet, call the graph **SMSALES**. Lotus will save the image in a file called SMSALES.PIC on the default drive.

2. Now that the graph has been created, you can name this graph from within the /Graph menu. Press **N** for Name. You'll next see the /Graph Names menu:

    MENU

    Use Create Delete Reset Table
    Make a named graph current

3. Type **C** to create a new graph. At the prompt fill in the name of the graph. For Smithton, let's call this graph **SALES BAR** and press **Enter**. The current settings will be saved in the name you provided.

    - The **Use** command will retrieve those settings at a later time.
    - To delete the graph settings from a named graph in the worksheet, use the **Delete** option.
    - The **Reset** option deletes *all* named graphs from the current worksheet Names list.
    - The **Table** option places a list of named graphs in the worksheet at a specified location.

4. The final step is to quit from the /Graph menu. Save the current worksheet, using the /**FS** command. Remember that not only are the cell expressions, formats and column widths saved with the worksheet, but so too are the Print settings and all named graph settings. *Don't neglect this step!*

PRINTING THE GRAPH: LOTUS PRINTGRAPH MODULE

Because the original versions of Lotus were designed for use with a minimally equipped personal computer, the Lotus system was broken into separate modules to conserve RAM. The modules were described in an earlier chapter. So far we have used just the 1-2-3 module. **PrintGraph** is responsible for printing the graph that was previously saved in a .PIC file.

To enter PrintGraph, first leave the 1-2-3 module with the /**Quit** command. From the Lotus Access System menu, choose PrintGraph.

```
1-2-3  Printgraph  Translate  Intall  Exit
Print 1-2-3 Graphs
```

PrintGraph may also be started directly from the DOS prompt if your system permits it. Type **PGRAPH** at the DOS prompt to start PGRAPH in this way.

Printing the graph from PrintGraph involves five steps:

1. Confirm that the hardware settings are correct.
2. Select the graph image (.PIC file) to be printed.
3. Make any changes in size or print fonts.
4. Select the printer to be used, and print resolution.
5. Adjust the printer paper, and print the graph.

The main PrintGraph screen is shown in Figure 6-13. The values shown in the PrintGraph screen will depend upon your computer installation. These reflect a hard disk computer with Lotus installed on the C: drive in the 123 subdirectory. The selected printer is an IBM Graphics Printer in low resolution.

Selecting the Graph Image

The default subdirectory for graph images is shown in the PrintGraph screen in Figure 6-14. If this doesn't agree with the subdirectory you chose when you saved the graph image in the .PIC file, you must change it in PrintGraph with the Settings command, discussed in the following section.

To select an image, press **I** for Image-Select. Lotus will display a list of all the .PIC files stored on the indicated subdirectory. Our image file, SMSALES, is listed on this screen. Use the arrow keys to move the cursor to the correct file, then press the space bar to lock in that choice. A pound sign (#) will appear in

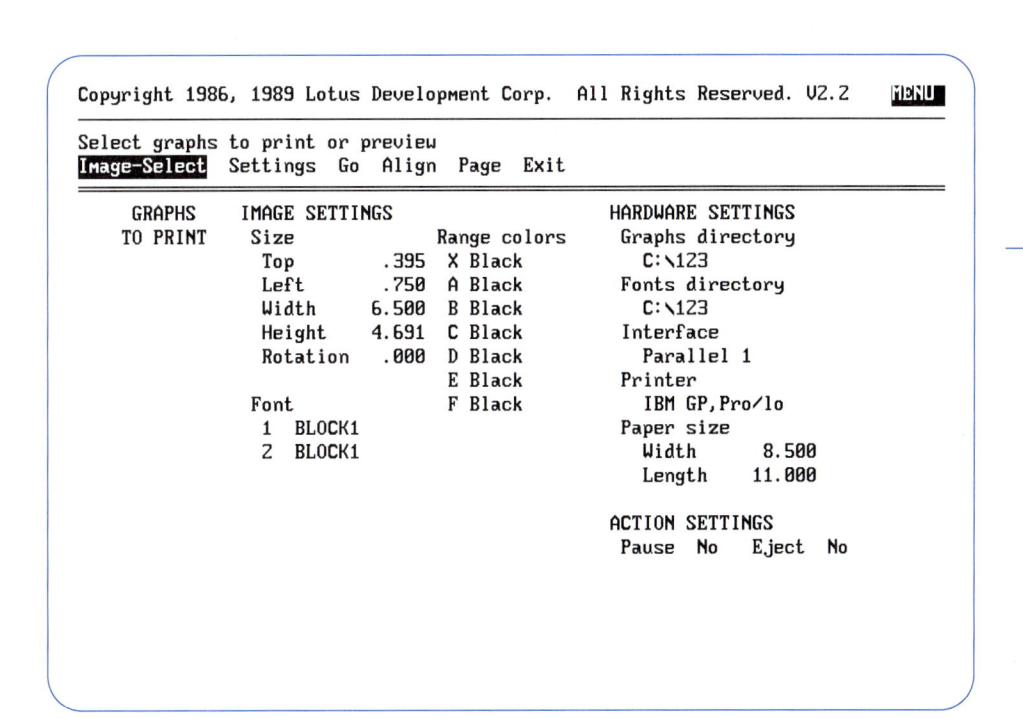

```
Copyright 1986, 1989 Lotus Development Corp.  All Rights Reserved. V2.2    MENU

Select graphs to print or preview
Image-Select  Settings  Go  Align  Page  Exit

   GRAPHS    IMAGE SETTINGS                      HARDWARE SETTINGS
   TO PRINT  Size              Range colors      Graphs directory
             Top        .395   X Black             C:\123
             Left       .750   A Black           Fonts directory
             Width     6.500   B Black             C:\123
             Height    4.691   C Black           Interface
             Rotation   .000   D Black             Parallel 1
                               E Black           Printer
             Font              F Black             IBM GP,Pro/lo
             1 BLOCK1                            Paper size
             2 BLOCK1                              Width      8.500
                                                  Length    11.000

                                                ACTION SETTINGS
                                                  Pause No    Eject No
```

FIGURE 6-13

Main Lotus PrintGraph Screen

FIGURE 6-14

PrintGraph Image-Select Screen

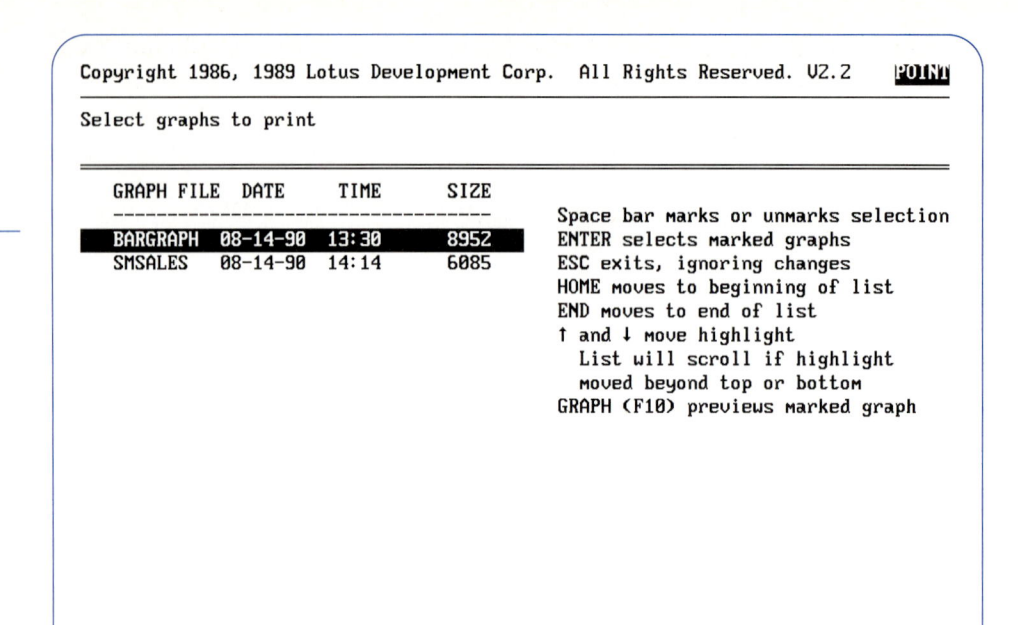

```
Copyright 1986, 1989 Lotus Development Corp.   All Rights Reserved. V2.2   POINT
Select graphs to print

    GRAPH FILE   DATE      TIME     SIZE
    ─────────────────────────────────────       Space bar marks or unmarks selection
    BARGRAPH    08-14-90   13:30    8952        ENTER selects marked graphs
    SMSALES     08-14-90   14:14    6085        ESC exits, ignoring changes
                                                HOME moves to beginning of list
                                                END moves to end of list
                                                ↑ and ↓ move highlight
                                                  List will scroll if highlight
                                                  moved beyond top or bottom
                                                GRAPH (F10) previews marked graph
```

front of the selected file. Lotus permits us to select several files at once for printing in a batch, but we will just choose SMSALES for this print job. Press **Enter** to return to the main menu.

Selecting PrintGraph Options

The most commonly chosen graph printing options are size of graph and type of printer. The **Settings** option of the main PrintGraph module will allow us to make changes in the settings.

MENU
```
Specify graph size, fonts, and colors
 Image  Hardware Action Save Reset Quit
```

The first choice, **Image**, allows you to change the default image size and fonts used in the graph. Graphs can be printed in full page, half-page or manually-chosen size. Because the time to print a graph is directly proportional to its size, it is usually desirable to choose a smaller graph size. The Size menu is shown below.

MENU
```
Size graph for full page automatically
 Full  Half Manual Quit
```

Full-page graphs are printed sideways on 8.5 by 11 inch paper, while half-page graphs are printed normally. As you might guess, you can fit two half-page graphs on the same sheet of paper. Manually chosen graphs allow you to choose the vertical and horizontal size of the graph, along with its location on the page. You can also rotate the graph on the page.

To select the half-page size for our graph, enter the **SISH** command (Settings Image Size Half) from the main PrintGraph menu. To return to the main menu, press the **Q** command (quit) three times.

Lotus offers several fonts for the titles and labels of graphs. You may select one font for the large, First Title, and a different font for the remaining characters in the graph. The Lotus manual shows print samples of each font. The default font is usually BLOCK1, and is used in printed samples in this textbook unless otherwise noted. The table below lists fonts by name. In each case the number "2" following a font indicates it is darker than the preceding font.

Font Name	Font Name
BLOCK1	LOTUS
BLOCK2	ROMAN1
BOLD	ROMAN2
FORUM	SCRIPT1
ITALIC1	SCRIPT2
ITALIC2	

Unless you are using a high-resolution printer setting, it is recommended that you not change the fonts used on the graph. The normal draft mode (low resolution) tends to reproduce elaborate fonts poorly.

The **Hardware option** allows us to change where graphs are stored and to change the selected printer. Use it if you saved your .PIC file to a different subdirectory (or drive) than the one shown in PrintGraph.

To change the graphs directory or the selected printer, enter the **Settings** menu and select **Hardware**. You'll see the following menu:

MENU

Specify directory containing graphs
Graphs-Directory Fonts-Directory Interface Printer Size-Paper Quit

If you choose the **Graphs-Directory** option, Lotus will prompt for the drive and subdirectory name where your .PIC files are stored. If you choose the **Printer** option, you will see a list of all the printers that have been installed for your system. With dot matrix printers there will be a phrase "Low Density" or "High Density" following the printer name. High-density printers take up to four times longer to print one graph, and should be avoided for all but the final draft of an important graph. [Note: Because high-resolution graphs require extra resources, some schools choose not to install these printer options.] In most cases the default selection will be appropriate for your graph. [Note: If you don't see your printer listed, it may emulate one of the listed printers. A frequent choice in such circumstances is the Epson FX series.]

Printing the Graph

With the graph image selected, and all other printer settings made, it is time to prepare the printer. If you are not already in the main PrintGraph menu, press **Quit** the proper number of times to return there. You can use the **Align** command to reset the Lotus line counter to zero and adjust the paper to the top of the printer page. When ready to print, press **Go**. Lotus will flash the **WAIT** mode indicator while the printer is busy. Half-page low-resolution graphs take approximately 2 to 3 minutes to print. Full-page high-resolution graphs may take longer than 10 minutes, but these times depend upon the speed of your printer.

At the completion of printing, you can use the **Page** command to issue a page-eject to the printer. If you print another graph, Lotus will leave a short space between graphs. To leave PrintGraph, use the **Exit** command. If you entered PrintGraph through the Lotus Access System, you will return to that menu. If you entered via the DOS prompt, you will again see the DOS prompt.

Chapter 6 — Lotus Graphs

FIGURE 6-15

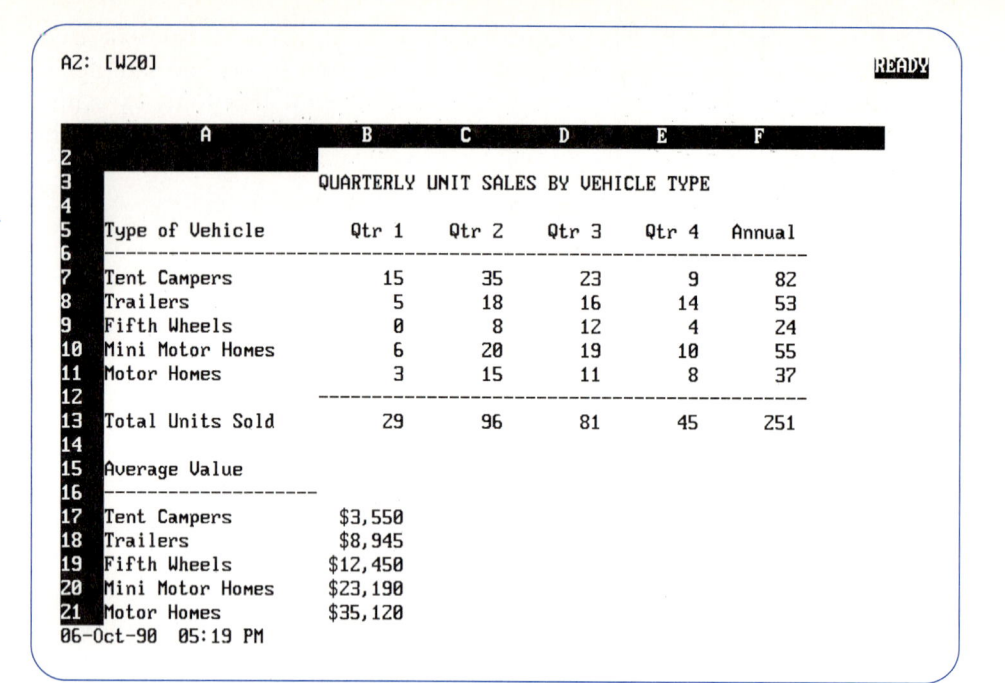

SMRVSALE Example Worksheet

```
A2: [W20]                                                      READY

            A           B         C         D         E         F
  2
  3                    QUARTERLY UNIT SALES BY VEHICLE TYPE
  4
  5    Type of Vehicle   Qtr 1     Qtr 2     Qtr 3     Qtr 4     Annual
  6    ----------------------------------------------------------------
  7    Tent Campers        15        35        23         9        82
  8    Trailers             5        18        16        14        53
  9    Fifth Wheels         0         8        12         4        24
 10    Mini Motor Homes     6        20        19        10        55
 11    Motor Homes          3        15        11         8        37
 12                        ----------------------------------------
 13    Total Units Sold    29        96        81        45       251
 14
 15    Average Value
 16    ------------------
 17    Tent Campers      $3,550
 18    Trailers          $8,945
 19    Fifth Wheels     $12,450
 20    Mini Motor Homes $23,190
 21    Motor Homes      $35,120
 06-Oct-90  05:19 PM
```

Example: Creating and Printing a Graph

Smithton sales personnel have compiled sales statistics from the past four quarters showing unit sales by type of vehicle. The data are shown in the Lotus spreadsheet in Figure 6-15. We wish to prepare a bar graph showing unit sales by quarter for all five vehicle types. Make sure you have entered 1-2-3.

1. If you have a copy of the data disk, retrieve the file called SMRVSALE.WK1 with the /**FR** command.

2. The next step is to enter the /Graph menu, so press /**G**.

3. Press **T** to specify the graph Type, then **B** to select Bar.

4. For this graph the X-range is the four quarters. Press **X** to select the X-range. Enter the X-range as **B5..E5** and press **Enter** to complete the entry.

5. The graph will have five Y-variables, ranges A–E. Let's enter the first one, then see what the graph looks like. To select the A-range, type **A**, then enter the cell range. You could use the Point method to highlight the cell range, **B7..E7**, and press **Enter**. Or, type the range coordinates directly. The Point method has the advantage of visually confirming that the highlighted cells are indeed those that you want to plot.

6. To see the graph so far, press **V** for View. The graph is represented in Figure 6-16.

7. Next select the **B**, **C**, **D** and **E** ranges in the same manner as before. The cell references for these quarterly sales figure ranges are in rows 8, 9, 10 and 11 respectively: **B8..E8**, **B9..E9**, **B10..E10**, and **B11..E11**.

8. Again, type **V** to view the graph. Notice that the bars are narrower as more data series are plotted. The new graph is shown in Figure 6-17.

9. The title for the graph will be entered next. Press **O** to enter the Options menu. Press **T** to activate the Titles menu. Press **F** to specify

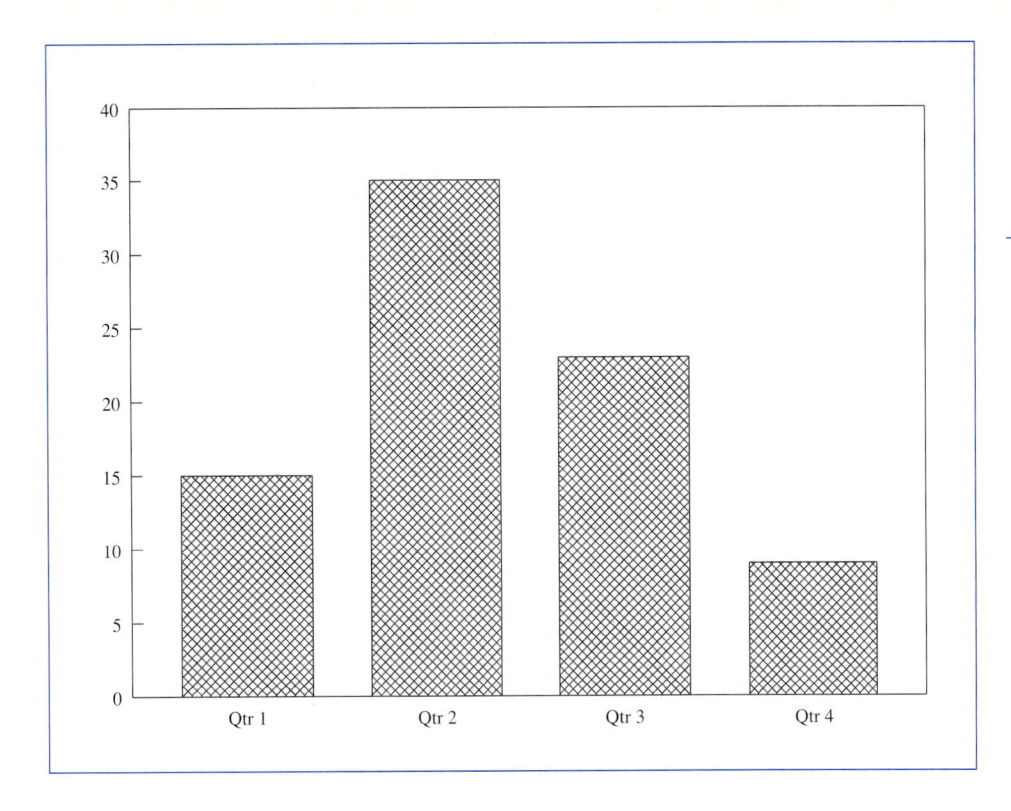

FIGURE 6-16

Graph After Step 6

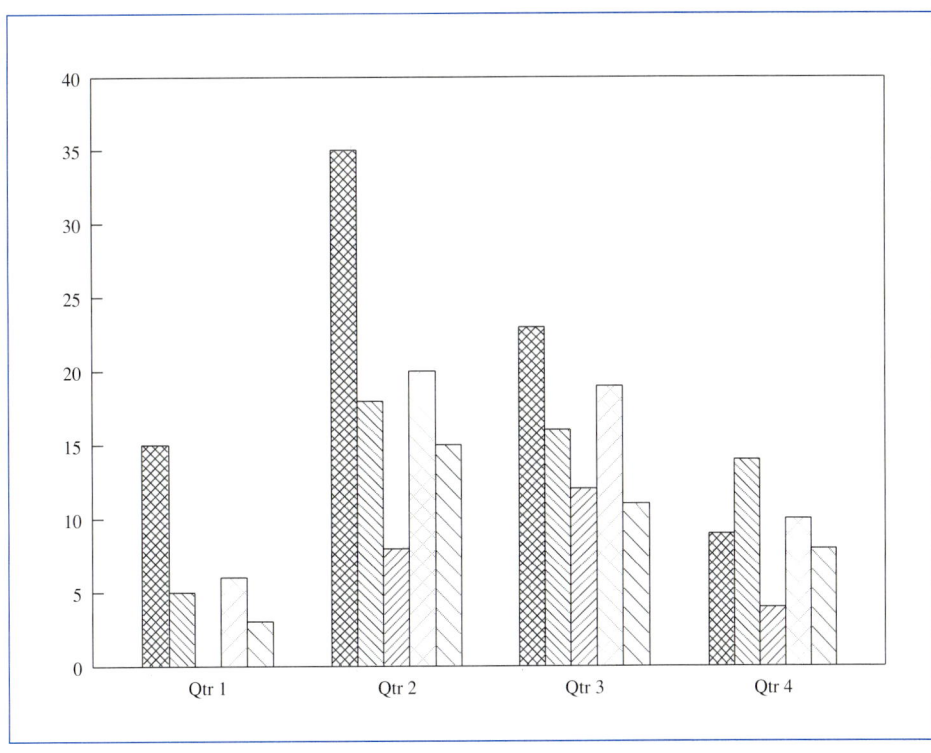

FIGURE 6-17

Graph After Step 8

the First title. Then enter **SMITHTON RV SALES, INC.** and press **Enter** to complete the entry.

10. Press **T** to specify another Title. Press **S** to enter the Second title as **Unit Sales by Quarter**. Press **T** again, then press **Y** to enter the Y-axis title as **Unit Sales**.

11. Press **Q** to Quit the Options menu and return to the main Graph menu. Type **V** to view the graph's progress.

Chapter 6 — *Lotus Graphs*

FIGURE 6-18

Completed Graph Settings Sheet for Example

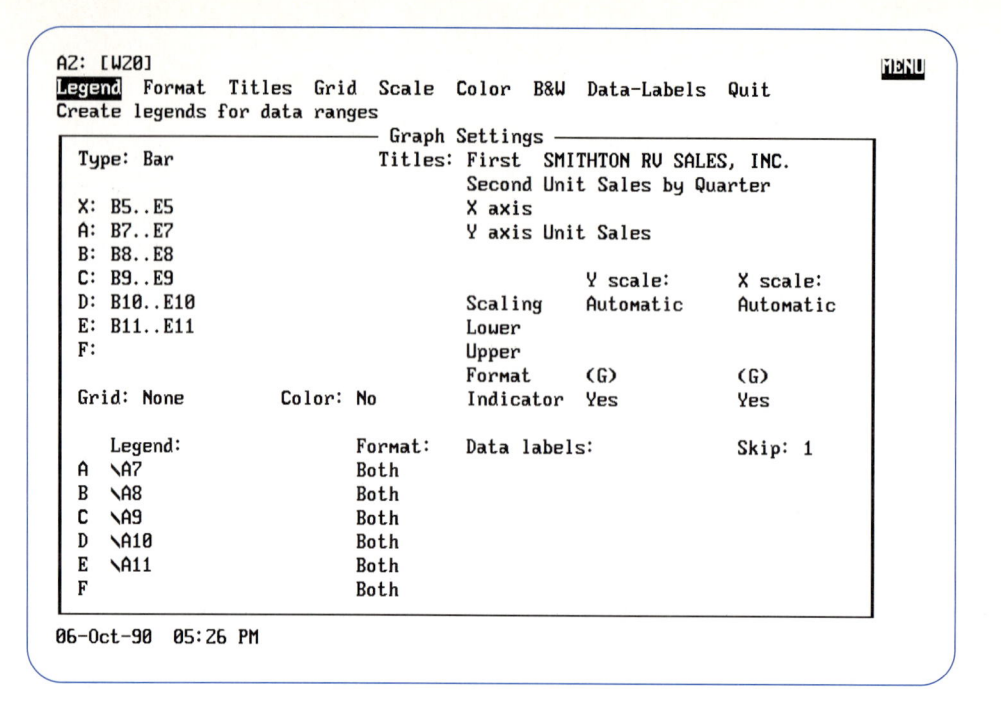

```
A2: [W20]                                                          MENU
Legend  Format  Titles  Grid  Scale  Color  B&W  Data-Labels  Quit
Create legends for data ranges
                          ─── Graph Settings ───
  Type: Bar                   Titles: First  SMITHTON RV SALES, INC.
                                      Second Unit Sales by Quarter
  X: B5..E5                           X axis
  A: B7..E7                           Y axis Unit Sales
  B: B8..E8
  C: B9..E9                                    Y scale:      X scale:
  D: B10..E10                         Scaling  Automatic     Automatic
  E: B11..E11                         Lower
  F:                                  Upper
                                      Format   (G)           (G)
  Grid: None     Color: No            Indicator Yes          Yes

    Legend:                   Format:        Data labels:     Skip: 1
  A  \A7                      Both
  B  \A8                      Both
  C  \A9                      Both
  D  \A10                     Both
  E  \A11                     Both
  F                           Both

06-Oct-90  05:26 PM
```

12. Next we should enter the Data Legend for the A–E ranges. From the main graph menu press **O** to activate the Options menu, then press **L** to select the Legend menu.

13. Press **A** to enter the A-range legend. Instead of typing in the name of the vehicle, use the existing label in cell A7 by typing \A7. Do the same for ranges B, C, D and E with cells **A8** through **A11**. Don't forget to precede the cell reference with the backslash key, or the legend will appear as the letters in the cell reference. The Graph settings appear in Figure 6-18.

14. Press **Q** to return to the main Graph menu. Press **V** to view the graph on the screen. The final graph is shown in Figure 6-19.

15. Save the graph image by entering **S**. Give the file name **SMBARS**.

16. To save the graph settings in the worksheet, use the **Name** command. At the Name menu, type **C** to create a new graph name. At the graph name prompt, enter **UNIT SALES BAR** and press **Enter**.

17. Finally, press **Q** to exit from the Graph menu. Use the **/FS** command to save the worksheet as **SMRVSALE**.

18. Enter the **/Quit** command to leave the 1-2-3 module,

19. From the Lotus Access Menu press **P** to enter PrintGraph.

20. Use the **Image-Select** option to select the SMBARS.PIC file you just saved. Move the cursor to that file in the list and press **Enter** to mark it for printing.

21. Check the PrintGraph status screen for appropriate printer, and make changes if needed with the **Settings** menu.

22. Finally, if the printer is ready, press **G** to begin printing your graph. After it is printed, use the **Page** command to feed the graph out of the printer, and **Exit** from PrintGraph.

FIGURE 6-19

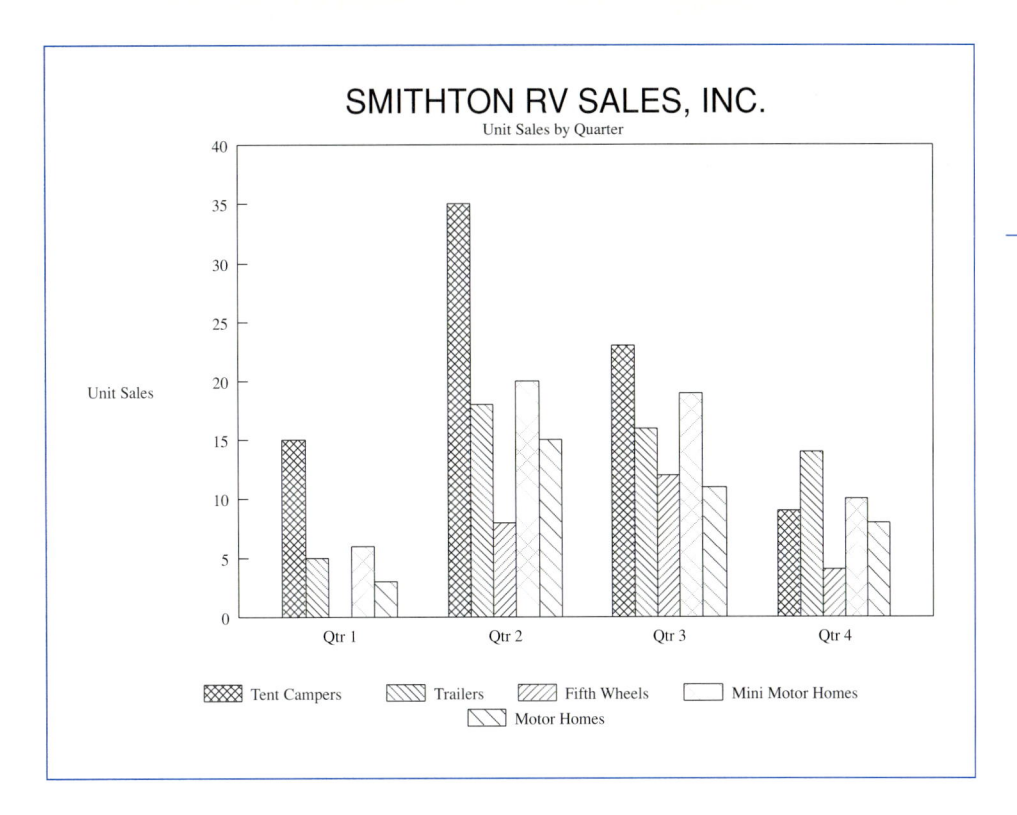

Completed Example Graph

After you have created and saved a graph with 1-2-3, you can use Allways to print a copy of the graph. Allways will not create the graph itself but allows you to print the graph (on the same page as the worksheet itself) without loading PrintGraph. The basic procedure is as follows:

1. Create the graph in 1-2-3 as usual, saving the graph image as a .PIC file.
2. Attach Allways and invoke this add-in.
3. Activate the Allways /Graph menu and add the graph .PIC file to the worksheet.
4. Select print settings such as font and font size, print colors, and page margins.
5. Issue the Allways /Print command and select print options such as print range, printer settings, resolution and number of copies.
6. Print the graph with Allways.
7. Quit Allways, returning to 1-2-3.
8. Save the worksheet as a .WK1 file.

PRINTING GRAPHS WITH ALLWAYS

Example: *Printing a Graph with Allways*

In this example we will place the sales SMBARS.PIC graph (created in the previous example) into the SMRVSALE worksheet. We will assume that Allways has been installed at your computer lab.

1. Begin Lotus as usual and select the 1-2-3 module. Retrieve the SMRVSALE.WK1 file from the data disk with the **/FR** command.

FIGURE 6-20

Main Allways Display Screen

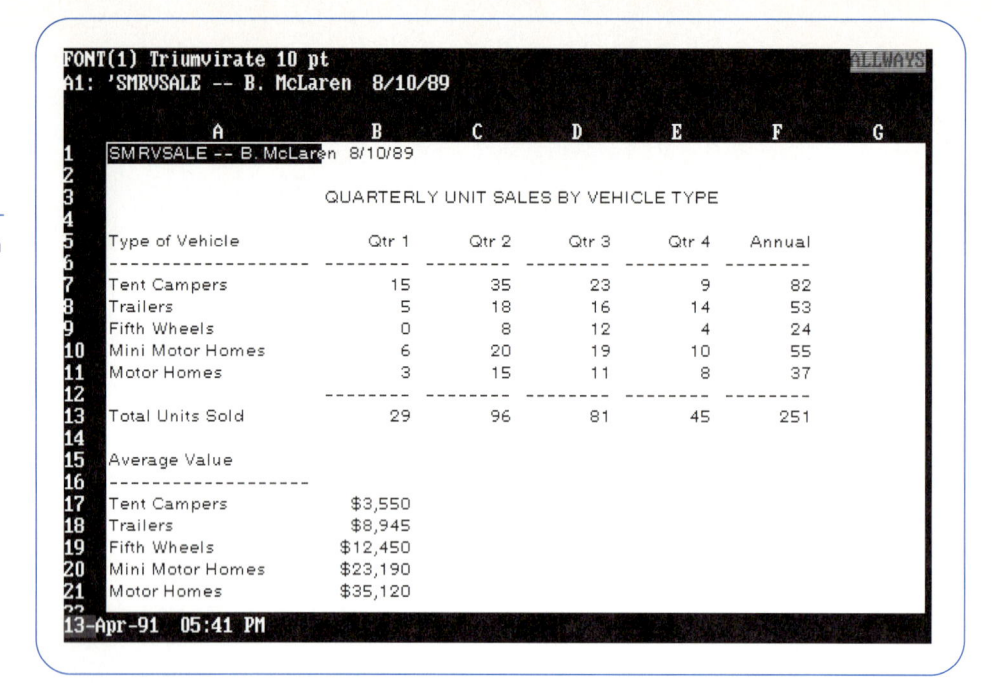

2. To attach the Allways add-in, press **/AA** and select ALLWAYS.ADN from the menu. Press **7** to assign Allways to the Alt-F7 function key. Press **Q** to return to 1-2-3.

3. After making any desired changes to the SMRVSALE worksheet, activate Allways by pressing **Alt-F7.** You'll see the main Allways display screen shown in Figure 6-20.

4. Use the arrow keys to move the cursor to cell C15. Alternatively, you can use the **F5** Goto key just as in 1-2-3.

5. We'll place the graph at cell C15. Activate the Allways Graph menu by pressing **/G.**

6. Press **A** to Add the graph to the worksheet. When presented with the list of .PIC files, move the cursor to SMBARS.PIC and press **Enter.**

7. You will be asked to specify the range for the graph. Use the arrow keys to highlight the range **C15..F25** and press **Enter.** Press **Q** to quit from the /Graph menu.

8. If the graphics display mode is activated, you will see the image of the graph on the screen as shown in Figure 6-21.

9. If you see a shaded box rather than the graph image on the screen, press **/D** to activate the Allways Display menu; press **G** to select Graphs and choose **Yes** to display graphs.

10. At this point you could modify such graph settings as the font and page margins with the /GS command. We will use the default settings of Block1 font and the standard margins.

11. Press **/P** to activate the Allways Print menu. Press **R** to select the Range and S to Set the print range. When asked to enter the print range, type **A1..F25** and press **Enter.** Allways will highlight the print range with a dotted line. Press **G** (Go) to send the output to the printer. The final output is shown in Figure 6-22.

FIGURE 6-21

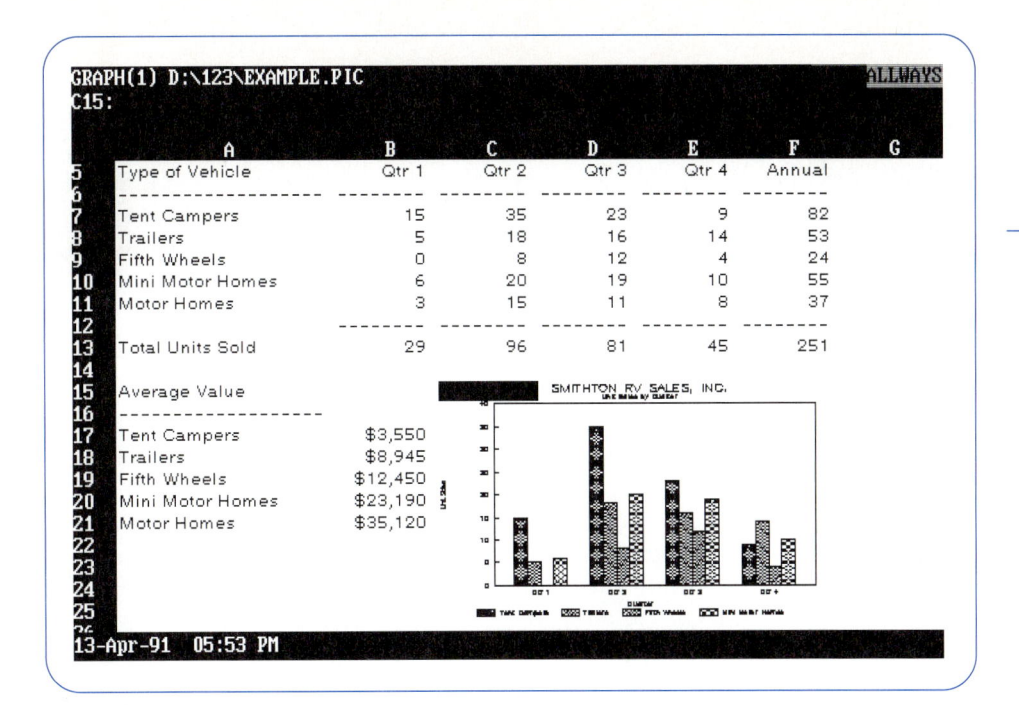

Allways Display of Worksheet and Graph

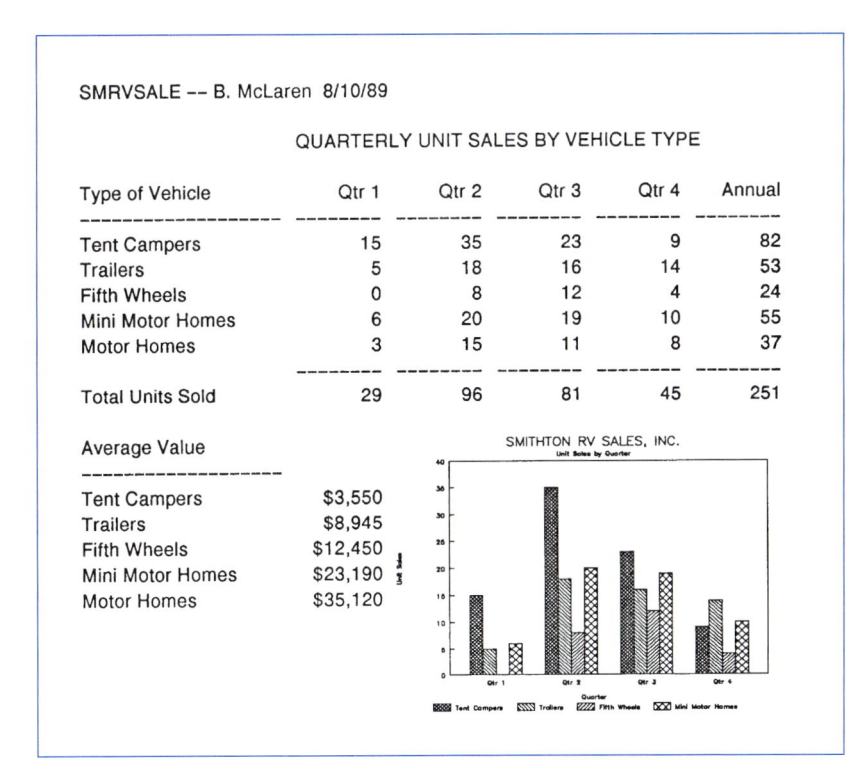

FIGURE 6-22

Final Output of Worksheet and Graph

12. Press **/Q** to quit from Allways back to 1-2-3. Press **/FS** to save the worksheet and the Allways settings.

The final copy of the Allways-produced graph is too small to be easily read. Use the /Graph Settings Range command to move the graph to a larger range of cells. You could also use Allways to add features to the worksheet such as a larger font size for the worksheet title, lines and shading. These steps are left as an exercise.

CHAPTER REVIEW

Creating Lotus Graphs

Lotus graphs, the second part of 1-2-3, provide a valuable means of interpreting numeric data. Graphs can quickly be created within the 1-2-3 module. Lotus provides five different types of graphs: line graphs, X-Y graphs, bar graphs, stacked bar graphs, and pie charts. You can change graph type with a few keystrokes and display the data in an alternative manner. Up to six Y-variable data ranges can be plotted on the same graph in Lotus. They are designated by the letters A–F. The letter X designates the X-variable.

Graph Settings

Lotus offers numerous graph settings to customize the graph. Titles identify the purpose of the graph and the meaning of the axes. First and Second titles appear at the top of the graph, while X and Y titles appear adjacent to the axes. Data legends are used to describe the individual Y-variable ranges and appear below the X-axis. Short legends are preferred so they will fit. Data labels are used to display on the graph the value of the cell that is plotted at each point. Titles and legends may be entered directly or you can use labels from actual worksheet cells by prefacing the cell address with a backslash character.

Scales, Formatting the Axes, and Drawing Grid Lines

Ordinarily the scales are chosen automatically to match the highest and lowest values plotted. You can override with manual settings for upper and lower values on the scales. Lotus typically uses Fixed format to display axis values, but any of the regular format types can be selected. Horizontal and vertical grid lines can be added to a graph to make it easier to read values against the axis scales.

Naming and Saving the Graph

Up to 10 graphs can be saved with each worksheet file. The Name command is used to create a new graph or use an existing graph. The Save command will place a printable image of the graph on the default disk; this image can be printed with the Lotus PrintGraph module at a later time. After naming the graph settings and saving the graph image, you must save the worksheet file to save the settings permanently.

Printing the Graph

PrintGraph is used with Lotus to print the image of the graph that was saved in 1-2-3. Images are selected through a menu option; one or more can be printed in the same batch. Settings are modified through another menu option. You can change the graph size and its orientation on the page, as well as the printer type and print resolution. Low-resolution, half-page graphs are recommended to expedite printing. Larger graphs take proportionally more time to print, and high-resolution graphs print very slowly. Lotus offers 11 different print fonts for graphs.

Using Allways to Print a Graph

The Allways add-in product can be used to place a .PIC graph file in the worksheet and print both the worksheet and accompanying graphs at the same time, without using PrintGraph. The graph must first be created with 1-2-3 and the results saved in a .PIC file. Many of the printing options available in PrintGraph are also found in Allways, such as choice of font, size, print colors used, and page margins.

DISCUSSION QUESTIONS

KEY TERMS

bar chart	grid lines	PrintGraph
data labels	Hardware option	Save graph settings **(/GS)**
data legend	high-low-close graph	stacked bar chart
data range	line graph	titles
Graph Options Grid command **(/GOG)**	manual graph size	View command **(/GV)**
	mixed graph	X-range
Graph Options Scale command **(/GOS)**	named graph settings	X-Y graph
	picture file (PIC file)	Y-range
graph type	pie chart	

DISCUSSION QUESTIONS

1. List the five types of graphs available with Lotus 1-2-3. Which is best for showing how a variable moves over time? Which is best for showing how parts of a whole are comprised?

2. Explain the purposes of the /Graph Name command. Why should you name a graph?

3. Describe the meaning of each of the following /Graph commands and Options:
   a. Save
   b. Titles Second
   c. Legend
   d. Data-Labels
   e. Grid
   f. Scale Manual
   g. Format .. Symbols.

4. Why must you save the worksheet after having saved the graph image as a .PIC file?

5. Why is the PrintGraph module distinct from the 1-2-3 module in Releases 2.01 and 2.2?

6. Explain the relationship between graph size, printer resolution, and printing time in PrintGraph. What are the recommended settings for these options?

7. Suppose you saved the graph as a .PIC file on a diskette in the B drive, but find the default graphs directory in PrintGraph is on the C drive. How do you change the default directory to your diskette in the B drive within PrintGraph?

8. Explain the role of the Page and Align commands in the main PrintGraph menu.

9. Explain the purpose of the following items from the PrintGraph settings sheet of Figure 6-13:
   a. Graphs directory   C:\123
   b. Printer   IBM GP,Pro/1o
   c. Font 1   BLOCK1
   d. Rotation   .000
   e. Eject   No.

10. Give the keystrokes necessary to accomplish the following:
    a. change the graph size to half-page
    b. change to a high-resolution printer setting
    c. select a graph called CATS
    d. select two graphs, CATS and DOGS, to be printed at the same time, one after another
    e. select a font called ITALIC2 for Font1

11. Explain the advantages of Allways over PrintGraph for printing graphs.

12. Suppose you have loaded a large worksheet into 1-2-3 and tried but were unable to attach and invoke Allways. The UNDO and MEM status indicators are lit at the bottom of the 1-2-3 screen. What do these mean? What can be done?

EXERCISES

1. Use the data in Figure 6-23 to prepare and print a Lotus bar graph. The Dean of the School of Business has supplied the statistics for current enrollments within majors, as shown.

   Use the Major column as X-range, the 1985 column as the A-range, and the 1989 column as the B-range. Your graph should have appropriate titles and legend. No grid is necessary. Name the graph **MAJOR BAR** and save it along with the spreadsheet. Also save the image of the graph as **MAJBAR.PIC** and print it as a half-page graph.

2. Use the same data from the previous problem, reset graph settings and create a pie chart for 1989 enrollments. This time highlight the increase in MIS enrollments by exploding that wedge in the pie chart. (Hint: Place a value above 100 in the cell adjacent to the 1989 MIS enrollment figure and define a B-range for the graph to include that cell.) Name this graph **MAJPIEX** and save it along with the worksheet. Save the graph image as **MAJPIEX** and print a half-page graph.

3. On-time performance data of U.S. airlines in July and June, 1989, is shown in Figure 6-24. (Source: *Wall Street Journal,* September 8, 1989, p. B3).

   Prepare and print a Lotus bar graph showing the on-time performance for all 13 airlines in both months. The First title for the graph should be **On-Time Performance**, and the Second Title is **Arriving Within 15 Minutes of Schedule**. Use appropriate Y-axis title and legends.

FIGURE 6-23

Sample Data for Exercise 1

```
              CURRENT ENROLLMENTS -- SCHOOL OF BUSINESS

                                    In 1985             In 1989
         Major                    No. Students        No. Students
         Accounting                    659                 525
         Administrative Systems        152                 136
         Business Administration       895                 920
         Management                    190                 165
         Marketing                     250                 345
         MIS                            80                 275
```

EXERCISES

4. The Smucker Investment Company has assembled selected financial data on foreign exchange, shown in the Figure 6-25. (Source: *Business Week*, July 17, 1989, p. 6.) Data show foreign currency units per US dollar. If you have the data disk, the file is called FOREXCH.WK1.

    a. Prepare a Lotus 1-2-3 bar graph using the first four currencies as the X-range. The three prices for each are the A-, B- and C-ranges. Use **SMUCKER INVESTMENTS** as the First title, and **Foreign Exchange** as the Second title. The Y-axis title is **Exchange Rates** and the X-axis title is **Currency**. Legends are the three column headings above the ratios. Print a copy of the graph.

    b. Add the French Franc to the bar graph and print a new copy. Why did the size of the other graphs change?

5. The Deveraux Company from Ottawa has gathered quality control data for the M9 assembly line. Prepare a line graph for the data shown in Figure 6-26. Use horizontal grid lines for your graph. The First title is **DEVERAUX COMPANY** and the Second title should be **Average Batch Weight**. Y-axis title is **Weight in Kilograms**, and X-axis title is **Batch Number**. Use Manual scale settings for the Y-axis, with Lower limit of 0.4 and Upper limit of 0.6, with (Fixed,3) for the Y-axis scale format.

6. The local APICS Chapter #211 statement for the Fall Seminar is shown in Figure 6-27. You are to print a pie chart showing Revenue Breakdown by category. Explode the segment showing Net Profit. Use different

Airline	July '89	June '89
America West	89.4%	90.8%
Eastern	86.0	80.1
Southwest	85.4	75.8
American	83.8	76.2
Alaska	82.2	80.4
Continental	80.0	72.5
TWA	79.8	78.6
Delta	79.1	72.0
Northwest	77.6	75.1
Pan American	73.9	64.4
US Air	72.2	69.4
Piedmont	67.6	62.8
United	62.3	63.0

FIGURE 6-24

Sample Data for Exercise 3

Foreign Exchange	Latest Week	Week Ago	Year Ago
German Mark	1.88	1.96	1.82
British Pound	1.62	1.56	1.71
Canadian Dollar	1.19	1.20	1.21
Swiss Franc	1.61	1.69	1.52
French Franc	6.39	6.66	6.13
Japanese Yen	138	143	132
Mexican Peso	2,508	2,501	2,300

FIGURE 6-25

Sample Data for Exercise 4

Chapter 6 — Lotus Graphs

FIGURE 6-26

Sample Data for Exercise 5

Batch	Weight
1	0.428
2	0.422
3	0.420
4	0.431
5	0.428
6	0.435
7	0.440
8	0.490
9	0.512
10	0.513
11	0.522
12	0.509

FIGURE 6-27

Sample Data for Exercise 6

Category	Amount
Meals	$752.07
Postage	338.00
Printing	348.10
Speaker Fees	500.00
Speaker Plaque	121.38
Net Profit	869.75

shading for adjacent segments of your graph. Use appropriate titles to describe the graph.

7. Retrieve the previous worksheet file and name the graph settings as **REVENUE-PIE**. Then change to a bar graph type and print a copy. Save the graph settings of the latter graph as **REVENUE-BAR**.

8. Using the **REVENUE-PIE** pie graph from the previous problem, print graphs with the following PrintGraph settings.

   a. Print a full-page graph in the low resolution printer setting. Change the print font to Forum before printing.

   b. Choose the manual image size and print the graph with Top at .75, Left at 1.25, Width of 4.046 and Height of 5.6 inches. Rotate the graph 270 degrees. Remember that the proper height/width ratio to maintain a circular pie chart is 1.385. When you choose a rotation of 90 or 270 degrees the ratio should be width/height. Use the Italic-1 font for your graph.

   c. If permitted at your computer lab, print a half-page graph with a high-density printer setting. Use the Reset command to return all other settings to the default values. Compare this graph with the others you have printed.

9. Redo exercise 1 using Allways to place the graph on the worksheet. Print a copy of the worksheet with the graph on the same page.

10. Redo exercise 5 using Allways to place the graph on the worksheet. Use Allways to print a copy of the worksheet with the graph.

CHAPTER 6 PROJECT
HCP INCORPORATED ANNUAL REPORT

Corporate Relations staffers at HCP are in the process of preparing final copy for the 1990 annual report. They have the financial results for the past ten years and wish to present it in a suitable manner. They know it will require a mixture of text and graphs but weren't sure how to display the data in a pleasing and informative manner. Historical data are shown in Figure 6-28 and are contained in a Lotus worksheet file named HCP.WK1 on the data diskette. Additional data are shown in other tables in Figure 6-28.

Prepare a presentation-quality table showing the historical data using Allways. The current year's figures should be highlighted in the table. The four account headings appearing above each group of account titles should appear in italic type and be bold. Any other formatting or style changes that would help in presenting this material should be implemented.

Prepare a set of graphs to display the Quarterly stock price data. Use Allways to display the the information from the bar graphs on the same output page as the actual data itself. Print that portion of the worksheet.

Prepare separate 1-2-3 bar graphs that illustrate the ten-year trends in Sales, Net Income, Earnings per Share, and Dividends per Share. Add formatting and other options as needed to carefully describe the information shown in the graphs. Make sure your graphs appear in chronological order by year, from 1981 to 1990. Is there any way to improve the visual appearance of these graphs? How might you add annotations to the graphs?

FIGURE 6-28

Sample Data for Chapter 6 Project, Contained in File HCP.WK1 on Data Disk

```
HCP -- Annual Report Data for Ten Years Ending 1990

HISTORICAL DATA

For the Year (dollars in millions)   1990     1989     1988     1987     1986     1985     1984     1983     1982     1981

Net Sales                          $2,796.6 $2,669.7 $2,317.8 $1,933.1 $1,636.1 $1,812.8 $1,515.5 $1,243.4 $1,234.3 $1,155.4
Gross Income                          979.8    996.9    861.8    665.1    517.3    676.8    589.0    465.5    476.5    454.5
Selling, General and Admin Expenses   505.2    467.0    426.0    362.4    318.4    307.2    292.0    250.4    236.7    224.0
Income from Operations                474.6    519.9    435.8    302.7    198.9    369.6    297.0    215.1    239.8    230.5
Interest Expense                     (21.6)   (16.2)   (16.2)   (16.4)   (15.6)   (13.6)   (12.2)   (10.9)   (13.0)   (14.2)
Other Income, Net                       2.3     15.5     10.9      7.7      9.2      6.7      7.8      9.3     14.2      6.8
Income Before Income Taxes            455.3    529.2    430.5    294.0    192.5    362.7    292.6    213.5    241.0    223.1
  % of Sales                           16.3     19.8     18.6     15.2     11.8     20.0     19.3     17.2     19.5     19.3
Income Taxes                          174.4    210.1    180.8    129.7     84.5    161.4    129.5     94.6    106.2     99.4
Net Income                           $280.9   $319.1   $249.7   $164.3   $108.0   $201.3   $163.1   $118.9   $134.8   $123.7
  % of Sales                           10.0     12.0     10.8      8.5      6.6     11.1     10.8      9.6     10.9     10.7
Net Income Per Share                  $2.63    $2.96    $2.31    $1.52    $1.00    $1.87    $1.52    $1.10    $1.25    $1.15
Cash Dividends                        128.1    107.8     91.8     80.0     77.7     68.9     57.4     50.3     43.2     36.0
Cash Dividends Per Share             $1.200   $1.000   $0.850   $0.740   $0.720   $0.640   $0.533   $0.466   $0.400   $0.333
Capital Expenditures                  252.1    220.3    171.8    151.7    198.5    255.7    127.6    121.9    108.9    113.3
Depreciation and Amortization         180.3    158.5    142.1    125.3     96.4     75.1     63.3     58.6     50.5     43.7
Research, Development and Engineering 253.0    238.0    204.0    170.0    160.0    163.0    133.0    112.0    111.0    104.0


At December 31 (dollars in millions)

Working Capital                      $711.7   $700.9   $625.3   $475.5   $356.1   $389.4   $446.5   $415.6   $410.7   $363.0
Property, Plant and Equipment, Net    953.8    894.6    865.4    793.6    750.2    620.4    461.9    413.5    362.9    323.4
Total Assets                        2,529.8  2,375.5  2,082.1  1,786.9  1,549.3  1,487.4  1,238.4  1,076.3  1,025.4    928.7
  % Return on Assets                   11.5     14.3     12.9      9.9      7.1     14.8     14.1     11.3     13.8     14.0
Long-Term Debt                         69.5     82.8     71.4     46.3     36.1     27.3     46.9     53.0     56.1     50.1
Total Debt                            284.0    224.8    187.1    191.4    188.8    202.3     95.6    103.4     94.1    102.3
Shareholders' Equity                1,625.4  1,521.3  1,348.6  1,134.9    996.9    923.2    800.9    714.5    660.5    577.7
  % Return on Equity                   17.9     22.2     20.1     15.4     11.2     23.4     21.5     17.3     21.8     23.1
Shareholder's Equity Per Share       $15.27   $14.16   $12.54   $10.50    $9.23    $8.57    $7.45    $6.64    $6.13    $5.35
Backlog                              $489.0   $475.0   $384.0   $326.0   $307.0   $340.0   $374.0   $254.0   $253.0   $248.0
Number of Employees                  24,400   24,100   22,000   21,800   22,800   24,500   21,300   19,750   19,650   18,650
Floor Space (millions sq. feet)         9.0      9.0      8.9      8.9      9.0      8.7      7.9      7.3      7.0      6.3
Shares of Stock Outstanding (millions)106.5    107.4    107.5    108.1    107.9    107.7    107.5    107.7    107.8    108.0


Annual Stock Price Range

High                                 49.375   54.250   71.500   45.000   37.875   39.500   39.000   23.500   20.875   18.750
Low                                  40.000   40.500   34.125   32.875   27.500   26.125   22.000   15.125   14.500   11.000


Quarterly Stock Price Range           1st Q    2nd Q    3rd Q    4th Q

1990 High                            49.375   44.125   47.250   47.500
1990 Low                             41.000   40.250   40.500   40.000

1989 High                            54.250   52.000   52.000   45.750
1989 Low                             40.500   42.875   40.500   40.625
```

7

Data Management with Lotus 1-2-3

Objectives

After completing this chapter, you should be able to:

- Define a Lotus database and explain how data records are stored in a worksheet.
- Create a simple Lotus database.
- Explain how to sort a set of database records in 1-2-3.
- Discuss the input, criteria, and output ranges used for data queries.
- List the four Lotus data query operations, and perform a simple query.
- Explain how to use the database @-functions.
- Discuss Lotus data tables and prepare a one-parameter data table.
- Understand the concept of regression and do a simple regression.

Chapter 7 — Data Management with Lotus 1-2-3

INTRODUCTION

Data management concepts are introduced in this chapter, along with a discussion about the way Lotus stores data in the worksheet. The data fill and sort commands are illustrated. Various data query options are presented, along with a discussion of the cell ranges needed for queries. The data regression command is illustrated. The database @-functions are also covered in the chapter. Finally, the data table commands are presented.

LOTUS DATA MANAGEMENT

Lotus 1-2-3 can be useful in managing lists of things. It can sort the list of items or locate items that have certain data values or characteristics. Although some people refer to this capability, the "3" in 1-2-3, as database management, a better description is a **list manager**.

Databasics with 1-2-3

Data Storage in the Worksheet

Data is stored in the worksheet in rows, in a contiguous block. Each row represents a **record**, or a set of attributes of an item or object. **Fields** occupy columns in the data area. A field is a single attribute or measurement about an object. For example, we could view a student gradebook as a set of data. Each student (a record) will occupy one row in the spreadsheet. For each student we will store several scores (each a field) in that row. When we manipulate the records, such as sorting them, we will want to move all the fields associated with that record at the same time.

Lotus requires that all data be present in the worksheet so that it can all be processed at the same time. True database programs store data on an external disk file, meaning that the size of the database is essentially unlimited. dBASE IV can handle up to one billion records. Because the size of the worksheet in Lotus is limited by the amount of random access memory (RAM) available, Lotus databases are quite limited in size. In fact, with a standard 640 KB of RAM, only a few hundred records fit within a single worksheet. Thus Lotus is better suited for shorter lists of data. For systems with expanded memory, larger worksheets can be accommodated. Future versions of Lotus are likely to have more space for storing data records. Some competing spreadsheet products such as VP Planner now offer this feature, as discussed at the end of the spreadsheet section of this text.

The /Data Menu

Several commands are accessible through the **/Data** menu, shown below.

```
                                                                  MENU
    Fill  Table Sort Query Distribution Matrix Regression Parse
    Fill a range with a sequence of values
```

- **Fill** instructs Lotus to automatically fill consecutive cells with incremental numbers, say payment numbers from 1 to 36 or interest rates from .08 to .12 by .005 increments. Because it is used frequently in preparing worksheets, the **Fill** operation is discussed immediately below.

- The **Sort** and **Query** commands are closely related, and are discussed in the following sections.

- The **Regression** and **Table** options are discussed later.

- **Distribution** is used for counting the number of observations that fall in certain categories.

- The **Matrix** option will multiply two matrices together or invert a matrix.

- The **Parse** option is used when importing data into a worksheet and is covered in Chapter 9.

Filling Data Cells

The /**Data Fill** (/**DF**) command saves time by automatically filling consecutive cells with incremental values. You must specify the beginning and ending values for the cell range, and the incremental value between cells, and Lotus will quickly fill the range. For example, we can fill cells A30 through A47 with the values 1 through 18. From the /Data menu, press **F** for Fill. You will be asked to enter the fill range, **A30..A47**. Then Lotus will prompt for the Start value (**1**), the Step Size or increment (**1**), and the Stop value (**8191** is the default value). Lotus will fill those cells indicated until either the Stop value is reached or the end of fill range is reached, whichever comes first. The screen shows in Figure 7-1 the results of the /Data Fill *after* the command has been executed.

To fill fractional values, simply give the Step size as a decimal value. For the interest rate example above, the Start value is .08, the Step is .005, and the Stop value is .12. Lotus can also fill a range of cells by decrementing, using a negative Step size. Be sure that the Start value is greater than the Stop value if using a negative step size.

Sorting Data Records

Lotus will rapidly sort rows according to **key field** values in those rows. You can choose one or two key fields to sort upon. The **primary key** is the more important field, and the **secondary key** can be used to break ties. For example, suppose we are sorting a list of customers by state and, within each state, by zip code. The primary key would be state, and the secondary key would be the column containing the zip code.

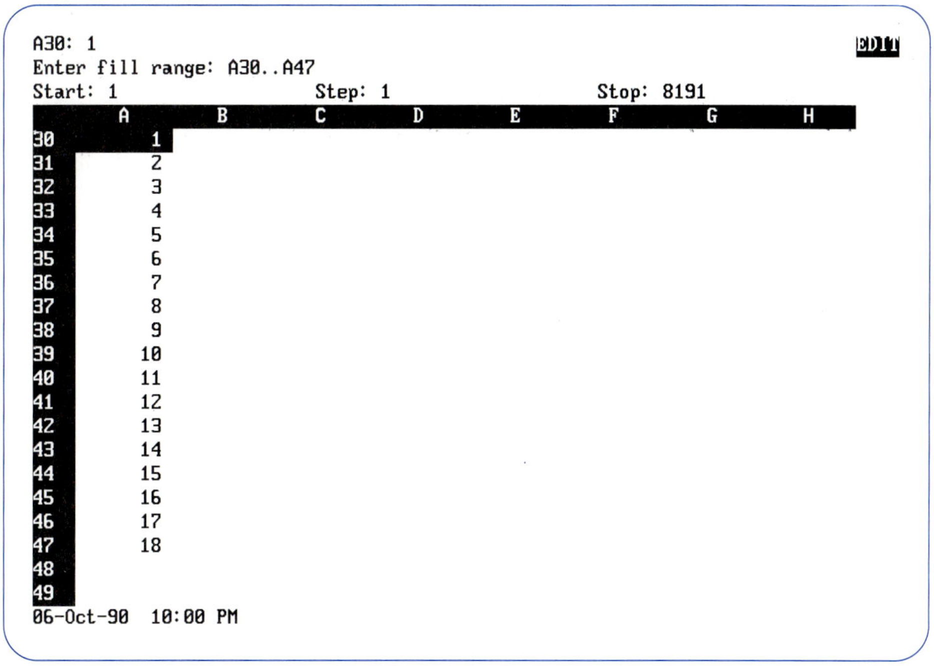

FIGURE 7-1

Data Fill Example (Press **/DF**)

Sorts can be done in **ascending** (increasing) or **descending** (decreasing) **order**. The default is for descending order. Remember that label cells will be sorted according to the computer's code for each character in the cell, beginning at the first character position. If you inadvertently place a space in front of a cell entry, it will be sorted where the space would place it, not where its first true character belongs. The sorting order for cells is:

- space character
- digits
- letters (lowercase come first but in alphabetical order: a A b B c C etc.)
- value cells

Lotus would place these cells in the following ascending order:

```
 adams
1234 (a label)
4567 (a label)
Able
Adams
baker
Baker
BAKER
blood
Charlie
    1234 (a value)
    4567.8 (a value)
```

The second cell is actually a label cell, entered as **'1234** while the last cell is a value cell. Descending order sorts would be in just the reverse order. Sorts are done in-place, meaning the input rows are replaced with the sorted rows.

When doing a sort you must provide the input sort cell range, then specify primary and, optionally, secondary key columns. For each key give the sorting order: **A** is for ascending, and **D** is for descending. If there are column headings, do *not* include those rows as part of the sort range or the column headings will be sorted, too. Be sure to include the *entire* sort range: if you inadvertently omit a column from the range, that column will not be sorted along with the rest of the data items from each record, and the data will be irretrievably mixed. Hint: save the worksheet *before* sorting.

Example: Sorting in Lotus

Suppose the following data represents customers for Smithton, and you wish to sort them by state and then by zip code. The worksheet is called SMCUST.WK1 if you have a copy of the data disk.

1. Retrieve the **SMCUST** worksheet shown in Figure 7-2 with the **/FR** command.

2. To do this sort, give the **/Data** (**/D**) command, then press **S** to enter the Sort menu. The Settings Sheet will display just beneath the sort menu.

```
Data-Range Primary-Key Secondary-Key Reset Go Quit
Select records to be sorted
```

CREATING DATA QUERIES

205

```
A1: [W14] 'SMCUST -- B. McLaren  8/11/89                         READY

         A             B          C      D         E       F
  1  SMCUST -- B. McLaren  8/11/89
  2
  3  SMITHTON RECREATIONAL VEHICLE SALES, INC.
  4              CUSTOMER LIST
  5                                Primary-key    Secondary-key
  6  Customer      Date of Sale  State Zip Code Vehicle
  7  Bellinger, D.   28-Feb-89   IN    46226 Tent Camper
  8  Ammerman, P.    09-Nov-88   OH    44106 Trailer          Data-range
  9  Cottingham, W.  07-Jun-89   IN    47907 Mini-Motor
 10  Wheeler, K.     24-Nov-87   IN    47803 Fifth Wheel
 11  Lindeman, P.    03-Nov-88   IL    66604 Tent Camper
 12  Moore, G.       30-Nov-87   NY    20202 Tent Camper
 13  Delainey, Y.    16-Feb-89   IN    46712 Trailer
 14  Kistner, F.     11-Aug-87   IL    61200 Motor Home
 15  Belvedere, J.   08-Mar-88   NY    20678 Mini-Motor
 16
 17
 18
 19
 20
06-Oct-90  05:43 PM
```

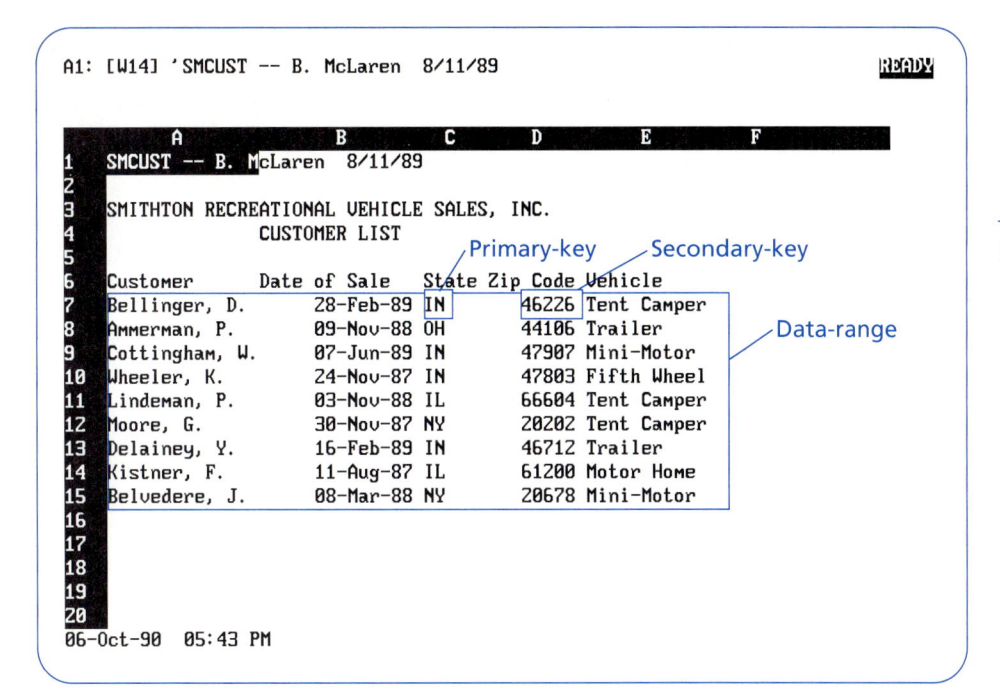

FIGURE 7-2

SMCUST Worksheet for Sort Example

3. Press **D** to specify the Data-range, then enter the cell range **A7..E15** and press **Enter** to complete the entry. If you do not specify the entire data range, Lotus may perform an incomplete sort.

4. Press **P** to select the Primary-Key column, and enter **C7** to specify State. Any cell in that column within the data range is acceptable. The sort order is Ascending, so press **A** at the next prompt.

5. Next press **S** to select the Secondary-Key column. Enter cell **D7** to specify zip code. The sort order is again Ascending.

6. While watching the data range cells, press the **G** key for Go and Lotus will immediately sort the range you specified. The sorted range is shown in Figure 7-3.

Lotus holds the previous Sort settings in memory. The **Reset** option is used to "turn off" the settings you previously selected. If you want to do another sort with different keys, choose the **R** option first to erase previous settings, then enter other parameters normally.

CREATING DATA QUERIES

A data **query** typically requests that records that match certain criteria be identified. Lotus data queries permit the user to **Find** records, **Delete** records, or **Extract** records that match the condition(s) specified. A fourth option, **Unique**, will keep only the first of several identical records; others are not retained. The /Data Query menu is shown below. Its setting sheet also appears beneath the menu on the screen.

MENU

```
Input  Criteria Output Find Extract Unique Delete Reset Quit
Specify range that contains records to search
```

FIGURE 7-3

Example Worksheet After Sorting on State and Zip Code (Press **/DS**)

```
A1: [W14] 'SMCUST -- B. McLaren  8/11/89                        READY

         A              B          C      D       E        F
 1  SMCUST -- B. McLaren  8/11/89
 2
 3  SMITHTON RECREATIONAL VEHICLE SALES, INC.
 4           CUSTOMER LIST
 5
 6  Customer       Date of Sale   State  Zip Code Vehicle
 7  Kistner, F.    11-Aug-87      IL     61200    Motor Home
 8  Lindeman, P.   03-Nov-88      IL     66604    Tent Camper
 9  Bellinger, D.  28-Feb-89      IN     46226    Tent Camper
10  Delainey, Y.   16-Feb-89      IN     46712    Trailer
11  Wheeler, K.    24-Nov-87      IN     47803    Fifth Wheel
12  Cottingham, W. 07-Jun-89      IN     47907    Mini-Motor
13  Moore, G.      30-Nov-87      NY     20202    Tent Camper
14  Belvedere, J.  08-Mar-88      NY     20678    Mini-Motor
15  Ammerman, P.   09-Nov-88      OH     44106    Trailer
16
17
18
19
20
06-Oct-90  05:45 PM
```

Types of data queries include the following:

- The **Find** operation will move the cursor to the first row in the data range that matches the specified criteria, and light the **FIND** mode in the upper right corner. You can use the up or down arrow keys to move the cursor only to other rows that match the criteria specified.

- The **Delete** operation will remove rows from the input range that match the criteria range. You can confirm or cancel the command before each record is deleted.

- **Extract** is probably the most common /Data Query command. It copies matching records from the input range to the output range according to the field names specified in the first row of the output range. It is the most complicated of the commands, but once mastered, provides a powerful means of producing custom reports.

- **Unique** is useful when there are duplicate data records in the input range. Only the first record of each identical group is copied to the output area. If you have worked with a set of data over time it is not uncommon to have duplicate records. Although they could be processed by hand, the Unique command can accomplish this quickly.

Query Data Ranges: Input, Criteria, Output

Lotus uses up to three data ranges when processing a user data query. These ranges specify where the data records are stored within the worksheet, where the criteria or conditions for including records are stored, and where records that match the query are to be placed.

- The **input range** contains the data rows *and* the column headings that serve as field names. The input range is comparable to the sort data-

CREATING DATA QUERIES   207

range, except the field names must now be included. The field names will be used to identify the fields.

- The **criteria range** specifies the field names and the conditions necessary for the record to be processed. Lotus uses a **query-by-example** (QBE) technique for specifying criteria. For simple criteria, the user need just include a condition similar to the one desired. For example, to have all the Indiana customers, the phrase **IN** could be placed in this range. More complex criteria are also possible, such as values greater than a certain figure. Lotus also lets you specify "and" and "or" conditions, such as tent camper sales AND date of sale during 1988. Examples follow at the end of this section.

- The **output range** specifies the field names and the worksheet area where the resulting records that match the criteria are to be placed. Only the listed fields in the output range are copied to the output area, and in the order shown in the first row of the output range. You should be sure to leave enough rows for all matching records to be placed, or an error message will appear. The output range is not used with **Find** and **Delete** queries.

You must be very careful to spell field names precisely the same way whenever they are referenced in these ranges. An extra blank, even at the end of the field name, will confuse Lotus.[1]

Example: Building a Query Find

We will use the Smithton customer worksheet to demonstrate /**Data Query**. This example will use the Find command to locate all tent camper customers.

1. You should retrieve a copy of the file, SMCUST.WK1, used in the previous sorting example.

2. The first step is to create the criteria range. The field name is **Vehicle** and the matching value is **Tent Camper**. Lotus ignores upper-/lowercase differences when matching labels, but different spellings will produce no match. The field name goes in cell A17, and the matching value goes just below it. At the READY mode, place the criteria range in cells **A17..A18**.

    ```
    Vehicle
    Tent Camper
    ```

3. The next step is to activate the /Data Query menu by typing /**DQ**.

4. Before executing the Find command, we must specify the input and criteria data ranges. Press **I** for input range, and enter **A6..E15** as the cell range. The criteria range is specified by pressing **C**, then entering **A17..A18** and pressing **Enter**. Both ranges could be specified by the POINT highlight method: move the cursor to the first cell in the range, press the period key to anchor the beginning of the range, then move the cursor to the last cell in the range and press **Enter**. See Figure 7-4.

---

[1] To check whether the field name cell has an extra blank at the end, move the cursor to that cell and press Edit, F2. The cursor should appear immediately after the last character in the cell.

FIGURE 7-4

Sample Worksheet with Criteria Range

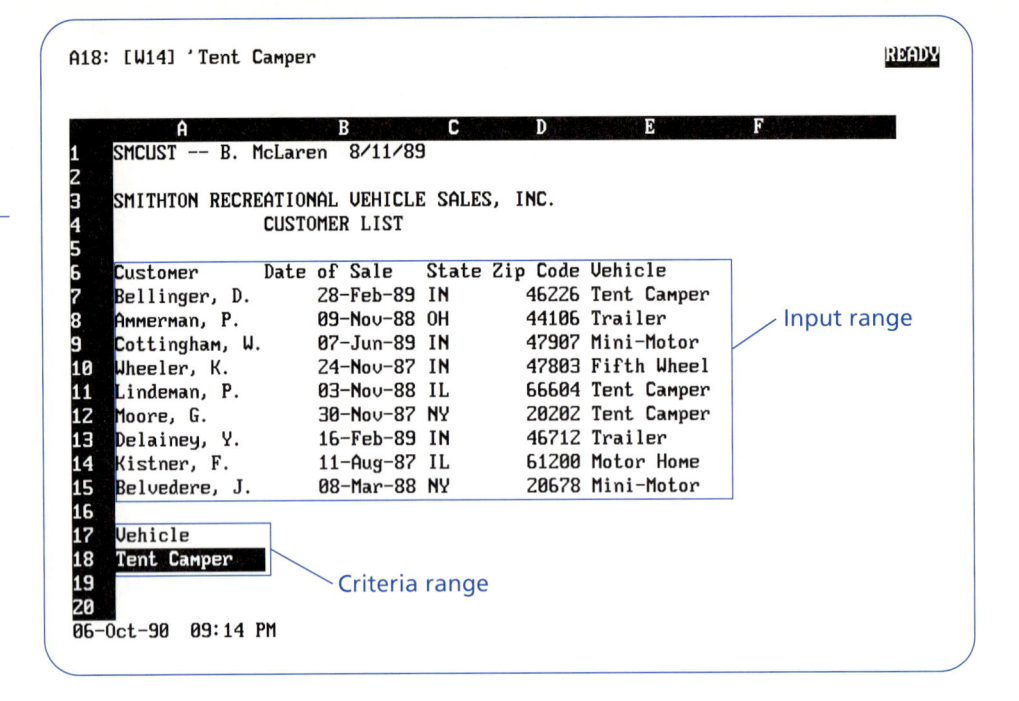

```
A18: [W14] 'Tent Camper                                          READY

         A              B           C     D         E         F
 1  SMCUST -- B. McLaren  8/11/89
 2
 3  SMITHTON RECREATIONAL VEHICLE SALES, INC.
 4              CUSTOMER LIST
 5
 6  Customer       Date of Sale  State Zip Code Vehicle
 7  Bellinger, D.    28-Feb-89   IN      46226  Tent Camper
 8  Ammerman, P.     09-Nov-88   OH      44106  Trailer           ─ Input range
 9  Cottingham, W.   07-Jun-89   IN      47907  Mini-Motor
10  Wheeler, K.      24-Nov-87   IN      47803  Fifth Wheel
11  Lindeman, P.     03-Nov-88   IL      66604  Tent Camper
12  Moore, G.        30-Nov-87   NY      20202  Tent Camper
13  Delainey, Y.     16-Feb-89   IN      46712  Trailer
14  Kistner, F.      11-Aug-87   IL      61200  Motor Home
15  Belvedere, J.    08-Mar-88   NY      20678  Mini-Motor
16
17  Vehicle
18  Tent Camper                        ─ Criteria range
19
20
06-Oct-90  09:14 PM
```

5. Next press the **F** key for **Find**. The cursor will move to the first record matching the criteria. (If this doesn't occur, check to see if you have spelled field names properly, and have specified the proper data ranges. Make sure the data types match—a value field must have a value in the criteria expression.)

6. To view the next record that matches the criteria, use the ↓ key. Lotus will beep when you try to go beyond the final matching record. The ↑ key allows you to view earlier matching records.

7. Press the **Esc** key to leave FIND mode and return to the Query menu.

8. If you need to make changes to the criteria range, **Quit** the Query menu and return to READY mode.

Advanced Criteria Expressions

While extremely powerful, Lotus QBE queries are difficult to master. This section will present several criteria examples to illustrate construction of more advanced queries. Remember to include all the columns of the criteria range when entering the criteria cell range in the query.

We can retrieve the records having zip codes starting with 6 or higher by using the ">" character in the criteria expression. We could use the following criteria to accomplish this query:

```
Zip Code
+D7>59999
```

We can use the @DATE function to access dates within a certain range. Recall that @DATE(89,1,1) represents January 1, 1989. We might use the following criteria to specify sale dates in 1989:

```
Date of Sale
+B7>=@DATE(89,1,1)
```

The entry **+B7** refers to the *first* cell value in the input range, and the >= operator means that this cell must be greater than or equal to the January 1, 1989, date. When you enter the expression, Lotus substitutes a "1" for the condition in cell A18, as shown below.

```
Date of Sale
            1
```

The 1 is the "answer" to the logical expression: because cell B7 reflects a 1989 sale, this expression is "true", and Lotus keeps track of that value as 1. If cell B7 reflected a sale prior to 1989, the condition would be "false," and Lotus indicates that value with a 0.

Suppose we wanted two conditions to be true at the same time. Our criteria range would consist of two columns and two rows. To specify Indiana customers who bought tent campers (State=IN AND Vehicle=Tent Camper), we'd use the following criteria range in adjacent columns.

```
State          Vehicle
IN             Tent Camper
```

This criteria range specifies that *both* conditions must be true in order for the record to match the criteria. If you examine our customer database, you'll find that only a single record matches this criteria—the first customer.

You can also create an "OR" criteria range—one where matching either of two conditions is sufficient to qualify a record. We can use the same criteria, but this time place **Tent Camper** on the row *below* the **IN** state value:

```
State          Vehicle
IN
               Tent Camper
```

Be sure to change the range reference to include the extra row in the criteria range. Any record matching *either* condition will qualify in the query. How many records from our database meet these criteria? (Answer is 6 records.)

Next we'll demonstrate how to specify a range of values in the criteria range. We'd like to find those customers having made purchases during 1988. In other words, Date of Sale *after* December 31, 1987, and *before* January 1, 1989. We might try the following criteria expressions:

```
Date of Sale      Date of Sale
+B7>@DATE(87,12,31)       +B7<@DATE(89,1,1)
```

Will this query give us the proper results? If you enter it, you'll find that Lotus only uses the *first* Date of Sale condition, and ignores the second. We need to introduce the **#AND#** operator, and place both conditions in the same cell:

```
Date of Sale
+B7>@DATE(87,12,31)#AND#B7<@DATE(89,1,1)
```

If you try this query, the proper rows will be selected. The **#OR#** operator may also be used to connect two conditions. The AND term specifies that both conditions must be true in order for the overall condition to be true. The OR term signifies that either side may be true in order for the overall condition to be met.

Example: Building a Query Extract

For this illustration we will use a more complicated criteria expression than before, and copy the selected records to another area of the worksheet. We wish to identify those customers having tent campers or those who purchased in 1987 or earlier.

1. Retrieve the SMCUST.WK1 file from the data disk.

2. Next set up the criteria range. Place **Vehicle** in cell A17 and **Date of Sale** in cell B17. There will be two rows below the field names, indicating that if either expression is true for a particular record, it will be selected. The criteria will be placed in cells **A17..B19**.

   ```
   Vehicle         Date of Sale
   Tent Camper
                   +B7<@DATE(88,1,1)
   ```

3. The result of the condition in cell B19 is false for the first record, represented by a 0 in that cell in Figure 7-5. (True values are represented by a 1.) The Output range must have the field names of the columns we wish to appear in the selected data area. We will specify Customer, Date of Sale, and Vehicle in cells A20, B20, and C20. You should list the fields in the order you wish them to appear. The modified worksheet will look like Figure 7-5.

4. Activate the Query menu at the READY mode by typing **/DQ**. Identify the Input range (**I**) as before, **A6..E15**. The Criteria range (**C**) occupies cells **A17..B19**. The Output range (**O**) will go in cells **A20..C20**.

5. When ready, press **E** to execute the Extract command. The records selected will be copied to the output area where they can be further analyzed, graphed or printed.

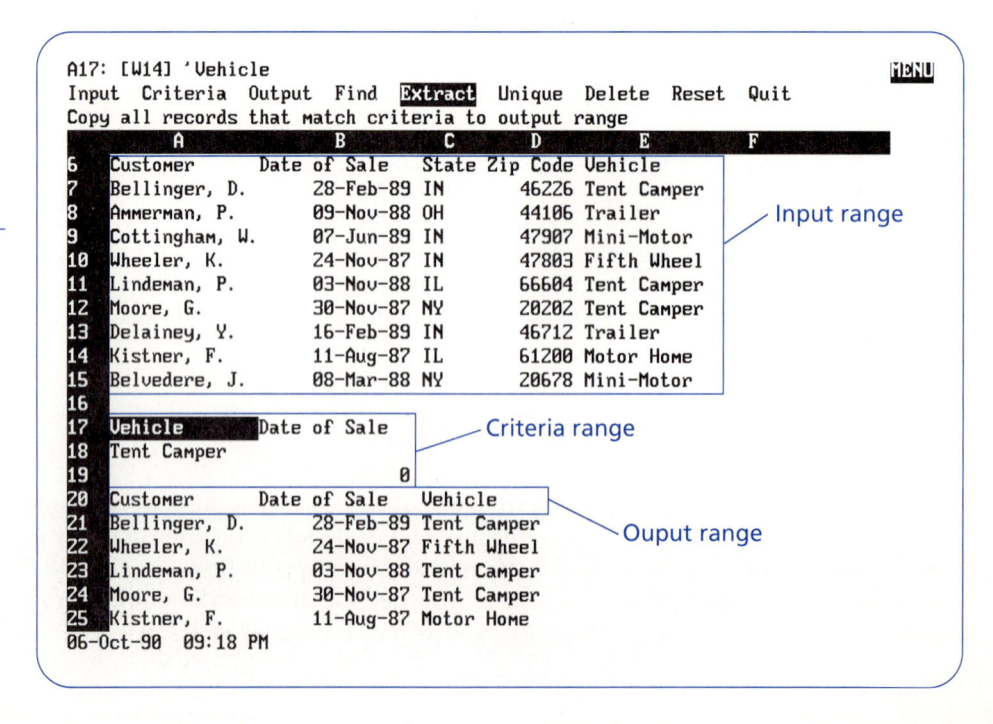

FIGURE 7-5

Query Extract Example Worksheet Showing Data Ranges

```
A17: [W14] 'Vehicle                                           MENU
Input Criteria Output Find Extract Unique Delete Reset Quit
Copy all records that match criteria to output range
       A              B           C       D       E          F
 6  Customer       Date of Sale  State  Zip Code  Vehicle
 7  Bellinger, D.   28-Feb-89    IN      46226    Tent Camper
 8  Ammerman, P.    09-Nov-88    OH      44106    Trailer            ← Input range
 9  Cottingham, W.  07-Jun-89    IN      47907    Mini-Motor
10  Wheeler, K.     24-Nov-87    IN      47803    Fifth Wheel
11  Lindeman, P.    03-Nov-88    IL      66604    Tent Camper
12  Moore, G.       30-Nov-87    NY      20202    Tent Camper
13  Delainey, Y.    16-Feb-89    IN      46712    Trailer
14  Kistner, F.     11-Aug-87    IL      61200    Motor Home
15  Belvedere, J.   08-Mar-88    NY      20678    Mini-Motor
16
17  Vehicle        Date of Sale                   ← Criteria range
18  Tent Camper
19                     0
20  Customer       Date of Sale  Vehicle
21  Bellinger, D.   28-Feb-89    Tent Camper      ← Ouput range
22  Wheeler, K.     24-Nov-87    Fifth Wheel
23  Lindeman, P.    03-Nov-88    Tent Camper
24  Moore, G.       30-Nov-87    Tent Camper
25  Kistner, F.     11-Aug-87    Motor Home
06-Oct-90   09:18 PM
```

Database Statistical @-Functions

Lotus provides several more @-functions that make use of the input and criteria ranges associated with the /**Data Query** command. These functions will *only* consider records from the input area that meet the conditions specified in the criteria range. These functions each begin with **@D** to distinguish them from the similar statistical functions without the D prefix.

In each function, the parameters include the input range ("input"), column "offset" and criteria range ("crit"). The offset parameter refers to the column number of the value referenced from the left side of the input range. An offset of 0 thus refers to the first column.

@DAVG(input,offset,crit)	Calculates the average of non-blank cells in the input range that match the criteria range.
@DCOUNT(input,offset,crit)	Counts the number of non-blank cells in the input range that match the criteria range.
@DSUM(input,offset,crit)	Sums the values in the input range that match the criteria range.
@DMAX(input,offset,crit)	Returns the largest value from the input range that meets the criteria range.
@DMIN(input,offset,crit)	Returns the smallest value from the input range that meets the criteria range.
@DSTD(input,offset,crit)	Calculates the population standard deviation of cells that meet the criteria range.
@DVAR(input,offset,crit)	Calculates the population variance of cells that meet the criteria range.

Example: *Using Database Statistical Functions*

To illustrate the database statistical functions we will need the SMDSTAT.WK1 worksheet with numeric cells, shown in Figure 7-6.

1. Retrieve this worksheet from the data disk using the /**FR** command.

2. The highlighted cell (B18) contains the expression

   ```
   @DAVG(A6..C15,2,A17..A18)
   ```

3. As the criteria range in cells A17..A18 is changed, the @DAVG value will also change. For example, if we replace **Tent Camper** with **Trailer**, the average becomes $9,372.50. What would happen if we left the Vehicle type in cell A18 blank? ($14,384.89 appears, the average of all records. If the criteria value is left blank, all records meet that criteria.)

4. What if we wished to find the *largest* Trailer sale? Place **Trailer** in the Vehicle type cell, **A18**. The @-function would be **@DMAX(A7..C15,2,A17..A18)**. The answer is $9,800.

DATA TABLES

Lotus provides a powerful tool for quickly creating "what-if" scenarios in a worksheet. **Data tables** allow you to substitute one or two parameters into complex formulas, creating a table of alternative values that are based upon those parameters. For example, we might wish to substitute a range of interest rates into an expression to determine the monthly payment on a particular

FIGURE 7-6

Sample Worksheet for Database Statistical Functions

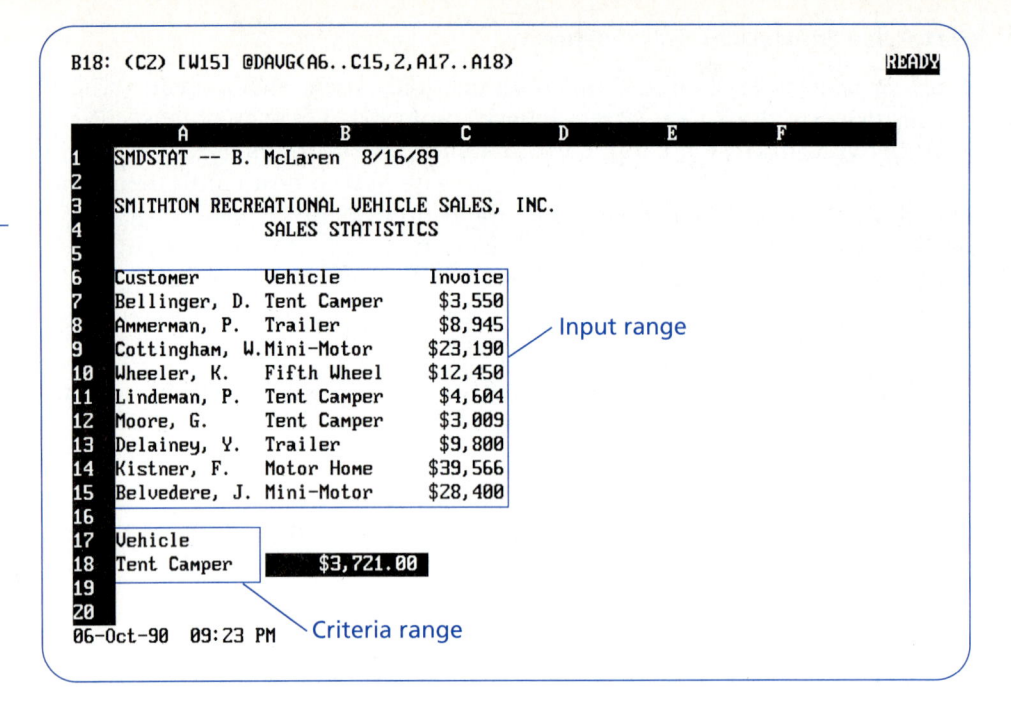

```
B18: (C2) [W15] @DAVG(A6..C15,2,A17..A18)                    READY

         A              B           C         D       E       F
 1  SMDSTAT -- B. McLaren  8/16/89
 2
 3  SMITHTON RECREATIONAL VEHICLE SALES, INC.
 4                SALES STATISTICS
 5
 6  Customer       Vehicle       Invoice
 7  Bellinger, D.  Tent Camper    $3,550
 8  Ammerman, P.   Trailer        $8,945       ─ Input range
 9  Cottingham, W. Mini-Motor    $23,190
10  Wheeler, K.    Fifth Wheel   $12,450
11  Lindeman, P.   Tent Camper    $4,604
12  Moore, G.      Tent Camper    $3,009
13  Delainey, Y.   Trailer        $9,800
14  Kistner, F.    Motor Home    $39,566
15  Belvedere, J.  Mini-Motor    $28,400
16
17  Vehicle
18  Tent Camper    $3,721.00
19
20
06-Oct-90  09:23 PM          ─ Criteria range
```

recreational vehicle. We may also wish to vary the number of months in the loan, creating a two-dimensional table showing payments for combinations of interest rate and length of loan.

To use the /Data Table feature, you must first create the model expression which refers to the base parameters in other cells. Next define the range of cells where the substitute parameters lie. Finally, create the output table by executing the /Data Table command. An example follows.

Example: *One-Parameter Data Table*

The finance manager at Smithton wishes to create a table showing the monthly payment that corresponds to a series of possible interest rates, between 7 and 12 percent. The loan will be over four years, or 48 months. The amount borrowed for this example will be $8,000. The current annual percentage rate is 9.5%, or .095/12 per month. Figure 7-7 shows the spreadsheet.

1. Start with an empty worksheet and create the label entries shown in cells A1, B3, and A5–A8, B5–B7, D5, and D6.

2. Remember that to calculate a monthly payment, you must provide the interest rate per month and the term of the loan in months. Type this expression in cell B8:

   @PMT(B5,B6/12,B7*12)

3. Before creating the data table, we need to enter the interest rate values that will be substituted into the payment expression. Use the **/Data Fill** command (**/DF**) to place the annual interest rate values in cells **D8..D16**. The Start value is **.08**, the Step size is **.005**, and the Stop value is **.12**.

4. Use the **/Range Format** command to format the interest rate values as percentages with one decimal place. The spreadsheet should look like Figure 7-7.

```
B8: (C2) [W15] @PMT(+B5,+B6/12,+B7*12)                              READY

         A                B            C        D        E        F
 1   SMDTABLE -- B. McLaren  8/16/89
 2
 3                    SMITHTON PAYMENT TABLE
 4
 5   Principal              $8,000        Interest
 6   Interest Rate           9.5%         Rate
 7   Term (years)              4
 8   Monthly Payment        $200.99        8.0%
 9                                         8.5%
10                                         9.0%
11                                         9.5%
12                                        10.0%
13                                        10.5%
14                                        11.0%
15                                        11.5%
16                                        12.0%
17
18
19
20
06-Oct-90  09:26 PM
```

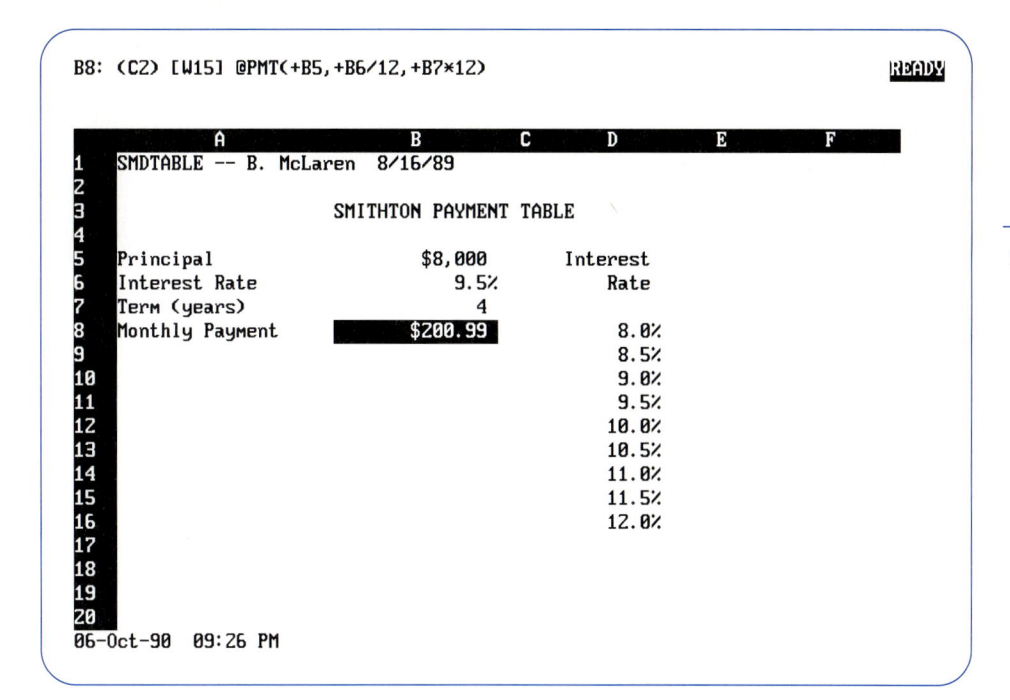

FIGURE 7-7

Sample Worksheet for One-Parameter Data Table

5. Next add the **Monthly** and **Payment** labels in column E, cells **E5..E6**. Place in cell E7 the cell reference of the formula that we wish to substitute into: **+B8**. Use the **/RFT** command to range format cell E7 as Text.

6. Finally we are ready to create the data table. From the READY mode, press **/DT** to activate the Data Table command.

7. Because we are going to substitute a single parameter into the payment formula, type **1** to use the 1-parameter table. When Lotus prompts for the table range, specify cells **D7..E16**. You must include both the column of parameters and the formula reference in your table range.

8. Next Lotus will ask for input cell 1 (the parameter to be substituted for). Reply with cell **B6**, the interest rate for the original formula.

9. When you press **Enter**, Lotus will immediately fill the table with monthly payment amounts for each interest rate. The finished table is shown in Figure 7-8 with the payment amounts formatted as currency type with 2 decimal places.

Example: Two-Parameter Data Table

Let's extend the one-parameter table to the two-parameter case. We will use three loan lengths for this table: 3, 4 and 5 years.

1. Using the SMDTABLE.WK1 spreadsheet from the previous example, let's add a section for the two-parameter table. In cells D20..D21 place the label for **Interest Rate**. In cell F21 place the label **Loan Term (years)**.

2. In cells E22..G22 place the values **3**, **4**, and **5** to reflect loans of those lengths. Repeat step 3 from the previous example for cells D23..D31.

3. Again place the expression **+B8** in cell D22, reflecting the formula into which we will be substituting interest rate and term. Format cell D22 as text

FIGURE 7-8

One-Parameter Data Table Example

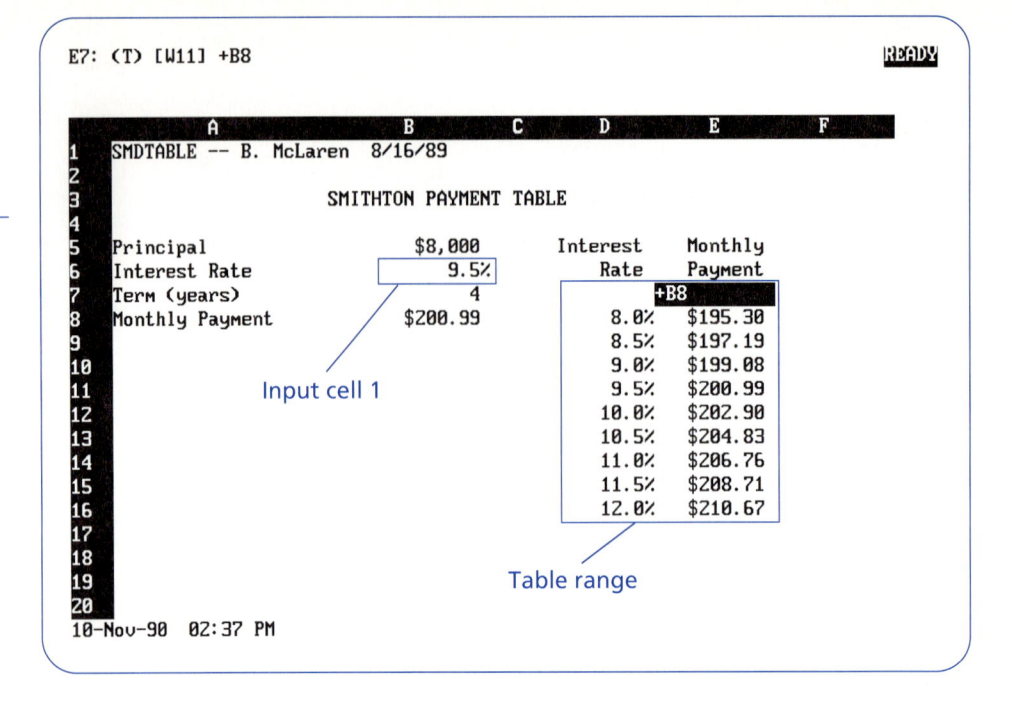

```
E7: (T) [W11] +B8                                          READY

              A           B          C       D        E         F
    1  SMDTABLE -- B. McLaren  8/16/89
    2
    3                    SMITHTON PAYMENT TABLE
    4
    5  Principal          $8,000           Interest   Monthly
    6  Interest Rate       9.5%              Rate    Payment
    7  Term (years)         4                +B8
    8  Monthly Payment    $200.99           8.0%     $195.30
    9                                       8.5%     $197.19
   10                                       9.0%     $199.08
   11              Input cell 1             9.5%     $200.99
   12                                      10.0%     $202.90
   13                                      10.5%     $204.83
   14                                      11.0%     $206.76
   15                                      11.5%     $208.71
   16                                      12.0%     $210.67
   17
   18
   19                                           Table range
   20
   10-Nov-90  02:37 PM
```

with the **/RFT** command. That portion of the spreadsheet will look like Figure 7-9.

4. To fill the table with values, from the READY mode type **/DT** to activate the Data Table command. This time press **2** to reflect a two-parameter data table.

5. The Table Range and other settings are retained from the first data table: press **R** to Reset those settings. The Table range will be cells **D22..G31**. As before, the table range includes the parameters to be substituted into the payment formula and the formula reference itself in cell D22. Note that for two-parameter data tables that formula is placed *above* the first parameter cells. (In the one-parameter data table this reference was placed immediately to the right of the first parameter column.)

6. Input cell 1 will be the interest rate cell, **B6**. Input cell 2 is the loan term, cell **B7**.

7. When you press **Enter** after the last entry, Lotus will immediately fill those cells with payments for combinations of interest rate and term. The spreadsheet in Figure 7-10 shows the results of the /DT2 command; the payment amounts are left unformatted. Notice that the payment ranges from $162.21 for a low-rate, long-term loan to $265.71 for a high-rate, shorter-term loan, all for the same vehicle.

You could, of course, copy the payment expression and substitute the interest rate and term into each formula. But the /Data Table command offers a quick means of doing the same thing with just a few keystrokes. Note that the cells in the Data tables are not formulas and thus will *not* change automatically if you change one of the parameters: you will have to execute the **/DT** command again to see the effects of those changes.

FIGURE 7-9

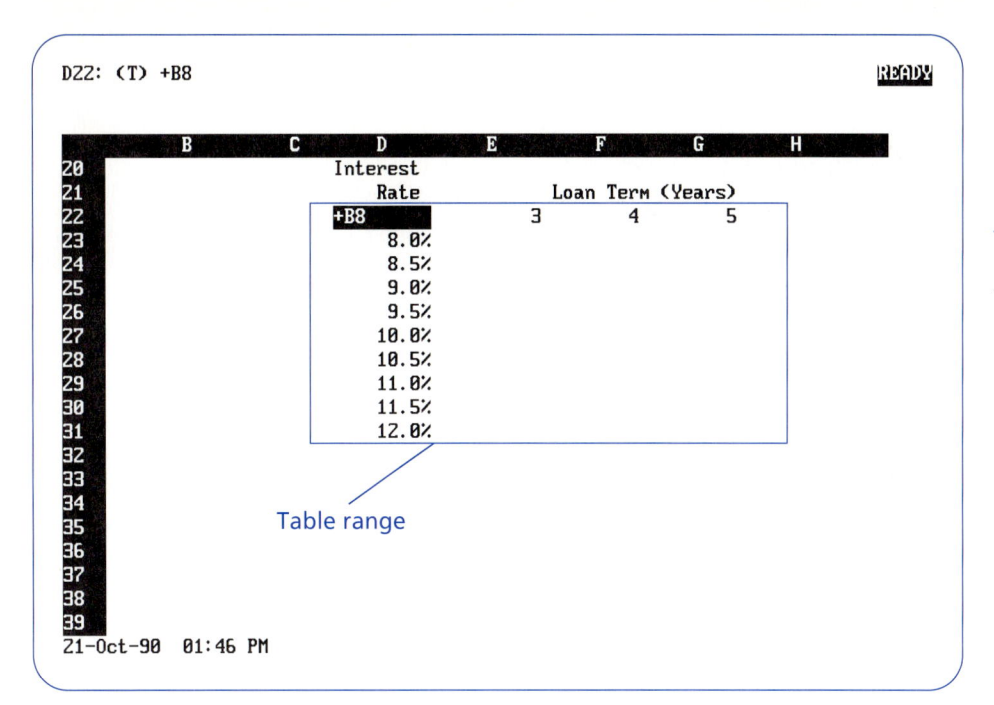

Portion of the Worksheet for the Two-Parameter Data Table Example

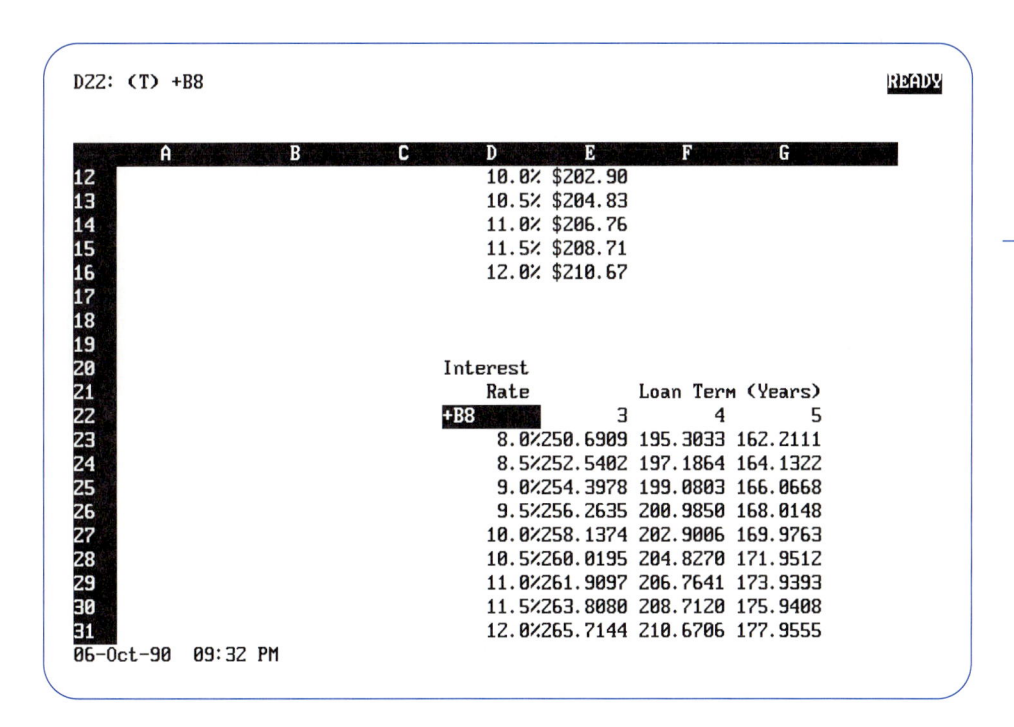

FIGURE 7-10

Payment Amounts Created by Lotus **/Data Table 2** Command

Regression is a useful statistical procedure in which you infer a relationship between two variables, Y and X. Often used for forecasting or predictive purposes, the regression will provide a formula for Y in terms of X: Y = A + BX. A and B are known as the regression coefficients. Thus if we know something about the value of X, the formula may yield knowledge about the value of Y. Lotus will perform the tedious mathematical calculations necessary in regression.

Before discussing the Lotus commands, we can explore regression concepts for a sample situation. Suppose we have collected data about camper sales

OTHER DATA COMMANDS

Regression with 1-2-3

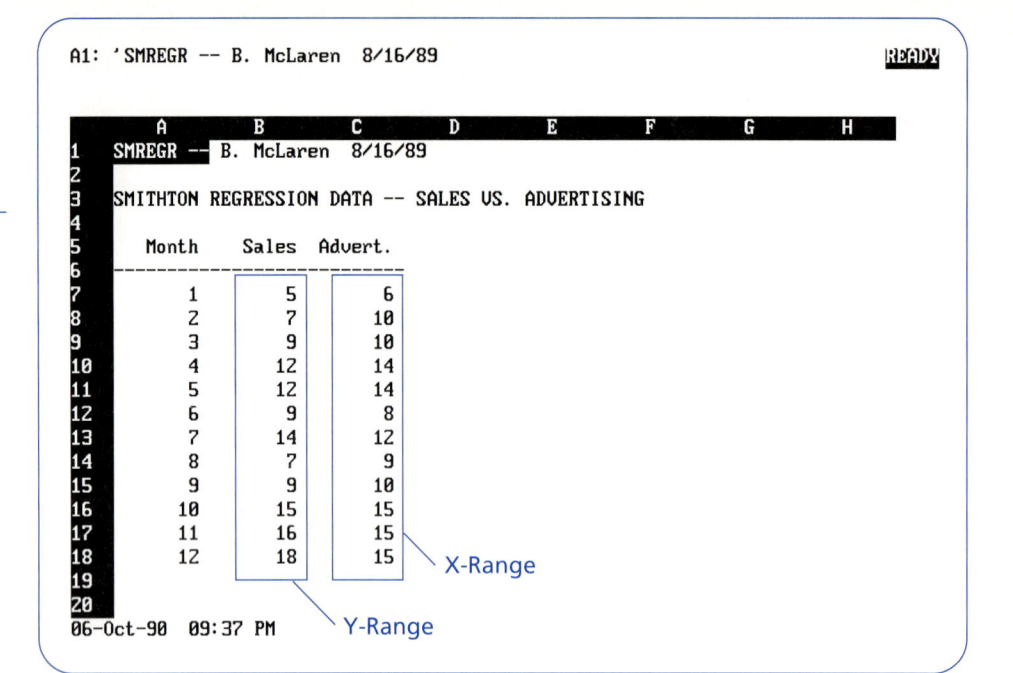

FIGURE 7-11

Regression Data

```
A1: 'SMREGR -- B. McLaren  8/16/89                              READY

       A         B        C       D        E        F        G        H
1  SMREGR --  B. McLaren  8/16/89
2
3  SMITHTON REGRESSION DATA -- SALES VS. ADVERTISING
4
5      Month     Sales    Advert.
6  ----------------------------
7        1        5         6
8        2        7        10
9        3        9        10
10       4       12        14
11       5       12        14
12       6        9         8
13       7       14        12
14       8        7         9
15       9        9        10
16      10       15        15
17      11       16        15
18      12       18        15          X-Range
19
20                         Y-Range
06-Oct-90  09:37 PM
```

and television advertising. Sample data are shown in Figure 7-11 for the SMREGR.WK1 spreadsheet.

Performing a Simple Regression

We would like to explore the relationship between advertising and sales. Intuitively, it seems that the relationship should be positive. Presumably, more advertising should increase sales of campers. We can use a Lotus graph to examine the relationship between these variables. The graph type should be **XY**, with Advertising as the **X** variable and Sales as the **Y** variable. Use the **/GOFGS** command (/Graph Options Format Graph Symbols) to remove the lines connecting the points. The graph is shown in Figure 7-12.

To do the regression, from the READY mode press **/DR**. The Regression menu is shown below.

```
                                                                MENU
   X-Range  Y-Range Output-Range Intercept Reset Go Quit
   Specify independent variables (X range)
```

The **X-range** in the regression is the variable we have control over, or knowledge of. In this case, that is the Advertising. The **Y-range,** or Sales, is the variable we are trying to predict. The **Output-range** is the upper left corner cell of the area where you wish to put the results of the regression analysis. The results table requires 9 rows and at least four columns, so be sure to place it in an unused part of the worksheet—it will overwrite any cells that it occupies. The **Reset** command is used to undo all of the regression settings. **Go** causes Lotus to do the calculations with the current settings.

To do this regression, press **X** and enter **C7..C18** for the X-range. Then press **Y** and respond with **B7..B18** for the Y-range. The **Output** area will be cell **E5**. Press **G** to do the regression. The results are shown in Figure 7-13.

OTHER DATA COMMANDS

217

SMITHTON RV SALES, INC.
Sales Versus Advertising

[Scatter plot of Sales vs. Advertising with data points]

FIGURE 7-12

Graph of Sales Versus Advertising

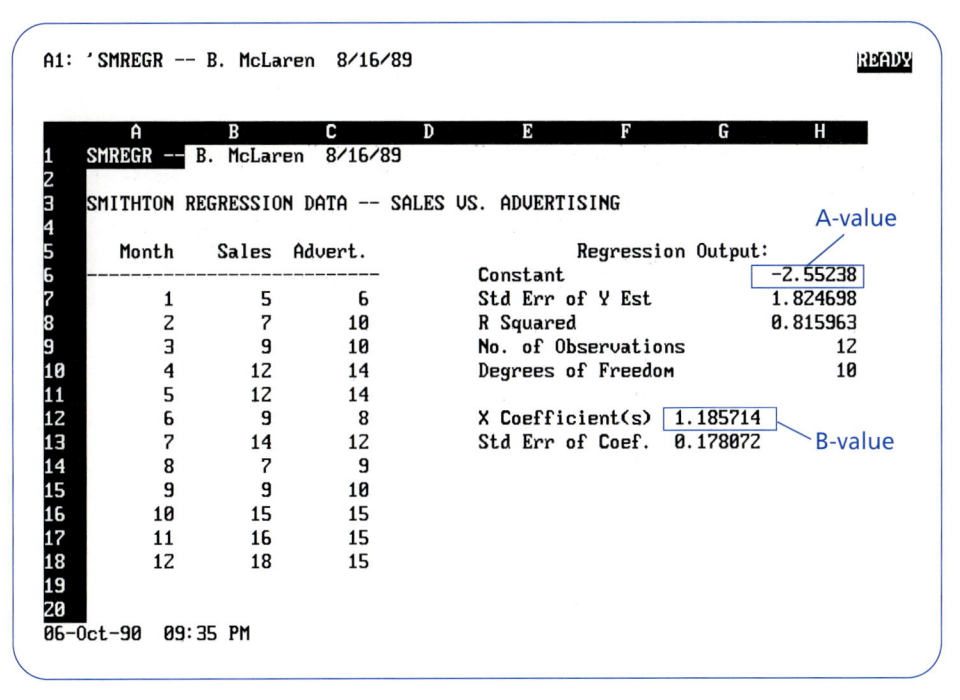

```
A1: 'SMREGR -- B. McLaren  8/16/89                          READY

      A        B       C       D       E       F       G       H
1  SMREGR -- B. McLaren  8/16/89
2
3  SMITHTON REGRESSION DATA -- SALES VS. ADVERTISING
4                                                        A-value
5     Month    Sales   Advert.              Regression Output:
6     ------   -----   ------         Constant              -2.55238
7       1        5       6            Std Err of Y Est      1.824698
8       2        7      10            R Squared             0.815963
9       3        9      10            No. of Observations        12
10      4       12      14            Degrees of Freedom         10
11      5       12      14
12      6        9       8            X Coefficient(s)      1.185714
13      7       14      12            Std Err of Coef.      0.178072    B-value
14      8        7       9
15      9        9      10
16     10       15      15
17     11       16      15
18     12       18      15
19
20
06-Oct-90  09:35 PM
```

FIGURE 7-13

Results of Lotus Regression Command (Press **/DR**)

Interpreting the Regression Results

The regression expression Y = A + BX can be determined from the regression table. The A term is the regression **constant**, shown in cell H6, or –2.55238. The B term is known as the **X coefficient**, shown in cell G12, or 1.185714. Thus Y = –2.55238 + 1.185714*X. To use the regression to predict Sales, we can substitute a value for Advertising into the equation. Assume Advertising for Month 13 will be 16. We might predict that Sales for that period will be –2.55238 + 1.185714*16, or 16.419.

We could draw another graph to examine the regression line estimate, using the regression equation from above. Adding column D, we can use the expression in cell D7 as **+$H$6+C7*$G$12**. We can copy that formula to cells D8..D18. Why did the H6 and G12 cell references use the dollar signs? (Absolute cell references are used in the copy command.) We can graph this column as variable B in the same graph as before. Refer to Figure 7-14.

The other numbers in the regression output are used to interpret that regression statistically. The **R Squared** term, 0.815963, reflects the R^2 statistic, or the percentage of variation in Sales that is "explained" by Advertising alone. The 81% figure indicates that most of the variation in Sales is explained by our regression equation. Other statistics are explained in statistics textbooks.

Performing a Multiple Regression

The **simple regression** explained above refers to using a single X-variable in the regression equation. A **multiple regression** uses two or more X-variables. In the two-variable case, the regression equation would be $Y = A + B_1*X_1 + B_2*X_2$. You must locate the two X-variables in contiguous columns, then tell Lotus that the X-range occupies both columns. The regression output will be very similar, except that there will be another column to the right of the first X-coefficient; the first value is B_1, and the second is B_2.

One would typically use more than one explanatory (X) variable to improve the accuracy of the regression. The R-squared statistic usually increases as more variables are added, but the statistical significance of the regression may not improve. Further information about multiple regression may be found in any standard statistics textbook.

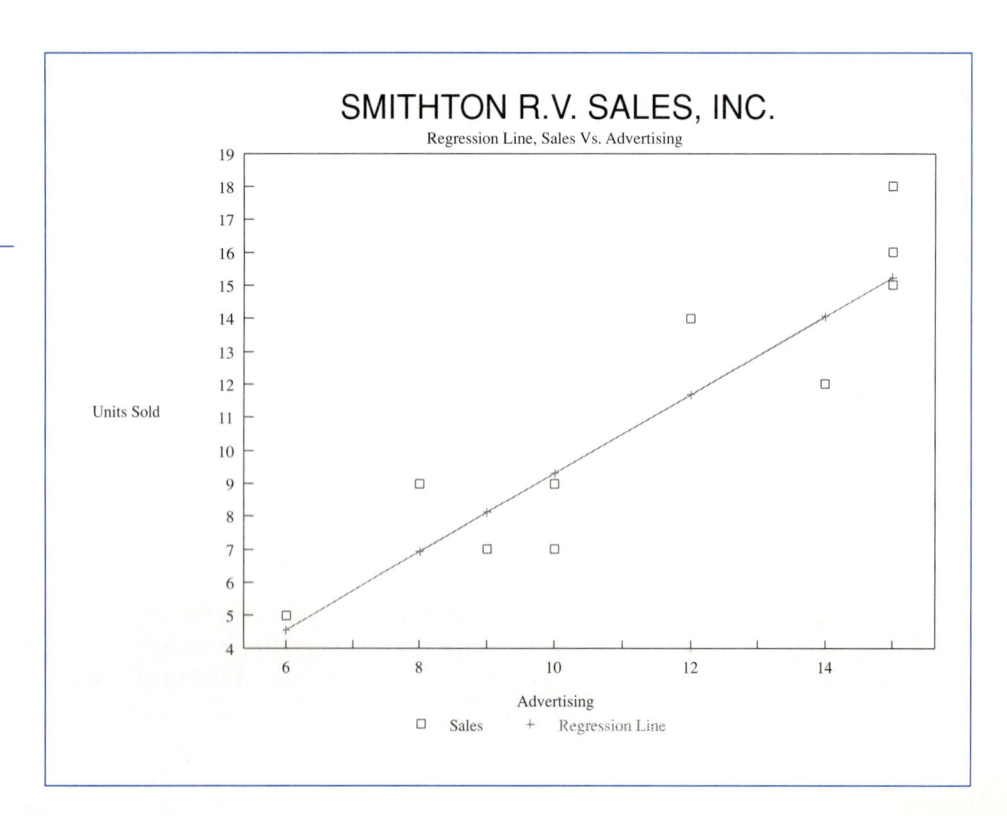

FIGURE 7-14

Illustration of Regression Line

Data Distribution

The **/Data Distribution** command can be used to tally the number of cells falling into a particular range of values. For example, we might wish to count the number of students having a grade point average between 2.5 and 3.0, 3.0 and 3.5, and so forth.

To use this command you must prepare a column for the **bin range,** or interval ranges. The bin range will contain the upper value for each range, entered in ascending order. Lotus will place the count tallies in the column to the right of the bin range so it should be blank to start.

Enter the values into the worksheet. They may reside in a column, a row, or a rectangular cell range. Issue the **/DD** command and provide the **values range** where these cells reside. When prompted, give the bin range. Lotus will examine each cell in the value range and tally it in the column adjacent to the bin range. Items are placed in the smallest bin whose bin range value is greater than or equal to the item value.

Example: Using the Data Distribution Command

We will tally the data distribution of the invoice amounts from the SMDSTAT.WK1 worksheet used in the database statistical function example earlier in this chapter.

1. Retrieve this worksheet from the data disk using the **/FR** command. Figure 7-6 shows this worksheet before the distribution columns are added.

2. Use the **/Data Fill** command to add the bin range values from 5000 to 50000 in cells E7 to E16, or enter them individually.

3. Press **/DD** to activate the Data Distribution menu. When prompted, the values range is **C7..C15**. The bin range is **E7..E16**.

4. As soon as you press **Enter** after the bin range, Lotus places the counts in column F cells just to the right of the bin range, as shown in Figure 7-15. For instance, the 3 in cell F7 means there were three cells less than or

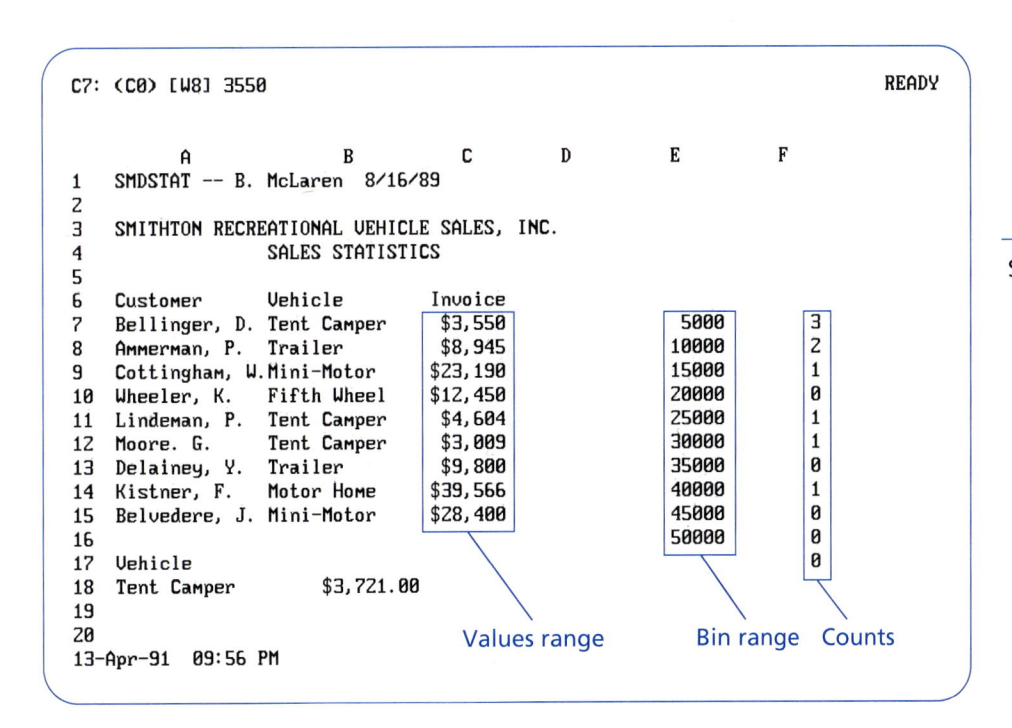

```
C7: (C0) [W8] 3550                                              READY

         A              B              C         D        E        F
 1  SMDSTAT -- B. McLaren  8/16/89
 2
 3  SMITHTON RECREATIONAL VEHICLE SALES, INC.
 4              SALES STATISTICS
 5
 6  Customer       Vehicle        Invoice
 7  Bellinger, D.  Tent Camper     $3,550            5000      3
 8  Ammerman, P.   Trailer         $8,945           10000      2
 9  Cottingham, W. Mini-Motor     $23,190           15000      1
10  Wheeler, K.    Fifth Wheel    $12,450           20000      0
11  Lindeman, P.   Tent Camper     $4,604           25000      1
12  Moore. G.      Tent Camper     $3,009           30000      1
13  Delainey, Y.   Trailer         $9,800           35000      0
14  Kistner, F.    Motor Home     $39,566           40000      1
15  Belvedere, J.  Mini-Motor     $28,400           45000      0
16                                                 50000      0
17  Vehicle                                                    0
18  Tent Camper           $3,721.00                            0
19
20                           Values range     Bin range   Counts
13-Apr-91  09:56 PM
```

FIGURE 7-15

Sample Worksheet for Data Distribution Example

equal to 5000. The 2 in cell F8 means there were two cells greater than 5000 but less than or equal to 10000. The final 0 in cell F17 means there were no values greater than the last bin range value of 50000.

Matrix and Parse Commands

The other /Data operations are used less frequently, and will only be briefly mentioned here.

- The **Matrix** option can be used to multiply two matrices or to invert a square matrix. These operations are not frequently used by business students, but may be useful in statistics or in other applications such as engineering or science.

- The **Parse** operation is helpful in converting data transferred by the /File Import command from another source into Lotus 1-2-3. You can specify a format line that can convert long labels into several columns of labels or numbers. Examples of **Parse** and the **/File Import** command appear in Chapter 9.

CHAPTER REVIEW

Lotus Data Management

The Data management options comprise the third part of Lotus 1-2-3. Data are stored in the worksheet in row form: each row comprises a record, and the columns delineate data fields. Because all of the data must reside in the worksheet in the computer's RAM, Lotus databases are limited by the amount of memory in the computer. In general, only small size databases can be used with Lotus 1-2-3 unless extra memory has been added.

The /Data Menu

A number of useful commands are accessed through the /Data menu. The Fill command permits you to fill consecutive cells with incremental values, saving time and improving accuracy. The increment, or step size, can be fractional or less than zero. Rows can be sorted on one or two key fields with the Sort command. Sorting can be done in descending or ascending order.

Creating Data Queries

Data queries allow the user to identify records that match specified criteria. Data queries use an input range to describe the field names and data values in the database. The criteria range contains the field names and conditions for inclusion in the query. The output range is used for copying records that match the criteria. It specifies the fields that are to be copied.

Types of Data Queries

The Find operation moves the cursor to the first record in the database that matches the criteria. Up and down arrow keys move the cursor to other matching records. The Delete command will permanently delete from the input range any records that match the criteria range. The Extract command will copy any records that match the criteria range to the output range where they can be further analyzed, graphed or printed. The Unique command copies only the first of any identical records that match the criteria into the output area.

Advanced Criteria Expressions

Criteria conditions that appear on the same line must all be met for the overall condition to be satisfied. Criteria on separate lines are used when the record qualifies if any of the criteria conditions are met. AND and OR conditions for a field can be specified in compound conditions.

Database Statistical @-Functions

There are seven additional @-functions that use the input and criteria ranges to select records for inclusion. These functions all begin with @D and apply only to records that meet the criteria range conditions.

Data Tables

Data tables offer a powerful tool to systematically substitute one or two parameters into a cell formula, creating "what-if" tables. After providing a model formula and sample values that are used in the formula, you can build a column or row with values that are to be substituted into the formula. Then the Data Table command will populate the table with values of the formula.

Regression with 1-2-3

Regression is easily accomplished with Lotus. The graphing feature allows you to view potential relationships among the data series. After specifying the X and Y variable ranges, the computer calculates the A and B regression coefficients. The regression equation $Y = A + BX$ can be used to predict values of Y given known values for X. Regression is particularly useful in forecasting applications. Lotus can perform simple or multiple regressions.

Other /Data Commands

Other Data operations include Distribution, Matrix, and Parse. The Distribution command will count the number of values that fall within a particular cell range. Matrix is used to multiply or invert matrices. Parse is useful in breaking up long labels that have been imported with the /File Import command.

KEY TERMS

#AND# operator	Data Find command	Parse
#OK# operator	**(/DQF)**	primary key
@D function	data range	query
ascending order	Data Sort command **(/DS)**	query-by-example (QBE)
bin range	data table	record
constant	descending order	regression
criteria range	field	secondary key
Data Distribution command **(/DD)**	input range	simple regression
	key field	values range
Data Extract command **(/DQE)**	list manager	X coefficient
	matrix	X-range
Data Fill command **(/DF)**	multiple regression	Y-range
	output range	

DISCUSSION QUESTIONS

1. Define the following data terms as they pertain to data management with Lotus 1-2-3:
   a. record
   b. field
   c. primary and secondary keys
   d. ascending.

2. Give the necessary commands to place the values 1 to 36 in cells A10 through A45. How would the command be changed to accommodate the values 36 to 1 in cells A10 through A45?

3. Assuming a descending order sort, how would the following cells be ordered?
   a. Money
   b. moonie
   c. moon
   d. '12990 (label)
   e. 12990 (value)
   f. ABC Foods (leading blank character).

4. Explain why you do not include the field names row in the data range for doing sorts.

5. Explain the purpose of the four kinds of Data Query operations: Find, Delete, Extract, Unique.

6. Why do we use the term "query-by-example" to explain the technique used in Lotus 1-2-3 for setting up data queries?

7. Suppose you have the Smithton Customer database set up with one additional field, INVOICE, in column F. Provide the Criteria Range for each of the following conditions:
   a. Sales above $4,000
   b. All Tent Campers or Trailers
   c. Tent Campers at any price, or Trailers less than $6,000
   d. Indiana customers who have purchased a Motor-Home
   e. Any sales made in February of any year (Hint: use the @MONTH function)
   f. Sales *not* made in Indiana (Hint: set up a condition with <> and put double quotes around IN).

8. Discuss why you would use the @D-functions instead of the similar @-functions without the D prefix.

9. What is a Lotus data table? Why is it used instead of copying the expression manually into the same cells?

10. Suppose you have used Lotus to do a simple regression, with the following Output. The X value for next period is known to be 20.

```
          Regression Output
Constant                    12.093564
Std Err of Y Est             3.011264
R Squared                    0.123456
No. of Observations                 8
Degrees of Freedom                  6

X Coefficient(s)            -1.82635
Std Err of Coef.             1.87456
```

    a. What is the regression equation, Y = A + BX?

    b. What would we expect Y to be in the next period?

    c. Is this a "good" regression? Why?

11. Briefly explain the meaning of the following /Data operations.

    a. Distribution

    b. Parse

    c. Matrix.

EXERCISES

1. Use the /Data Fill command to create the following ranges. Print the resulting worksheet, and write the start, step, and stop values beneath the bottom cell in each range.

    a. Cells A4 to A20 are to be filled with increasing even numbers beginning with 100.

    b. Cells B4 to B20 are to be filled with interest rates starting with 2.9% with .2% as the increment. Use the Percent format with one decimal place.

    c. Cells beginning at C4 are to be filled with loan principal amounts beginning at $10,000, going to $70,000, with $5,000 added to each cell.

    d. Cells D4 to D12 should contain decreasing numbers, beginning with 50, with a step size of -10.

    e. Cells beginning at E4 should contain the dates of 10 consecutive Mondays, beginning with September 11, 1989. Format the cells as Date-1 format.

2. Load the data for the Wabash Animal Hospital from the file called WABASH.WK1 on the data disk (Figure 7-16). We will use this database for the following simple queries. You should print the portion of the worksheet that contains your criteria and output ranges. It is not necessary to print the data rows, although you should print out a copy of the entire worksheet to examine while you prepare and test the queries.

    a. Extract the Date, Owner, and Treatment for all charge Status customers.

    b. Extract the Owner and Pet Type for all Grooming Treatments.

FIGURE 7-16

Sample Data for Exercise 2

```
WABASH--B. McLaren 9/9/89

WABASH ANIMAL HOSPITAL DATABASE

Date       Status      Owner       Pet Type    Invoice   Treatment
08-Nov-88  Paid        Smith       Cat            23     Immunization
08-Nov-88  Paid        Fredericks  Dog            18     Immunization
09-Nov-88  No Charge   Ottinger    Hamster         0     Physical
09-Nov-88  Paid        Hollar      Dog            19     Grooming
10-Nov-88  Paid        Robey       Porcupine      57     Trauma
10-Nov-88  Paid        Rupert      Fish            6     Checkup
12-Nov-88  No Charge   Crow        Dog             0     Follow-up
12-Nov-88  Paid        Bauer       Dog            19     Grooming
12-Nov-88  Charge      Hier        Cat           192     Surgery
14-Nov-88  Charge      Jetson      Cat            46     De-claw
15-Nov-88  Paid        Bell        Cat            19     Grooming
15-Nov-88  Paid        Vanderling  Skunk          33     De-scent
16-Nov-88  Charge      Giltner     Dog           129     Neuter
16-Nov-88  Paid        Butwin      Bird           12     Checkup
17-Nov-88  Charge      Kelly       Cat            18     Immunization
17-Nov-88  Charge      Newsome     Dog            23     Immunization
18-Nov-88  Charge      Azart       Cat            46     De-claw
18-Nov-88  Paid        Williams    Dog            20     Checkup
18-Nov-88  Paid        Dooley      Dog            36     Allergies
19-Nov-88  Pending     Whalen      Snake          18     Checkup
19-Nov-88  Charge      Green       Rabbit         13     Immunization
19-Nov-88  Pending     Cheswick    Cat            19     Grooming
19-Nov-88  Charge      Thump       Cat            89     Surgery
19-Nov-88  Paid        Mijir       Dog            73     Neuter
19-Nov-88  Paid        Palmer      Dog            24     Immunization
19-Nov-88  Charge      Elliott     Guinea Pig     11     Checkup
```

    c. Extract the Date and Owner for all visits before November 16, 1988.

    d. Extract the Owner and Invoice for Dog or Cat Pet Types, and show the output range in alphabetical Owner order. (Hint: Sort your output range after the extract.)

    e. Extract the Owner and Treatment for Immunization Treatments to Dogs.

3. Using the data file from the previous problem, print the data input range area in the order given by the following sort instructions. Sorts should be in ascending order unless otherwise indicated.

    a. Sort the input range in alphabetical order according to the owner's name.

    b. Sort the input range in order by treatment type.

    c. Sort the input range by pet type (primary order) and by treatment type (secondary order).

d. Sort by invoice amount in descending order (primary key) and by date (descending order as secondary key).

4. Use the @D-functions to answer the following queries about the Wabash Animal Hospital database. You should print the criteria range and the result of the function. Write the exact function next to the cell containing its result.

   a. Determine the overall average Invoice amount for all visits.

   b. Calculate the maximum Invoice for Dogs.

   c. Find the number of dog and cat visits in the database.

   d. Determine the average cost for the non-dog visits.

   e. Find the average visit cost for the period November 10–16, 1988.

5. Ben Moore has recently been promoted to a new marketing position with a company that compensates sales personnel on a commission basis. The base salary is $12,500 with a 7% commission on sales above $100,000. Prepare a one-parameter data table for Ben that will illustrate possible total salary amounts for varying sales amounts. Your data table should include sales amounts from $120,000 to $200,000 in $10,000 increments. For example, for sales of $130,000, total salary would be 12500 + (130000 – 100000)*.07. Avoid using commas in Lotus cell expressions, but all money amounts should be formatted with Currency format and no decimal places.

6. Modify the previous problem to account for two commission rates. The base rate of 7% is used for sales amounts less than $150,000. For the portion of sales above that amount, the commission rate increases to 8.4%. For example, the commission for sales of $160,000 would be 12500 + 50000*.07 + (160000–150000)*.084. Use the @IF function in the base cell expression to test the sales amount. Your solution should use a one-parameter data table, and a single base formula. Also print the cell formulas for your worksheet.

7. You are to build a two-parameter data table for the Valley State Bank that will calculate the cumulative interest for a mortgage loan of varying interest rates and length of loan. Assume the loan principal is $50,000. Cumulative interest can be found by subtracting the loan principal from the total payments amount. The annual interest rate should vary from .08 to .12 by .005 increments. The loan lengths should be 15, 20, 25, and 30 years, representing the second parameter in the data table. As an example calculation, the loan payment for a $50,000 loan over 20 years at 10.5% is about $499.19. Total payments over the life of the loan are 20*12*499.19 or $119,805.60. Therefore the cumulative interest is $119,805.60 – $50,000 or $69,805.60. Print out cell formulas for your worksheet.

8. The Anderson Motor Freight Company is trying to forecast demand over the next five years. They have accumulated time-series data for total pounds shipped from the past ten years, shown in Figure 7-17. They have asked you to prepare a least squares linear regression model that might be used to predict demand for the next five years. Use the Lotus /Data Regression command to build a worksheet for this purpose. Use the **a** and **b** values directly from the model in your forecasts for years 11–15. Comment on the validity of your forecast results, based upon the statistical results of the regression. Also print a line graph showing the 10 years of data.

FIGURE 7-17

Sample Data for Exercise 8

Year	Demand (in thousands of pounds)
1	20,400
2	24,200
3	26,700
4	25,900
5	27,100
6	30,200
7	28,800
8	31,000
9	31,400
10	30,200

FIGURE 7-18

Sample Data for Exercise 9

Sales	Year	Advertising	CPI	Price
18,406	1	220	1.050	2.19
25,690	2	245	1.060	1.99
25,700	3	250	1.060	2.05
30,440	4	270	1.090	1.89
27,450	5	275	1.120	2.15
29,350	6	260	1.080	1.99

Is it possible to plot your regression equation ($Y = a + bX$) on the same graph? Explain.

9. International Chemical Corporation recently hired you as market research analyst in their Consumer Chemicals Division. They have collected some market and economic data possibly related to demand for their new biodegradable trash bag product. The data are shown in Figure 7-18 for the past few years.

   a. Prepare and print an XY graph relating Sales and Advertising. Use symbols only in the plot. Does there seem to be a relationship between these items?

   b. Use the Lotus /Data Regression command to prepare a multiple regression analysis of sales for the product. The independent variables for this regression are Year, Advertising, Consumer Price Index, and Price. What is the multiple regression equation?

   c. Suppose that next year the Advertising budget was 280, the CPI expected at 1.07, and the Price at 2.04. What would be the expected Sales? Do you have confidence in your forecast? Why?

10. Use the WABASH.WK1 database file discussed in Exercise 2 to prepare a data distribution tally. Print a copy of the worksheet for part a and for part b.

a. Prepare a data distribution for the Invoice amount of this worksheet. Your bin ranges should be from $0-24.99, $25-49.99, $50-74.99 and so forth, in $25 increments.

b. Prepare a second data distribution showing the number of visits on each day, from November 8, 1988 through November 19, 1988. Remember that the bin range must be a numeric amount entered in ascending order. How does Lotus store dates internally, before they are formatted?

Because many customers have been interested in refinancing their home loan, the Mortgage Loan Department wants to evaluate different loan options using Lotus 1-2-3 templates. Three worksheet templates are needed for different purposes. Each template should be carefully labelled, and have instructions for its use.

CHAPTER 7 PROJECT
PEAK STATE BANK
MORTGAGE LOAN
DEPARTMENT

PAYMENT

The PAYMENT template is a large data table which shows the interest rate going down the left, and the term going across the top. Interest rates are to vary by 0.5%, from 8.0% to 13.0%. Term will vary from 15 to 30 years in one-year increments. The body of the table should be the monthly payment for a $1 loan. To find the monthly payment for a particular mortgage, locate the proper combination of rate and term, then multiply the table figure by the principal of the mortgage. Because this will be a very wide table, you must determine a way of organizing and printing the data. Remember to format the cells to include a sufficient number of decimal places.

AMORT

This template will take a set of loan factors (principal, interest, term) and prepare a loan amortization table for each payment, giving the amount going to pay principal and interest, the cumulative interest, and the remaining balance of the loan. Calculate the loan payment and round to the nearest penny. The loan factors should be placed in a parameter block above the table, and used in the cell expressions in the table. For the first table, assume these factors:

```
Principal = $80,000    Interest = 10.75%    Term = 20 years
```

In addition to the amortization table, you should prepare a line graph showing the remaining balance at the end of every year of the loan. Use horizontal grid lines, and plot the data with symbols only. Because Lotus requires that plotted values reside in contiguous cells, you will need to move the year-end values to another location in the worksheet.

ACCEL

For this template you will use the same parameters from the AMORT table. For this loan the customer will pay *1/2 of the regular payment* every two weeks, thus making 26 half-payments during the year. The net effect is to make an extra month's payment each year, thus retiring the loan earlier. Redo the amortization table to calculate the cumulative interest for this accelerated payment plan and determine when the loan is repaid. Compare these values with those from the regular loan.

8

Lotus Macros and Advanced Spreadsheet Topics

Objectives

After completing this chapter, you should be able to:

- Explain the advantages of using macros.
- Create and execute a simple keystroke macro.
- Create an autoexecute macro.
- Create a menu macro.
- Describe various add-in products that can be installed within Lotus 1-2-3.
- Compare Lotus 1-2-3 Release 2.2 with other Lotus releases.
- Discuss other competing spreadsheet programs.

INTRODUCTION

This chapter describes the use of Lotus **macros**—stored keystrokes that can be "played back" at any time. A macro is a set of instructions to be performed, just like any computer program. Macros save time and improve accuracy. They are particularly useful with repetitive operations and for large spreadsheets. You can build custom menus with Lotus macros, including the moving-bar command line with prompt or help messages below, similar to the usual Lotus command menus.

There is a large market for third-party programs—those that are added into (**add-ins**) Lotus itself and become part of Lotus command menus. Some might argue that these programs make up for shortcomings in the Lotus 1-2-3 program, while others say they increase the usability of Lotus. Several add-in products are discussed, including the HAL natural-language interface that makes it easier to interact with Lotus. Add-in products are available to provide word processing capability within Lotus, to link to databases, and to analyze the worksheet expressions for possible errors.

MACROS AND THE LOTUS COMMAND LANGUAGE

Macros are an alternative way to perform Lotus commands and functions. Stored as labels in one or more cells in the worksheet, macros contain commands, text and numbers. They can be executed from the keyboard or called from another macro. Macros can:

- Save time because keystrokes need only be entered one time.

- Reduce errors because the keystrokes have been entered correctly when the macro was created.

- Allow relatively untrained individuals to use complex worksheets.

- Provide additional help messages when using menu macros.

- Access certain programming commands that are available within macros that cannot be accessed from the keyboard.

- Autoexecution macros can begin executing as soon as a worksheet is retrieved, or when the 1-2-3 module is loaded.

Overview of Macro Applications

The simplest and most common kind of macro is the **keystroke macro**. It holds the same keystrokes you would type when entering a command or filling cells with data. Keystroke macros can be used to format a range of cells, to print a certain range in the worksheet with selected print options, to save the worksheet, or to accomplish a host of other actions. For example, you might create a macro to save the worksheet, convert the cells to Text format, print the worksheet with Cell-formulas, then retrieve the original worksheet:

1. Save the worksheet: **/FS <filename> Enter**

2. Change cell formats to Text: **/RFT <cell-range> Enter**

3. Print the resulting worksheet: **/PPR <cell-range> Enter AGPQ**

4. Retrieve the original worksheet with its range formats: **/FR <filename> Enter.**

Of course, there are some details missing from these steps. No actual file name is given for the Save or Retrieve commands. The range for the text cell format is not given, nor is the range for the Print command. We'll return to this macro later in the chapter.

More complicated macros present menus of user commands that are used just like the built-in Lotus 1-2-3 commands. The macro presents a series of choices on line 2 at the top of the screen, in the Control Panel. The line just below contains a help message or other useful prompt for selecting that command. The user can move the cursor to each command choice; the next line changes as the cursor moves to another choice. **Menu macros** allow an inexperienced person to use a complicated spreadsheet by offering structured choices to the user. It is much easier to select from a limited set of choices than to remember the choices without a menu.

A third type of macro can do **programming** operations, most of which are not available from the keyboard. The Lotus command language offers macro commands for looping, conditional testing based upon user inputs, and branching. Whole systems can be constructed with menu macros that call upon keystroke macros to complete a specific task.

Creating a Simple Macro

There are several steps in creating a simple keystroke macro.

- You must first design the worksheet, choosing where the data will be located and selecting a location for the macro that will not interfere with any data.

- Next the macro itself should be designed *on paper*, based upon the desired function(s).

- To test the design, you should then execute the keystrokes as regular commands, noting the specific keystrokes needed to accomplish the task.

- Then enter the macro in one or more adjacent cells in the same column. Documentation for the commands in each cell should be placed in the column immediately to the right of the macro cells.

- Finally, select a range name for the macro. Lotus macro names consist of the backslash (\) and a single letter, A–Z, or the digit 0. Examples include \F, \P, \0. Release 2.2 offers the same one-character naming convention, but also allows longer range names for macros. For example, in Release 2.2 you could use descriptive names such as PRINT, SAVE, and POST ENTRIES as macro names.

Macros can be tricky for new users, and usually require **debugging** before they will work. Debugging involves testing the macro, locating any incorrect keystrokes and making any necessary changes. Lotus will ordinarily run the macro at full speed, stopping only at errors or when the macro is finished. You can slow it down for debugging purposes, using the STEP mode. More on this will appear later in this chapter.

Executing a Macro

To run a macro after it has been entered in the worksheet, hold down the **Alt** key and press the letter of the macro's name. Release 2.2 users can run longer-named macros by pressing **Alt-F3**, then typing the macro's name and pressing **Enter**. No special indicators are lit unless you are executing the macro in single-step mode for debugging purposes, in which case the **STEP** indicator lights. The macro will follow instructions vertically within that column in your worksheet until it reaches a blank cell.

232 Chapter 8 — Lotus Macros and Advanced Spreadsheet Topics

Example: *Simple Range Formatting Macro*

In this example we will use a macro to format the cells in the original Smithton spreadsheet. We want to format the range C7..E17 as Fixed with no decimal places. The macro should be placed to the right and below the spreadsheet so that the two will not interfere with each other in case rows or columns are inserted or deleted.

1. Retrieve the **SMITHRVP.WK1** file from the data disk. It should appear like the one in Figure 8-1.

2. We will pick cell AA30 as the starting point for the macro. Press **F5** (Goto) and type **AA30** as the location. Press **Enter** to complete the Goto entry.

3. The keystrokes for accomplishing the range formatting would be /RFF0 <Enter> C7..E17 <Enter> if typed on the keyboard. The first Enter completes the 0 decimal places entry, while the second completes the cell range entry. Lotus uses the **tilde** (~) as a substitute for the **Enter** key in a macro. We will call the macro \F, short for the formatting macro. The name of the macro is not considered a part of the macro, but is placed to the left of the first cell of the macro as part of the documentation. Put **'\F** in cell AA30. Don't forget the beginning single apostrophe.

4. The macro itself is short enough to go into a single cell, AB30. The contents of the macro will be:

   '/RFF0~C7..E17~
   Note: The sixth character is zero.

   The apostrophe (single quote) character at the beginning of the macro indicates that this is a label cell. What would happen if you forgot to start with the apostrophe? (Lotus would execute the slash command immediately, bringing up the command menu, not storing it in the current cell.)

5. Because the macro is wider than the default column width of column AB, we should widen the column. Go to cell AB30, press **/WCS**. When prompted for the new column width, type **15** and press **Enter**. This is not a part of the

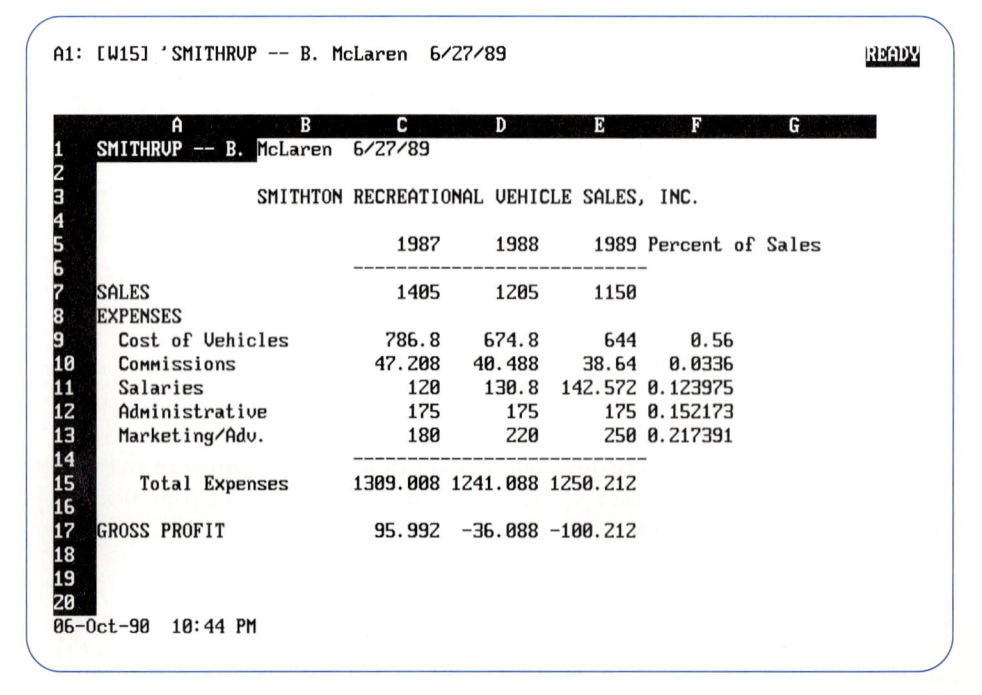

FIGURE 8-1

Unformatted Worksheet Before Macro Has Executed

```
A1: [W15] 'SMITHRVP -- B. McLaren  6/27/89                          READY

         A           B          C          D          E       F        G
 1  SMITHRVP -- B. McLaren  6/27/89
 2
 3              SMITHTON RECREATIONAL VEHICLE SALES, INC.
 4
 5                         1987       1988       1989 Percent of Sales
 6                         ----       ----       ----
 7  SALES                  1405       1205       1150
 8  EXPENSES
 9    Cost of Vehicles     786.8      674.8       644      0.56
10    Commissions          47.208     40.488     38.64    0.0336
11    Salaries             120        130.8     142.572  0.123975
12    Administrative       175        175        175     0.152173
13    Marketing/Adv.       180        220        250     0.217391
14                         ----       ----       ----
15    Total Expenses      1309.008  1241.088  1250.212
16
17  GROSS PROFIT            95.992   -36.088  -100.212
18
19
20
06-Oct-90  10:44 PM
```

macro, but will let us see all of the keystrokes in that cell when the documentation comments are added in cell AC30.

6. Place the comment **Format Expense cells as Fixed** in cell AC30.

7. Next we must name the macro. Enter the **/RNC** (/Range Name Create) command. At the Enter name prompt, type **\F** as the range name and press **Enter**. The cell range is a single cell, **AB30**. The macro range does not include the name label in cell AA30 or the comments in cell AC30.

8. Before you execute the macro, move the cursor to cell A1 by pressing the **Home** key. To run (execute) the macro, hold down the **ALT** key and press the **F** key. If all is well, the cells will appear in Fixed format, rounded up or down as needed, with no decimal places. If you have an error, recheck the expression in cell AB30. Don't forget the two tildes (~) in the macro expression.

Example: Modifying a Simple Macro

In the previous example we neglected to format the Percentages cells as Percent formats. We will use the same worksheet. We need to add a second line to the macro.

1. Go to cell AA30 (**F5 AA30**). Add the following expression in cell AB31:

   '/RFP1~F9..F13~

2. Put the comment **Format Percentage cells as Percent** in cell AC31. Double-check the spelling in both cells.

3. You need to add the second row to the macro cell range. Enter the **/RNC** command and specify **\F** as the range name. When prompted for the range, enter **AB30..AB31**. Remember—don't include the macro name label or the comments in the cell range. The macro should appear in the spreadsheet as in Figure 8-2 below.

```
AA30: '\F                                                      READY

         AA          AB              AC          AD          AE          AF          AG
30   \F          /RFF0~C7..E17~    Format Expense cells as Fixed
31               /RFP1~F9..F13~    Format Percentage cells as Percent
32
33
34
35
36
37
38
39
40
41
42
43
44
45
46
47
48
49
07-Oct-90   01:16 PM
```

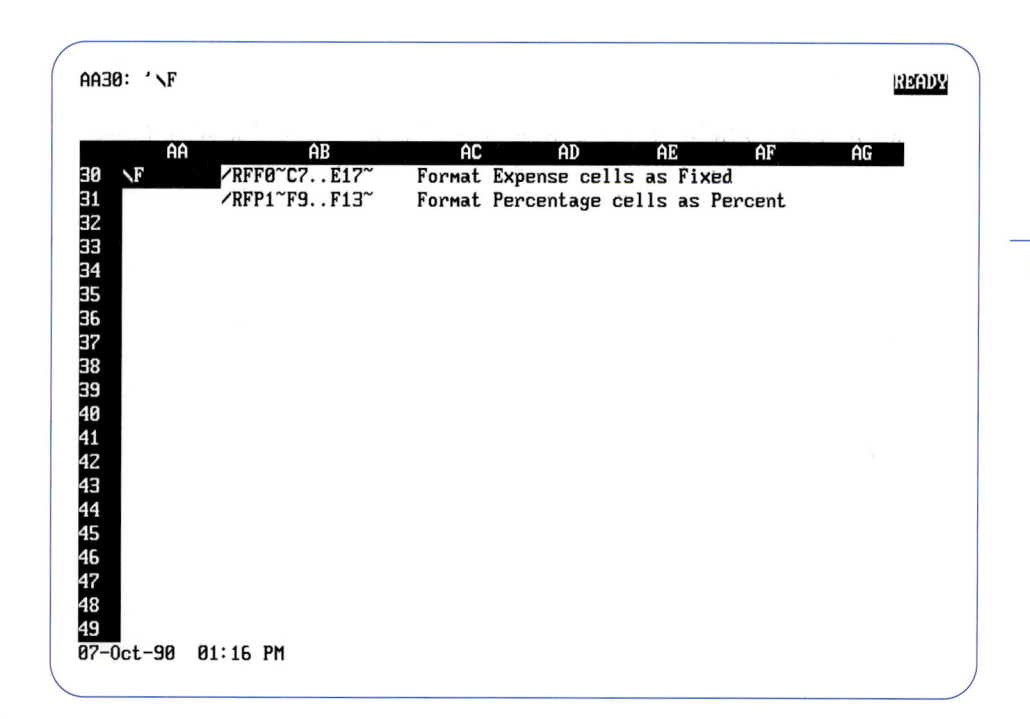

FIGURE 8-2

Format Macro Instructions

Chapter 8 — Lotus Macros and Advanced Spreadsheet Topics

FIGURE 8-3

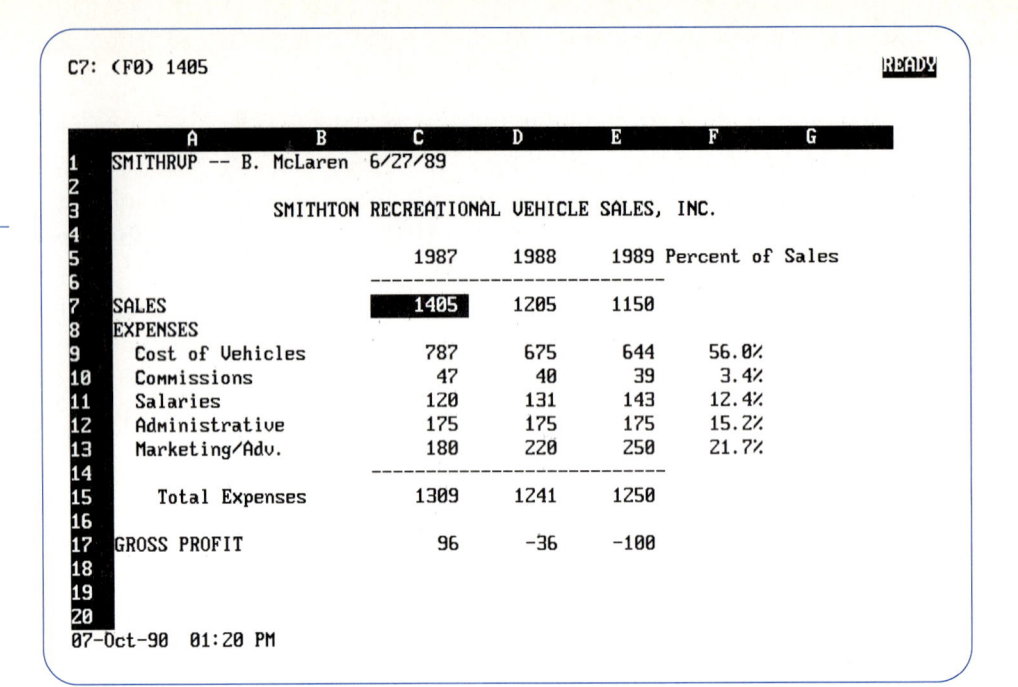

Results of \F Macro

```
C7: (F0) 1405                                                    READY

          A        B        C        D        E        F        G
 1 SMITHRUP -- B. McLaren 6/27/89
 2
 3                  SMITHTON RECREATIONAL VEHICLE SALES, INC.
 4
 5                        1987     1988     1989 Percent of Sales
 6                        ----------------------------
 7 SALES                   1405     1205     1150
 8 EXPENSES
 9    Cost of Vehicles      787      675      644     56.0%
10    Commissions            47       40       39      3.4%
11    Salaries              120      131      143     12.4%
12    Administrative        175      175      175     15.2%
13    Marketing/Adv.        180      220      250     21.7%
14                        ----------------------------
15    Total Expenses       1309     1241     1250
16
17 GROSS PROFIT              96      -36     -100
18
19
20
07-Oct-90  01:20 PM
```

4. Return to the A1 cell (**Home**) and press **Al**t F to run the macro. The spreadsheet should be formatted in Figure 8-3. If you add up the 1989 Expenses, they total 1251. But the spreadsheet's total is 1250. Why don't they match? (Even though the numbers appear as rounded values, Lotus uses the un-rounded numbers internally when adding cells together.)

Example: A Printing Macro

Next we will prepare a more complicated macro to print the spreadsheet with several print options. The macro will print the cells in range A1..G17, skip three lines, then print the macros and comments (cell range AA30..AG39) beneath the spreadsheet. It will change the left margin from 4 to 2, and change the top margin from 2 to 6.

The macro is shown in Figure 8-4, along with comments. Note that we have divided this longer macro into separate lines where only a single task is accomplished in each line. Debugging is much simpler if you follow this principle. We will name the macro \P, and can run it by typing **Alt-P**.

Several additional comments are needed for this macro. The first Clear command is used to eliminate any previous print settings. The Options command leads to choosing Left and Top Margin settings. The Align command will zero out the line counter so that Lotus will print a full page. The "LLL" command will skip three lines after the first printout. For the second part of the report, we clear only the Range settings. We have added the P (Page) command on the last line, just after the G, to skip to the top of the next page after printing. The report should look like Figure 8-5 after the macro executes.

Release 2.2 Learn Feature

Release 2.2 of Lotus has a **Learn feature** that will automate the process of entering keystrokes. Because it is easy to make mistakes in entering (as labels) the keystrokes directly into the macro cells, the Learn feature should greatly

```
AA33: '\P                                                    READY

          AA        AB          AC      AD      AE      AF      AG
     33   \P      /PPCA         Print to printer, clear all settings
     34           RA1..G17~     Range is A1..G17
     35           OML2~MT6~Q    Select left and top margins
     36           AGLLL         Align printer, print (Go), skip 3 lines
     37           CR            Clear range setting only
     38           RAA30..AG39~  Range for macro cells, including comments
     39           GPQ           Print (go) and quit to READY
     40
     41
     42
     43
     44
     45
     46
     47
     48
     49
     50
     51
     52
     07-Oct-90  01:20 PM
```

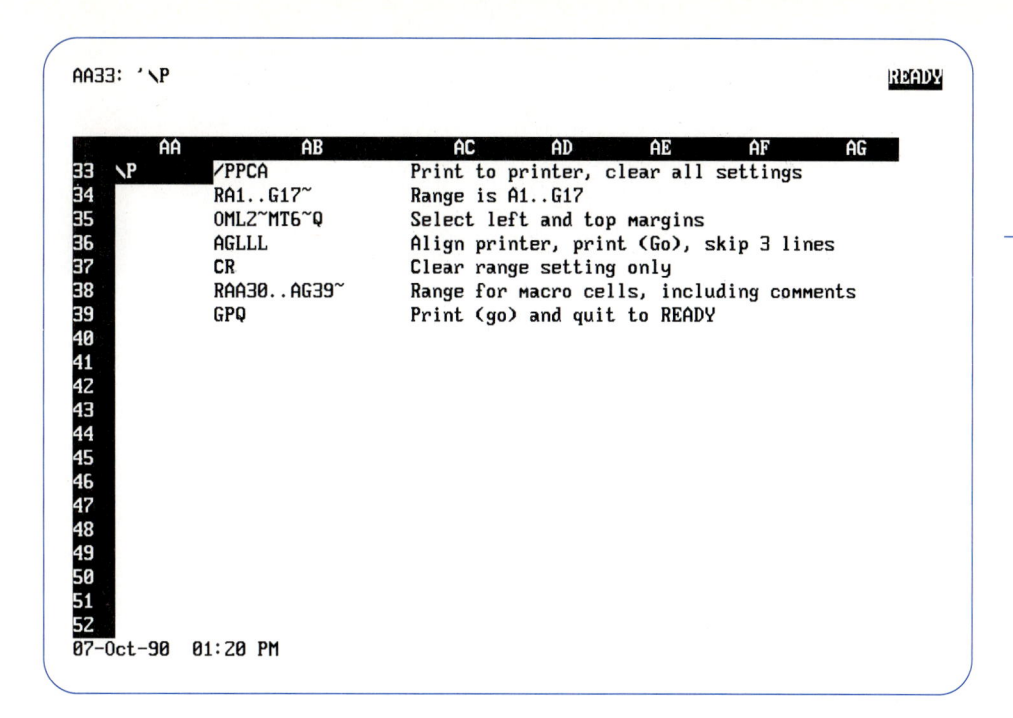

FIGURE 8-4

Printing Macro Instructions

reduce the potential for errors. This new function will memorize keystrokes as you execute the desired keystrokes and commands. You must choose a location on the worksheet for Lotus to store your keystrokes with the **/Worksheet Learn Range** command, then move the cursor to that cell where you would ordinarily begin entering commands. Press **Alt-F5** to begin recording your keystrokes. Enter commands as you would normally. To turn off the recording feature, press **Alt-F5** again. We'll demonstrate the Learn feature in an example.

Example: *Creating a Macro Using the Learn Feature*

In this example we will use the Lotus Release 2.2 Learn feature to create a graph macro. The example will use the same Smithton worksheet.

1. If you have not already retrieved the **SMITHRVP.WK1** worksheet, do so with the **/FR** command.

2. We will place the macro near the worksheet only to illustrate how the graph is prepared. Press **/WL** to activate the Worksheet Learn menu. Press **R** to specify Range, then enter **A22..A32**. This allows for the macro to be placed in a vertical column in those cells.

3. Press **Alt-F5** to activate the Learn feature. The LEARN indicator will appear in the bottom row of the 1-2-3 display. All keystrokes you make will be placed in the worksheet at the Learn range specified in step 2. Enter the following graph commands:

4. Press **/G** to start the graph menu. Press **R** for Reset, then **G** to clear all graph settings. Press **T** for Type, then **B** to indicate Bar graph.

5. Press **X** to enter the X-range, then enter **C5..E5** to specify the Year labels as the X-range. Press **Enter** to complete the entry.

6. Press **A** to specify the A-range, then enter **C7..E7** to specify the 1987 Sales amounts as the A-range. Press **Enter** to complete the entry.

FIGURE 8-5

Printout After \P Print Macro Executes

```
SMITHRV -- B. McLaren   6/27/89

           SMITHTON RECREATIONAL VEHICLE SALES, INC.

                      1987    1988    1989 Percent of Sales
                      ----------------------------
SALES                 1405    1205    1150
EXPENSES
   Cost of Vehicles    787     675     644    56.0%
   Commissions          47      40      39     3.4%
   Salaries            120     131     143    12.4%
   Administrative      175     175     175    15.2%
   Marketing/Adv.      180     220     250    21.7%
                      ----------------------------
   Total Expenses     1309    1241    1250

GROSS PROFIT            96     -36    -100


\F       /RFF0~C7..E17~    Format Expense cells as Fixed
         /RFP1~F9..F13~    Format Percentage cells as Percent

\P       /PPCA             Print to printer, clear all settings
         RA1..G17~         Range is A1..G17
         OML2~MT6~Q        Select left and top margins
         AGLLL             Align printer, print (Go), skip 3 lines
         CR                Clear range setting only
         RAA30..AG39~      Range for macro cells, including comments
         GPQ               Print (Go), eject page and quit to READY
```

7. Next press **O** to enter the Options menu, then **T** to activate the Title menu. Press **F** to specify the First title, and enter **Sample Graph Macro**. Press **Enter** to complete the entry.

8. Press **T** to use the Title menu, then **Y** to specify the Y title. Type **Sales** and press **Enter**.

9. Press **Q** to Quit from the Options menu, then **V** to View the graph.

10. Press **S** to Save the graph, then give **SMGRAPH** as its name. Press **Enter** to complete the entry. Press **Q** to leave the /Graph menu.

MACROS AND THE LOTUS COMMAND LANGUAGE

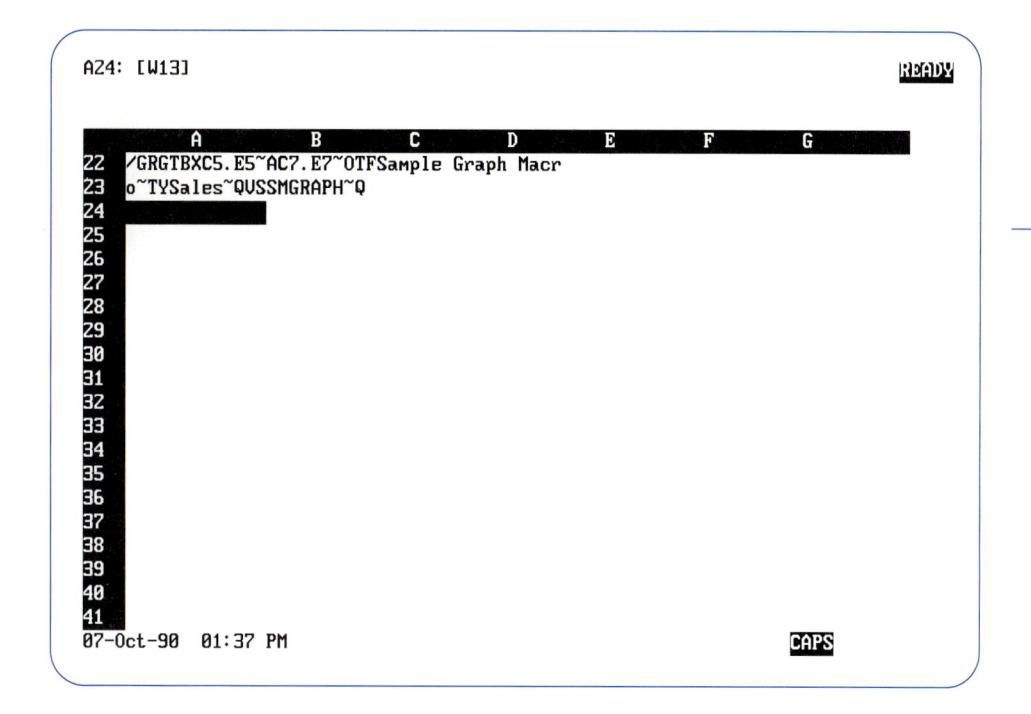

```
A24: [W13]                                              READY

          A         B        C        D       E       F       G
22  /GRGTBXC5.E5~AC7.E7~OTFSample Graph Macr
23  o~TYSales~QUSSMGRAPH~Q
24
25
26
27
28
29
30
31
32
33
34
35
36
37
38
39
40
41
07-Oct-90  01:37 PM                                    CAPS
```

FIGURE 8-6

Sample Graph Macro Created with Lotus Learn Feature

11. Now that the macro is complete, press **Alt-F5** to terminate Learn mode. The LEARN indicator will disappear.

12. Use the **/RNC** command to name the macro. When prompted for the name, enter **MACRO GRAPH** and press the **Enter** key. The range for this macro will be **A22..A22**. (Only the first cell of the macro must be named.)

13. To execute the macro, press **Alt-F3**. When prompted for the name, type **MACRO GRAPH** and press **Enter**. You should see the screen blink as the /Graph commands are executed. Lotus will pause after displaying the graph. Press any key to continue.

14. The macro will finish by saving the image of the graph as a .PIC file. If the file already exists, you'll see a Cancel or Replace prompt message. Choose **Replace** and the new image will replace the existing one.

15. The macro will look like Figure 8-6.

Debugging a Macro

Because Lotus macros are tricky to enter, many macros may not run properly at first. *Debugging* involves diagnosing errors and fixing them, usually an iterative process that takes several tries. The usual indication of an error is the Lotus "beep" and possibly the ERROR mode indicator in the upper right corner when you try to run the macro. To fix the errors, interrupt the macro and return to READY mode by typing **Ctrl-Break**. If possible, obtain a printed copy of the macro as it is entered in your worksheet, and study the listing for errors. Leaving out a tilde (or inserting an unneeded one) is responsible for many macro failures.

Lotus offers a **single-step mode** in which the macro executes a single keystroke at a time. This mode allows you to view the results of the macro after each command, and may pinpoint the error. To invoke the STEP mode, press **Alt-F2** *before* you execute the macro. You should see STEP in the status line area at the bottom of the screen. Release 2.2 users will also see the current macro cell in the lower left corner, with the next macro instruction highlighted. To single-step through the macro, press the space bar and the next macro keystroke will execute. When you discover where the error lies, interrupt execution of the macro by typing **Ctrl-Break** and return to READY mode. Then edit the macro cell as you would any cell. Once fixed, you can execute the macro with the **Alt** key as before. You remain in single-step mode until you turn it off with **Alt-F2**.

The Lotus Command Language

The three simple keystroke macros just described consist of the usual Lotus keystrokes. There are many powerful commands available for more complicated macros. These commands consist of Lotus keywords surrounded by curly braces: { }.

Keyboard Macro Commands

Each of the function keys and cursor keys has an equivalent command keyword, shown in Figures 8-7 and 8-8. The commands marked with an asterisk can have a repeat count inside the braces: {down 3} is equivalent to {down} {down} {down} but saves space in the macro line.

For example, you might wish to use the {graph} command to display the current graph settings using the data in the worksheet. The {abs} command can be used just like pressing the **F4** function key to convert a relative cell address to an absolute address. The {bigright} command can move the display over one screen at a time, just as the **Ctrl-Right** command does. The {query} command will display the results of the most recent /**Data Query** command. Likewise, the {table} command will construct a Data Table using the most recent instructions.

Advanced Macro Commands

There are 50 **advanced macro commands** available in Release 2.2 in addition to the keyboard commands. In general, their format is similar to the previous commands: {command}. Some of the instructions use arguments which also appear within the braces, separated from one another by commas: {command arg1, arg2}.

The commands can be broken into several categories.

- **Data Manipulation commands** will place data into cells or erase cells.

- **File Manipulation commands** are useful when writing to or reading from a text file.

- **Flow Control commands** manipulate the sequence of macro cells, including branching, looping, conditional branching, and ending a macro.

- **Interactive macro commands** handle communications with the user, including user inputs, custom menus, and suspending macro execution.

- **Screen Control commands** manipulate display of various portions of the screen, including the worksheet frame, Control Panel, mode indicator, and the worksheet area.

A few of the more useful commands are described below. Refer to the Lotus manual for details on other available commands. Two dots after the command name {commandname ..} mean that arguments may follow the command. The comments may describe the arguments.

{?}	Suspends macro execution to let the user respond to or complete an entry. Pressing **Enter** will restart the macro.

Keystroke	Meaning	Macro Command
BkSp	Backspace	{backspace} or {bs}
Ctrl-←	Big Left	{bigleft}
Ctrl-→	Big Right	{bigright}
Del	Delete	{delete} or {del}
↓	Down	{down}* or {d}
End	End	{end}
Esc	Escape	{escape} or {esc}
Home	Home	{home}
←	Left	{left}* or {l}
PgDn	Page Down	{pgdn}
PgUp	Page Up	{pgup}
Enter	Return	~
→	Right	{right}* or {r}
↑	Up	{up}* or {u}

* A count can be added, as in {down 3}

FIGURE 8-7

Keyboard Macro Commands

Keystroke	Meaning	Macro Command
F4	Absolute Reference	{abs}
F9	Calculate	{calc}
F2	Edit Cell	{edit}
F5	Goto	{goto}
F10	Graph	{graph}
F1	Help	{help}
F3	Name	{name}
F7	Query	{query}
F8	Table	{table}
F6	Window	{window}

FIGURE 8-8

Function Key Macro Commands

{subroutine} — Will call the macro called "**subroutine**". After reaching a {return} command or a blank cell, control returns to the calling macro. See {branch}.

{beep} — Sounds the beep in the computer. Can add a tone-number argument (1, 2, 3, or 4) to vary the tone.

{branch loc} — Jump to the cell address or range name given by "**loc**" and continue executing macro commands. {branch} is frequently used with the {if} command to conditionally execute different sections of the macro. Control does not return to the point of the {branch} command.

{breakon} — Enables use of **Ctrl-Break** command to terminate macro execution.

{breakoff}	Disables use of **Ctrl-Break** command to terminate macro execution.
{for c,start,stop,step,sub)	Creates a for-loop with successive calls to the subroutine called "**sub**". "**c**" is the counter cell address which begins at value "**start**", continues until "**stop**" is reached, and uses the "**step**" size at each iteration. For example, **{for A7,1,10,2,SUB9}** will call the subroutine "**SUB9**" 5 times. The counter begins at **1** and is stored in cell **A7**. Each time through the loop **2** is added to the counter, until the counter is greater than **10** (taking on the values 1, 3, 5, 7, and 9).
{getlabel prompt,loc}	The **prompt** message will be displayed in the Control Panel and the macro will wait until the user enters a label and presses Enter. The label will be placed in the cell address given by "**loc**". Enclose the prompt message in quotes.
{getnumber prompt,loc}	Similar to {getlabel}, this command prompts for a numeric value to be entered by the user and places it in the specified cell address "**loc**".
{if cond}..	If the condition given by "**cond**" is true, the command immediately following the {if} in the same cell is executed next. Otherwise, control passes to the command immediately below the {if}. The **cond** condition is a Lotus logical expression such as +C7>10.
{let loc,entry}	Places **entry** (value or label) in the cell location given by "**loc**". Entry may be an expression or a constant. Differs from the {get..} commands in that {let} doesn't get the value from the user.
{menubranch loc}	Displays a custom menu in the Control Panel starting in the first cell given by "**loc**". User can move the cursor to various choices in the menu and see help/prompt messages about each. Pressing **Enter** (or the first letter) while highlighting a given choice in the menu will cause 1-2-3 to execute the macro code beneath that cell. See menu example.
{menucall loc}	Same as {menubranch} except that after the menu choice at cell "**loc**" executes, control is returned to the macro command that called the menu.
{quit}	Stops a macro immediately, and user regains keyboard control. A blank cell in a macro has the same effect as {quit}.
{return}	Finishes execution of a subroutine and returns control to the cell beneath the command that called the subroutine when used with {subroutine} and {menucall}. Continues next loop iteration when used with {for}.

{wait time} Suspends macro execution and displays WAIT mode indicator until "**time**" specified. For example, **{wait @ now + @ time (0, 0, 10)}** will wait 10 seconds from now. When that time occurs, the macro continues execution normally. **Ctrl-Break** will function during the wait interval unless {breakoff} is in effect.

Creating a Menu Macro

We will create a custom menu macro that gives the user four choices in the same kind of moving-bar menu used in 1-2-3 menus:

- Print the worksheet.
- Save the worksheet.
- Exit from the macro back to the READY mode.
- Quit from 1-2-3.

Overview of Menu Macros

The macro commands are shown in Figure 8-9. The menu macro consists of two parts, the \M menubranch macro and the menu area starting in cell AB44. The menu area consists of three parts:

- The capitalized words in row 44 for each choice will appear in the Control Panel as a user menu.
- A descriptive message from row 45 will appear beneath the menu as we use the cursor to highlight a menu choice.
- The instructions associated with each menu choice appear beneath row 45. Each macro will execute the commands within its column until an empty cell or {menubranch} command is reached.

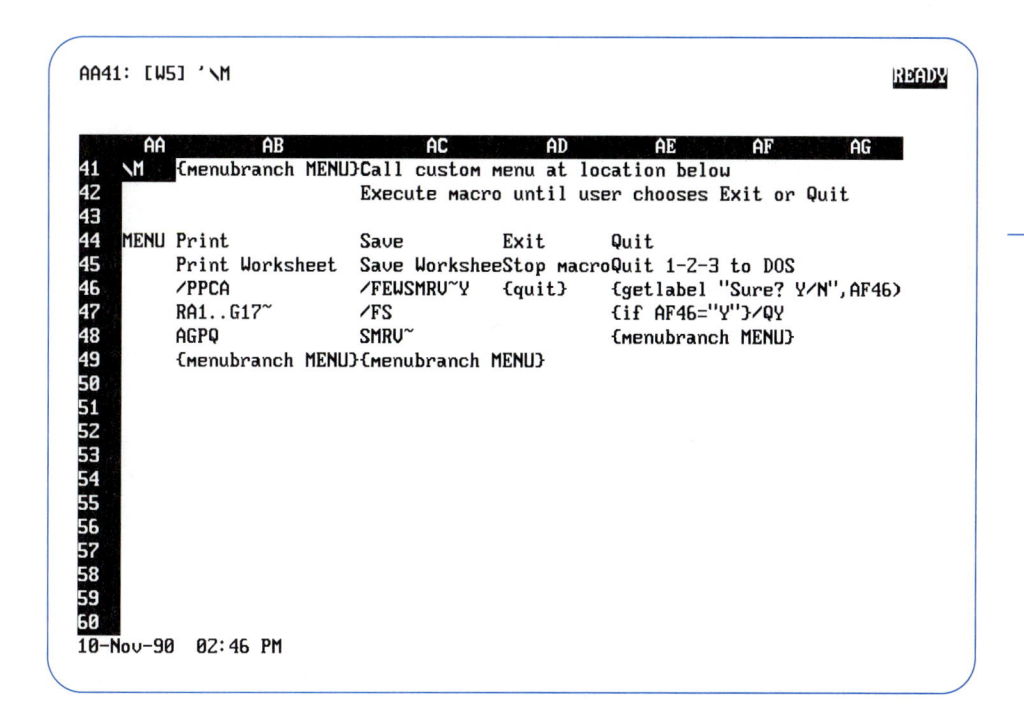

```
AA41: [W5] '\M                                                    READY

       AA        AB             AC           AD         AE        AF        AG
41    \M     {menubranch MENU}Call custom menu at location below
42                             Execute macro until user chooses Exit or Quit
43
44    MENU Print             Save         Exit       Quit
45         Print Worksheet   Save WorksheeStop macroQuit 1-2-3 to DOS
46         /PPCA             /FEWSMRU~Y   {quit}     {getlabel "Sure? Y/N",AF46}
47         RA1..G17~         /FS                     {if AF46="Y"}/QY
48         AGPQ              SMRU~                   {menubranch MENU}
49         {menubranch MENU}{menubranch MENU}
50
51
52
53
54
55
56
57
58
59
60
10-Nov-90  02:46 PM
```

FIGURE 8-9

Menu Macro Instructions

FIGURE 8-10

Print Macro Instructions

```
Print                    Menu line choice
Print Worksheet          Help/prompt line for Print choice
/PPCA                    Clear all print settings
RA1..G17~                Range for printing
AGPQ                     Align printer, go, page eject, quit /P menu
{menubranch MENU}        Go back to main menu
```

FIGURE 8-11

Save Macro Instructions

```
Save                     Menu line choice
Save Worksheet           Help/prompt line for Save choice
/FEWSMRV~Y               Erase existing SMRV file, if any
/FS                      Save file
SMRV~                    File name is SMRV
{menubranch MENU}        Go back to main menu
```

It is difficult to provide documentation with menu macros because the four choices in the menu must be in adjacent columns. Below we will show each macro separately with descriptive comments about each step. The MENU range name refers to the upper left cell of the menu area, in this case cell AB44.

The Print Macro

The first macro choice is **Print**, similar to the first print macro developed earlier. Shown in Figure 8-10 with additional comments *not included in the worksheet,* it ends with another {menubranch MENU} command which displays the main menu again.

The Save Macro

The second macro choice is to **Save** the file. The macro is written so that it will work properly whether the SMRV file already exists on the default drive or not. It first attempts to erase the SMRV.WK1 file. The **Y** response at the end of the **/File Erase Worksheet** line will either confirm erasing the file, or will clear the error message that will appear if SMRV.WK1 does not already exist. Then the file can be saved normally. The Save macro ends with a return to the main menu. The Save macro is shown in Figure 8-11.

The Exit Macro

There are two ways to end the menu macro—exit from the macro back to the READY mode, or quit from 1-2-3 back to DOS. The code in Figure 8-12 will process the request to exit the macro by using the {quit} command. There is no need for the {menubranch MENU} command at the end because the {quit} will stop the macro's execution. The {quit} command merely returns to READY mode, not out of 1-2-3.

FIGURE 8-12

Exit Macro Instructions

```
Exit                              Menu line choice
Stop macro, Return to READY       Help/prompt line for Exit choice
{quit}                            End macro execution
```

FIGURE 8-13

Quit Macro Instructions

```
Quit                              Menu line choice
Quit 1-2-3 to DOS                 Help/prompt line for Quit choice
{getlabel "Sure? Y/N",AF50}       Enter response, save in cell AF50
{if AF50="Y"}/QY                  Only quit if AF50 holds "Y"
{menubranch MENU}                 Otherwise return to main menu
```

The Quit Macro

The Quit choice will issue the /**Quit** command to leave 1-2-3. Because this is a serious step, the macro asks the user to confirm that choice by answering the "Sure? Y/N" prompt. The answer is stored in an empty cell, AF50. The next line will issue the /**QY** command only if cell AF50 contains "Y"; otherwise, the macro returns to the main menu. Note in Figure 8-13 that the file is *not* saved before the worksheet is closed. You might wish to add the commands necessary to accomplish this here, just before the /**QY** command is given. Be sure you have saved the worksheet file containing the macro before you test the Exit option! If you entered 1-2-3 through the Lotus Access System, the macro will quit to the Access Menu, not all the way back to DOS.

Autoexecute Macros

When a worksheet containing a macro with the special name \0 (zero, not "oh") is retrieved, that macro is automatically run by 1-2-3. This kind of macro can be used to display a menu macro or do other start-up processing commands with no intervention by the user. **Autoexecute macros** are particularly helpful for inexperienced users.

The special name **AUTO123.WK1** is reserved for a worksheet that is automatically loaded into memory whenever 1-2-3 is started. This worksheet must be saved in the default directory in order for it to be automatically loaded. If the AUTO123.WK1 file contains a \0 macro, that macro will also automatically execute whenever Lotus is started.

You may also begin 1-2-3 by specifying on the command line **–w** and the name of the worksheet file to load automatically. For example, typing at the DOS prompt **123 –wSMRV** would start 1-2-3 and load the SMRV.WK1 file. If that worksheet contains a \0 macro, it will execute automatically as soon as 1-2-3 is loaded, provided the /Worksheet Global Default Autoexec (/**WGDA**) setting is Yes.

COMPANION SPREADSHEET PRODUCTS

Because of the widespread use of Lotus 1-2-3, numerous products have been developed to augment its use. Many of these products are called *add-ins*, reflecting their implementation inside Lotus 1-2-3, and appear as additional Lotus commands. Others are used with Lotus worksheet or graph files. The Lotus Development Corporation has officially adopted one add-in product, Allways, and includes it with all copies of Release 2.2 and copies of Release 2.01 shipped after mid-1988. Other products are sold separately.

Allways

This add-in product provides special formatting and presentation-quality printing capabilities with Lotus worksheets and graphs. Because it installs as an add-in, Allways can be called up from READY mode like other Lotus commands, usually with the **Alt-F7** keystroke. Allways requires a personal computer with at least 512K of conventional memory and a hard disk. It must be installed before it can be used. Check with your computer lab consultant for availability at your site. Allways examples appear in Chapters 5 and 6.

Sideways

It is very difficult to print spreadsheets that are wider than the standard paper width. Lotus will print them in pieces which can be cut apart and taped together—the "tile" approach. The Sideways product is able to print wide worksheets sideways down the paper by turning the output ninety degrees and using the printer's graphics mode. Sideways is an excellent tool for wide spreadsheets that are fairly shallow, say up to 40 rows.

HAL—The Natural Language Analyzer

This extra-cost add-in enables you to use English-like commands to 1-2-3 instead of the usual ones. HAL will carry out the command for such things as entering data, formulas, / commands and editing cells. HAL recognizes certain key words such as Enter, Type, Draw, Plot, Show, Fix and Format. HAL commands are preceded with the backslash (\) character. For example, **format row 10 like row 6** will accomplish a range format of row 10. While HAL makes entering commands easier, it provides few additional features.

Spreadsheet Notes and Word Processors

Some packages add word processing capabilities to 1-2-3. 4WORD provides such capabilities within 1-2-3, placing text within an ordinary worksheet. You can insert and delete text, set tabs and margins, move or copy blocks of text, and link a document with values from Lotus cells. Most common word processing capabilities are present with 4WORD, including the ability to merge printer documents based upon data values stored in Lotus worksheets. 4WORD documents can be saved or printed with the usual Lotus /File and /Print commands. In-Word is a similar word processing add-in.

Another useful add-in is Note-It Plus, a cell note utility. Modeled after the popular 3M Post-it™ notes, the notes can be attached to any cell in the worksheet. Ordinarily invisible, you can pop them up at the touch of a key to reveal comments or special instructions for the contents of a cell or use of the spreadsheet. This tool is particularly useful for spreadsheets that are used by many people or that may be used over a long period of time, when cell expressions may be forgotten or confused.

Database Linkers

The data records in Lotus databases must be contained within the computer's conventional memory. Although expanded memory can provide additional storage capability, records must still be imported into Lotus before the /Data commands can be used. There are several products which will automatically link database records from popular third-party database packages such as dBASE. These add-ins let you retrieve appropriate records directly into 1-2-3, without exiting from Lotus. They provide the advantage of large database capacity (using the computer's disk drive and the native database program) and easy retrieval of records into Lotus worksheets. Some products even allow you to make changes to the external database while working in 1-2-3. Examples of database linkers include 4Views, Silverado, and @BASE.

Spreadsheet Analyzers

There is a tendency to complete development of a complicated spreadsheet with minimal testing, particularly by users who are not trained in programming and debugging techniques. Because spreadsheets are increasingly used in critical decision-making situations, it is important to verify that cell formulas are correct and summary information is correct.

Spreadsheet analysis programs such as The Auditor or Cambridge Spreadsheet Analyzer can help in this important phase. They can be used to look for common mistakes and omissions such as a circular cell reference or a numeric cell expression that refers to label cells or @SUM formulas whose ranges don't include all contiguous filled cells.

A New England company had constructed a worksheet to help in preparing a bid proposal. One portion of the spreadsheet detailed the company's projected expenses for the project, with an @SUM at the bottom of the column. The analyst inadvertently added another row of cost information *below* the last cell included in the @SUM expression. When the spreadsheet was recalculated, the new item was not included in the @SUM range and thus was not added to the sum. After being awarded the job and discovering its error, the company was not successful in petitioning to be reimbursed for the overlooked cost factor because of their error.

Some of the analysis programs can provide a "bird's eye view" of large spreadsheets, showing the cell categories on one sheet of paper. You can see where formulas, constants, labels, macros, blank and other cell types are located. This is very useful when designing large spreadsheets that extend beyond a few pages in size. Macro developers will appreciate knowing addresses of cell ranges in the worksheet. This view might discover the common error of having a constant value in the middle of a series of formula cells. Some of these products provide cross-references that can trace the contents of a cell back to previous references.

Another important benefit is the ability to print out cell expressions within the matrix of rows and columns. Because the Lotus /Print option for printing cell formulas is awkward to use, the matrix printout can help uncover errors in cell expressions.

Graphing Packages

Lotus graphs are somewhat limited for presentation purposes. There are several graphing programs that start with Lotus worksheets or .PIC files and add sophisticated features. Lotus Freelance Plus and Harvard Graphics are perhaps the best-known packages. You can create the data within Lotus and use the Lotus graph facility to create test graphs. Once the data are prepared and confirmed, the separate graphing programs are used to enhance the graphs.

The graphing programs are able to output to a wide variety of devices, including color printers, plotters, film recorders and the usual dot matrix and laser printers. Graphs can be printed in very high resolutions and with full color where needed. Slide shows can display consecutive charts on a monitor or video projector for live presentations to groups. Additional graph types are available with these packages, and several graphs can be displayed on the same sheet.

Symbols and other art work can be superimposed on the graphs to create emphasis and special effects.

Spreadsheet Compilers These products translate the finished worksheet into an executable file that can be used without Lotus itself. The resulting program closely resembles the original worksheet. Macros can be run and graphs can be created. However, the user cannot change cell formulas with a compiled spreadsheet, protecting the original expressions. Because a copy of Lotus is not necessary, more users can use the compiled spreadsheet at little additional cost to the organization.

Compiled spreadsheets would be easier to use than the original and the user need not be trained in Lotus 1-2-3. Recalculations may work faster with a compiled spreadsheet. Examples of **spreadsheet compilers** are Baler and @Liberty.

Decision Analysis Tools Two innovative products, SuperTree and @Risk, treat decision making under uncertainty. SuperTree performs spreadsheet sensitivity analysis, decision analysis, and risk analysis by organizing "what-if" tests to vary parameters in the spreadsheet. @Risk is a true 1-2-3 add-in and allows the user to evaluate models of uncertain situations through simulation across user-supplied probability distributions for uncertain quantities. The resulting risk analyses and profiles are presented graphically. The benefits of Lotus' quick calculations in what-if scenarios, combined with the expected value functions for solving decision trees, are a powerful tool in solving an important class of business problems.

Optimizing Products Optimizing add-ins allow you to add the power of linear programming and goal-seeking algorithms to your spreadsheet. These products will determine the best solution that optimizes an objective function and meets constraints. What-If Solver and What'sBest! are examples of this kind of add-in.

Financial Add-Ins Although Lotus 1-2-3 comes with many built-in financial functions (covered in Chapter 4 of this text), these add-in products add specialized @-functions for solving more sophisticated financial problems such as bond calculations, adjustable rate mortgages and complex cash flow problems. Financial @nalyst and Financial Toolkit are the best-known of this group of add-ins. The Budget Express helps you build a consolidated budget spreadsheet from several files. Instant Analyst provides the ability to set up financial ratio calculations quickly.

Forecasting Add-Ins ForeCalc, Tomorrow, and Trendsetter Expert help you prepare forecasts with Lotus 1-2-3 using exponential smoothing and other mathematical techniques. These mathematical techniques can also be implemented directly in 1-2-3 without using the add-in but require some expertise on the part of the modeler.

Other Utilities These add-ins save time and in some cases, allow you to recover damaged spreadsheet files. P.D.Queue is a print spooler that allows you to print large spreadsheets in the background while doing working on other jobs. Up to 99 jobs can be stored in its buffer memory, including Allways. Rescue Plus can help you restore damaged Lotus spreadsheets. There are several products that make writing and debugging macros easier. Macro Editor/Debugger is designed for macro programmers building large systems. Worksheet Archive System is a sort of super-Undo utility: it keeps track of changes made to a spreadsheet and lets you restore a previous version.

COMPATIBILITY WITH OTHER LOTUS 1-2-3 VERSIONS

Earlier Releases: 1a, 2, 2.01

The first widely used version of Lotus 1-2-3 was Release 1a. Version 1a was issued in 1983 and quickly became the number one selling software product in the industry. Release 1a worksheets had the .WKS file extension and required greater storage space than later versions. All later releases of Lotus 1-2-3 are able to automatically retrieve and translate earlier file types. Version 1a is not able to read worksheet files created by later versions.

In 1985 Release 2 was issued; version 2.01 fixed some errors in release 2. A more compact file storage method was used and the .WK1 file extension was standard. The extensive macro command language from the Lotus Symphony product was added to 1-2-3. Additional translation capabilities were added to the Access Menu, along with a comprehensive tutorial module called View. Support for EGA and VGA video displays was also added to the package. Users with expanded memory (EMS) cards could build larger worksheets than the standard 640K RAM would allow. Other new features of Release 2 included the built-in multiple regression command and several new string functions. Release 2 also provided password protection for worksheet files that encrypts them on the disk. More international format types were added for date and time values. Copy protection was removed from release 2.01 in 1988.

Release 2.2

In 1988 Lotus announced a new version of 1-2-3 to replace Release 2. As development progressed, it became clear that two new versions of 1-2-3 would be developed. Version 2.2 was designed to run on personal computers with modest hardware requirements, including the 8088-based IBM PC and compatibles. Release 3 was aimed at 80286-based personal computers with more memory and disk space.

While this textbook focuses on Release 2.2, nearly all of the commands and menu screens are compatible with earlier versions. The 2.2 version brings several new features: improved macro development tools including the learn facility and enhanced step mode for debugging, minimal recalculation to reduce waiting time, network support, file linking for using values from other worksheets in the current worksheet, and improved graphics. Many command settings have been consolidated in Group screens for easier reference. The included Allways add-in program provides presentation quality printing for outputs and graphs.

Release 2.2 uses the same worksheet file format and .WK1 extension as Release 2. The add-in products designed for Release 2 will also work with Release 2.2. The add-in manager in 2.2 will make it easier to use these third-party products. Release 2.3 was announced as this book went to press; see Chapter 10.

Release 3.0

The Release 3.0 version is similar to earlier versions but offers numerous new features. Because it is a significantly larger program, more hardware resources are necessary to run it. You must have an 80286, 80386 or 80486 microprocessor; release 3.0 will not run on an 8088- or 8086-based computer. To run under DOS, it also requires a minimum of 1 megabyte of memory, divided into 640K of conventional memory and at least 384K of extended memory. For OS/2 users, at least 3 MB of memory is needed. Version 3.0 of 1-2-3 requires a hard disk drive with about 3.5 MB of free space, and a graphics video display.

Previous versions of 1-2-3 were text-based, using the built-in fixed-size character set to represent information on the screen. Release 3.0 uses a graphics mode to represent all screens, allowing different character sets to be used in worksheets and graphs.

A key advantage of Release 3.0 is its ability to handle **three-dimensional worksheets**. The top "page" is the usual 256-columns-by-8192-rows spreadsheet. Release 3.0 adds 254 more pages, identified by a letter in the upper left corner. Cells are identified by three coordinates. For example, **A:B7** is cell B7 on page A. It is possible to reference ranges that include several pages. The range **A:B7..C:B10** represents the block of cells B7, B8, B9, and B10 on pages A, B, and C.

Three-dimensional worksheets are useful when consolidating the results of several sheets into a single summary worksheet. Place the individual worksheets on consecutive pages in Release 3.0, with the summary sheet on top. Use cell expressions that reference the other pages in the consolidation worksheet. You can **link** cell values from other worksheet files into the current spreadsheet with the file-linking feature. When you issue the Link-Refresh command the current cell will be updated with the referenced values. Release 2.2 also offers the file link capability as discussed in Chapter 5.

Release 3.0 allows you to reference records from external database files, including dBASE, in cell expressions and in the /Data commands. Thus the data does not have to reside in the spreadsheet itself. There are changes in some of the /Data commands that will make it easier to use.

A new worksheet file format is used in Release 3.0. The default file extension is .WK3 for Release 3.0 files. Existing files with the old .WK1 file format are automatically read by Release 3.0 so no translation is necessary. You can save files in the .WK3 or .WK1 formats. Most macros written for earlier versions will run properly in Release 3.0 unless they rely upon cursor movement to select / command options.

Release 3.0 graphics are improved. There are new graph types and you can print the graph directly from 1-2-3: PrintGraph is no longer needed. You can display the graph in a window next to the worksheet and cell changes are immediately reflected in the graph. You can create two Y axes and logarithmic scaling is also available for the Y-axis. There are more /Graph options available.

Recalculations in Release 3.0 take place in the **background**, enabling you to immediately work with the worksheet instead of watching the WAIT indicator blink until all **recalculations** are finished. Priority is given to recalculating the cells on the current screen display.

Printing also takes place in the background with Release 3.0. Your print jobs join the print queue, as with WordPerfect, and you can change their print priority in the queue. There are some new /Print options for changing print font and type size.

You can add comments to Release 3.0 cell expressions and notes to range names. Thus unusual formulas or important messages to a user can be accommodated directly. There is a **mapping** command that gives an overview picture of the worksheet. With the map you can see which cells are constants, labels, or formulas.

The **Undo** feature introduced with Release 2.2 is included with 3.0. Lotus will also warn the user to save the worksheet if you quit or attempt to erase the unsaved worksheet.

There are some new macro commands available with Release 3.0, along with the ability to store macros in any file open in memory. Thus you can create macro libraries that may be used with any worksheet, not just the one they were stored within.

Release 3.1 and 3.1+

Release 3.1 adds spreadsheet publishing features with WYSIWYG, similar to the Allways add-in for version 2.2. It works with Windows 3.0 or with DOS. More graph types and @-functions are provided with release 3.1. Chapter 10 contains a more-thorough discussion of Releases 3.1 and 3.1+, including examples.

OTHER SPREADSHEET PROGRAMS

The first microcomputer-based spreadsheet program was VisiCalc, released in 1978. VisiCalc was extended to several computers, including the Apple II family and 8080- and Z80-based computers running the CP/M operating system. A version was even ported for the IBM PC. Lotus 1-2-3 was closely modeled after VisiCalc but with significant improvements. Many spreadsheet programs are available today, but Lotus still retains a majority of the market share. Most competing programs offer significant Lotus compatibility, including the ability to read Lotus worksheets and run Lotus macros.

Lotus Work-Alikes: VP-Planner and Twin

These two products were introduced in the middle 1980s as lower-cost substitutes for Release 1a of Lotus. Twin had greater use in the educational market, while VP-Planner enjoyed some commercial success. New releases kept pace with Lotus revisions. VP-Planner Plus is compatible with many features of Lotus versions 2.2 and 3.0. Its multi-dimensional spreadsheet and external database facilities are powerful tools. Most Lotus commands and macros work the same way with these work-alike programs. Additional choices can be found in some screens, so macros should utilize command-letter choices rather than use cursor key selection. VP-Planner Plus offers an alternative pull-down menu system as well as the usual moving-bar menus. The latest version, VP-Planner 3D, features three-dimensional worksheets and improved graphics. Unlike Lotus 1-2-3 Release 3.0, VP-Planner 3D will run on an 8088-based PC with as little as 384K RAM. Lotus Development Corporation sued the publisher of VP-Planner, claiming it used copyrighted menus and screens. In a milestone 1990 legal settlement, VP-Planner was taken off the market and is no longer sold.

Level III is the latest Twin release, functionally equivalent to Lotus Release 2. It can support multiple spreadsheets in memory, equivalent to a three-dimensional worksheet. It can read Lotus .WKS and .WK1 worksheets and will run most macros unchanged.

Quattro and Quattro Pro

Released by Borland Software, Quattro is another lower-cost alternative to Lotus 1-2-3. Quattro menus closely resemble the Lotus menus, but an alternative customizable system is also available. Quattro's graphics are a significant improvement over Release 2.2 of Lotus. Like Release 2.2, it uses minimal recalculation to reduce waiting time.

A more sophisticated version called Quattro Professional is designed to compete with features of Lotus Release 3.0, yet work on a standard 512K 8088-based computer with at least 4 megabytes of hard disk space. This product adds enhanced graphics, spreadsheet consolidation, and database links to its base features. Quattro Professional has built-in presentation-quality printing and graphic capabilities. Quattro Pro 3.0 was released just as this book went to press.

Microsoft Excel

First developed for the Macintosh computer, Excel has been ported to the IBM-compatible world. Users familiar with the Macintosh version will have few troubles using the IBM version. Excel was written for Microsoft Windows and is a graphic-based spreadsheet program. It requires at least an 80286 microprocessor, like Lotus 3.0, and works better with extra memory. A mouse is also recommended. Excel is able to read most worksheet file formats, and can save worksheets in the Lotus .WK1 format as well. Lotus macros will not run in Excel without first being translated by an Excel utility. Excel menus were not designed to be compatible with Lotus menus, unlike all of the other spreadsheet programs reviewed in this section.

Excel is a powerful program with features equivalent to those found in Lotus Release 3.0. It uses a presentation-quality WYSIWYG screen display that is somewhat similar to that found in Allways. You can load several worksheets in separate windows and reference values from several worksheets at one time. It also has good consolidation capabilities. Excel graphics are also quite good, better than those in Lotus Release 3.0.

SuperCalc

SuperCalc is one of the earliest spreadsheet products still being sold today. The current product is SuperCalc 5, highly compatible with Lotus Release 2.2. Its graphics are very high quality, with numerous graph types not found in Lotus 1-2-3. SuperCalc has a multiple-spreadsheet capability similar to Release 3.0's page feature, although with some limitations. Supercalc also includes a set of auditing tools.

Engineers and scientists will appreciate the advanced analysis tools built into SuperCalc. There are linear, quadratic and cubic regression commands, as well as additional functions for complicated mathematical expressions.

Other Spreadsheets

Most integrated software systems come with a spreadsheet program. The spreadsheet in Lotus Symphony is very similar to the 1-2-3 product, sharing its better features with 1-2-3. First Choice, Framework, Smart, and Enable also have spreadsheets, although generally more limited than the separate spreadsheet packages discussed here.

Some vendors are marketing minicomputer and mainframe-based spreadsheet software. Designed for multi-user access, these spreadsheets can accommodate very large worksheets, larger than most personal computers. Recalculations can be done very quickly and links with data stored on the central database can be handled without first transferring the data to the personal computer. You must have an appropriate terminal to effectively use such a system because the screen must be continually updated during a normal session.

CHAPTER REVIEW

Macros and the Lotus Command Language

Macros are programs of stored keystrokes and commands that save time and reduce errors. Repetitive keystrokes can be replayed whenever needed. Untrained individuals can use an unfamiliar spreadsheet through macros that provide custom menus with help and prompt messages. Autoexecution macros can begin working as soon as the worksheet is retrieved. Programming commands can be embedded in macros to build loops, test certain conditions, and branch to subroutines. Any / command can be placed in a macro.

Creating a Macro

Creating macros can be difficult for new users. Macros should be located in a section of the worksheet away from regular cells. The steps or instructions in a macro are stored as labels in consecutive vertical cells in a column. The macro will stop at a blank cell. Although not a part of the macro itself, documentation comments are usually placed in the column to the right of the macro statements. The name of the macro is created as a range name. The first cell of the macro is given a special range name consisting of the backslash character followed by a single letter or the digit zero. Lotus 2.2 allows use of longer range names for macros. The \0 name is used for the autoexecution macro. To execute a macro, hold down the Alt key and press the letter of the macro name. The Lotus Learn feature can be used to automatically enter keystrokes into a macro.

Executing a Macro

After the macro is entered in the worksheet, it can be run in the single-step mode for debugging purposes by pressing the Alt-F2 command. Pressing any key will advance the macro's execution by a character at a time. Lotus 2.2 displays the macro statement currently being executed in the lower left corner of the display. Normal execution speed can resume if Alt-F2 is entered again.

The Lotus Command Language

Most of the keyboard keys can be entered in a macro with a special keyword, enclosed in braces. For example, the right arrow cursor key can be represented as {right}. The F4 function key is {abs}. The Enter key is represented as the tilde, ~. The command to stop a macro's execution is {quit}. There are 50 advanced macro command statements in addition to the keyboard keys.

Companion Spreadsheet Products

Many products that augment Lotus 1-2-3 have been introduced. Some of these, called add-ins, actually install inside 1-2-3 and are as easy to use as regular Lotus commands. One such product, Allways, brings typeset-quality text to worksheet outputs and graphs. Lotus has bundled Allways with latter deliveries of Release 2.01 and all copies of 2.2. HAL is a natural language analyzer that lets you enter Lotus commands and cell entries with English-like phrases. Other products provide word processing capabilities within 1-2-3. A particularly useful add-in allows you to attach explanatory notes to a cell, much like the popular Post-It notes on paper.

Database Linkers, Spreadsheet Analyzers and Compilers, Graphing Packages, Decision Analysis Tools, Optimizing, Financial, and Forecasting Tools

Other products enable use of third-party databases from within 1-2-3. These utilities let you retrieve specified records or link values from those records directly into a Lotus worksheet. Spreadsheet analyzers help the spreadsheet developer check for errors and possible problems in large worksheets. Graphing packages can enhance Lotus graphs by adding more graph types, presentation-quality and output on more devices, including color printers and film recorders. Spreadsheet compilers eliminate the need for Lotus 1-2-3 by creating stand-alone programs out of worksheets. They protect cells by preventing the cell expressions from being changed. Decision analysis tools permit decision trees to be integrated with data in 1-2-3 worksheets. Financial tools provide additional @-functions for solving complex financial problems. Optimizing add-ins solve linear programming problems set up within Lotus spreadsheets.

Compatibility with Other Lotus 1-2-3 Versions

There have been several releases of Lotus 1-2-3 since its introduction in 1983. Release 1a was the first widely used version. Release 2 arrived two years later and added better macro capabilities and multiple regression capability, along with large spreadsheet support through expanded memory. Release 2 was quickly followed by 2.01, fixing some errors and providing compatibility with more hardware types. In 1989 two new versions of 1-2-3 were released. Version 2.2 is for less-demanding situations and runs on most IBM compatibles with an 8088 or better microprocessor and at least 320K RAM. It closely resembles Release 2.01 but adds network support, improved macro capabilities, minimal recalculation, file linking and improved graphics. Release 2.2 also introduces Group setting screens that make it easier to enter worksheet commands and settings. Release 2.2 uses the same .WK1 worksheet file format as Release 2. There is a new Undo feature that lets you remove changes made since the last time in the Ready mode. Allways was bundled in with all copies of Release 2.2.

Release 3.0 Features

Release 3.0 was the other new release in 1989. Although it requires a faster microprocessor and more memory, Release 3.0 brings many new desired features. Three-dimensional worksheets consisting of stacked pages can be created, with the page letter added to cell range references. You can also refer to values from other worksheet files. Release 3.0 uses a new worksheet file format with a .WK3 file extension, but will automatically read .WK1 files. The menus in Release 3.0 are very similar to earlier releases. Printing takes place in the background to save time. Release 3.0 also supports the Undo command.

Other Spreadsheet Programs

Numerous companies have released Lotus 1-2-3 compatible spreadsheet products. VP-Planner, Twin, and Quattro Pro will read Lotus worksheet files, will execute 1-2-3 macros and have menus nearly identical to Lotus 1-2-3. SuperCalc has evolved over time into a strong competitor to Lotus, adding some new features. Perhaps the biggest competitor to Lotus is Excel, a graphical spreadsheet based upon the Windows user interface. Excel offers superior graphics with some Lotus compatibility, although the menus are not compatible.

KEY TERMS

add-ins	keystroke macro	screen control commands
advanced macro commands	Learn feature (Alt-F5)	single-step mode
Allways	link	spreadsheet analysis programs
autoexecute macro	Lotus Command Language	spreadsheet compiler
background recalculation	macros	three-dimensional worksheets
data manipulation commands	mapping	tilde
debugging	menu macro	Undo
file manipulation commands	programming	/Worksheet Learn Range command
flow control commands	recalculations	
interactive commands	Release 2.01	
	Release 2.2	
	Release 3.0	
	Release 3.1	

DISCUSSION QUESTIONS

1. Define the concept of the macro in Lotus worksheets. Why are macros useful?

2. Discuss the three categories of Lotus macros. Give an application for each kind of macro.

3. Explain how to create a macro. Describe the steps in executing a keyboard macro.

4. What is an autoexecution macro? How is it created?

5. How do you name a macro? How is it saved permanently?

6. Discuss the single step mode for debugging a macro. How do you return to normal macro execution?

7. Give the Lotus macro instruction for the following keyboard keys:
    a. **F2**
    b. **Enter**
    c. **F10**
    d. **PgUp**
    e. **Ctrl-Left**
    f. **F9**
    g. **Esc.**

8. Explain the purpose of the following command language statements:
    a. {branch PRINT}
    b. {PRINT}
    c. {getlabel "Enter Cust. ID#:",H34}
    d. {let AC14,1249/41}
    e. {if HOURS>40}{OVTIME}
       {REGTIME}
    f. {menubranch MAIN}.

9. Explain why the Release 2.2 macro Learn facility would be useful in creating keystroke macros. If you have Release 2.2, use the Lotus Help command to find out more about Learn.

10. Define the concept of an "add-in" product for 1-2-3. Why do they make Lotus 1-2-3 more useful?

11. Give a brief explanation of each of the following add-in product categories:
    a. natural language analyzer
    b. spreadsheet word processor
    c. database linker
    d. graphing package.

12. Describe the benefits of the Allways add-in product.

13. Explain why we need to take advantage of the tools found in spreadsheet analyzers. Give examples of the kinds of analysis possible with these products.

14. What new features are available with Lotus 1-2-3 Release 3.0? Discuss the hardware requirements for Release 2.2 and Release 3.0.

15. Discuss features of the main competing spreadsheet programs available for IBM-compatible personal computers.

EXERCISES

1. Create a simple keystroke macro that places the label '   **HALDER LOAN COMPANY** in cell A4, then places the cursor in cell A6. Your macro should write **Year** in cell A6, **Payment** in cell B6, and **Balance** in cell C6. These column headings should be right-justified in each cell. The macro should be called **\H** and should start in cell AA1. Print a copy of the worksheet area and the macro instructions.

2. Add the data shown in Figure 8-14 to the Halder worksheet created in the previous problem. The formula in cell C8 will appear as a value on your worksheet, not the formula as shown.

   Create a second keystroke macro, called **\C**, that will copy the formula found in cell C8 to cells C9..C12 and format that column as Comma with two decimal places. Place documentation comments in the column adjacent to the macro steps. Print the worksheet and the macro instructions.

3. Create a macro called **\P** that will print the Halder worksheet from the previous problem. Your keystroke macro should print only the loan table cell range, not the macro itself. Be sure to clear all print settings as part of the macro. Document the steps in your macro in the adjacent column. Print the macro instructions manually.

4. Modify the \P macro from the previous problem to ask the user whether they would like to see cell formulas. Use cell A20 to hold the Yes/No answer to the {getlabel} prompt, and an {if} statement to invoke cell formulas if requested. Document your macro instructions in an adjacent column. Use the single-step mode to test your macro.

5. Manually create a Loan Table as shown in Figure 8-15 (don't use a macro to build the table entries). Be sure to use formulas to create the table entries where indicated. If you have the data disk, retrieve the HALDER2.WK1 file.

   The Payment cell uses the @PMT function. The Cumulative Interest is determined by multiplying the Payment times the Term in months, and subtracting the initial Principal of the loan.

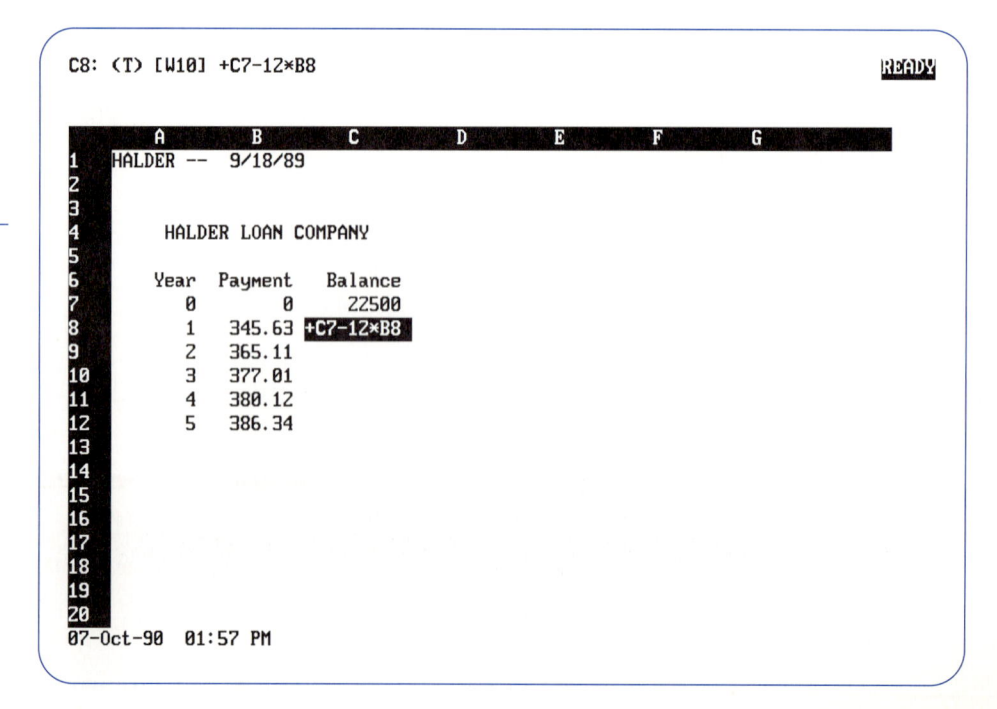

FIGURE 8-14

Sample Data for Exercise 2

```
C8: (T) [W10] +C7-12*B8                                        READY

        A         B         C         D         E         F         G
 1  HALDER --  9/18/89
 2
 3
 4         HALDER LOAN COMPANY
 5
 6      Year   Payment   Balance
 7        0         0     22500
 8        1    345.63  +C7-12*B8
 9        2    365.11
10        3    377.01
11        4    380.12
12        5    386.34
13
14
15
16
17
18
19
20
07-Oct-90  01:57 PM
```

Create a macro that will present the user with prompts for each of the loan parameters: Principal, Interest, Term. Your macro should calculate the Payment and Cumulative Interest and print the Loan Table. You should also submit a printed copy of the macro and its documentation.

6. Add to the previous problem by creating a Loan Amortization Table. See Figure 8-16. The Amount To Interest cell uses the previous month's Remaining Balance multiplied by the monthly Interest Rate. The Amount to Principal is the Payment minus the Amount to Interest. The new Remaining Balance is the previous period's Balance less the Amount to Principal. Use absolute cell addresses when referring to items in the parameter block. The last few rows are shown in the horizontal window in

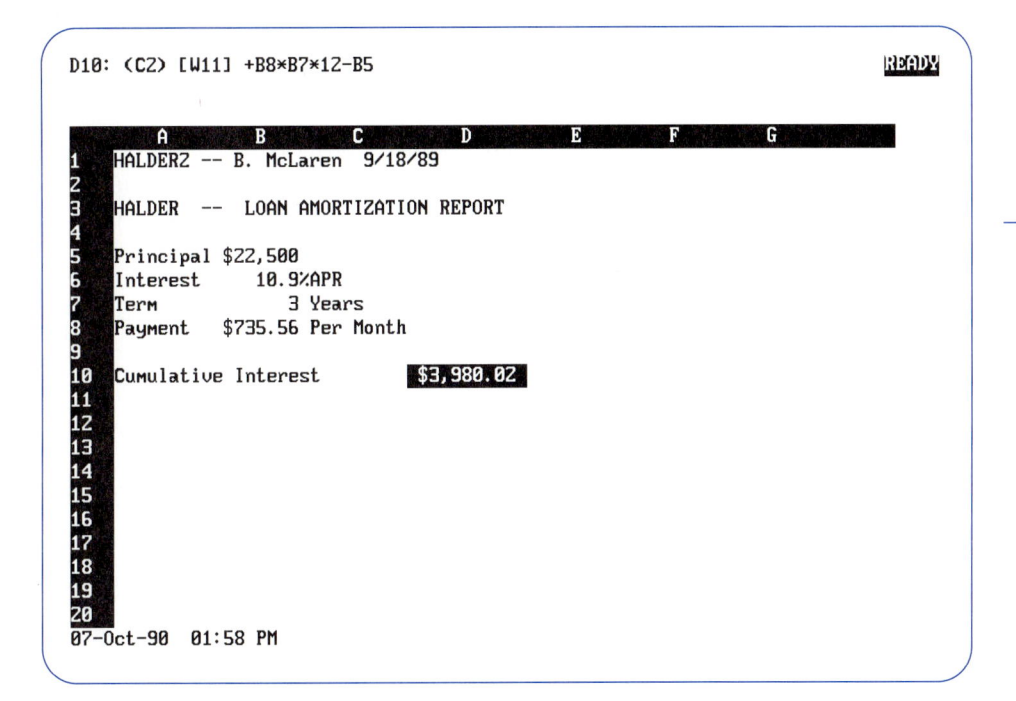

```
D10: (C2) [W11] +B8*B7*12-B5                                    READY


         A         B        C          D        E      F      G
 1  HALDER2 -- B. McLaren  9/18/89
 2
 3  HALDER   --   LOAN AMORTIZATION REPORT
 4
 5  Principal  $22,500
 6  Interest       10.9%APR
 7  Term            3 Years
 8  Payment    $735.56 Per Month
 9
10  Cumulative Interest           $3,980.02
11
12
13
14
15
16
17
18
19
20
07-Oct-90  01:58 PM
```

FIGURE 8-15

Sample Data for Exercise 5

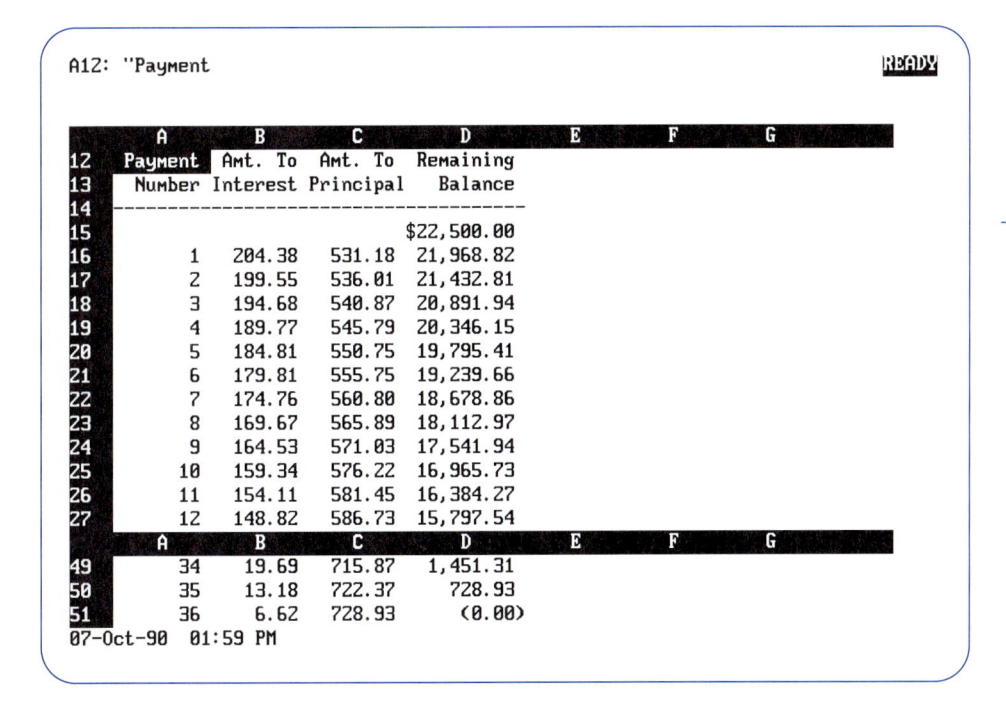

```
A12: "Payment                                                    READY


         A         B        C          D        E      F      G
12   Payment   Amt. To  Amt. To   Remaining
13   Number    Interest Principal  Balance
14   ------------------------------------
15                                $22,500.00
16      1       204.38   531.18    21,968.82
17      2       199.55   536.01    21,432.81
18      3       194.68   540.87    20,891.94
19      4       189.77   545.79    20,346.15
20      5       184.81   550.75    19,795.41
21      6       179.81   555.75    19,239.66
22      7       174.76   560.80    18,678.86
23      8       169.67   565.89    18,112.97
24      9       164.53   571.03    17,541.94
25     10       159.34   576.22    16,965.73
26     11       154.11   581.45    16,384.27
27     12       148.82   586.73    15,797.54
         A         B        C          D        E      F      G
49     34        19.69   715.87     1,451.31
50     35        13.18   722.37       728.93
51     36         6.62   728.93        (0.00)
07-Oct-90  01:59 PM
```

FIGURE 8-16

Sample Worksheet for Exercise 6

the bottom of the figure. If you have the text data disk, this material is stored in a file called HALDER3.WK1. If you move the cursor to cell A12, you can do a /File Combine which will load the entire HALDER3 file at that cell.

Save the combined worksheet on your own disk as HALDER4.WK1.

7. Prepare a menu macro to accomplish the following tasks with the HALDER4 worksheet:
   - Enter New Loan Parameters.
   - Print the Worksheet.
   - Save the Worksheet (under a new name).
   - Quit the Macro.

   a. First lay out the macro on paper, designing where the main menu will appear and where any subroutines will be placed. Determine names for parts of your macro.

   b. Next determine the overall steps of the macro, writing them by hand in pseudocode fashion. In other words, write down the purpose of each step, not the specific instructions of each macro. Also determine appropriate range names for parts of the loan table that would be useful in the macro.

   c. Enter the subroutine macros first and test them out by executing each one individually, before running the menu macro.

   d. Finally enter the menu macro itself and test the macro. How will you handle the problem of loan terms other than three years? Remember that the amortization table was only created for three-year loans.

   e. Print a copy of the macro and its documentation. If possible, submit a diskette containing a copy of the macro to your instructor.

8. Modify the HALDER4 menu macro of the previous problem by adding a second level menu macro for the Print choice in the main menu. From the Print choice, there are three further choices:
   - Print the Loan Parameters Only.
   - Print the Loan Table (Parameters and Amortization).
   - Print the Amortization Table Only.

   Thus your original menu macro should call another menu macro. Fully document all steps.

9. Retrieve the data for the Wabash Animal Hospital from the file called WABASH.WK1 on the data disk (used in exercise 10 from in the previous chapter). The first few rows of the worksheet are shown in Figure 8-17.

   Create a menu macro that will accomplish the following tasks:
   - Sort the data by Date, Pet Type, Owner, and Invoice.
   - Print the database.
   - Quit the macro.

   Fully document your steps and submit a printed copy of the macro.

10. If you have Lotus Release 2.2, use the Learn command to create a macro automatically. Your macro should create and view a bar graph using the data in Figure 8-18.

CHAPTER 8 PROJECT   **257**

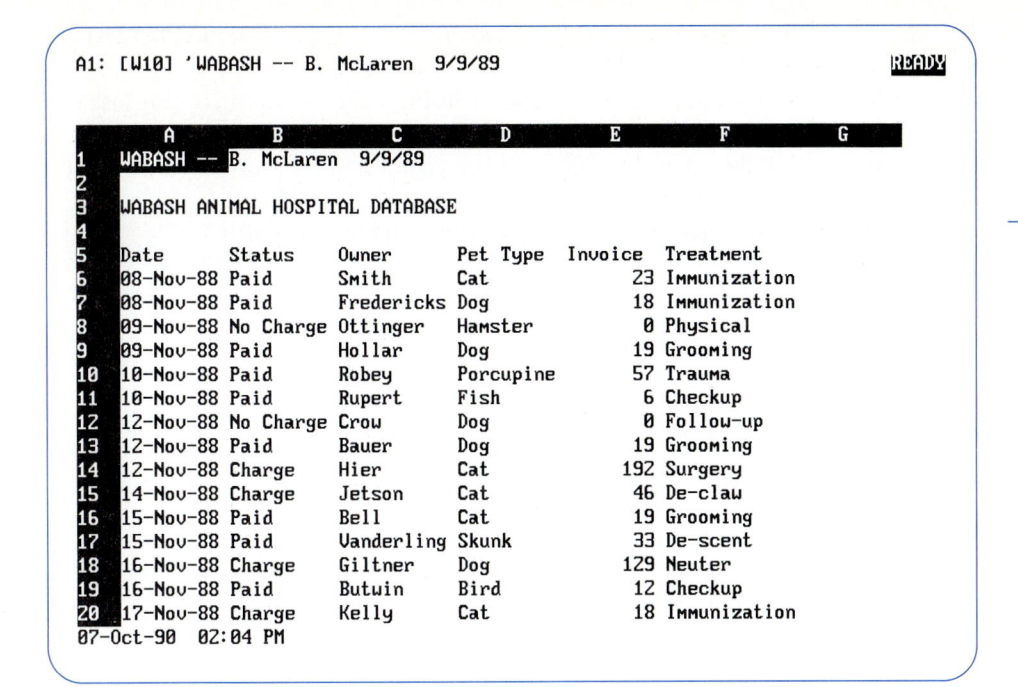

```
A1: [W10] 'WABASH -- B. McLaren  9/9/89                          READY

        A         B         C         D         E         F         G
 1  WABASH -- B. McLaren  9/9/89
 2
 3  WABASH ANIMAL HOSPITAL DATABASE
 4
 5  Date      Status    Owner     Pet Type  Invoice   Treatment
 6  08-Nov-88 Paid      Smith     Cat            23   Immunization
 7  08-Nov-88 Paid      Fredericks Dog           18   Immunization
 8  09-Nov-88 No Charge Ottinger  Hamster         0   Physical
 9  09-Nov-88 Paid      Hollar    Dog            19   Grooming
10  10-Nov-88 Paid      Robey     Porcupine      57   Trauma
11  10-Nov-88 Paid      Rupert    Fish            6   Checkup
12  12-Nov-88 No Charge Crow      Dog             0   Follow-up
13  12-Nov-88 Paid      Bauer     Dog            19   Grooming
14  12-Nov-88 Charge    Hier      Cat           192   Surgery
15  14-Nov-88 Charge    Jetson    Cat            46   De-claw
16  15-Nov-88 Paid      Bell      Cat            19   Grooming
17  15-Nov-88 Paid      Vanderling Skunk         33   De-scent
18  16-Nov-88 Charge    Giltner   Dog           129   Neuter
19  16-Nov-88 Paid      Butuin    Bird           12   Checkup
20  17-Nov-88 Charge    Kelly     Cat            18   Immunization
07-Oct-90  02:04 PM
```

FIGURE 8-17

Sample Data for Exercise 9

Network	Nominations	Awards
ABC	85	13
CBS	96	27
Fox	12	4
NBC	103	25
PBS	32	0

FIGURE 8-18

Sample Data for Exercise 10

The graph title should be **41st Annual Emmy Awards** with the second title as **Awards By Network**. Add legends for the A and B ranges. Your macro should also save the graph as **EMMY41.PIC**. Quit back to the READY prompt at the end of your macro.

Add the documentation steps manually once you have stored the macro in your worksheet.

11. Using the same worksheet data as the previous problem, create an autoexecution macro named \0 that places the current date in the second cell below "PBS" and formats that cell as Date-1 format. Be sure to save your worksheet with the \0 macro installed, then Retrieve it to be sure that the macro works. Submit a printed copy of the \0 macro.

A group of college friends has formed an investment club for the purpose of combining capital and spreading risk among more investments. The group needs to prepare a monthly statement for members. One of the group's founders sketched out the statement shown in Figure 8-19. The top part of the form is a

CHAPTER 8 PROJECT
PORT HURON
INVESTMENT GROUP

member's monthly statement, and the bottom section describes the Port Huron portfolio, shown in Figure 8-20.

Your job is to prepare a Lotus macro system that would allow the form to be updated with changes in the PH portfolio, the member's monthly transaction amount, and the group's share value. The portfolio now consists of the securities listed in Figure 8-20.

The group also has cash of $2,600. There are 5 members, and a total of 1327.4419 shares between the members. The current share value is $18.53. You may choose the names and addresses of the group. The number of shares and amount invested per member are shown in Figure 8-21.

FIGURE 8-19

Port Huron Statement Format

```
                    P O R T    H U R O N    P O R T F O L I O

================================================================
Partner:   <partner name>              Soc Sec Number: xxx-xx-xxxx
           <partner address>           Phone Number:  (xxx)xxx-xxxx
           <partner city, state, zip>
================================================================
Transaction    Transaction    Share      Shares This      Shares In
   Date          Amount       Value      Transaction       Account
-----------   -----------    -----      -----------      --------
January         xxx.xx        xxx.xx      xxx.xxxx        xxx.xxxx
February
March
April
May
June
July
August
September
October
November
December

              Amount Invested:            xxxx.xx
              Shares Purchased:           xxx.xxxx
              Current Share Value:        xxx.xx
              Value of Account:           xxxx.xx
              Percent of Gain or Loss:    xx.xx%

================================================================

                 P O R T    H U R O N    P O R T F O L I O

                                           Purchase     Recent
Qty       Investment             Symbol     Price        Price
---       ----------             ------    --------     -------
xxx    xxxxxxxxxxxxxxxxxxxxx     xxxxxx    xxxx.xx      xxxx.xx
xxx    xxxxxxxxxxxxxxxxxxxxx     xxxxxx    xxxx.xx      xxxx.xx
xxx    xxxxxxxxxxxxxxxxxxxxx     xxxxxx    xxxx.xx      xxxx.xx
```

Qty	Investment	Symbol	Recent	Purchase
120	Buckhorn Mfg.	BHM	$45.50	$41.875
25	Zlippel Bonds	ZLPL	124.75	106.50
50	KPW Corporation	KPW	3.25	4.50
100	Ted Oil Company	TEDO	19.50	15.25
300	Seelyville Electric	SEEE	20.00	20.00
150	Boston Beans	BB	35.375	38.25

FIGURE 8-20

Port Huron Securities Portfolio

Member	# Shares	Total Invested
Member 1	218.3585	4,000.00
Member 2	124.7564	2,145.00
Member 3	340.0811	5,790.00
Member 4	79.2376	1,400.00
Member 5	565.0083	9,620.00

FIGURE 8-21

Port Huron Member Shares

9

Integrating the Tools

Objectives

After completing this chapter, you should be able to:

- Understand how data can be shared between the three software packages.
- Move print files between Lotus and WordPerfect.
- Transfer data records from dBASE to WordPerfect.
- Translate dBASE data to Lotus 1-2-3 format.
- Merge print in WordPerfect using data from Lotus or dBASE.

INTRODUCTION

This textbook has illustrated Lotus 1-2-3 version 2.2, the most popular electronic spreadsheet software package. This chapter presents ways in which we can benefit by transferring data between Lotus and two other popular software programs, WordPerfect 5.1 and dBASE IV. Each package is able to manipulate data in certain ways that other packages cannot. WordPerfect is a word processing package, maintaining data in a rectangular grid. dBASE IV is a database management program, storing data in fields and rows.

Lotus comes with a data conversion program to translate data from one file format to another. WordPerfect and dBASE each have their own translation features. In addition, each is able to read data directly under certain conditions.

Although Lotus 1-2-3 will print tables in hardcopy format, we can print the report to a disk file which can be retrieved into a WordPerfect document. The same is true with dBASE IV reports. We may also wish to do merge printing in WordPerfect with data transferred from Lotus or dBASE.

The Lotus Translate utility is able to read files in several other formats and convert them to the .WK1 spreadsheet file type. With the /File Combine and /File Import commands we can read data from other spreadsheet files and from plain text (ASCII) files. dBASE is able to import and export data directly from several file types, including the Lotus .WK1 format and plain text files.

This chapter will present examples showing how to exchange data between all three packages; we assume you already know how to use them.

Exchanging Data Between Software Packages

It is not uncommon to transfer data from one package to another. Each package stores data in a different native format, and native format files usually cannot be directly read by another package. Most of the software packages provide a **translate** or **conversion program** to assist in this process. The originating package may also have an optional file format menu so it may save data in an appropriate format. All of the packages covered in this text will also save data in plain text or ASCII files. Most of the formatting information found in the file is usually deleted when the data file is saved as a text file.

Types of Data Transfers

We have already discussed some kinds of data transfers in earlier chapters. Lotus 1-2-3 reports may be saved as a .PRN file for later Retrieval into a WordPerfect document. We can do the same with dBASE reports and WordPerfect. It is possible to Import text data into a Lotus worksheet. dBASE will allow records to be Appended from text files. We can list six different types of transfers using just these three packages. The first three transfers are perhaps the most common, but all are used.

- Lotus to WordPerfect
- dBASE to WordPerfect
- dBASE to Lotus
- WordPerfect to Lotus
- WordPerfect to dBASE
- Lotus to dBASE.

We may also wish to transfer data to other kinds of packages, such as desktop publishing or graphics programs. The rest of this section will describe transfers *from* Lotus, dBASE, and WordPerfect, as well as transfers *to* each package, beginning with WordPerfect.

WordPerfect has two internal Save modes. The regular or **native format** is prepared with the **F10** Save or **F7** Exit/Save commands; the text format is prepared with the **Ctrl-F5** Text In/Out command. For those who need backward compatibility, WordPerfect 5.1 can also convert files directly to WordPerfect 4.2 and 5.0 formats with the **Ctrl-F5** command.[1] [Note: WordPerfect 5.0 and 5.1 will automatically convert a WordPerfect 4.2 document when it is retrieved with the **Shift-F10** Retrieve command.]

Some programs are capable of reading WordPerfect files directly. The Grammatik IV grammar checker package not only can read this format directly, but it can also insert changes directly into the original file. Ventura Publisher 2.0 and PageMaker will also read WordPerfect files directly. To keep the original file safe, you should only use a *copy* of the original file for such applications.

TRANSFERRING DATA FROM WORDPERFECT

Neither Lotus nor dBASE can directly read or translate WordPerfect native files, so the text format is typically used to transfer data to these programs. Any tabs, indents, center or flush right codes are replaced by an equivalent number of spaces in the text file version of the document. Other formatting codes such as bold, underline, fonts, and merge codes are stripped out of the text file. None of the graphics boxes are saved in the text file, even if they contain text lines. The text within the graphics box is not saved in the text file. Footnotes and endnotes are not included in the text file.

Saving Documents in Text (ASCII) Format

Example: *Creating a Text File with WordPerfect*

Suppose you have created a table of names and addresses and wish to convert these to text or ASCII format. That table looks like the box in Figure 9-1. Suppose you wish to send these names to Lotus or dBASE, and intend to save the data as an ASCII file.

1. Make sure you have saved the data file as a regular WordPerfect document. We'll assume you used the name **MEMBERS.WP**. The .WP file extension will help to remind us that this is a WordPerfect format file.

2. From within WordPerfect, enter the **Ctrl-F5** command and select option **1** DOS Text.

3. From the next menu select option **1** Save, and WordPerfect will ask for the file name to save the document as. Reply **MEMBERS.TXT** and press **Enter**.

4. WordPerfect will save your membership list as a plain text file on the default drive; the .TXT extension will remind you that this is the ASCII version. [Note: Do *not* use the same file name and extension for both versions of the file.]

An auxiliary program called CONVERT.EXE accompanies WordPerfect and will convert between several file types. While CONVERT will not translate directly to Lotus 1-2-3 or dBASE IV, it will translate to an intermediate file type

WordPerfect CONVERT Program

---

[1] WordPerfect 5.0 can convert to version 4.2 file formats with the **Ctrl-F5** command.

FIGURE 9-1

Sample Data for Text Transfer Example

Williams, Carolyn	1883 Huron Way	Spencer	IN 47460
Smith, Robert	Box 220, RR 51	Otterbein	IN 47970
Muraska, Eric	155 Keane Lane	Terre Haute	IN 47803
Osmon, Randy	899 N. 9th Street	Terre Haute	IN 47807
Green, Janet	2307 Highland Drive	Clinton	IN 47842
McCune, Michael	3404 Marquette	Terre Haute	IN 47804
Todd, Bernard	1246 Lafayette Ave	Pimento	IN 47822
Whitlock, Jane	543 Nancy Lane	Indianapolis	IN 46226
Joslin, Wallace	2956 S. 8th Street	Seelyville	IN 47878
Moore, Edith	RR 53	Greencastle	IN 46135
Gauer, Harold	2214 Lakeview	Sullivan	IN 47591
Hughes, Samuel	410 E. Tennessee	Zionsville	IN 46077
Josephs, Cameron	8745 Newsom Drive	South Bend	IN 46522

which can be imported by Lotus or dBASE. The CONVERT program will convert *from* WordPerfect 5.1 to the following file formats:

- IBM DCA format (revisable form and final form)
- Navy DIF (private Navy format)
- WordStar 3.3 and 4.0 format
- MultiMate Advantage II
- Seven-bit transfer format (to send WP file with modem)
- ASCII text file (duplicates Text In/Out function)
- Spreadsheet DIF format (from WP secondary merge format).

CONVERT will also convert the following file formats *into* WordPerfect 5.1 format:

- IBM DCA
- Navy DIF (private Navy format)
- WordStar 3.3 and 4.0
- MultiMate Advantage II
- Seven-bit transfer format (WP files received by modem)
- WordPerfect 4.1 format

```
Mr. William Hassler{END FIELD}
Starcraft Industries, Inc.{END FIELD}
2804 East 19th Street{END FIELD}
Jonesville, IN 45678{END FIELD}
Budget Planner{END FIELD}
{END RECORD}
================================================================================
Ms. Sally Hansen{END FIELD}
French Public Accounting{END FIELD}
188 Poplar Street{END FIELD}
Sheybogan, WI 56234{END FIELD}
Accounting Trainee{END FIELD}
{END RECORD}
================================================================================




Field: 1                                              Doc 1 Pg 1 Ln 1" Pos 1"
```

FIGURE 9-2

WordPerfect Merge Format File for CONVERT Example

- Mailmerge (to WP secondary merge format)
- Spreadsheet DIF (to WP secondary merge format)
- Microsoft Word 4.0 (only with WordPerfect 5.1)
- DisplayWrite (only with WordPerfect 5.1).

For transfers to Lotus 1-2-3, the ASCII and Spreadsheet DIF formats are recommended. The example below discusses how the **DIF format** can be created from the WordPerfect CONVERT program.

Example: *Converting a WordPerfect Merge File to DIF Format*

The CONVERT.EXE program is a separate program that is run from the DOS prompt. You must have first created the WordPerfect document in secondary merge file format and saved it.

1. From DOS, change to the directory where the CONVERT program is stored (usually the directory where WordPerfect is stored). Type **CONVERT** at the DOS prompt and press **Enter**.

2. We'll assume the file to be converted is called EMPLOY.SEC and stored on the A: drive. When DOS asks for the name of the Input File, provide the pathname of the file: **A:EMPLOY.SEC** and press **Enter**. This file is shown in Figure 9-2.

3. You'll next be asked for the Output File, so enter a name and the drive you wish it to be stored in. Call the new file **A:EMPLOY.DIF**.

4. Next you'll see the Convert menu as shown in Figure 9-3A. Select **1** (WordPerfect to Another Format), then choose **8** (WordPerfect Secondary Merge to Spreadsheet DIF) in Figure 9-3B and press **Enter**.

5. After a few seconds, WordPerfect will inform you that the conversion has been completed.

FIGURE 9-3A

CONVERT Screen for DIF Conversion Example

```
Name of Input File? EMPLOY.SEC
Name of Output File? EMPLOY.DIF

0 EXIT
1 WordPerfect to another format
2 Revisable-Form-Text (IBM DCA Format) to WordPerfect
3 Final-Form-Text (IBM DCA Format) to WordPerfect
4 Navy DIF Standard to WordPerfect
5 WordStar 3.3 to WordPerfect
6 MultiMate Advantage II to WordPerfect
7 Seven-Bit Transfer Format to WordPerfect
8 WordPerfect 4.2 to WordPerfect 5.1
9 Mail Merge to WordPerfect Secondary Merge
A Spreadsheet DIF to WordPerfect Secondary Merge
B Word 4.0 to WordPerfect
C DisplayWrite to WordPerfect

Enter number of Conversion desired 1
```

FIGURE 9-3B

CONVERT Screen for DIF Conversion Example After Selecting option 1

```
Name of Input File? EMPLOY.SEC
Name of Output File? EMPLOY.DIF

0 EXIT
1 Revisable-Form-Text (IBM DCA Format)
2 Final-Form-Text (IBM DCA Format)
3 Navy DIF Standard
4 WordStar 3.3
5 MultiMate Advantage II
6 Seven-Bit Transfer Format
7 ASCII Text File
8 WordPerfect Secondary Merge to Spreadsheet DIF

Enter number of output file format desired 8
```

Example: *Create a WordPerfect Secondary Merge File from a Mail Merge File*

Many software packages create a merge data file in the **mailmerge** format. While not directly usable by WordPerfect, the Mailmerge format can be converted to Secondary merge format with the WordPerfect CONVERT program.

1. From the DOS prompt, enter **CONVERT** to begin the conversion. The input file name will be **HABITAT.TXT** while the output file will be named **HABITAT.SEC** to reflect its use as a secondary merge file.

2. At the first CONVERT menu select CHOICE **9**, Mailmerge to WordPerfect Secondary Merge File.

```
Name of Input File? C:\DBASE\HABITAT.TXT
Name of Output File? HABITAT.SEC

1 WordPerfect to another format
2 Revisable-Form-Text (IBM DCA Format) to WordPerfect
3 Final-Form-Text (IBM DCA Format) to WordPerfect
4 Navy DIF Standard to WordPerfect
5 WordStar 3.3 to WordPerfect
6 MultiMate Advantage II to WordPerfect
7 Seven-Bit Transfer Format to WordPerfect
8 WordPerfect 4.2 to WordPerfect 5.1
9 Mail Merge to WordPerfect Secondary Merge
A Spreadsheet DIF to WordPerfect Secondary Merge
B Word 4.0 to WordPerfect
C DisplayWrite to WordPerfect

Enter number of Conversion desired 9
Enter Field delimiter characters or decimal ASCII values enclosed in {}
, <Enter>
Enter Record delimiter characters or decimal ASCII values enclosed in {}
{13}{10}  <Enter>
Enter Characters to be stripped from file or press Enter if none
"  <Enter>
C:\DBASE\HABITAT.TXT Converted to HABITAT.SEC
```

FIGURE 9-4

CONVERT Screen for Mailmerge Conversion Illustration

3. The CONVERT program will prompt you to provide the field delimiter character (that separates fields); type a comma and press **Enter**.

4. You'll next be asked to provide the character that ends a record. Type {13}{10} to signify the carriage return and line feed that end each line of the text file, and press **Enter**. (Type the { } brace characters *and* the numbers inside the braces.)

5. The next prompt asks which characters are to be stripped from the file. Type in the double quote character, ", and press **Enter**.

6. When CONVERT is finished, you'll be told that the conversion is complete. Figure 9-4 illustrates the sequence of steps in this example.

If another package is capable of creating a document in the WordPerfect 4.2, 5.0, or 5.1 formats, WordPerfect can read it automatically[2] when the file is retrieved with the **Shift-F10** command. Text format files can be read with the **Ctrl-F5** Text In/Out command. Any other file format must first be converted before it is usable.

TRANSFERRING DATA TO WORDPERFECT

The **Ctrl-F5** Text In/Out command is used to read text files as well as to save files in text format. From the main WordPerfect screen press **Ctrl-F5**. You'll see the following menu.

Reading a Text File with WordPerfect

1 **D**OS Text; **2** **P**assword; **3** Save **A**s; **4** **C**omment; **5** **S**preadsheet: **0**

Choice **1** will take you to the DOS Text menu where files can be saved or retrieved in text format.

1 **S**ave; **2** **R**etrieve (CR/LF to [Hrt]); **3** R**e**trieve (CR/LF to [SRt] in HZone): **0**

---

[2] WordPerfect 5.0 is able to Retrieve and convert version 5.1 files provided they do not use any of the word processing features unique to version 5.1.

Depending upon the type of text file, you may wish to retrieve it with choice 2 or 3. Choice **2** will convert any carriage return/line feed combination it encounters to a hard return, signifying the end of a paragraph to WordPerfect. Lines that must retain their format, such as Lotus .PRN files, will use choice 2. Choice **3** will convert the end-of-line carriage return/line feed characters to *soft* returns. With choice 3 you can later adjust margins or modify the text, and WordPerfect will automatically wrap the lines as needed. With the latter choice you will have to manually insert end of paragraph hard returns.

Example: *Reading a Lotus Text File*

Suppose we have already created a Lotus .PRN file called SMITH.PRN, and wish to insert it into the middle of an existing WordPerfect document.

1. Start WordPerfect. Before retrieving the text file, move the cursor to the document location where the Lotus .PRN file is to be placed.

2. Then press **Ctrl-F5** to bring up the Text In/Out menu. Press **1** to bring up the DOS Text menu, then **2** to retrieve the file.

3. When WordPerfect prompts for the filename, enter the complete pathname, including the drive and directory where the document is stored. On hard-disk computers this might be **C:\123\SMITH.PRN**; on a floppy disk computer this might be **A:SMITH.PRN** on the data disk.

4. The resulting integrated text is shown on this page. WordPerfect will insert the print file as if you had typed the text in from the keyboard, but will place a hard return after each line. [You might wish to use the **Alt-F3** Reveal Codes command to see the HRt codes at the end of each line.] If the report is too wide for your current margins you might wish to temporarily adjust the margins as needed. If the table falls across a page boundary, you might wish to insert a hard page break above the report, or use the **Alt-F4** Block command to define the report as a block, then use the **Shift-F8** command to protect the block.

```
SMITH -- B. McLaren 6/27/89
             SMITHTON RECREATIONAL VEHICLE SALES, INC.

                          1987          1988          1989
                       ---------------------------------------
SALES                     1405          1205          1150
EXPENSES
   Cost of Vehicles       786.8         674.8          644
   Salaries               120           130.8          142.572
   Administrative         175           175            175
   Marketing/Adv.         180           220            250
                       ---------------------------------------
   Total Expenses         1261.8        1200.6         1211.572
GROSS PROFIT              143.2         4.4            -61.572
```

Example: *Reading a Text File with Soft Returns*

For this example we will read a text file into WordPerfect and convert the hard returns to soft returns. We know that the file is called ACME.TXT, stored on the data disk.

```
Dear Irwin:

    Congratulations on signing the contract with Acme
Systems for your computer-based inventory/order entry
system. I am impressed by your dedicated efforts to learn
as much as possible about distributor systems in a short
period of time. In fact, the references you obtained from
other distributors and from manufacturer representatives
made the decision process much more straight-forward.

    I plan to be available in the future should you require
more assistance, but expect to be somewhat less involved
now that the purchase decision has been made. Good luck
with your data planning efforts and the July 11-12 course.

Sincerely,

Larry Gardner
Consultant

LG
```

FIGURE 9-5

Sample Text for Soft Return Retrieval

1. Start WordPerfect as usual, and with the cursor in the desired location for the new text, press the **Ctrl-F5** Text In/Out command.

2. At the next menu press **1** to enter the DOS Text menu. Because we wish to have the document inserted with soft returns, press **3**. WordPerfect will prompt you for the file name. Enter **ACME.TXT** and press **Enter**. (Also give the drive letter and directory if this file is not on the default directory.)

3. The sample text is shown in Figure 9-5. WordPerfect uses the **hyphenation zone** area to determine whether a line should have a hard return or a soft return at the end. If the line ends within the current hyphenation zone, it will have a soft return at the end. Otherwise there will be a hard return code. The default hyphenation zone is 10% of the line length, and may be changed with the **Shift-F8 1** Format Line command. If you make changes in the text retrieved with this method, any lines ending in a soft return will be automatically reformatted to fit the current line margins.

Importing a Lotus Worksheet File Directly

WordPerfect 5.1 is able to import a Lotus worksheet (.WK1) file directly, without going through convert or having Lotus output to a .PRN file. WordPerfect will import it into a WordPerfect table or directly into the document without the table grid lines. To use this feature, press **Ctrl-F5** (Text In/Out) and select **5** to indicate spreadsheet. Press **1** to Import and and you will see the menu shown in Figure 9-6. At the Spreadsheet Import screen press **1** to name the file. Choice **3** is used to determine whether a WordPerfect table or plain text is to be used to receive the spreadsheet. Choice **4** is used to perform the import.

FIGURE 9-6

WordPerfect Spreadsheet Import Screen (Press **Ctrl-F5 F 1**)

```
Spreadsheet: Import
    1 - Filename
    2 - Range
    3 - Type              Table
    4 - Perform Import
```

Example: *Importing a Spreadsheet Into a WordPerfect Table*

We will import a Lotus spreadsheet file called SMITH.WK1, stored on the data disk, into a WordPerfect table.

1. Start WordPerfect as usual and move the cursor to the desired location in the WordPerfect document to receive the spreadsheet.

2. Activate the Text/In command by pressing **Ctrl-F5**. Select Spreadsheet by pressing **5**, then Import by pressing **1**. Refer to the menu in Figure 9-6.

3. We'll assume the spreadsheet file is stored on the A drive. Press **1** and fill in the file name **A:SMITH.WK1** and press **Enter**. We will import the entire file range so leave the Range option unchanged.

4. Press **4** to Perform the import. You should see the same text as in the previous example, this time in a WordPerfect table. The table is shown in Figure 9-7.

Inserting a Lotus Graph Image into a Graphics Box

WordPerfect is able to directly read a number of graph image file types, including the Lotus .PIC file format. For those graph types that cannot be read directly, there is a graph file conversion program that comes with the WordPerfect 5.1 package. This text will not cover the graph conversion program, but more information is available in the WordPerfect Reference Manual.

The basic steps in importing a graphic image into WordPerfect include creating a graphic box, then providing the name of the file to be inserted into the box.

Example: *Importing a Lotus Graph into WordPerfect*

Suppose that we have a Lotus graph (see Figure 9-8) image stored in a file called EMMY41.PIC, and wish to insert it into a document called Emmy.

FIGURE 9-7

Table Created by WordPerfect

```
SMITH -- B. McLaren   6/27/89

          SMITHTON RECREATIONAL VEHICLE SALES, INC.

                              1987         1988         1989
                           ---------    ---------    ---------
SALES                        1405         1205         1150
EXPENSES
   Cost of Vehicles          786.8        674.8        644
   Salaries                  120          130.8        142.572
   Administrative            175          175          175
   Marketing/Adv.            180          220          250
                           ---------    ---------    ---------
   Total Expenses            1261.8       1200.6       1211.572

GROSS PROFIT                 143.2        4.4          -61.572
```

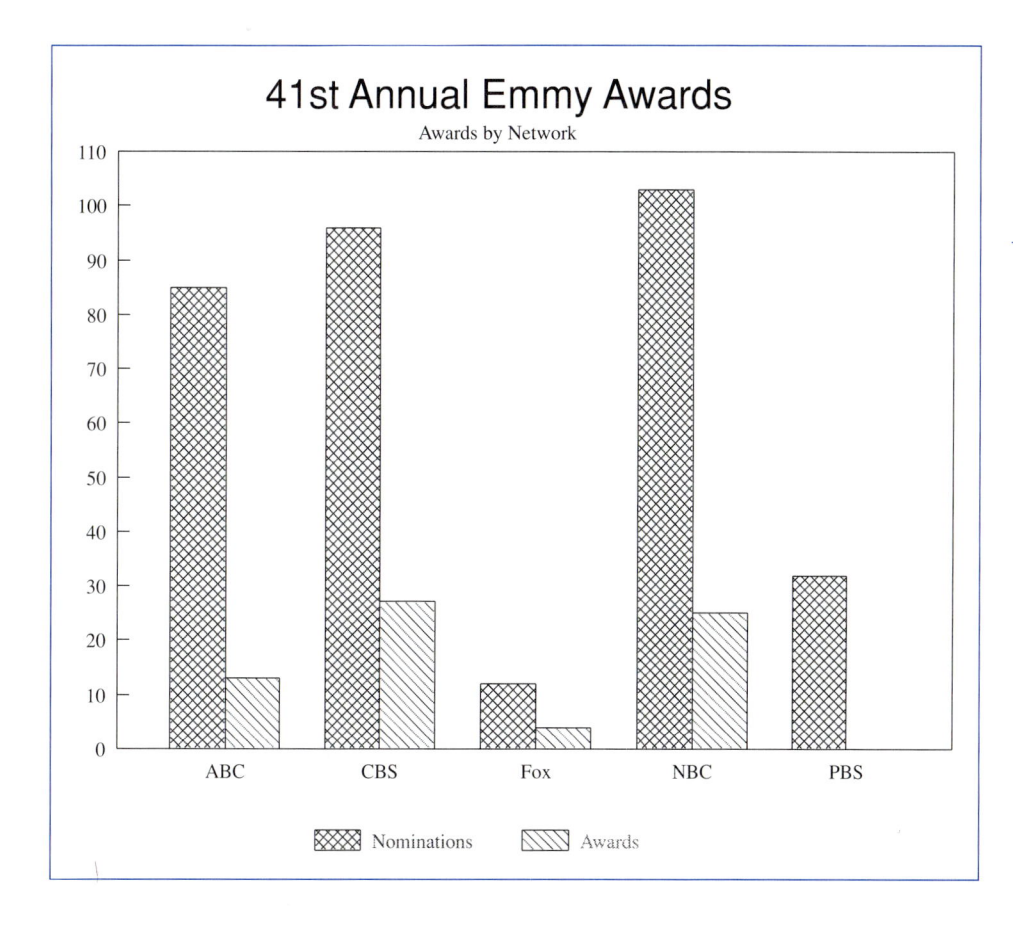

FIGURE 9-8

Sample Lotus .PIC File in Graphics Box

41st Annual Emmy Awards
Awards by Network

[Bar chart showing Nominations and Awards for ABC, CBS, Fox, NBC, PBS]

1. In WordPerfect, retrieve the EMMY document and move the cursor to the end. Press **Alt-F9** to view the Graphics menu.

2. Choose **1** to select Figure type and **1** to Create the graphic box.

3. From the Graph screen select **1** to enter the filename. Specify **EMMY41.PIC** (along with its location) and press **Enter**. Press **Enter** to leave Graphics.

4. WordPerfect will choose the size according to the image and the Horizontal Position selected, and place the graph on the page. The resulting graph is displayed below. Remember that WordPerfect supports three levels of print resolution (Draft, Medium, High), which will affect how the image is ultimately printed. Use View Document to see the page.

TRANSFERRING DATA FROM LOTUS 1-2-3

Lotus 1-2-3 will save data in several internal formats. The native format is the .WK1 file, and the text format is a .PRN file. Graph images are stored in a .PIC file which can be read by WordPerfect and some other packages such as Harvard Graphics and Ventura Publisher.

Creating a Lotus Text (.PRN) File

To create a text file from 1-2-3, issue the **/Print File** command (**/PF**) and provide the proper range to be printed. Lotus will use the current margins when printing to the printer or a file, so be sure the margins are wide enough to fit the lines on the page. Many users will wish to change the margins to zero within 1-2-3 and allow the destination package (usually the word processor) to do the line formatting.

Any other Print Options that are set, such as borders, headers and footers, will also be added to the .PRN file. Turn them off if they are not desired. You can use the **Unformatted** option (**/PFOOU**) to suspend printing of headers, footers and page breaks.

Example: *Printing to a Disk File*

In this example we will create the SMITH.PRN file that was discussed earlier.

1. First start 1-2-3 and retrieve the SMITH.WK1 file with **/FR**.

2. To print the worksheet to a file, issue the **/PF** command. When prompted for the name, reply with **SMITH** and press **Enter**; Lotus will fill in the .PRN file extension when the file is created. [Note: You can use a different file extension if desired—fill it in with the file name before you press **Enter**.]

3. Next Lotus will present the setting sheet for the print screen, as shown in Figure 9-9.

4. Select the **Range** option, and enter the print range as usual, in this case **A1..G17**.

5. Clear the margins by pressing the Options command (**O**) then **M** for Margins. In the Margins menu press **N** for None—this resets the left margin to 0, and the right margin to 240. Press **Q** to return to the main print menu.

6. To change the print type to unformatted, press **OOU** from the main print menu, then press **Q** to return to the main print menu.

7. Finally, press **G** (Go) to send the worksheet to the print file. This will only take a few seconds.

```
A1: 'SMITH -- B. McLaren  6/27/89                            MENU
Range Line  Page  Options  Clear  Align  Go  Quit
Specify a range to print
                    ─── Print Settings ───
   Destination:  D:\123\SMITH

   Range:

   Header:
   Footer:

   Margins:
     Left 4      Right 76    Top 2    Bottom 2

   Borders:
     Columns
     Rows

   Setup string:

   Page length:  66

   Output:       As-Displayed (Formatted)

28-Sep-90  09:20 PM
```

FIGURE 9-9

Lotus /Print File Screen (Press **/PF**)

8. You can **Quit** from the Print menu and return to the READY mode. If you save the worksheet at this point, the modified print settings will also be saved. Generally it is better to save the worksheet before you print to a file.

Using the Lotus Translate Module

Like WordPerfect, Lotus has a translation module that will convert between several file formats. The Translate module is accessed from the Lotus Access menu, not from 1-2-3. You must first save the worksheet file from 1-2-3, then Quit from 1-2-3. The Lotus Access menu is displayed in Figure 9-10.

The Translate module can convert a Lotus spreadsheet file to the following spreadsheet file formats:

- Lotus 1-2-3 Release 1a
- Lotus 1-2-3 Release 2, 2.01, and 2.2
- Lotus 1-2-3 Release 3.0
- dBASE II
- dBASE III, III PLUS, and IV
- Spreadsheet DIF format
- Symphony 1.0
- Symphony 1.1, 1.2, and 2.0

Release 2.2 files use the same format as Release 2 and 2.01. The following formats can be translated to the Lotus format:

- Lotus 1-2-3 Release 1a
- Lotus 1-2-3 Release 2, 2.01, and 2.2
- dBASE II

FIGURE 9-10

Lotus Access Menu (Translate Module)

```
1-2-3  PrintGraph  Translate  Install  Exit
Transfer data between 1-2-3 and other programs

                    1-2-3 Access System
                    Copyright  1986, 1989
                  Lotus Development Corporation
                      All Rights Reserved
                         Release 2.2

The Access system lets you choose 1-2-3, PrintGraph, the Translate utility,
and the Install program, from the menu at the top of this screen.  If
you're using a two-diskette system, the Access system may prompt you to
change disks.  Follow the instructions below to start a program.

o  Use → or ← to move the menu pointer (the highlighted rectangle
   at the top of the screen) to the program you want to use.

o  Press ENTER to start the program.

You can also start a program by typing the first character of its name.

Press HELP (F1) for more information.
```

- dBASE III, III PLUS, and IV
- Spreadsheet DIF format
- Multiplan
- Symphony 1.0
- Symphony 1.1, 1.2, and 2.0
- VisiCalc.

Example: *Translating from DIF to WK1 Format*

For this example we will take the EMPLOY.DIF file created in an earlier WordPerfect example and convert it to .WK1 format for Lotus Release 2.2.

1. Begin Lotus normally but do not go into 1-2-3. To use the Translate module, press **T** from the Access menu.

2. You will see the TRANSLATE FROM screen, shown in Figure 9-11, where Lotus asks you to name the type of file you wish to translate. Select the **DIF** file type by moving the cursor to that line and pressing **Enter**.

3. After you make the FROM selection, Lotus will present the TRANSLATE TO screen, shown in Figure 9-12, where you can select the type of file to translate to. Not all TO formats are available, depending upon which FROM format is chosen. From the TO screen select Release 2.2 as the desired format.

4. You will next see a screen asking for the name of the .DIF file. If the **EMPLOY.DIF** file is already shown on the screen, move the cursor to the file and press **Enter**. Otherwise follow the instructions on the screen to change to the directory where the .DIF file is stored.

5. Next you will provide a name for the new .WK1 file. Use **EMPLOY.WK1** as the name. Use the **Columnwise** version, indicating that the cells were stored in the .DIF file by column. Refer to Figure 9-13

TRANSFERRING DATA FROM LOTUS 1-2-3

```
         Lotus  1-2-3  Release 2.2 Translate Utility
   Copr. 1985, 1989  Lotus Development Corporation  All Rights Reserved

What do you want to translate FROM?

       1-2-3   1A
       1-2-3   2, 2.01 or 2.2
       dBase II
       dBase III
       DIF
       Multiplan (SYLK)
       Symphony  1.0
       Symphony  1.1, 1.2 or 2.0
       VisiCalc




              Highlight your selection and press ENTER
                Press ESC to end the Translate utility
                Press HELP (F1) for more information
```

FIGURE 9-11

Translate FROM Menu

```
         Lotus  1-2-3  Release 2.2 Translate Utility
   Copr. 1985, 1989  Lotus Development Corporation  All Rights Reserved

Translate FROM: DIF            What do you want to translate TO?

                                      1-2-3   1A
                                      1-2-3   2, 2.01 or 2.2
                                      Symphony  1.0
                                      Symphony  1.1, 1.2 or 2.0




              Highlight your selection and press ENTER
           Press ESC to return to the source product menu
                Press HELP (F1) for more information
```

FIGURE 9-12

Translate TO Menu

6. Press **Y** to perform the translation. Lotus will report that the conversion is completed. Press the **Esc** key two times to return to the Access menu.

7. To be sure that the original .DIF file is readable as a .WK1 file, go into the **1-2-3** module and retrieve the newly created EMPLOY.WK1 file. The EMPLOY.WK1 file is shown in Figure 9-14. Wider columns would show the complete data values. We could do further analysis on this data with Lotus, if desired.

FIGURE 9-13

Lotus Translate Screen for DIF Translation

```
                Lotus  1-2-3  Release 2.2 Translate Utility
         Copr. 1985, 1989 Lotus Development Corporation  All Rights Reserved

 Translate FROM: DIF                    Translate TO: 1-2-3 2.2

 Source file: D:\WP51\EMPLOY.DIF

 Target file: D:\WP51\EMPLOY.WK1




            Edit the target file specification if necessary and press ENTER
                     Press ESC to select a different source file
                       Press HELP (F1) for more information
```

FIGURE 9-14

Converted EMPLOY.WK1 File

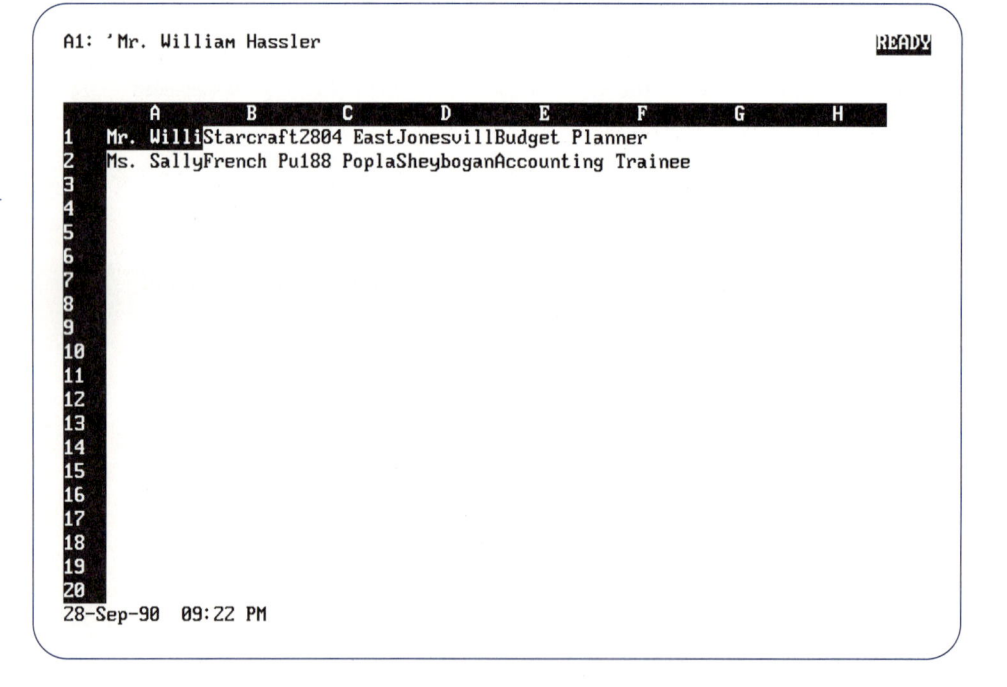

```
 A1: 'Mr. William Hassler                                              READY

         A     B     C     D     E     F     G     H
  1   Mr. WilliStarcraft2804 EastJonesvillBudget Planner
  2   Ms. SallyFrench Pu188 PoplaSheyboganAccounting Trainee
  3
  4
  ...
 20
 28-Sep-90  09:22 PM
```

Example: *Translating from WK1 to DBF Format*

This example will illustrate the process of converting a Lotus .WK1 worksheet file to the dBASE .DBF format. We will use a veterinarian database file, WABASH.WK1. A portion of that file is shown in Figure 9-15.

For .WK1 to .DBF translations, the Translate program requires that the first row of the file (or a named data range) contains valid dBASE-like field names, and the second row contains data values.

```
A1: [W10] 'WABASH -- B. McLaren  9/9/89                              READY

           A         B         C         D         E       F         G
    1  WABASH -- B. McLaren  9/9/89
    2
    3  WABASH ANIMAL HOSPITAL DATABASE
    4
    5  Date      Status    Owner     Pet Type  Invoice Treatment
    6  08-Nov-88 Paid      Smith     Cat            23 Immunization
    7  08-Nov-88 Paid      Fredericks Dog           18 Immunization
    8  09-Nov-88 No Charge Ottinger  Hamster         0 Physical
    9  09-Nov-88 Paid      Hollar    Dog            19 Grooming
   10  10-Nov-88 Paid      Robey     Porcupine      57 Trauma
   11  10-Nov-88 Paid      Rupert    Fish            6 Checkup
   12  12-Nov-88 No Charge Crow      Dog             0 Follow-up
   13  12-Nov-88 Paid      Bauer     Dog            19 Grooming
   14  12-Nov-88 Charge    Hier      Cat           192 Surgery
   15  14-Nov-88 Charge    Jetson    Cat            46 De-claw
   16  15-Nov-88 Paid      Bell      Cat            19 Grooming
   17  15-Nov-88 Paid      Vanderling Skunk         33 De-scent
   18  16-Nov-88 Charge    Giltner   Dog           129 Neuter
   19  16-Nov-88 Paid      Butwin    Bird           12 Checkup
   20  17-Nov-88 Charge    Kelly     Cat            18 Immunization
   28-Sep-90  09:22 PM
```

FIGURE 9-15

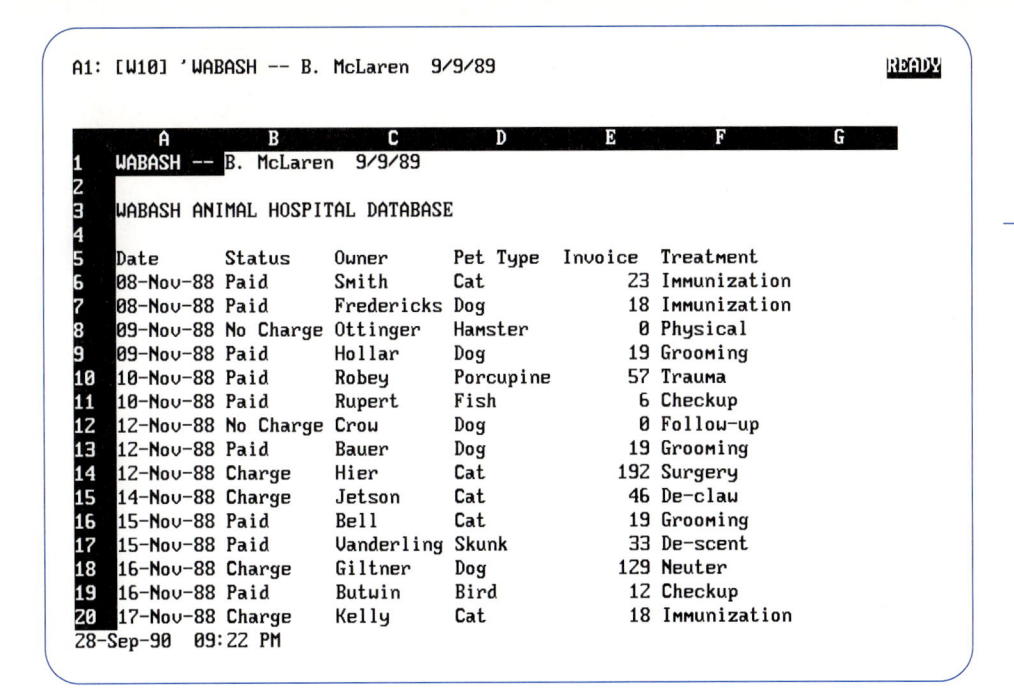

WABASH.WK1 Database Spreadsheet

1. In 1-2-3, retrieve the **WABASH.WK1** file. Create a range name to represent the database portion of the worksheet. Press **/Range Name Create** to create the named range. The range name is **DATA,** which represents the data in cells A1..F31. Change the width of column F to 12 characters. Save the WABASH worksheet file as usual with the **/FS** command.

2. After 1-2-3 has saved the data in the new file, **Quit** from 1-2-3. From the Lotus Access menu press **T** to enter the Translate module.

3. In Translate, select the **1-2-3 2, 2.01, 2.2** FROM option, and the **dBASE III** TO option. The FROM filename is **WABASH.WK1** and we'll choose **WABASH.DBF** for the TO name. You will see a help screen of instructions. Press **Esc** to continue.

4. Next you'll be asked to choose either the entire worksheet or a named range to translate. Select **Range**. When prompted for the range name, reply **DATA** and press **Enter**.

5. Lotus will create the WABASH.DBF file, displaying a chart showing percentage of completion. Press **Esc** two times to leave the Translate module.

The data transfer commands of the Lotus 1-2-3 /File menu are briefly summarized below:

- **Retrieve**   Replace the current worksheet in memory with a .WK1 file retrieved from the disk.

- **Save**   Saves the entire worksheet as a .WK1 file.

- **Combine**   Merge another .WK1 file into the current worksheet at the cursor location. Options are to **Copy**, **Add**, or **Subtract** merged cell values.

- **Xtract**   Copy a portion of the worksheet to a new .WK1 file.

TRANSFERRING DATA TO LOTUS 1-2-3

Combining Information into a Lotus 1-2-3 Worksheet

- **Import**   Merge a text file into the current worksheet at the cursor location. Options are to enter each row as **Text**, or break **Numbers** into separate columns. If the Text option is used, the **/Data Parse** command can be used to break the text into individual fields.

Release 2.2 also allows cell values from other worksheets to be **linked** to the current worksheet by using the **+<<filename.WK1>>celladdress** expression. The latter method requires no steps by the user to obtain the cell value from the worksheet stored on disk—the cell value is automatically fetched when the worksheet containing the link expression is retrieved, or when the **/File Admin Link** command is issued.

Importing Text Information into a Lotus 1-2-3 Worksheet

The **/File Import** command is able to bring text data into a 1-2-3 worksheet at the cursor location. You can select the **Text** option where each line of the text file (terminated by a carriage return and line feed) is placed into the first cell of a row in the worksheet. This is appropriate where the merged data is primarily text data. The **/Data Parse** command can be used to break a long label into separate columns, as shown in the example below.

Example: Importing a Text File into 1-2-3

This example will bring the EMPLOYEE.TXT database file into Lotus 1-2-3. You can assume that the original EMPLOYEE.DBF file was copied to a text file, as explained in the dBASE sections of this chapter. The EMPLOYEE.TXT file contains all fields for the full database of 18 records.

1. To merge the data from this file, open up a 1-2-3 worksheet and position the cursor at the location where the merged data is to be placed. In this case we'll place the data at the A1 cell.

2. Then issue the **/File Import** command. Next 1-2-3 will ask you to select between Text and Numbers. Pick **Text** for this example.

3. When prompted, enter the name of the merge file; in this case, type **EMPLOYEE.TXT** and press **Enter**. The first part of the spreadsheet will look like that shown in Figure 9-16.

Example: Parsing Data with 1-2-3

The spreadsheet looks just fine, but if you move the cursor to cell A3 you will see that the entire row of values has been placed into that cell. Adjacent columns are empty. To break the data into individual columns, you must use the **/Data Parse** command.

1. Move the cursor to cell A3, then press **/DP**.

2. Press **Enter** on the **Format-Line** menu choice, then select **Create**.

3. Based upon the format of the values in the first data row (where the cursor was placed initially), 1-2-3 will create a tentative format line that will be used to divide the information in the input column into separate fields. That format line may need to be edited, especially if there are spaces within any of the field values. The initial format line is shown in Figure 9-17. You can press the **F6** Window key in 1-2-3 to temporarily remove the settings sheet and see the underlying worksheet.

```
A1:                                                          READY

         A        B          C        D          E       F        G        H
    1
    2  Record#  EMP_NAME            DEPT        HIRE_DATE   SALARY COMMENTS TIT
    3     1     Williams, John      Accounts    10/01/76   19500.00 MEMO
    4     2     Johnson, Catherine  Personnel   12/17/81   14600.00 MEMO
    5     3     Schmidt, James      Finance     02/01/70   33000.00 MEMO
    6     4     Taylor, Donna       Management  08/22/86   29600.00 MEMO
    7     5     Anderson, Henry     Operations  06/19/82   22450.00 MEMO
    8
   ...
   20
   28-Sep-90  09:23 PM
```

FIGURE 9-16

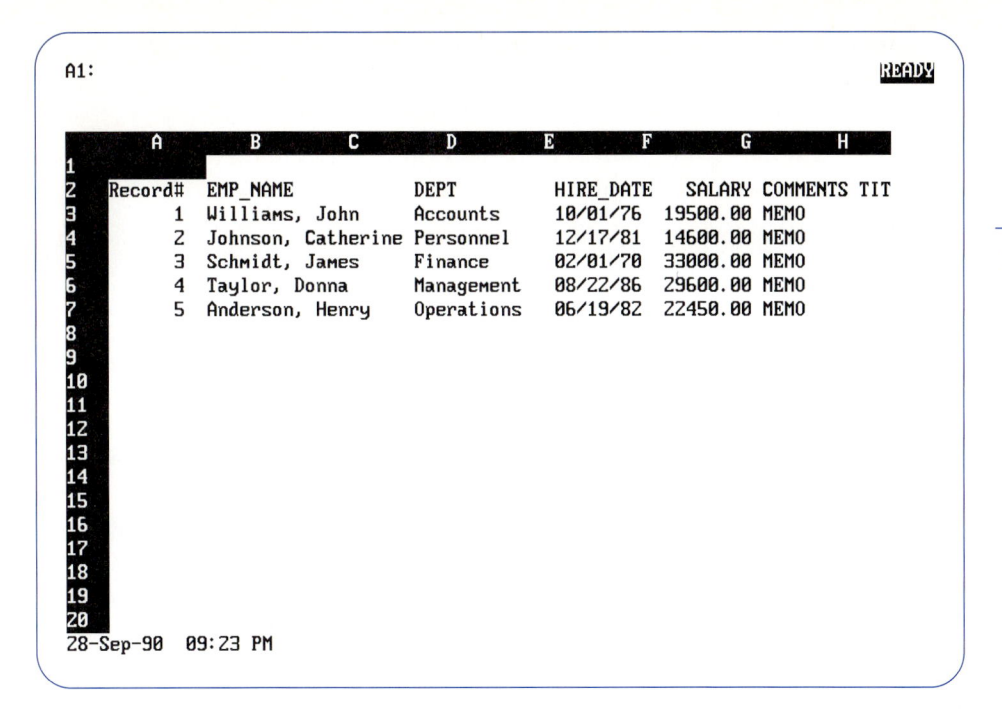

Spreadsheet Imported from Text File

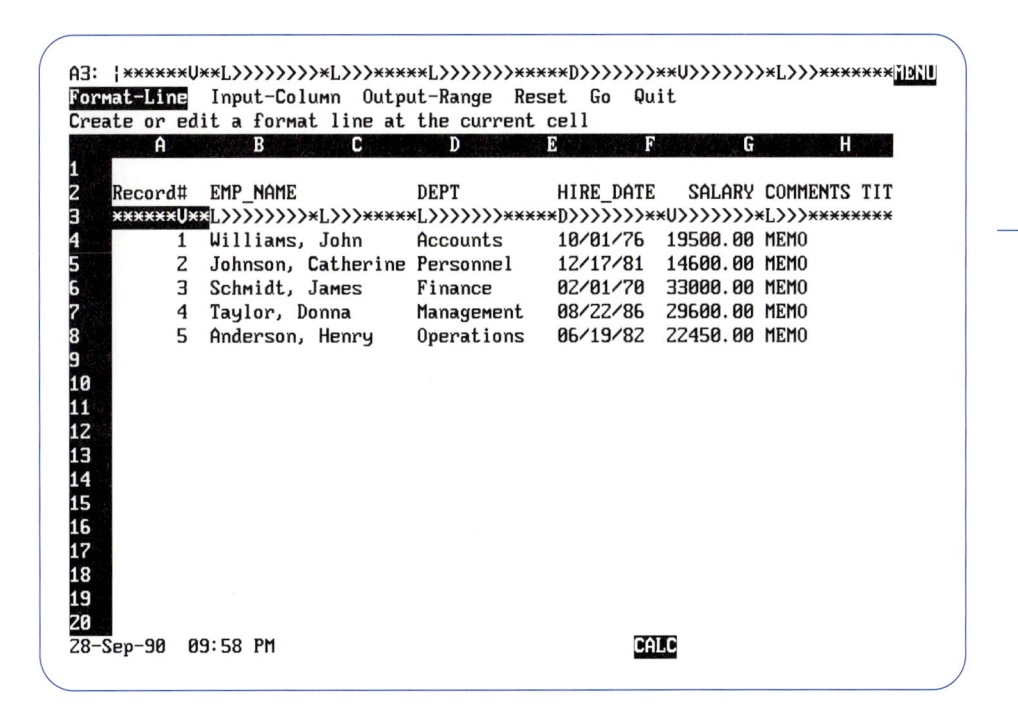

```
A3: |******U**L>>>>>>>*L>>>*****L>>>>>>*****D>>>>>>>**U>>>>>>>*L>>>*******  MENU
Format-Line  Input-Column  Output-Range  Reset  Go  Quit
Create or edit a format line at the current cell
         A        B          C        D          E       F        G        H
    1
    2  Record#  EMP_NAME            DEPT        HIRE_DATE   SALARY COMMENTS TIT
    3  ******U**L>>>>>>>*L>>>*****L>>>>>>*****D>>>>>>>**U>>>>>>>*L>>>*******
    4     1     Williams, John      Accounts    10/01/76   19500.00 MEMO
    5     2     Johnson, Catherine  Personnel   12/17/81   14600.00 MEMO
    6     3     Schmidt, James      Finance     02/01/70   33000.00 MEMO
    7     4     Taylor, Donna       Management  08/22/86   29600.00 MEMO
    8     5     Anderson, Henry     Operations  06/19/82   22450.00 MEMO
    9
   ...
   20
   28-Sep-90  09:58 PM                               CALC
```

FIGURE 9-17

Parse Format Line Created by 1-2-3

4. A complete discussion of format line symbols is given in the Lotus Reference Manual. The format line begins with the special character, |. The **V** represents a value item, and the **L** a label item. The > symbol is used to denote the extent of the field. The **D** shows a possible date field, and the * means to use that extra space (if needed) when breaking data into individual fields. We need to make several corrections to the format line.

5. While still in the /Data Parse menu, select **Format-Line** again, this time choosing **Edit**. Move the cursor to the desired spot with the arrow keys and

make the corrections. Press the **Ins** key as needed to switch between Insert and Overtype modes. The record number field is not needed, so we'll fill that field with **S** characters to skip it altogether.

6. The employee name field is broken at the comma between last and first names, so we'll replace the ***L** with two **>** symbols to make it one field.

7. Finally, the MEMO field did not copy from the dBASE file so replace that field with all **S** characters.

8. When finished editing, press **Enter** to leave EDIT mode. The new format line is shown in Figure 9-18.

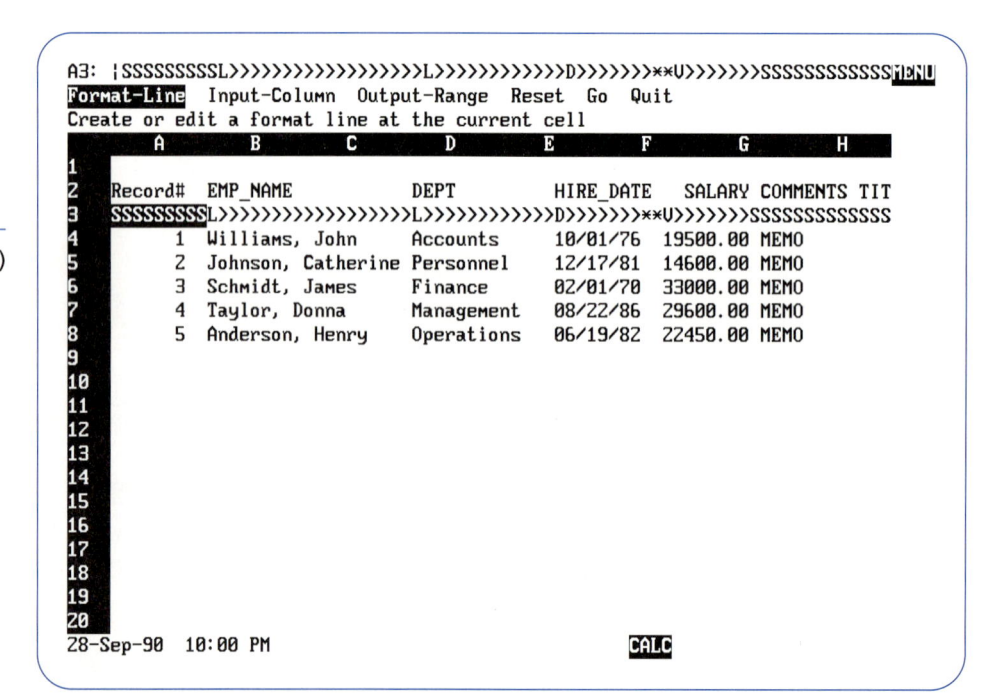

FIGURE 9-18

Revised Format Line (Row 3) for /Data Parse Example

```
A3: |SSSSSSSSSL>>>>>>>>>>>>>>>>L>>>>>>>>>>>>D>>>>>>>**U>>>>>>SSSSSSSSSSSSSMENU
Format-Line  Input-Column  Output-Range  Reset  Go  Quit
Create or edit a format line at the current cell
           A         B            C          D         E        F       G       H
 1
 2       Record#   EMP_NAME       DEPT       HIRE_DATE  SALARY  COMMENTS TIT
 3       SSSSSSSSSL>>>>>>>>>>>>>>>>L>>>>>>>>>>>>D>>>>>>>**U>>>>>>SSSSSSSSSSSSS
 4           1     Williams, John    Accounts     10/01/76   19500.00  MEMO
 5           2     Johnson, Catherine Personnel   12/17/81   14600.00  MEMO
 6           3     Schmidt, James    Finance      02/01/70   33000.00  MEMO
 7           4     Taylor, Donna     Management   08/22/86   29600.00  MEMO
 8           5     Anderson, Henry   Operations   06/19/82   22450.00  MEMO
 9
10
11
12
13
14
15
16
17
18
19
20
28-Sep-90   10:00 PM                                          CALC
```

FIGURE 9-19

Parsed Data for Example

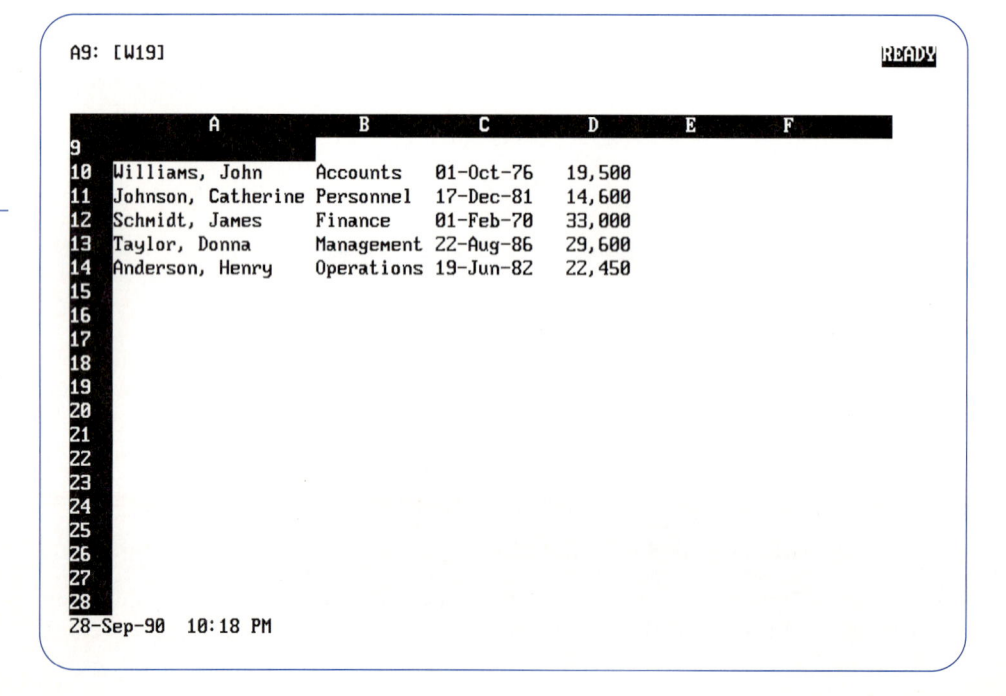

```
A9: [W19]                                                        READY

           A            B            C          D         E        F
 9
10    Williams, John    Accounts    01-Oct-76   19,500
11    Johnson, Catherine Personnel  17-Dec-81   14,600
12    Schmidt, James    Finance     01-Feb-70   33,000
13    Taylor, Donna     Management  22-Aug-86   29,600
14    Anderson, Henry   Operations  19-Jun-82   22,450
15
16
17
18
19
20
21
22
23
24
25
26
27
28
28-Sep-90   10:18 PM
```

9. Finally we are ready to actually parse the data. You must specify the **Input-Column** range, in this case **A3..A8**. The **Output-Range** can be given as **A10..F14**.

10. Press **Go** and the data will be copied to the output range as specified by the format line.

11. After widening columns A and B, and formatting the date and salary fields, the data will look like Figure 9-19.

TRANSFERRING DATA FROM dBASE IV

Because the dBASE III/IV file format is well known,[3] many other packages are able to read or convert those formats directly. The Lotus Translate program can convert from dBASE to any of the 1-2-3 file formats. Although WordPerfect cannot convert the .DBF file format directly, other forms such as Spreadsheet .DIF are common to both packages.

Using the COPY TO Command to Export Data

The dBASE **COPY TO** command can be used to copy information from one file to another. The syntax of this command is

```
COPY TO <filename> [[TYPE] <filetype>]
```

The <filetype> is taken from the following table (file types *not* available in dBASE III PLUS are marked):

Filetype	Meaning
(Omitted)	Uses dBASE IV .DBF format.
DBASEII	The dBASE II .DB2 file format (not in III PLUS).
DELIMITED	Each field is right-trimmed and the values are enclosed in quotations. Uses .TXT extension.
DIF	Spreadsheet .DIF format.
FW2	Framework II file format (not in III PLUS).
RPD	RapidFile file format (not in III PLUS).
SDF	Standard data format where fields are fixed-length and run together with no space between. Uses .TXT extension.
SYLK	Multiplan SYLK file format.
WKS	Lotus 1-2-3 Release 1a file format.

From the dot prompt you should open a database file as usual. If an index is in use the records will be ordered according to the controlling key field. Then issue the **COPY TO** command, specifying the destination file name and the type of destination file. The word **TYPE** is optional, as indicated by the square brackets in the syntax expression above. If no filetype is specified, the destination file will have the dBASE IV .DBF format.

---

[3] There are minor differences between the file formats of dBASE III and IV, but for most purposes they are interchangeable. dBASE III+ is able to read dBASE IV data files provided no features specific to dBASE IV are used..

Example: Create an SDF Text File with the COPY TO Command

For this example we will create a text file using the COPY TO command from the dBASE dot prompt. We need to use the **EMPLOYEE.DBF** file from the data disk.

1. From the dot prompt, issue the command **USE EMPLOYEE**. dBASE will open the database file and position the record pointer at the top of the file.

2. Then issue the command **COPY TO EMP1 SDF** and press **Enter**. dBASE will report the number of records copied and display the next dot prompt. The text file EMP1.TXT will be created on the default drive.

3. You can display the file by using the dBASE **TYPE EMP1.TXT** command. Note that with the SDF filetype the fields are packed together with no spaces between field values. The date field is converted to YYYYMMDD format with this copy option. Figure 9-20 shows these commands.

Example: Create a WKS File with the COPY TO Command

This example creates a Lotus 1-2-3 (Release 1a) worksheet file using the COPY TO command.

1. As in the previous example, give the **USE EMPLOYEE** command from the dot prompt to open the database file.

2. Then give the **COPY TO EMP2 WKS** command. dBASE will copy the records, creating a new file called EMP2.WKS on the default drive. You cannot TYPE a worksheet file, but it can be read directly into Lotus 1-2-3 with the 1-2-3 /**File Retrieve** command. The memo field is not copied to the .WKS file, but the dates are correctly converted to the Lotus date format.

3. The Lotus worksheet is shown in Figure 9-21 after columns are widened to show the data.

Creating a Text File with the dBASE IV LIST TO FILE Command

It is also possible to use the dBASE IV **LIST TO FILE** command to create a text file. The LIST command will copy the fields and field names for all records to the text file unless otherwise specified. All of the usual LIST options are available including the **FOR** and **WHERE** clauses, and a field list to indicate the fields and their order in the new file. If the TO FILE option is not included, the records will be listed only on the display. The LIST TO FILE command results in a file that is quite similar to the COPY TO SDF command, except that there is a space between field values and the field names are printed first. The record number is also placed in the file unless the keyword **OFF** is placed at the end of the **LIST** command line. This command is not available in dBASE III PLUS.

Example: Create a Text File with the LIST TO FILE Command

This example will create the EMPLOYEE.TXT text file that was used in the Lotus /File Import example.

FIGURE 9-20

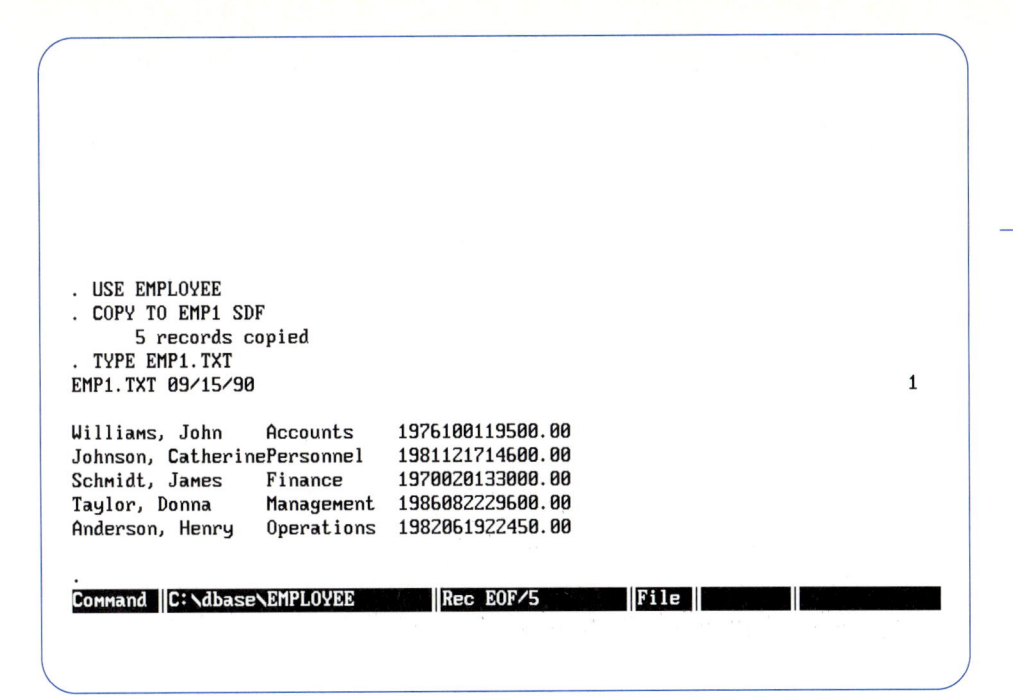

Illustration of Creating an SDF File from dBASE

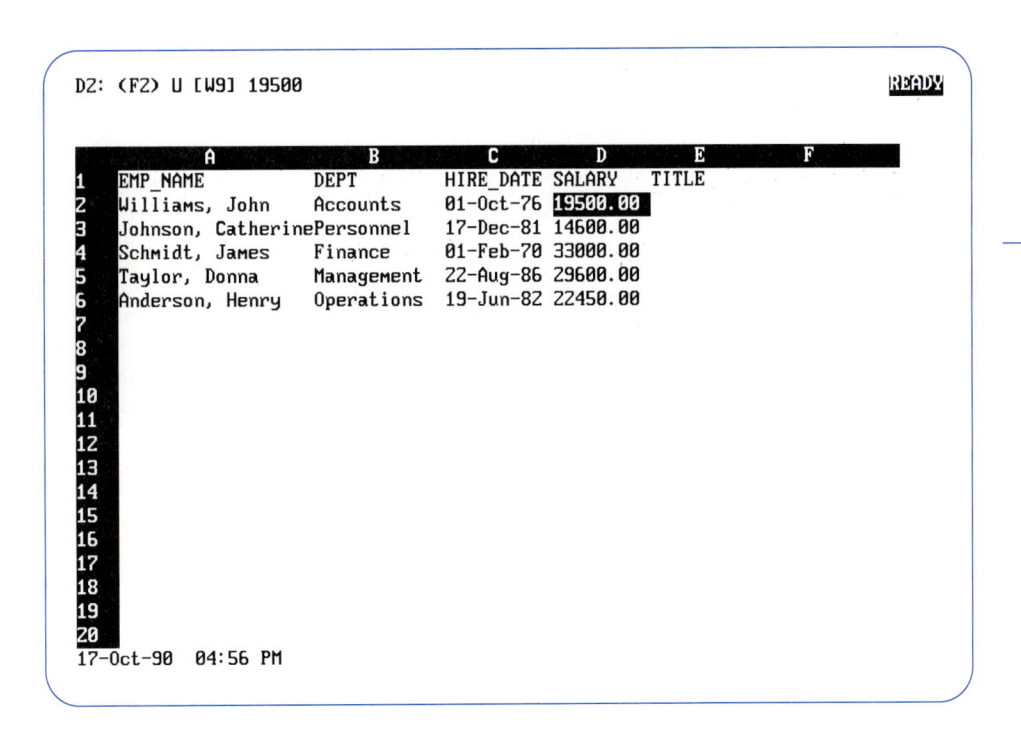

```
. USE EMPLOYEE
. COPY TO EMP1 SDF
     5 records copied
. TYPE EMP1.TXT
EMP1.TXT  09/15/90                                      1

Williams, John      Accounts      1976100119500.00
Johnson, Catherine  Personnel     1981121714600.00
Schmidt, James      Finance       1970020133000.00
Taylor, Donna       Management    1986082229600.00
Anderson, Henry     Operations    1982061922450.00
.
```

Command │ C:\dbase\EMPLOYEE │ Rec EOF/5 │ File

FIGURE 9-21

EMP2.WKS File Converted from EMPLOYEE.DBF

```
D2: (F2) U [W9] 19500                                    READY

        A                    B           C         D        E      F
1   EMP_NAME              DEPT         HIRE_DATE  SALARY   TITLE
2   Williams, John        Accounts     01-Oct-76  19500.00
3   Johnson, Catherine    Personnel    17-Dec-81  14600.00
4   Schmidt, James        Finance      01-Feb-70  33000.00
5   Taylor, Donna         Management   22-Aug-86  29600.00
6   Anderson, Henry       Operations   19-Jun-82  22450.00
7
...
20
17-Oct-90  04:56 PM
```

---

1. As before, issue the **USE EMPLOYEE** command from the dot prompt.

2. Then give the **LIST TO FILE EMPLOYEE** command. dBASE will list the records on the screen and will copy them to a text file called EMPLOYEE.TXT.

3. You can issue the **TYPE EMPLOYEE.TXT** command to display the text file as shown in Figure 9-22.

Chapter 9 — Integrating the Tools

FIGURE 9-22

Illustration of LIST TO FILE Example

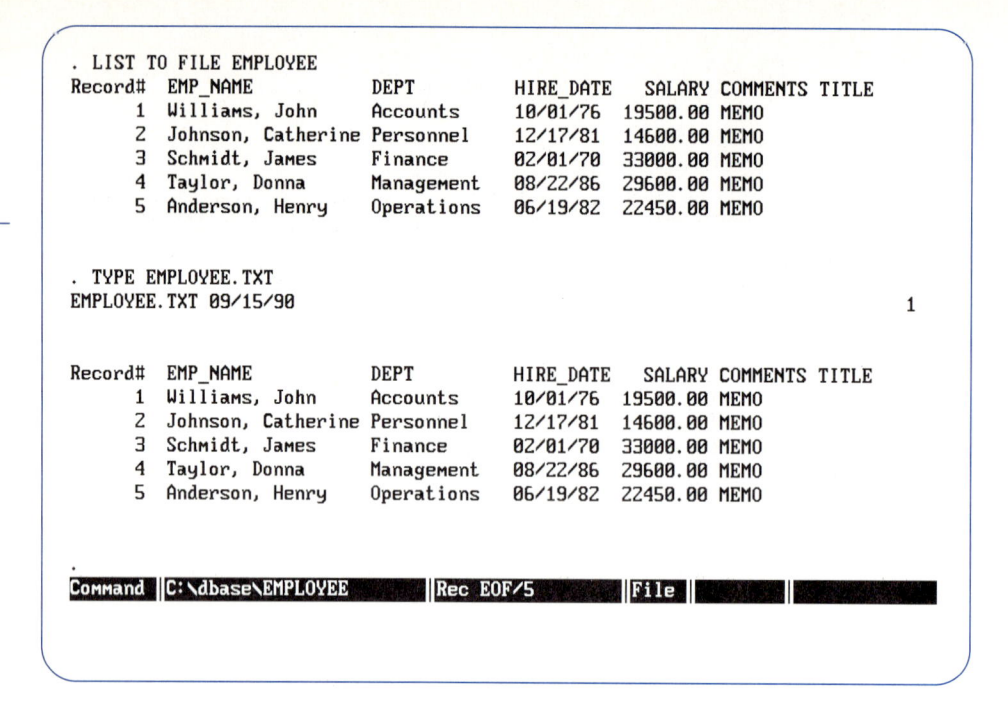

```
. LIST TO FILE EMPLOYEE
Record#  EMP_NAME           DEPT         HIRE_DATE   SALARY   COMMENTS TITLE
      1  Williams, John     Accounts     10/01/76    19500.00 MEMO
      2  Johnson, Catherine Personnel    12/17/81    14600.00 MEMO
      3  Schmidt, James     Finance      02/01/70    33000.00 MEMO
      4  Taylor, Donna      Management   08/22/86    29600.00 MEMO
      5  Anderson, Henry    Operations   06/19/82    22450.00 MEMO

. TYPE EMPLOYEE.TXT
EMPLOYEE.TXT 09/15/90                                                        1

Record#  EMP_NAME           DEPT         HIRE_DATE   SALARY   COMMENTS TITLE
      1  Williams, John     Accounts     10/01/76    19500.00 MEMO
      2  Johnson, Catherine Personnel    12/17/81    14600.00 MEMO
      3  Schmidt, James     Finance      02/01/70    33000.00 MEMO
      4  Taylor, Donna      Management   08/22/86    29600.00 MEMO
      5  Anderson, Henry    Operations   06/19/82    22450.00 MEMO

.
Command   C:\dbase\EMPLOYEE          Rec EOF/5      File
```

Exporting Data from the dBASE IV Control Center

The same data export options are available with the Control Center Menu Bar. From the main Control Center screen press the **F10** key to activate the Menu Bar. Move the cursor to the **Tools** bar and select the *Export* line. The menu shows each of the file types available from the COPY TO command, along with the resulting file extension. The *Text fixed-length fields* choice is the SDF file type discussed earlier. That display is shown in Figure 9-23. To select a choice, use the arrow keys to move the cursor to the desired line and press **Enter**.

Next dBASE will prompt for the name of the file you wish to copy. A new file with the same name but the appropriate extension will be created, and all records from the first file are copied. Note that you cannot create a file with a new name from the Control Center Export command. The destination file must be listed in the file name prompt box that appears next. In this context the COPY TO command issued from the dot prompt offers more flexibility.

Example: *Create a Delimited (MailMerge) File*

Suppose we wish to create a mailmerge format file for export to a word processor that will merge print customized letters.

1. For this file we will use the HABITAT.DBF file, so from the dBASE Control Center select **HABITAT** from the Data panel.

2. Then activate the Menu Bar with the **F10** key, and select the *Export* line of the **Tools** pull-down menu.

3. Move the cursor to the *Character delimited {"}* line and press **Enter**. Press **Enter** again at the next menu when dBASE shows you the possible delimiting characters—this selects the double quotation symbol to surround each data field.

FIGURE 9-23

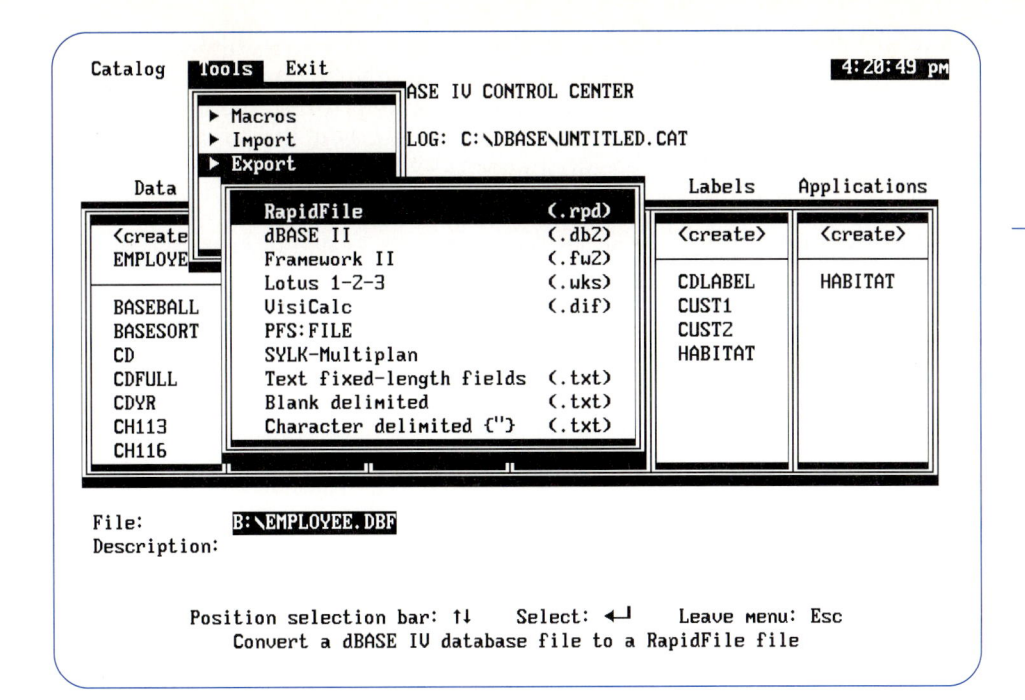

dBASE IV Export Menu

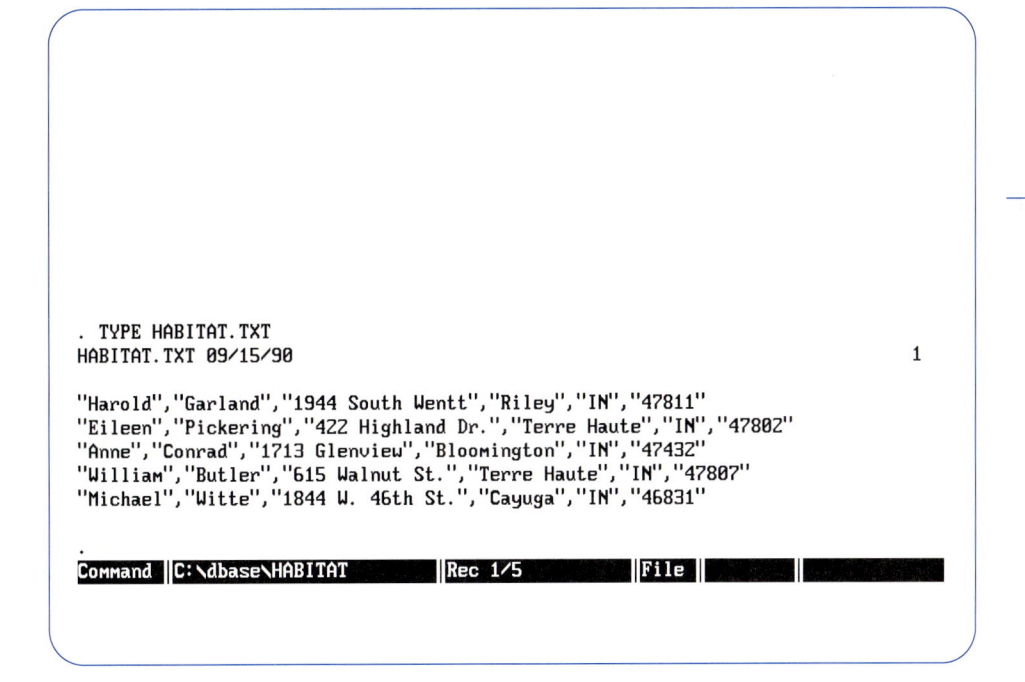

FIGURE 9-24

Contents of Delimited (MailMerge Format) File

4. Select **HABITAT** from the filename list. dBASE will create a new file called HABITAT.TXT that will contain the records. Each field is enclosed in quotations, and fields are separated with a comma. Each record is terminated with a carriage return and line feed. The contents of that file are shown in Figure 9-24.

TRANSFERRING DATA TO dBASE IV

There are several ways to add data to dBASE IV database files. The direct method is to issue the **APPEND** command and type the data in at the keyboard. Of course, if the data already exist in another file, it would seem desirable to **APPEND FROM** that file. In fact, dBASE supports several file import protocols, in addition to importing data from other dBASE IV .DBF files.

Using the APPEND FROM Command with Other Files

The **APPEND FROM** command will add data to the end of the current data file from the named file in the command line. You must already have a file structure in use before using APPEND FROM. The syntax of this command is:

```
APPEND FROM <filename> [[TYPE] <filetype>]
```

The <filetype> is taken from the following table (file types not available in dBASE III PLUS are marked):

Filetype	Meaning
(Omitted)	Uses dBASE IV .DBF format.
DBASEII	The dBASE II .DB2 file format (not in III PLUS).
DELIMITED	Each field is right-trimmed and the values are enclosed in quotations. Uses .TXT extension.
DIF	Spreadsheet .DIF format.
FW2	Framework II file format (not in III PLUS).
RPD	RapidFile file format (not in III PLUS).
SDF	Standard data format where fields are fixed-length and run together with no space between. Uses .TXT extension.
SYLK	Multiplan SYLK file format.
WKS	Lotus 1-2-3 Release 1a file format (not Release 2.x files).

Importing Data from Other Files

The dBASE **IMPORT FROM** command is used to translate from various file types, including Lotus Release 2.x .WK1 files. No structure need be created before issuing the command. It will create a database file with the same name as the original file, using the .DBF extension. The field names will be A, B, C, etc. You can change the field names using the MODIFY STRUCTURE command after importing the data values. The syntax of the command is:

```
IMPORT FROM <filename> [[TYPE] <filetype>]
```

The <filetype> is taken from the following table (dBASE III PLUS supports only the PFS type):

Filetype	Meaning
(Omitted)	Uses dBASE IV .DBF format.
PFS	PFS:File format.
DBASEII	dBASE II .DBF format.
FW2	Framework II file format.
RPD	RapidFile file format.
WK1	Lotus 1-2-3 Release 2.x format.

TRANSFERRING DATA TO dBASE IV

FIGURE 9-25

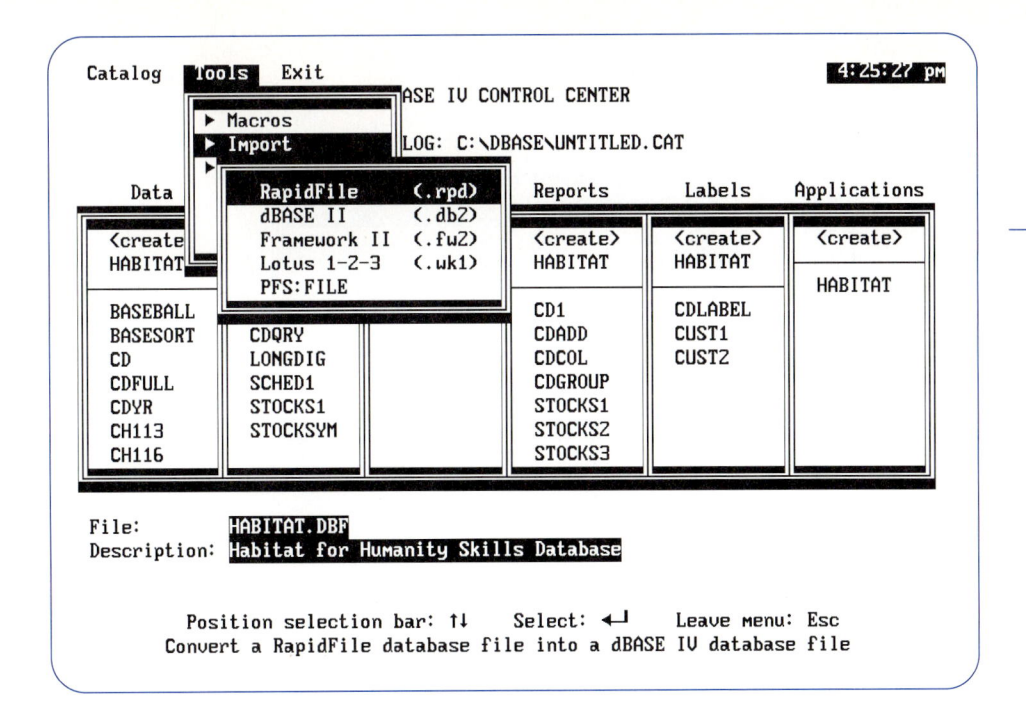

dBASE IV Import Menu

The previous command is issued from the dot prompt. You can achieve the same results from the Control Center. To activate the Control Center import facility, press **F10**, then select the *Import* line from the **Tools** bar. The Import menu is shown in Figure 9-25. The Control Center offers conversion from the following file types:

Filetype	Meaning
RPD	RapidFile file format.
DB2	dBASE II format.
FW2	FrameWork II format.
WK1	Lotus 1-2-3 Release 2, 2.01, 2.2 format.
PFS	PFS:File file format.

The Import procedure is similar to Export, except that you are given a list of files from which to choose a source of data. You may need to change to the directory where the data file of the specified type is stored. With 1-2-3 files be sure to save the worksheet with column widths sufficient to display all the data in a cell, otherwise dBASE will import only the data that fits within the column width.

There is another way to add data to a file. From the Database Design screen (**Shift-F2** from the main Control Center screen) activate the Menu Bar with **F10** and move to the **Append** bar. The three choices there are:

- Enter records from keyboard
- Append records from dBASE file
- Copy records from non-dBASE file.

The last choice allows input from the same kinds of files that were available for export in the previous section. The full screen is shown in Figure 9-26. Note that the only Lotus 1-2-3 files that may be appended from this screen are .WKS files. The **Import** Menu Bar command can also import .WK1 files.

FIGURE 9-26

dBASE Append Menu–
Copy Records

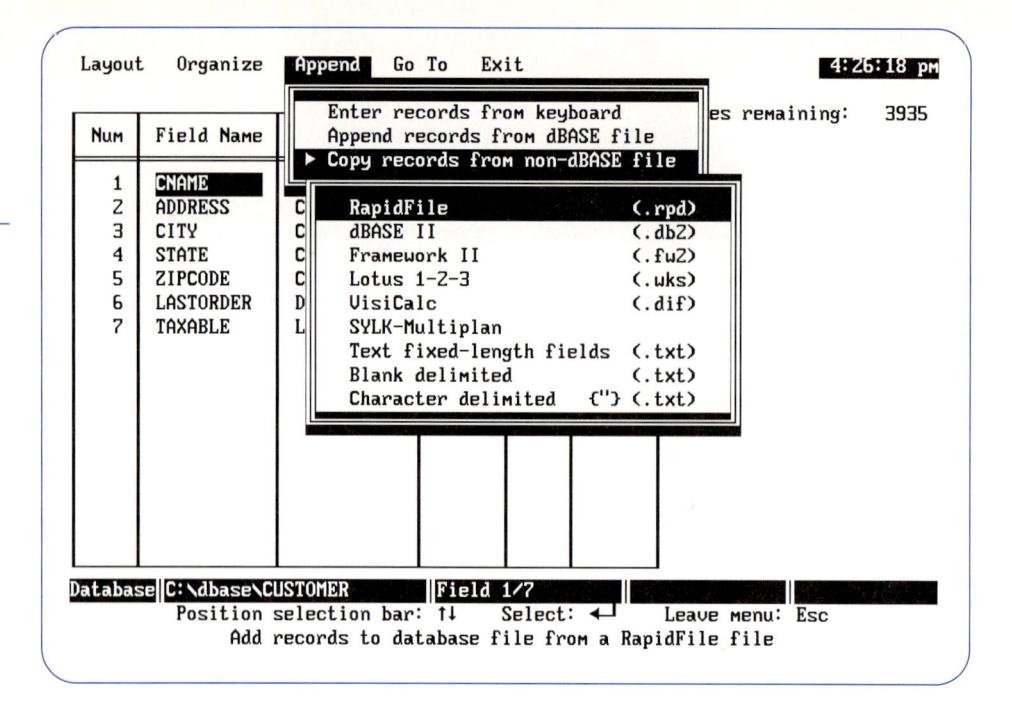

```
 Layout    Organize   Append    Go To    Exit               4:26:18 pm
                       Enter records from keyboard       es remaining:  3935
   Num   Field Name   Append records from dBASE file
                    ▶ Copy records from non-dBASE file
    1   CNAME
    2   ADDRESS    C    RapidFile              (.rpd)
    3   CITY       C    dBASE II               (.db2)
    4   STATE      C    Framework II           (.fw2)
    5   ZIPCODE    C    Lotus 1-2-3            (.wks)
    6   LASTORDER  D    VisiCalc               (.dif)
    7   TAXABLE    L    SYLK-Multiplan
                        Text fixed-length fields  (.txt)
                        Blank delimited           (.txt)
                        Character delimited {"}   (.txt)



 Database│C:\dbase\CUSTOMER       │Field 1/7
           Position selection bar: ↑↓    Select: ↵     Leave menu: Esc
               Add records to database file from a RapidFile file
```

Example: Adding Records from Another dBASE File

It is possible to add records from another dBASE III PLUS or IV database file. Data will be copied from fields with the same names. No data is copied from fields that don't have the same names. For this example we will add records to a CUSTOMER database from another database file called PROSPECT.DBF, merging the two together into a single database. The contents of PROSPECT.DBF are shown in Figure 9-27. Note that the last field does not exist in the CUSTOMER database, and that several of the fields are of different lengths.

1. To merge the two files together, first open the **CUSTOMER** file from the dBASE Control Center.

2. Then press **Shift-F2** to open the Database Design screen. Activate the Menu Bar with **F10** and select the *Append records from dBASE file* line of the **Append** pull-down menu.

3. Next dBASE will display a list of all the .DBF files in the current directory; move the cursor to **PROSPECT.DBF** and press **Enter** to select it. Its four records will be appended to the end of the CUSTOMER file.

4. The CUSTOMER file will look like Figure 9-28. The final four records (those without last order dates) came from the PROSPECT file.

When adding records from an SDF text file, you must be aware of the structure of the target database file. The fields must be arranged in the same order in the target database file and in the text file. Fields are filled according to the number of characters in the field width. If the first field is 15 characters wide, the first 15 characters in the text file will be placed in the first field. With a

Records Organize Fields Go To Exit

CNAME	ADDRESS	CITY	STATE	ZIPCODE	REFERENCE
Mostichello, B,	226 Woodside Drive	Chicago	IL	60606	SP22
Frederick, R.	2444 Ashton Street	Urbana	IL	63204	SM07
Kellerman, F.	40 Wall St.,Suite 18	New York	NY	10012	BA09
Jenkins, S.	4509 Pendleton Lane	Anderson	IN	46588	IS001

Browse | C:\dbase\PROSPECT | Rec 1/4 | File

FIGURE 9-27

Contents of PROSPECT Database

Records Organize Fields Go To Exit

CNAME	ADDRESS	CITY	STATE	ZIPCODE	LASTORDER	TA
Jones, B.	244 19th St.	Wabash	IN	47521	06/21/89	Y
Hollar, W.	1804 Thames	Richmond	IN	46154	10/15/89	N
Anderson, M.	Box 128	Vincennes	IN	48231	02/01/88	Y
Snow, B.	605 Ohio St.	Terre Haute	IN	47807	09/13/89	Y
O'Reilly, W.	1332 Western	Cory	IN	47823	09/30/89	N
Mains, W.	2199 West Laurin	Princeton	IN	47233	06/12/72	Y
Mostichello, B,	226 Woodside Drive	Chicago	IL	60606	/ /	
Frederick, R.	2444 Ashton Street	Urbana	IL	63204	/ /	
Kellerman, F.	40 Wall St.,Suite 18	New York	NY	10012	/ /	
Jenkins, S.	4509 Pendleton Lane	Anderson	IN	46588	/ /	

Browse | C:\dbase\CUSTOMER | Rec 1/10 | File

FIGURE 9-28

Results of Append Operation

delimited data text file, each field receives the next delimited value from the text file.

A better way to handle text transfers into dBASE is to first determine the structure implied by the fields as they appear in the text file, then create that structure in a temporary dBASE database file. Next import the data into the temporary database file. The database file can then be appended to the designated target database file using the *Append records from dBASE file* option.

FIGURE 9-29

Contents of ACCOUNTS.TXT and Structure of TEMPCUST.DBF

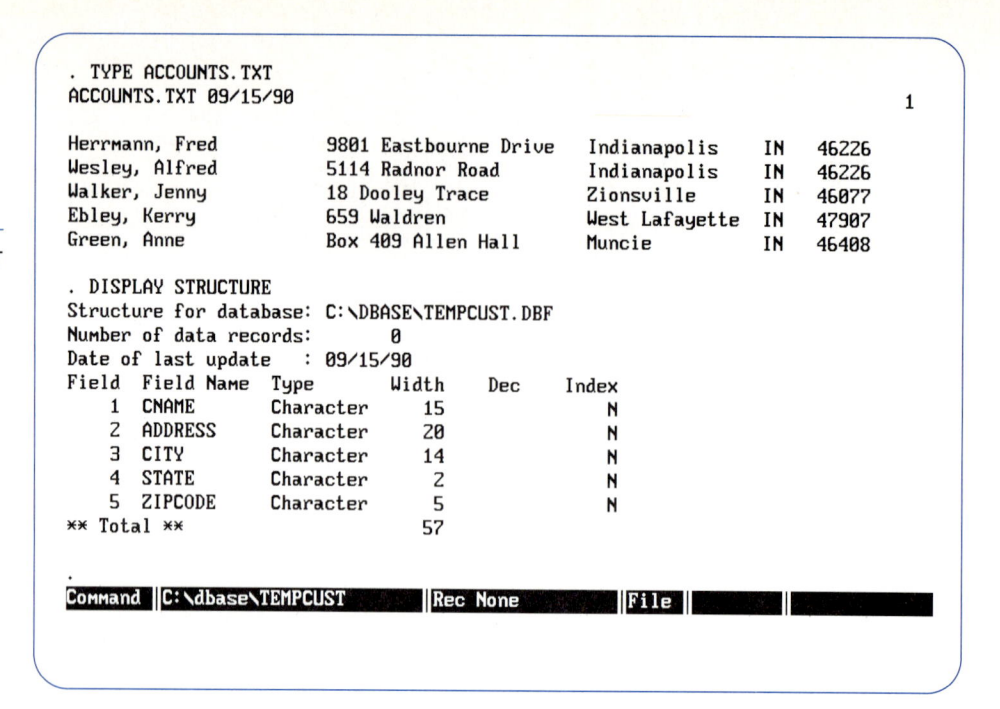

```
. TYPE ACCOUNTS.TXT
ACCOUNTS.TXT  09/15/90                                                    1
   Herrmann, Fred      9801 Eastbourne Drive   Indianapolis    IN   46226
   Wesley, Alfred      5114 Radnor Road        Indianapolis    IN   46226
   Walker, Jenny       18 Dooley Trace         Zionsville      IN   46077
   Ebley, Kerry        659 Waldren             West Lafayette  IN   47907
   Green, Anne         Box 409 Allen Hall      Muncie          IN   46408
. DISPLAY STRUCTURE
Structure for database: C:\DBASE\TEMPCUST.DBF
Number of data records:         0
Date of last update   : 09/15/90
Field  Field Name  Type        Width   Dec   Index
    1  CNAME       Character      15           N
    2  ADDRESS     Character      20           N
    3  CITY        Character      14           N
    4  STATE       Character       2           N
    5  ZIPCODE     Character       5           N
** Total **                       57
.
```
`Command` `C:\dbase\TEMPCUST` `Rec None` `File`

Example: Adding Records from a Text File

Suppose we have the following text data stored in a file called ACCOUNTS.TXT. That file is shown in Figure 9-29 with a tentative file structure for the temporary file which is called **TEMPCUST**. Note that the field names are the same as those in the CUSTOMER.DBF file, in anticipation of merging the ACCOUNTS data into that file. But the field widths were chosen to match the text data as it appears in the ACCOUNTS.TXT file.

1. To merge the two files together, change to the Database Design screen in dBASE (**Shift-F2** from the Control Center) and activate the *Copy records from non-dBASE file* line of the **Append** pull-down menu.

2. Then select *Text fixed-length records* and press **Enter**.

3. The text file that contains our data is **ACCOUNTS.TXT**. Move the cursor to that file and press **Enter**. The data will be merged into the TEMPCUST file.

4. Next, select the **CUSTOMER** file from the Data panel in the Control Center, then switch to the Database Design screen.

5. Activate the Menu Bar, then choose the *Append records from dBASE file* line of the **Append** option of that menu.

6. Select the **TEMPCUST** file from the list of files, and press **Enter**. The fields from the TEMPCUST file will be appended to the end of the CUSTOMER file. Of course, there will be blank values for those fields that were not present in the TEMPCUST file.

KEY TERMS

291

CHAPTER REVIEW

Exchanging Data Between Software Packages

The three software packages studied in this book are able to exchange information in many ways. Each is able to save and retrieve data in the plain text, or ASCII format. But to retain formatting and other special characteristics, the native file format of the package should be used. WordPerfect is able to save documents in the native 5.1, 5.0, and 4.2 file formats. Lotus 1-2-3 uses the .WK1 format, and dBASE IV saves data to .DBF files.

Transferring Data form WordPerfect

WordPerfect will save to a text file or WP 4.2 file with the Ctrl-F5 Text In/Out command. The same command permits importation of a text file. If the usual F10 Save or F7 Exit commands are used to save the document, the WP 5.1 format is chosen.

WordPerfect Convert Program

Each package is equipped with a conversion or translation program that can accommodate numerous file formats. The WordPerfect CONVERT.EXE program handles eight formats, including .DIF, WordStar, MultiMate II, and Mailmerge. WordPerfect will import graphic images in several formats, including Lotus .PIC files and the popular .TIF and .PCX graphic formats.

Transferring Data from Lotus 1-2-3

The Lotus Translate module handles 10 formats, including other 1-2-3 and Symphony formats, dBASE, .DIF, and Multiplan files. The /Print File command is used to create a text file, and the /File Import will read a text file into the current worksheet. Unusually formatted text lines can be broken into individual columns by use of the /Data Parse command.

Transferring Data from dBASE IV

dBASE IV will export and import using ten different file types, including several text-type formats. The COPY TO and APPEND FROM commands are used from the dot prompt, while the **Tools** menu of the Menu Bar is use from the Control Center.

KEY TERMS

1-2-3 .PRN format
1-2-3 .WK1 format
1-2-3 .WKS format
APPEND FROM command
ASCII (text) file
conversion (translate)
   program
COPY TO
/Data Parse
dBASE .DBF format
dBASE .TXT format
delimited file
.DIF format

Exit (**F7**)
export
/File Combine
/File Import
/File Xtract
fixed-length fields
hyphenation zone
IMPORT FROM
link expression
Lotus Translate module
mailmerge format
native format

/Print File command
Save (**F10**)
SDF format
soft return
Text In/Out (**Ctrl-F5**)
unformatted option
WordPerfect CONVERT
   program
WP 4.2 format
WP 5.1 format
WP secondary merge
   format

DISCUSSION QUESTIONS

1. Discuss reasons for transferring data between the following modules. Give an example of the kind of data that might be transferred in each case.
    a. Lotus 1-2-3 to WordPerfect
    b. dBASE to 1-2-3
    c. dBASE to WordPerfect
    d. WordPerfect to dBASE
    e. dBASE to WordPerfect secondary merge.

2. Explain the meaning of the term **text (ASCII) file**. Why is it important for file transfers?

3. Describe the use of the CONVERT program packaged with WordPerfect. What file formats are supported by this program?

4. Suppose you had a program that would proofread and edit word processing documents, but did not support the WordPerfect 5.1 format. Discuss options that you might have in exporting the document to this software.

5. List the steps involved in placing a Lotus .PIC file inside a WordPerfect graphics box. Be explicit.

6. Suppose you have a colleague who is using a database program such as dBASE and you wish to use some of the data in a Lotus 1-2-3 worksheet. Discuss options that you might have in transferring that data to your worksheet.

7. Discuss the procedure to transfer data records from dBASE to WordPerfect for merge printing purposes. Be explicit.

8. WordPerfect offers two options when importing text files into a document. Define these options, and discuss the differences between them.

9. Compare the following 1-2-3 /File commands:
    a. **Retrieve**
    b. **Combine**
    c. **Import**
    d. **Save**
    e. **Xtract**.

10. Explain the differences between the 1-2-3 Text and Numbers /File Combine options.

11. Discuss the purposes of the **/Data Parse** command in 1-2-3. Describe a situation in which it would be useful.

12. Describe the Lotus 1-2-3 Release 2.2 link expression, and how it is useful in transferring data between worksheets.

13. List the file format types available with the dBASE IV Export and Import commands.

EXERCISES

1. Using WordPerfect, prepare the text in Figure 9-30 as a document.
    a. Save the document normally using the name **QUOTE.WP**.
    b. Save the document as a DOS text file named **QUOTE.TXT**.

FIGURE 9-30

Text for Exercise 1

```
                 Spectrum Computer Sales
                  3269 Westbourne Drive
                  Indianapolis, IN 46245
                       (555) 555-4321
                                (insert current date here)


   TO:      Boyer Machine Tool Company
            2278 Statesman Road
            Charlotte, VT 02316

   RE:      RFQ #18234-90

   We are submitting the following bid for the CAD workstation
   specified in the above-named Request for Quotation. The
   hardware model selected is based upon a close examination of
   your needs and represents, in our opinion, an excellent
   choice. The warranty period for this equipment is one year
   from date of delivery, FOB Indianapolis. We will, at our
   option, repair or replace defective hardware.

       1 CompuVal 386/20 Personal Computer with 4 MB RAM
       1 CADMaster Video Adapter with Full Page Display
       1 150 MB Landway Hard Drive with SCSI Interface
       1 HP Series III Laser Printer

   The total bid, including delivery and setup at your premises,
   is $14,844.00. This bid will expire 30 days from the date at
   the top of this form.
```

2. Use Lotus 1-2-3 to prepare a financing plan for the quotation of the previous problem. Assume that the buyer must pay 20% as a down payment, financing the rest over four years at 11.2%. Your 1-2-3 report should include an explanation of all assumptions used, the monthly payment over that time period, the total amount of all payments, and the cumulative interest paid over the life of the loan.

   a. Save the worksheet normally as **FINQUOTE.WK1**.
   b. Print to a text file, using the name **FINQUOTE.PRN**.
   c. Insert the Lotus report at the end of the WordPerfect **QUOTE.WP** document created in the previous problem, and print the merged document.

3. Make a copy of the file called **SAMPLE.DIF** from the demo disk accompanying this text, and use the Lotus Translate module to convert it to the .WK1 format. Retrieve it into a Lotus worksheet and print the contents. You may need to adjust column widths and change cell formats before printing the final copy.

FIGURE 9-31

Suggested Structure for Exercise 6

```
NAME         Character    20
TITLE        Character    18
SALARY       Numeric       6
DEPARTMENT   Character    18
HIRE_DATE    Date          8
```

4. Make a copy of the file called **SAMPLE.DIF** from the demo disk accompanying this text, and convert it to WordPerfect secondary merge format. Use the name **SAMPLE.WP**. Print a copy of the SAMPLE.WP file as it appeared after it was converted. The numeric fields may appear in scientific notation, such as 2.850000000000000E+04. Written in normal format, this is 28500 and represents the salary. 3.242200000000000E+04 is the Lotus version of the hire date, or 32422. Is there a way to maintain the date in its usual format, such as October 6, 1988, when doing the conversion?

5. Use the **SAMPLE.WK1** file created in Exercise 3 to build a bar graph showing salaries for the employees. Select appropriate titles. Save the graph settings in a file called **SAMPLE.PIC**. Then create a one-page WordPerfect document that describes the graph, and insert the graph into a graphic box in the document, similar to the example of this chapter. Print the document in the highest graph resolution possible with your printer.

6. From dBASE import the data from the **SAMPLE.WK1** file you created in exercise 3. Because the first row of the spreadsheet contains the field names, you will need to delete the first record of the new database, or remove it from the .WK1 file. A possible structure for the database file is shown in Figure 9-31.

7. Use the **SCHED.DBF** file from the data disk accompanying this text to Export data to Lotus 1-2-3. For this exercise you should prepare a text fixed-length fields (SDF) file in dBASE, then use the /File Import command within 1-2-3. Use the 1-2-3 Text option, and save the file as **SCHED.WK1**. Print a copy of this database file.

8. Using the **SCHED.WK1** file from the previous problem, create a parse format that will break the values in column A into separate fields. Print this portion of the worksheet. Then use the /Data commands to do the following. Print the results for each part of the problem.

    a. Sort the rows by instructor name.

    b. Extract only the classes meeting on MW or MWF.

    c. Extract the MIS classes and sort those by time of day.

    d. List all classes meeting in room SB 106 or SB 108.

    The dBASE structure for this file is shown in Figure 9-32.

9. Use the Lotus Translate facility to convert the **SCHED.DBF** file into a 1-2-3 Release 2.2 file called **SCHED2.WK1**. Use dBASE III as the input file format. Retrieve that file in 1-2-3 and print its contents. Note that the column widths have been modified to fit the field widths.

```
Structure for database: C:\DBASE\SCHED.DBF
Number of data records:      39
Date of last update    : 10/30/89
Field   Field Name   Type        Width   Dec   Index
    1   PREFIX       Character       3           N
    2   NUMBER       Character       3           N
    3   SECTION      Numeric         2           N
    4   LIMIT        Numeric         3           N
    5   INSTRUCTOR   Character      15           N
    6   TIME         Character       5           N
    7   DAY          Character       3           N
    8   ROOM         Character       7           Y
    9   TITLE        Character      30           N
   10   DOCTORATE    Logical         1           N
** Total **                         73
```

FIGURE 9-32

Sample Structure for Exercise 8

```
Structure for database: C:\DBASE\CUSTOMER.DBF
Number of data records:      14
Date of last update    : 11/20/89
Field   Field Name   Type        Width   Dec   Index
    1   CNAME        Character      15           N
    2   ADDRESS      Character      20           N
    3   CITY         Character      14           N
    4   STATE        Character       2           N
    5   ZIPCODE      Character       5           N
    6   LASTORDER    Date            8           N
    7   TAXABLE      Logical         1           N
** Total **                         66
```

FIGURE 9-33

Sample Structure for Exercise 10

10. In this exercise we will use the **CUSTOMER.DBF** file to create a mail merge file that will be imported into WordPerfect secondary merge format. From dBASE Export the data using the Character delimited format; use the default double quote {"} character as the delimiter. From the DOS prompt run the CONVERT program to create a new file called **CUSTOMER.WP** in secondary merge format. Remember that the CONVERT program will ask for the field delimiter character, which is the comma. The record delimiter characters are **{13}{10}**. The character to be stripped out is the double quote, or ". Print the resulting WordPerfect file. The structure of the CUSTOMER.DBF file is shown in Figure 9-33.

11. Use WordPerfect to create a letter to be sent to each customer in the **CUSTOMER.WP** file. The letter may be of your choosing, but should include all of the fields from the file. Merge the letters, and print the first six letters. Each should be on a separate page. You may need to review the coverage of merge printing with WordPerfect.

CHAPTER 9 PROJECT
STUDENT VOLUNTEER AGENCY

Prepare a dBASE IV database containing information about students interested in doing volunteer work for the college community. Use the following job categories: tutoring, homebound visitation, park cleanup, small business assistance, hospital assistant, recreation instructor, and general help. Be sure to capture complete mailing information for each volunteer. Other personal data might include previous service, hours available per week, college major, and special skills. The database should be split into several tables. Suggestions include a table to hold mailing information about students, another table to hold job categories, and perhaps a table to store information about student skills.

Discuss the various kinds of reports and letters that can be prepared from this database. Describe situations in which the data might be transferred to other microcomputer software packages. Are there situations in which a spreadsheet might be useful?

10

Working with Lotus 1-2-3 Release 2.3 and 3.1

Objectives

After completing this chapter, you should be able to:

- Explain the system hardware and software requirements for Releases 2.3 and 3.1.
- Discuss the new features of Release 2.3 that were not available in Release 2.2.
- Explain the multi-dimensional worksheet features of Release 3.1.
- Describe the spreadsheet publishing features available with the WYSIWYG add-in program.
- Discuss the new graphing and printing features of Release 3.1.
- Explain the worksheet analysis capabilities of Release 3.1.
- Describe the automatic cell formatting and /Data operations new to Release 3.1.
- Comment about the compatibility of Release 3.1 worksheets with other Lotus 1-2-3 versions.

INTRODUCTION

The Lotus Development Corporation has continued to develop new versions of its 1-2-3 product for different hardware platforms. The two 1-2-3 versions for DOS have been upgraded to 2.3 and 3.1. The low-end 2.3 release will run on any 8088-based IBM-compatible microcomputer, while the 3.1 release requires at least an 80286 microprocessor. Specific hardware requirements are discussed within each section.

The 2.3 release introduces new spreadsheet publishing features with its WYSIWYG display, mouse support, and additional graph types. Release 3.1 provides for three-dimensional worksheets, much-enhanced graph capabilities, and the WYSIWYG interface.

Both Lotus versions share the traditional / commands of earlier versions. Users familiar with Lotus Release 2.01 or 2.2 should have little trouble moving to the newer releases. Although there are some additional choices in the Release 3.1 / commands, most Release 2.2 keyboard macros will work with few changes.

LOTUS 1-2-3 RELEASE 2.3

This Lotus version was released in the summer of 1991 as this book went to press, so only a summary of the improvements is included. Although numbered as a minor upgrade to Release 2.2, Lotus 2.3 adds enhancements in the area of spreadsheet publishing with multiple fonts and graphing capabilities. It shares the .WK1 worksheet file format with Release 2.2. Additional features are explained below.

System Requirements

A replacement for Release 2.2, Release 2.3 will run on 8088-based IBM-compatible PCs with at least 384 KB of RAM and DOS 2.1 or later. Users who want to use the WYSIWYG interface will need at least 512 KB of RAM. A hard disk drive with at least 2 MB of free space is required to use the basic features of Lotus 2.3; 5 MB of free space is necessary to use all features of Release 2.3. As with previous versions, a graphics monitor (high-resolution preferred) is needed for displaying graphs and viewing the WYSIWYG display. Personal computers with an 80286 or higher microprocessor will perform significantly faster.

Overview of New Features

This version is quite similar to Release 2.2. The Release 2.3 editing window is shown in Figure 10-1. Most of the / commands work in the same manner in both versions.

Release 2.3 shares some of the newer features of Release 3.1, including the WYSIWYG facility for spreadsheet publishing. Similar to Allways in Release 2.2, **WYSIWYG** provides the ability to use multiple fonts, underlining, bold, italics, and shading. WYSIWYG allows you to place a graph in a worksheet so that both can be printed at the same time. Unlike Allways, WYSIWYG menus and 1-2-3 menus are accessible at the same time; WYSIWYG uses the : prefix, while 1-2-3 uses the / key. You can annotate WYSIWYG worksheets and graphs with lines, boxes, arrows, and freehand drawing. A detailed WYSIWYG example appears in the Lotus Release 3.1 section of this chapter.

Release 2.3 includes three new graph types including horizontal bar graph, high-low-close-open (HLCO), and mixed line/bar graphs. You can select three-dimensional aspects for bar graphs and can place a box around graphs.

Release 2.3 provides limited **on-sheet word processing** within 1-2-3. You can choose left, centered, or right-justified text with word wrap to fit text within a space on the worksheet. This release supports search and replace functions within a text block. Figure 10-2 illustrates the use of this feature.

For long outputs, Release 2.3 provides a kind of **background printing** in which you send the output to an encoded printer file. This file can be printed

FIGURE 10-1

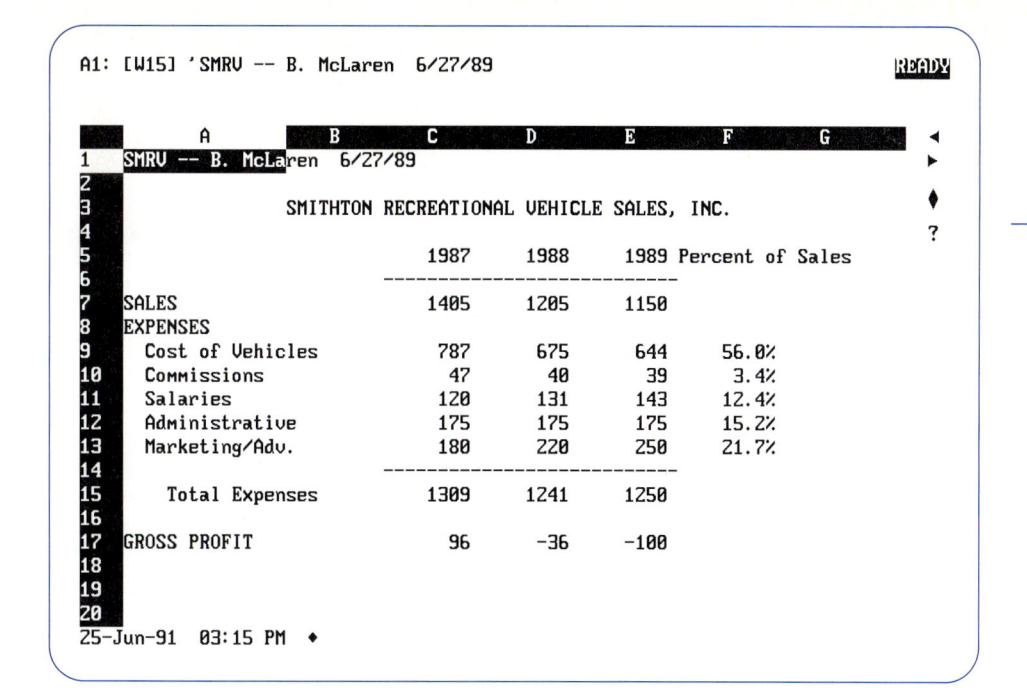

Main Editing Display of Lotus 1-2-3 Release 2.3

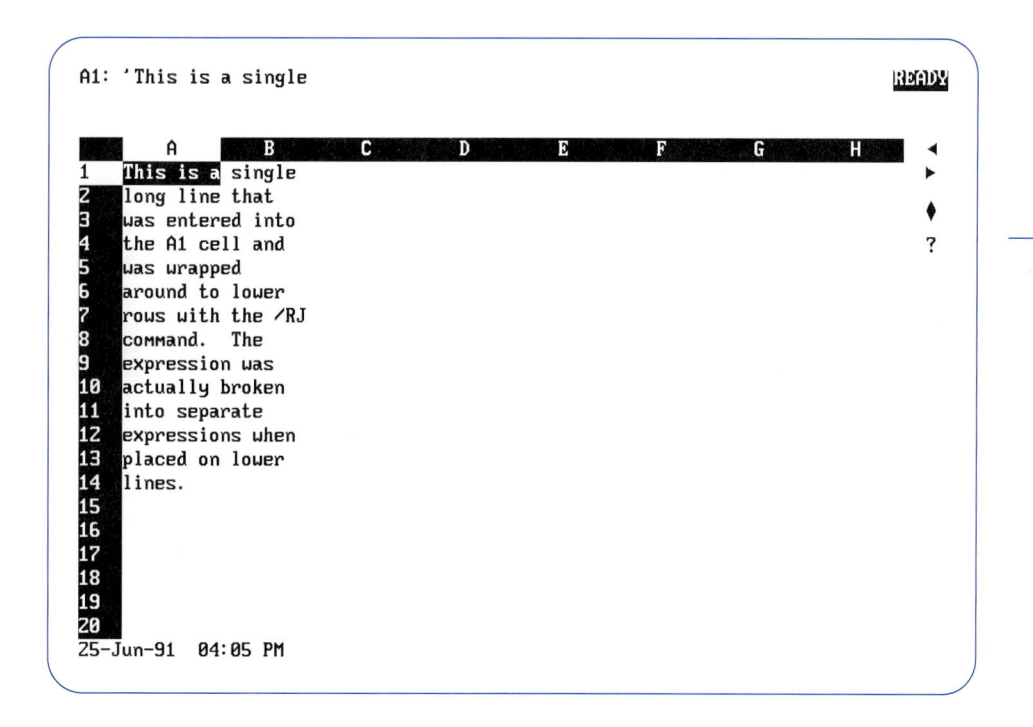

FIGURE 10-2

Word Wrap Feature (**/RJ**)

later in the background from the DOS prompt, or while 1-2-3 executes, using a supplied terminate-and-stay-resident (TSR) printing program. The **/Print File** command in previous Lotus versions only produced an ASCII text file that did not include the special printing control codes needed to activate special print features.

For this version Lotus has added an **auto-compression** facility in which large outputs can be printed on a single page by using a small print font. Lotus will automatically adjust the font size, provided your printer supports downloaded fonts or graphical printing. This feature is available from the 1-2-3 READY mode and does not require WYSIWYG.

Chapter 10 — Working with Lotus 1-2-3 Release 2.3 and 3.1

There is a built-in **file viewer** that allows you to see the contents of Lotus worksheet and other files without leaving 1-2-3. Based on the Lotus Magellan software that is available separately, the file viewer saves time when you are looking for a specific worksheet file but cannot remember its name. Figure 10-3 shows the use of the file viewer.

An **auditing** feature has been included with Release 2.3. You can examine cell contents, trace expressions to other cells, and check for circular references. The Auditor screen is shown in Figure 10-4.

Minimal recalculation speeds worksheet entries by recalculating only those cells affected by changes made in the worksheet. Lotus 2.3 employs a better

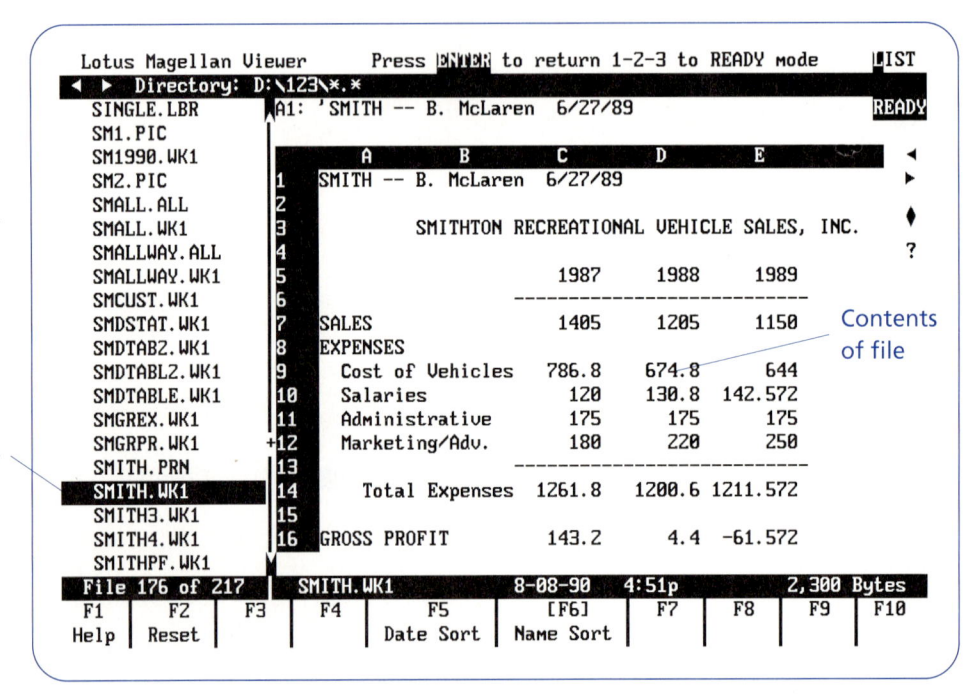

FIGURE 10-3

Lotus File Viewer Display

FIGURE 10-4

Release 2.3 Auditor Menu Display

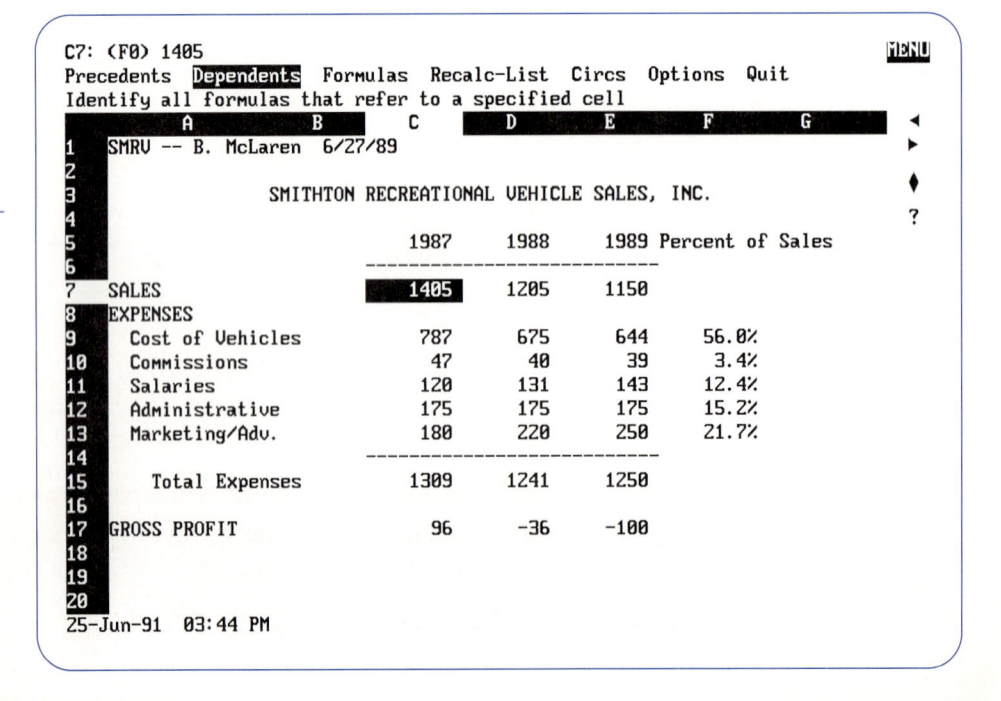

memory management method for large spreadsheets, using up to 12 MB of RAM. More detailed context-specific help screens now appear in **pop-up help windows** instead of the full-screen help displays in previous versions. A sample help box appears in Figure 10-5.

This release comes with **mouse support**. Moving the mouse into the Control Panel automatically brings up the slash command menu. You can use the mouse to select menus, highlight cell ranges, and change column widths.

Release 2.3 comes with on-line tutor add-in programs for 1-2-3 and WYSIWYG. These programs have numerous sample files and can be used from within 1-2-3 or from the DOS prompt. Figure 10-6 shows the 1-2-3-Go! tutorial screen.

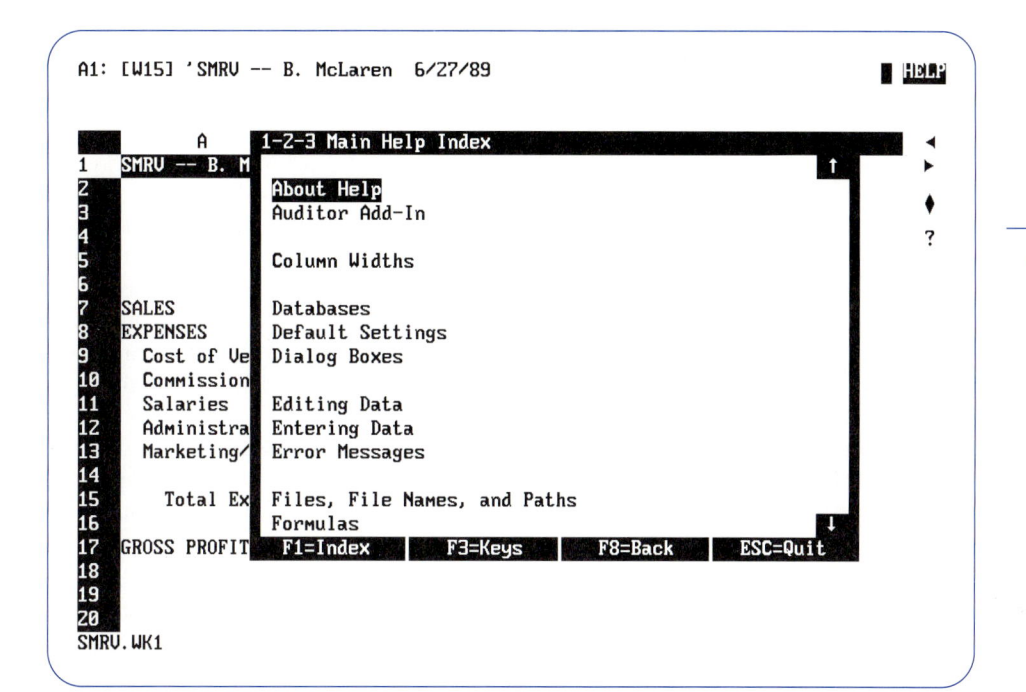

FIGURE 10-5

Release 2.3 Main Help Box

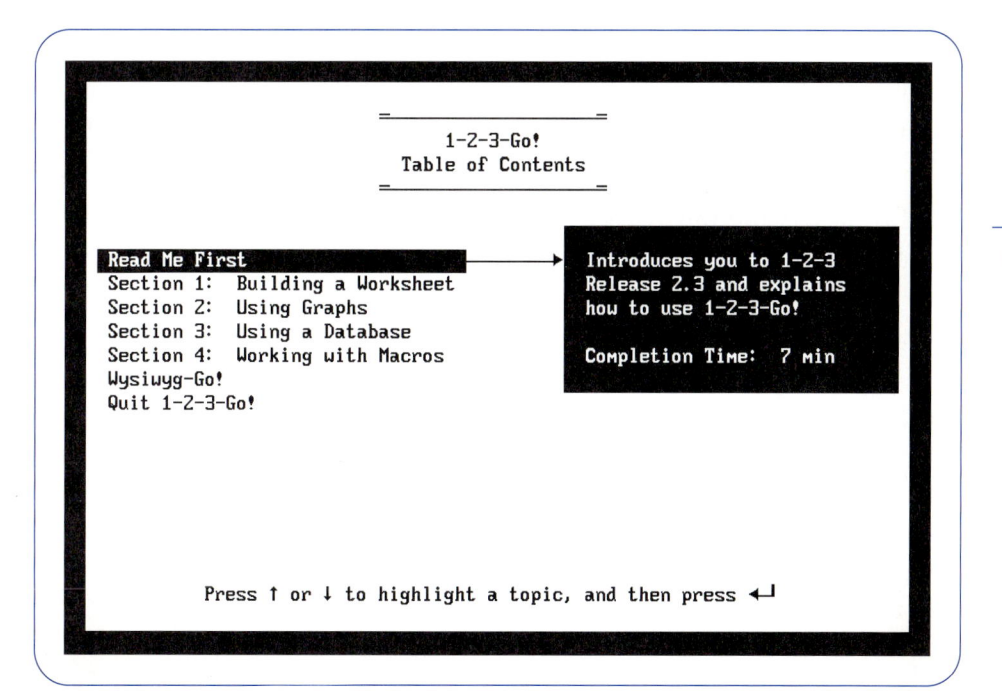

FIGURE 10-6

Release 2.3 1-2-3-Go! Tutor Program Opening Screen

LOTUS 1-2-3 RELEASE 3.1

This version of Lotus 1-2-3 was released in late 1990 and replaces Release 3.0. It adds the WYSIWYG spreadsheet publishing capability and will run under Windows 3.0. Most of the other 3.1 features were introduced with Release 3.0. A brief discussion of the Release 3.0 features appears in Chapter 8 of this book.

System Requirements

Release 3.1 requires an 80286 or higher microprocessor and at least 1 megabyte of RAM to run. This 1 MB consists of 640 KB of conventional RAM and at least 384 KB of extended RAM. Some computers devote a portion of RAM beyond 1024 KB for copying the BIOS and/or video ROMs (called **shadow RAM**), and thus may require additional RAM beyond 1 MB to run Lotus 3.1. This version of Lotus requires at least DOS 3.0 and a hard drive with 5 MB of free space available. A graphics-based monitor is required to use Release 3.1's WYSIWYG facility; Hercules, EGA, and VGA monitors work best with the WYSIWYG display.

Overview of New Features

New File Types

Lotus 3.1 uses the **.WK3 file extension** as the default when saving worksheets. Releases 2.2 and 2.01 are unable to read this format. If you anticipate the need to transfer Release 3.1 files to earlier versions, save the file as a .WK1 type by adding those characters as a file extension when saving the file. You can also use the Translate facility of Release 3.1 to convert an existing .WK3 file to another format. Release 3.1 will automatically read .WK1 and .WK3 files when you use the /**File Retrieve** command.

Graphs can be printed from within the 1-2-3 module, so .PIC files are no longer necessary. Release 3.1 is able to save graph images in the PIC format as well as in a new format called **.CGM graph files**, which are easily transported to other programs. The .TMP file format is used for temporary storage when Lotus does not have enough memory to complete a function. The .TMP files are erased automatically when you exit from 1-2-3. An encoded file with the .ENC extension is produced when you print to an encoded file. **Encoded printer files** can be sent directly to the printer at a later time.

Multiple Worksheets Per File

Release 3.1 is capable of three-dimensional worksheets consisting of multiple two-dimensional **pages** or **sheets**. These worksheet pages are designated by letters A, B, and so on. You can have up to 256 worksheets in memory at one time, subject to memory limitations. **Multiple sheets** can be used to hold detailed data with the top (A) sheet for consolidating the subsheets. Different sheets might represent a sales territory, product line, or time period. A group of three sheets might be used to hold budget, actual, and variance figures.

To insert another worksheet into memory, use the /**Worksheet Insert Sheet** command, select either the **Before** or **After** option, and the number of worksheets you intend to insert. The new worksheets are given the appropriate letter and placed before or after the current worksheet. The letter of the current sheet appears in the box above row 1. You can use the GROUP mode to copy the settings of the current worksheet into all other sheets, if appropriate.

To move to another worksheet, use **Ctrl-PgUp** or **Ctrl-PgDn** to move to a higher or lower worksheet letter. For example, if you are in worksheet C and press **Ctrl-PgUp** one time, you will move to worksheet D; from sheet D, press **Ctrl-PgDn** three times and you will move to worksheet A. Lotus will beep if you cannot move to a sheet in the requested direction, just as it beeps when you have moved the cursor to column A or row 1 and continue to press the left or up arrow keys.

FIGURE 10-7

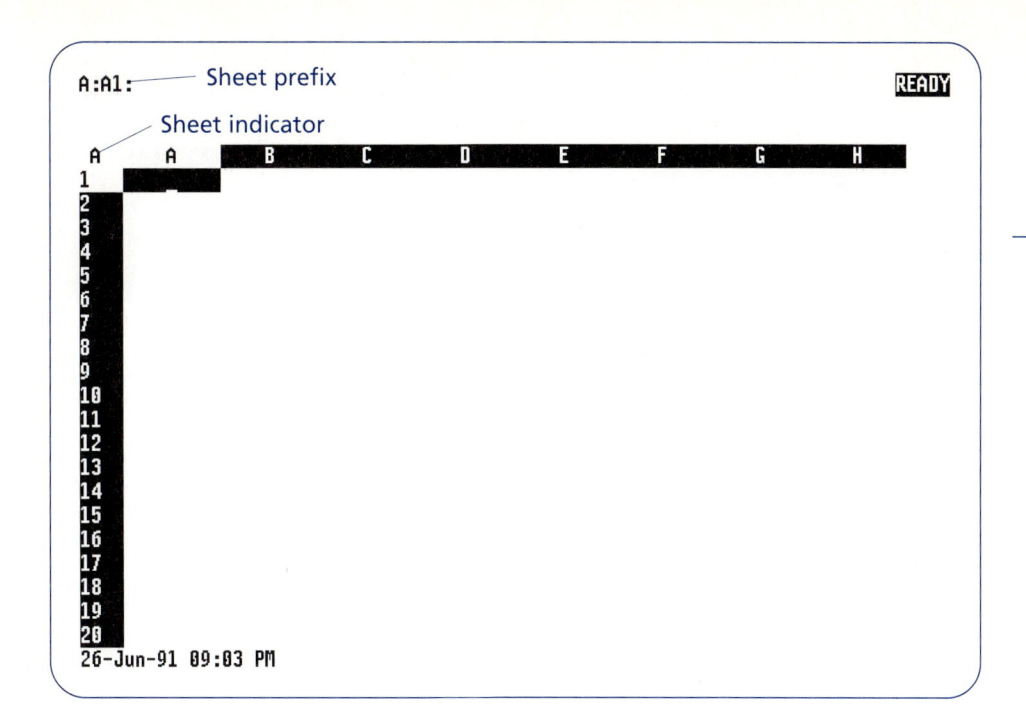

Release 3.1 Edit Screen

Of course, the worksheets are *not* saved permanently unless you use the **/File Save** command. Multiple worksheets are saved in a single worksheet file. To add an existing worksheet file before or after the current sheet, use the **/File Open** command, providing the appropriate file name when prompted. (The **/File Retrieve** command will replace *all* of the multiple worksheets in memory with the retrieved file.)

Lotus 3.1 cell references now contain the letter of the page of the worksheet in front of the normal column/letter designation. Thus **A:B5** refers to cell B5 in the first page. **C:A1..C:A10** refers to the top ten cells in the first column of the third worksheet page. Figure 10-7 shows an empty Release 3.1 edit screen.

You can create a **perspective window** that allows you to view six lines from each of three worksheets on the screen at one time by using the **/Worksheet Window Perspective (/WWP)** command. To return the to normal display of one worksheet, use the **/Worksheet Window Clear** command. You can also use the familiar horizontal or vertical windows to display two sheets on the screen at one time.

Example: *Preparing a Multiple Worksheet*

The 1993 School of Business budget has been prepared by three departments. You will develop a means of combining the three spreadsheets into one School of Business worksheet through using multiple worksheets.

1. Begin Release 3.1 as usual. Prepare the A sheet as shown in Figure 10-8. Column A must be widened to 24 characters to accommodate the wide account titles.

2. Issue the **/Worksheet Insert Sheet** command and insert **After** the current worksheet **3** sheets. They will be labeled B, C, and D. Lotus will leave you in sheet B, the first new sheet. The sheet indicator in the left corner of the worksheet frame will be B.

3. Give the **/File Combine Copy Entire-File** command (**/FCCE**) to place a new file in the current sheet. The file name is **MISBUD.WK3** and should be found on the data disk.

FIGURE 10-8

Master Budget Worksheet A

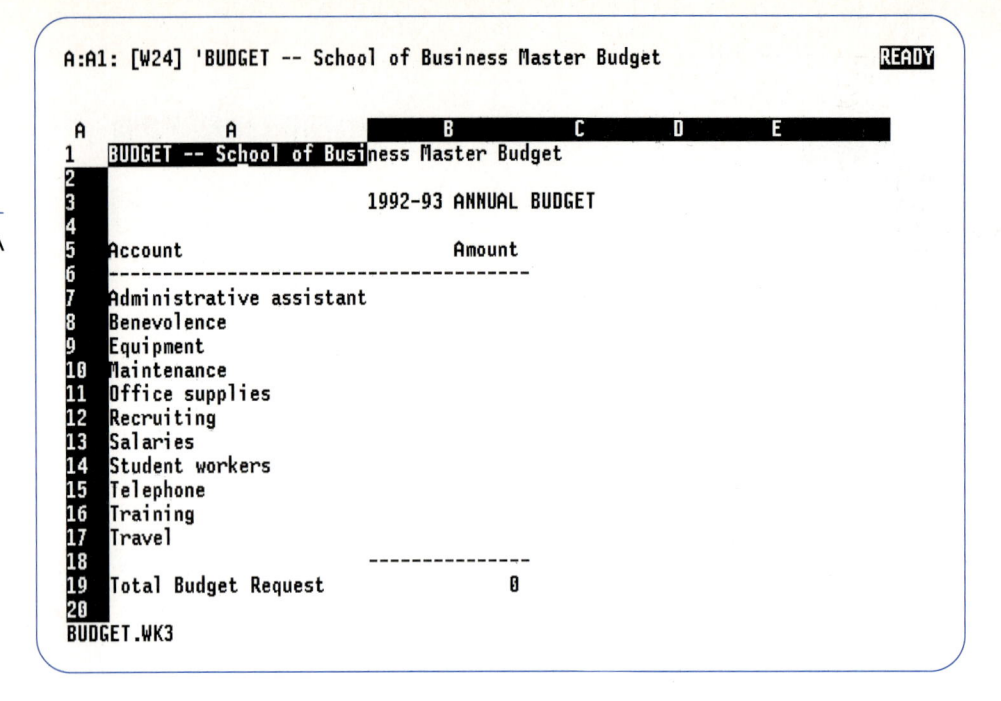

```
A:A1: [W24] 'BUDGET -- School of Business Master Budget          READY

     A              A               B         C         D    E
                BUDGET -- School of Business Master Budget
  1
  2
  3                        1992-93 ANNUAL BUDGET
  4
  5             Account                  Amount
  6             ------------------------------------
  7             Administrative assistant
  8             Benevolence
  9             Equipment
 10             Maintenance
 11             Office supplies
 12             Recruiting
 13             Salaries
 14             Student workers
 15             Telephone
 16             Training
 17             Travel
 18                                      ---------------
 19             Total Budget Request              0
 20
BUDGET.WK3
```

4. Use **Ctrl-PgUp** to change to the C sheet. Repeat step 3 with the **MGTBUD.WK3** file.

5. Press **Ctrl-PgUp** to move to the D sheet. Repeat step 3 with the **ACCTBUD.WK3** file.

6. Press **Ctrl-PgDn** three times to move back to the A sheet. In cell A:B7 type the expression **@SUM(B:B7..D:B7)** and press **Enter**. Format this cell as currency type with no decimal places by typing **/RFC0 Enter Enter**.

7. Next copy the formula to other rows in the master budget worksheet. Press **/Copy** and specify the From: range as **A:B7..A:B7**. The To: range is **A:B8..A:B17**.

8. Move to cell A:B19 and enter the formula: **@SUM(B7..B17)**. Format this cell as currency with no decimal places by typing **/RFC0 Enter Enter**. The worksheet should look like Figure 10-9.

9. Finally we will save the entire worksheet as one file called BUDGET92. Press **/File Save** and give **BUDGET92** as the file name.

10. To be sure that Lotus saved all pages in the worksheet, issue the **/File Retrieve** command and retrieve **BUDGET92**. Give the **/Worksheet Window Perspective** command and you should see the A, B, and C sheets. Press **Ctrl-PgUp** and the perspective view will now include sheets B, C, and D.

WYSIWYG Graphical Display

The WYSIWYG feature is implemented as an add-in that can be activated with the **Alt-F10** Add-In command. Similar to the Allways add-in that came with Release 2.2, the WYSIWYG add-in permits use of different text fonts, proportional spacing, underlining, bold, italics, shading, and boxes in Lotus worksheets.

FIGURE 10-9

BUDGET92.WK3 Worksheet

```
A:A1: [W24] 'BUDGET -- School of Business Master Budget          READY

       A                    B           C        D       E
 1  BUDGET -- School of Business Master Budget
 2
 3                   1992-93 ANNUAL BUDGET
 4
 5  Account                    Amount
 6  ------------------------------------
 7  Administrative assistant   34,550
 8  Benevolence                   750
 9  Equipment                  26,600
10  Maintenance                 3,900
11  Office supplies             3,000
12  Recruiting                  7,950
13  Salaries                1,772,800
14  Student workers            11,700
15  Telephone                   1,650
16  Training                    1,500
17  Travel                     24,500
18                          ----------
19  Total Budget Request    $1,888,900
20
BUDGET92.WK3
```

The WYSIWYG add-in accompanies Releases 2.3, 3.0, and 3.1; it becomes the standard graphical interface tool for DOS versions of Lotus 1-2-3. [Note: A Windows version of Lotus, called **1-2-3/W,** is planned for release in late 1991 or early 1992. 1-2-3/W will have a different graphical interface that is consistent with other Windows 3.0 software applications.]

Often referred to as **spreadsheet publishing**, WYSIWYG improves the appearance of the worksheet. By using a small font you can display more information on one printed page. Using WYSIWYG and other Lotus 3.1 features it is possible to embed graphs and text in the middle of a worksheet page without leaving Lotus. WYSIWYG information is saved in a .FM3 file.

In WYSIWYG you can access all of the Lotus / commands and still remain in the WYSIWYG mode; in Allways you had to leave the Allways mode to do worksheet commands. To bring up the WYSIWYG command menu, press the colon (:) key. You can also set up Lotus to be able to use a mouse to bring up the WYSIWYG menu.

The main WYSIWYG **:** **menu** is shown in Figure 10-10. There are nine commands available:

- The **Worksheet** command is used to set column widths and row heights. You can place page breaks with this command.

- **Format** is used to apply special formatting characteristics such as text font, bold or italic, underline, worksheet color, horizontal and vertical lines, shading, and drop shadows to the right and below a range. Standard text fonts include Swiss, Dutch, Courier, and Xsymbol. Samples are shown in Figure 10-11.

- The **Graph** menu permits you to place an existing Lotus graph or .PIC file in the worksheet. This command is also used to edit and enhance the graph's appearance, including the ability to add annotations to the graph. Edit tools include text, lines, polygons, arrows, rectangles, ellipses, and freehand drawing.

FIGURE 10-10

Release 3.1 WYSIWYG Menu (:)

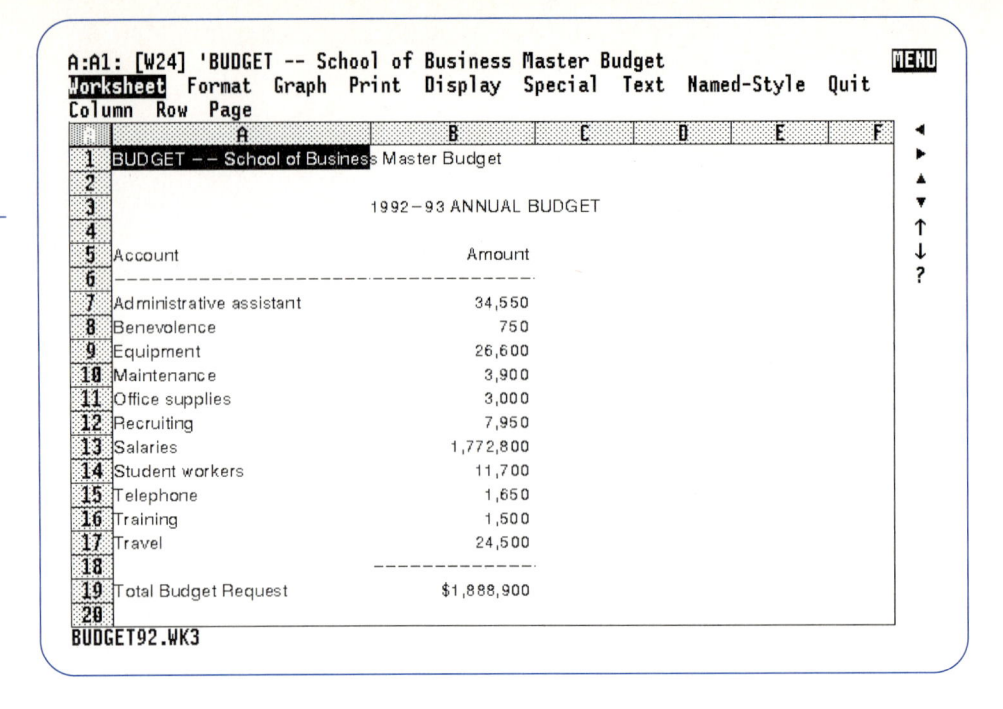

```
A:A1: [W24] 'BUDGET -- School of Business Master Budget         MENU
Worksheet Format Graph Print Display Special Text Named-Style Quit
Column  Row  Page
     A                          B              C         D         E         F
 1  BUDGET -- School of Business Master Budget
 2
 3                      1992-93 ANNUAL BUDGET
 4
 5  Account                       Amount
 6  ------------------------------------
 7  Administrative assistant      34,550
 8  Benevolence                      750
 9  Equipment                     26,600
10  Maintenance                    3,900
11  Office supplies                3,000
12  Recruiting                     7,950
13  Salaries                   1,772,800
14  Student workers               11,700
15  Telephone                      1,650
16  Training                       1,500
17  Travel                        24,500
18                             ----------
19  Total Budget Request       $1,888,900
20
BUDGET92.WK3
```

FIGURE 10-11

Sample WYSIWYG Text Fonts

Swiss 14 point text font   ABCDEFGH1234567890

Dutch 14 point text font   ABCDEFGH1234567890

Courier text font   ABCDEFGH1234567890

Xsymbol set:
➡➢➣➤➥⇨⇩⇪⇫⇬⇭➮➯➱➲➳➴➵➶➷➸➹⑤⑥⑦⑧⑨⑩❶❷❸❹

- **Print** sends a printed copy of the worksheet to the chosen destination after the layout is established. This command prints the worksheet and its graphs if they have been placed in the worksheet. Lotus 3.1 has no PrintGraph module—all graphs can be printed from the /Print or :Print menus.

- The **Display** command is used to control how the worksheet appears on the screen while in WYSIWYG mode. You can add grid lines, change background and foreground colors, and zoom in on certain parts of the worksheet.

- The **Special** command is used to copy or move a set of WYSIWYG format specifications from one range to another, or from one worksheet file to another file.

- **Text** lets you add long labels to text ranges and provides some limited formatting control. This command allows you to add paragraphs to the worksheet without leaving Lotus.

- The **Named-Style** menu lets the user define a group of WYSIWYG format specifications and name it as a style. The style can be used in later WYSIWYG worksheets.

- **Quit** returns you to the Ready mode. You may enter WYSIWYG or 1-2-3 / commands in this mode. To clear the WYSIWYG add-in from memory, use the **Alt-F10** Add-In command and select **Clear**.

Example: *Creating a WYSIWYG Worksheet*

In this example we will use WYSIWYG to create the same enhanced Smithton worksheet that was developed in Chapter 5 with Allways. The final output will use different type fonts, italics, shading, and some lines to highlight the results. The worksheet file, SMRV.WK1, is found on the data diskette that accompanies this textbook.

1. Change to the Lotus 3.1 drive and subdirectory and type **123** to start Lotus 1-2-3. At the Ready mode, press **Alt-F10** to activate the Add-In menu.

2. Press **L** to select Load an add-in. At the next prompt, select the WYSIWYG.PLC add-in and press **Enter**. At the next menu select **No-Key**. After a few moments you will see the WYSIWYG display. Press **Q** to return to WYSIWYG Ready mode.

3. Next, press **/FR** to retrieve the SMRV.WK1 worksheet file from the data disk. Press **Esc** once or twice to clear the default drive and subdirectory, then key in the drive and **SMRV** file name. For instance, if the data disk is in the A drive, you would type **A:SMRV.WK1** and press **Enter**. You should see the WYSIWYG display with the SMRV worksheet in place. Lotus shows the file name in the lower left corner.

4. First we will mark the title to appear in a larger font. Move the cursor to cell B3 and press **:F** to activate the Format menu.

5. Press **F** to select the Font option. Move the cursor to font 2 (Swiss 14 point) and press **Enter**.

6. At the next prompt, use the → key to highlight the **A:B3..A:F3** cell range. Remember that Lotus places the A: in front of the cell addresses to indicate that this is the top worksheet. Press **Enter** to complete the range entry for the new font.

7. At this point WYSIWYG will redisplay the worksheet title in large letters, but it is no longer centered over the spreadsheet. We can use the Lotus / Move command to move the label to cell A3. Press **/M** to activate Move. The From range is **A:B3..A:B3**. The To range is **A:A3..A:A3**. WYSIWYG will move the worksheet title to the first column.

8. Next use the italic format for the column headings and Expense categories. Move the cursor to cell C5 and press **:FIS** to set the italic font option. At the range prompt type **C5..F5** and press **Enter**. [Note: The sheet letter does not have to be entered in cell ranges—Lotus assumes the current worksheet. The remaining ranges in this example will omit the sheet letter.] The italic effect is seen immediately in the display. The first line of the Control Panel shows the phrase {Italics} before the cell expression in cells with the Italic format.

FIGURE 10-12

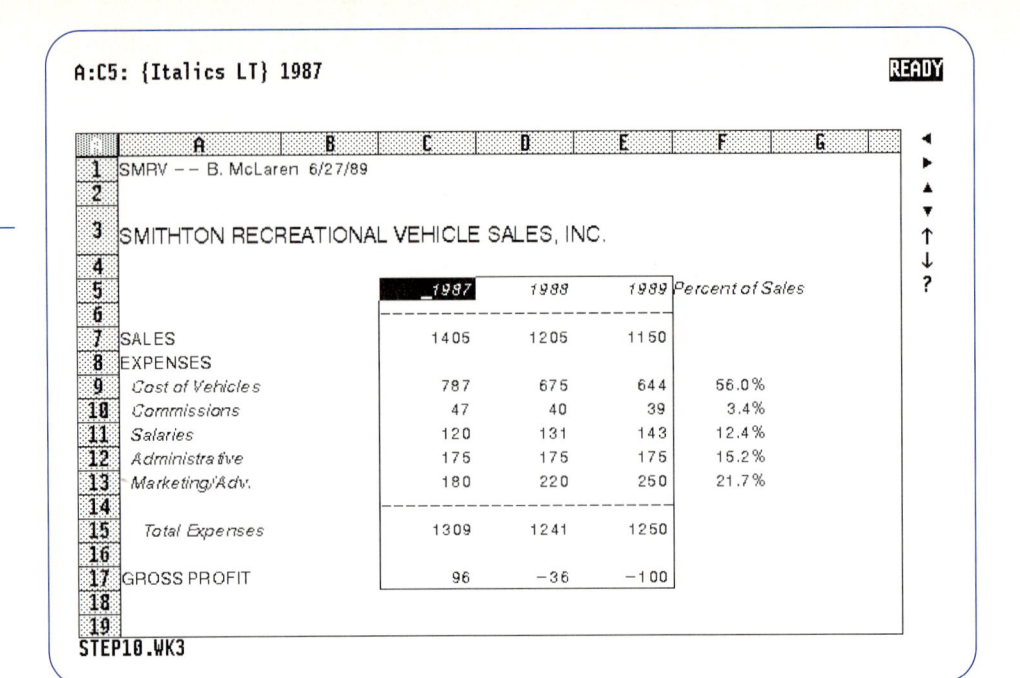

WYSIWYG Screen After Step 10

```
A:C5: {Italics LT} 1987                                          READY

         A         B         C         D         E         F         G
  1  SMRV -- B. McLaren 6/27/89
  2
  3  SMITHTON RECREATIONAL VEHICLE SALES, INC.
  4
  5                          1987      1988      1989  Percent of Sales
  6                        --------------------------
  7  SALES                   1405      1205      1150
  8  EXPENSES
  9    Cost of Vehicles       787       675       644      56.0%
 10    Commissions             47        40        39       3.4%
 11    Salaries               120       131       143      12.4%
 12    Administrative         175       175       175      15.2%
 13    Marketing/Adv.         180       220       250      21.7%
 14                        --------------------------
 15    Total Expenses        1309      1241      1260
 16
 17  GROSS PROFIT              96       -36      -100
 18
 19
STEP10.WK3
```

9. Repeat the previous step for the expense category labels. Move the cursor to cell A9. Press **:FIS** to set the italic font. Press the down arrow key six times, highlighting the range A9..A15, and press **Enter** to complete the entry.

10. Now draw a box around the numbers in the worksheet. Move the cursor to the first cell to be included, C5. Issue the **:FL** command to activate the Line format. Press **O** to select Outline, then use the down and right arrow keys to highlight the cell range **C5..E17** and press **Enter**. Figure 10-12 shows the WYSIWYG display and the SMRV worksheet to this point.

11. You can use WYSIWYG to shade sections of the worksheet. Move the cursor to cell C5. Press **:FS** to activate the Shade menu. Press **L** to select the Light shading. At the range prompt, enter **C5..C17** and press **Enter**. WYSIWYG shades the cells in column C. Repeat with cells **E5..E17** to shade column E.

12. It is a good habit to save the worksheet periodically. To save this sheet, press **/FS** and give the name as **SMRVWYS**. Using a different name means that the changes we are making will not interfere with the original copy of the SMRV.WK1 worksheet. Lotus saves this worksheet with the new .WK3 file extension and creates another file called SMRVWYS.FM3 containing the WYSIWYG format instructions.

13. Move the cursor to cell F5. Use the **:WCS** command to set the width of column F. Press **Enter** to select column F, then type **14** and press **Enter**. You could also use the left and right arrow keys to adjust the width visually.

14. Move the cursor to cell C6. We want to remove this row and replace the row of hyphens by underlining row 5 entries. Press **/WDR** to delete row 6. Press **Enter** to confirm that A:C6..A:C6 is the correct entry. Move the cursor to cell C13 and repeat the procedure to delete row 13: **/WDR Enter**.

15. Move the cursor to cell C5 and press **:FL** to activate the Line format. Press **B** to indicate the bottom of the cells are to be lined. Use the right arrow key to highlight the range **C5..E5** and press **Enter**.

16. Move the cursor to cell C12 and repeat the above procedure to place a line below cells **C12..E12**. Type **:FLB** and give the range as **C12..E12**.

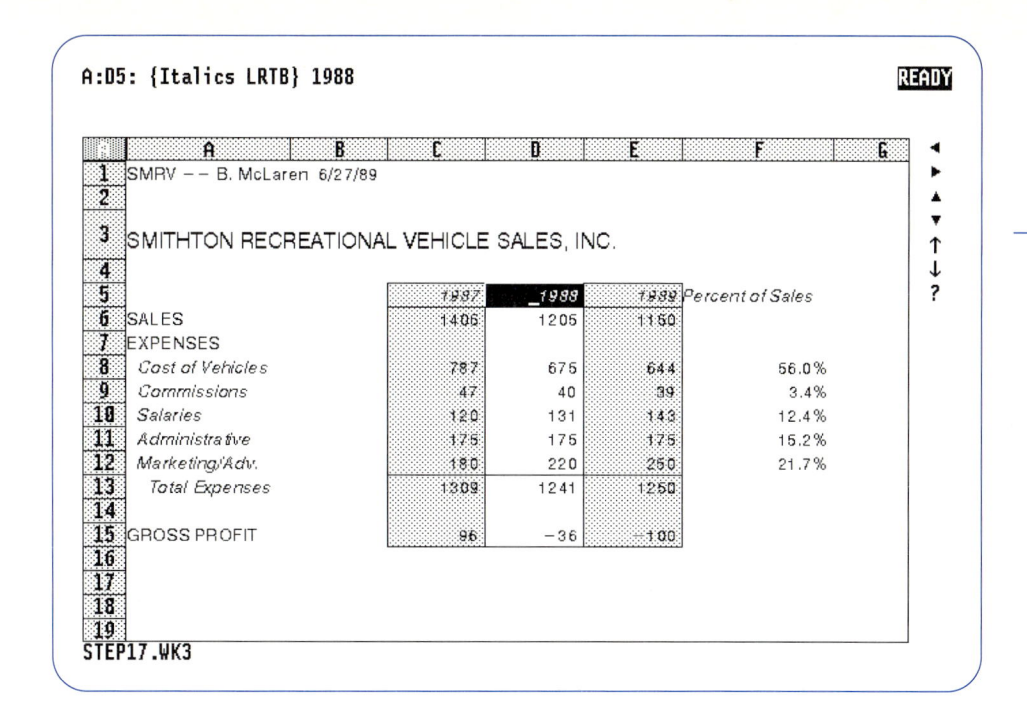

FIGURE 10-13

Final WYSIWYG Screen for SMRV Example

FIGURE 10-14

Output from WYSIWYG Example

17. To further highlight the middle year, we will add vertical lines to the left and right of the 1988 figures. Move the cursor to cell D5, then press **:FL** to activate the Line menu. Select **Left** and enter **D5..D15** as the cell range. With the cursor still in cell D5, press **:FL** and select **Right**. Specify **D5..D15** as the cell range and press **Enter**. WYSIWYG will place vertical lines between the columns. [Note: You could also use the :Format Line Outline choice for cell range D5..D15 and achieve the same results.] The final screen appears in Figure 10-13.

18. Finally you are ready to print the worksheet with WYSIWYG. Press **:P** to activate the Print menu. Press **RS** to Set the print Range, then enter **A3..F16** as the print range. WYSIWYG highlights the printed portion of the worksheet; to temporarily remove the settings sheet and see the worksheet underneath, press **I**. To replace the worksheet with the print settings sheet, press **I** again. Then press **G** for Go, and WYSIWYG will print the worksheet. If it will be printed in graphics mode on a dot matrix printer, it may take longer than usual to print. The completed worksheet as printed by a laser printer appears in Figure 10-14.

New Graph Features

Release 3.1 brings two new graph types and numerous options. The **HLCO graph** type refers to High-Low-Close-Open, often used to display stock market prices. The **Mixed graph** type allows mixing bar and line chart types on the same graph. Examples of these graphs appear in Figures 10-15 and 10-16.

The HLCO graph type uses data ranges A, B, C, and D for the high values, low values, closing values, and opening values, respectively. The Mixed graph

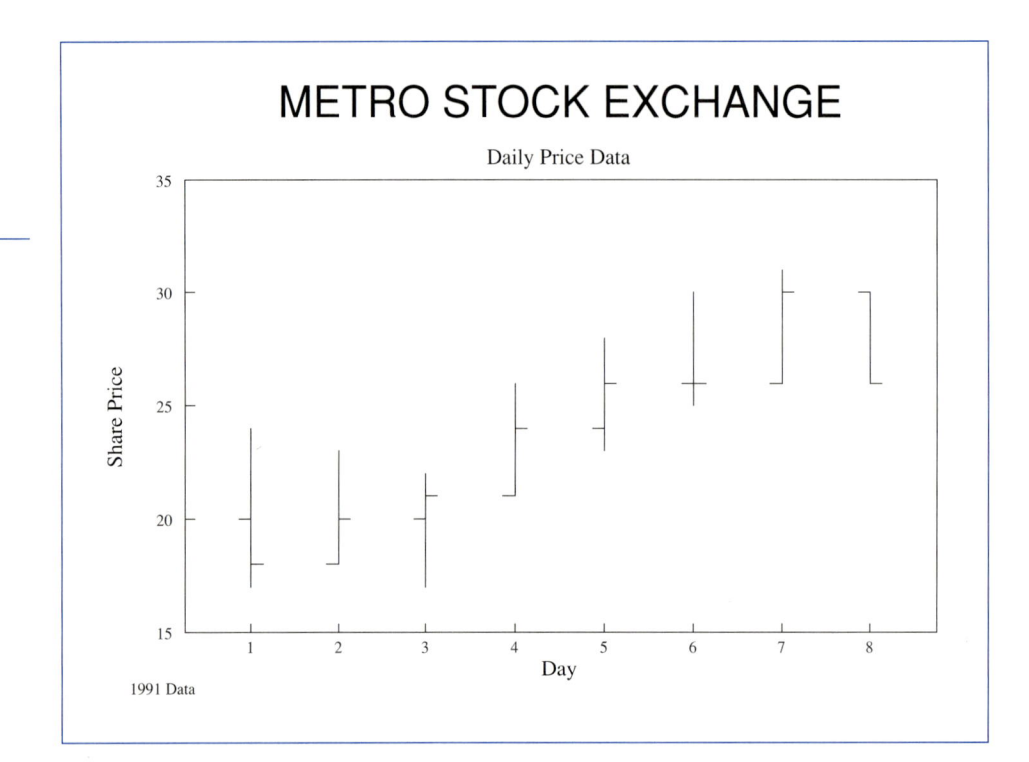

FIGURE 10-15

HLCO Graph Example

FIGURE 10-16

Mixed Graph Type Example

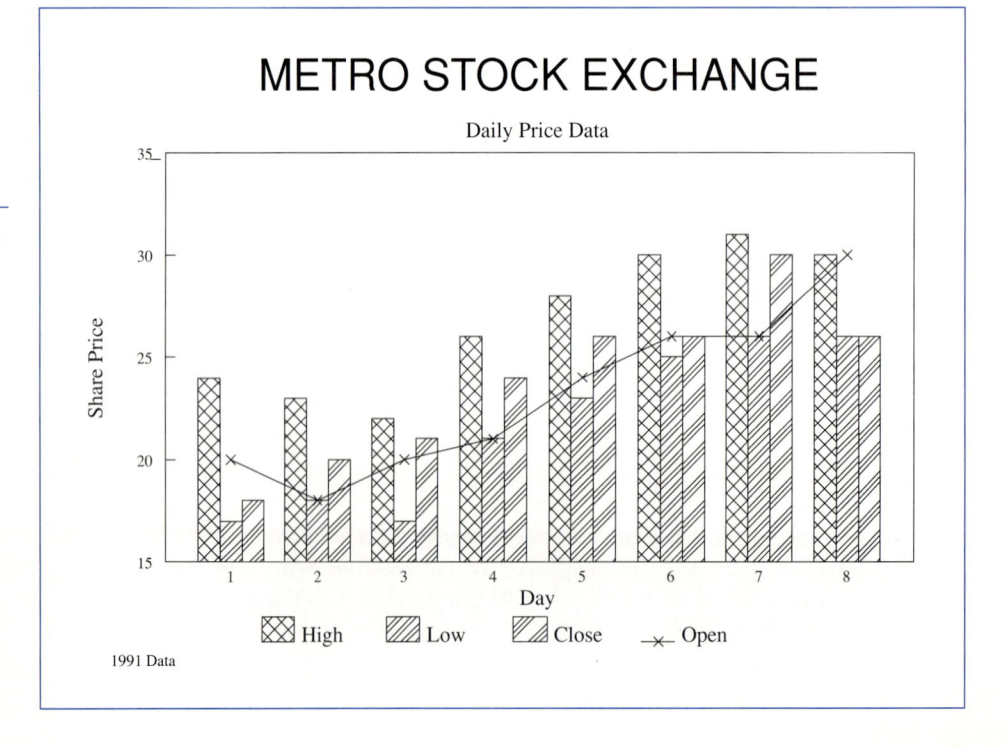

type uses the A, B, and C ranges for bar graph data and the D, E, and F ranges for the line graph data.

The **Features** option of the /Graph menu provides several new settings for Release 3.1 graphs including use of a second Y-axis.

- **Vertical** provides for the standard configuration of the X-axis along the bottom of the graph and the Y-axes at the left and right edges of the graph.

- **Horizontal** places the graph on its side with the X-axis along the left edge and the Y-axes at the top and bottom of the graph.

- **Stacked** works with the Line, Bar, Mixed, and XY graphs to stack the data ranges on top of one another. You can also turn off the stacked feature so that the data ranges appear next to one another.

- **100%** instructs Lotus to display the data ranges as a percentage of their total or to display data ranges with their original values.

- **2Y-Ranges** is used to assign one or more data ranges to a second Y-axis that appears at the right edge of a vertical graph. The second Y-axis is helpful when the magnitudes of values in the data ranges are different. Figure 10-17 shows an example of a graph with two Y-ranges.

You can add one or two footnote lines at the lower portion of the graph with the new Lotus release. Use the **/Graph Options Title** command and select **Note** for the first line and **Other-Note** for the second footnote line. The text in the footnotes appears in the same size as the scale titles

This release offers more precise control over colors, shading or cross-hatching, fonts, and text size for graphs. The **/Graph Options Advanced** command will provide access to these settings. This option can also be used to fill areas in line graphs between the lines.

Release 3.1 also allows you to create a **graph window** to display the worksheet and the graph on the screen at the same time. Any changes made in the

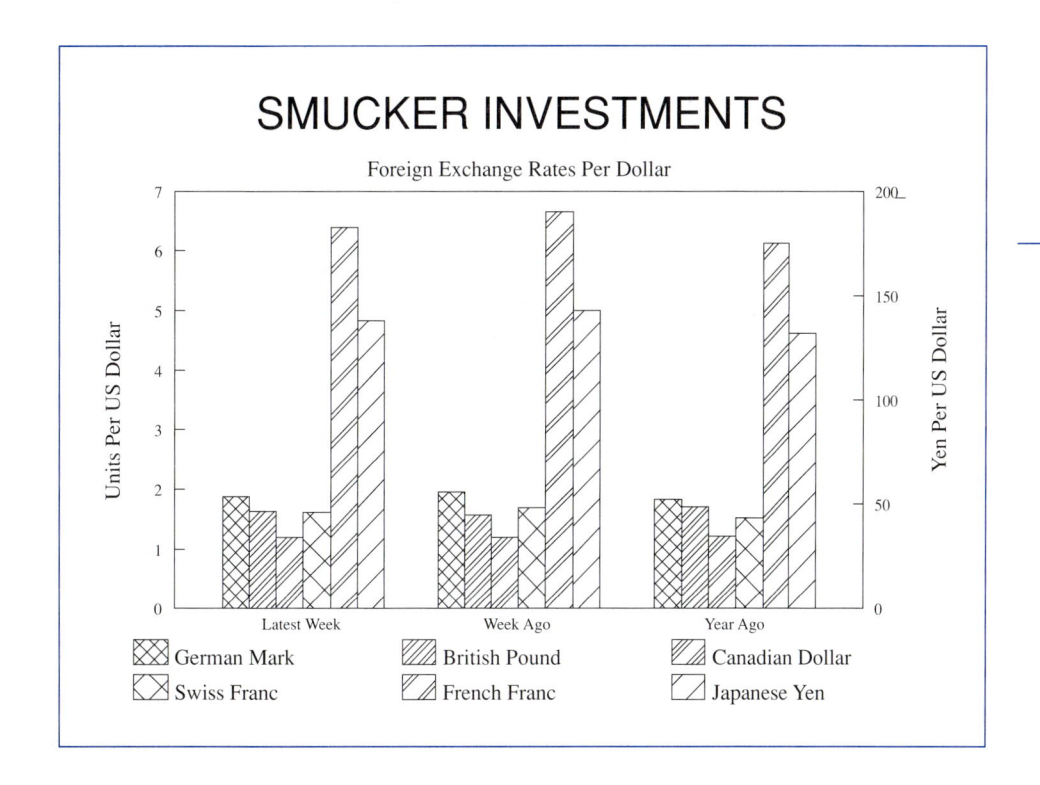

FIGURE 10-17

Second Y-Axis Example

worksheet are instantaneously reflected in the graph. Use the /**Worksheet Window Graph** command to open the window; the graph will be displayed in the right window and the worksheet in the left window. To close the window use the /**Worksheet Window Clear** command.

Print Features

As described above, the WYSIWYG facility provides spreadsheet publishing capability for Lotus 1-2-3. Multiple fonts in different sizes can be used to make the printed worksheet more attractive and to fit more on the page. If you choose not to use WYSIWYG, the /**Print** command offers menu choices for using normal, compressed, and expanded print for the worksheet without having to provide setup strings. You can choose from normal or compressed vertical spacing to place more lines on a page. You can choose between the default **portrait mode** and **landscape mode** for horizontal printing, provided your printer is capable of printing in landscape mode. Dot matrix printers use graphics printing, while ink jet and laser printers usually have built-in landscape fonts. Figure 10-18 shows a worksheet printed by a laser printer using the Lotus landscape orientation. The output also includes the worksheet frame.

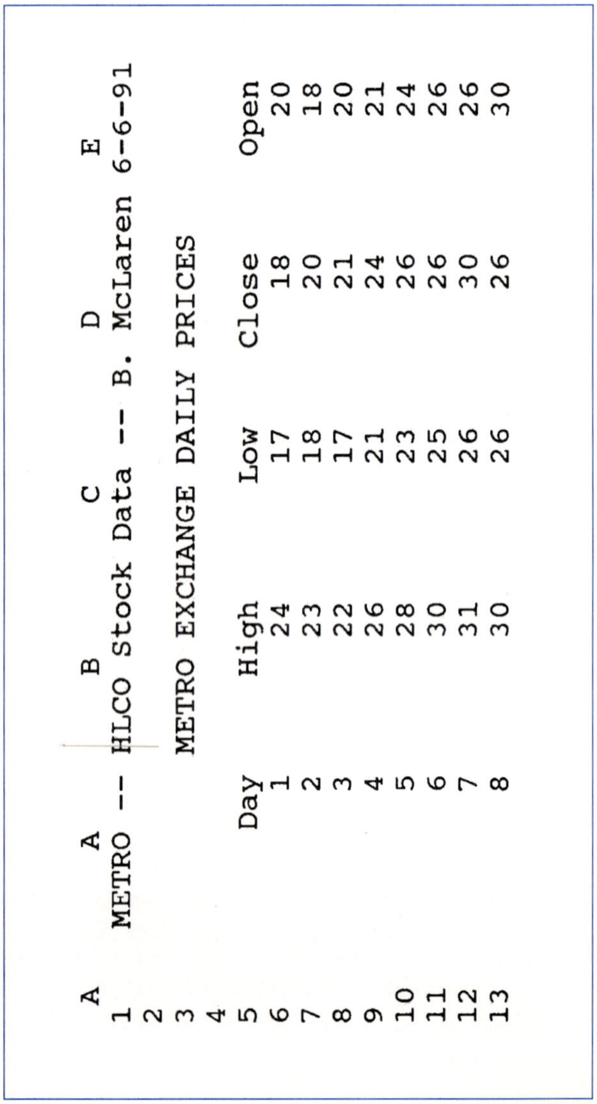

FIGURE 10-18

Worksheet Printed in Landscape Orientation

```
          A       B              C         D            E
   1   METRO -- HLCO Stock Data -- B. McLaren 6-6-91
   2
   3           METRO EXCHANGE DAILY PRICES
   4
   5   Day   High    Low     Close   Open
   6    1     24      17      18      20
   7    2     23      18      20      18
   8    3     22      17      21      20
   9    4     26      21      24      21
  10    5     28      23      26      24
  11    6     30      25      26      26
  12    7     31      26      30      26
  13    8     30      26      26      30
```

A particularly useful feature of Release 3.1 is its background printing. You select the print range and various options as usual, then start printing. The **PRT** status indicator will appear in the lower part of the screen to indicate that a print job is working. Instead of waiting for the complete output to print, you can return to Ready mode and edit the worksheet. Lotus will print the worksheet as a background operation. You can set a high or low priority for the print operation; a high priority causes the job to be printed sooner at the expense of slower response time while you move around and edit the worksheet. Any changes made during this editing session will not be reflected in print jobs already started. You can **suspend a print job** now and later **resume** it, useful if the printer is needed for another purpose.

Release 3.1 is able to print graphs from the **/Print** menu, eliminating the need for a PrintGraph module. Most of the PrintGraph options are found in the **/Print Options Advanced** menu, although they are organized differently. You may print the current graph or a named graph; there is no need to create a .PIC file (or the new .CGM file format) unless you want to transfer those graph images to another application. For instance, the Lotus graph .PIC files in this book were transferred to a desktop publishing program directly, rather than using a printed copy of the graph.

Lotus 3.1 adds a sample print feature that demonstrates the capability of your printer to produce various text fonts and graphs. Use the **/Print Sample Go** command to produce this four-page output. The sample output is similar in nature to the PRINTER.TST document that accompanies WordPerfect. After changing printer settings you can reprint the sample output to learn the effects. You do not specify a print range or any print options when selecting the sample output.

You can specify multiple print ranges and/or graphs, then print them all with a single **Go** command. Separate the print ranges with a semicolon. For example, **A1..A19;DETAIL;B:A1..F35** prints the A1..A19 range from the current worksheet, then prints the range named DETAIL from the current worksheet, then prints the range A1..F35 from the B: worksheet. If you place a graph name preceded by an asterisk in the print range, it will print on the page along with the worksheet text without having to use the WYSIWYG feature.

It is also possible to print column letter and row number borders (called the **worksheet frame**) with the worksheet for easier reference. Use the **/Print Options Borders** command to select the borders for the output.

Worksheet Analysis and Debugging Features

Along with the ability to print row and column borders is the **spreadsheet map** feature of Release 3.1. Use the **/Worksheet Window Map Enable** command to convert the display to map mode in which each cell appears as a two-character representation of the contents. Labels appear as a double quote ("), numeric constants as a pound sign (#), and formulas appear as a plus sign (+). With the standard 25 x 80 display you can see from cell A1 to cell AJ20. As you move the cursor to a particular cell, its contents appear in the Control Panel at the upper left. Press **Esc** to return to the normal mode. The SMRV worksheet map view is shown in Figure 10-19.

Release 3.1 allows you to add a **cell comment** to the end of a cell expression for documentation purposes. After entering the cell expression, type a semicolon, then type the comment. The correct value of the cell expression will appear in the worksheet. When you move the cursor to the cell containing the comment, the comment appears in the Control Panel at the upper left. Printing cell formulas also prints any comments you have attached to the cells. The following expression illustrates use of a cell comment: **(B14-40)*$A$7*1.5; Overtime hours pay calculation.**

FIGURE 10-19

Map View of the SMRV.WK1 Worksheet

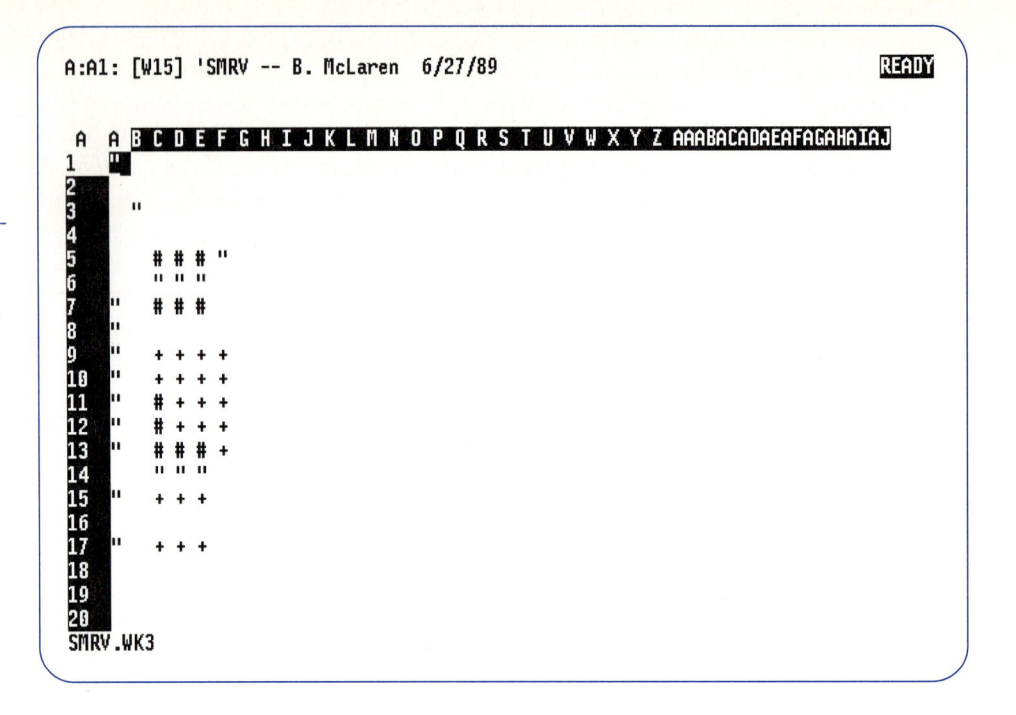

```
A:A1: [W15] 'SMRV -- B. McLaren  6/27/89                    READY

   A A BCDEFGHIJKLMNOPQRSTUVWXYZ AAABACADAEAFAGAHAIAJ
 1    "
 2    "
 3    "
 4
 5        # # # "
 6        " " "
 7    "   # # #
 8    "
 9    "   + + + +
10    "   + + + +
11    "   # + + +
12    "   # + + +
13    "   # # # +
14    "   " " "
15    "   + + +
16
17    "   + + +
18
19
20
SMRV.WK3
```

In a similar fashion you can create a **range comment**. Use the /**Range Name Note Create** command to create the note, then use the /**Range Name Note Table** command to create a table of range names and the accompanying notes. The /**Range Name Table** command does not produce the note.

Automatic Cell Formatting

A new feature of this version of Lotus is that you can give **automatic format** information when the cell entry is made, rather than having to use the /**Range Format** command *after* the cell values are entered. To use this feature, issue the /**Range Format Other Automatic** command and specify the cell range to be formatted. Lotus uses the (A) indicator for this format type. Then, when you enter a cell value, type the formatted value. Lotus will scan the entry and determine which format type you intended. Examples follow:

Cell Entry	Format	Explanation
123.46	(F2)	Fixed, 2 decimal places
$123	(C0)	Currency, 0 places
$12,345.20	(C2)	Currency, 2 places
ABC	(L)	Label
6.02E+23	(S2)	Scientific, 2 places
04:12	(D9)	Date type 9 (time)
06/13/91	(D4)	Date type 4
89.1%	(P1)	Percentage, 1 place
12,245	(,0)	Comma, 0 places

You can display negative cell values in a different color using the /**Range Format Other Color** command. Lotus adds a minus sign to the format indicator in the Control Panel. For instance, **(F2-)** means fixed format with 2 decimal places and negative values will appear in red.

Another new format command allows you to enclose a range of cells in parentheses, regardless of their value. When you have set this format, Lotus places () inside the format indicator. Thus, **(F2())** means that this cell will appear in fixed format with two decimal places and will have parentheses around it.

The **/Range Format Other Label** command instructs Lotus to convert cell expressions to labels as they are entered. This would be valuable when entering expressions within a macro and eliminates the need to press the quote key before entering the expression. This format type is indicated by **(L)**. Thus if you entered **+B4/$B$89** in a cell with the Label format, Lotus would place a single quote character in front of it and consider it a left-justified label, not a value expression.

New /Data Options

Lotus now allows you to have up to 255 sort keys for sorting. Previous versions allowed only two key fields, primary and secondary. This release has an **Extra-Key** option in the **/Data Sort** menu.

For **/Data Query** operations you can create a calculated column for the output range in addition to using existing field names. The first row in the column should contain an expression involving one or more field names from the input data range. When the Extract query is executed, Lotus will calculate the expression for records that qualify for the query and place the result in the calculated column.

Lotus 3.1 is able to access data from **external tables** (non-Lotus) that are created with database management programs such as dBASE III Plus. The **/Data Query Extract** command is used to retrieve data from the table. The query requires that you specify input, criteria, and output ranges before records can be retrieved. You must first create a link to the external database with the **/Data External Use** command and assign it to a Lotus range name. The range name for the external table will be the input data range. With the connection to the external table established, retrieve the database field names with the **/Data External List Fields** command and place them in the worksheet. Copy these field names to a row in the worksheet, then place any criteria beneath that row for records to be retrieved. The output range row should list the field names for which you want data. Then execute the **/Data Query Extract** command; the qualifying records from the external table will be placed in the worksheet's output range. Lotus also has the capability of placing data into an existing external table and can create a new external table.

Previous Lotus versions allowed use of one-parameter and two-parameter tables to perform what-if analysis. This release of 1-2-3 can prepare data tables with three input variables using the **/Data Table 3** command.

Release 3.1 Macro Changes

Like Release 2.2, this version is able to record up to 512 bytes of keystrokes for later use in a macro. The **Alt-F2** Erase command is used to begin the recording feature. As you enter commands, they are captured in a memory buffer. When you are ready to place the keystrokes in the worksheet, issue the **Alt-F2** command again and select the **Copy** option. Lotus will display the saved keystrokes on the screen. You can then edit the keystrokes and, when ready, highlight the portion of the keystrokes you want to place in the worksheet. Lotus will prompt you to indicate the range in which you want to store the recorded keystrokes. Unlike Release 2.2, this version allows you to make changes and select only the desired keystrokes from those that were recorded.

There are a few new macro commands in Release 3.1 and some new arguments in existing macro commands. Most of the new commands deal with moving between pages in multiple worksheet files and with accessing new function key commands.

Although Release 3.1 shares most of the same / command options with previous Lotus versions, Release 2.2 macros that make use of the specific location of a menu choice may not work properly in 3.1. In other words, macros should always execute a command option by its first character, not by relying on cursor keystrokes to reach that option within a particular menu. Older macros with label names that are the same as a Release 3.1 macro command must be changed.

Other Changes

This release of Lotus 1-2-3 brings some new @-functions. There are several database functions that work with external database tables. The **@D360(start-date,end-date)** function calculates the number of days between two dates assuming 360 days per year, and is sometimes used in financial analysis. Several functions work with multiple worksheets. The new **@STDS(list)** and **@VARS(list)** statistical functions calculate the sample standard deviation and variance of numbers in a list; previous **@STD()** and **@VAR()** functions calculate the population standard deviation and variance. The **@INFO()** function returns various information about the operating system and worksheet status.

For users with large worksheets that take some time to recalculate, this version of Lotus offers **background recalculation,** which allows you to continue to edit the worksheet while recalculations are being performed. Previous Lotus versions forced the user to wait until all calculations were performed. On color monitors the **CALC indicator** appears in red when Lotus is doing a background recalculation; a blue CALC indicator means that you should press **F9** to perform a manual recalculation. For users with monochrome monitors, a white CALC means background recalculations are taking place; a reverse video (black letters on white background) CALC indicator refers to the need to perform a manual recalculation.

Because most users have a high-resolution graphical display with their system, Release 3.1 was designed to display more than the usual 20 rows on the screen at a time. Only the CGA and EGA with 64 KB video memory options are limited to 20 rows. Of course, displaying more than 20 rows reduces the size of the characters in the worksheet and make it somewhat more difficult to read. Up to 50 rows and 132 characters across can be displayed. Use the **INSTALL** command to change to a higher resolution screen.

This release has **search and replace** capabilities. Issue the **/Range Search** command and provide the cell range to examine. Lotus will prompt you to enter the target search text. It can highlight the occurrence within the range of that text or can substitute a new value for it.

Compatibility with Other Lotus Versions

Because Release 3.1 is able to read .WK1 and .WK3 files, there is excellent upward compatibility from previous versions. The Lotus manual recommends that you save files in .WK3 format because they will load faster than other versions. Lotus does *not* modify the disk file containing the .WK1 worksheet as it is retrieved into Release 3.1.

If you intend to take Release 3.1 worksheet files to Release 2.x (2.3, 2.2 or 2.01), save the file in the .WK1 format by appending that extension to the end of the file name when you save it. Because many of the new features have no counterparts in Release 2.x, some changes will be made when the file is saved. Previous versions allowed only 240 characters per cell, so longer expressions may be lost. [Note: Long expressions from translated Release 3.1 worksheets are accepted by 2.x, but if you edit a cell with such an expression, any characters past the 240th are dropped when you save the edited cell expression.] Incompatible @ functions are replaced by the @? function followed by a list of the arguments of the function; these cells will evaluate as @NA. If you read the .WK1 file *back* into Release 3.1 the @? functions are correctly reconstructed.

Any notes attached to range names or cell expressions are dropped when the file is translated into the .WK1 format. New /Print and /Graph settings are also eliminated. The automatic format is changed to the Release 2.x default format type. Multiple worksheet files must be converted to separate .WK3 files before they are saved. (The Lotus TRANSLATE program will automatically convert a multiple-sheet file into separate .WK1 files.) If there are incompatibilities detected when a .WK3 file is saved in .WK1 format, the ERROR mode indicator is lit to indicate that information was lost.

Release 3.1 calculates values to 18 digits whereas previous versions used 15 digits. This could lead to slightly different results for the same worksheet. Previous versions will truncate decimal places for a value that is too wide to fit in the current cell width. Release 3.1 will round off the last digit that fits within the cell width. All versions of Lotus use the maximum number of digits internally when performing calculations, regardless of how the value is displayed on the screen.

Lotus 1-2-3 Release 3.1 Plus

Although Release 3.1 Plus was not officially released as this book went to press, it will add to Release 3.1 the file viewer and auditor features from Release 2.3. Another important addition is the Solver capability in which Lotus varies an input cell in order to produce a desired result in another cell. Release 3.1 Plus will probably replace Release 3.1, just as Release 2.3 will replace Release 2.2.

CHAPTER REVIEW

Lotus 1-2-3 Release 2.3

Introduced in summer 1991, Release 2.3 replaced Release 2.2 as the low-end spreadsheet package for use with 8088 microcomputers. Although it closely resembles Release 2.2, the newer version adds some important new features. Its WYSIWYG facility provides improved spreadsheet publishing capabilities and provides compatibility with Release 3.1. Other new features include a spreadsheet auditor and an auto-compress function that automatically formats and prints with a small font so that a large spreadsheet fits on a single page.

Release 2.3 offers three new graph types (Horizontal Bar, High-Low-Close-Open, and Mixed Line/Bar) for better display of data. A built-in file viewer allows you to see the contents of worksheet and other disk files without leaving 1-2-3. This version also provides background printing, useful with long outputs.

Lotus 1-2-3 Release 3.1

This Lotus version replaced Release 3.0 in late 1990. Release 3.1 adds WYSIWYG spreadsheet publishing and compatibility with Microsoft Windows 3.0. Version 3.1 requires an 80286 or better microprocessor with 640 KB conventional RAM, 384 KB or more of extended memory, and a hard drive with 5 MB of free space.

Multiple Worksheets

Release 3.1 provides access to three-dimensional worksheets with up to 256 sheets in memory at one time. The sheets are lettered, beginning with A. Cell ranges may be prefixed with the sheet letter followed by a colon, then the normal cell address. Thus B:D4 refers to cell D4 in sheet B. Expressions may refer to cells on other sheets. Applications include consolidating data from multiple territories or time periods.

WYSIWYG Graphical Display

Although similar to Allways, the WYSIWYG facility offers much improved spreadsheet publishing capabilities. With WYSIWYG you can select different text fonts with proportional spacing, text size, underlining, bold, italics, lines, and shading for the printed worksheet. You can annotate worksheets with freehand drawing, lines, arrows, boxes, and other shapes. The WYSIWYG menu is accessed with the : prefix and can be used in combination with the usual 1-2-3 / commands without leaving WYSIWYG mode. You can place Lotus graphs in the worksheet with WYSIWYG and print them together with text material.

New Graph Features

Release 3.1 introduced the High-Low-Close-Open and Mixed Bar/Line graph types. HLCO graphs are used to display stock market information in a special format. Mixed graphs can display three data ranges of bar graphs and three data ranges of line graphs, all on the same graph page. Also included in this release are the ability to display two Y-range scales, useful when the data values to be plotted are not taken from the same scale magnitude. Graphs can be printed in the usual vertical manner or rotated in a horizontal fashion. Release 3.1 is able to print graphs from within 1-2-3, eliminating the need for a PrintGraph module. (WYSIWYG is not necessary to print graphs within Release 3.1.) You can open a graph window in the worksheet, displaying the worksheet and a graph on the screen simultaneously. Any changes made to the worksheet are seen immediately in the graph.

Print Features

Release 3.1 provides /Print menu control for selecting normal, compressed, and expanded fonts, so that you don't have to memorize complicated setup printer control strings. You can select the normal portrait mode for output or rotate the output 90 degrees to print in landscape mode. Release 3.1 offers automatic background printing so that you can return to editing the worksheet instead of waiting for the printer to finish the output. You can specify multiple print ranges and graph names in one range command, then print them with a single Go command. There is a built-in sample print capability so that you can determine the text and graphics printing capabilities of your printer.

Worksheet Analysis and Debugging Features

Release 3.1 provides a mapping facility in which you can view a summary of large worksheets on the screen. In map mode each cell is represented by a two-character symbol for label, numeric constant, or formula. The map will help in documenting location of ranges, tables, and macros. In 3.1 you can append a comment to a cell expression for documentation purposes. The comment must be preceded by a semicolon and appears in the Control Panel of the main worksheet display when you move the cursor to a specific cell. Comments can also be placed with range names and displayed in a range name table.

Automatic Cell Formatting

With this release you can activate an automatic range format type and assign a cell format when the cell value is entered. When you enter the cell expression, its format can be interpreted and that cell given the appropriate format type. Lotus can display negative numbers in color or enclose them in parentheses. For entering macro keystroke commands, Release 3.1 has a Label cell format in which cell expressions are always considered as labels rather than interpreted by their first character.

New /Data Options

Release 3.1 permits up to 255 sort keys. You may now create calculated columns for the output range in a Data Query Extract operation. Data from external database files such as dBASE III PLUS may be linked to a Data Query and read directly into Lotus without going through a transformation first. Although somewhat cumbersome, this procedure may facilitate access to large databases in a single step. Release 3.1 also provides for a three-parameter data table where there are three input variables.

Release 3.1 Macro Changes

Most macros from earlier Lotus versions will run in Release 3.1 with few or no changes. There are a few new macro commands that correspond to new features in this version. Macros that will be used in a different Lotus version should be written to select / command options by their first character rather than by use of cursor keys. The macro learn feature of Release 2.2 is replaced by an improved record capability. Up to 512 characters can be captured in a memory buffer, edited, then stored in a cell range.

Other Changes

There are a few new @-functions for working with external databases and statistical analysis. Release 3.1 employs background recalculation to permit worksheet editing while other cells in the worksheet are recalculated. The CALC indicator has two functions—one to show that background recalculation is taking place and the other to show that a manual recalculation should be done before viewing or printing the worksheet.

Depending on the hardware you have, more than 20 and up to 50 rows can be displayed on the screen, with 132 characters across. Release 3.1 offers search and replace functions with the /Range Search command.

Compatibility with Other Versions

Release 3.1 is able to read worksheet files from all previous Lotus versions. It saves worksheet files in the .WK3 format by default, but you can use the .WK1 extension to save a file in the Lotus 2.2 format. When you save Release 3.1 worksheets as .WK1 files, features available only in .WK3 files are not retained. Graph image files are saved either as .CGM or .PIC format files; the .CGM format allows easier transfer to other graphics programs such as desktop publishing. Because Release 3.1 uses 18 digits internally when performing calculations, three more digits than prior versions, worksheets may display slightly different results.

Lotus Release 3.1 Plus

Not officially released as this book went to press, the new 1-2-3 version will have the file viewer and auditor features from Release 2.3, along with all the features of Release 3.1. It will have the ability to solve backward to arrive at a particular cell value by manipulating input cell values.

KEY TERMS

1-2-3/W	graph window	range comment
auditing	HLCO graph	Release 2.3
auto-compression	landscape mode	Release 3.1
automatic format	: menu	Release 3.1 Plus
background printing	minimal recalculation	search and replace
background recalculation	mixed graph	shadow RAM
CALC indicator	mouse support	sheets
cell comment	multiple sheets	spreadsheet map
.CGM graph file	on-sheet word processing	spreadsheet publishing
encoded printer file	pages	suspend/resume print job
external table	perspective window	.WK3 file extension
extra-key sort option	pop-up help windows	worksheet frame
file viewer	portrait mode	WYSIWYG

DISCUSSION QUESTIONS

1. Discuss the system requirements for Release 2.3 and Release 3.1 of Lotus 1-2-3. Your answer should include microprocessor, memory, and hard drive requirements.

2. Describe the major new features of Release 2.3 that are *not* available in Release 2.2.

3. Explain how a worksheet created in Release 3.1 could be used by someone with Releases 2.2 or 2.3. Are there any incompatibilities between the versions?

4. What is meant by the term *three-dimensional worksheet?*

5. Discuss the meaning of the following new Lotus commands:
    a. **Ctrl-PgDn**
    b. **/Worksheet Window Perspective**
    c. **Alt-F10**
    d. **:**
    e. **/Print Encoded**

6. Explain the following WYSIWYG features:
    a. **:Display** menu options
    b. **:Named-Style** options
    c. **:Format Italics**
    d. **:Graph Edit** tools
    e. drop shadow format

7. Discuss the new /**Graph** features available in Release 3.1.

8. Discuss the new /**Print** features available in Release 3.1.

9. Describe the automatic format capability in Release 3.1. List the format type that Lotus would determine for the following cell entries:
   a. 123,233.12
   b. $12.41
   c. 23.44%
   d. 3.14159E+00
   e. 07/04/92
   f. 14:23
   g. This is a comment.

10. Discuss the new /**Data** features available in Release 3.1.

11. Compare the Release 2.2 macro learn feature with the keystroke record method of Release 3.1. Which is preferred for recording macros, and why?

12. Explain the meaning of the following Release 3.1 functions.
    a. @D360()
    b. @STDS()
    c. @VARS()
    d. @VAR()

13. Discuss the changes anticipated for Lotus Release 3.1 Plus.

EXERCISES

1. Start Lotus Release 3.1 and create the spreadsheet in Figure 10-20. The Hammacker Corporation wants to prepare a Portfolio Statement as shown in the figure. Fill in columns E and F with appropriate expressions. Column E is calculated by multiplying the number of shares by the market price. Calculate the Purchase Cost in each security based upon purchase price and number of shares. Column F is the total gain or loss, i.e., Current Value less Purchase Cost. Use appropriate formatting to display the financial values in the worksheet. Save the worksheet under the name **HAMMPORT.WK3** and obtain a printed copy.

```
                  HAMMACKER PORTFOLIO REPORT

Name of           Purchase Purchase   Market   Current    Gain/
Security            Price  Quantity   Price     Value     Loss
---------         ---------------------------------------------
ABM Gold Corp.      4.875      50     2.875
Duff & Phelps       8.125     100     8.500
Student Mkt. Assn.  3.125     100     3.750
Wiser Oil Company  15.250     100    15.000
GM Zero Coupon Bon 93.500      10   116.125
                                             -------------------
TOTAL                                              0         0
                                             ===================
```

FIGURE 10-20

Spreadsheet for Exercise 1

FIGURE 10-21

First Quarter Data for Exercise 2

```
              First Quarter Sales

              SALES
                Charters              $9,076
                Package Del.          12,224
                Air Ambulance         13,543
                Crop Dusting           4,120
                Special Missions      13,451
                                    ---------
                                     $52,414
```

2. Prepare a multiple worksheet for the Air Direct Company. The top sheet should contain the annual sales figures. Sheets B-E will contain quarterly sales data that will be consolidated on the top sheet. Figure 10-21 shows the general format for the first quarter results. Remaining quarterly results are contained in files called AIRDQ2.WK1, AIRDQ3.WK1, and AIRDQ4.WK1, stored on the data disk. Use the **/File Combine** command to place the quarterly spreadsheets into existing sheets. Save the entire worksheet as **AIRD.WK3** and obtain a printed copy showing the top sheet.

3. This exercise requires that WYSIWYG be installed on your computer. Retrieve the GRAM.WK1 worksheet file from the data disk. Attach WYSIWYG and use it to prepare the following items:

   a. Use the 14-point Swiss font for the first two title lines. Keep them roughly centered over the report. You may need to move the first title line to column A; leave the second title line in column B.

   b. Delete the row of hyphens beneath the column headings. Use WYSIWYG to place a line below the column headings.

   c. The column headings should be in italics.

   d. Alternating sets of five price lines of the report should be shaded to improve viewing legibility. That is, the August 24–28 lines should appear unshaded, August 29–September 2 lines should be shaded, and so on.

   e. Place an outline around the highest price cell in each column.

   f. Print a copy of the worksheet with WYSIWYG.

   g. Save the revised worksheet under the name **GRAM3**.

4. The Deveraux Company from Ottawa has gathered quality control data for the M9 assembly line, shown in Figure 10-22. Add a column that measures the three-period moving average batch weight. There will be no moving average for periods 1 and 2; for period 3 the three-period average would be (0.428+0.422+0.420)/3. For period 4 the moving average would include periods 2 through 4, and so on.

   Prepare a mixed graph that shows the individual batch weights as bars and the moving average as a line. The first title is **DEVERAUX COMPANY** and the second title is **Average Batch Weight**. The Y-axis title is **Weight in Kilograms** and the X-axis title is **Batch Number**. Use (Fixed,3) format for the Y-axis scale.

Batch	Weight
1	0.428
2	0.422
3	0.420
4	0.431
5	0.428
6	0.435
7	0.440
8	0.490
9	0.512
10	0.513
11	0.522
12	0.509

FIGURE 10-22

Sample Data for Exercise 4

5. Repeat the problem from Exercise 4 using WYSIWYG. Select appropriate fonts to display the worksheet. Print the data and the graph on the same worksheet.

6. Load the HAMMPORT.WK3 worksheet you created in Exercise 1 and activate the map mode. Give the meaning of each of the symbols in the map. [Note: Unless your computer has been set up to print graphics screens, the **Shift-PrtSc** command cannot be used to print the contents of the worksheet map. Users with CGA displays may be able to use the **Shift-PrtSc** command because those monitors do not use graphics mode to display the worksheet.]

7. Provided your printer is capable of printing in landscape mode, load the SMRV.WK3 worksheet from the data disk and obtain printed copies in both portrait and landscape orientations. Compare the quality of the characters in each output.

8. Activate the keystroke recorder with **Alt-F2** and record the keystrokes necessary to load and print the BUDGET.WK3 worksheet from the example called "Preparing a Multiple Worksheet," earlier in this chapter. Then copy those keystrokes to cell A21 of a new worksheet. Print a copy of the worksheet containing the stored keystrokes.

CHAPTER 10 PROJECT
HCP INCORPORATED ANNUAL REPORT

Corporate Relations staffers at HCP are in the process of preparing final copy for the 1990 annual report. They have the financial results for the past ten years and want to present it in a suitable manner. They know it will require a mixture of text and graphs but aren't sure how to display the data in a pleasing and informative manner. Historical data are shown in Figure 10-23 on the following page and are contained in a Lotus worksheet file named HCP.WK1 on the data diskette. Additional data are shown in other tables in the same figure.

Prepare a presentation-quality table showing the historical data using WYSIWYG. The current year's figures should be highlighted in the table. The four account headings appearing above each group of account titles should appear in italic type and be bold. Any other formatting or style changes that would help in presenting this material should be implemented.

Prepare a set of graphs to display the quarterly stock price data. Use WYSIWYG to display the information from the bar graphs on the same output page as the actual data itself. Print that portion of the worksheet.

Prepare separate 1-2-3 bar graphs that illustrate the ten-year trends in sales, net income, earnings per share, and dividends per share. Add formatting and other options as needed to carefully describe the information shown in the graphs. Make sure your graphs appear in chronological order by year, from 1981 to 1990. Is there any way to improve the visual appearance of these graphs? How might you add annotations to the graphs?

FIGURE 10-23

Sample Data for Chapter 10 Project, Contained in File HCP.WK1 on Data Disk

```
HCP -- Annual Report Data for Ten Years Ending 1990

HISTORICAL DATA

For the Year (dollars in millions)      1990      1989      1988      1987      1986      1985      1984      1983      1982      1981

Net Sales                            $2,796.6  $2,669.7  $2,317.8  $1,933.1  $1,636.1  $1,812.8  $1,515.5  $1,243.4  $1,234.3  $1,155.4
Gross Income                            979.8     996.9     861.8     665.1     517.3     676.8     589.0     465.5     476.5     454.5
Selling, General and Admin Expenses     505.2     467.0     426.0     362.4     318.4     307.2     292.0     250.4     236.7     224.0
Income from Operations                  474.6     519.9     435.8     302.7     198.9     369.6     297.0     215.1     239.8     230.5
Interest Expense                        (21.6)    (16.2)    (16.2)    (16.4)    (15.6)    (13.6)    (12.2)    (10.9)    (13.0)    (14.2)
Other Income, Net                         2.3      15.5      10.9       7.7       9.2       6.7       7.8       9.3      14.2       6.8
Income Before Income Taxes              455.3     529.2     430.5     294.0     192.5     362.7     292.6     213.5     241.0     223.1
  % of Sales                             16.3      19.8      18.6      15.2      11.8      20.0      19.3      17.2      19.5      19.3
Income Taxes                            174.4     210.1     180.8     129.7      84.5     161.4     129.5      94.6     106.2      99.4
Net Income                             $280.9    $319.1    $249.7    $164.3    $108.0    $201.3    $163.1    $118.9    $134.8    $123.7
  % of Sales                             10.0      12.0      10.8       8.5       6.6      11.1      10.8       9.6      10.9      10.7
Net Income Per Share                    $2.63     $2.96     $2.31     $1.52     $1.00     $1.87     $1.52     $1.10     $1.25     $1.15
Cash Dividends                          128.1     107.8      91.8      80.0      77.7      68.9      57.4      50.3      43.2      36.0
Cash Dividends Per Share               $1.200    $1.000    $0.850    $0.740    $0.720    $0.640    $0.533    $0.466    $0.400    $0.333
Capital Expenditures                    252.1     220.3     171.8     151.7     198.5     255.7     127.6     121.9     108.9     113.3
Depreciation and Amortization           180.3     158.5     142.1     125.3      96.4      75.1      63.3      58.6      50.5      43.7
Research, Development and Engineering   253.0     238.0     204.0     170.0     160.0     163.0     133.0     112.0     111.0     104.0


At December 31 (dollars in millions)

Working Capital                        $711.7    $700.9    $625.3    $475.5    $356.1    $389.4    $446.5    $415.6    $410.7    $363.0
Property, Plant and Equipment, Net      953.8     894.6     865.4     793.6     750.2     620.4     461.9     413.5     362.9     323.4
Total Assets                          2,529.8   2,375.5   2,082.1   1,786.9   1,549.3   1,487.4   1,238.4   1,076.3   1,025.4     928.7
  % Return on Assets                     11.5      14.3      12.9       9.9       7.1      14.8      14.1      11.3      13.8      14.0
Long-Term Debt                           69.5      82.8      71.4      46.3      36.1      27.3      46.9      53.0      56.1      50.1
Total Debt                              284.0     224.8     187.1     191.4     188.8     202.3      95.6     103.4      94.1     102.3
Shareholders' Equity                  1,625.4   1,521.3   1,348.6   1,134.9     996.9     923.2     800.9     714.5     660.5     577.7
  % Return on Equity                     17.9      22.2      20.1      15.4      11.2      23.4      21.5      17.3      21.8      23.1
Shareholder's Equity Per Share         $15.27    $14.16    $12.54    $10.50     $9.23     $8.57     $7.45     $6.64     $6.13     $5.35
Backlog                                $489.0    $475.0    $384.0    $326.0    $307.0    $340.0    $374.0    $254.0    $253.0    $248.0
Number of Employees                    24,400    24,100    22,000    21,800    22,800    24,500    21,300    19,750    19,650    18,650
Floor Space (millions sq. feet)           9.0       9.0       8.9       8.9       9.0       8.7       7.9       7.3       7.0       6.3
Shares of Stock Outstanding (millions)  106.5     107.4     107.5     108.1     107.9     107.7     107.5     107.7     107.8     108.0


Annual Stock Price Range

High                                   49.375    54.250    71.500    45.000    37.875    39.500    39.000    23.500    20.875    18.750
Low                                    40.000    40.500    34.125    32.875    27.500    26.125    22.000    15.125    14.500    11.000


Quarterly Stock Price Range            1st Q     2nd Q     3rd Q     4th Q

1990 High                              49.375    44.125    47.250    47.500
1990 Low                               41.000    40.250    40.500    40.000

1989 High                              54.250    52.000    52.000    45.750
1989 Low                               40.500    42.875    40.500    40.625
```

Appendices

A **A PC Buyer's Guide** 328

B **DOS Commands** 339
   Internal DOS Command Summary
   External DOS Command Summary

C **Lotus 1-2-3 Commands** 341
   Lotus 1-2-3 Cursor Movement Commands
   Lotus 1-2-3 Keyboard Macro Commands
   Lotus 1-2-3 Function Key Macro Commands
   Statistical @-Functions
   Mathematical @-Functions
   Financial @-Functions
   Depreciation @-Functions
   Date and Time @-Functions
   If and Lookup @-Functions
   String @-Functions
   Lotus Alphabetic Quick Reference
   Lotus 1-2-3 Command Tree
   Lotus 1-2-3 Printgraph Command Tree
   Allways Command Tree

Appendix A
A PC Buyer's Guide

COMPONENTS OF THE DECISION

There are many alternatives for buying personal computer hardware and software today. While prices and features are constantly changing, there are certain issues to consider in addition to the current model selection. The purchasing process can be broken down into five phases:

1. Determine what applications you want to do with the microcomputer.
2. Decide the kinds and brands of the software you need.
3. Choose the most appropriate hardware that runs the software chosen.
4. Interview vendors about support, price, and product availability.
5. Make the purchase and install the equipment.

Many people are more concerned with steps 3 and 5, without giving the other three enough thought. This textbook focuses on IBM and compatible computer applications, but the steps above apply to all kinds of computers.

SOFTWARE SELECTION

Most people want to do word processing with their computer, and there are more word-processing-software applications than any other kind. Spreadsheet and database applications are also very popular. Telecommunications applications using a modem are common. Some users may wish to do programming, in BASIC, Pascal, or another programming language. This text has introduced the most popular software packages used with IBM-compatible personal computers. The final chapter in each application section compared other popular competing products with the covered software.

Many popular software packages require a hard disk. Some require a graphics video adapter. Because most vendors will not accept a software package for return after it has been opened, read the "fine print" before breaking the seal. Some vendors have a demonstration copy you can try before buying. Be sure to examine carefully the memory and operating system version required for the package. For IBM users the minimal hardware configuration would include 512 KB RAM and DOS 3.2 or higher. Macintosh users would want at least one megabyte of RAM. Additional RAM may be needed to run certain programs.

One consideration for choosing software is the availability of training, user support, and other reference materials. If your school has standardized on a particular product, it is usually desirable to choose that product unless it doesn't fulfill your needs. Another issue consists of transferring data from one application to another. Most of the popular packages can exchange data freely—be certain your chosen brands can do so if this is expected. There is a chapter in this book about exchanging data between applications.

Word Processing Packages

The most popular full-featured word processing packages are WordPerfect, WordStar, Microsoft Word, XYWrite, and Multimate Advantage. This textbook features WordPerfect 5.1, the top-selling word processing package. There are many packages with fewer features. They require less hardware and may be easier to learn. pfs-Write is an easy-to-learn package. **Integrated software** packages such as First Choice, Framework, and Enable have embedded word processing capabilities. Integrated software packages typically combine word processing, spreadsheet, database, graphics, and telecommunications features into a single program with common menus.

Spreadsheets

Spreadsheet packages have less variety than word processors. Lotus 1-2-3 has a large market share, more than 65%. This textbook demonstrates spreadsheet concepts using release 2.2 of Lotus 1-2-3. It is the dominant brand in use today. But there are several excellent alternatives, most of which are compatible with Lotus files and with most Lotus commands. SuperCalc 5, Quattro, Twin, and VP Planner are full-featured programs that go beyond Lotus Release 2.2. Microsoft's Excel runs only on an 80286 or 80386 microprocessor, and offers many new spreadsheet capabilities.

Database Software

Database management programs range from inexpensive file managers like PC-FILE or File Express to multi-user relational database systems like dBASE, Paradox and R:Base. dBASE is the best selling package, but doesn't dominate the database market as Lotus 1-2-3 does the spreadsheet market. Database management software is quite versatile, ranging from simple mailing list applications to complete, menu-driven systems. Each application should be carefully examined before deciding what to purchase. There are several dBASE imitators ("clones") available, including dBXL and Foxbase, for those who want a comparable package for less money.

Shareware and Public Domain Software

Occasionally "free" software is bundled along with certain computer brands. Such software may not be a bargain, particularly if it differs from the standard brands supported on campus or elsewhere. Be sure this software satisfies the needs you established earlier. Shareware is another inexpensive source of software, available from vendors like Public Brand Software or from local computer clubs or libraries. Catalogs describing this software are available free. Some of the software is in the **public domain,** contributed by other users without expectations of payment for the programs. Some of the software is distributed on the **shareware** basis: copy it freely, but make a nominal payment to the program's author if it is used after the trial period. There is some remarkable software available on this basis, including ProComm, an excellent intelligent terminal program. Good educational programs are also available through this distribution method.

Educational Versions

Educational, or student, versions of software are available at very low cost (often included in the price of a textbook) and serve a purpose in learning how to use a package. These versions may not be useful in regular applications, either due to license restrictions or because of size and feature limitations. Usually only limited documentation accompanies the disk. Once the learning period is over, a full working copy should be purchased. Upgrades are sometimes available—check the fine print accompanying the educational disk.

Copyrights and Software Piracy

Most software available today is licensed to a single user. Copying it for another user is a violation of the Federal copyright law. The term **software piracy** is used to describe the act of copying software illegally. Most universities have significant penalties for those who make illegal copies of software. Ethical use of software is the responsibility of each user.

CHOOSING HARDWARE

Once the software choices are made, you can consider hardware. Most users will know early in the process whether they want an IBM compatible machine, an Apple Macintosh, or some other family of microcomputers. Business users have traditionally chosen the IBM line, while elementary education users have focused on Apple II products. The Macintosh became popular with the advent of desktop publishing, but all computers can be used with virtually all applications with proper software. Of course, there are some fundamental differences between IBM compatibles and the Macintosh.

The Mac made an important contribution with its user interface, based upon graphical images (icons) that represent functions in graphical menus. The user can maneuver a mouse to move the cursor to the desired function icon, and depress the mouse button ("click") on it. Most Macintosh software is designed with the same architecture; that is, once you've learned one Mac package, others are very similar. Some people dislike having to move their hand from the keyboard to manipulate the mouse, but many appreciate the ease of communicating with a program. In fact, many software designers have used Mac features in IBM compatible software. Microsoft's Windows and DESQview utilize the graphical approach. PageMaker, a desktop-publishing program, works the same way in the Mac and the IBM versions. With the OS/2 Presentation Manager following closely the Macintosh interface, icon/graphical presentations can be achieved in the IBM world. This textbook focuses on IBM-compatible computers and related buying issues.

Microcomputer magazines are an excellent source of information on available products and vendors. *PC Magazine* regularly offers detailed reviews on products. Their printer review issues are exceptional. Other good IBM-related magazines include *Personal Computing, InfoWorld, PC World,* and *Byte*. The top two Macintosh magazines are *Mac User* and *Mac World*. There are many specialty magazines dealing with specific markets or kinds of products, and even magazines dealing with a single product like *WordPerfect The Magazine*. Another good source of information is a local computer users' group. Many communities have such groups, organized locally to help members learn more about computing. You might check with the local library or school for information about meeting times and membership.

Hardware buying decisions include type of drives (hard, floppy, storage capacity, speed), type of display adapter and monitor, central processing unit CPU type and speed, amount of RAM (conventional, expanded), desktop or portable/laptop, cabinet style and number of expansion slots, and number of I/O ports. Many users will buy a mouse, which requires either a spare serial port or a bus card.

A complete system includes the computer itself with sufficient memory (minimum 512 KB but preferably 640 KB or more), 1 or 2 disk storage devices (floppy or hard drive), serial and parallel ports for mouse and printer, video adapter, display monitor (monochrome or color, but matching the video adapter), printer cable and printer (dot matrix, ink jet, or laser), and perhaps a surge protector or modem. Since the entire system is rarely packaged together in one bundle, you will have to make some choices. Keep in mind that the software chosen will dictate certain hardware requirements. It is recommended that a hard disk be part of the configuration if budget allows the extra $200-$400 cost. A perplexing issue involves 3.5-inch versus 5.25-inch floppy disk drives. Most newer machines come with the 3.5-inch size but older machines probably have the larger drive. Software is available in both sizes, and some publishers include both size diskettes in the box. This decision depends in part on those with whom you will be exchanging information. One solution is to install both sizes of floppy drives in the same computer; the second floppy drive costs about $100.

Hardware Manufacturers

There are many manufacturers of IBM-compatible personal computers, most priced competitively. IBM offers a complete selection of personal computers. Other well-known companies such as Hewlett-Packard, AT&T, Unisys, and NCR offer similar personal computers, but there are numerous new companies with good products. Compaq is one of the fastest growing companies in U.S. history, reaching the $1 billion sales level faster than any other firm. Zenith Data Systems has a complete line of personal computers and has extensive sales agreements with the federal government and with educational institutions. Tandy sells excellent personal computers and has a well-developed hardware support network. Several mail-order vendors, including CompuAdd and Dell Computers, offer good equipment at attractive prices. Most of these machines advertise complete IBM compatibility and will run virtually all software designed for IBM personal computers.

Selecting the System Unit

With the IBM PC family nearly a decade old, there are many compatible models available. The original IBM PC and XT used the 8088 microprocessor, and have been discontinued for several years. But many clone vendors still sell 8088 machines. This processor is capable of running most applications software, but some newer packages like Microsoft's Excel spreadsheet require an 80286 processor. The 8088 will handle routine chores like word processing well, although certain tasks such as spell checking or global search-and-replace will work more slowly on an 8088 machine. In some cases a faster hard drive can make up for a slower processor. But computation-intensive applications, such as large spreadsheets, will be considerably slower on an 8088 machine. An 8087 numeric co-processor chip can speed up the calculations if the software is written to recognize the presence of the chip. The 8088 is an 8/16 processor; it uses an 8-bit data bus for data transfers between memory and the CPU, and accomplishes 16-bit internal calculations. When purchasing expansion boards for an 8088 computer, choose the 8-bit variety. The 8088 can access up to 1 MB of memory, but cannot run the OS/2 operating system.

A faster replacement was introduced in 1985. The IBM AT featured an 80286 processor and a 16-bit data bus. It also can handle some 32-bit internal calculations and is significantly faster than the PC and XT. While 8-bit expansion boards can be used with an AT, critical components such as disk controller and expansion memory should be the 16-bit variety. Another change with the AT was inclusion of high-density, 1.2-MB, 5.25-inch disk drives, making backups of larger hard-disk drives easier. This machine will run spreadsheet software up to 4 times faster than an XT, but word processing will not be speeded up comparably. The 80287 numeric co-processor can be added to these machines to speed up numeric calculations. Most experts believe that 8088 machines will eventually disappear, and the AT-class 286 machines will become the low end of the market. There are many AT clone products available.

IBM introduced its PS/2 line of microcomputers in 1987. Bundled with 3.5-inch disk drives, they are much smaller in size than previous models. The line-up consists of XT-like 8086 models (similar in performance and capabilities to 8088 models), several 80286 machines, and several 80386 and 80386SX machines. New high-end models support the 80486 microprocessor. Designed for easy customer configuration and with an advanced data bus, these machines represent IBM's current offerings. Unlike earlier models, expansion cards for older models will not work in the PS/2 line. However, more options were made standard on these machines and fewer expansion boards are needed.

Portable Computing: Laptops

Most vendors offer a complete line of computers, including portable and laptop computers. Virtually as powerful as the desktop models, the portables come with full 640 KB memory, 3.5-inch floppy drive, graphics video adapter, and a monochrome liquid crystal display (LCD), and can be ordered with hard-disk drive and modem. Expansion room is limited, but some models permit you to add more EMS memory or hook up an expansion cabinet for additional boards. Laptop computers come with a rechargeable nicad battery good for 2 to 4 hours of computing. The battery can be recharged overnight. Laptops range in weight from 6 pounds to 15 pounds, and can be used anywhere. Some ultra-light units are small enough to fit inside a briefcase. The portable computers, usually larger than the laptops, typically require AC power and may have a better resolution screen. Portables can weigh up to 20 pounds and are ill-designed for extensive carrying.

Floppy-Disk Drives

Most users should purchase the drive size (3.5- or 5.25-inch) that is used at their school or organization. The previous standard 5.25-inch drive is still popular, but today's smaller computers usually come with the 3.5-inch size. Some may wish to have both size drives in their computer, as shown in Figure A-1. Those users who need to exchange information between computers with incompatible drives can use file transfer software such as LapLink and send data between the computers' serial or parallel ports.

FIGURE A-1

Personal Computer with Both 3.5" and 5.25" Drives.

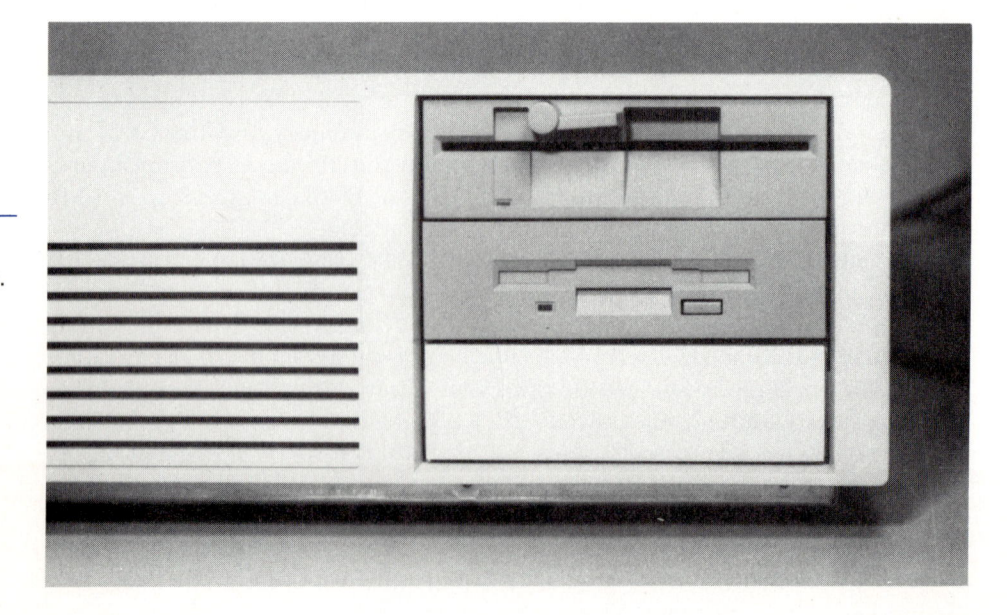

Hard-Disk Drives

Hard disk drives come in two physical sizes, 5.25-inch or 3.5-inch width. The system unit will dictate whether the larger size will fit in the drive bay. The capacity of the disk is given in megabytes, typically 20, 30, 40, 60, or more. Capacity of the drive depends on the number of disk surfaces, number of tracks, and recording density. The newer RLL (run length limited) drives can store 50% more bits in the same space by using magnetic recording more efficiently. Hard drives require a controller card and cables to connect the two units. The controller card installs in an expansion slot in the system unit, or may be built into the motherboard, or main circuit board. Some hard drives require a special type of controller card—it is best to purchase a matched set (hard-disk, controller card, cable) to insure compatibility between drive and controller. Larger disk drives may use the newer ESDI or SCSI interfaces, providing for much faster data transfer between the drive and the CPU. Again, special controller adapters are needed to use these drive types. ESDI and SCSI drives are somewhat more expensive than the standard drives.

The speed of a hard drive depends on two factors: number of bits transferred by the disk controller and track access time. The 286 and 386 computers come with a 16-bit disk controller and data transfers are much faster. The 8088 and 8086 computers use the slower 8-bit controller. Track access time, given in milliseconds, tells how long the disk read heads take to move halfway across the drive. XT-class drives are more than 60 milliseconds, while AT drives are 30-40 milliseconds. Newer drives offer track access times of less than 20 milliseconds.

Dot Matrix Printers

Dot matrix printers begin at under $200 and are the bargain of the microcomputing world. Items to consider when buying a dot matrix printer are number of pins in the print head (9 or 24), rated print speed (in both draft and near-letter quality modes), paper-handling abilities (paper width, continuous-form tractor feed, ability to print envelopes, sheet feed capability, and printer emulations). To take advantage of all the printer's features, your software must either have an installation option for that specific printer model, or the printer must emulate another standard printer type that is available with your software. Ribbon cost and number of characters per ribbon are also important—some printers will automatically re-ink the ribbon while it is used, allowing the ribbon to print darker for a longer time. Another consideration is the ease of selecting print styles (fonts) from the front panel. Epson and Panasonic printers have easy-to-use controls. While 9-pin printers are typically $150 less than 24-pin models, they are much slower in near-letter quality (NLQ) modes because they must make two or more passes to create characters. The 24-pin models slow down when in NLQ mode but typically print at half of the draft speed; 9-pin models print at less than one-fourth of draft speed. Compare the output samples shown in Figure A-2.

Virtually all printers come with a parallel interface, connecting to the parallel port on the computer. Some models can be ordered with an optional serial interface. The parallel method is much faster—an important consideration when printing graphics. A sizable printer buffer can speed printing by storing print characters from the computer and allowing the printer to print while the computer is doing something else. While most dot matrix printers can print multi-part forms (several sheets of paper with carbon paper between), only heavy-duty printers do a credible job of printing more than two copies at once. In fact, before purchasing a printer you should carefully estimate the print load expected of the printer: some printers are rated for occasional use, typically no more than 25% duty cycle. This means the printer should be expected to be

FIGURE A-2

Standard, 9-pin NLQ, and 24-pin NLQ Printer Output.

```
This is an example of draft quality on a 9-pin Panasonic dot
matrix printer. ABCDEFGHIJKLMNOPQRSTUVWXYZ 1234567890
abcdefghijklmnopqrstuvwxyz !#$%&*()


This is an example of near-letter quality on a 9-pin Panasonic
dot matrix printer. ABCDEFGHIJKLMNOPQRSTUVWXYZ 1234567890
abcdefghijklmnopqrstuvwxyz !#$%&*()


This is an example of a near-letter quality with an Epson 24-pin
dot matrix printer. ABCDEFGHIJKLMNOPQRSTUVWXYZ 1234567890
abcdefghijklmnopqrstuvwxyz !#$%&*()
```

FIGURE A-3

Hewlett-Packard ink jet printer output.

```
This is a sample sentence printed on an ink jet printer at highest
quality. ABCDEFGHIJKLMNOPQRSTUVWXYZ 1234567890 abcdefghijklmnopqrs
tuvwxyz#$^&%*()
```

printing only two hours out of each eight hours, and not for two hours in a row. Fortunately, most printers have a built-in thermal sensing device that slows down or turns off the printer if it senses the print head is becoming overloaded and too hot.

Ink Jet Printers

Ink jet and laser printers provide 300 by 300 dots-per-inch print resolution, with near-typeset print quality (see Figure A-3). As non-impact printers, neither is able to print multi-part forms. Ink jet printers are priced at much less than lasers, and print more slowly. The best-known manufacturer of ink jet and laser printers is Hewlett-Packard. Most applications software can be installed for use with either kind of printer. The HP ink jet emulates some of the HP laser printer's commands, but some print capabilities cannot be done by the ink jet printer due to limitations in the technology. The ink jet printer offers better print quality than either dot matrix or daisy wheel, at faster speeds. It may not have the durability for high-volume use that other printers might have.

FIGURE A-4

Laser printer sample ouptut.

```
This is an example of a Hewlett-Packard laser printer.
ABCDEFGHIJKLMNOPQRSTUVWXYZ 1234567890 abcdefghijklmnopqrstuvwxyz
!#$%&*()
```

Laser Printers

The HP Laserjet family of laser printers has become the world standard. In 1988 HP sold more than one billion dollars worth of these printers. Laser printers excel at providing high quality printing at high speeds. Although the price is beginning to fall, both for the printer and for supplies, laser printers are more expensive than other types. Many people underestimate the per-page cost of using a laser printer. However, its ability to turn out desktop publishing documents has placed it high on the want list at many organizations. The laser printer is able to print normally across the page, called **portrait mode.** It is also able to print sideways, along the long side of a page, called **landscape mode.**

Laser printers come with several print fonts built in, and additional fonts can be added either by purchasing a font cartridge or by installing downloadable soft fonts. Soft fonts are stored on the host computer's hard disk, then are sent through the printer cable and stored in the memory of the laser printer as long as it is turned on. The applications software can be programmed to change fonts quickly. Like the dot matrix printer, the laser printer can automatically change fonts and type sizes on the same page without user intervention. Laser printers do an excellent job of printing forms with different type sizes. Figure A-4 is an example of laser printer output.

Laser printer buying decisions include type of printer emulation, print speed, amount of printer memory, and additional font capability. **PostScript printers** use the high-level PostScript language to represent print information, requiring much less data be transmitted through the printer cable but relying more upon the printer itself to do formatting. PostScript printers accept more powerful editing commands and usually come with many built-in print fonts. Although non-PostScript-compatible printers are less expensive, they tie up the host computer longer to do image formatting and translation. You can purchase PostScript adapters for some non-PostScript printers. Print speed is generally given in pages per minute, with 6 or 8 being the most common speed. Some printers will print both sides of the paper at the same time, but are more expensive. Another feature is the number of paper trays in the printer: most printers have a single tray with only a single kind of paper loaded. This makes printing two-page correspondence (with letterhead as page one and plain paper for later pages) more difficult. Printer memory is generally given as 512 KB or 1 MB. Additional memory is necessary to hold additional soft fonts or to print full-page graphics. The minimum practical memory size for desktop publishing is 1.5 MB for non-PostScript laser printers, and more with PostScript printers. Font cartridges typically cost about $200 and offer a dozen print fonts. Soft fonts are a little less costly but are less convenient because they must be downloaded each time the printer is turned on. Font cartridges are instantly available at printer power-up and take up no printer memory.

Most laser printers have a replaceable print/toner cartridge containing a new light-sensitive print drum, black toner, and other critical components necessary to maintain good quality print. The cartridge lasts 3000-4000 pages, depending on type of printing and amount of toner used. The printer will signal when it is time to replace the cartridge. Per-page cost with a laser printer is 4 to 5 cents, including the cost of paper.

SELECTING A VENDOR

The next step is choosing a vendor. Caution is in order because not all vendors are able to provide necessary support. Mail order prices are generally 20-30% lower than local computer store prices, although this is not always the case. Some mail order vendors can provide installation support and ongoing assistance, but not many have extensive customer assistance. For mail order purchases, who pays the shipping and insurance charges? Is there a surcharge for using a credit card? Is the company well-known and in business for some time? Will they accept COD deliveries, or do they require pre-payment? What is the typical delivery time? Another nagging issue is the availability of local service and support for equipment purchased by mail order—some computer stores are unwilling to service equipment they did not sell.

Local computer stores are able to explore your needs and determine the proper equipment for you. Avoid the store that immediately shows you rows of hardware—if you purchase locally expect individual assistance. Local vendors should be willing to discuss complete system needs first. Expect to have your computer set up, with all optional equipment installed and tested, before accepting delivery. Mail order vendors rarely offer this service. Also expect some instruction on how to start up the computer and do routine tasks. Most vendors do so willingly, if asked, although some also offer fee-based training classes for more elaborate instruction.

Warranty Considerations

Explore the warranty options with your vendor. Do they have a no-questions-asked return policy for the first 30 days? This is especially useful for mail-order purchases. How long is the manufacturer's warranty period? Does it cover parts and labor, or just parts? Does the vendor have on-site repair technicians? Do they offer a loaner machine while your equipment is in the shop? Do they stock an adequate supply of replacement parts, or will your machine need to be shipped elsewhere for repair? Is the brand a well-known one, likely to exist in the future? Will they continue to stock accessory parts, even if they discontinue the computer line? For mail order vendors, do they have a technical support telephone line? Is it free?

Trouble-shooting problems can be a difficult task. Most hardware problems turn out to be operator problems, some of which can be fixed over the phone. For those who are afraid to "roll up their sleeves" and work with the computer's innards, local support and hand-holding may be in order. Because many local computer stores cannot provide substantial software assistance, and because software does not require "repair" like hardware does, mail order software purchases are very popular. Some mail order vendors even provide next-day deliveries. (For example, PC Connection, a mail order company located in New Hampshire, offers next-business-day air freight deliveries for just a few dollars per order.)

Software Purchases

Software is available locally and from mail order outlets, but local vendors may not have the software expertise needed to justify the higher local price. Regrettably, most computer stores sell hardware first, and include software afterwards.

Perhaps you can negotiate a system price to include software from a local vendor. Be sure the vendor sells the most current release of the software you have chosen. Ask whether the store's personnel can help in using the software. Do they offer more than one brand in a given category? Mail order suppliers sell more software than do local outlets, and offer a larger selection.

MAKING THE PURCHASE

The final step is to make the purchase and install the system. Have your vendor connect all equipment and test the computer before it leaves the store. Some computer problems may occur shortly after the item is installed, and the vendor can repair or exchange the defective part before you take it home. Your vendor may agree to **burn-in** the computer, running it for a day or two in the shop to assure all is working properly. Keep all receipts and packing materials; should equipment have to be returned, the original box is the best means of protection.

Information about setting up a new computer may be found in Chapter 2 of this textbook, and in the sections about applications software. Most the software packages have special "Getting Started" instructions that make installing the software relatively easy.

AFTER THE PURCHASE: GETTING HELP

The primary source of help with your computer will probably be the documentation that comes with the computer. A careful reading of the manuals may pinpoint problems with the system. Another good source of information about your system is the vendor who sold it to you. Local computer stores sometimes offer courses for new owners. Check with your vendor about seminars and other group activities. Mail order computer companies often have a support group available via toll-free telephone. Most prefer that you call while sitting at the computer so that diagnostic procedures can be tried immediately. Take notes when you talk to the support department, whether it be in person or by telephone.

The documentation accompanying software packages you have purchased is another excellent source of information. Many packages have a Getting Started section for new users, and some offer tutorials on paper or through the computer. Before calling the software vendor's technical support group, read the manual carefully. Some packages have a troubleshooting section that may answer your questions.

A good way to find out what other people are doing is to join a user group. Check with a local computer store for the names of local groups. Specialized groups supporting different hardware families exist in many towns. Contacts made via user groups can bring individuals together with common interests. Some groups offer informal classes and seminars.

Books and magazines are an important source of information. Magazines are more current but don't have the depth that a book can offer. Many libraries subscribe to the more popular computer publications. Otherwise, check your bookstore for magazines and books.

CARING FOR THE MICROCOMPUTER SYSTEM

There are some good practices to follow when setting up the computer system. Be careful to not block any of the ventilation ports in the system unit. Keep the computer away from heat sources or high humidity. Avoid dust and smoke around the computer area. The desk or table it sits upon should be sturdy enough to support the computer and all its devices.

Make sure there are an adequate number of electrical outlets for plugging in components. Most computers will have power cords for the system unit, monitor, and printer. Other devices like external modems may also need to be plugged in. You may wish to purchase a power strip with multiple outlets that would allow the components to be plugged into a single wall outlet. Better power adapters have filtering circuits that remove some of the electrical noise that may appear on the power line. More filtering is obtained with higher-cost power strips. Some power adapters offer **surge protection** for lightning and other power surges that may occur during storms. The best practice is to unplug computer and other electronics equipment during electrical storms. Don't forget to unplug the modem from the telephone line.

The computer needs little or no regular maintenance. Avoid eating and drinking around the computer so that spills on the keyboard or system unit don't occur. The monitor's screen will attract dust because of a static electricity charge on its surface. Turn off the monitor before cleaning the surface with a damp cloth. Avoid touching the surface of the monitor while in contact with any diskettes or the inside of the system unit. These components are particularly sensitive to static discharges.

Your printer manual will give suggestions for printer maintenance. The ribbon should be changed at the suggested interval or whenever it appears worn or frayed. You might wish to write the date on the ribbon cartridge when it is installed as a reminder of the ribbon's age. Vacuum the paper dust inside the printer and clean the case with a soft damp cloth. Periodical cleaning of the carriage shaft may also be needed.

Floppy disks should be stored in a safe place. Use the boxes that blank diskettes came in or a plastic disk storage box. 5.25-inch floppy diskettes should be stored vertically; 3.5-inch diskettes may be stacked because their rigid plastic shell gives better protection to the disk inside. Keep floppy disks away from magnetic fields and extreme heat or cold. Avoid spilling liquids on a diskette, or on any other part of the computer.

Avoid using the original disks after making a backup copy. For greater protection, hard-disk backup disks should be stored in a different location than the computer. That way an accident such as fire or water damage would not harm both the hard drive and the backup disks.

You should examine insurance policies to assure that the new equipment is properly covered. Regular homeowner's policies offer limited coverage, depending on usage. Inexpensive riders can be added for complete coverage, even away from home. It's wise to check before theft or storm damage occurs.

KEY TERMS

burn-in	portrait mode	shareware
integrated software	PostScript printers	software piracy
landscape mode	public domain	surge protection

Appendix B
DOS Commands

INTERNAL DOS COMMAND SUMMARY

Command	Purpose
BREAK	Allows or disables Ctrl-C interrupt of program
CHDIR (CD)	Change default directory
CLS	Clears the display screen
COPY	Copy specified file(s)
d:	Change default drive to specified letter
DATE	Display and set the current date
DEL (ERASE)	Delete specified file(s)
DIR	List files in a directory
EXIT	Exit the command processor
MKDIR (MD)	Create a new subdirectory
PATH	Set command file search path
PROMPT	Change DOS command prompt
RENAME (REN)	Rename a file
RMDIR (RD)	Remove a subdirectory
SET	Set environment variable
TIME	Display and set the current time
TYPE	Display contents of a file on the screen
VER	Show the DOS version number
VOL	Displays the disk's volume label

EXTERNAL DOS COMMAND SUMMARY

Command	Purpose
APPEND	Set a search path for data files
ASSIGN	Assign a drive letter to a different drive
ATTRIB	Set or display file attributes
BACKUP	Back up files from one disk to another
CHKDSK	Check directory for errors, also display free RAM and disk space remaining
COMMAND	Start the DOS command processor
COMP	Compare the contents of two files
DISKCOMP	Compare the contents of two disks
DISKCOPY	Copy contents of one disk
EXE2BIN	Convert .EXE files to binary format
FC	Compare files, display differences
FDISK	Configure and initialize hard disk
FIND	Locate a specific text string
FORMAT	Prepare a new disk for storing data
GRAFTABL	Load a table of graphics characters
GRAPHICS	Prepare DOS to print graphics screens
JOIN	Join a disk drive to a path
LABEL	Display and change disk volume label
MODE	Set operating characteristics for devices such as monitor and I/O ports
MORE	Display screen of output at a time
PRINT	Print contents of file
RECOVER	Recover from errors in file
REPLACE	Replace previous version of file with new version of same name
RESTORE	Restores files that were previously backed up
SORT	Sorts data in ascending or descending order
SUBST	Substitute a string for a path
TREE	Display subdirectory structure and file names
XCOPY	Copies files and subdirectories

Appendix C
Lotus 1-2-3 Commands

LOTUS 1-2-3 CURSOR MOVEMENT COMMANDS

Command	Meaning
↑	Move cursor up one row
↓	Move cursor down one row
←	Move cursor left one column
→	Move cursor right one column
PgUp	Move display up 20 rows (one screen)
PgDn	Move display down 20 rows (one screen)
Ctrl-←	Move display left one screen
Ctrl-→	Move display right one screen
Home	Move cursor to A1 cell location
End Home	Move cursor to lower-right corner of sheet
End ↑ / ↓	Moves cursor to last (un)filled cell in the up/down direction from current cell
End ← / →	Moves cursor to last (un)filled cell in the left/right direction from current cell
(F5) <cell>	Go directly to indicated cell address
ScrollLock "on"	When ScrollLock is on, arrow commands cause the screen to move instead of the cursor.

LOTUS 1-2-3 KEYBOARD MACRO COMMANDS

Keystroke	Meaning	Macro Command
BkSp	Backspace	{backspace} or {bs}
Ctrl-←	Big Left	{bigleft}
Ctrl-→	Big Right	{bigright}
Del	Delete	{delete} or {del}
↓	Down	{down}* or {d}
End	End	{end}
Esc	Escape	{escape} or {esc}
Home	Home	{home}
←	Left	{left}* or {l}
PgDn	Page Down	{pgdn}
PgUp	Page Up	{pgup}
Enter	Return	~
→	Right	{right}* or {r}
↑	Up	{up}* or {u}

* A count can be added, as in {down 3}

LOTUS 1-2-3 FUNCTION KEY MACRO COMMANDS

Keystroke	Meaning	Macro Command
F4	Absolute Reference	{abs}
F9	Calculate	{calc}
F2	Edit Cell	{edit}
F5	Goto	{goto}
F10	Graph	{graph}
F1	Help	{help}
F3	Name	{name}
F7	Query	{query}
F8	Table	{table}
F6	Window	{window}

STATISTICAL @-FUNCTIONS

@AVG(range)	Calculates the average (mean) of the non-blank cells in the range.
@COUNT(range)	Counts number of non-blank cells in the range.
@MAX(range)	Returns the maximum value in the range.
@MIN(range)	Returns the minimum value in the range.
@STD(range)	Calculates the population standard deviation of cells in the range.
@SUM(range)	Sums cell values in the range.
@VAR(range)	Calculates the population variance of cells in the range.

MATHEMATICAL @-FUNCTIONS

@ABS(value)	Absolute value of a number.
@EXP(value)	Take e to the power in value (e^{value}).
@INT(value)	Take integer part of value (largest integer less than or equal to value.)
@LN(value)	Natural logarithm (base e) of value.
@LOG(value)	Common logarithm (base 10) of value.
@MOD(value, divisor)	Returns remainder of value divided by divisor.
@RAND	Random number between 0 and 1.
@ROUND(value, places)	Rounds value to the indicated number of decimal places.
@SQRT(value)	Square root of value.

FINANCIAL @-FUNCTIONS

@CTERM(interest,fv,pv) — The number of periods at the given interest rate for an initial present value to grow to a future value; there are no periodic cash flows with this function.

@FV(payment,interest,term) — The future value amount equivalent to making the indicated payment each period for term periods at the interest rate given; this assumes periodic cash flows.

@IRR(estimate,cashflow range) — Lotus converts a series of uneven cash flows in the given range to an annual rate of return, using the estimate as a starting point.

@NPV(rate,cashflow range) — Net present value of a series of cash flows in the cell range given a discount rate.

@PMT(principal,interest,term) — Periodic payment to amortize a loan over term periods at the given interest rate for the principal amount borrowed.

@PV(payment,interest,term) — Calculates the present value of term equal payments at the specified interest rate.

@RATE(fv,pv,n) — Returns the periodic interest rate for an initial present value to grow to a future value over n periods.

@TERM(payment,interest,fv) — Calculates the number of periods necessary for periodic payments to grow to a future value at a given interest rate.

DEPRECIATION @-FUNCTIONS

@SLN(cost,salvage,life) — Returns annual depreciation for an asset of given cost and residual salvage value over life years, using the straight-line method.

@DDB(cost,salvage,life,per) — Returns depreciation for a specific period using the double-declining balance method.

@SYD(cost,salvage,life,per) — Returns depreciation for a specific period using the sum-of-the-years-digits method.

DATE AND TIME @-FUNCTIONS

@DATE(year,month,day) — Converts the year value, month value, and day into a Lotus date number. Year is entered as the last two digits, and the month is entered as a number from 1 to 12. For years above 1999, add 100 to the last two year digits. Lotus handles dates through December 31, 2099.

@DATEVALUE(datetext) — Converts date text to a Lotus date number. Date is entered as "DD-MMM-YY" where MMM is the three-letter month abbreviation and YY is the last two digits of the year. The quotes must be included.

@NOW — Returns current date and time as a Lotus date number. The value changes every time the spreadsheet is recalculated.

@TIME(hour,minute,sec) — Converts the hour value, minute value and second value into a Lotus time number.

@TIMEVALUE(timetext) — Converts time text to a Lotus time number. Time text is entered as "HH:MM:SS" and quotes must be given.

@SECOND(timenumber) — Converts a time number into the number of seconds (0–59).

@MINUTE(timenumber) — Converts a time number into the number of minutes (0–59).

@HOUR(timenumber) — Converts a time number into the number of hours (0–23).

@DAY(datenumber) — Converts a date number into the day (1–31).

@MONTH(datenumber) — Converts a date number into the month (1–12).

@YEAR(datenumber) — Converts a date number into the year (0–199).

IF AND LOOKUP @-FUNCTIONS

@IF(cond,true expr,false expr) — If condition is true, cell will contain the true expression; otherwise, it will contain the false expression.

@VLOOKUP(value,table range,offset column) — Vertical lookup table. Returns entry from offset column of proper row of table range.

@HLOOKUP(value,table range,offset row) — Horizontal lookup table. Returns entry from offset row of the proper column in table range.

STRING @-FUNCTIONS

@FIND(str,string,start)	Locate the starting position of substring str in overall string, beginning in start position. Returns 0 if str is not found.
@LEFT(string,length)	Returns the left-most length number of characters from string.
@LENGTH(string)	Number of characters (including embedded blanks) in string.
@LOWER(string)	Converts string to all lower-case characters.
@MID(string,start,length)	Returns substring of given length from specified string beginning at start position.
@PROPER(string)	Converts character at beginning of each word in string to upper-case.
@REPEAT(str,number)	Repeats given string str a specified number of times.
@REPLACE(string,start,length,str)	Replaces length characters in string with str beginning at start.
@RIGHT(string,length)	Returns right-most length characters from string.
@STRING(number,places)	Converts the value in number to a string with specified decimal places.
@TRIM(string)	Trims trailing blanks from string.
@VALUE(string)	Converts a string to a value. String must be an acceptable number form. (Example: "1989")

LOTUS ALPHABETIC QUICK REFERENCE

Topic	Keystrokes (all in 1-2-3 unless noted)
Absolute addresses	Press **F4** key to add $ to cell expression
Access System	Enter **LOTUS** at DOS prompt
Allways	**/AA** to attach an add-in
Automatic recalculation	**/WGRA** (default when Lotus starts)
Cell formulas	**/PPOOC** to activate cell-formulas printout
Change column width	**/WGC** for global column change; **/WCS** for single column; **/WCCS** for column-range
Change default directory	**/FD** for session-long change; **/WGDD** for permanent change (then must choose **U** to update)
Combine files	**/FC**
Copy cell expressions	**/C**
Correcting errors	**F2** in Ready mode
Create a graph	**/G** then specify **Type**, variable ranges (**X**, **A-F**) and options; **View** graph then **Save** image
Create a range name	**/RNC**
Database features	**/DS** for sort; **/DF** for data fill; **/DQ** for data queries; **/DT** for data look-up tables
Data Distribution	**/DD** then specify data values, bin range
Data Fill	**/DF** then specify range, begin, step, end values
Dates	Number of days since December 31, 1899
Delete a column or row	**/WDC** or **/WDR**
Display a graph	In 1-2-3 Ready mode press **F10**; **/GV** in /Graph menu; in PrintGraph press **I**, then mark file with **#**, press **F10**
Edit cell expression	**F2** in Ready mode or while entering expression
Erase a cell	**/RE** to erase a cell or a range of cells
File commands	**/F** in 1-2-3; use **Settings** menu in Print-Graph
Fill cells	See Data Fill
Format a cell	**/RF** then specify format type and decimals
Functions	Begin with **@** and are used in cell expressions
Graphing	**/G** in 1-2-3 to create and save graph; in PrintGraph select graph image and print
Help messages	**F1** to obtain context-specific help in any menu

Topic	Keystrokes (all in 1-2-3 unless noted)
Insert a column or row	**/WIC** or **/WIR**
Install module	**I** at Lotus Access menu (change hardware setup)
Justify Labels	Use **'** for left, **"** for right, **^** for centered; **/RLL**, **/RLR** or **/RLC** to change existing labels
Learn Mode (macros)	**/WLR** to define a learn range; **Alt-F5** to record keystrokes
Linked cells	Use **+<<filename>>cellref** expression
List filenames	**/FL** then specify type of file
Macro Execute	Press **Alt-** with letter of macro range name
Macro Learn	**/WLR** to create range; **Alt-F5** to record keystrokes
Macro single step mode	**Alt-F2** to turn on step mode; **Alt-F2** cancels
Manual recalculation	**/WGRM**
Mode indicator	First key in cell expression determines mode: Value, Label or Menu
Move cell expression	**/M**
1-2-3 module	**1** at Lotus Access menu
Options	Print options **/PPO**; Graph options **/GO**
Page break	Move cursor to desired cell, then **/WP**
Print worksheet	**/PP** then specify range and options
Print graph	**/GS** to save image in 1-2-3; select image and print in PrintGraph
PrintGraph module	**P** at Lotus Access menu
Protect Cells	**/WGPE** to activate protection; **/WGPD** to disable protection.
Queries	**/DQF** for Find, **/DQE** for Extract, **/DQU** for Unique, **/DQD** for Delete operations
Quit 1-2-3	**/Q** then confirm; use **Exit** command in Access menu
Quit PrintGraph	**Exit** command
Range commands	**/RF** for format, **/RE** for erase, **/RN** for range names, **/RJ** for label justify
Recalculate worksheet	In manual recalc mode press **F9** key
Recalculation	**/WGR** then specify Manual or Automatic options
Relative addresses	Default in cell expresions without $

Topic	Keystrokes (all in 1-2-3 unless noted)
Retrieve worksheet	**/FR** to retrieve entire worksheet; **/FC** to retrieve another worksheet into current one
Save worksheet	**/FS** to save entire worksheet; **/FX** to save portion of worksheet; **/PF** to save values of worksheet in text file
Settings sheet	Holds settings for Status, Print, Graphing; press **F6** to go between settings sheet and worksheet
Setup codes (printing)	**/PPOS** then specify control codes; **\015** is usual compressed print code on dot matrix printers
Single step mode	**Alt-F2** to toggle on, off (macro execution)
Sort rows	**/DS** then specify data range, key fields
System DOS prompt	**/S** for DOS prompt; type **EXIT** to return to 1-2-3
Titles in graph	**/GOT** then specify **First**, **Second**, **X-axis** or **Y-axis**
Titles in print	**/PPOH** for header or **/PPOF** for footer
Titles in worksheet	**/WT** to set vertical or horizontal title
Translate module	**T** at Lotus Access Menu
View current graph	**/GV** or **F10** key

LOTUS 1-2-3 COMMAND TREE

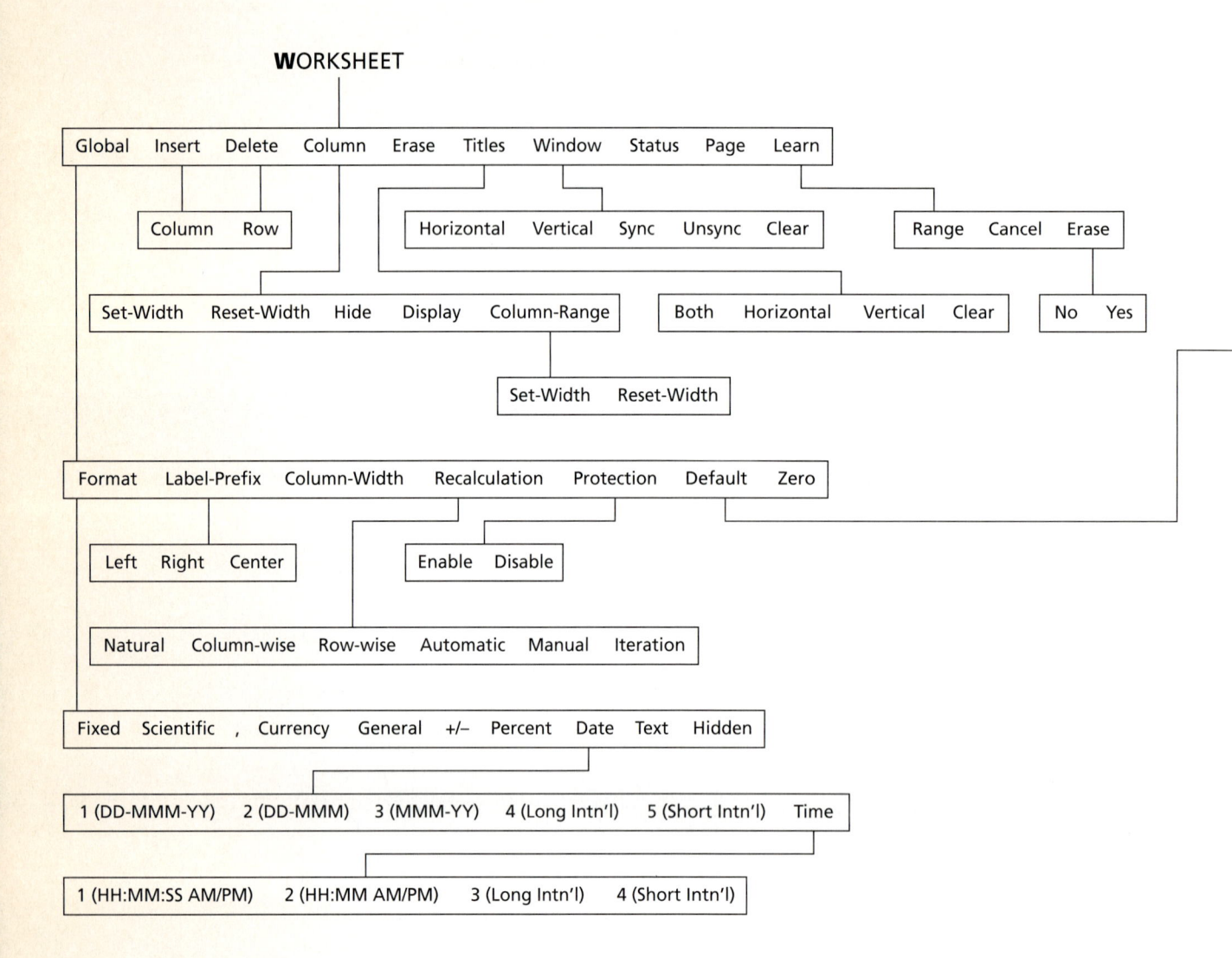

WORKSHEET

Global   Insert   Delete   Column   Erase   Titles   Window   Status   Page   Learn

Insert/Delete: Column   Row

Titles: Horizontal   Vertical   Sync   Unsync   Clear

Learn: Range   Cancel   Erase

Column: Set-Width   Reset-Width   Hide   Display   Column-Range

Titles Clear options: Both   Horizontal   Vertical   Clear

Erase: No   Yes

Column-Range: Set-Width   Reset-Width

Global: Format   Label-Prefix   Column-Width   Recalculation   Protection   Default   Zero

Label-Prefix: Left   Right   Center

Protection: Enable   Disable

Recalculation: Natural   Column-wise   Row-wise   Automatic   Manual   Iteration

Format: Fixed   Scientific   ,   Currency   General   +/–   Percent   Date   Text   Hidden

Date: 1 (DD-MMM-YY)   2 (DD-MMM)   3 (MMM-YY)   4 (Long Intn'l)   5 (Short Intn'l)   Time

Time: 1 (HH:MM:SS AM/PM)   2 (HH:MM AM/PM)   3 (Long Intn'l)   4 (Short Intn'l)

LOTUS 1-2-3 COMMAND TREE

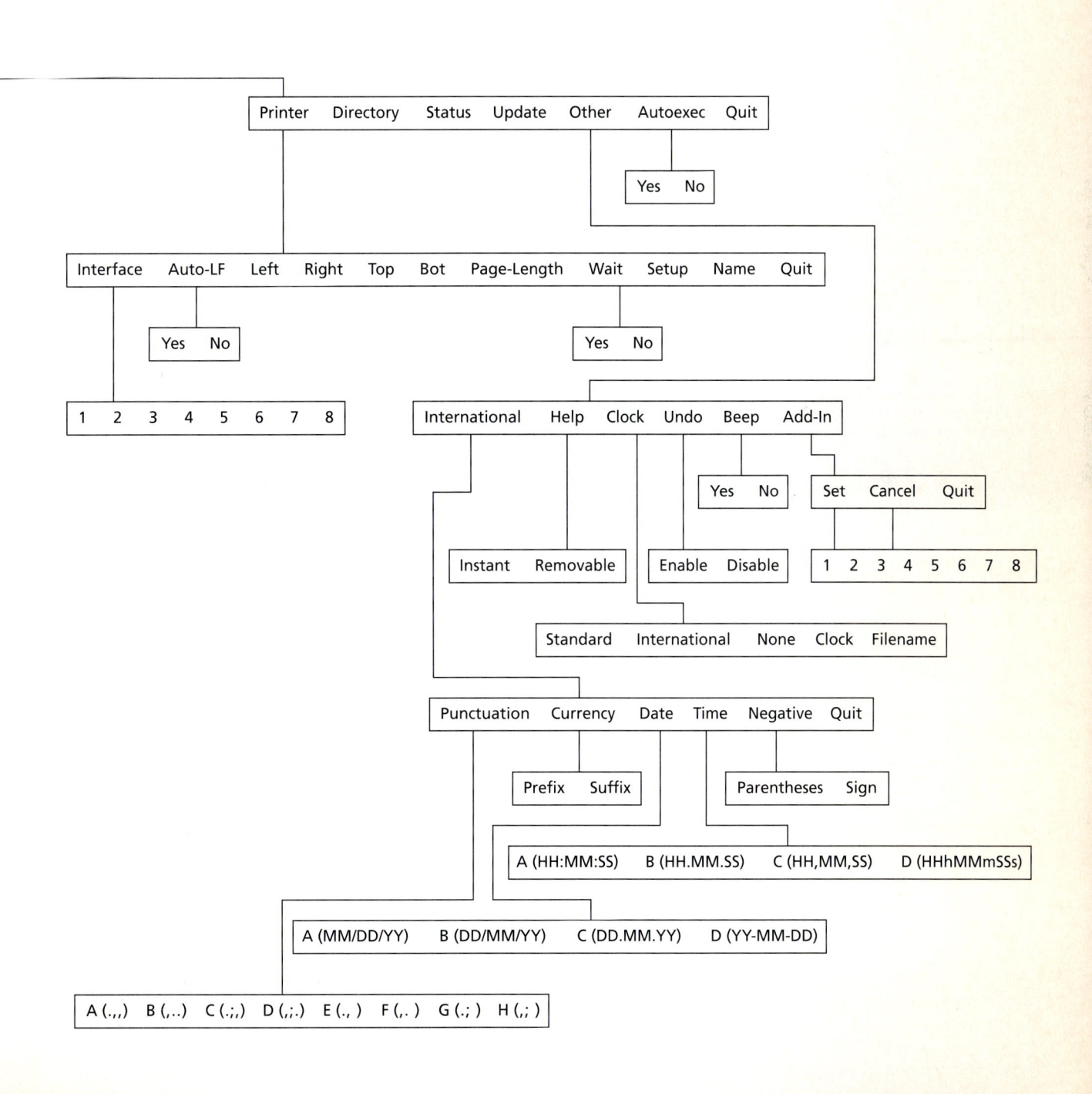

351

```
                    ┌─────────────────────────────────────────────────────────────┐
                    │ Printer  Directory  Status  Update  Other  Autoexec  Quit │
                    └──┬──────────────────────────────────────┬─────────┬────────┘
                       │                                      │         │
                       │                                      │      ┌──┴──────┐
                       │                                      │      │ Yes  No │
                       │                                      │      └─────────┘
  ┌────────────────────┴──────────────────────────────────────┴──────────────────────┐
  │ Interface  Auto-LF  Left  Right  Top  Bot  Page-Length  Wait  Setup  Name  Quit │
  └────┬─────────┬───────────────────────────────────────────┬──────────────────────┘
       │         │                                           │
       │     ┌───┴─────┐                                  ┌──┴──────┐
       │     │ Yes  No │                                  │ Yes  No │
       │     └─────────┘                                  └─────────┘
  ┌────┴────────────────────┐
  │ 1  2  3  4  5  6  7  8 │                  ┌──────────────────────────────────────────────┐
  └────────────────────────┘                  │ International  Help  Clock  Undo  Beep  Add-In │
                                              └──┬──────────────┬──────┬──────┬──────────┬───┘
                                                 │              │      │      │          │
                                                 │              │      │   ┌──┴──────┐ ┌─┴──────────────────┐
                                                 │              │      │   │ Yes  No │ │ Set  Cancel  Quit │
                                                 │              │      │   └─────────┘ └──┬─────────────────┘
                                                 │          ┌───┴──────┴────┐             │
                                                 │          │ Instant  Removable │    ┌────┴───────────────────┐
                                                 │          └──────────────┘      │ 1  2  3  4  5  6  7  8 │
                                                 │                  ┌──────────────────────────────────────────┐
                                                 │                  │ Standard  International  None  Clock  Filename │
                                                 │                  └──────────────────────────────────────────┘
                                     ┌───────────┴────────────────────────────────────────────┐
                                     │ Punctuation  Currency  Date  Time  Negative  Quit    │
                                     └────┬────────────┬───────┬──────┬──────────┬──────────┘
                                          │            │       │      │          │
                                          │        ┌───┴─────┐ │  ┌───┴──────────────┐
                                          │        │ Prefix  Suffix │  │ Parentheses  Sign │
                                          │        └─────────┘ │  └──────────────────┘
                                          │                    │
                                          │                ┌───┴────────────────────────────────────────────────────┐
                                          │                │ A (HH:MM:SS)   B (HH.MM.SS)   C (HH,MM,SS)   D (HHhMMmSSs) │
                                          │                └────────────────────────────────────────────────────────┘
                                          │        ┌───────────────────────────────────────────────────┐
                                          │        │ A (MM/DD/YY)   B (DD/MM/YY)   C (DD.MM.YY)   D (YY-MM-DD) │
                                          │        └───────────────────────────────────────────────────┘
                     ┌────────────────────┴─────────────────────────────────────────┐
                     │ A (.,,)  B (,..)  C (.;,)  D (,;.)  E (.,)  F (,.)  G (.;)  H (,;) │
                     └──────────────────────────────────────────────────────────────┘
```

Appendix C — Lotus 1-2-3 Commands

RANGE

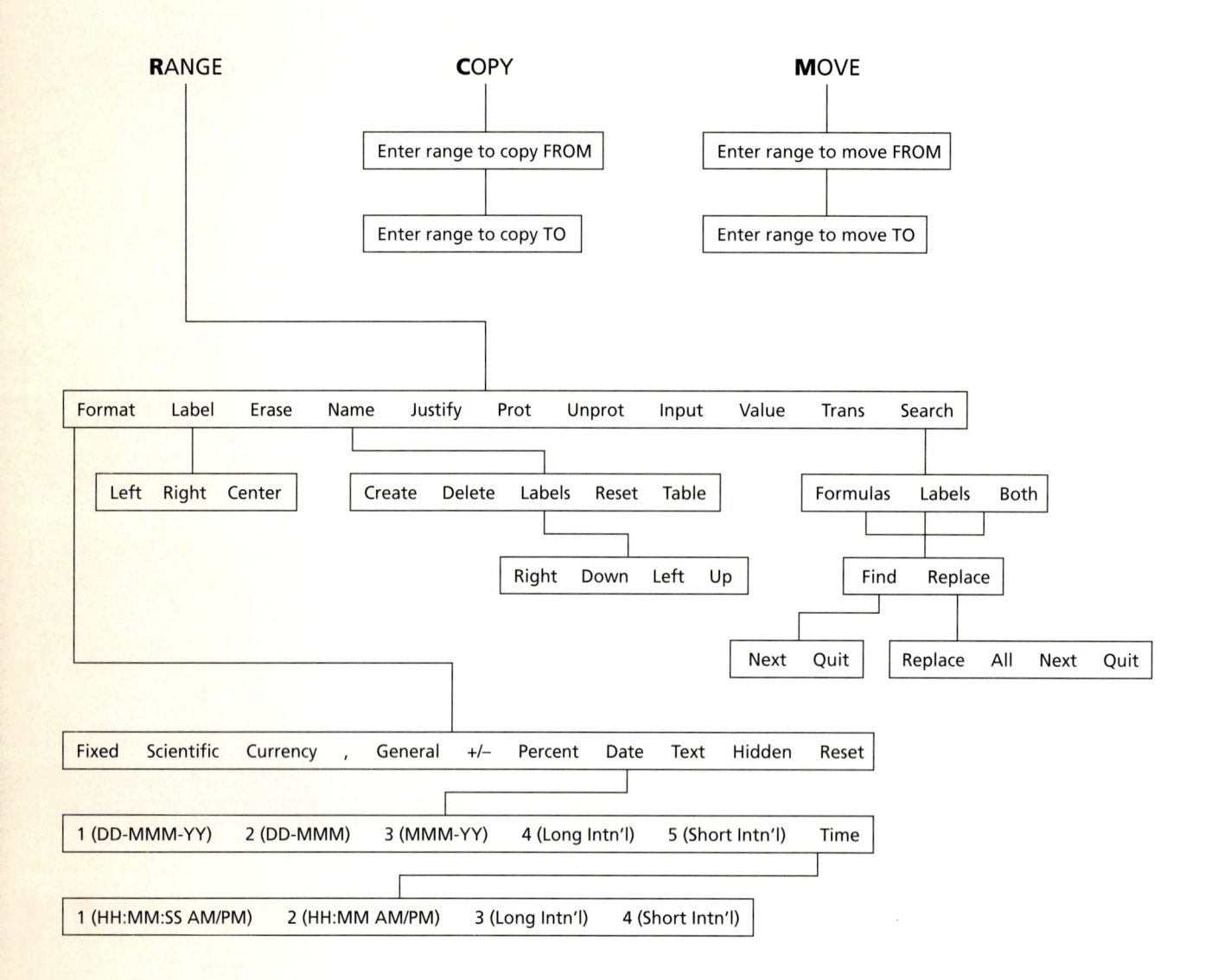

COPY
- Enter range to copy FROM
- Enter range to copy TO

MOVE
- Enter range to move FROM
- Enter range to move TO

Range submenu: Format · Label · Erase · Name · Justify · Prot · Unprot · Input · Value · Trans · Search

- Label: Left · Right · Center
- Name: Create · Delete · Labels · Reset · Table
  - Labels: Right · Down · Left · Up
- Search: Formulas · Labels · Both
  - Find · Replace
    - Find: Next · Quit
    - Replace: Replace · All · Next · Quit

Format: Fixed · Scientific · Currency · , · General · +/− · Percent · Date · Text · Hidden · Reset

Date: 1 (DD-MMM-YY) · 2 (DD-MMM) · 3 (MMM-YY) · 4 (Long Intn'l) · 5 (Short Intn'l) · Time

Time: 1 (HH:MM:SS AM/PM) · 2 (HH:MM AM/PM) · 3 (Long Intn'l) · 4 (Short Intn'l)

LOTUS 1-2-3 COMMAND TREE

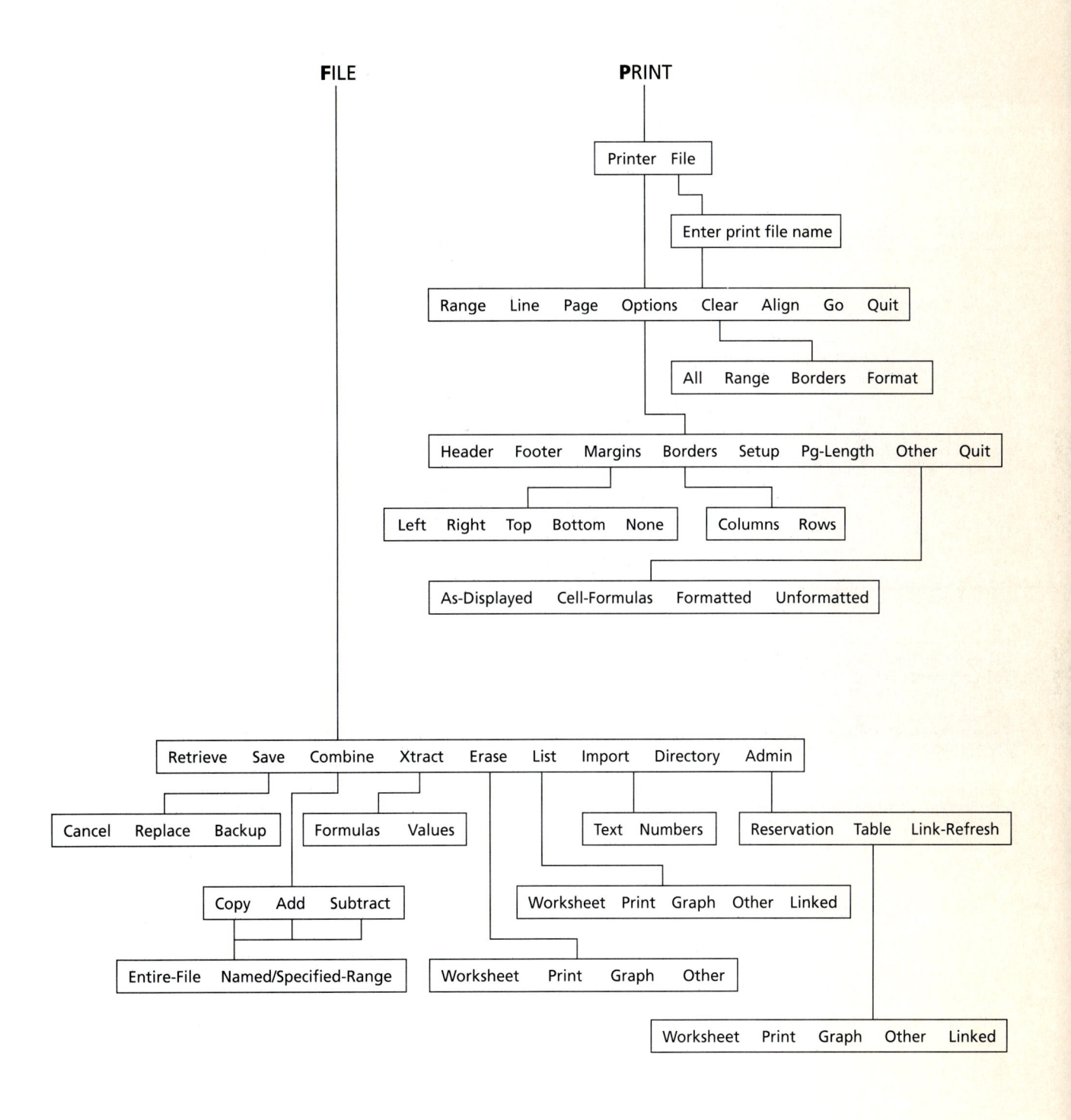

FILE

PRINT

- Printer   File
  - Enter print file name
- Range   Line   Page   Options   Clear   Align   Go   Quit
  - All   Range   Borders   Format
- Header   Footer   Margins   Borders   Setup   Pg-Length   Other   Quit
  - Left   Right   Top   Bottom   None
  - Columns   Rows
- As-Displayed   Cell-Formulas   Formatted   Unformatted

Retrieve   Save   Combine   Xtract   Erase   List   Import   Directory   Admin

- Cancel   Replace   Backup
- Formulas   Values
- Text   Numbers
- Reservation   Table   Link-Refresh
- Copy   Add   Subtract
- Worksheet   Print   Graph   Other   Linked
- Entire-File   Named/Specified-Range
- Worksheet   Print   Graph   Other
- Worksheet   Print   Graph   Other   Linked

GRAPH

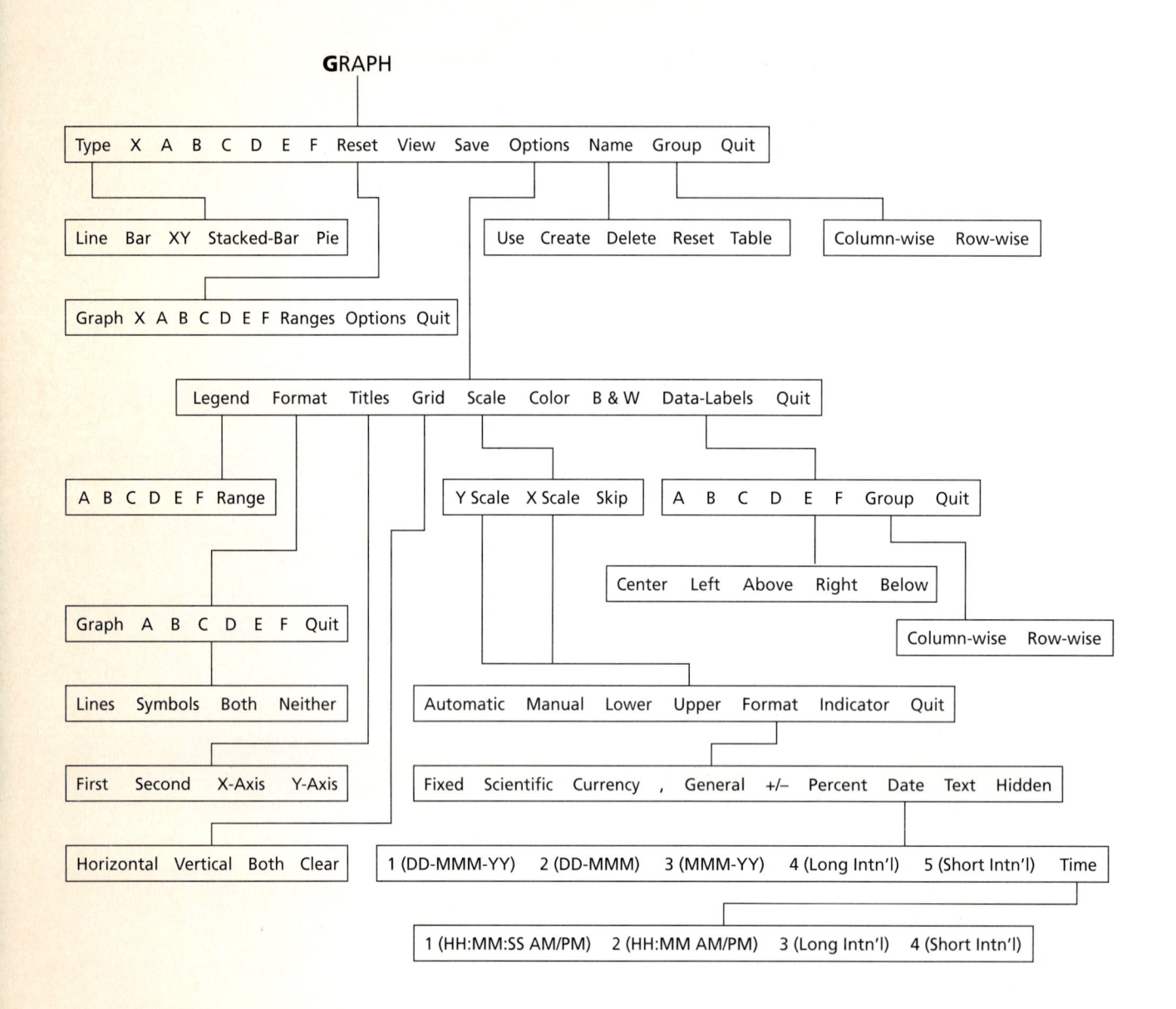

- **Type** X A B C D E F Reset View Save Options Name Group Quit

  - Line Bar XY Stacked-Bar Pie

  - Graph X A B C D E F Ranges Options Quit

    - Legend Format Titles Grid Scale Color B & W Data-Labels Quit

      - A B C D E F Range

      - Graph A B C D E F Quit

      - Lines Symbols Both Neither

      - First Second X-Axis Y-Axis

      - Horizontal Vertical Both Clear

      - Y Scale X Scale Skip

        - Automatic Manual Lower Upper Format Indicator Quit

          - Fixed Scientific Currency , General +/– Percent Date Text Hidden

            - 1 (DD-MMM-YY) 2 (DD-MMM) 3 (MMM-YY) 4 (Long Intn'l) 5 (Short Intn'l) Time

              - 1 (HH:MM:SS AM/PM) 2 (HH:MM AM/PM) 3 (Long Intn'l) 4 (Short Intn'l)

      - A B C D E F Group Quit

        - Center Left Above Right Below

        - Column-wise Row-wise

  - Use Create Delete Reset Table

  - Column-wise Row-wise

LOTUS 1-2-3 COMMAND TREE

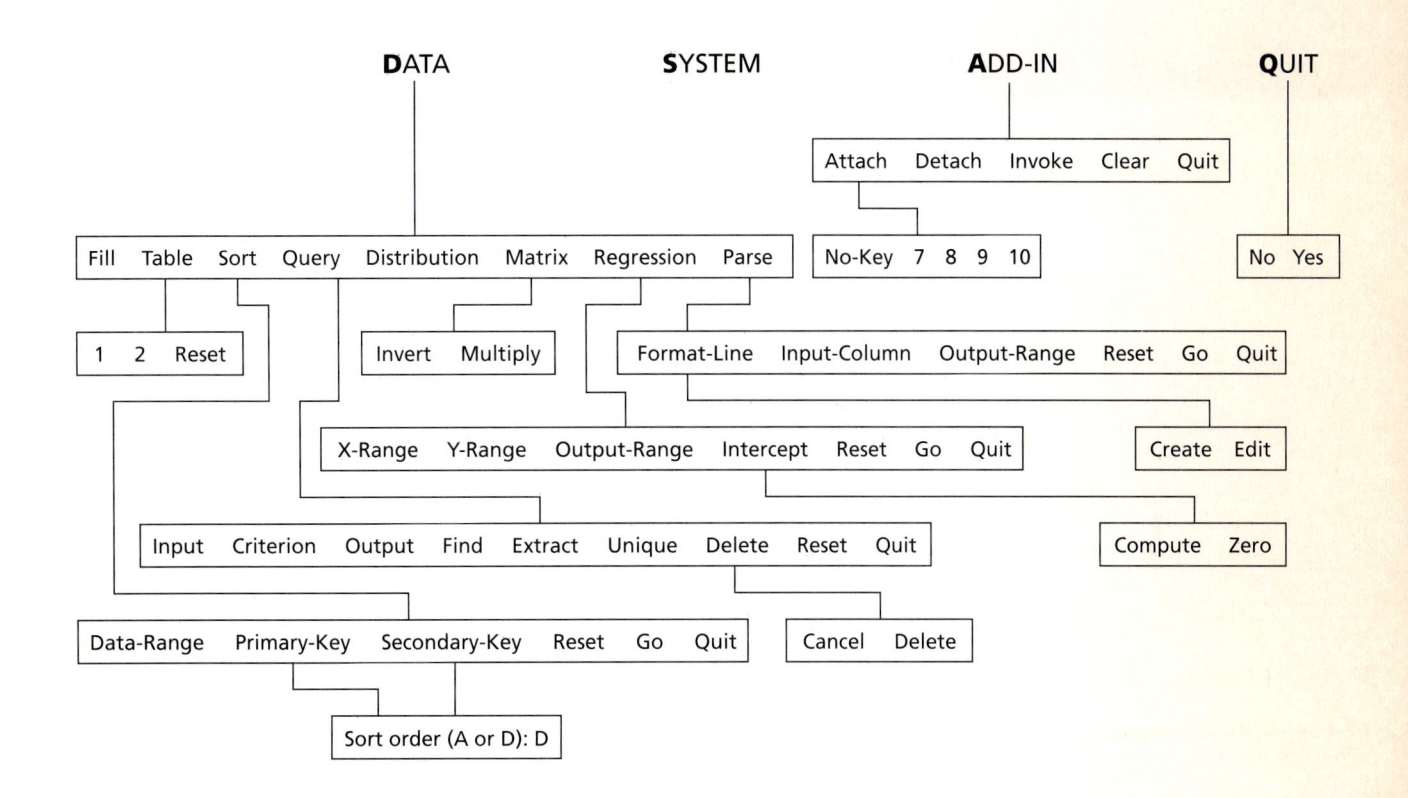

DATA   **S**YSTEM   **A**DD-IN   **Q**UIT

ADD-IN: Attach, Detach, Invoke, Clear, Quit

DATA: Fill, Table, Sort, Query, Distribution, Matrix, Regression, Parse

Attach: No-Key, 7, 8, 9, 10

QUIT: No, Yes

Table: 1, 2, Reset

Matrix: Invert, Multiply

Parse: Format-Line, Input-Column, Output-Range, Reset, Go, Quit

Regression: X-Range, Y-Range, Output-Range, Intercept, Reset, Go, Quit

Format-Line: Create, Edit

Query: Input, Criterion, Output, Find, Extract, Unique, Delete, Reset, Quit

Intercept: Compute, Zero

Sort: Data-Range, Primary-Key, Secondary-Key, Reset, Go, Quit

Delete: Cancel, Delete

Primary-Key / Secondary-Key: Sort order (A or D): D

LOTUS 1-2-3 PRINTGRAPH COMMAND TREE

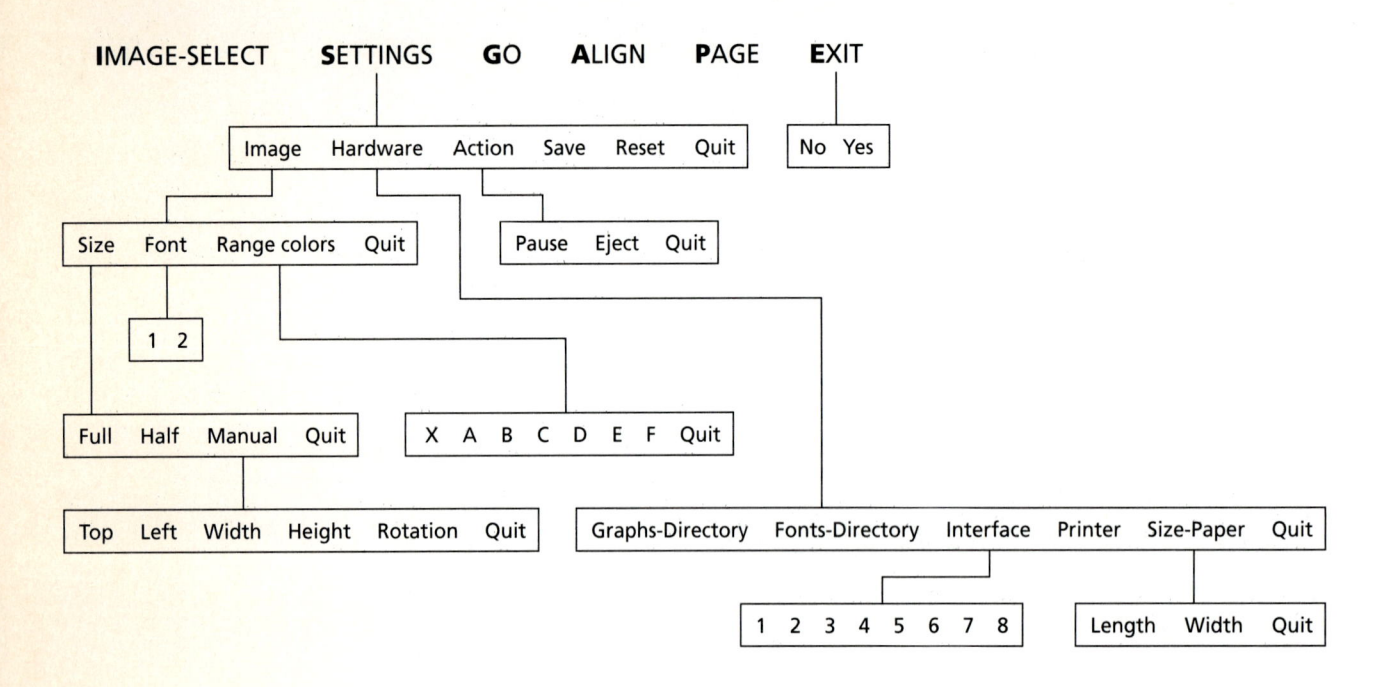

IMAGE-SELECT   **S**ETTINGS   **G**O   **A**LIGN   **P**AGE   **E**XIT

Under SETTINGS: Image   Hardware   Action   Save   Reset   Quit

Under EXIT: No   Yes

Under Image: Size   Font   Range colors   Quit

Under Action: Pause   Eject   Quit

Under Font: 1   2

Under Size: Full   Half   Manual   Quit

Under Range colors: X   A   B   C   D   E   F   Quit

Under Manual: Top   Left   Width   Height   Rotation   Quit

Under Hardware: Graphs-Directory   Fonts-Directory   Interface   Printer   Size-Paper   Quit

Under Interface: 1   2   3   4   5   6   7   8

Under Size-Paper: Length   Width   Quit

ALLWAYS COMMAND TREE

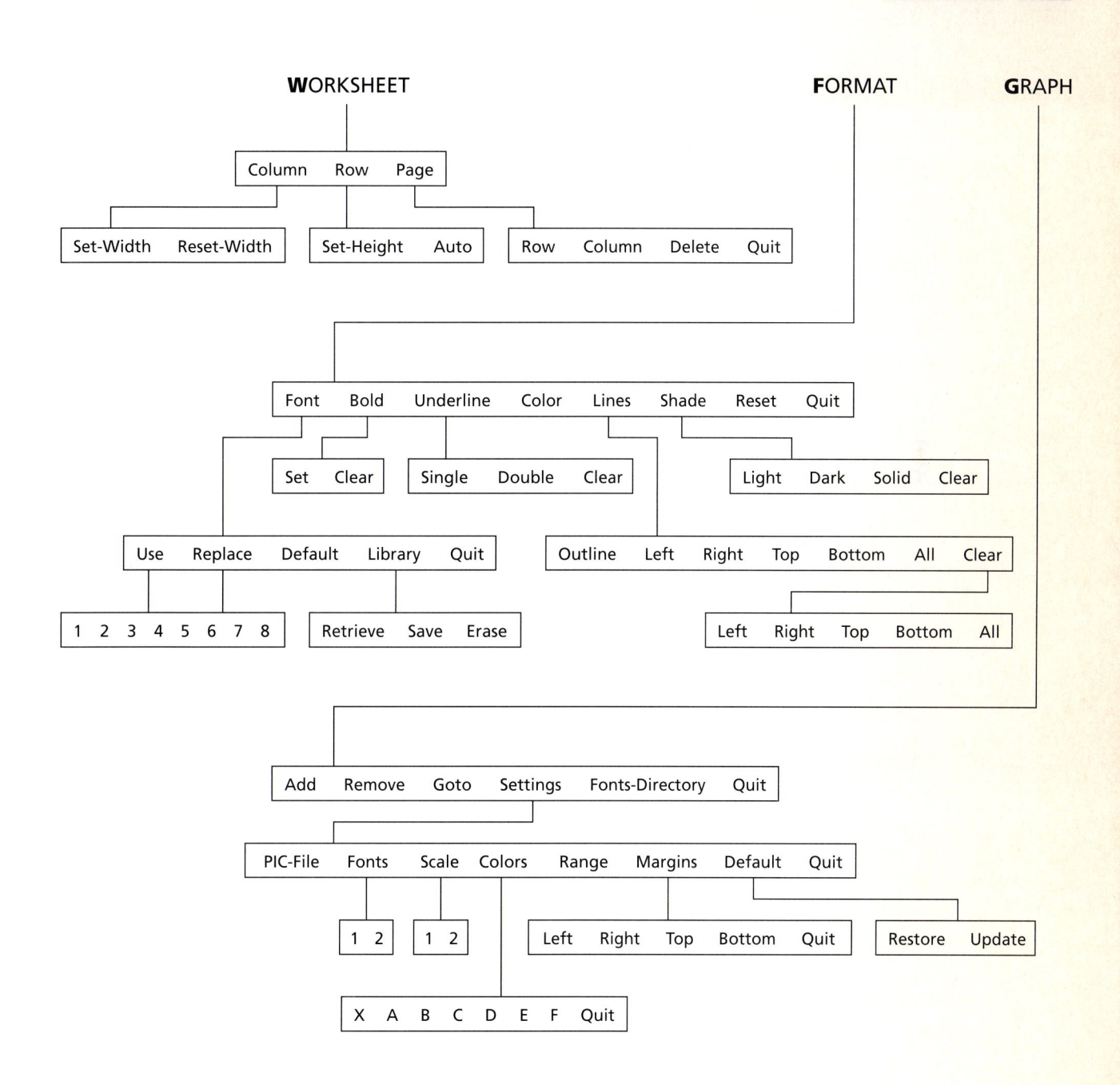

WORKSHEET

- Column | Row | Page
  - Set-Width | Reset-Width
  - Set-Height | Auto
  - Row | Column | Delete | Quit

FORMAT

- Font | Bold | Underline | Color | Lines | Shade | Reset | Quit
  - Set | Clear
  - Single | Double | Clear
  - Light | Dark | Solid | Clear
- Use | Replace | Default | Library | Quit
  - 1 2 3 4 5 6 7 8
  - Retrieve | Save | Erase
- Outline | Left | Right | Top | Bottom | All | Clear
  - Left | Right | Top | Bottom | All

GRAPH

- Add | Remove | Goto | Settings | Fonts-Directory | Quit
  - PIC-File | Fonts | Scale | Colors | Range | Margins | Default | Quit
    - 1 2
    - 1 2
    - Left | Right | Top | Bottom | Quit
    - Restore | Update
    - X A B C D E F Quit

Appendix C — Lotus 1-2-3 Commands

LAYOUT

- Page-Size
  - 1 2 3 4 5
- Margins
  - Left Right Top Bottom Quit
- Titles
  - Header Footer Clear Quit
    - Header Footer Both
- Borders
  - Top Left Bottom Clear Quit
    - Top Left Bottom All
- Options
  - Line-Weight Grid Quit
    - Normal Light Heavy
    - No Yes
- Default
  - Restore Update
- Library
  - Retrieve Save Erase
- Quit

PRINT

- Go
- File
- Range
  - Set Clear
- Configuration
  - Printer
    - 1 2
  - Interface
    - 1 2 3 4 5 6 7 8
  - Cartridge
    - 1 2 ... 13
  - Orientation
    - Portrait Landscape
  - Resolution
    - 1 2 3 4
  - Bin
    - 1 2
  - Quit
- Settings
  - Begin End First Copies Wait Reset Quit
    - No Yes
- Quit

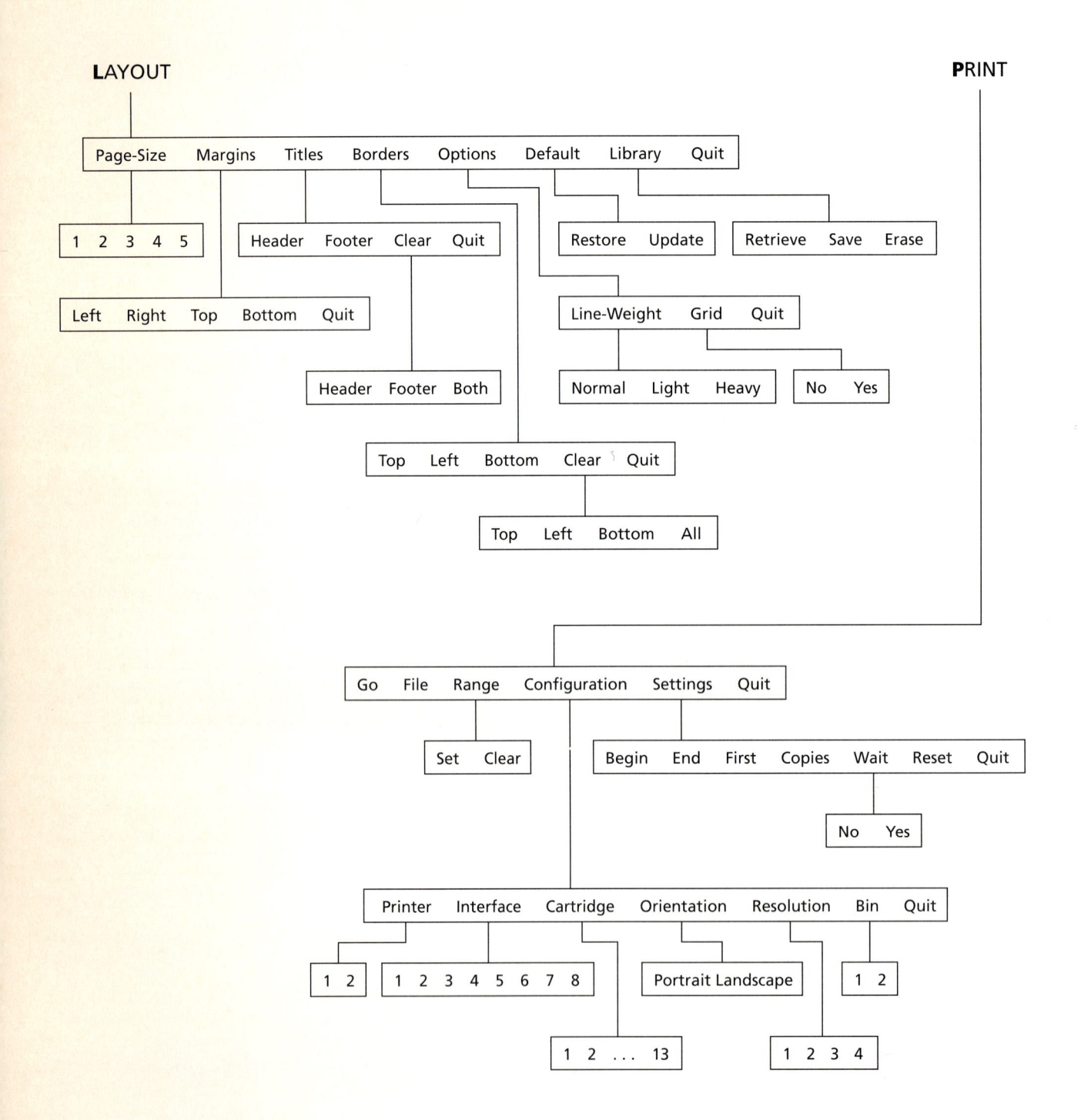

ALLWAYS COMMAND TREE

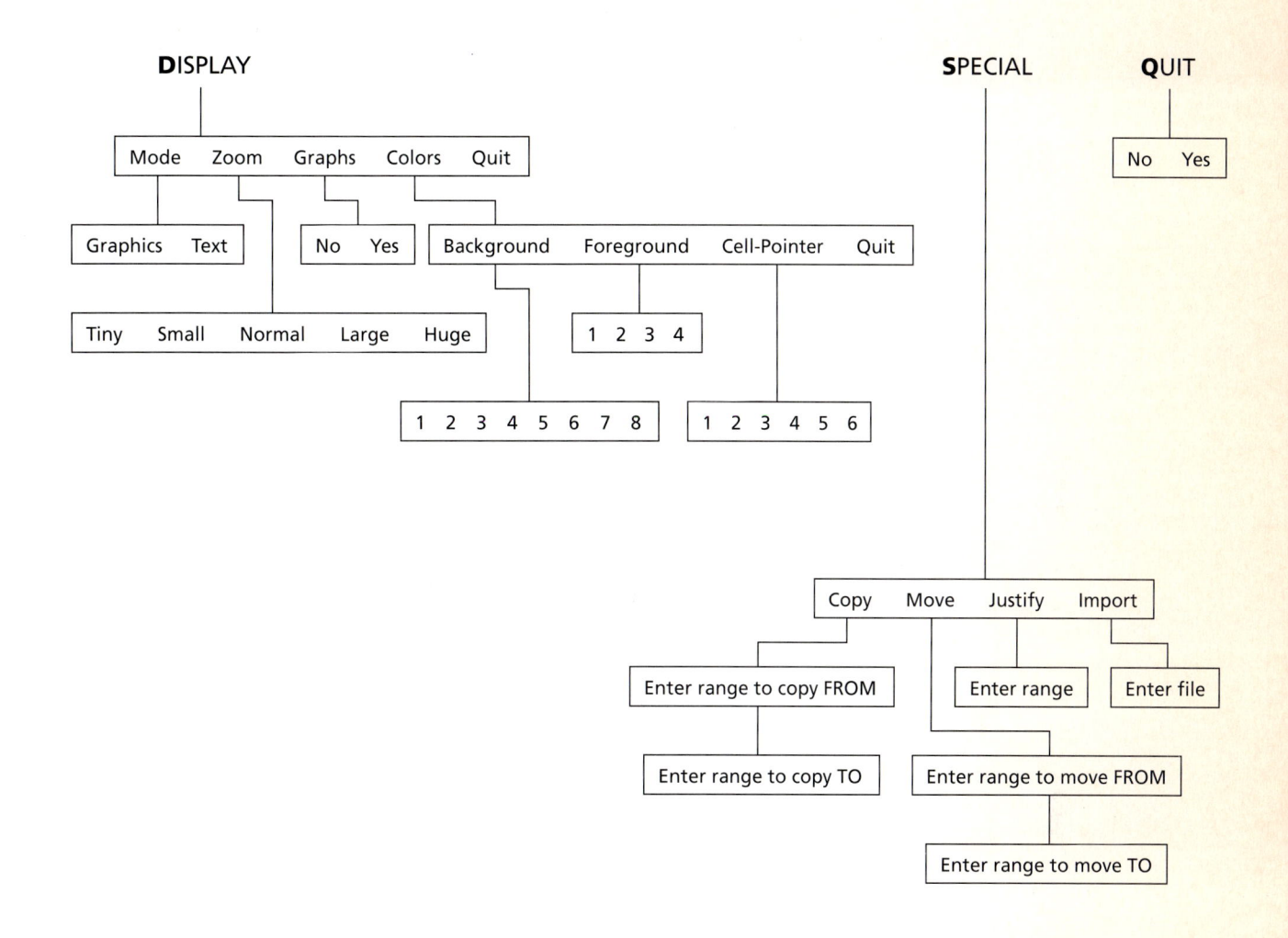

DISPLAY

- **Mode**
  - Graphics
  - Text
- **Zoom**
  - Tiny
  - Small
  - Normal
  - Large
  - Huge
- **Graphs**
  - No
  - Yes
- **Colors**
  - Background: 1 2 3 4 5 6 7 8
  - Foreground: 1 2 3 4
  - Cell-Pointer: 1 2 3 4 5 6
  - Quit
- **Quit**

SPECIAL

- **Copy**
  - Enter range to copy FROM
  - Enter range to copy TO
- **Move**
  - Enter range to move FROM
  - Enter range to move TO
- **Justify**
  - Enter range
- **Import**
  - Enter file

QUIT

- No
- Yes

Index

Abort (Ctrl-Break) command, 79, 237
@ABS, 122
Absolute address, 106-107, 108
Accelerator board, 24, 60, 331
Access:
    menu, 72-73, 185
    time, 333
Accounting applications, 6
Add-in products, 88, 244-246
Address:
    absolute, 106-107, 129
    cell range, 73, 83, 108
    relative, 106
Align right. *See* Label prefix
Allways, 160-163, 189-191, 244
Alt key, 17, 74, 160, 231, 306, 317
Amortization table, 139
Analog signals, 21
Anchor cell range, 83
AND filter condition, 209
Append, 286
Append records, 286-290
Apple Macintosh, 7, 9, 27, 58, 66, 330
Archive file attribute, 53
Arithmetic:
    operations, 78
    precedence, 78-79
Arrow keys. *See* Cursor movement
Ascending order, 204
ASCII file. *See* Text file
As-Displayed option, 157
ASSIGN command, 62
Asterisk (*):
    cell overflow, 114
    wildcard character, 37, 86, 146
@ date character, 155
@-functions, 121-130
@Base, 245
@Liberty, 246
@Risk, 246
ATTRIB command, 52, 62
Auditor, 245, 302
Autocompression, 301

AUTOEXEC.BAT file, 51, 53
Autoexecution macro, 243
Automatic recalculation, 116-118
@AVG, 122

Background:
    printing, 248, 300-301, 315
    recalculation, 248
Backslash (\) key, 81, 179, 231, 243
Backspace key, 33, 77, 79
Backups:
    DOS BACKUP, 48, 58, 62
    for hard disks, 15, 58, 338
    Lotus, 147
Baler, 246
Bar graph:
    Lotus, 173, 187
    stacked bar, 173
BASIC, 7
Basic input/output system (BIOS), 10, 30
Batch files, 53-56
    creating, 54
    examples, 55
Baud rate, 21
Bin range, 219
Bit (binary digit), 10
Bold, 160, 306-307
Boot disk, 30, 71
Boot files, 30-31, 38
Boot sequence, 30-32
    cold boot, 30, 35
    warm boot, 35, 71
Borders, 155, 315
Boxes, 161-162
Braces ({ }), 238, 267
BREAK command, 61
Budget Express, 246
Buffers, 50
Built-in functions, 121-130, 318
Burn-in, 337
Bus, 7, 11
Business applications, 4
Byte, 10

Cable, 25
CALC mode indicator, 75, 118, 318
Cambridge Spreadsheet Analyzer, 245
Cancel command. *See* Escape
CapsLock key, 17, 35, 74
Caret (^), 78, 115
Carrier signal, 21
Cartridge (cassette) tape, 15
Cell:
    absolute, 106-107, 108
    addresses, 73, 77, 304-305
    borders, 155
    comment, 315
    contents, 73
    copying, 104
    edit (F2), 74, 79, 88
    erase, 79
    formatting, 80, 109-114
    formulas, 73, 75, 78-79, 157, 305
    from range, 104
    moving, 105
    range, 83, 154
    range names, 108-109
    relative, 106
    to range, 104
    type, 78
Cell formats, 109-114, 316-317
    automatic, 316
    color, 317
    comma, 110
    currency, 110
    date, 111
    fixed, 109-110
    general, 109, 110, 111
    global default, 111
    hidden, 110, 111
    percent, 110, 111
    +/−, 110, 111
    reset, 112
    scientific, 111, 316
    text, 113-114, 157
    time, 111
Cell-formulas option, 157
Cell labels, 115-116
    centered (^), 115

INDEX

Cell labels (continued)
   left ('), 80, 115
   repeating (\), 81, 115
   right ("), 115
   spilling over, 114
Centered label, 115
Central processing unit (CPU), 7, 330
Changing default disk drive, 33, 71, 85, 86, 144-145
Characters:
   repeating, 81, 115
   valid file name, 36, 146-147
   wildcard, 37, 148
CHDIR (or CD) command, 46, 61, 71
Chip, 8
CHKDSK command, 43, 62
Circular reference, 75
Clock speed, 8, 330
Clone, 331
CLS command, 52
Cold boot, 30, 35
Colon (:):
   command, 307
   drive separator, 36
Color graphics adapter (CGA), 16
Color monitor, 16-17, 330
Columns:
   deleting, 103-104
   inserting, 101-103
   width, 114-115
Combining files, 86
Comma format, 110-111, 129
COMMAND.COM file, 30, 71, 87
Command language, macro, 238-241
Command line startup options, 243
Command line template, 52
Comment lines. *See* Documentation
Compaq, 331
Compatibility, IBM, 331
COM ports, 55
Compound conditions, 209
CompuAdd, 331
Computer-assisted design (CAD), 6, 20
Computer crime, 330
CONFIG.SYS file, 50
Consolidation, 150-153, 248, 304-306
Control key (Ctrl), 17, 76
Control Panel, 73-76, 115, 237, 241, 315
Conventional memory. *See* Memory
Convert program. *See* Translate
Coprocessor, 331
Copying:
   DOS COPY command, 40, 48, 50, 54
   Lotus formulas, 87, 104-106
Correcting errors, 79
@COUNT, 122

Criteria range, 207-209, 212
@CTERM, 123
Ctrl-Alt-Del (warm boot), 35, 71
Ctrl key, 17, 76
Ctrl-Break, 79, 237
Ctrl-PgDn, Ctrl-PgUp, 304
Ctrl-PrtSc, 35
Currency format, 110-111
Current cell indicator, 73
Cursor, 18, 73
Cursor movement, 76-77, 239
Customizing Lotus. *See* Installing Lotus
Cylinder, 38

Daisy wheel printer, 20
Data:
   fill, 202-203
   range, 206
   table, 211-215, 317
Database:
   Lotus, 70, 88, 201-220
   management software, 4
   statistical functions, 211
@DATE, 125, 208
Date:
   arithmetic, 125
   functions, 125-126
   number, 125
@ date character, 155
DATE command, 32-33, 75
@DATEVALUE, 125
@DAVG, 211
@DAY, 126
dBASE III PLUS/IV, 6, 202, 276, 282-284, 290, 317
@DCOUNT, 211
@DDB, 125
Debugging, 7, 231, 237-238
Default disk drive, 33, 40, 85, 144-145
DEL command, 42
Del key, 17, 35, 52
Delete query, 205-206
Deleting:
   characters, 79
   files, 147-149
   rows and columns, 100-104
   undeleting (Undo), 75
Delimited file, 284
Delimiter, 267
Depreciation functions, 126
Descending order, 204
Designing worksheet, 100
Desktop publishing (DTP), 6
DESQview, 58
Destination drive, 40, 42, 43, 48, 49
Diagonal design rule, 100, 104

Digital signals, 21
DIR command, 38, 40, 52
Directories, 38-40, 44-48
   change in DOS (CD), 46, 71
   change in Lotus, 144-145, 183
   create in DOS (MD), 46, 145
   current or default, 38, 47, 85, 144-145
   displaying, 38, 40, 45
   PATH DOS command, 47
   remove in DOS (RD), 46
   subdirectories, 44-48
   TREE DOS command, 45, 62
DISKCOMP command, 43, 62
DISKCOPY command, 42, 62
Disk directory, 38-40
Disk drive, 12-15, 332-333
   changing drives in DOS, 33
   changing drives in Lotus, 144-145, 183
   choosing, 330-331
   default, 33, 40, 71, 85, 144-145
   directory, 38-40
   floppy drive, 12-14, 71, 87
   fragmentation, 50
   hard drive, 14-15, 44-50, 333
Diskette:
   capacity of, 12-13, 332
   care and handling, 13-14, 337-338
   formatting in DOS, 37-38
Disk operating system. *See also* DOS
   DOS 3.3, 59, 61
   DOS 4, 59
   DOS 5, 59
   OS/2, 25, 59
   Unix, 60
   Windows, 58
Distribution command, 219-220
@DMAX, 211
@DMIN, 211
Documentation, 100, 157, 315-316
Dollar sign ($):
   Lotus absolute cell reference, 106-107, 108
   Lotus currency cell format, 111
DOS, 30-55, 71, 75, 88, 153, 243
   AUTOEXEC.BAT, 51
   batch files, 53-56
   booting computer, 30-32
   COMMAND.COM, 30
   command line template, 52
   command summary, 61-62
   CONFIG.SYS, 50
   default drive, 33, 40
   DESQview, 58
   directory, 38-48
   DOS 3.3, 59, 61
   DOS 4, 59
   DOS 5, 59

INDEX

editing keys, 52
EDLIN program, 55
environment, 58
external commands, 62
file extensions, 36
file names, 36
hidden files, 30-31
IBMBIO.COM and IBMDOS.COM, 31
internal commands, 61
IO.SYS and MSDOS.SYS, 31
MS-DOS, 30-55
OS/2, 59-60
PC-DOS, 30
prompt, 31-47, 55, 183, 243
shell, 56, 57, 58, 153
Unix, 60
Windows, 58
DOS commands:
    BACKUP, 48, 58
    changing drive, 33
    CHDIR (CD), 46, 71, 145
    CHKDSK, 43
    CLS, 54
    COPY, 40, 48, 52, 54
    Ctrl-Alt-Del, 35
    Ctrl-PrtSc, 35
    Ctrl-Z, 52
    DATE, 32-33, 75
    Del key, 52
    DEL (or ERASE), 42
    DIR, 38, 40
    directory, 38-40
    DISKCOMP, 43
    DISKCOPY, 42
    ECHO, 53
    Esc key, 52
    external, 62
    FDISK, 45
    FORMAT, 37-38, 45
    GOTO, 54
    IF, 54
    Ins key, 52
    internal, 61
    MKDIR (MD), 46, 145
    PATH, 47
    PAUSE, 54
    PRINT, 41
    PROMPT, 47
    PrtSc, 35
    REM, 54
    RENAME, 42
    RESTORE, 49
    RMDIR (RD), 46
    Shift-PrtSc, 35
    summary of, 61-62
    TIME, 32, 75
    TREE, 45
    TYPE, 41
    XCOPY, 49

DOS prompt, 31, 47, 55, 175
DOS utilities:
    Norton Utilities, 53-56
    PC Tools, 53, 57, 58
Dot matrix printer, 18-19, 163, 333-334
Double density, 13
Download fonts, 160-161. *See also* Laser printer
Draw lines, 307
Driver software, 51
Drives. *See* Disk drive
@DSTD, 211
@DSUM, 211
@D360, 318
@DVAR, 211
Duty cycle, 333
Dynamic RAM (DRAM). *See* Memory

ECHO command, 53
EDIT mode indicator, 74, 79
Edit window (screen), 73, 76, 300-301, 305
Editing:
    DOS, 52
    Lotus cell (F2), 74, 79, 88, 207
EDLIN program, 55
Educational versions, 329
Electronic spreadsheet, 4, 70. *See also* Lotus 1-2-3
Encoded printer file, 304
End key, 35, 75, 76, 77, 155
Enhanced graphics adapter (EGA), 16
Enter key, 33, 71, 77
Environment, DOS, 58
Equations. *See* Cell formulas
ERASE (DEL) command, 42
Erasing files:
    DOS, 42
    Lotus, 147-149
Ergonomics, 16
Error:
    message, 61
    mode indicator, 74
Esc key, 17, 34, 52, 77, 79, 144, 146-147
ESDI, 333
Ethics in computing, 330
Excel. *See* Microsoft
Exiting:
    Access menu, 87, 243
    Allways, 191
    Lotus 1-2-3 (/Q), 86, 243
    PrintGraph, 183, 188
    WYSIWYG, 309
@EXP, 122
Expanded memory (EMS), 24
Expansion card, 11, 12, 331-332
Expansion slot, 7, 11

Export, 284-285
Extended memory (XMS), 24, 51
Extension. *See* File name extension
External DOS commands, 62
External modem. *See* Modem
Extract query, 205-206

Facsimile (fax) card, 22-23
FC command, 52
FDISK command, 45
Field, 202
File:
    attributes, 38, 53
    backup, 48, 58, 62, 147
    names, 36, 86, 146
    naming, 36
    operations in Lotus, 144-154
    path, 47
    retrieving, 82
    saving, 79
    transfer, 260-291
    translating. *See* Translate
    viewer, 302
File name extensions, 36
    .ADN (Lotus), 161
    .ALL (Lotus), 163
    .BAK (Lotus), 86, 147
    .BAT (DOS), 36
    .CGM (Lotus 3.1), 304, 315
    .COM (DOS), 36
    .DBF (dBASE), 273-274, 281
    .ENC (Lotus 3.1), 304
    .EXE (DOS), 36
    .FM3 (Lotus 3.1), 307
    .PIC (Lotus), 147, 181, 315
    .PLC (Lotus 3.1), 309
    .PRN (Lotus), 147, 158
    .WKE (Lotus), 85, 146
    .WK1 (Lotus), 85, 146, 247, 304, 319
    .WK3 (Lotus 3), 85, 146, 248, 304, 319
    .WKS (Lotus), 85, 146, 247
    .TMP (Lotus 3.1), 304
    .TXT (Text), 263, 267, 278, 282
Fill cells, 203
Film recorder, 21
Filter condition, 207-209
Financial @nalyst, 246
Financial functions, 123
Financial Toolkit, 246
@FIND, 130
Find query, 205-208
Floppy disks, 12-14, 27, 37, 332. *See also* Diskette
    2-inch, 12
    3.5-inch, 12
    5.25-inch, 12
    8-inch, 12
    as backup media, 15

Flush right label, 116
Font:
    Allways, 160-161
    cartridge, 335
    graph, 184-185
    Lotus 2.3, 301
    PostScript, 335
    soft, 161
    WYSIWYG, 306-307
Footer, 155
Forecalc, 246
FORMAT command, 37-38, 45
Formatted option, 157
Formatting:
    cell, 109-114
    disk, 37-38
    low-level, 45
Form feed, 84, 154, 158, 185
Formulas:
    editing, 74, 79, 88
    entering, 77-79
    expressions, 78
    precedence operations, 78-79
4Views, 245
4Word, 244
Fragmented disk drive, 50
Freelance Plus, 245
Full page graph, 184
Function keys, 17, 88-89, 107, 160, 231, 235, 237, 238, 239, 306, 317
Functions, Lotus, 70, 121-130, 211, 318
    database statistical, 211
    date and time, 125-126
    depreciation, 124-125
    financial, 123-124
    logical, 126-129
    mathematical, 122-123
    nested, 127
    statistical, 121-122
    string, 129-130
@FV, 123

Game port, 11
General format, 110
Global:
    cell format, 109
    column width, 114-115
    label prefix, 116
    settings, 111-112
GOTO (F5), 77
Graph:
    Allways, 189-191
    axes, 172
    bar chart, 173, 187
    creating, 172, 176-177
    data labels, 179

    data legends, 178
    data ranges, 172
    fonts, 184-185
    format option, 181
    grid, 180-181
    high-low-close-open, 174, 300, 312
    horizontal bar, 300
    legend, 178
    line, 173
    mixed, 174, 300, 312
    module, 70
    naming, 182
    options, 178-181
    .PIC file, 181-182
    pie, 173
    presentation, 6
    printing, 185, 188, 189
    PrintGraph, 182-189
    resolution, 183, 185
    saving, 181-182
    scales, 179-180
    select-image, 183
    settings sheet, 179
    size, 184
    stacked bar, 173, 313
    titles, 178
    type, 173-175, 300, 312
    viewing, 177, 186, 189-191
    X-axis and Y-axis, 172, 178, 313
    X-Y, 173
Graphical user interface (GUI), 66
GRAPHICS command, 53
Graphics quality, 185
Graphing applications, 6
Grid option, 180-181

HAL, 244
Half-page graph option, 184
Hard copy, 22
Hard disk, 12, 14-15, 27, 333
    backup, 15, 58, 338
    booting the computer, 31
    preparing, 44-45
    subdirectories, 44-47
    type of, 333
Hard page break (::), 158
Hardware:
    accelerator board, 24, 60, 331
    bus, 7, 11
    cartridge (cassette) tape, 15
    choosing, 230-236
    diskette, 12, 14, 332
    expansion slots, 7, 11
    floppy drive, 12, 27, 37, 332
    hard drive, 14-15, 27, 333
    keyboard, 12, 17, 33
    local area network (LAN), 23
    manufacturers, 331

    memory, 7, 10, 23, 24
    microcomputer, 4
    microprocessor, 7, 8, 24, 247, 329, 331
    modem, 21, 25, 27
    monitor, 12, 16
    motherboard, 7
    mouse, 12, 18
    pointing device, 18
    ports, 11, 21
    printers, 18-21, 27
    RAM, 10, 23-25
    scanner, 22
    surge protector, 25
    system unit, 7-11
    video adapter, 12, 16
Harvard Graphics, 245
Header, 155
Help feature (F1), 77-78, 303
Hewlett-Packard, 334-335
Hidden:
    column, 110, 115
    file, 30, 31, 53
High density, 13
High-Low-Close-Open (HLCO) graph, 174, 300, 312
High memory, 24
@HLOOKUP, 127-129
Home key, 17, 35, 76, 83, 155
Horizontal:
    title, 119
    underline (Allways), 162
    window, 120
Hot key sequence, 51
@HOUR, 126

IBM:
    AT, 11, 33, 331, 333
    clone, 331
    compatible, 4, 59, 329, 331
    PC, 4, 11, 33, 331
    PS/2, 9, 11, 16, 332
    XT, 11, 13, 333
IBMBIO.COM and IBMDOS.COM, 31
IF command, 53
@IF, 126-127
Import:
    data, 153
    dBASE, 286-290
    Lotus, 150-151, 277-281
    spreadsheet in WordPerfect, 268-272
    See also Translate
Indicators:
    mode, 73, 74, 86, 185, 231, 237-238, 279
    status, 73, 75-76
@INFO, 318

INDEX

Initialize:
    disk, 37, 45
    printer, 156
Initial settings, 72
Ink jet printer, 19, 161, 334
Input device:
    joystick, 12, 18
    keyboard, 12, 17, 27, 33, 34
    light pen, 18
    mouse, 12, 18
    scanner, 22
    trackball, 18
Input/Output (I/O) port, 7, 10-11, 27
Input range, 206, 212
Insert mode:
    DOS, 52
    Lotus, 79
Inserting:
    rows and columns, 100-103
    text. *See* Typeover
Ins key, 17, 35, 52, 79
@INT, 122
Installing Lotus, 72, 300, 304
Integrated circuit, 8. *See also* Chip, Microprocessor
Internal DOS commands, 61
Internal modem. *See* Modem
IO.SYS and MSDOS.SYS, 31
@IRR, 123
Italics, 160, 307, 309

Joystick, 12, 18
Justification:
    Center, 115-116
    Left, 115-116
    Right, 115-116

Keyboard, 12, 17, 27
    84-key, 17, 33
    101- key expanded, 17, 34
    numeric keypad, 17-18
    template, 88-89
Keys, sorting, 203
Kilobyte (KB), 10, 13

Label:
    cell type, 78
    prefix, 115-116
LABEL command, 53
Landscape mode, 314, 335
Language, programming, 7
Laptop computer, 27
Laser printer, 19-20, 335-336
    advantages of, 335
    Allways, 161, 163
    fonts, 161-163
    HP-compatible, 20, 335

    memory for, 335
    PostScript, 335
    toner cartridge, 20, 25, 336
    WYSIWYG, 307
Learn feature (Alt-F5) for macros, 234-237, 317
@LEFT, 130
Left justification, 115-116
@LENGTH, 130
Letter-quality printer, 19
Light emitting diode (LED), 17, 35
Light pen, 18
Line:
    counter, 84, 154, 185
    drawing, 161-163, 307
    graph. *See* Graph
    option, 154
Linked spreadsheet, 147, 151-152
Liquid crystal display (LCD), 332
List files (F3) command, 147, 149
List manager, 202
@LN, 122
Local area network (LAN), 23
Lock key indicators, 73, 74
@LOG, 122
Logical functions, 126-129
Lookup functions, 127-128
Lotus 1-2-3 version 2.2, 68-259, 269-281
    absolute address, 106-107
    Access system, 72-73, 87, 185
    /Add-In command, 88
    addresses, 77
    Allways, 160-163, 189-191
    ascending vs. descending order, 204
    automatic vs. manual recalculation, 116-118
    built-in functions, 121-130, 211
    cell entry, 77-78
    column width, 109, 114-115
    combining files, 150-151
    command language, 238-241
    companion products, 244-246
    Control Panel, 73-76, 77, 115, 237, 241
    /Copy command, 87, 104-106
    correcting errors, 79
    creating graphs, 172
    cursor movement, 76-77
    /Data command, 88, 201-220, 317
    database features, 201-211
    data table, 211-215
    default directory, 71, 85, 86, 144-145
    deleting rows and columns, 100, 103-104
    designing worksheet, 100
    edit cell, 74, 79, 88

    entering cell expressions, 77-79, 244
    /File command, 85-86, 144-154
    formatting cells, 109-114
    function keys, 88-89, 107, 117
    functions, 70, 121-130, 211
    /Graph command, 88, 171-189
    graphing, 171-191
    help feature, 77
    inserting rows and columns, 101-103
    Install module, 72
    labels, 77-78
    linked cells, 151-152
    macros, 100, 230-243
    mode indicator, 73
    /Move command, 87, 105
    moving-bar menu, 75
    1-2-3 module, 71-72
    parsing data, 278-281
    /Print command, 83, 87, 154-163
    PrintGraph module, 72
    protecting cells, 118
    queries, 205-211, 317
    QuickStart, 71-88
    /Quit command, 86
    /Range command, 87, 108-114, 116, 118
    range names, 108-109
    recalculation, 116-118
    regression, 215-220
    retrieving worksheet file, 86, 146
    saving worksheet file, 85, 146-147, 149-150
    settings sheet, 83, 154, 177
    setup string, 156
    slash (/) commands, 76, 87-88
    sorting, 203-205, 317
    Symphony, 250
    /System command, 88
    titles, 119-120
    Translate module, 72, 273-277
    values, 77-78
    versions, 247-248, 300, 304
    window, 120
    /Worksheet command, 75, 87, 111, 114, 116-120, 145
Lotus 1-2-3 Release 2.3, 247, 300-303
    overview of new features, 300
    system requirements, 300
Lotus 1-2-3 version 3.1, 248, 304-319
    automatic cell formatting, 316
    /Data options, 317
    /Graph features, 312
    macro enhancements, 317
    /Print features, 314-315
    version 3.1+, 319
    worksheet analysis feature, 315-316
    WYSIWYG features, 306-312
Lotus Access System, 72-73, 87, 185

INDEX

Lotus-compatible packages, 249-250
Low-level formatting, 45
@LOWER, 130

Mace Utilities, 58
Macintosh, Apple, 7, 9, 27, 58, 66, 330
Macro Editor/Debugger, 246
Macros:
    autoexecute, 243
    creating, 231, 241
    debugging, 231, 237-238
    DOS batch file, 54-55
    executing, 231-232
    keystroke, 230
    Learn feature, 234-237
    Lotus, 100, 230-243, 317-318
    Lotus command language, 231, 238-241
    menu, 231, 241-243
Magnetic disk, 12
Magnetic tape drive, 15
Mailmerge format, 266-267, 284-285
Mail-order vendors, 336-337
Maintenance, 338
Manual:
    graph size, 184
    recalculation, 75, 118
Mapping, spreadsheet, 248, 315
Margin commands, 156
Mathematical functions, 122-123
Matrix command, 220
@MAX, 122
Megabyte (MB), 10, 13
Megahertz (MHz), 8
Memory, 7, 10. *See also* RAM, ROM
    chip, 8
    conventional, 24, 51, 328, 330
    DRAM, 10, 24
    expanded (EMS), 24, 330
    extended (XMS), 24, 51
    for laser printer, 335
    Lotus requirements, 71, 75, 202, 247, 300, 304
    pages, 58
    primary, 7, 10
    secondary, 12
    shadow RAM, 304
    SIMM, 10
Memory-resident. *See* Terminate-and-stay-resident
Menu macro, 231, 241-243
Micro channel architecture (MCA), 11
Microcomputer, 4
    IBM-compatible, 4, 328-330
    magazines, 330, 337
Microprocessor, 7, 8, 24, 332
    Intel, 8

Motorola, 8
    numeric coprocessor, 8, 331
    80286, 8, 24-25, 59, 247, 329, 332
    80386, 8, 24-25, 59, 247, 329, 332
    80386SX, 8, 24-25, 59, 332
    80486, 8, 24-25, 59, 247, 332
    8087, 331
    8088, 8, 24-25, 59, 247, 331
Microsoft:
    DOS, 25, 33
    Excel, 249-250
    Windows, 58
@MID, 130
@MIN, 122
Minimal recalculation, 116, 302
Minus (–) key, 78, 81
@MINUTE, 126
Mixed graph type, 174, 300, 312
MKDIR (MD) command, 46
@MOD, 122
MODE:
    command, 53
    indicator, 73, 74, 86, 185, 231, 237-238, 279
Modem, 21-22, 25, 27
    external, 21
    fax card, 22
    internal, 21
Module, Lotus:
    Install, 72
    1-2-3, 71, 72
    PrintGraph, 72, 181-189
    Translate, 72, 273-277
Monochrome graphics adapter (MGA), 16
@MONTH, 126
Motherboard, 7
Mouse, 12, 18, 303, 307, 330
Move Lotus cell, 87, 104-105
Moving-bar menu, 75-76
MS-DOS, 30-55. *See also* DOS
Multiple:
    regression, 218
    worksheet, 304-306
Multitasking, 56, 58

Natural (recalculation) order, 116-117
Near-typeset quality, 19
Near-letter quality, 19, 333
Nesting functions, 127
Network:
    interface card, 23
    local area network, 23
    log-on, 31
    server, 23
Notebook computer, 12
Note-It Plus, 244

Notes for graphs, 313
@NOW, 125
@NPV, 123
Numbering pages, 155
Numeric coprocessor, 8, 331
Numeric keypad, 17-18, 74
NumLock key, 17, 34, 74

On sheet word processing, 300
One-parameter data table, 212-213
1-2-3-Go! tutorial, 303
Operating system, 30. *See also* DOS
Optical scanner. *See* Scanner
Options menu:
    graph, 178-181
    print, 155
    PrintGraph, 184-185
OR filter conditions, 209
OS/2, 25, 59-60
Output devices:
    film recorder, 21
    monitor, 16
    plotter, 20
    printer, 18, 27
Output range, 207, 216
Overtype, 75, 79. *See also* Typeover

Page:
    break, 158
    feed, 84, 154, 185
    length, 156
    memory, 58
    numbering, 155
    sheet in 3D worksheet, 304-306
Parallel port, 11, 55
Parameters, startup, 243
Parentheses in expressions, 78-79
Parsing data, 220, 278-281
PATH command, 47
Pathname, 47
PAUSE command, 53
PC Connection, 336
PC-DOS, 30
PC Tools, 53, 57, 58
P.D. Queue, 246
Percent:
    batch file parameter, 53
    format type, 110-111, 129
Period (.) key, 83
Peripheral devices, 7, 12-21
Personal computer (PC), 4
Personal improvement programs, 6
Perspective window, 305
PGRAPH.EXE, 183
PgUp and PgDn keys, 17, 35, 76, 304
Pie chart. *See* Graph

Pixel, 16
Plotter, 20
Plus (+) key, 78, 81
@PMT, 123
Pointer. *See* Cursor movement
Pointing device, 18
Pop-up help, 303
Portable computer. *See* Laptop
Portrait mode, 314, 335
Ports:
    COM, 11, 55
    game, 11
    I/O, 7, 10, 11, 27
    parallel, 11, 55
    serial, 11, 21
PostScript. *See* Laser printer
Pound sign (#), 155, 183
    use in compound expressions, 209
Power-on self-test (POST), 31
Power supply, 7
Presentation graphics, 6, 21, 161
Preview graph, 177, 189
Primary:
    key, 203
    memory. *See* Memory
Printer, 18-21, 27
    daisy wheel, 20
    dot matrix, 18-19, 156, 163, 183, 311, 333-334
    ink jet, 19, 161, 334
    laser, 19-20, 156, 161, 163, 311, 337-338
    plotter, 20
Printer driver, 51. *See also* Graph, Quality
PrintGraph module, 72, 181-189, 308
    options, 184-185
    printing graph, 185
    selecting image, 183
Printing:
    DOS PRINT file command, 41
    DOS screen, 35
    Lotus graphs, 185, 189-191
    Lotus cell formulas, 157
    Lotus worksheet, 84-85, 154-157, 160-163
Print resolution, 183, 185
Print Screen (PrtSc) command, 35
Print spooler, 51
Processing unit, 7
Productivity software, 4
Program, 7
Programming, 7
Project management software, 6
Prompt, DOS, 31, 47
PROMPT command, 47
@PROPER, 130

Proportional spacing, 161, 307
Protecting cell expressions, 118
PrtSc command, 17
Public Brand Software, 329
Public domain software, 329. *See also* Shareware
Pull-down menu, 249
@PV, 124

Quality, print, 183
Query, Lotus, 205-211
    criteria range, 207-209
    delete, 206
    extract, 210
    find, 207
    input range, 206
    output range, 207
    QBE, 207
    unique, 206
Question (?) wildcard character, 37
Quit Lotus, 86
QWERTY keyboard, 12

Random access memory (RAM), 7, 10, 23-25, 58
RAM disk, 51
@RAND, 122
Range:
    comment, 316
    formatting, 109-114, 116
    names of, 108-109
@RATE, 124
Read-only file attribute, 53
Read-only memory (ROM), 10
Read/write access slot, 13
READY mode, 73, 74, 86, 279
Recalculation, 75, 116-118
    automatic, 117
    background, 248
    manual, 75, 118
    minimal, 116, 302
    natural sequence, 116
Record, 202
RECOVER command, 53
Recreational applications, 6
Regression, 215-220
Relative addresses, 106. *See also* Absolute addresses
Releases of 1-2-3:
    1a, 247
    2, 2.01, 247
    2.2, 68-259, 269-281
    2.3, 247, 300-303
    3.0, 247-248
    3.1, 248, 303-319
    3.1+, 248, 319
    Windows, 307

REM command, 54
RENAME (REN) command, 42
@REPEAT, 130
@REPLACE, 130
Reset button, 35
RESTORE command, 49
Restoring deleted text (Undo), 75, 160
Retrieving a file, 86, 146
Return (Enter) key, 33, 71, 77
Rescue Plus, 246
@RIGHT, 130
Right justification, 115
RMDIR (RD) command, 46
Root directory, 44
@ROUND, 110, 123
Row and column borders, 84
Rows:
    deleting, 103-104
    inserting, 101-103
R-Squared, 218

Saving:
    backup option, 85-86
    blocks (Xtract), 149
    file, 85, 146-147
    replacing, 86
Scanner, 22
Scientific format, 111
Scroll Lock key, 17, 74, 76
SCSI, 333
Search and replace, 318
Search path, 47
@SECOND, 126
Secondary key, 203
Secondary storage, 12
Serial port, 11, 21, 55
Server (network), 23
Settings sheet, 83, 154
Setup string, 156
Shading, 160, 162, 307, 310
Shadow RAM, 304
Shareware, 329
Shell (DOS), 56, 57, 58
Shift key, 17
Shift-PrtSc, 35
Shift-Tab, 33, 76
Sideways, 244
Silverado, 245
Simple regression, 218
Signal bus, 7, 11
Single in-line memory module (SIMM), 10
Single step mode, 74, 231, 237-238
Slash (/) key, 75, 300

INDEX

@SLN, 124
Software, 4, 328-332
    piracy, 330
Sorting, 203-205, 317
Source drive, 40, 42, 43, 48, 49
Spreadsheet, 4
    map, 315. *See also* Auditor mode, 74
Spreadsheet publishing, 160, 307
@SQRT, 123
Stacked bar graph. *See* Graph
Starting Lotus, 71, 243
Statistical functions, 121-122
Status indicators, 73, 75-76
STEP mode (Alt-F2), 74, 231, 237-238
@STD, 122, 318
@STDS, 318
@STRING, 130
String functions, 129-130
Subdirectories, 44-47. *See also* Directories
@SUM, 82, 108, 122, 245
SuperCalc, 250
Supertree, 246
Supplemental dictionary, 11
Surge protector, 25, 338
Suspend print job, 315
@SYD, 125
Symphony, 250
System:
    boot disk, 30
    file attribute, 38, 53
    unit, 7-11, 35

Tab key, 17, 33, 76
Telecommunications, 58
Template, function key, 88-89
Temporary DOS session (/S), 88, 153-154
@TERM, 124
Terminal emulation, 6, 10
Terminate-and-stay-resident (TSR), 51
Text:
    file, 55, 158, 263, 267-269, 278, 282-283, 290
    formatting, 160, 307
The Auditor, 245
Three-dimensional worksheet, 248, 304-306
Tilde (~), 232-233
@TIME, 126
TIME command, 32
@TIMEVALUE, 126
Titles:
    graph option, 178
    worksheet, 119
Toggle, 17, 35
Tomorrow, 246
Toner cartridge. *See* Laser printer
Top margin, 156
Track, 37, 333
Trackball, 18
Translate:
    CONVERT.EXE (WordPerfect), 263-267
    dBASE to Lotus, 282
    dBASE to mailmerge, 284
    dBASE to SDF, 282
    dBASE to text, 282-283
    DIF to Lotus, 274
    Lotus to dBASE, 276
    Lotus to .PRN text, 272
    Lotus .PIC to WordPerfect, 270
    Lotus .PRN to WordPerfect, 268
    Lotus .WK1 to WordPerfect, 269, 270
    mail merge to WordPerfect merge, 266
    module (Lotus), 273-277
    text to dBASE, 290
    text to Lotus, 278
    text to WordPerfect, 267-269
    WordPerfect merge to DIF, 265
    WordPerfect to text, 263
TREE command, 45
Tree structure. *See* Directories
Trendsetter Expert, 246
@TRIM, 130
Tutorial, 303
Twin, 249
Two-parameter data table, 213-214
TYPE command, 41, 54
Type of Lotus cell, 78
Typeface. *See* Font
Typeover mode, 52, 75

Underline, 162
Undo command (Alt-F4), 75, 160
Unformatted:
    cell. *See* General format
    print option, 157
Uninterruptible power supply, 25
Unique query, 205-206
Unix, 60
Upgrade, 331
User group, 337
Utility software, 51, 56-58

@VALUE, 130
VALUE indicator, 78
@VAR, 122, 318

@VARS, 318
Vendor, selecting, 336-337
VER command, 53
Versions, software, 59, 61, 247-248
Vertical:
    title, 119
    window, 120
Video adapter, 12, 16
Video graphics adapter (VGA), 16
    monitor, 12, 16
    Super VGA, 16
@VLOOKUP, 127-129
VOL command, 53
Volume label, 38
VP Planner, 249

WAIT mode indicator, 74, 84, 86, 185
Warm boot, 35, 71
Warranty, 336
What-if planning, 246
What-If Solver, 246
What's Best!, 246
Wide directory, 40
Wildcard template:
    DOS, 37, 40, 41
    Lotus, 86, 146
Window, Lotus, 119-120
Windows, Microsoft, 58
WordPerfect, 263-272
    Convert program, 263-267
    graphics, 270
    import spreadsheet, 269, 270
    merge printing, 266
    text file, 263
Word processing, 4, 244, 300, 329
Word wrap, 300
Worksheet. *See* Spreadsheet
Worksheet Archive System, 246
Worksheet:
    design, 100
    status, 111
Write-protected, 13, 38
WYSIWYG, 161, 248, 300, 304, 306-311

XCOPY command, 49
XGA video adapter, 16
X-range, 172, 216
Xtract command, 149
XY Graph. *See* Graph

@YEAR, 126
Y-range, 216

Zenith Data Systems, 331